Evaluation is for making it work.

If it works . . .
Notice and nurture.

If it doesn't work . . .
Notice and change.

Sourcebook

Casebook

Program Evaluation

A PRACTITIONER'S GUIDE FOR TRAINERS AND EDUCATORS

ROBERT O. BRINKERHOFF

DALE M. BRETHOWER

TERRY HLUCHYJ

JERI RIDINGS NOWAKOWSKI

Kluwer-Nijhoff Publishing
Boston   The Hague   Dordrecht   Lancaster
a member of the Kluwer Academic Publishers Group

Distributors for North America:
Kluwer·Nijhoff Publishing
Kluwer Boston, Inc.
190 Old Derby Street
Hingham, Massachusetts 02043, U.S.A.

Distributors outside North America:
Kluwer Academic Publishers Group
Distribution Centre
P.O. Box 322
3300 AH Dordrecht, The Netherlands

Library of Congress Cataloging in Publication Data
Main entry under title:

Program evaluation: a practitioner's guide for trainers and
educators: sourcebook and casebook

(Evaluation in education and human services)
1. Educational accountability. 2. Educational
accountability—United States—Case studies.
I. Brinkerhoff, Robert O. II. Series.
LB2806.P77 1983   379.1′54   81-14913
ISBN 0-89838-121-5

Program evaluation: a practitioner's guide for trainers and
educators: A sourcebook.

(Evaluation in education and human services)
1. Evaluation research (Social action programs)—
Handbooks, manuals, etc. 2. Educational accountability
—Handbooks, manuals, etc. I. Brinkerhoff, Robert O.
II. Series
HV11.P739 1983   361.6′1   82-16213
ISBN 0-89838-120-7

Printed in the United States of America.

Contents

About these Materials

Introduction to the Package

Program Evaluation: A Practitioner's Guide was developed by the Evaluation Training Consortium (ETC) project at the Evaluation Center, Western Michigan University. The ETC project was funded by the U.S. Office of Special Education from 1972 to 1982; it has developed program evaluation procedures for use by teacher educators and delivered training to thousands of professionals across the United States. The mission of the ETC has been to improve the evaluation capabilities of projects and programs engaged in preparing personnel to work with special and regular education clients and pupils. This package of materials is intended to carry forward that mission, and help educators to help themselves improve educational practice.

This set of materials is for use in training, teacher education, and other professional development programs and projects in private and public agencies, public schools and colleges and universities. They are designed to help individuals or groups in their own work, and they can be used to train others.

The package has the following parts:

(1) Sourcebook, which contains chapters of guidelines, resources and references for each of 7 key evaluation functions.
(2) Casebook (bound together with Sourcebook), which is a collection of twelve stories about evaluation applied to real-life projects and programs in different settings. These show people planning, conducting and using evaluation.
(3) Design Manual, which contains a programmed set of directions, worksheets, examples, and checklists to help you design an evaluation for a particular use.

Conceptual Basis

These materials are about designing, conducting, and using evaluation, but their underlying assumption is that evaluation should be useful for improving current and/or future training efforts. While these materials are meant to help you do evaluation well, we believe that evaluation is not worth doing at all unless you can use it to make training better, or to better invest training resources.

Good training, whether preservice or inservice, must satisfy four conditions:

(1) Training must be directed toward worthwhile goals.
(2) Training strategies must be theoretically sound, reflect good practice, be feasible, and make optimum use of available resources.
(3) Implementation of training must be efficiently managed and responsive to emerging problems and changing conditions.
(4) Recycling decisions (i.e., to terminate, continue, curtail or expand training) should be based on knowledge of impacts of training, the extent to which training outcomes are in use, and the worth of training. These decisions should be responsive to continuing and emerging needs and problems.

These criteria are not independent, and each is important to another. Training designs must be not only potent but they must be directed toward worthwhile goals; good designs can serve as guides to implementation, and implementation is facilitated by good design; and, well-implemented training is most likely to have positive outcomes. Also, these criteria are functionally related in a cycle which repeats as training programs grow and develop:

Cycle of Training Functions

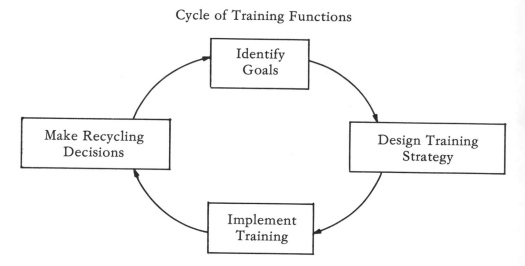

Evaluation activities are what tie these training functions together. Different kinds of evaluations are done during each of these training function stages to ensure that the function is carried out as well as it can be.

Table 1 shows the different kinds of evaluation we have defined and portrayed in these materials. The *Casebook* provides examples of these different uses; the *Sourcebook* will help you learn about options and guidelines for doing these different kinds of evaluation. The *Design Manual* can help you design an evaluation to serve one or more of these evaluation purposes.

Evaluation Purposes Related to the Key Training Program Functions

Key Training Function	Evaluation Purposes and Uses
1. Identify worthwhile training goals	Assess needs, validate goals, prioritize goals, identify constraints and problems related to goals for training
2. Design effective training strategies	Assess alternative strategies, compare training designs, identify criteria to judge designs, determine feasibility and potential for success
3. Effectively implement training	Monitor and control program operation, identify problems and revision needs, determine whether objectives are achieved, document costs and activities
4. Decide whether to terminate, continue, curtail or expand training	Determine usage and application, identify emerging and continuing needs, determine benefits of training, identify problems and revision needs to enhance training usage

How the Materials Are Organized

The *Sourcebook* is organized by major evaluation function:

(1) focusing an evaluation and clarifying its purpose
(2) designing an evaluation
(3) collecting information
(4) analyzing information
(5) reporting: interpreting and using evaluation findings
(6) managing evaluation activities
(7) evaluating evaluation efforts

Each function is defined, then the several key decisions needed to complete the function are explained. The *Sourcebook* contains examples, guidelines, criteria and checklists you can use to do more effective evaluation. It also includes references to other books and resources that can be useful in evaluating training programs.

The *Casebook* contains twelve case-examples. Each is a story about evaluation within a particular training program. The case examples, designed to portray evaluation applications of different types in different settings, were contributed by field practitioners and written in conjunction with ETC staff. They are fictional accounts but based on actual programs and uses of evaluation. Each case-example is annotated to highlight the seven major evaluation functions as set forth in the *Sourcebook*. This is done to show how these functions differ according to particular program needs and settings. Following each case is a set of review and discussion questions to help extend the lessons available in the case-example.

The *Design Manual* contains worksheets, directions, and guidelines for designing an evaluation. Its organization is similar to the *Sourcebook,* as it helps you produce different parts of an overall evaluation design. Each section presents an example of the design product needed; gives you worksheets, directions, and aids for producing that document; and provides a checklist for assessing your work.

You can use the *Design Manual* to produce:

(1) an evaluation overview
(2) an outline of evaluation questions
(3) an information collection plan
(4) an analysis and interpretation plan
(5) a management plan
(6) a report plan
(7) a plan for evaluating your evaluation

Suggestions for Using the Materials

There is no one particular order in which these materials are meant to be used. You could begin in any of the three parts, using them alone or in combination. Where you begin and how you use the materials depends on what you want to use them for. We'll suggest some possible options and applications here. You could follow one or more of these, or simply look through the materials and make up your own way of using them.

Remember that you can use these materials by yourself or in conjunction with a group. Or, you could use these materials to train other people in evaluation.

Some Options

1. To learn about how evaluation could be used to help with particular problems, you could read some of the case-examples. Use the guide below to see which cases relate to certain problems.

some common uses/problems	relevant case-examples (numbers listed are from Casebook Table of Contents)
–putting together an inservice workshop or program	–L-1, L-2, C-2
–designing, conducting a needs assessment	–L-1, C-1, C-5
–looking at child-change as a result of inservice (worth of training)	–L-4
–managing a new project	–C-2
–evaluating services provided from an agency	–S-3

some common uses/problems	relevant case-examples (numbers listed are from Casebook Table of Contents)
–improving curriculum and courses	–C-1, C-5
–proposal evaluation	–S-2
–monitoring programs, improving services	–S-1, S-3, L-3
–looking for evidence of impact and worth	–L-4, S-3, C-3, L-2
–improving an evaluation	–C-4

2. To learn more about evaluation applications in your setting: read the case-examples for your setting (state agency, local school, college).
3. To learn more about evaluation in general and how it fits in with training: read the *Sourcebook* and discuss a few cases with yourself or others.
4. To complete some evaluation design work for a program you're working on: use the *Design Manual.*
5. To become more knowledgeable and proficient in evaluation: read the *Sourcebook* (then try some more evaluation work!).
6. To train others:
   (1) Read the *Sourcebook* yourself and use it as the basis for training.
   (2) Select some case-examples from the *Casebook* for participants to read and discuss.
   (3) Have participants work on evaluation designs using the *Design Manual.*

Acknowledgments

The ideas and procedures described in this package of materials have evolved in ways too circuitous and interwoven to be accurately described. For us the "authors" to attach our names to them is as brazen perhaps as the fixing of a zoologist's name to a newly discovered snail; the zoologist, at least, makes no claim to creation.

We can quite clearly dedicate this work to Malcolm M. Provus, creator of the Discrepancy Evaluation Model, who initiated the project from which these materials came. His vision and impetus enabled the Evaluation Training Consortium (ETC) to survive beyond his untimely death in 1975. We can quite clearly, too, state that the work of dozens of ETC staff members from years past, advisors and friends is reflected in virtually every page. And finally, the several thousand teacher educators who labored in ETC workshops have inspired and shaped all that is between these covers.

With this labyrinthian progenesis recognized, let us humbly but more precisely try to point out credit and blame.

The four whose names appear on the books' covers stand jointly responsible for the materials. We worked together on all parts, though leadership was partitioned among us on the several pieces. Jeri Ridings Nowakowski brought forth the *Sourcebook*, as well as editing a section of the *Casebook*. Terry Hluchyj and Dale Brethower collaborated on the *Design Manual*. Bob Brinkerhoff, Director of ETC since 1975, wrote parts of and edited all of the books, kibitzed, harassed and midwived the entire effort.

Working closely with the primary authors during the last two years of the project were ETC staff members Ann Hallawell and Bob Olsen, who edited each a Casebook section and assisted with many other parts as well. Also ably assisting were graduate assistants Dick Frisbie and Laurie Rudolph.

Dan Stufflebeam, Director of the College of Education's Evaluation Center at Western Michigan University, provided critical reviews and administrative guidance throughout the project. Jim Sanders and Bob Rodosky played similar roles, reviewing draft after draft.

Becky Fitch, ETC project secretary, typed more drafts than she or any of us care to remember before being lured from Michigan's fiscal wastelands to booming Texas. Amy Leftwich saved us. We are indebted to Becky and Amy for their cheerful patience and sure skills.

Since its inception in 1972, the ETC project has been blessed with the support of an especially able Advisory Board. Bruce Balow, now at the University of Minnesota but once a USOE official, helped begin the project and has given invaluable leadership and counsel for eleven years. Hanging in with Bruce for the full eleven also was Vic Baldwin. Rounding out this current board, all of whom guided our work on the materials, are Helen

Almanza, Jeanie Crosby, Egon Guba, Bruce Irons and John Johnson. Past board members of noteworthy long service since 1972 are: Roger Kroth, Marty Martinson, Hugh McKenzie, and Dick Whelan.

There are many others whose help we acknowledge.

Early in this work's development, we visited several training sites to learn and be told about current needs and problems. Persons who graciously arranged for and hosted these visits were: Margaret Arbuckle, Ed Blackhurst, Phil Burke, Larry Carmichael, Stan Fagen, John Mathey, Herb Prehm, Hugh Watson, Daun Dickie, Deane Crowell, Rose Hicks, Vicki LaBrie and Mike Wilhelm.

Abe Nicolaou and Stacia Farrell conducted literature reviews and context studies early in the material's development. Ariah Lewy from Israel, during a visit to Michigan reviewed our plans and provided helpful development guidance. Providing a crucial panel review in January 1981 were:

College and university	Local school	State agency
Dwight Allen	Margaret Arbuckle	Vic Baldwin
Bruce Balow	Paula Tissot	Cy Freston
Ed Blackhurst	Kathy Byers	Dee John
Egon Guba	Phil Cartwright	Carol Lacey
Steve Lilly	Steve Checkon	Alex Law
Glen Vergason	Jim Collins	Bill Schipper
	Bruce Irons	

Jay Millman and Wayne Welch joined Jim Sanders and Dan Stufflebeam in a marathon review of cases which dramatically shaped their revision.

The next-to-final draft of the materials were reviewed by Fred Baars, Egon Guba, John Hansen, John McLaughlin, Nancy Zimpher and Tom Ryan in early 1982.

The entire package was submitted to an extensive field test in November 1981 and again in January 1982, coordinated by Vic Dotson of the ETC. Field testers were:

Fred Appelman	James Impara	Nancy Spinner
Kathleen Bolland	David Kazen	Sandra K. Squires
Jane R. Braden	Cynthia L. Knorr	Diane Treadway
Ruth V. Burgess	William Lee	Diana Trehary
Janice R. Duncan	Marvin Lew	Elaine M. Walsh
Kathryn Dunn	George Madaus	Miriam O. Williams
Robert Flexer	Kenneth R. Olson	
Janet Freese	Michael Plog	

Finally, we should acknowledge the institutional support provided to the ETC from 1972–1978 at the University of Virginia and 1978 to 1982 at Western Michigan University. The Division of Personnel Preparation of the U.S. Office of Special Education provided funding for the project, ably overseen by project officer Jim Siantz.

EVALUATION: WHAT IS IT?

David Nevo

Different people mean different things when they use the word "evaluation." They might also "do" evaluation in different ways, use it for different purposes, or even use different standards to decide what a good evaluation should look like. If you want to pinpoint what someone means, you have to find out a number of things.

Here are ten questions that will help you summarize what is mean when someone talks about evaluation. You can use the ten questions to find out what others have in mind when they talk about or ask you to do evaluation. Most important, these ten questions will help you clarify what *you* mean when you use the word "evaluation," or how you will define it the next time you use it.

1. How is evaluation defined? What are the unique features of an evaluation? How do you know when you see one? How does it differ from things such as "measurement" or "research?"

Is evaluation administering tests and questionnaires? Providing information for decision makers? Determining whether goals have been achieved? Assessment of merit? Or something else?

2. What is evaluation for? Why do evaluation? What is the purpose of evaluation? What functions does it serve? Is it done to serve decision making? To demonstrate accountability? For accreditation or certification? To motivate people? To change and improve programs? Or for some other reason?

3. What are the objects of evaluation? What could or should be evaluated? Are the "things" that are to be evaluated students, teachers, projects, programs, institutions or something else?

4. What aspects and dimensions of an object should evaluation investigate? What questions should be addressed about whatever is being evaluated? What types of information should be gathered? Are the aspects of the object that should be evaluated resources, impacts or outcomes, processes or implementation, staff and client transactions, goals and plans, costs and benefits, needs, organizational characteristics, or something else?

5. What criteria should be used to judge an object? How are you going to interpret the findings? How should value meaning be assigned to collected information? How will you decide if the object is "good" or "bad?" Should the criterion be achievement of stated goals, adherence to plans, responding to identified needs, achievement of social goals or ideals, comparison with alternative objects, adherence to laws and guidelines, conformity with audience expectations, or something else?

6. Who should be served by an evaluation? Who is the client? Who is the audience for the evaluation? Whose information needs does it serve? Is it done for yourself, your students, the staff, the funding agency, the general public, or someone else?

7. What steps and procedures are involved in doing an evaluation? How do you start an evaluation and how do you proceed? What are the major stages of an evaluation project? Is there a "best" sequence for conducting an evaluation?

8. What methods of inquiry should be used in evaluation? How do you collect information? What kind of inquiry design should be used in evaluation? Is the "best" methodology for evaluation tests and questionnaires, panels of experts, experimental design, surveys and correlational studies, ethnographies and case studies, "jury" trials, naturalistic approaches, or some other approach?

9. *Who should do evaluation?* What kind of evaluator should you employ? What kind of skills should an evaluator have? What should be the authority and responsibilities of an evaluator? Should the evaluation be done by a professional evaluator, an internal or external evaluator, an evaluation specialist or an expert in the field to be evaluated, regular staff, or someone else?

10. *By what standards should evaluation be judged?* How do you know what is a good evaluation? What are the characteristics of a well-done evaluation? How do you evaluate an evaluation? Should evaluation be practical and useful, provide accurate and reliable information, be realistic, prudent and frugal, be conducted legally and ethically, be objective and scientific, or should it be something else?

As mentioned earlier in this section, the ten questions can be used for various purposes, but there are two ways in which the ten questions can be particularly useful:

· *Use them to organize your own perception of what evaluation is.*
· *Use them to understand what others mean when they refer to evaluation.*

SOME ANSWERS TO THE TEN QUESTIONS FROM THE EVALUATION LITERATURE

Your acquaintance with some major evaluation approaches will help you to develop your own perception of evaluation and its main concerns.

1. *How is evaluation defined?* Many definitions of evaluation can be found in the literature. One well-known definition, originated by Ralph Tyler, perceives evaluation as *the process of determining to what extent the educational objectives are actually being realized* (Tyler, 1950, p. 69). Another widely accepted definition of evaluation has been that of *providing information for decision making* suggested by various leading evaluators, such as Lee Cronbach (1963), Dan Stufflebeam (*Stufflebeam, et al., 1971) or Marvin Alkin (1969). Malcolm Provus, the originator of Discrepancy Evaluation (1971), defined evaluation as *the comparison of performance to some standards to determine whether discrepancies existed.* In recent years, a considerable amount of consensus has been reached among evaluators regarding the definition of evaluation as *the assessment of merit or worth* (Scriven, 1967; Glass, 1969; Stufflebeam, 1974). A joint committee on standards for evaluation, comprised of seventeen members representing twelve organizations associated with educational evaluation, published their definition of evaluation as *the systematic investigation of the worth or merit of some object* (Joint Committee, 1981, p. 12). Such a definition, which points to the judgmental character of evaluation might create a considerable amount of anxiety among potential evaluees and raise resistance among opponents of evaluation. Obviously, a nonjudgmental definition of evaluation might be accepted in a more favorable way by evaluees and clients. However, it may be unrealistic to create positive attitudes towards evaluation by ignoring the fact of judgment as its major and inevitable feature. Another approach intended to develop positive attitudes towards evaluation might be to demonstrate its constructive functions within the various domains of education.

2. *What is evaluation for?* Scriven (1967) was the first to suggest the distinction between *formative evaluation* and *summative evaluation*, referring to two major roles or functions of evaluation, although he was probably not the first one to realize the importance of such a distinction. Later on, referring to the same two functions, Stufflebeam (1971) suggested the distinction between *proactive evaluation intended to serve decision making* and *retroactive evaluation to serve accountability.* Thus, evaluation can serve two functions. In its formative function, evaluation is used for the improvement and development of an ongoing activity (or program, person, product, etc.). In

its summative function, evaluation is used for accountability, certification, selection or continuation.

A third function of evaluation, which has been less often treated by evaluation literature, should also be considered. This is the *psychological or socio-political* function of evaluation. In many cases it is apparent that evaluation is not serving only formative purposes nor is it being used solely for accountability or other summative purposes. However, it may have a major use to increase awareness of special activities, motivate desired behavior of evaluees, or promote public relations. Regardless of our personal feelings about the use (or misuse) of evaluation for this purpose, we cannot ignore it.

Obviously, there are no "right" or "wrong" functions of evaluation, and more than one function can be served by an evaluation. There also might be more than these three evaluation functions. However, different functions can be served by different evaluation methods.

3. What are the objects of evaluation? Almost any training entity can serve as an object of evaluation. While some, like students or faculty, have always been popular objects of evaluation in education, others, like projects, programs, curricular materials, or educational institutions, have presently become favorite objects of educational evaluation. Two major conclusions can be drawn from the review of evaluation literature:

(a) almost anything can be an object of evaluation and evaluation should not be limited to the evaluation of students or faculty;
(b) the clear identification and delineation of the evaluation object is an important part of the development of any evaluation design.

It is very important that you determine what is "the thing" that you want to evaluate. This will help you decide what kind of information you should collect, and how you should analyze it. It helps keep an evaluation focused. And, clear object identification helps clarify and resolve value conflicts and potential threat among stakeholders and others likely to be affected.

4. What aspects and dimensions of an object should evaluation investigate? After an evaluation object has been chosen, a decision has to be made regarding the various aspects of the object that should be evaluated. Earlier approaches to evaluation focused mainly on results or outcomes. Thus, to evaluate an educational object (e.g., a workshop) would mean to evaluate the quality of the results of its functioning (e.g., participant's achievements). In recent years, some interesting attempts have been made to extend the scope of evaluation variables in various evaluation models (Stake, 1967; Stufflebeam, 1969, 1974; Stufflebeam, et al., 1971; Alkin, 1969; Provus, 1971). Stufflebeam's CIPP Model, for example, suggests that evaluation focus on four aspects of an evaluation object: (1) its *goals*; (2) its *design*; (3) its *process of implementation*; and (4) its *outcomes*. According to this approach a complete evaluation of an educational project, for example, would be an assessment of (a) the merit of its goals, (b) the quality of its plans, (c) the extent to which those plans are being carried out, and (d) the worth of its outcomes.

You should not *confuse "outcome evaluation" with "summative evaluation" nor "process evaluation" with "formative evaluation." "Outcome evaluation" is an evaluation focused on* outcomes; *"process evaluation" is one focused on* process rather than outcomes—*both of them could be either formative or summative.*

5. What criteria should be used to judge an object? To choose the criteria to be used to judge an evaluation object or any of its aspects is one of the most difficult tasks in educational evaluation. Those who think that evaluation should only attempt to determine whether goals have been achieved make this task easy for themselves by ignoring partially the issue of evaluation criteria. What they do is use "goal achievement" as the evaluation criterion without necessarily having justified or investigated the intrinsic worth of the goals. What about trivial goals or all kinds of "stated objectives" that may not be worth achieving? Should they be used as evaluation criteria?

Nonetheless, the *achievement of (important!) goals* is one possible basis for evaluation criteria. Alternative bases for evaluation criteria might be: *identified needs* of actual and potential clients, *ideals or social values,* known *standards* set by experts or other relevant groups, or the *quality or efficiency in comparison to alternative objects.*

There seems to be agreement among most evaluation experts that the criterion (or criteria) to be used for the assessment of a specific object must be determined within the specific context of the object and the function of its evaluation. While in many cases the evaluators do not or should not have the authority to choose among the various alternative criteria, *it is the evaluators' responsibility that such a choice be made, and they should be able to provide a sound justification for the choice,* made by them or by somebody else.

6. *Who should be served by an evaluation?* If evaluation is to be useful at all, it has to be useful to some specific *client* or *audience.* Most evaluation literature does not suggest which is the "most appropriate" audience for evaluation, but three important propositions can be found in writings regarding this issue. They are:

(1) An evaluation can have more than one client or audience.
(2) Different evaluation audiences might have different evaluation needs.
(3) The specific audiences for an evaluation and their evaluation needs have to be clearly identified at the early stages of planning an evaluation.

Differences in evaluation needs might be reflected in many ways: by the kind of information to be collected, the level of data analysis to be used, or the form of reporting the evaluation results. Sometimes it is impossible to serve all identified evaluation needs, and a decision has to be made regarding the specific evaluation needs to which the evaluation will respond.

7. *What steps and procedures are involved in doing an evaluation?* The process of doing an evaluation might differ according to the theoretical perception guiding the evaluation. A theoretical approach perceiving evaluation as an activity intended to determine whether goals have been achieved (Tyler, 1950) might recommend the following evaluation process:

(1) Stating goals in behavioral terms
(2) Developing measurement instruments
(3) Collecting data
(4) Interpreting findings
(5) Making recommendations

Another approach, perceiving evaluation as providing information for decision making (Stufflebeam, et al., 1971) might use an evaluation process including:

(1) Identification of information needs of decision makers
(2) Collection of relevant information
(3) Providing evaluative information to decision makers

Or, an evaluation aiming to build staff awareness, commitment and knowledge might proceed through many cycles of:

(1) Identifying problem areas
(2) Defining staff expectations and value positions
(3) Collecting performance information
(4) Providing discrepancy reports to staff and helping resolve conflicts

While there seems to be no agreement among evaluation experts regarding the "best" process to follow when conducting an evaluation, most of them would agree that all evaluations should include a certain amount of interaction between evaluators and their audiences at the outset of the evaluation, to identify evaluation needs, and at its conclusion, to communicate its findings. *Evaluation cannot be limited to the technical activities of data collection and analysis.*

8. What methods of inquiry should be used in evaluation? While challenging the usefulness of various research methods for evaluation studies (Provus, 1971, Stufflebeam, et al., 1971), recent years have also introduced a variety of methods of inquiry into the field of evaluation. In addition to traditional experimental and quasi-experimental designs (Campbell and Stanley, 1963) naturalistic methods (Guba and Lincoln, 1981; Patton, 1980), jury trials (Wolf, 1975), system analysis, and many others became legitimate methods for the conduct of evaluation. Some methodologists still advocate the superiority of certain methods, but overall there seems to be more support among evaluators for a more eclectic approach to evaluation methodology. Such an approach seeks to find the best method or set of methods for meeting a particular evaluation purpose, rather than assume that one method is best for all purposes.

9. Who should do evaluation? Becoming a professional group, evaluators devoted a lot of attention to identifying the characteristics of "good" evaluators and appropriate ways to train them. To be a competent and trustworthy evaluator one needs to have a combination of a wide variety of characteristics. These include: technical competence in the area of measurement and research methods, understanding of the social context and the substance of the evaluation object, human relations skills, personal integrity, and objectivity as well as characteristics related to organizational authority and responsibility. Since it is difficult to find one person possessing all those qualifications, it often becomes necessary to conduct an evaluation by a team, or choose the person with the most appropriate characteristics for a specific evaluation task.

The evaluation literature suggests two important distinctions that should be taken into account when deciding who should do an evaluation. The first is the distinction between an *internal evaluator* and an *external evaluator*. An internal evaluator of a project is usually one who is employed by the project and reports directly to its management. Obviously, the internal evaluator's objectivity as well as external credibility might be different from those of an external evaluator who is not directly employed by the project and/or enjoys a higher degree of independence.

The second distinction is between a *professional evaluator* and an *amateur evaluator*. This distinction, suggested by Scriven (1967), refers to two different foci of training and expertise rather than to a value judgment regarding the quality of an evaluator. An amateur evaluator is usually one whose major professional training is not in evaluation and whose involvement in evaluation represents only part of the job description. A professional evaluator is one with extensive training in evaluation and whose major (or even only) responsibility is the conducting of evaluation. While the amateur evaluator's technical evaluation skills might be less than those of a professional evaluator, the amateur might have a better understanding of the project's unique evaluation needs and be able to develop better rapport with the members of the evaluated project.

These two distinctions are independent; there may be an internal-amateur evaluator, an external-amateur, an internal-professional evaluator, etc.

10. By what standards should evaluation be judged? Several attempts have been made during the recent years to develop standards for evaluation of educational activities. Boruch and Cordray (1980) analyzed six sets of such standards and reached the conclusion that there has been a a large degree of overlap and similarity among them. The most elaborate and comprehensive set of standards and the one based on the largest amount of consensus is probably the set developed and published by the Joint Committee on Standards for Educational Evaluation (Joint Committee, 1981). These standards have been developed by a committee of seventeen members, chaired by Dr. Daniel Stufflebeam, which represented twelve professional organizations associated with educational evaluation. Thirty standards divided into four major groups have been suggested by the committee: *utility* standards (to ensure that evaluation serves practical information needs); *feasibility* standards (to ensure that evaluation be realistic and prudent); *propriety* standards (to ensure that evaluation be conducted legally and ethically); and *accuracy* standards (to ensure that evaluation reveal and convey technically adequate information). Table 1 lists the 30 standards.

No single evaluation is expected to meet all of the standards, and the degree of agreement among evaluators regarding the relative importance of the various standards is still to be determined. However, the comprehensive set of standards and the rationale on which they have been developed provide an invaluable source for major issues ato be considered in developing an evaluation and assessing its quality.

Lee J. Cronbach (1980) raises the consideration that standards related to the conduct of the evaluation may not be as important as those related to its consequences. This viewpoint suggests that the "best" evaluation is that which has a positive effect on program improvement.

Table 1 Thirty Standards for Evaluation

A. *Utility Standards*
1. Audience identification
2. Evaluator credibility
3. Information scope and selection
4. Valuational interpretation
5. Report clarity
6. Report dissemination
7. Report timeliness
8. Evaluation impact

B. *Feasibility Standards*
1. Practical procedures
2. Political viability
3. Cost effectiveness

C. *Propriety Standards*
1. Formal obligation
2. Conflict of interest
3. Full and frank disclosure
4. Public's right to know
5. Rights of human subjects
6. Human interaction
7. Balanced reporting
8. Fiscal responsibility

D. *Accuracy Standards*
1. Object identification
2. Context analysis
3. Described purposes and procedures
4. Defensible information sources
5. Valid measurement
6. Reliable measurement
7. Systematic data control
8. Analysis of quantitative information
9. Analysis of qualitative information
10. Justified conclusions
11. Objective reporting

THE PERCEPTION OF EVALUATION YOU FIND IN THESE MATERIALS

This introductory chapter has intended to help you think about evaluation and understand more about what others—and *you*—mean by evaluation. It has presented several different views and definitions that demonstrate a fairly broad range of expressed and potential opinion. But, this doesn't mean we don't have a more unified approach to evaluation to which we subscribe. This perception is a combination of our interpretations of several conceptualizations of evaluation and our experience in helping others conduct evaluations of training and development programs. We do not consider our perception as being the "right" perception of evaluation or even the best possible one. However, *we* find it logically sound and very useful.

In general, we believe that evaluation should be part and parcel of any training or professional preparation effort. You can't do training well without doing some evaluation of needs and goals, designs, implementation activities, and immediate and longer term effects of training. We see evaluation as functional. It is done for a reason, and that reason is to serve training efforts. Above all else, evaluation should be useful, and it should be used to make better decisions about key aspects of training programs. Here, then, is how we would respond to the ten questions in light of these materials.

1. How is evaluation defined? Evaluation is systematic investigation of various aspects of professional development and training programs to assess their merit or worth.

2. What is evaluation for? Evaluation should serve the development, implementation and recycling needs of training programs. It should be used for one or more purposes; to improve a particular program (formative); for accountability or selection (summative); to motivate, increase knowledge and gain support of staff and others (psychological).

3. What are the objects of evaluation? While we think most any entity can be an evaluation object, in these materials, the objects and training programs and/or their component parts.

4. What aspects and dimensions of an object should evaluation investigate? To best serve training programs, evaluation should focus on goals and needs, training designs, implementation and transactions, and effects of training.

5. What criteria should be used to judge an object? The following criteria should be considered when evaluating training efforts: (a) a responsiveness to needs, ideals and values; (b) optimal use of available resources and opportunities, (c) adherence to effective training practices, and (d) achievement of intended and other (important!) objectives and goals. Multiple criteria should most often be used.

6. Who should be served by an evaluation? Evaluation should serve the information needs of actual and potential stakeholders in the evaluation object. Evaluation should carefully identify these stakeholders and determine their needs and interests.

7. What steps and procedures are invovled in doing an evaluation? Evaluation must include decisions and action in regard to seven (7) functions: (1) focusing the evaluation; (2) designing the evaluation; (3) collecting information; (4) analyzing information; (5) reporting information from and about the evaluation; (6) managing the evaluation; and (7) evaluating the evaluation. They are not necessarily pursued in the order shown, and one often recycles among them. The *Sourcebook* is devoted to guidelines and options for doing these seven functions.

8. What methods of inquiry should be used in evaluation? We think an eclectic approach is best. Evaluation should use inquiry methods from the behavioral sciences and related fields as they are appropriate to a particular setting and evaluating purpose. At the present state of art an a priori preference for any specific method of inquiry is not warranted.

9. Who should do evaluation? Evaluation should be conducted by individuals or teams possessing: (a) extensive competencies in research methodology and data analysis techniques; (b) understanding of the social context and the unique substance of the evaluation object; (c) the ability to maintain correct human relations and develop rapport with individuals and groups involved in the evaluation; and (d) a conceptual framework to integrate all the abovementioned capabilities.

10. By what standards should evaluation be judged? Evaluation should strike for an optimal balance in meeting standards of: (a) utility (to be useful and practical); (b) accuracy (to be technically adequate); (c) feasibility (to be realistic and prudent); and (d) propriety (to be conducted legally and ethically). An evaluation not worth doing is not worth doing well.

REFERENCES

Alkin, M.C. "Evaluation Theory Development." Evaluation Comment 2, 1969: 2-7.

Alkin, M.C. quoted in *Educational Research & Development Report*, Volume 3, Number 1, Winter 1980, pp. 8-12.

Boruch, F.R. and Cordray, D.S. *An Appraisal of Educational Program Evaluations: Federal, State and Local Agencies.* Evanston, IL: Northwestern University, 1980.

Brinkerhoff, R.O. Evaluation of Inservice Programs. *Teacher Education and Special Education.* Vol. III, No. 3, Summer, 1980. pp. 27-38.

Campbell, D.T. and Stanley, J.C. "Experimental and Quasi-Experimental Designs for Research of Teaching." In N.L. Gage (Ed.), *Handbook of Research on Teaching.* Chicago: Rand McNally, 1963.

Cronbach, L.J. "Course Improvement through Evaluation." *Teachers College Record* 64, May 1963: 672-683.

Cronbach, L.J., Ambron, S.R., Dornbusch, S.M., Hess, R.D., Hornik, R.C., Phillips, D.C., Walker, D.E., and Weiner, S.S. *Toward Reform of Program Evaluation.* San Francisco: Jossey-Bass, 1980.

Dornbusch, S.M. and Scott, W.R. *Evaluation and the Exercise of Authority.* San Francisco: Jossey-Bass, 1975.

Glass, G.V. *The Growth of Evaluation Methodology.* Research paper no. 27. Boulder, CO: Laboratory of Educational Research, University of Colorado, 1969 (mimeo).

Guba, E.G. and Lincoln, Y.S. *Effective Evaluation.* San Francisco: Jossey-Bass, 1981.

Joint Committee on Standards fo Educational Evaluation, *Standards for Evaluations of Educational Programs, Projects and Materials.* New York: McGraw-Hill, 1981.

Nevo, D. "The Evaluation of a Multi-Dimensional Project." In A. Lewy *et al., Decision Oriented Evaluation in Education: The Case of Israel.* Philadelphia: International Science Services, 1981.

Patton, M.Q. Qualitative Evaluation Methods. Beverly Hills, CA: Sage Publications, 1980.

Provus, M.M. *Discrepancy Evaluation.* Berkeley, CA: McCutchan, 1971.

Scriven, M. "The Methodology of Evaluation" in R.E. Stake (Ed.), *Curriculum Evaluation*, AERA Monograph Series on Evaluation, No. 1. Chicago: Rand McNally, 1967.

Stufflebeam, D.L., Foley, W.J., Gephart, W.J., Guba, E.G., Hammond, R.L., Merriman, H.O., and Provus, M.M. *Educational Evaluation and Decision-Making.* Itasca, IL: Peacock, 1971.

Stufflebeam, D.L. *Meta-Evaluation.* Occasional Paper Series, The Evaluation Center, Western Michigan University, December 1974.

Tyler, R.W. *Basic Principles of Curriculum and Instruction.* Chicago, IL: University of Chicago Press, 1950.

Wolf, R.L. "The Use of Judicial Evaluation Methods in the Formation of Educational Policy." *Educational Evaluation and Policy Analysis*, 1, 1979: 19-28.

Worthen, B.R. and Sanders, J.R. *Educational Evaluation: Theory and Practice.* Belmont, CA: Wadsworth Publishing Co., 1973.

INFLUENCES ON SPECIAL EDUCATION EVALUATION

Bruce Balow and *Robert Brinkerhoff*

The history of special education in the United States is much like that of many of its clients: an outsider attempting to move into the mainstream. Education of handicapped children has had to prove its value time and again, to the children it teaches, and more difficult, to the larger educational system, and more difficult yet, to society.

Much of what makes special education special in some measure influences the nature and purpose of the evaluation programs relating to the handicapped. Special education is more often oriented to basic life skills than is education for others: its procedures are highly individualized and resource intensive, and more recently, highly data based. Handicapped education can move painfully slowly, and since results are sometimes marginal at best, special education is emotionally costly and frustrating. The influences these and other characteristics of special education have on evaluation go beyond evaluation of direct intervention programs. These influences extend in an unbroken line to activities and programs that prepare professionals who provide educational services.

In this brief chapter, we explore the specialness of special education, and show how evaluation of programs that prepare personnel who may work with the handicapped should attend to special needs. First, the history of special education is briefly reviewed; then, we move to consider consequences for evaluation.

HISTORY

It can be argued that the history of education is the history of society. That is, it is part and parcel of the culture, occasionally influencing but more often being influenced by larger events in society. The placement, care, and education of handicapped children is reflected in and by those larger events.

In the late 1800's an agrarian nation found productive uses for the mentally handicapped without taking particular note of them as deviant, disabled or different. Severely handicapped persons were placed in residential schools that were categorical in nature and limited in availability, and there was little optimism about curing handicaps.

Through the early 1900's institutions increased in size and in number, segregation of the handicapped increased in popularity, and the protection of society came on strongly as social policy. By 1926, 29 states had sterilization laws covering the mentally retarded, the mentally ill, and epileptics.

Perhaps 25% of the population graduated from high school in the period around the 1920's, and while there continued to be a few noteworthy programs of special classes in public schools, handicapped children and others who were poor achievers in the schools were not well accommodated. The vast majority of the population attained no more than a grade school education, and many of the handicapped were simply excluded from school.

The great depression and World War II kept the United States preoccupied for fifteen years, and there is little evidence of particular progress in the education; of handicapped children during those years. However, the 1940's and that war established a launching pad in this country for the greatest and longest sustained economic boom in history. It entirely changed the outlook and the educational status of most of our people. People learned other ways of thinking, other life styles, other ideas; in short, we became better educated. And following that war, millions of young people, who had never previously considered vistas beyond high school graduation and employment in their home town, went on to post-high-school education and personal-social and geographic mobility with opportunity and unprecedented prosperity.

Concurrently, there was an enormous expansion of special education programs in the public schools, for the most part following a "special class" model. But many handicapped children, especially those most severely handicapped, continued to be excluded from school. With society in general becoming more open, more sophisticated, more involved in the political process, and more increased belief in the power of education, parents of handicapped children and their allies began to press effectively for legislation mandating the inclusion of handicapped children in public schools.

A strong belief in the power of education to lead to individual and group prosperity and to solve the social welfare ills of the nation increased through the 1950's and the 1960's. In the 1960's, in a period of enormous prosperity, the United States government under President Johnson turned markedly toward attempts to improve social welfare through education. Mr. Johnson obtained from the Congress more federal appropriations for education than had been true in the previous 100 years together. Similarly, for children's welfare and public health activities, he obtained record increases and expenditures. The Civil Rights Movement was strong and moving rapidly at that time, the youth movement was strong and gaining strength, and the contemporary movement for equal rights for women was in its early beginnings. Improvements in circumstances for the handicapped were beginning to come as well, but only in small amounts with limited visibility. However, local school board decisions, local community decisions, and state and federal legislation began to include handicapped, and colleges and universities responded with increased attention to teacher education for handicapped children. From a very few training programs attending to the needs of teachers of handicapped in the 1940's, there were 40 personnel preparation programs by the 1950's and 400 such programs by the 1970's. Many of the teacher education programs were a direct result of specific federal financing aid for preparation of teachers of handicapped children.

By 1965 the United States had enjoyed for some years an economic paradise believed by many at that time to be essentially permanent. There was steady growth, low unemployment, and a low rate of inflation. The president had set a principal goal of abolishing poverty and, at the same time, many people believed that American free enterprise and American democracy would be able to do so, not only in this country, but around the world. We are now a nation of urban sophisticates, yet naive enought to hold such a belief. That belief disintegrated in the late 1970's.

The 1970's was a decade of litigation and legislation. Integration of handicapped children in regular public schools and in regular classes to the extent possible, zero rejection, thus including the serverely handicapped in the public schools, the development of due process procedures, IEP's, a range of service provisions for handicapped children, nondiscriminatory assessment, parental participation in decision processes and similar requirements of the schools all came about as a result of federal and state legislation and numerous actions in state and federal courts. The society was receptive, parents led, and professionals began to fulfill on the expectations promulgated.

The 1970's may well have been the watershed of widely shared economic prosperity in the United States and, with that economic change, a similar parallel watershed in the provision of free, appropriate public education to the handicapped. While much of the evidence to support or deny such a concern will likely become clear in the immediate future, the early portents are troublesome.

An apparent change of social values in the 1980's, reflected by political decisions, which have the effect of reducing requirements for inclusion of handicapped persons in the mainstream of society and which tend to reduce their claim on educational resources, are more than a cause for concern. They are that, to be sure, but they are also a reason for increased attention to the collection and distribution of evidence that the education of handicapped children is neither charity nor a holding tank, but an investment with remarkable payoff in social and economic value.

There is a strong expectation that the education of handicapped children must constantly prove itself in order to be accepted as a normal part of schooling and society. This is due to several factors: (1) special education curriculum is sometimes different and more labor intensive; (2) regular education colleges are often skeptical; (3) special education requires a lengthy political process to obtain significant amounts of money over and beyond what is required for educating pupils who are not handicapped; and (4) special educators' own expectations for children's growth and progress is limited.

Limited resources may be provided on the basis of charity, but substantial resources come about only on the basis of investment. In a growing, expanding and prosperous economy there is far greater willingness to expend resources on problematic or "unproven" areas of social welfare but, in a contracting economy and inward turning culture, the danger is that without extraordinarily strong evidence as to the effectiveness of activities for marginal contributors, the decision makers will cut back on those resources and those commitments. The early portents from the current political leadership in this country show a very strong move in the direction of financial retrenchment for expenditures to educate the handicapped and show also a considerable willingness to reduce the regulatory requirements for inclusion and education of such persons.

Possibly more important even than that area of concern, is that the long history of involvement of parents and others in the development and financing of programs for handicapped children has rightly led to strongly held expectations about the use of resources allocated to such programs, the progress of children included in those programs and the overall effectiveness of the program. Those expectations, together with our own enlightened self-interest, strongly call for information routinely obtained through evaluation procedures.

The outcomes and expectations for handicapped children have often been less global, more specific, more narrowly task oriented and detailed than is true for nonhandicapped children. When expectations are relatively limited, it is important to note small changes, often difficult to observe, in order to understand whether progress is occurring.

The audiences interested in the education of handicapped children are oftentimes more actively concerned than are the audiences concerned with the education of nonhandicapped. Parents and handicapped persons have had to work quite hard to obtain special programs and therefore they maintain a strong interest and concern for what occurs in those programs. Legislators oftentimes take an active interest in handicapped children because they frequently allocate special sums of money for the purpose. Accountability demands in special education tend to be high, not only for those reasons, but because not all allied professionals are convinced, a priori, that specific programs for handicapped children are likely to be successful.

Special education is more similar to regular education than it is different. Nonetheless, differences are significant and by their nature often call for information about resource allocation, program procedures, and results. Because handicapped children frequently make very slow progress, teachers and other direct service persons need data to help them make daily decisions. Because the content of special education programs is often the skills learned by normal children in the normal course of growing up, decision makers need evidence demonstrating that those life functions are effectively taught.

EVALUATION OF PREPARATION PROGRAMS FOR TEACHERS OF THE HANDICAPPED

It can be argued that it is no more necessary to evaluate programs for teachers of handicapped children than for any other aspect of teacher education. If professional competence were the only criterion, that would be true, but educating handicapped children is more difficult, costly, and controversial than general education—and the audiences, our critics, are more active, better informed, and more watchful. Among these critics are the financing agencies that, on occasion, give off signals that they regard special education as outside of the normal responsibility of the public educational system. Clearly, it is in the best interest of teacher-educators engaged in preparation of special education personnel to analyze program designs, identify program deficiencies, establish accountability information, measure the competence of program graduates, and estimate cost-benefit results of our programs.

Professional competence is, of itself, sufficient reason for careful, detailed evaluation of professional preparation programs in special education. While it can be argued (though questionably) that teachers of normal children do not particularly need to be highly skilled because the children will learn in any event, surely no one would argue that case with respect to handicapped children. If handicapped children are to learn effectively or as effectively as they are capable of learning, the teacher is responsible for a degree of skill in managing the learning process. That skill will only come about if the teacher preparation program is comprehensive and highly effective. Those outcomes in turn will only be true if the program staff knows the effect of program components on student attitude, knowledge, and skill. The idea that knowledge is power is as true in teacher education as it is anywhere else. A key source for this knowledge is evaluation of our teacher education programs.

No one in or near public education today is unaware of recent litigation in which the school's provision of education and services to children has been legally challenged. A prevailing interpretation of laws has been that the school may not be legally accountable for the outcomes of education, but that it certainly is responsible to assure that persons providing services (e.g., teachers, clinicians) are qualified to do so. This has sometimes resulted in court-ordered inservice training. While this legal aspect is probably not a wholly sufficient reason for evaluating personnel training, evaluation of personnel training seems a prerequisite to a defensible argument that the staff is qualified; this would apply to the evaluation of preservice as well as inservice education of personnel.

The current state-of-the-art of evaluation is not sufficiently well developed that one can present much in the way of a ironclad case that recipients of professional training are, in fact, competent. But, one can certainly present data about what and how much training has been delivered and received, logical and empirical rationale for training content, and data about training effects (e.g., knowledge acquired) and perceptions of trainees as to skills practiced and mastered. In short, one can construct a dramatically more defensible argument for professional competence with, rather than without, training evaluation information.

EVALUATION AND STAFF DEVELOPMENT

Finally, the special nature of special education requires evaluation as part and parcel of preservice and inservice education efforts. In fact, when evaluation comes full circle and provides information about effects and outcomes of teaching or clinical intervention, evaluation *is* professional development.

Special education is, like all other kinds of education, an imperfect art. While there is much we know about teaching and learning, there remains much we do not know. And, what we do is always less than we know. Practice inevitably lags behind knowledge, because knowledge dissemination is incomplete and because the facts of our daily work-life are such that we hurry, are harried, forget, and act impulsively more often than we like. We know more about how to swim with grace and power and certainly want to, but keeping our heads about water is a demanding concern and can take nearly all our time.

When evaluation becomes a more regular and systematic part of educational endeavors, knowledge becomes greater. We learn more about the effects we have and are better able to change, to try, and then to improve what gets done. When such information is regularly provided to program staff, practice almost inevitably improves as a sort of biofeedback process. And as staff are provided with more information about results—particularly in a field like special education where results are slow and hard to come by—work becomes more satisfying.

Good professional development does not just transfer professional knowledge from sellers to buyers, it creates professional knowledge and competence from everyday professional experience. Evaluation is a necessary ingredient in this process.

The Sourcebook

READER'S GUIDE TO THE SOURCEBOOK

The Sourcebook that follows divides evaluation into seven functional areas:

1. Focusing the Evaluation
2. Designing the Evaluation
3. Collecting Information
4. Analyzing & Interpreting Information
5. Reporting Information
6. Managing Evaluation
7. Evaluating Evaluation

Within these seven major functions, the Sourcebook identifies 35 critical questions and tasks.

The Sourcebook is intended to be a supplement to the Casebook and the Design Manual. It focuses on decisions evaluators commonly need to make and provides options and procedural suggestions to guide evaluation performance. References are included so that you can study any topic in further detail.

To use the Sourcebook, turn to the *Contents Grid* that follows. This grid summarizes the major functions, critical questions, and evaluation tasks discussed in the Sourcebook. Page numbers are provided to locate the discussion within the Sourcebook. An abbreviated guide precedes each functional area in the Sourcebook. It summarizes critical questions found in the section and topics discussed within them.

Each question addressed in the Sourcebook proposes some options for the evaluator in dealing with a question or issue, provides alternative procedures available to accomplish the evaluation tasks related to the issue, and finally, provides guidelines and criteria that help the evaluator determine whether the job has been done adequately.

A number of tables and figures have been included to efficiently summarize information, examples have been provided, and each major functional area concludes with a reference section.

Function	Key Issues	Tasks	Page Numbers
Focusing the Evaluation	1. What will be evaluated?	1. Investigate what is to be evaluated	7-15
	2. What is the purpose for evaluating?	2. Identify and justify purpose(s)	16-19
	3. Who will be affected by or involved in the evaluation?	3. Identify audiences	20-22
	4. What elements in the setting are likely to influence the evaluation?	4. Study setting	23-26
	5. What are the crucial evaluation questions?	5. Identify major questions	27-30
	6. Does the evaluation have the potential for successful implementation?	6. Decide whether to go on with evaluation	31-36
Designing Evaluation	1. What are some alternative ways to design an evaluation?	1. Determine the amount of planning, general purpose, and degree of control	37-42
	2. What does a design include?	2. Overview evaluation decisions, tasks, and products	43-58
	3. How do you go about constructing a design?	3. Determine general procedures for the evaluation	59-63
	4. How do you recognize a good design?	4. Assess the quality of the design	64-71

Function	Key Issues	Tasks	Page Numbers
Collecting Information	1. What kinds of information should you collect?	1. Determine the information sources you will use	77-83
	2. What procedures should you use to collect needed information?	2. Decide how you'll collect information	84-88
	3. How much information should you collect?	3. Decide whether you need to sample and, if so, how	89-94
	4. Will you select or develop instruments?	4. Determine how precise your information must be and design a means to collect it	95-99
	5. How do you establish reliable and valid instrumentation?	5. Establish procedures to maximize validity and reliability	100-107
	6. How do you plan the information collection effort to get the most information at the lowest cost?	6. Plan the logistics for an economical information collection procedure	108-115
Analyzing and Interpreting (Evaluation)	1. How will you handle returned data?	1. Aggregate and code data if necessary	119-122
	2. Are data worth analyzing?	2. Verify completeness and quality of raw data	123-126
	3. How will you analyze the information?	3. Select & run defensible analyses	127-144
	4. How will you interpret the results of analyses?	4. Interpret the data using prespecified and alternative sets of criteria	145-147
Reporting	1. Who should get an evaluation report?	1. Identify who you will report to	151-153
	2. What content should be included in a report?	2. Outline the content to be included	154-158

Function	Key Issues	Tasks	Page Numbers
	3. How will reports be delivered?	3. Decide whether reports will be written, oral, etc.	159-164
	4. What is the appropriate style and structure for the report?	4. Select a format for the report	165-167
	5. How can you help audiences interpret and use reports?	5. Plan post-report discussions, consultation, follow-up activities	168-169
	6. When should reports be scheduled?	6. Map out the report schedule	170-173
Managing	1. Who should run the evaluation?	1. Select, hire, and/ or train the evaluator	176-180
	2. How should evaluation responsibilities be formalized?	2. Draw up a contract or letter of agreement	181-186
	3. How much should the evaluation cost?	3. Draft the budget	187-190
	4. How should evaluation tasks be organized and scheduled?	4. Draft a time/task strategy	191-196
	5. What kinds of problems can be expected?	5. Monitor the evaluation and anticipate problems	197-200
Evaluating Evaluation (Meta-evaluation)	1. What are some good uses of meta-evaluation?	1. Determine whether you need to meta evaluate; if so, when	205-207
	2. Who should do the meta evaluation?	2. Select a meta evaluator	208-209
	3. What criteria or standard should you use to evaluate the evaluation?	3. Select or negotiate standards	210-217
	4. How do you apply a set of meta-evaluation criteria?	4. Rank order standards, determine compliance	218-220

Focusing the Evaluation

Focusing evaluation is the progressive specification of what and how you are going to evaluate. Like focusing a camera, focusing an evaluation demands that a number of variables be considered simultaneously. This section provides information about which variables to consider in order to focus your evaluation. Generally, these variables include: the "object" being evaluated (what your camera will be focused upon); the purpose for evaluating; the people who should be considered; the background or setting and its effect on the evaluation; and the important questions the evaluation must answer to serve its purpose.

Remember that focusing involves progressive attempts; expect initial drafts and discussions to be general—even vague. And, as sequential plans become more and more detailed, continue to ask whether the evaluation is still worth the effort and cost. Not every evaluation that is contemplated should be undertaken.

WHEN FOCUSING DECISIONS GET MADE

Focusing marks the beginning of the evaluation process and design. The decisions outlined in this chapter must be reviewed regularly to accommodate changes in the object being evaluated, its setting, and the people involved. You need to consider these decisions for any kind of evaluation, whether it's to meet an external funding requirement, to improve a program, or for some other purpose.

WHAT WILL BE EVALUATED?

The object of an evaluation is whatever you are investigating—it can be a program, a project, a three-day inservice, materials, or even another evaluation. In short, anything can be the "object" of an evaluation. In this book, the objects of evaluation are related to training and include curriculum programs, inservice workshops, and demonstration projects.

The task of identifying and describing the object to be evaluated seems simple and straightforward; it is often neither. In fact it is one of the most difficult and important evaluation responsibilities you will face. This is true for two reasons: (1) the object (e.g., a program) is not static—it grows, is affected by external and internal events, and, in short, constantly changes; and (2) the object looks different depending upon perspective (e.g., an administrator would see a program in one way, a client in another). It is necessary to describe and get agreement about what is being evaluated in order to design an evaluation. And if there is little agreement about what an object is or does, it might be premature to evaluate unless the purpose of the evaluation is to better describe and understand the object.

SOME KINDS OF TRAINING OBJECTS THAT CAN BE EVALUATED	· course · workshop · workshop series · curriculum · management system · trainer selection · certification system · self-instructional materials · logistic system · degree program · service provision · texts, materials · information management system · needs assessment process · consultant services · proposal solicitation and funding process · staff retreat · staff development program · seminar · filing and record keeping system · evaluations of training · training clearinghouse functions · conferences · meetings · symposia

FEATURES TO INCLUDE IN DESCRIBING AN OBJECT OF EVALUATION	WHO	Actors	Who's involved? Who are the key decision makers and leaders, the funders, the personnel implementing the program and being served by the program; who are the advocates and adversaries, interested luminaries?
	WHY	Goals	What goals and objectives are intended, or appear to be pursued? Are there conflicting goals? What needs are being addressed?
	WHAT	Components	Is there a model or description of the object; how many separate components are included and do they interact?
		Activities	What kinds of activities are included; what services are being provided; how many maintenance or internal administrative services are provided?

	Resources	What are the available benefits and opportunities? Consider budget, manpower, facilities, use of volunteer time, expert review or guidance, use of materials, machinery, communication systems, personnel, etc.
	Problems	Generally, what appears to be the biggest constraint in the eyes of key stakeholders (dept. chair, faculty, students, dean)? Would you concur?
WHEN	Timeline	How long has the object been around? What does its history look like, and what kind of future is it anticipating? How long does it have to accomplish short and long range goals?
WHERE	Setting	What in the setting influences the object? Where does it fit into the larger organization, the political network? What and who can it be influenced by?

WHERE TO GO TO FIND OUT ABOUT AN OBJECT

TO DOCUMENTS

Letters of commendation or criticism
Presentations by staff
Attitude surveys
Existing performance data
Staffing profile
Materials produced (pamphlets, syllabi, guidelines, manuals)
Request for Proposal (RFP)
Proposal
Audit reports
Mission/goals statement
Budget
Organizational chart
Management plan
Reports
Communications between project and funding agency
Job descriptions
Minutes of advisory or management groups
Evaluations (accrediting reports)
Public relations releases
Media coverage

TO RELEVANT AUDIENCES

Sponsors

Policy Makers

Staff

Clients

Professional

Taxpayers
Funding agents
Federal agents
State education departments
Accrediting groups
Central administrations
University cabinets
Boards of education
Program planners
Present and past staff
Students
Parents
General public
Community agencies
Professional associations
Professional journals
Other educational agencies

WAYS TO DESCRIBE OBJECTS   One or more of the following strategies can be used to describe what you are evaluating.

STRATEGY   Pert charts

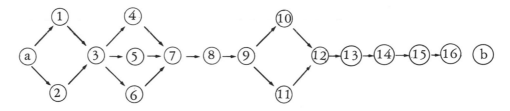

Activity or Procedure	Subgoal or Event
1. Search literature for attitude scales	a. Start scale development
2. Review attitude scaling procedures	1. Complete search
3. Select procedure to be used	2. Complete review
4. Construct scale items	3. Complete selection
5. Assemble prototype scale	4. Complete item construction
6. Arrange field test of prototype scale	5. Complete scale assembly
	6. Complete arrangements

WHAT IT TELLS YOU   program activities, sequencing of tasks

STRATEGY   Management Plan (And Budget)

Activity	Personnel Responsible	Person Days	October 1 2 3 4	November 1 2 3 4	December 1 2 3 4
OBJECTIVE 1: 1. Develop research questions	Schmidt Simon Trumper	14			
2. Determine data collection procedures (includes development of instrumentation) 3. Develop analysis plan	Simon Schmidt Feldt	15 7			

WHAT IT TELLS YOU   chain of responsibility, schedule, planned use of resources

STRATEGY   Existing Evaluation Approaches

Countenance by Robert Stake: Gathering a full range of descriptive and judgmental information about an object.

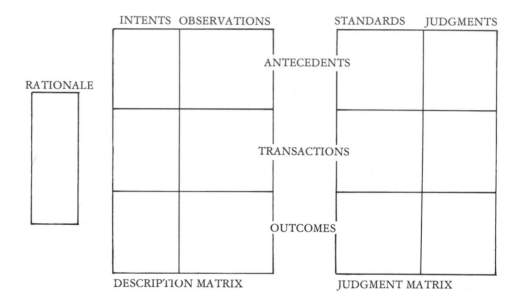

WHAT IT   When you use Countenance to describe an object, you might look at the
TELLS YOU   following:

· **rationale**–for the training program
· **antecedents**–conditions that exist prior to training (willingness, skill level, interest)
· **transactions**–the instructional/delivery process
· **outcomes**–consequences of training (e.g., knowledge, transfer, relearning)
· **judgments**–of training approach, of trainer, of materials
· **intents**–what trainers or educators intended the program to do
· **observations**–what observers perceive to be happening
· **standards**–what stakeholders expect
· **judgments**–how valuable the program is in the eyes of judges and other audiences

STRATEGY   *CIPP* by Daniel Stufflebeam: Describing the context, input, process, and products of a program

	CONTEXT EVALUATION	INPUT EVALUATION	PROCESS EVALUATION	PRODUCT EVALUATION
OBJECTIVE	To define the institutional context, to identify the target population and assess their needs, to identify opportunities for addressing the needs, to diagnose *problems* underlying the *needs* & to judge whether proposed objectives are sufficiently responsive to the assessed needs.	To identify & assess *system capabilities*, alternative program *strategies*, procedural designs for implementing the strategies, budgets, & schedules, programs.	To identify or predict, in process, *defects* in the procedural design or its implementation, to provide information for the preprogrammed decisions, and to record & judge procedural events & activities.	To collect descriptions & judgments of outcomes & to relate them to objectives & to context, input, & process information, & to interpret their worth & merit.
METHOD	By using such methods as system analysis, survey, document review, hearings, interviews, diagnostic tests, & the Delplir technique.	By inventorying & analyzing available human & material resources, solution strategies, & procedural designs for relevance, feasibility & economy. And by using such methods as literature search, visits to "misicle workers," advocate teams, & pilot trials.	By monitoring the activity's potential procedural barriers & remaining alert to unanticipated ones, by obtaining specified information for programmed decisions, by describing the actual process, & by continually interacting with & observing the activities of project staff.	By defining operationally & measuring outcomes criteria, by collecting judgments of outcomes from stakeholders, & by performing both qualitative & quantitative analyses.
RELATION TO DECISION-MAKING IN THE CHANGE PROCESS	For deciding upon the *setting* to be served, the *goals* associated with meeting needs or using opportunities, & the *objectives* associated with solving problems, i.e., for *planning* needed changes. And to provide a basis for judging outcomes.	For selecting *sources of support*, solution *strategies* & procedural *designs*, i.e., for *structuring* change activities. And to provide a basis for judging implementation.	For *implementing* and *refining the program design and procedure*, i.e., for effecting *process control*. And to provide a log of the actual process for later use in interpreting outcomes.	For deciding to *continue, terminate, modify, or refocus* a change activity, & present a clear record of effects (intended & unintended, positive & negative).

WHAT IT TELLS YOU   If using CIPP as an organizer to approach a training program, you might study the following.

· the context
· needs/opportunities
· problems underlying needs

· human and material resources
· alternative service strategies
· system capabilities
· barriers to service delivery
· delivery process
· programmed decisions
· program outcomes
· outcomes in light of objectives
· objectives in light of standards or comparisons
· outcomes in light of context, input, and process information

STRATEGY   *Program Goals or Objectives*

For example, here is a set of objectives for a training program.

TRAINING RECIPIENT CHANGE VARIABLE ANALYSIS FORM

Recipient	Immediate Objectives	Job/Usage Objectives	Ultimate Outcomes
Who will receive training?	What skills, knowledge or attitudes will be changed as a result of training?	What use will be made of the training on the job?	What person, product, or organizational change will eventually result?
Special Education Teachers	Awareness of problems and concerns of regular teachers in teaching handicapped students	Increased planning with regular teachers for implementing individual educational plans	Exceptional children receiving more appropriate educational experiences in the least restrictive environment
	Increased skills in the interpretation and utilization of strategies for individual planning	Improved implementation of individual educational plans	
Building Teams	Knowledge of: - Consultation process	Improved coordination of resources used within the schools	Exceptional children receiving more appropriate educational experiences in the least restrictive environment
	Skills in: - Problem solving and diagnostic procedures	Provision of building-level technical assistance and consultation upon request	

STRATEGY   Systems Analyses

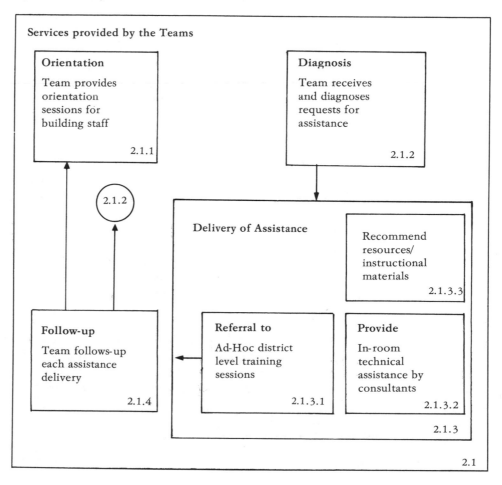

WHAT IT TELLS YOU   components of project, functional relationships among components, inter-relationships, key decision points

STRATEGY   Organizational Charts

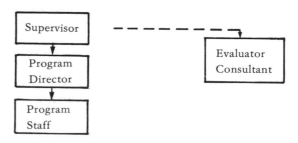

WHAT IT TELLS YOU   staff responsibilities, chain of command, unit and sub-unit organization

STRATEGY   ● *Personal Viewpoints, Observations, Histories*

Log 4/7/82
        9:15 a.m.

Today was the third and final day of training. W. was noticeably tired and it took almost an hour for the group to get started into their concluding activities.

3:30 p.m.

. . . as evaluation forms were being collected, a spontaneous conversation among trainees indicated a real sense of accomplishment (e.g., "my chairman won't believe I'm coming back with a set of specific training objectives and an evaluation plan"; and "I've never been to a more valuable workshop . . . in fifteen years this has been the best.") However, as the group leader officially began the evaluation discussion, trainees got side-tracked on their disappointment with the simulation exercise earlier. In particular, they didn't like the person walking them through the simulation. Unfortunately, W. did not hear the positive comments made earlier.

5:30 p.m.

. . . three trainees asked if they could purchase extra sets of the materials. Every set, including the extras on the supply table, were taken. A list was begun by one trainee and passed around; nine persons requested that the training be offered again within the next year.

WHAT IT TELLS YOU   perceptions of the object from experts, interested or experienced audiences, or objective observers

TIPS FOR MAINTAINING A GOOD DESCRIPTION OF THE OBJECT

Seek Multiple Viewpoints	Try to get multiple perspectives and descriptions of the object.
Use Independent Observers	Confirm what you are finding by an objective observer (one-day visit by an evaluation or content specialist).
Plan for Direct Observation	Directly observe the program or make use of other outside observers.
Listen for Repetition	Pay attention to issues brought up repeatedly across information sources and audiences.
Plan Ongoing Review	Keep a log to continue to note changes in the object throughout the evaluation.

EXAMPLE OF AN OBJECT DESCRIPTION   See "What Does a Design Include?" for the complete evaluation design of this workshop.

The object of the evaluation is a workshop developed and delivered by the ETC Project. It is a three-day workshop which gives participants intensive training in evaluation and time to work on their own evaluation designs. Participants are from professional development and teacher preparation programs in colleges and universities and local and state educational agencies. The Project received funding from the federal Office of Special Education to develop the materials used in the workshop, but must rely on registration fees to cover some delivery costs. The Project is based at a University Evaluation Center which is interested in insuring quality and coordinating the Project with its other activities.

How the Workshop Works

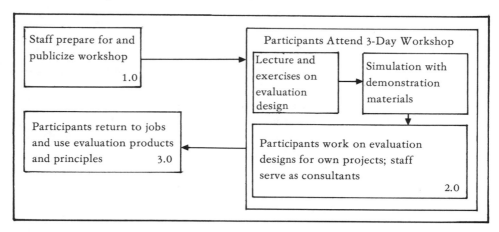

WORKSHOP AGENDA

Day One

9:00– 9:30	Introduction
9:30–10:30	Evaluation design exercise
10:30–12:00	Discussion: Review of Decision Areas from *Sourcebook*
12:00– 1:00	Lunch
1:00– 2:30	Participants read selected case
2:30– 3:30	Small group exercise: Participants analyze case using Decision Areas
3:30–4:30	Summary Review

Day Two

9:00– 9:30	Introduction to the Design Manual
9:30–12:00	Participants (each with own Design Manual) complete Products #1 and #2
12:00– 1:00	Lunch
1:00– 2:30	Exercise and lecture: Measurement Planning
2:30– 4:30	Participants complete Products #3 and #4

Day Three

9:00–10:00	Lecture and demonstration: Reporting
10:00–11:00	Participants complete Product #5
11:00–12:00	Panel discussion: Management
12:00– 1:00	Lunch
1:00– 3:30	Participants complete Products #6 and #7
3:30– 4:00	Wrap-up

WHAT IS THE PURPOSE FOR EVALUATING?

The general purpose for evaluating should be clear. To determine the most appropriate evaluator and evaluation strategy, it's important to know why the evaluation is taking place. Will the evaluation be used to find a problem, solve a problem, provide ongoing information, or judge the success of the program? Knowing the general reason for evaluating will help you determine the strategy for generating specific evaluation questions.

Deciding on the purpose for an evaluation is probably the single most important decision initially made about the evaluation. And while there is generally one overriding or central purpose to be served by evaluation, you will find that different audiences will have different reasons for wanting the same evaluation. Accordingly, audiences will intend to use the results differently.

Multiple purposes and hidden or conflicting agendas should be investigated and negotiated openly at the outset so that useful information can be provided to key stakeholders. You can promote this by doing some of the following:

· clearly define, document and disseminate the general purpose
· determine whether there are other purposes or objectives
· rank order purposes and objectives
· determine whether there are resources to meet multiple purposes and, if so, which ones will be met

GENERAL EVALUATION PURPOSES RELATED TO TRAINING PROGRAMS		Purposes for objects being planned, developed, or recently implemented	Purposes for objects that have been around through several rounds of revision
	Goals or needs	· to establish goals or needs · to evaluate the soundness of goals or validate needs · to rank goals or needs · to seek opportunities	· to determine whether goals and needs have been met · to evaluate the soundness of goals · to identify the goals and needs that guided the object · to seek unused opportunities
	Design	· to assess a system and its resources · to select a design · to clarify roles or resolve conflicts related to the design · to compare alternative designs · to locate problems that are keeping the design from working	· to determine the adequacy of the design that was used · to assess how well the design was developed and implemented · to compare the design to alternatives not used

GENERAL EVALUATION PURPOSES RELATED TO TRAINING PROGRAMS *(continued)*		Purposes for objects being planned, developed, or recently implemented	Purposes for objects that have been around through several rounds of revision
	Implementation and process	· to determine the adequacy of a given design . · to help staff implement the program · to help staff make incremental improvements · to identify strengths and opportunities · to diagnose problems · to assure that the design is operating as planned	· to determine whether program was run as planned and, if so, if it was worthwhile · to identify and describe problems that developed · to examine the relationship of what occurred to observed outcomes · to identify the effective or durable relationships involved in program delivery
	Products and Outcomes	· to determine immediate outcomes and initial effects · to determine what outcomes are appropriate to expect · to determine the quality of intermediate products · to monitor resources and impact	· to assess the quality of outcomes · to determine what outcomes were achieved · to determine whether intended outcomes were achieved · to determine cost effectiveness · to uncover side effects · to determine utility of the program
	Recycling	· to improve the object for future implementation · to determine how worthwhile it is · to determine whether it is what it intended to be · to determine whether it is worth the resources it will consume	· to determine whether it was worthwhile to consumers and other key audiences · to determine whether it did what it intended to do · to compare actual outcomes to needs · to determine whether it was worth the resources it consumed · to determine if the program is a viable competitor

CRITERIA FOR DEFENSIBLE PURPOSES

A defensible purpose is:

Clear   the purpose is understood by key audiences

Accessible   the evaluation purpose has been documented and disseminated to those who might be affected by the evaluation or have a right to know about it

CRITERIA FOR DEFENSIBLE PURPOSES *(continued)*

Useful	the commitment to use the evaluation information is real and the action to be taken anticipated
Relevant	the information need the evaluation is meeting has been identified and could serve the program
Humane	given the political and fiscal support, it is realistic to believe that evaluation can be successfully implemented without harming people involved or affected
Compatible	evaluation seems to be congruent with the principal goals of the program, its staff, the larger institutional setting, and the target audience
Worthwhile	the potential benefits of the evaluation justify its likely costs

---

COMMON PITFALLS THAT CAN UNDERMINE EVALUATION OF TRAINING

Not every evaluation conceived should be undertaken; and sometimes there is little reason to evaluate. For example:

· when the evaluation will be designed to justify a decision that has already been made
· when the evaluation information cannot be ready until after key decisions are made about the program
· when there is no clear explanation of how and by whom the evaluation information will be used
· when someone (or some group) is likely to be seriously and unjustifiably hurt through the evaluation process
· when information like that which is to be gathered already exists and is not being used
· when the normal growth process of a new program might be stifled by premature evaluation
· when control over writing and editing of the evaluation report cannot be established and nonindependence is likely
· when it is apparent that the evaluation will use resources (time, personnel, money) without providing commensurate help or benefits
· when the evaluation will alienate or polarize staff at a time when cohesion is imperative
· when it is likely that the evaluation information will not be technically accurate or credible to key audiences

---

EXAMPLE OF EVALUATION PURPOSES IN THE CASEBOOK

Evaluation Purposes and Uses	Case-example from Casebook
Assess needs, validate goals, prioritize goals, identify constraints and problems related to goals for training	Case L1 Case S2 Case S1
Assess alternative strategies, compare training designs, identify criteria to judge designs, determine feasibility and potential for success	Case C1 Case C4 Case S2 Case L2

EXAMPLE OF EVALUATION PURPOSES IN THE CASEBOOK
(continued)

Evaluation Purposes and Uses	Case-example from Casebook
Monitor and control program operation, identify problems and revision needs, determine whether objectives are achieved	Case C5 Case L3 Case S3 Case C2
Determine usage and application, identify emerging and continuing needs, determine benefits of training, identify problems and revision needs to enhance training usage.	Case C3 Case L4 Case S3

L = local school
C = college or university
S = state agency

WHO WILL BE AFFECTED BY OR INVOLVED IN THE EVALUATION?

Evaluation affects both the object and all those who have a stake in the object. Because this is true, multiple groups are going to be interested in the evaluation. It is important to identify these "stakeholders" in the evaluation as they will provide the basis for some of the evaluation questions generated later. Evaluators cannot meet relevant needs unless they know who will use the evaluation and how.

It's usually not possible to accommodate all the identified audiences for an evaluation. It soon becomes necessary to think about whose information needs can be reasonably accommodated. This makes it necessary to rank order audiences and their concerns. A measure of how adequately you have identified audiences is the degree to which the needs of key stakeholders are reflected in your design.

Don't be fooled into thinking that audience issues are completed after you have determined the initial evaluation questions. To keep an evaluation useful and relevant, evaluators return to audiences, literally and figuratively, throughout the life of an evaluation.

TYPES OF EVALUATION AUDIENCES TO CONSIDER

Persons sponsoring or commissioning the evaluation.
Persons who will make decisions based upon the results of the evaluation.
Persons in the target group from whom information is being gathered.
Persons involved in planning or creating the program being evaluated.
Persons involved in running the program or project (the object) being evaluated.
Persons interested in the evaluation object (advocates and critics).
Persons who have a right to the information (in evaluations funded with public dollars, this can include everyone. Especially it refers to legislators, taxpayers, parents, and stakeholders who should know about the evaluation because of their responsibility for the target group.)
Persons whose roles might be affected by evaluation results and decisions.

WAYS OF IDENTIFYING RELEVANT AUDIENCES

Conversations with key program staff to identify:

program advocates
program critics
influential decision makers

Conversations with those outside the program to identify:

support for the program (economical, political)
special interest groups
controversial issues and stakeholders

Observations of program activities to identify:

formal and informal leaders
personnel responsible for work
personnel with authority to make decisions

Analysis of documents that define audiences and describe their stake in the program:

organizational charts
budget allocations
program materials

WAYS OF RANK-ORDERING AUDIENCES

By Degree of Involvement

The more directly affected the audience is by the evaluation, the more defensible their request for information, and the more important their involvement.

By Commitment and Ability to Use

The greater the potential that there is a commitment and ability to use the information, the more defensible the request.

By Request of Key Decision Maker/Sponsor

The information requests of the audiences identified by sponsors and key decision makers are ranked high because of expected follow through.

Interest in the Evaluation

Information requests of interested audiences often should be met. The greater the interest, the greater the attempt to service information needs through the evaluation.

WAYS OF INVOLVING AUDIENCES THROUGHOUT EACH STAGE OF THE EVALUATION

Focusing Evaluation
· audiences help identify key stakeholders
· audiences' perspectives of object documented
· audiences generate questions
· audiences educated about evaluation process and use
· evaluation questions reviewed by key audiences

Designing Evaluation
· audience needs are responded to in the design and choice of evaluator
· audiences identified in the design are appropriate (e.g., to give information, collect information, interpret results)

Information Collection
· audiences' information requirements considered
· audiences' information requests rank ordered
· audiences' role in information collection negotiated and practical
· key audiences are used as information sources

Information Analysis
· audience issues are key to determining level and type of analysis
· analyses are shared with key audiences
· interpretations are made in light of multiple perspectives
· audiences are given the opportunity to discuss and react to findings

WAYS OF
INVOLVING
AUDIENCES
THROUGHOUT
EACH STAGE OF
THE EVALUATION
(continued)

Reporting Information

· dates for audience information needs are identified
· ongoing evaluation activities are shared with key audiences
· audiences suggest in advance information that would be of interest to them; areas for recommendations; and displays and graphs that would be useful
· reports are delivered to relevant audiences in time for their use
· follow-through activities are planned based upon audience needs (e.g., post-report discussions, press releases, training)

Managing Evaluation

· audiences are treated humanely and kept informed throughout
· interruptions of regular activities are kept to a minimum for key audiences

Meta-evaluation

· audiences interested in the evaluation of the evaluation are identified and the report is shared with them

WHAT ELEMENTS IN THE SETTING ARE LIKELY TO INFLUENCE THE EVALUATION?

It is important to pay attention to the general setting of an evaluation. Generally, you want to know if the setting is stable and conducive to evaluation. Especially, you want to find out if evaluation is likely to be sabotaged or if it will be expected to function in a non-supportive environment. Understanding and describing key elements in the setting promotes a realistic design and productive coexistence between evaluation and setting.

In addition to influencing the evaluation, the setting also influences the object you are evaluating. It will be important to find out how elements in the setting (e.g., politics, economics, social patterns) impact the object in order later to interpret the evaluation.

When the success or failure of a program is reported, one piece of crucial information is the degree to which events in the setting were responsible. Others who want to adapt and use the findings of the evaluation must determine the effect the setting had on overall results and then judge how similar or dissimilar that setting is to their own.

In a small-scale evaluation, the program director/evaluator might spend only a few hours thinking about influences in the setting and how to attend to them in the design. In larger-scale evaluations, the object being evaluated and its setting might be thoroughly investigated to decide whether the evaluation should be undertaken. There is both reason and time in any evaluation to investigate the setting well enough to prevent front-end problems in the design.

A practical and ethical concern is determining how evaluation will affect the setting. If the costs are too great, it is possible that the evaluation should be reconsidered, rescheduled, or relocated. If these are not options, then certainly the evaluation will have to be sensitively designed to respond to a hostile or unstable setting.

EVENTS TO LOOK FOR IN THE SETTING	INFLUENCES	EVALUATION IMPLICATIONS
	Organizational Politics	Is there political support for the evaluation? Are there opponents? How secure is the object within the organization?
	Program Leadership	Who has control over the program, formally and informally; what goals do they have for the program's future? How does the evaluation fit those goals?
	Professional Influences	How supportive are professional groups of the evaluation? Will you need to deal with union representatives? What will their agenda be?
	History	How mature and stable is the object to be evaluated? Has there been a tradition of self-appraisal and evaluation use? Is the object stable enough to withstand evaluation? What information already exists?

IMPLICATIONS OF SETTING FOR THE EVALUATION DESIGN *(continued)*	INFLUENCES	EVALUATION IMPLICATIONS
	Organizational Setting	Where does the program fit into the larger organizational network? Which decision makers can impact it? What kind of information could jeopardize the object?
	Economics	How secure is the fiscal support system for the program and the evaluation? Have funds been allocated? Will a written commitment of fiscal support be forthcoming?
	Communication and Social Patterns	How much disaffection (interpersonal conflict) is likely to result? Is the evaluation controversial to staff; are there apparent factions emerging as a result of its being discussed? What does the "normal" social pattern look like?
	Legal Guidelines	Are there legal restrictions (rights of human subjects) that will limit collection of desired information? Are there professional or institutional rulings that affect evaluation procedures? Will the object be affected by pending legislation?
	Resources	Will there be available resources to support the evaluation: e.g., skilled personnel, facilities, time, supportive climate, access to support services, access to personnel? Is there likely to be a change in resources that will affect the program?

WAYS OF INVESTIGATING THE SETTING	Conversations with key audiences	key authority figures formal/informal leaders program advocates program critics target audiences influential members persons responsible for target audience persons servicing target audience evaluation clients
	Conversations with specialists	legal consultants district/university lawyer legislators professional evaluator independent observer internal evaluator administative/political consultant union leader state department personnel dean
	Observations of the setting	social interactions climate or general atmosphere attitudes of specific personnel professional practices protocol followed efficiency and cooperation political camps existing resources facilities available and their quality support services provided budget allocations

Analysis of documents	management documents organization charts budgets funding guidelines programmatic materials proposal management plan materials used/produced historical data minutes of meetings media coverage memos and program communiques	
Interaction with existing groups	policy groups advisors client group management team staff group	

PROBES FOR INTERVIEWING KEY AUDIENCES	Probe about the object (e.g., program or project)	How well do you think things are going? Are most people supportive? Do you have the resources you need? Have things changed much over the past? (staff, goals, outcomes, support) What problems have you run into? How do you see the program's future?
	Probe about the evaluation	Do you think the evaluation will be useful? Who will use it? Will it cause problems? For whom? What do you think will be done with the results? What will happen to the program without the evaluation?

IMPLICATIONS OF SETTING FOR THE EVALUATION DESIGN	DESIGN DECISION	IMPLICATIONS OF THE SETTING
	Evaluator	Could an internal evaluator stay independent in this setting? Would an external evaluator be accepted or believed? Would a team be preferable?
	Information Collection	Is the setting conducive to close evaluator/audience interaction? Will it be possible to collect information to answer key evaluation questions? Is there more than one information source? What kinds of resources can be counted on?
	Information Sources	Are there influences in the setting that are likely to prevent access to information sources (people, documents, meetings, etc.)? What sources will be available? How much relevant information already exists?
	Information Analysis	What kind of evidence is likely to make a difference in this setting? Traditionally, what information has been produced and how? Who will be influential in interpreting data?

IMPLICATIONS OF SETTING FOR THE EVALUATION DESIGN *(continued)*	DESIGN DECISION	IMPLICATIONS OF THE SETTING
	Reporting	Is there a "no-win" situation for the report? Who will read the report; who will use it; who will be affected by it; when will it be needed to be of use? Who might want to edit it and can editing be prevented if necessary?
	Managing	What kinds of resources will be available? Who will help, be available for help? Who should receive a contract agreement? How much time will be spent in managing events related to the setting, such as political infighting or administrative protocol.
	Evaluating the Evaluation	Can outside evaluators be brought in at any time? Should they be? How credible will the evaluation be if it is not evaluated? Who is likely to insist that it isn't? What kind of evaluator would be credible in the setting?

WHAT ARE THE CRUCIAL QUESTIONS THE EVALUATION MUST ADDRESS TO ACHIEVE ITS PURPOSE?

It is important to establish the general questions the evaluation will address. As the evaluation design matures, you will carefully rethink and refine the questions to make sure you have the best set. When you finally collect information you can return to update, add, and revise these questions depending on timeline and resources.

Evaluation questions are the basic building blocks for the evaluation. The questions stakeholders would like to see answered by the evaluation influence the kind of information that should be gathered, and the type of information gathered and the means of gathering it, in turn, determine analysis options. Evaluation questions, then, are key to the whole information process.

Evaluations are apt to suffer from too many rather than too few questions. Much worse than too many questions are insignificant questions. Evaluators are responsible for identifying or helping audiences identify the crucial questions related to the evaluation purpose. If, for instance, the purpose of an evaluation is to *"assess the effectiveness of the newly installed training program in order to make improvements,"* the evaluation questions might include:

1. Does the new program cost more or less per trainee?
2. Has trainee performance improved with the new training?
3. Is the new training program getting necessary administrative support?
4. How do trainers feel about the new training program?
5. How do trainees like it?
6. How valid are the competencies being taught?
7. Are some parts of the training more effective than others?

Initial evaluation questions can be gathered from audiences through conversations, interviews, surveys, and group meetings. (See also Audiences in this chapter.) Different audiences will be interested in different questions. "Training effectiveness," for instance, may translate into cost effectiveness to an administrator, positive trainee reactions to training staff, relevant information to a trainee, and better skills to a supervisor. Some audiences will find certain questions far more relevant to achieving the purpose of the evaluation than others.

To generate specific evaluation questions you must understand the general evaluation purpose and have some agreement about what is to be evaluated. For example, when you evaluate training are you evaluating its goals, the workshop, staff, outcomes, or all of these? And, you must know who will need to be involved so that their questions can be answered.

METHODS FOR DEFINING EVALUATION QUESTIONS

METHODS

1. *Analysis of the Object*: Identify key functions in the object and their critical interdependencies to highlight critical paths, major milestones, dependencies, etc. Evaluation questions are keyed to critical junctures, potential weak points, areas of staff concern, points of critical function, or key objectives and goals.

2. *Use of Theoretical Frameworks*: The object of evaluation is interpreted in light of a particular theoretical model, such as a change model, an evaluation model, learning theory, etc. Evaluation questions are derived from the model's key points and assumptions.

3. *External Expertise and Experience*: Experts in the area of the evaluation object identify evaluation questions of importance; literature review of similar evaluation; review of similar programs.

4. *Interaction with Key Audiences*: Discuss the evaluation with audience members. Ask what questions they want answered or what they believe is most important to investigate.

5. *Definition of the Purpose for Evaluation:* Do a logical, definitional analysis of the purposes for the evaluation. Identify the set of questions

EXAMPLE
(based on a hypothetical workshop)

1. The evaluator did a systems analysis of the workshop, defining components in terms of their inputs, process, and outputs. The staff reviewed this analysis, then generated evaluation questions in 3 categories:
   a. Where are breakdowns most likely to occur?
   b. Where is there the most disagreement as to the soundness of the design?
   c. What are the most important objectives?

2. A review of training and evaluation literature turned up two "models" that seemed especially relevant. Rummler's* posed 4 major questions:
   a. Did the participants like it?
   b. Did they learn it?
   c. Did they use what they learned?
   d. Did using what they learned make a difference?
   Stufflebeam's CIPP model** suggested a different set of concerns:
   a. Are the goals valid?
   b. Is the design a good one?
   c. Is the design well implemented?
   d. Were the goals achieved?
   Using these models, the evaluation came up with evaluation questions pertinent to the 2 day workshop.

3. The evaluator called a consultant friend who recommended 3 evaluation reports from similar workshops. These were reviewed, and they suggested some good evaluation questions.

4. The evaluator interviewed several key audience members: the training director, the superintendant, a school board member, and a few potential participants. Based on their interests and needs, some key evaluation questions were defined.

5. A staff meeting was held to brainstorm evaluation questions that seemed related to the purposes for the evaluation. This list was then synthesized to remove overlap and duplica-

METHODS FOR DEFINING EVALUATION QUESTIONS *(continued)*

METHODS

which, if addressed, would meet each purpose.

6. *"Bonus" Questions*: Given that you're going to do an evaluation anyway, are there some questions you can pursue that will be worthwhile, perhaps for research, public relations, marketing, etc.?

EXAMPLE
(based on a hypothetical workshop)

tion. Then a Q-sort technique was used to assemble a set of questions that most agreed defined the purpose of the evaluation.

6. The evaluator and project director discussed some opportunities presented by the evaluation. They decided it might be useful to explore whether participants who enrolled in order to meet recertification requirements were more or less successful than "volunteer" attendees, as these requirements were currently under state scrutiny.

* Brethower, K.S., & Rummler, G.A., "Evaluating Training," *Improving Human Performance Quarterly*, 1977, 5 pp. 107–120.
** Stufflebeam, Daniel L. in Worthen & Sanders Educational Evaluation: Theory and Practice, Jones Publishing, Ohio, 1973, pp. 128–150.

ASSESSING EVALUATION QUESTIONS IN LIGHT OF THE INFORMATION THEY WILL PRODUCE

Evaluation questions generate information and so should be assessed in light of the quality and type of information they will produce. To assess questions in light of their information yield, it is necessary to forecast or think ahead toward some other evaluation decisions.

Evaluation Questions
1. identified
2. rank ordered
3. as a set, they are relevant, important, comprehensive, balanced, and realistic.

What will be reported back to audiences
1. How might the information gathered be displayed, interpreted, and reported to answer questions?
2. What kind of report(s) might be necessary for different audiences?
3. When do audiences need information to answer questions?

How information could be analyzed
1. Would information to answer questions be qualitative or quantitative, or both?
2. What methods are available to analyze these kinds of data?
3. What or whose criteria would be used to judge the results?

Information that could be gathered
1. What information sources are available to answer these questions (e.g., people, test scores, documents)?
2. What methods might be used to gather information from these sources (e.g., interviews, testing, document review)?
3. What instruments or tools might be used (e.g., interview protocols, achievement test, checklist)?

EXAMPLES OF EVALUATION QUESTIONS FOR A 2-DAY INSERVICE WORKSHOP ABOUT SCHWARTZIAN THEORY	Questions related to aspects of the object	Questions for a "new" object (i.e., being planned or recently implemented)	Questions for an "old" object (i.e., been around awhile perhaps through several rounds of revision)
	Goals or Needs	What problems are teachers having with handicapped children? What kinds of training do teachers want? What time and other constraints exist among the target population? To what extent do teachers value the planned workshop objectives?	Are the identified needs still valid? Did the workshop address the 3 goals intended? What needs do attendees have?
	Program Design	Is Design A more practical than Design B? Is Design C any good? Are there sufficient resources for the chosen design? Are these exercises needed to meet the learning goals? What do teachers think of the design?	Is the design specific and practical enough for replication by satellite sites? What elements of the workshop are least productive? Is the new shorter design feasible? potent? Why don't other teachers attend the sessions?
	Implementation or Processes	Did trainers use Schwartzian Methods correctly? Who attended the session? Were Day 1 objectives met? What problems did trainers encounter? How many people attended optional sessions?	What problems are being encountered by new training staff? Who attends? Are attendance rates consistent across times and locations? Does the Day 2 afternoon session help with problem solving?
	Products or Outcomes	Did teachers' knowledge of Schwartz's Theory increase? How well can teachers use Schwartz techniques? Are graduates using Schwartz Techniques in their classrooms?	What are effects on pupils of teachers' use of new methods? What other uses or misuses are being made of workshop acquired methods? Do people who receive less workshop training perform less well than others?
	Recycling Decisions	How much did the session cost? Do graduates consider the session worthwhile? Are Principals supporting graduates' efforts to use new methods?	What are the costs and benefits to attendees of using the new methods? To what extent is the workshop reaching the population? What continuing needs and problems exist despite the workshop benefits?

ANALYZING AND RANK ORDERING EVALUATION QUESTIONS

Many times you generate more evaluation questions than you can answer. So, it becomes important to decide how you'll spend your resources and which questions you will answer. To do this, you can list a set of criteria that may be important in the rank-ordering process (like the key considerations listed across the grid). This allows you to illustrate not only which questions are being asked, but also to indicate the feasibility and importance of answering them. Such a display helps key audiences or the evaluator select the critical and practical evaluation questions.

General purpose: Assess the effectiveness of a two day inservice training.

Key Considerations

The Evaluation Questions	Who wants to know (nature/ number)	Could you make good use of infor- mation? (decision to be made)	How much would it cost to evaluate?	Are there existing procedures /info. available? (quality/ amount)	Can this infor- mation have impact on target audience?	How much time would be neces- sary to gather data?
Increased cost?						
Improved performance?						
Attitudes?						
Valid competencies?						
Some elements more effective than others?						
Well implemented?						
Graduates more effective?						

EVALUATE THE QUESTIONS AS A SET

- Questions are relevant to the purpose and will likely bring useful information.
- Questions are important, and they merit answering.
- Questions are comprehensive and cover core issues related to purpose.
- Questions are balanced and do not focus on a single program element.
- Questions are realistic and there are resources and means available to answer them.

Crucial evaluation questions can emerge throughout an evaluation, so it is important to regularly return to the evaluation questions to assess their appropriateness.

ANOTHER EXAMPLE OF EVALUATION QUESTIONS

EXCERPTED FROM CASE C-3 BY DALE BRETHOWER *

Course Design	Course Delivery	Course Outcomes
Are instructional procedures consistent with the relevant learning processes?	Are logistics well managed?	Are the course objectives being met?

Subquestions:

Course Design	Course Delivery	Course Outcomes
Are procedures relevant to cognitive domain? objectives consistent with principles and research findings? relevant to cognitive learning? Are procedures relevant to affective domain? objectives consistent with principles and research relevant to affective learning?	Are there systematic procedures for: scheduling faculties advertising the course preparing, producing, and/or ordering materials scheduling media, etc. scheduling out-of-class meetings, etc. prompt return of student work managing production of tests, surveys, etc. managing student records etc.	Do students like the course? Do they achieve the objectives? Do they use what they learn?

*See Casebook

DOES THE EVALUATION STAND A GOOD CHANCE OF BEING IMPLEMENTED SUCCESSFULLY?

Not every evaluation conceived should be undertaken so you must consider whether evaluation is worth the resources. Anticipating problems increases the evaluation's potential for success. This chapter provides a checklist to help you rethink issues previously introduced and to anticipate issues that lie ahead. It also provides you with a listing of products that might be useful in responding to relevant items on the checklist.

CHECKLIST OF EVALUATION CONCERNS RELATED TO POTENTIAL FOR SUCCESS	Questions to consider	Sources of evidence
	Can the evaluation object be identified?	description using existing information (proposal, organizational or management plan) and further discussions and observation using relevant audiences
	Has the object been described from a number of different value perspectives?	
	Is the evaluation object relatively stable and mature? What kind of evaluation can it withstand?	
	Are there criteria available to interpret evaluation information?	established criteria, e.g., program objectives, comparison to like programs, needs assessment data, staff judgments
	Is the evaluation purpose clear and defensible, and has it been shared with key stakeholders?	statement of evaluation purpose and rationale disseminated
	Have the events in the setting that are likely to influence the evaluation been identified?	description of setting including interviews with those in organization who can affect program
	Is the setting conducive to or supportive of evaluation (e.g., political support)?	
	Would disruptions caused by the evaluation be tolerable?	
	Have audiences who will be affected or involved been identified?	list of primary and secondary audiences
	Have key stakeholders' needs and questions been identified?	list of key evaluation questions
	Are questions for the evaluation important and worth answering?	
	Is someone available to do the evaluation who has some basic skills in conducting evaluations?	criteria for selection of evaluator documented
	Will the evaluation's credibility be jeopardized by evaluator bias?	
	Is there economic support for the evaluation?	draft of budget
	Are there procedures available to answer the evaluation questions?	lists of possible information collection procedures
	Are there criteria to interpret answers?	list of criteria to be used to interpret answers to questions has been drafted
	Is it feasible to complete the evaluation in the allotted time?	draft management plan (personnel, timeline, tasks)
	Is there a commitment to implement sound evaluation?	
	Is there some agreement about criteria to judge the success of the evaluation?	choice of evaluation criteria (e.g., Joint Committee *Standards*) specified
	Can a written agreement (memo or contract) be negotiated to document the considerations about evaluation goals, responsibilities, resources, and criteria?	draft of contract

REFERENCES

Guba, E.G. & Lincoln, Y.S. *Effective Evaluation: Improving the Usefulness of Evaluation Results Through Responsive and Naturalistic Approaches.* San Francisco: Jossey-Bass, 1981.

Joint Committee on Standards for Educational Evaluation. *Standards for Evaluation of Educational Programs, Projects, & Materials.* New York: McGraw-Hill, 1981.

Martin, Marilyn A. A framework for identifying information needs for evaluation planning, *Instructional Aids Series*, No. 4, Evaluation Center, College of Education, Western Michigan University, Kalamazoo, Michigan 49008, April, 1976.

Smith, Nick L. Evaluability assessment: a retrospective illustration and review, *Educational Evaluation and Policy Analysis, 3*, January–February, 1981.

Yavorsky, Diane K. *Discrepancy Evaluation: A Practitioner's Guide.* Evaluation Research Center, University of Virginia, 1978.

Designing Evaluation

WHAT IT IS

Evaluation design is both a process and a set of written products or plans. An evaluation design can be a loosely constructed emerging plan or a predetermined and fairly rigid blueprint for the evaluation. Whether the evaluation is planned "as it goes" or is carefully choreographed in advance, it includes: progressive focusing; collecting information; analyzing information; reporting information; managing and, often, evaluating evaluation.

Even though evaluations are essentially made of the same elements, some are distinctly better than others. In this chapter differences in approaching evaluation design are described and criteria for judging designs discussed. It is important to note at the outset that there are a number of perspectives about the best way to evaluate, and not infrequently they are at odds. This chapter provides you with some alternative ways to think about and to plan evaluation.

WHEN DESIGN DECISIONS ARE MADE

A number of important decisions often have been made before evaluators sit down to draft a design document for an evaluation. These decisions, covered in Focusing the Evaluation, are actually the beginning of the design. They are the decisions that help evaluators progressively focus their attention on what audiences want evaluated and why. (To review the checklist of concerns related to focusing, turn back to p. 32–33.) Any evaluation design typically must be readjusted over time. As problems arise and changes take place in the object being evaluated, the design must stay responsive to new needs.

To design evaluation using this sourcebook, you should remember that designing entails collection, analysis, and reporting of evaluation information. This means you will need to use other chapters in the Sourcebook to flesh out your evaluation design in detail. Also, consider using the **Design Manual**, the companion piece constructed to help readers complete their own evaluation design.

WHAT ARE SOME ALTERNATIVE WAYS TO DESIGN EVALUATION?

While every evaluation design is essentially made of similar elements, there are many ways to put those elements together. Below are three major decisions that determine the general approach to evaluation that you will be taking.

Fixed vs. Emergent Evaluation Design: Can the evaluation questions and criteria be finalized at the outset? If so, should they be?

Formative vs. Summative Evaluation: Is the evaluation to be used for improvement or to report on the worth of a program . . . or both?

Experimental and Quasi-Experimental Designs vs. Unobtrusive Inquiry: Is the evaluation going to include intervening into events (trying to manipulate environment, persons getting treatment, variables affected, etc.), or will it just "watch" events . . . or a little of both?

Answers to the questions listed above initially may not be clear cut. (For instance, you might attempt a quasi-experimental design that includes the use of unobtrusive inquiry.) Nonetheless, the categories represented by these broad decision areas reflect the amount and kind of front-end planning, the general purpose for evaluating, and the amount of control you'll want during the evaluation process. Deciding where you stand, even generally, on these issues will help you establish some preliminary benchmarks to help explain, guide, and judge evaluation tasks.

FIXED VS. EMERGENT EVALUATION DESIGNS

A fixed design is determined and systematically planned prior to the evaluation's implementation. The design likely is built around program goals and objectives and poses specific evaluation questions; it specifies information sources and collection and analysis plans and decides in advance which audiences will receive information for what purpose. While more structured than emergent evaluation, fixed or preordinate evaluation can also be readjusted to meet changing needs. Most formal evaluations in personnel preparation have been based upon preordained designs because program objectives were carefully fixed in advance by grants and proposals.

An emergent evaluation design readily responds to ongoing influences, evolving as it accommodates changing audiences, problems, and program activities. Emergent evaluation designs devote a good deal of time at the front end of the evaluation to *seeking* purposes and issues, as these are not initially specified or assumed.

FIXED DESIGNS	EMERGENT DESIGNS
greatest expenditure of evaluation resources in the design revolves around activities to specify questions, prepare and administer instruments, analyze the results, and formally report results to audiences	greatest expenditure of evaluation resources in the design is invested in observing the program and focusing further inquiry
evaluator uses program goals and objectives to identify evaluation questions for the design and stimulates relevant audiences to expand and refine these questions	evaluator does not stimulate audiences to think about program or evaluation issues as much as respond to what they say. Audiences determine the important issues and information needs for the "design."
communications between evaluator and audiences regarding the design are at regular intervals but typically formal and often written	communication between evaluator and audiences is formal and ongoing
information collection strategies specified typically involve formal instrumentation (tests, surveys, questionnaires, and rating scales) and can include research methods. Research criteria such as internal and external validity are considered important. The data gathered are often quantitative.	observation, case study, advocate team reports are examples of methods. Less "objective" and less obtrusive measures are taken and the responsive evaluator will sacrifice some precision in measurement for usefulness. Qualitative information is often gathered.
the design is usually drafted and shared with key stakeholders. While it can change, an attempt is made to adhere to initial objectives and plans.	the design continues to grow, change, and react to the setting. In a sense, it is never really finished.

FORMATIVE VS. SUMMATIVE EVALUATION

Formative evaluation is used to glean information to help improve a project, a curriculum, or inservice. It is structured for staff use and may sacrifice external credibility for usefulness. There are many who think the most defensible evaluation is formative evaluation.

Summative evaluation is designed to assess the worth of an object. It is often requested by funding agents, sponsors or administrators who must make fiscal cuts. Summative evaluation is used to make judgments about how worthwhile a program is in order to determine whether to keep it or license it; hence, the evaluation must have credibility for a number of audiences who will be affected by that decision. In funded areas of personnel preparation summative evaluation has been more common than formative evaluation. While less popular with program staff, summative evaluation does bring data to "go/no-go" decisions that must be made. How it is used, or whether it is used, depends upon the decision maker.

It is possible to build evaluations to provide ongoing information for improvement and information for judgments of worth. However, often formative and summative evaluation have conflicting purposes and cannot easily be reconciled in the same design. For example, if a program will stay or go based on an evaluation, few staff will be interested in improving as they anticipate the final report.

FORMATIVE	SUMMATIVE
evaluation resources expended on need areas identified by program staff	evaluation focuses on "success" variables considered important by sponsor or decision makers
evaluator is often part of program and works closely with program staff	external evaluator or review team frequently used, as internal evaluator is more likely to have a conflict of interest
any information collection strategy might be used but emphasis will be on turning over useful information quickly to make improvements	information collection strategy will maximize external and internal validity and might be gathered over a longer period of time
the evaluation design (fixed or emergent) is drawn up with staff and revised to meet their needs	the evaluation design (could be emergent but probably will be fixed) is drawn up to meet the needs of sponsors/key decision makers

EXPERIMENTAL AND QUASI-EXPERIMENTAL DESIGNS VS. UNOBTRUSIVE INQUIRY

Some evaluations use classic research methodology. In such cases, subjects are randomly selected or assigned, treatments are given, and measures of impact are taken. The purpose, if it's evaluation, is still to make a judgment about the worth of the object, e.g., a demonstration program or an early intervention strategy. When students or programs are randomly selected, it is possible to make generalizations to a larger population. It is, however, difficult and sometimes not ethical to intervene in an educational setting by selecting or sorting subjects or by giving or withholding treatments. Thus, the degree to which the setting can be manipulated and the degree to which such a strategy is considered sound is a major consideration at the outset of the evaluation.

In some cases, intervention is neither possible nor desirable. If events have already happened, evaluators must look at historical documents, study test scores, or analyze existing research. If it is important to evaluate a setting or a program so as to improve it, evaluators might choose to watch, talk with people, and keep a low profile so that the program they evaluate is not unduly threatened or changed by their appearance. Many methodologies (including observation, survey, meta analysis, case study and even interview) can be used in such a way as to minimize the evaluation's impact on people and events and maximize its reporting on the "what is."

RESEARCH DESIGN	NATURAL "UNOBTRUSIVE" INQUIRY
a good deal of resources go into the preparation for and administering of instruments to assess treatments; quantitative data typically gathered and statistical criteria used	evaluators spend more time on-site watching and talking to relevant audiences; multiple evaluation strategies and sources are used to increase the reliability of information gathered
statistical criteria focused on program outcomes are established at the outset and the design is formalized and left intact throughout	evaluator discusses issues with audiences; the degree to which evaluator issues are discussed depends on evaluator style
interaction with audiences is to formulate plan, gather information and report it back	interaction with audience is ongoing and informal
information collection strategies specified typically involve formal instrumentation (tests, surveys, questionnaires and rating scales) and can include research methods. Research criteria such as internal and external validity are considered important. The data gathered are often quantitative.	observation, case study, advocate team reports are examples of methods. Less "objective" and less obtrusive measures are taken and the responsive evaluator will sacrifice some precision in measurement for usefulness.
the design is usually drafted and shared with key stakeholders. While it can change, an attempt is made to adhere to initial objectives and plans.	the design may be finalized at the outset if program objectives are clear or it might be emergent and work toward identifying program goals

---

SOME EXISTING APPROACHES USEFUL IN TRAINING EVALUATION

It's possible to shop around for an existing evaluation model rather than attempt to invent your own. Since 1965 a number of evaluation approaches have been described and applied in varied settings. Below some of these approaches are briefly described. Remember that any existing approach or design must be thoughtfully retailored to fit a specific context.

GENERAL APPROACH	PURPOSES	RELEVANT MODELS AND REFERENCES
CONGRUENCY AND COMPLIANCE		
Actual program progress and activities are charted and compared to plans (designs, intentions) or to some external standards or criteria.	helping management keep a program on track documenting that plans and proposals were adhered to gaining accreditation,	Discrepancy Evaluation Model (DEM) Program Evaluation and Review Technique (PERT) Management by Objectives (MBO)

SOME EXISTING
APPROACHES
USEFUL IN
TRAINING
EVALUATION
(*continued*)

GENERAL APPROACH	PURPOSES	RELEVANT MODELS AND REFERENCES
CONGRUENCY AND COMPLIANCE	demonstrating compliance	Program Analysis of Service Systems (PASS) State Audits
DECISION-MAKING Information is collected pertinent to key developmental stages and steps (e.g., goal setting, program design) to help choose a course of action or see how well a program is progressing at any given point.	providing a data base for forecasted key decision points helping a program progress through certain developmental stages explaining or justifying why certain actions were taken	CIPP Evaluation Model Concerns-Based Adoption Model (CBAM) Discrepancy Evaluation Model (DEM) Impact Evaluation Model (IEM) NIN Child Change "Steps" Model
RESPONSIVE This identifies the critical audiences and stake-holders of a program, then helps get the information they need or want to use, judge, or benefit from the program.	enhancing support for and involvement in a program demonstrating good intentions and concern for audiences providing the worth of a program to its key stakeholders	R. Stake's "Responsive Evaluation" Guba & Lincoln, *Effective Evaluation*
OBJECTIVES-BASED Specific objectives are defined for each activity, then data are collected that will measure their achievement.	seeing whether activities produce what they're supposed to forcing specificity and clarity on program outcomes demonstrating performance	Goal Attainment Scaling R. Mager's *Preparing Instructional Objectives* R. Tyler's *Defining Educational Objectives*
ORGANIZATIONAL DEVELOPMENT Information about staff and project problems, expectations and progress are regularly collected, then fed back to staff.	help bring increasing knowledge and certainty about what's taking place, what's working and why help staff become more effective, productive, and satisfied identify staff development and organization development needs facilitate staff and project growth	Provus, *Discrepancy Evaluation* Brinkerhoff, "Training Evaluation" Shumsky, *Action Research*

SOME EXISTING APPROACHES USEFUL IN TRAINING EVALUATION *(continued)*	GENERAL APPROACH	PURPOSES	RELEVANT MODELS AND REFERENCES
	NATURALISTIC		
	Open, emergent inquiry into program activities and outcomes. Begins with little preconceived plan about evaluation questions, procedures, data collection, etc.	to determine what's really happening identify actual effects and consequences whether planned or not better understand the context of a program and the forces acting on it	Guba & Lincoln, *Effective Evaluation* Patton, *Qualitative Evaluation Methods*
	EXPERT-JUDGMENT		
	Information about program activities, resources, etc. is collected, then given to one or more "judges" who draw conclusions, make recommendations, etc.	get new ideas and perspectives on how to operate a program gain acceptance, credibility interpret and place a value on program outcomes	E. Eisner's Connoiseurship Judicial Evaluation Model Goal-free Evaluation
	EXPERIMENTAL		
	Outcome data are carefully specified and measured under controlled treatment conditions, after using control groups or statistical methods to assess and control error.	compare effects of one approach to another demonstrate cause-effect relationships; provide evidence that program is cause of outcomes identify correlates and relationships among key program variables gain validation from JDRP	Campbell and Stanley Cook and Campbell Joint Dissemination and Review Panel (JDRP)
	COST ANALYSIS		
	Program costs are defined and analyzed to determine how much was spent on what activities, and with what effects.	relate increments of outcomes to increments of cost document expenditures and costs facilitate replication efforts	Levin's "Cost Effectiveness Analysis"

WHAT DOES A DESIGN INCLUDE?

It is important to keep in mind that evaluation designs are comprised of the same elements or, as we refer to them, functions. These functions include focusing, collecting, analyzing, and reporting information, managing and evaluating the evaluation. Whether the design emerges or is fixed at the outset, it will contain these functions in one form or another. Adapted existing models and designs will also be constructed of these same basic functions, but they will put them together using different perspectives.

What makes evaluation designs different, or better, or more appropriate is how well these same basic functions are integrated and operationalized. Like a book with a well-blended plot, theme and setting, the sound evaluation design puts all the parts together well. Moreover, the sound evaluation design is useful for improving training.

There are a number of important decisions and corresponding tasks that must be resolved during the process of evaluation. Design decisions as well as design products that form an audit trail are described in this section. Remember, each evaluation design tells its own unique story; you do not need to include all considerations listed in this section, but you should have considered their influence on your design.

DESIGN DECISIONS AND TASKS In this book seven major evaluation activities have been described and 35 key decisions and tasks relating to these functions have been identified. Whether you choose to design your own evaluation or adapt an existing design, we recommend that you consider each decision listed in the following grid:

Function	Key Issues	Tasks	Page Numbers
Focusing the Evaluation	1. What will be evaluated?	1. Investigate what is to be evaluated	7–15
	2. What is the purpose for evaluating?	2. Identify and justify purpose(s)	16–19
	3. Who will be affected by or involved in the evaluation?	3. Identify audiences	20–22
	4. What elements in the setting are likely to influence the evaluation?	4. Study setting	23–26
	5. What are the critical evaluation questions?	5. Identify major questions	27–31
	6. Does the evaluation have the potential for success?	6. Decide whether to go on with evaluation	32–34

DESIGN DECISIONS AND TASKS *(continued)*	Function	Key Issues	Tasks	Page Numbers
	Designing Evaluation	1. What are some alternative ways to design an evaluation?	1. Determine the amount of planning, general purpose, and degree of control	37–42
		2. What does a design include?	2. Overview evaluation decisions, tasks, and products	43–58
		3. How do you go about constructing a design?	3. Determine general procedures for the evaluation	59–63
		4. How do you recognize a good design?	4. Assess the quality of the design	64–71
	Collecting Information	1. What kinds of information should you collect?	1. Determine the information sources you will use	77–83
		2. What procedures should you use to collect needed information?	2. Decide how you'll collect information	84–88
		3. How much information should you collect?	3. Decide whether you need to sample and, if so, how	89–94
		4. Will you select or develop instruments?	4. Determine how precise your information must be and design a means to collect it.	95–99
		How do you establish reliable and valid instrumentation?	Establish procedures to maximize validity and reliability	100–107
		5. How do you plan the information collection effort to get the most information at the lowest cost?	5. Plan the logistics for an economical information collection procedure	108–115
	Analyzing and Interpreting (Evaluation)	1. How will you handle returned data?	1. Aggregate and code data if necessary	119–122
		2. Are data worth analyzing?	2. Verify completeness and quality of raw data	123–126
		3. How will you analyze the information?	3. Select & run defensible analyses	127–144
		4. How will you interpret the results of analyses?	4. Interpret the data using prespecified and alternative sets of criteria	145–147
	Reporting	1. Who should get an evaluation report?	1. Identify who you will report to	151–153
		2. What content should	2. Outline the	154–158

DESIGN DECISIONS AND TASKS *(continued)*	Function	Key Issues	Tasks	Page Numbers
		be included in a report?	content to be included	
		3. How will reports be delivered?	3. Decide whether reports will be written, oral, etc.	159–164
		4. What is the appropriate style and structure for the report?	4. Select a format for the report	165–167
		5. How can you help audiences interpret and use reports?	5. Plan post-report discussions, consultation, follow-up activities	168–169
		6. When should reports be scheduled?	6. Map out the report schedule	170–173
	Managing	1. Who should run the evaluation?	1. Select, hire, and/or train the evaluator	176–180
		2. How should evaluation responsibilities be formalized?	2. Draw up a contract or letter of agreement	181–186
		3. How much should the evaluation cost?	3. Draft the budget	187–190
		4. How should evaluation tasks be organized and scheduled?	4. Draft a time/task strategy	191–196
		5. What kinds of problems can be expected?	5. Monitor the evaluation and anticipate problems	197–200
	Evaluating Evaluation (Meta Evaluation)	1. What are some good uses of meta-evaluation?	1. Determine whether you need to meta evaluate; if so, when	205–207
		2. Who should do the meta evaluation?	2. Select a meta evaluator	208–209
		3. What criteria or standards should you use to evaluate the evaluation?	3. Select or negotiate standards	210–217
		4. How do you apply a set of meta-evaluation criteria?	4. Rank order standards, determine compliance	218–220
		5. What procedures are used in meta-evaluation?	5. Select procedures for evaluating evaluations	221–222

DESIGN PRODUCTS   Design activities are guided by documents which outline evaluation tasks. Below is a listing of design products that leave a trail for others to study and evaluate the evaluation design. You may have all of these products or only some of them and they may be produced in any order.

DESIGN PRODUCTS
(continued)

Evaluation Function	Evaluation Products	Content Included
Focusing the Evaluation	Evaluation Overview	description of evaluation object and setting; listing of relevant audiences; evaluation questions and subquestions; evaluation criteria to judge success.
Collecting Information	Information Collection Plan	evaluation questions/sub-questions; variables of interest; information sources; instruments; collection methods; timeline.
Managing Information	Analysis Plan	type of information to be gathered; statistical/valuational criteria; interpretation strategy (who/how); type of analysis specified.
Reporting Information	Report Strategy	audiences to receive reports; number of reports; report content; report format (oral, written); report schedule.
	Follow Through Plans	plans for consultation with key audiences; inservice for staff; dissemination to outside audience.
Managing an Evaluation	Management Plan	tasks to be completed; timeline; personnel reponsible; budget.
	Evaluation Contract	specifies evaluator and evaluator responsibility; summarizes and documents the other evaluation products.
Evaluation of Evaluation	Meta Evaluation Plan	criteria to be used; persons to evaluate.

DESIGN ELEMENTS

Name	Definition	How Design Elements Fit Together in Good Evaluation
Object:	What gets evaluated	*Object* has interest or value to *Audiences*
Purpose:	What the evaluation is to accomplish; why it's being done	*Purpose* is clear, shared and defensible; there is some commitment to use information to be produced relative to *Object*; Some *Audiences* will benefit from *Purpose*
Audiences:	Who the evaluation is for and who will be involved	*Audiences* have an interest in the *Object* and would be willing to help generate and use evaluation information
Evaluation Questions:	Questions about the nature and value of some object which, if answered, could	*Evaluation Questions* are responsive to *Audience* interests or needs and are pertinent to the *Object* and its context

DESIGN ELEMENTS
(continued)

Name	Definition	How Design Elements Fit Together in Good Evaluation
	provide useful information	
Collected Information:	Information about the object or its context that has been aggregated and sorted	*Collected Information* is responsive to *Audiences*; reflects *Object* or context without distortion; and is useful for answering or generating *Evaluation Questions*
Information Collection Methods:	Ways information gets collected (observation, tests, etc.)	*Information Collection Methods* produce good *Collected Information* (as defined above) economically
Instruments:	Forms and records used in information collection	*Instruments* are suitable for *Information Collection Methods*
Analysis Methods:	Ways of understanding collected information	*Analysis Methods* are appropriate to *Collected Information* and will lead to answering or generating useful *Evaluation Questions*
Interpretations and Conclusions:	Values and meaning attached to collected information	*Interpretations and Conclusions* are justified by *Analysis Methods* and are responsive to *Purposes*
Reports:	Communications with audiences about the evaluation or its interpretations and conclusions	*Reports* clearly present *Interpretations and Conclusions* or other relevant information and are useful for *Audiences*
Report Methods:	How communications are made (oral, written, T.V. show, etc.)	*Report Methods* are appropriate for *Audiences* and report content

CHECKLIST FOR EVALUATION DESIGN

A. Clarity of Evaluation Focus
   1. Is there an adequate description of what (program, context, functions, products, etc.) is to be evaluated? (Object)
   2. Is the evaluation object relatively stable and mature? Do you know what kind of evaluation it can withstand? (Object, Purposes)
   3. Are the reasons for the evaluation specified and defensible? (Purpose)
   4. Is it clear what planning, implementing, redesign, judging, or other decisions and interests are to be served by the evaluation? (Purpose)
   5. Are all relevant evaluation audiences described? (Audiences)
   6. Are the criteria, values, and expectations that audiences will bring to bear in interpreting information known and described? (Audiences)

7. Have the events in the setting that are likely to influence the evaluation been identified? (Constraints)
8. Is someone available to do the evaluation who has some basic skills in conducting evaluations? (Constraints)
9. Is the setting conducive to or supportive of evaluation (e.g., political support)? (Constraints)
10. Would disruptions caused by the evaluation be tolerable? (Constraints)

B. Evaluation Questions
1. Have key stakeholders' needs and questions been identified?
2. Are questions for the evaluation important and worth answering?
3. Are questions sufficiently comprehensive? If addressed, would they meet the evaluation's purpose?

C. Information Collection
1. Are there procedures available to answer the evaluation questions?
2. Are the **kinds of information** to be collected logically related to the information needs?
3. Are the information collection procedures appropriate for the kinds of information sought?
4. Is the evaluation likely to provide accurate information?
5. Is the evaluation likely to provide timely information?
6. Is the evaluation likely to provide information sufficient to meet its purposes?
7. Is the evaluation likely to provide useful information to each audience?
8. Are the procedures compatible with the purposes of the evaluation?
9. Will information collection be minimally disruptive?

D. Analysis and Interpretation
1. Are information organization, reduction, and storage procedures appropriate for the information to be collected? Safe?
2. Are information analysis procedures specified and appropriate?
3. Are methods and/or criteria for interpreting evaluation information known and defensible?

E. Reporting
1. Are report audiences defined? Are they sufficiently comprehensive?
2. Are report formats, content and schedules appropriate for audience needs?
3. Will the evaluation report balanced information?
4. Will reports be timely and efficient?
5. Is the report plan responsive to rights for knowledge and information with respect to relevant audiences?

F. Management
1. Does the design provide for adequate protection of human privacy and other rights?
2. Are personnel roles specified and related to information collection and management requirements?
3. Is the evaluation likely to be carried out in a professional and responsible manner?
4. Is the evaluation likely to be carried out legally?
5. Has sufficient time been allocated for evaluation activities (instrument development, data collection, analysis, reporting, management)?
6. Are sufficient fiscal, human and material resources provided for?
7. Are personnel qualified to carry out assigned responsibilities?
8. Are intended data sources likely to be available and accessible?
9. Are management responsibilities and roles sufficient to support the evaluation?

**CHECKLIST FOR
EVALUATION
DESIGN**
(continued)

10. Is it feasible to complete the evaluation in the allotted time?
11. Can a written agreement (memo or contract) be negotiated to document the considerations about evaluation goals, responsibilities, resources, and criteria?
12. Are there provisions for redesigning or redirecting the evaluation as experience over time may indicate?

G. Evaluating the Evaluation
  1. Is there a commitment to implement sound evaluation?
  2. Is there agreement about criteria to judge the success of the evaluation?
  3. Will the evaluation's credibility be jeopardized by evaluator bias?
  4. Are there procedures planned to assess the quality of the evaluation's design, progress and results?
  5. Are there provisions for disseminating, reporting, interpreting and otherwise utilizing the results and experience of the evaluation?

**EXAMPLE OF AN
EVALUATION
DESIGN
(EXCERPTED FROM
DESIGN MANUAL,
APPENDIX B)**

INTRODUCTION

This appendix* contains a complete (all 7 Products) evaluation design. The example used is an evaluation design for a 3-day training workshop. To get extra mileage from this example, the 3-day workshop is an evaluation training workshop, in which the hypothetical participants learn about evaluation and produce evaluation designs using the Design Manual (it's a lot like a workshop the authors used to conduct).

So, this example gives you a look at all seven (7) products. It might also give you some ideas how you could use the companion Design Manual to train others.

PRODUCT 1: *Evaluation Preview*

What is to be Evaluated

The object of the evaluation is a workshop developed and delivered by the ETC Project. It is a three-day workshop which gives participants intensive training in evaluation and time to work on their own evaluation designs. Participants are from professional development and teacher preparation programs in colleges and universities and local and state educational agencies. The project received funding from the federal Office of Special Education to develop the materials used in the workshop, but must rely on registration fees to cover some delivery costs. The project is based at a University Evaluation Center which is interested in insuring quality and coordinating the project with its other activities.

HOW THE WORKSHOP WORKS

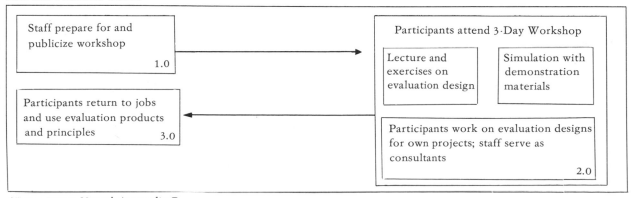

*From *Design Manual*, Appendix B

Day One		Day Two		Day Three	
9:00– 9:30	Introduction	9:00– 9:30	Introduction to the Design Manual	9:00–10:00	Lecture and demonstration: Reporting
9:30–10:30	Evaluation design exercise	9:30–12:00	Participants (each with own Design Manual) complete Products #1 and #2	10:00–11:00	Participants complete Product #5
10:30–12:00	Discussion: Review of Decision Areas from *Sourcebook*	12:00– 1:00	Lunch	11:00–12:00	Panel discussion: Management
12:00– 1:00	Lunch	1:00– 2:30	Exercise and lecture: Measurement Planning	12:00– 1:00	Lunch
1:00– 2:30	Participants read selected case	2:30– 4:30	Participants complete Products #3 and #4	1:00– 3:30	Participants complete Products #6 and #7
2:30– 3:30	Small group exercise: Participants analyze case using Decision Areas			3:30– 4:00	Wrap-up
3:30– 4:30	Summary Review				

Evaluation Purpose

The primary purpose is to produce information which can be used to redesign subsequent versions of the workshop. A secondary purpose is to provide impact and other accountability information to external audiences.

Audiences for the Evaluation

The primary audience is the staff, who want to conduct good, efficient training. Other audiences include: (1) the Federal Office whose primary interest is to see their funds well used to support a quality effort, and (2) the University Evaluation Center and Administration, who hope to promote coordination with other efforts and high quality, visible efforts.

Constraints

The project has a small amount of funds set aside for an internal evaluator (a part-time student). The staff prefer an internal evaluator with whom they can work closely but see the need for credibility of their self-evaluation work. The evaluation must involve participants (federal regulation) and be completed before the end of the funding period.

PRODUCT 2: *Outline of the Evaluation Questions*

Evaluation Questions	Subquestions	Audiences	Why the Question is Important
Who attended the workshops?	What are their: number? positions? organizational affiliations? evaluation experience?	OSE (funders) University Staff Project Director	The project will change organizations only if key leaders (e.g., deans, chairs) attend
Did participants think it was worthwhile?	Was it: interesting? useful?	OSE (funders) Staff	The "word-of-mouth" network is strong among participants; and, if they don't like it, they won't learn it
Were the learning objectives met?		OSE Staff Project Director	Needed to revise subsequent workshop and to guide any follow-up

PRODUCT 2: *Outline of the Evaluation Questions (continued)*

Evaluation Questions	Subquestions	Audiences	Why the Question is Important
What problems arose?	What problems were related to: preparation? delivery?	Staff Project Director	Staff expect some rough spots; the Director will base staff training on problem areas
How costly was it?	What did it cost? Are there savings possibilities?	University Project Director OSE	The project was funded on a per-participant estimate that cannot be exceeded over the entire workshop series
What uses were made of the training?	What were the: job applications? benefits and effects?	OSE Staff Project Director	This will serve as impact data and will be used as needs data in next year's proposal
Is the workshop content sound?	How sound is it from the point of view of: evaluation methodology? instructional design?	Staff Project Director University OSE	Needed for revision. And, OSE and the University expect to see high quality efforts.
Is the workshop responsive to needs?		OSE University Staff Project Director	The entire workshop proposal is based on identified needs for evaluation improvement

PRODUCT 3: *Information Collection: Overall Plan (A)*

Evaluation Questions and Sub-Questions

Information Collection Procedures	1. Who attended? a. number? b. position? c. organization?	2. Did they think it was worthwhile? a. interesting? b. useful?	3. Were learning objectives met?	4. What problems arose? a. preparation? b. delivery?	5. How costly was it? a. costs? b. potential savings?	6. What uses were made? a. actual uses? b. benefits?	7. Is the content sound? a. evaluation methods b. instructional design	8. Is it responsive to needs?
A. Participants (P's) complete registration forms at beginning of workshop	X							
B. P's complete brief questionnaire at end of first day		X						
C. Sample of P's (key respondent) discuss workshop		X	X	X (b)				X

Evaluation Questions and Sub-Questions

Information Collection Procedures	1. Who attended? a. number? b. position? c. organization?	2. Did they think it was worthwhile? a. interesting? b. useful?	3. Were learning objectives met?	4. What problems arose? a. preparation? b. delivery?	5. How costly was it? a. costs? b. potential savings?	6. What uses were made? a. actual uses? b. benefits?	7. Is the content sound? a. evaluation methods b. instructional design	8. Is it responsive to needs?
at end; staff members take notes								
D. Staff keep notes on P's use of materials, questions asked, problems			X	X (b)				X
E. External reviewers rate samples of evaluation designs produced at workshop			X					
F. At post-workshop meetings, staff discuss procedures for developing and producing materials and making arrangements			X (a)	X (b)				
G. Evaluator compiles cost and registration fees					X			
H. Staff members telephone interview sample of P's after training						X		X
I. Selected evaluation and instructional design experts review workshop materials							X	X
J. Evaluation and instructional design experts observe							X	

PRODUCT 3: *Information Collection: How Each Procedure Works (B)*

Procedure	Evaluation Questions Addressed	Schedule for Collection	Respondents	Sample	Instrument(s) Used
A. Participants (P's) complete registration forms at beginning of workshop	1	Beginning of workshop at registration	Workshop participants	All	Registration Questionnaire
B. P's complete brief questionnaire at end of first day	2	End of each of three days during workshop	Workshop participants	All	Reaction Form
C. Sample of P's (key respondent) discuss workshop at end; staff members take notes	2, 3, 4b, 8	Afternoon of last day of workshop	Workshop participants	8–12 selected by staff	Staff notes and Key Respondents Guide Sheet
D. Staff keep notes on P's use of materials, questions asked, problems	3, 4b, 8	Continuous during workshop	Staff	All	Staff Daily Log
E. External reviewers rate sample of evaluation designs during workshop	3	Ratings made two weeks after workshop	Evaluation consultant	3	Reviewer Rating Form
F. At post-workshop meetings, staff discuss procedures for developing and producing materials and making arrangements	4a	Continuous during preparation and delivery of workshop	Staff	All	Staff Daily Logs and other notes
G. Evaluator compiles cost and registration fees	5	1 week after workshop	N.A.	N.A.	None
H. Staff members telephone interview sample of P's after training	6, 8	2 months after workshop	Workshop participants	Approximately 1/3 of participants stratified by type of job setting	Interview Guide
I. Selected evaluation and instructional design experts review workshop materials	7, 8	Materials sent 1 week after workshop; replies completed in 3 weeks	Expert reviews	3 of each type	Reviewer's Guide Questions
J. Evaluation and instructional design experts observe	7	During workshop	Observers	1 of each type	None (observers take own notes)

PRODUCT 4: *Analysis and Interpretation Plan*

Evaluation Questions	Collection Procedure	Analysis Procedure	Evaluation Criteria	Procedures for Making Judgments
1. Who attended the workshop? a. number? b. positions? c. organizational affiliation? d. evaluation expert?	A. Participants (P's) complete registration forms at beginning of workshop.	Analyze questionnaire items regarding the four sub-questions to determine frequencies.	Number of P's needed to cover costs; 90% of participants should match characteristics of intended participants.	Evaluator compares findings to criteria.
2. Did P's think it was worthwhile? a. interesting? b. useful?	B. P's complete brief questionnaire at end of first day.	Analyze relevant questionnaire items to determine ratings of workshop elements. Content analyze staff notes taken during the discussion.	Average ratings of 3-0 or less on 5-pt. scale are considered very low.	Comparison of summarized findings with those from previous workshops.
	C. Sample of P's (key respondents) discuss workshop at end; staff members take notes.			
3. Were the learning objectives met?	C above			
	D. Staff kept notes on P's use of materials, questions asked, problems.	Content analyze staff notes to identify evidence that objectives used were not met. Summarize reviewers' rating sheets.	List of learning objectives ranked by importance. All major objectives should be achieved.	Evaluator compares all findings to criteria and presents own summary; reviewers' ratings also presented separately. Project Director makes final determination.
	E. External reviewers rate sample of evaluation designs during workshop.			
4. What problems arose? a. preparation? delivery? b. delivery?	C above for "b" D above for "b"	Content analyze notes from staff logs and discussion to identify problems, how they developed, and their effects.	Problems such as confusions about materials inadequate facility unproductive diversion from schedule.	Evaluator summarizes information; Project Director and staff review it at staff meeting. Consensus of staff sought.

PRODUCT 4: *Analysis and Interpretation Plan (continued)*

Evaluation Questions	Collection Procedure	Analysis Procedure	Evaluation Criteria	Procedures for Making Judgments
	F. At post-workshop meeting, staff discuss procedures for developing and producing materials and making arrangements. (for "a")			

5. How costly was it?
  a. cost?
  b. savings possibilities?
	G. Evaluator compiles cost and registration fees.	Compare expenditures to budget and to income from fees.	Were there unusual or unjustified expenditures?	Evaluator presents findings to Director who determines savings possibilities based upon comparisons to similar activities.

6. What uses were made of the training?
  a. job applications?
  b. benefits/effects?
	H. Staff members interview sample of P's after training.	Analyze items from interview schedule regarding uses of materials; determine types of uses and apparent effects.	Summary presented. No pre-set criteria established.	Staff discuss, reach consensus about adequacy, as compared to needs data. (Information reported to OSE for any judgments they choose to make.)

7. Is the workshop content sound?
  a. evaluation point of view?
  b. instructional design point of view?
	I. Selected evaluation and instructional design experts review workshop materials.	Compare workshop content to design criteria. Compare workshop operation to design criteria.	Experts selected so that one is familiar with project and at least one is nationally recognized but with no association with project or staff members.	Evaluator summarizes comparison of its content to criteria to identify strengths and weaknesses.

	J. Evaluation and instructional design experts observe workshops and make reports to staff.			
8. Is the workshop responsive to needs?	C above D above H above	Content analysis of staff notes and reports of expert reviews.	All major needs (identified when project began).	Evaluator compares findings to Needs Report.

PRODUCT 5: *Report Plan*

Audience	Content	Format	Date/Frequency	Event
OSE	Description of Project activities and plans; answers to questions 1–3, 5–8	Written report	60 days after funding year	End-of-the-year report
University	Description of Project activities and budget; answers to questions 1, 5, 7, 8	Written report	30 days after funding year	End-of-the-year report
Staff	Evaluation design	Meetings with written summary	2 months before workshop	Staff meeting
	Review of findings and implications; answers to questions 1–4, 6	Presentation by evaluator	2 weeks after workshop	Staff meeting
	Review of findings and implications; answers to questions 7, 8	Presentation by evaluator	2½ months after workshop	Staff meeting
Project Director	Same as for staff	(see above)	(see above)	(see above)
	Progress, problems, and next steps	Informal discussion	Every 2 weeks	Meeting
	Answers to questions 1–8	Written report	2½ months after workshop	Meeting

PRODUCT 6: *Management Plan*

Evaluation Workplan	Person Responsible	Feb	Mar	Apr	May	June	July	Aug
A. Design the evaluation								
· draft the design	Evaluation	X X						
· review	Director and staff		X					
· present to staff	Evaluator		X					
· revise	Evaluator		X X					
· have reviewed by consultant	Director (and consultant)		X X					
B. Develop procedures and instruments								
· draft registration from (Proc. A), questionnaire (Proc. B), and guidelines for expert review (Procs. E and J)	Evaluator		X	X				
· review	Director and staff			X				
· revise	Evaluator			X X				
· produce	Secretary				X			
· train staff for keeping notes on workshop process (Procs. C and D)	Evaluator				X			

PRODUCT 6: *Management Plan (continued)*

Evaluation Workplan	Person Responsible	Feb	Mar	Apr	May	June	July	Aug
develop interview schedule (Proc. A)	Evaluator					X X		
C. Collect information during workshop Procs. A, B, C, D	Staff and evaluator				X			
following workshop Proc. E send designs to reviewers	Evaluator					X		
reviews due						X		
Proc. F post-workshop meeting						X		
Proc. G compile budget information						X		
Proc. H interview a sample of P's							X	
Proc. I send material to reviewers					X			
reviews due						X		
D. Analyze information to answer questions 1–5, 7, 8	Evaluator					X X		
to answer question 6	Evaluator							X
E. Reports prepare summaries	Evaluator					X X		
staff meetings to report findings	Evaluator and Director					X		
meetings with Director	Evaluator and Director	X X	X X	X X	X X	X X	X X	X
write reports for Director's use in year-end reports	Evaluator							X
prepare meta-evaluation report	Consultant							X

Budget

Personnel

Evaluator (25% of $4,000 × ½ year)	$ 500
Consultant fees for 2 workshop observations ($100/day × 2 days × 2)	400
Consultant fees for reviews ($100 × 4)	400
subtotal	1,300

PRODUCT 6: *Management Plan (continued)*

Evaluation Workplan	Person Responsible	Feb	Mar	Apr	May	June	July	Aug

Travel and Lodgings

To Workshop for: 165
Evaluator (carfare = \$15, per diem = \$50 × 3 = \$150)
Consultant (2) (carfare = 50 × 2, per diem = \$60 × 3 × 2 = \$360)   460

subtotal   625

Material and Supplies

Office supplies   50
Copying   100
Postage   20

subtotal   170

TOTAL   \$2,095

PRODUCT 7: *Meta-Evaluation Plan*

Evaluation of Evaluation Design

Purpose: To demonstrate a credible and defensible design to funding agent, and to revise evaluation design as necessary.
Method: Send evaluation design to external consultant not affiliated with project; meet with consultant to review design.
Resources: Consultant fees, meeting time and space, checklist.
Criteria: Joint Committee *Standards*.

Evaluation of Progress

Purpose: To revise evaluation as necessary.
Method: Staff will meet with evaluator before, during and after workshop to discuss evaluation instruments and data collection.
Resources: None extra.
Criteria: Utility and accuracy of information.

Evaluation of Completed Evaluation

Purpose: To "certify" evaluation report and determine how to revise future evaluation work.
Methods: 1. Send evaluation report to external consultant who will append a Meta-evaluation Report.
2. Conduct meeting with staff and invited others to review the evaluation report, design and uses; discuss utility and worth.
Resources: Consultant fees; meeting time, promotion and space.
Criteria: Joint Committee *Standards*; utility and economy.

HOW DO YOU GO ABOUT CONSTRUCTING A DESIGN?

There are different ways of constructing an evaluation design. Some ways are better than others in particular situations, and there's probably no one way that's best in all situations. For example, sometimes it pays to act alone and unilaterally, and other times you should proceed in careful concert with others. In any case, you always need to attend to organizational conditions and needs, other people's interests and values, and the purposes that spawned the evaluation.

Designing an evaluation is rarely a linear, one-time-only process. Most often, the design grows iteratively. An architectural design grows much the same way. First, the architect produces a rough sketch (preferably on a tavern napkin). While nowhere near a detailed blueprint, the sketch proposes a complete solution to an architectural problem. It meets the client's needs, is responsive to the site and climate, and makes good use of available resources. Assuming all is "go" (and the project is not abandoned at this point), the architect will work with the client to produce several incremental versions of working drawings. These have more detail than the first napkin sketch and are still complete in that they represent the whole building. Sometimes construction begins now, depending on the skill and style of the builder. Or, one proceeds to make final blueprints which give sufficient detail to guide construction. The initial sketch foreshadowed the final blueprint, and the final blueprints, despite many incremental revisions, carry the vestiges of that first rough sketch.

There are at least four decisions that you should bear in mind as you construct your evaluation design. (Keep in mind the design products, decisions and tasks outlined in the preceding section. They are likely to be the grist of your evaluation design.)

· How much will you plan beforehand? Will you develop a detailed blueprint, or will you "play it by ear," beginning with only a rough sketch (or less) of a design?
· Who will be the evaluator? Who will be involved in the evaluation and who will have primary responsibility for its implementation? What kind of role will those evaluation persons play with staff and key decision makers?
· What will be the scope of your effort? Should you try for a small effort with modest payoff that is most likely to succeed? Or, should you bite off a bigger chunk, taking a greater risk but offering more impact?
· How will you decide when you have a good design? What are the criteria or standards by which all audiences will judge the design? To know if you've successfully arrived at a good evaluation design you must decide in advance what a "good design" looks like.

The first three issues are dealt with in this section. Selecting criteria to judge your evaluation design is a key issue and is highlighted in the section that follows.

DECIDING HOW
MUCH YOU
SHOULD PLAN
BEFOREHAND

Sometimes the amount of evaluation planning is determined by time, expertise, Request-For-Proposal (RFP) guidelines, or the evaluation "model" you have decided to use. In most circumstances, however, you need to determine when to do the bulk of your evaluation planning. Below are some considerations. See also the fixed vs. emergent design discussion on pp. 37–38.

THREE OPTIONS (Different Planning Approaches)

Planning Approaches	Benefits & Drawbacks
Plan in great detail before you begin. Specify carefully each step in the evaluation: what questions you'll address, how, who will get what information, when, and so on. Plan to follow your plan unless you absolutely have to deviate.	*Benefits* - People know what to expect. The plan can be used like a contract, to hold people accountable. Costs and time can be predicted and planned for. *Drawbacks* - Assumes a greater degree of knowledge and control than may exist. Doesn't allow for capitalizing on opportunities. Doesn't allow response to changes. Limits the conclusions to what can be predicted and prescribed.
Wing it. Plan as you go, following the evaluation as it leads you. Begin only with a general purpose, and don't commit yourself to particular questions, methods or interim objectives.	*Benefits* - Can capitalize on opportunity and respond to changing needs and conditions. Is more compatible with how programs and general experience operate. Mimics life. *Drawbacks* - Makes people nervous, which may affect cooperation. Hard to staff and budget. Difficult to get approval from administrators and participants who want more certainty.
Take the "Middle Road" Recognize the Two Planning Errors: 1. It's a mistake not to have a plan. 2. It's a mistake to follow your plan completely Plan as specifically as you can, but recognize, admit and plan for deviations. Be ready to take advantage of changes and respond to emerging needs	*Benefits* - Reduces anxiety among parties to the evaluation because direction and general procedures are known, allows allocation of resources, yet maintains and recognizes legitimacy of deviation, spontaneity. Encourages ongoing contact with audiences. Represents a rational humane approach. *Drawbacks* - Is hardest to do well. Becomes easy to get committed to plans and blind to needs for change. Requires tolerance for ambiguity.

DESIGN ELEMENTS
THAT SHOULD BE
CONSIDERED
BEFOREHAND AND
THOSE THAT CAN
BE LEFT FOR
LATER

Design elements you should almost always plan beforehand are . . .
· purposes for evaluating
· who will be involved as evaluators, judges and decision-makers
· the kinds of conclusions the evaluation will, and will not, draw
· audiences for the evaluation or process for identifying them

DESIGN ELEMENTS THAT SHOULD BE CONSIDERED BEFOREHAND AND THOSE THAT CAN BE LEFT FOR LATER *(continued)*

· resources available for the evaluation
· legal, organizational and other guidelines that will direct or affect the evaluation
· meta-evaluation procedures and standards
· begin/end dates
· report dates and audiences

Design elements you can define now, but are often OK or preferable to leave for later...
· instrument types and content
· information collection methods
· analysis methods
· verification and aggregation and coding steps
· report content
· report methods
· interpretation methods and criteria

INVOLVING AUDIENCES IN THE EVALUATION DESIGN

There are a number of strategies available to involve key stakeholders in designing evaluation. Regardless of the tactic you choose, it should help assure that the evaluation design is *defensible, clear, internally consistent*, and *mutually agreed upon*.

STRATEGY

1. Evaluator(s) do evaluation by themselves and informally, "in their head," rather than written or shared with others.

2. Evaluators do a rough draft of each product. They check it for accuracy, etc., as they interview others. Then they write up the product and get people to sign off on it.

3. Evaluators identify key persons from the evaluation audience for the project. They convene them for a planning session in which they (a) brainstorm through the process of doing a product, (b) break into subgroups to write parts of it, and (c) come back together to share, improve, and approve the resulting document.

4. Evaluators do a rough draft of each product. They use drafts as input into a session similar to that described for the third tactic. Audiences edit, modify, and sign off on it in the group session.

BENEFITS AND RISKS

1. Low effort and commonly done. Risks misunderstandings and overlooking something critical.

2. Moderate effort. Reduces risks by providing a written agreement up front. Risks overlooking something if people sign without really thinking it through.

3. Moderate to large effort. Shares risks, obtains full and early involvement of key persons. Lowers risk of overlooking something. Risks (a) not being able to get them to commit themselves that much or (b) uncovering/encountering serious conflicts early in the process. (That sometimes is a benefit rather than a risk!)

4. Moderate to large effort. Obtains early involvement but can be perceived as manipulative, if badly handled. Reduces risks of getting embroiled in conflict.

5. Evaluators form an advisory group that represents all audiences and involve them throughout in planning and reviewing.

5. Moderate to large effort. Sustains involvement and promotes acceptance and use. Can be volatile and slow the process. Government requires use of such groups.

KEY PERSONS INVOLVED IN EVALUATION DESIGN

You must decide at the outset who will be responsible for and involved in designing the evaluation. Until primary responsibility is clear, it will be difficult to make any of the important design decisions. See pp. 176–180 in the Management section of the Sourcebook for a lengthier discussion regarding evaluator selection.

Candidates for evaluator role
· internal staff member
· key decision maker
· external consultant
· ad hoc team including line and staff
· external team

Others you might think about involving in a design effort
· clients for the evaluation
· program staff
· program clients
· funding agents
· oversight boards
· consulting experts
· advocacy groups and special interest parties
· parents, community members
· legal experts, attorneys
· union representatives

Ways of involving others
· form advisory groups
· conduct open reviews and panels
· hire them (as consultants)
· interviews and visits
· sign-off lists
· public meetings
· joint working sessions
· task forces, teams

TRAINING AUDIENCES THROUGH THE EVALUATION DESIGN PROCESS

There are a number of *reasons* you may need or wish to train others as a part of their involvement in an evaluation design.

So they can *perform evaluation tasks* adequately. Tasks often requiring training are: generating key evaluation questions, information collection procedures, coding and verification, analysis, and interpretation.

So they can better use *evaluation results*. Such training might be in evaluation approaches and uses, limitations, decision making, problem-solving, ranking and valuing, etc.

So they will *support* evaluation efforts. Topics here might include: general evaluation uses and methods and limitations, or how a particular effort is designed or will proceed.

So they can *do their own* evaluation when you are through. This training might include any of the topics listed above.

DETERMINE THE SCOPE OF THE EVALUATION EFFORT

Decide whether you will start "Big" or "Small." This decision will be affected by a number of variables including resources, time, evaluation expertise, and magnitude of the problem for which the evaluation is to be

DETERMINE THE SCOPE OF THE EVALUATION EFFORT *(continued)*

used. Generally speaking, you are better off beginning modestly (especially if you are relatively inexperienced at formal evaluation) and growing carefully and incrementally. However some evaluations by virtue of what they are evaluating must be grand in scope.

Expenditure Possible	Low		High
Resources available, e.g., money, person hours, equipment, time	Evaluation will be bootlegged; no extra funds available	Budget can support some evaluation activities (person hours, Xeroxing, instrument development)	Substantial and separate support exists for the purpose of evaluation

Expertise Available	Minimal		Maximum
Skills needed, e.g., technical, conceptual, managerial, experiential	Evaluation must be done completely by existing staff who lack evaluation experience	Most of the evaluation will be done by staff; funds exist for training or an outside consultant	Funds and time exist to recruit and hire an experienced evaluator

Impact Anticipated	Small		Large
Magnitude of the impact, e.g., persons affected, dollars/resource allocation, expected system changes	Evaluation is done primarily to meet a mandate; unlikely that it will have any real impact	At least some of the program components are likely to be affected by the evaluation	The expectation is that the program will be drastically changed or aborted based upon evaluation results

HOW DO YOU RECOGNIZE A GOOD DESIGN?

Keep in mind that there are always a number of alternative designs that are appropriate for an evaluation problem. There isn't a single "right" design, nor is there an infallible design. In order to choose one design over another or to determine when an evolving design has reached maturity, you need to have decided what criteria your design should meet.

This section contains some alternative sets of criteria and standards for judging an evaluation design. Regardless of which set of evaluation criteria is adopted, adapted, or created, there will be tradeoffs when attempting to apply it. Because this is so, it pays to construct an evaluation design a number of different ways—varying design procedures to meet a maximum number of important design criteria.

A useful evaluation design targets on program problems or areas of concern for stakeholders. The design responds to where the program is at the time as well as where it wants to be. To do this, program needs identified by the evaluator as well as important audiences have had to be identified and ranked. The issues uncovered launch a number of evaluation questions that become the starting point for information collection.

After evaluators and stakeholders think through the information needed to address evaluation questions, they must respond to some practical and technical concerns. For instance, what problems might there be in getting information; how accurate will the information likely be; how tough will it be to analyze; how will it be used? Again, it is beneficial to draft several strategies for gathering information, varying the sources, procedures, and analysis. It is preferable to start modestly and grow only in relationship to expanding purposes or questions.

The best evaluation designs are practical; that is, they can be done within the constraints of the environment and your resources. And the most useful evaluations attend to people and how they might be affected by the evaluation. These qualities are more important than which format or method your evaluation design ultimately embraces. Your design, for instance, might take the form of a letter, a grid, a systems chart, or a story. It might include a case study, a series of observations, or a pre/post test. Whatever the format or method, it should consider the issues described in this section.

THE DESIGN CONSIDERS PRACTICALITY ISSUES   The most useful design might not turn out to be practical, or even possible. Look down the following list of issues and consider how they are being dealt with in your design.

Cost$$ **cost has been anticipated**
              · dollars, person hours and possible disaffection
              · projected benefits (number, type)

THE DESIGN CONSIDERS PRACTICALITY ISSUES *(continued)*

· cost of evaluation
· usefulness of evaluation
· audience reaction to cost
· time to complete the evaluation

Politics

you have thought about persons with special interests
· who will be interested in the findings, potential gains or conflicts for particular audiences
· control of final report and its release
· how bias will be limited in report (minority opinions sought)
· what kind of protocol must be anticipated (who must you see first, who must be involved, who is being excluded)
· who will use the information and under what circumstances might they *not* use it
· what groups can stop or change evaluation procedures with their disapproval (unions, professional organizations, clients, administrators)
· whether the contract has established timeline budget, renegotiation strategies and clear responsibility and authority for evaluation tasks

Procedures

the procedures are practical given the purpose
· the criticality of information need has been considered (you're not spending lots of dollars to get more of the same information)
· procedures are commensurate with purpose (finding out how good a 5-hour inservice is does not demand more time than the inservice)
· if the purpose changes, the procedure can change (you've anticipated the unexpected)
· procedures have been okayed by key stakeholders (e.g., teachers know they will hand out tests)

THE DESIGN ANTICIPATES THE QUALITY AND WORTH OF EXPECTED INFORMATION

There is no such thing as a flawless design. Further, there is no such thing as indisputable information. Begin with the assumption that regardless of what the information you turn over looks like, there will be varied interpretations.

Some logical questions to ask yourself:

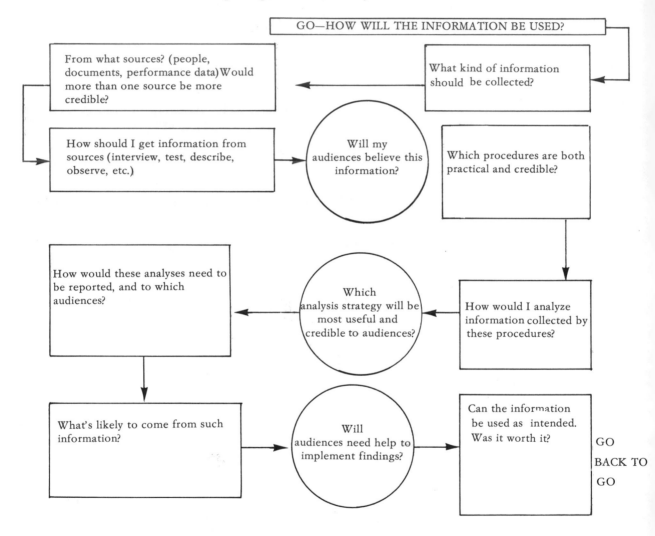

THE DESIGN IS SENSITIVE TO PEOPLE

Evaluations have sometimes been good for organizations and bad for the people in them. This "castor-oil" approach to evaluation has done a good deal of harm. The field of evaluation and professional evaluators do not promote hurtful evaluation; to the contrary, the best evaluations are more useful than harmful to people. Professional evaluation standards highlight

THE DESIGN IS SENSITIVE TO PEOPLE *(continued)*

the importance of human interactions and ethical considerations. So, being professional in evaluation is being considerate to those affected.

EVALUATION FUNCTION	PITFALLS AFFECTING PEOPLE
Focusing the Evaluation	people affected by evaluation aren't contacted, interviewed, or otherwise considered *result*: key questions not answered 　　　　　results not accepted
Information Collection	procedures involving target audience violate rights of human subjects (self-esteem, civil rights, due process, anonymity, informed consent) *result*: civil suit procedures cost valuable time of personnel and they reap no benefits *result*: disaffection and lack of cooperation procedures are obtrusive and cause people to change their behavior *result*: unrealistic data 　　　　　disruption of the setting
Information Analysis	analysis embarrasses individuals (individual results reported) analysis is too technical for audiences expected to use it analysis doesn't address critical questions of key audiences *result*: information is not valued or used
Reporting	audiences who helped get information aren't given a report audiences aren't given a chance to react to the report before and after its release (consider appending a minority report) the report's release affects people's jobs or plans some people's views are excluded in the report the report embarrasses individuals or units *result*: information is not likely to be used by affected groups
Managing Evaluation	people aren't considered when scheduling evaluation tasks (teachers' units are interrupted, the secretaries are asked to do work) an ill-planned budget forces personnel to work too hard for scant payoffs the person(s) evaluating misuse information being gathered (this includes storing it inappropriately, leaking confidences, or walking around with a smug I-know-something-you-don't expression on their face) *result*: everyone gets really aggravated

THE DESIGN
MEETS
PRESPECIFIED
CRITERIA

An evaluation design is judged from a number of different perspectives; for example, from the perspective of key decision makers, evaluators, program staff, funding agents, and outside observers interested in the evaluation, the program, or both. An evaluation design may not be judged "good" by all of its audiences. This is because as the design is strengthened in one area (e.g., technical adequacy) to meet the needs of some audiences, it makes necessary tradeoffs in other areas (e.g., cost or timeliness) that affect other audiences.

While few designs meet with everyone's approval, it is easier to construct a sound design with the use of criteria that define good evaluation designs. Below are examples of criteria for evaluation designs.

THE JOINT
COMMITTEE
STANDARDS

Standards for Evaluating Educational Programs, Projects & Materials suggests the following standards as most relevant to designing evaluation (See the section on Meta-Evaluation for more information about the Standards):

· Audience Identification
· Information Scope and Selection
· Valuational Interpretation
· Practical Procedures
· Formal Obligation
· Balanced Reporting
· Object Identification
· Described Purposes and Procedures
· Described Information Sources
· Valid Measurement
· Reliable Measurement
· Analysis of Quantitative Information
· Analysis of Qualitative Information
· Justified Conclusions
· Objective Reporting

SANDERS &
NAFZIGER
CRITERIA

The following list of criteria is from Sanders & Nafziger, "A Basis for Determining the Adequacy of Evaluation Designs."

I. Regarding the Adequacy of the Evaluation Conceptualization
    A. *Scope*: Does the range of information to be provided include all the significant aspects of the program or product being evaluated?
        1. Is a description of the program or product presented (e.g., philosophy, content, objectives, procedures, setting)?
        2. Are the intended outcomes of the program or product specified, and does the evaluation address them?
        3. Are any likely unintended effects from the program or product considered?
        4. Is cost information about the program or product included?
    B. *Relevance*: Does the information to be provided adequately serve the evaluation needs of the intended audiences?
        1. Are the audiences for the evaluation identified?

2. Are the objectives of the evaluation explained?
3. Are the objectives of the evaluation congruent with the information needs of the intended audiences?
4. Does the information to be provided allow necessary decisions about the program or product to be made?

  C. *Flexibility*: Does the evaluation study allow for new information needs to be met as they arise?
1. Can the design be adapted easily to accommodate new needs?
2. Are known constraints on the evaluation discussed?
3. Can useful information be obtained in the face of unforeseen constraints, e.g., noncooperation of control groups?

  D. *Feasibility*: Can the evaluation be carried out as planned?
1. Are the evaluation resources (time, money, and manpower) adequate to carry out the projected activities?
2. Are management plans specified for conducting evaluation?
3. Has adequate planning been done to support the feasibility of particularly difficult activities?

II. Criteria Concerning the Adequacy of the Collection and Processing of Information

  A. *Reliability*: Is the information to be collected in a manner such that findings are replicable?
1. Are data collection procedures described well enough to be followed by others?
2. Are scoring or coding procedures objective?
3. Are the evaluation instruments reliable?

  B. *Objectivity*: Have attempts been made to control for bias in data collection and processing?
1. Are sources of information clearly specified?
2. Are possible biases on the part of data collectors adequately controlled?

  C. *Representativeness*: Do the information collection and processing procedures ensure that the results accurately portray the program or product?
1. Are the data collection instruments valid?
2. Are the data collection instruments appropriate for the purposes of this evaluation?
3. Does the evaluation design adequately address the questions it was intended to answer?

III. Criteria Concerning the Adequacy of the Presentation and Reporting of Information

  A. *Timeliness*: Is the information provided timely enough to be of use to the audiences for the evaluation?
1. Does the time schedule for reporting meet the needs of the audiences?
2. Is the reporting schedule shown to be appropriate for the schedule of decisions?

  B. *Pervasiveness*: Is information to be provided to all who need it?
1. Is information to be disseminated to all intended audiences?
2. Are attempts being made to make the evaluation information available to relevant audiences beyond those directly affected by the evaluation?

IV. General Criteria

  A. *Ethical Considerations*. Does the intended evaluation study strictly follow accepted ethical standards?
1. Do test administration procedures follow professional standards of ethics?
2. Have protection of human subjects guidelines been followed?
3. Has confidentiality of data been guaranteed?

**SANDERS &
NAFZIGER
CRITERIA**
(continued)

B. *Protocol*: Are appropriate protocol steps planned?
   1. Are appropriate persons contacted in the appropriate sequence?
   2. Are department policies and procedures to be followed?

**OFFICE OF SPECIAL
EDUCATION**

The Office of Special Education and Rehabilitation Services, Handicapped Personnel Preparation Program (OSE) suggests the following guidelines for rating the adequacy of program evaluation designs. (U.S. Department of Education, 1981)

EVALUATION: Does the proposal describe an evaluation design which specifies:

a. An appropriate evaluation methodology used to judge the success of each project subcomponent?
b. The kinds of data to be collected for each subcomponent?
c. The criteria to be used to evaluate the result of the project?
d. Procedure for assessing the attainment of competence within the project?
e. A method to assess the contribution of project graduates
   1. toward meeting the needs of children INCLUDING the number of graduates prepared and placed by role;
   2. graduates' length of services; and
   3. graduates' proficiency as judged by employers?
f. A method for assessing the effectiveness and efficiency of project resource usage?
g. A method for assessing the impact of this project on related projects within the institution and the community?
h. At least annual evaluation of progress in achieving objectives?
i. At least annual evaluation of the effectiveness of the project in meeting the purposes of the program?
j. At least annual evaluation of the effect of the project on persons being served by the project, including any persons who are members of groups that have been traditionally underrepresented such as members of racial or ethnic minority groups and handicapped persons, etc.? (p. 35)

**RANK ORDER
DESIGN CRITERIA**

In order to judge an evaluation design: 1) criteria should have been identified (or negotiated) so it is clear how the design is to be judged; 2) stakeholders or independent consultants who will be assessing the design should be identified; and 3) ongoing priorities should be set should tradeoffs in criteria prove necessary down the road.

The Joint Committee *Standards* order the relevant standards for designing evaluation according to these major qualities:

1. usefulness
2. feasibility
3. propriety
4. accuracy

**RANK ORDER
DESIGN CRITERIA**
(continued)

This is one general breakdown of priorities. Each evaluation design should be guided by a set of priorities—they might be usefulness, timeliness, cost, minimal disaffection, maximum information in a prespecified area, technical quality, etc. Remember that it's not enough to have criteria to evaluate the design—you must think about which criteria are the most important in order to make necessary tradeoffs.

REFERENCES

Brethower, K.S. & Rummler, G.A. Evaluating training. *Improving Human Performance Quarterly*, 1977, 5, 107–120. (IEM)

Brinkerhoff, R.O. Evaluation of inservice programs. *Teacher Education and Special Education*. Vol. III, No. 3, Summer, 1980, pp. 27–38.

Campbell, D.T. & Stanley, J.C. Experimental and quasi-experimental designs for research on teaching. In N.L. Gage (Ed.), *Handbook of research on teaching*. Chicago: Rand McNally, 1963. (Also published as *Experimental and quasi-experimental designs for research*. Chicago: Rand McNally, 1966.)

Carroll, S.J., Jr., & Tosi, H.L., Jr. *Management by objectives: Applications and research*. New York: Macmillan, 1973.

Cook, T.D. & Campbell, D.T. *Quasi-experimentation: Design and analysis issues for field settings*. Chicago: Rand McNally, 1979.

Drucker, P. *The practice of management*. New York: Harper & Bros., 1954. (original MBO piece)

Eisner, E.W. *The perceptive eye: Toward the reform of education evaluation*. Invited Address, Curriculum and Objectives, American Educational Research Association, Washington, D.C. March 31, 1975. (Connoisseurship)

Federal Electric Corporation. *A programmed introduction to PERT*. New York: John Wiley & Sons, 1963.

Guba, E.G. & Lincoln, Y.S. *Effective evaluation: Improving the usefulness of evaluation results through responsive and naturalistic approaches*. San Francisco: Jossey-Bass, 1981.

Hall, G.E. Facilitating institutional change using the individual as the frame of reference. In J.K. Grosenick & M.C. Reynolds (Eds.), *Teacher education: Renegotiating roles for mainstreaming*. Minneapolis: National Support Systems Project, University of Minnesota, Council for Exceptional Children, & Teacher Education Division of CEC, 1978. (CBAM)

Joint Committee on Standards for Educational Evaluation. *Standards for evaluating of educational programs, projects, & materials*. New York: McGraw-Hill, 1981.

Kiresuk, T.J. & Lund, S.H. Goal attainment scaling. In C.C. Attkisson, W.A. Hargreaves, & M.J. Horowitz (Eds.), *Evaluation of human service programs*. New York: Academic Press, 1978.

Levin, H.M. Cost-effectiveness analysis in evaluation research. In M. Guttentag & E.L. Struening (Eds.), *Handbook of evaluation research* (Vol. 2). Beverly Hills: Sage, 1975.

Mager, R.F. *Preparing instructional objectives* (2nd ed.). Belmont, CA: Fearson, 1975.

Patton, M.Q. *Qualitative evaluation methods*. Beverly Hills: Sage, 1980.

Provus, M.M. *Discrepancy evaluation*. Berkeley, CA: McCutchan, 1971.

Provus, Malcolm. Evaluation of ongoing programs in the public schools systems, in *Educational evaluation: Theory into practice*. Edited by Blaine R. Worthen and James R. Sanders. Worthington, Ohio: Charles A. Jones Publishing Co., 1973.

Sanders, James R. & Nafziger, Dean H. A basis for determining the adequacy of evaluation designs, *Occasional Paper Series*, No. 6, Evaluation Center, College of Education, Western Michigan University, Kalamazoo, Michigan 49008, April, 1976.

Scriven, M.S. Pros and cons about goal-free evaluation. *Evaluation Comment*, 1972, 3.

Scriven, M.S. Goal-free evaluation. In E.R. House (Ed.), *School evaluation: The politics and process*. Berkeley, CA: McCutchen, 1973.

Shumsky, A. *The action research way of learning: An approach to inservice education*. New York: Bureau of Publications, Teachers College, Columbia University, 1958.

Stake, Robert E. The countenance of Educational Evaluation, in *Educational evaluation: Theory into practice*. Edited by Blaine R. Worthen and James R. Sanders. Worthington, Ohio: Charles A. Jones Publishing Co., 1973.

Stake, Robert E. Program evaluation, particularly responsive evaluation. *Occasional Paper Series*, No. 5, Evaluation Center, College of Education, Western Michigan University, Kalamazoo, Michigan 49008, November, 1975.

Stufflebeam, Daniel L. An introduction to the PDK book: Educational evaluation and decision-making, in *Educational evaluation: Theory into practice*. Edited by Blaine R. Worthen and James R. Sanders. Worthington, Ohio: Charles A. Jones Publishing Co., 1973.

Tallmadge, G.K. *Joint Dissemination and Review Panel Ideabook*. Washington, D.C.: U.S. Government Printing Office, 1977.

Thompson, E.K. (Ed.). *Using Student Change Data to Evaluate Inservice Education*. Bloomington, ILL: School of Education, Indiana University, 1981. (NIN "Steps")

Tyler, R.W. Some persistent questions on the defining of objectives. In C.M. Lindvall (Ed.), *Defining Educational Objectives*. Pittsburgh: University of Pittsburgh Press, 1964.

Wolf, Robert L. Trial by jury: A new evaluation method. *Phi Delta Kappan*, 1975, November.

Wolfensberger, W., & Glenn, L. *Program Analysis of Service Systems: A Method for the Quantitative Evaluation of human services*. (3rd Ed.) Vol. I: *Handbook*. Vol. II: *Field manual*. Toronto: National Institute on Mental Retardation, 1975.

Collecting Information

WHAT IT IS

This function involves gathering information to address the evaluation questions. Information sources can include people, documents, performance data, and observations of events. There are a number of methods to gather information including traditional measurement approaches such as tests, ratings, and frequencies, as well as investigative procedures like natural observation, ethnographic description, interviews, case studies, and literature review.

The most important issue related to information collection is *selecting* the most appropriate information or evidence to answer your questions. The information gathered must be relevant to the questions, and there must be enough information to provide convincing answers. Gathering too much information taxes the system and makes the evaluation costly and impractical. The aim is to collect enough information of the right kind at the lowest cost.

To plan information collection, evaluators must think about the questions to be answered and the information sources available. Moreover, they must think ahead to how that information could be analyzed, interpreted, and reported to audiences so it is credible and useful. Sound information collection entails looking ahead through the entire evaluation process to forecast what is likely to happen to the information collected (see Evaluation Questions, pp. 27–32). It also demands practical considerations about how information will be gathered (by whom, when) and how it will be monitored for continuing accuracy.

WHEN DECISIONS GET MADE

Plans for collecting information are usually made after evaluation questions have been posed. (Be wary when decisions about the appropriate information sources or methods precede decisions about what questions are important). After the evaluation is focused and the major questions drafted, a decision usually is made about the general type of information to collect. In most evaluations, information collection is cyclical. That is, some questions are posed which spur information collection. The information then triggers further questions which in turn demand more information collection. This process continues, growing incrementally more specific until sufficient certainty is reached.

WHAT KIND OF INFORMATION SHOULD BE COLLECTED?

The information you collect is the evidence you will have available to answer the evaluation questions. Poor evidence is information which cannot be trusted, is scant, or simply is not relevant to the questions asked. Good evidence, on the other hand, is information that comes from reliable sources by trustworthy methods to address important questions.

The task of selecting the appropriate information sources and methods is initially governed by practical concerns. That is, what's already available, how much money can you spend, what procedures are feasible? The information you finally decide to collect should be determined by what's possible and what best answers important questions. There will be tradeoffs, as you will see in the following sections.

SOME KINDS OF INFORMATION TYPICALLY COLLECTED IN TRAINING PROGRAMS	EVALUATIVE PURPOSES			
	To Decide on Goals	To Determine Strategies	To Determine Implementation: is it working?	Recycling: should it be continued?
Descriptive Information	characteristics of job descriptions, proposals, plans, reports current skill, knowledge levels, amount of training rates of use, production, incidences policies, rules patronage patterns kinds of clients served demographic data	characteristics of plans, proposals, user's guides, training manuals data about current services reports from commissions, task groups records of resources available, programs in use people's schedules, positions, jobs, rates demographic data research studies	records of use, attendance records of materials consumed, used, purchased, etc. transactions, behavior reactions nature and frequency of materials produced test scores performance levels pre/post changes	records of use, access rates, consumption effects on pupils, clients costs test scores of pupils, clients patterns of use, nature of use transactions follow-up activities, continued access and involvement case information

SOME KINDS OF
INFORMATION
TYPICALLY
COLLECTED IN
TRAINING
PROGRAMS
(continued)

EVALUATIVE PURPOSES *(continued)*

	To Decide on Goals	To Determine Strategies	To Determine Implementation: is it working?	Recycling: should it be continued?
Judgmental Information	expert opinions consumer preferences, wants beliefs, values criteria, laws, guidelines perceived priorities normative data	expert opinions user/trainee preferences, convenience, needs results of feasibility studies, pilot tests, research recommendations from task groups, leaders	opinions of trainees and trainers comparison of test scores to objectives, expectations. qualities of products produced in training expert opinions	opinions of graduates, users opinions of consumers, clients, pupils expert opinions quality of work samples benefits compared to costs

MAJOR SOURCES
OF EVALUATION
INFORMATION

People

how you might
get information
from them

whom you might seek as an information source

conversation
(face to face
or telephone)
structured
interviews
questionnaires
group
consensus
strategies,
e.g., Delphi
or Nominal
Group
Technique

those who originated the idea of the program, project or
activity
legislators, federal or state agency staff, university
administrators, department chairpeople committee
those who planned the actual "evaluation object": project
directors or team, ad hoc committee, instructors
the staff
those who will be held accountable for outcomes: deans,
chairpeople, instructors, principals, superindendents, etc.
those who will need to make decisions: administrators,
instructors, students, others
those whose needs are intended to be directly and
immediately served: students, pupils, teachers, etc.
those who are to benefit intentionally, but not immediately:
special education pupils, parents, school administrators,
other teachers
those who may be affected incidentally, positively, or
negatively: other faculty, non-included students, the public
those whose knowledge or expertise, independent of the
specific object being evaluated, may provide information or
insight in addressing the evaluation questions: former
teachers
trainees, other staff, experts

MAJOR SOURCES OF EVALUATION INFORMATION *(continued)*

Performance Data

how to get information
about performance

"eyeballing" data
statistical analysis (e.g., inferential,
   descriptive)
observation
rating (e.g., using multiple
   perspectives)
interview
survey
study of trends
content analysis

types to consider

---

test scores
observations of performance
achievement records
simulations
practice teaching
classroom behavior
social interaction
job success
problem solving skills
written/oral reports
work-samples

Documents

how to get information
using documents

---

counting numbers of documents (e.g.,
   letters to target audiences)
sorting into types (e.g., materials
   related to specific objectives)
content analysis
assessing quality of material
considering trends (e.g., watching for
   general changes in communication
   patterns)
gathering factual data (e.g., reading to
   find out dates, numbers, outcomes,
   etc.)
analysis using checklists

types to consider

---

proposals
requests for proposals
reports
schedules
minutes
memos
letters
course outlines
work samples (e.g., curricular
   materials)
student records
fiscal records
expenditure records

Context

how to get information
from the context

---

observe
interview stakeholders
read reports

things to consider

---

facilities
schedules
organizational patterns
management styles
political forces
economic realities
attitudes of personnel
protocols followed
informal/formal power structures
distribution of responsibility

SELECTING
INFORMATION
SOURCES
Once you know what information is available, there are some procedures that help you arrive at the information you should collect. In general, the more of these procedures you have the time and resources to complete, the more sure you'll be of collecting sound and useful information.

1. study what you are evaluating, its context, and related literature to determine what variables appear to be linked to effectiveness (see the previous chapter to review dimensions of an object and setting)
2. interview key stakeholders to determine what questions and variables they think are important
3. rank order the evaluation questions, and search for the variables that most likely would provide evidence to answer the questions
4. determine which sources would give you convincing information about a variable's effect on the program or whatever you are evaluating
5. list and review existing information sources (e.g., past reports, review documents used in program, find out what data is available)
6. select information sources based upon a predetermined set of criteria (see next section) and have this selection reviewed by key stakeholders

---

WHEN EVALUATION QUESTION ASKS ABOUT . . .   Some Potential Indicators Are . . .

WHEN EVALUATION QUESTION ASKS ABOUT...	Some Potential Indicators Are...		
Needs and Goals	characteristics of job descriptions, proposals, plans, reports policies, rules demographic data beliefs, values normative data	current skill, knowledge levels, amount of training patronage patterns expert opinions criteria, laws, guidelines nature and frequency of problems	rates of use, production, incidences kinds of clients served consumer preferences, wants perceived priorities
Training Strategies and Designs	characteristics of plans, proposals, user's guides, instructor's manuals records of resources available, programs in use training literature	data about current services people's schedules, positions, jobs, rates expert opinions results of feasibility studies, pilot tests, research	reports from commissions, task groups demographic data user/trainee preferences, convenience, needs recommendations from task groups, leaders
Implementation of Training	attendance rates and patterns usage of materials, resources perceptions of observers	trainer behavior perceptions of trainees transactions (verbal, other) wear and tear on materials	trainee behaviors perceptions of trainers discard rates and nature

WHEN EVALUATION QUESTION ASKS ABOUT... *(continued)*			
Immediate Outcomes	materials produced in training trainer ratings observer ratings	knowledge (i.e., test scores) trainee ratings self-report ratings	performance in simulated tasks pre/post changes in test scores
On-Job Usage of Training Outcomes	nature and frequency of usage peer opinions records of use, behavior	trainee perceptions observed behavior performance ratings	supervisor opinions quality of work samples test scores transactions of trainees with others
Impacts (Worth) of Training	changes in policies, rules, organization perceptions of clients patterns of use rates cost/benefit analyses	performance ratings performance of clients (e.g., test scores) opinions of experts, visitors, observers	promotion records perceptions of clients, peers, relatives consumer opinions quality of work samples treatment, sales records

---

DETERMINE IN ADVANCE THE CRITERIA INFORMATION SHOULD MEET

There are a number of considerations when selecting information; and, often, accommodating one consideration such as "cost effectiveness" forces you to trade off another such as "technical accuracy." It's up to evaluators and their audiences to prioritize criteria *their* information must meet. To help make those decisions, some criteria for evaluation information are listed below along with descriptions of information that meets such criteria, rationale for why criteria are significant, and some tips on what might be done to meet the criteria.

Criterion	Information that meets criterion	Significance of meeting criterion	Procedures for meeting criterion
Credibility	Information that is believable to audiences because it is accurate (see below), was produced by competent, trustworthy persons and interpreted in light of defensible criteria	Only information that can be trusted by audiences will be used	Selecting a competent evaluator who is considered skilled by important audiences. Interpreting the information from several value bases, or including minority reports
Practicality	Information produced by reasonable efforts that are not too costly or disruptive	Complex information sources and analyses can be costly and have little practical significance	Prioritize audience questions, adhere to fiscal and practical constraints

Criterion	Information that meets criterion	Significance of meeting criterion	Procedures for meeting criterion
Timeliness	Information produced in time to meet audience needs	Late information is useless to key stakeholders	Plan backwards; target the completion date and then determine lead time necessary to produce
Accuracy	Information that is relevant and trustworthy, and not flawed with errors due to collecting methods, processing or analysis	Inaccurate or flawed information not only misinforms but can mislead audiences	Monitor information, specify how and why it will be analyzed, bring in outside consultants to reanalyze complex or large data bases
Ease of analysis	Information that personnel have the capability (competence and support system) to analyze	You have to be equipped to analyze the information you collect	Anticipate the type of information and analysis you'll have; make sure you have access to someone who has experience in dealing with such analyses
Objectivity	Open and direct information which has not been unduly distorted by the personal or professional investments of evaluators or certain audiences	Information biased by a particular perspective is dismissed; even objective sections of reports perceived to be nonindependent are ignored	Multiple perspectives; multiple value bases reported; meta evaluations at certain stages; independent observers; reviews of reports; appended minority reports
Clarity	Unambiguous and understandable information	Highly technical reports, or sloppy reports, cannot be read or understood by audiences who need to use them	Give drafts to non-technical readers for review; keep rewriting for clarity; use summary sheets and graphs
Scope	Information that is broad enough to provide a credible answer to a question, but not so broad as to be diffuse or unmanageable	Excess information is costly and cumbersome; scant information leaves too many questions unanswered	Balance comprehensive information against information overload by rank ordering questions, feeding back information to see when you have

Criterion	Information that meets criterion	Significance of meeting criterion	Procedures for meeting criterion
			enough, producing quality not quantity
Availability	Existing data or data that are cheap and easy to get, e.g., records, reports, files, test scores, survey results, demographic data	Available data are usually free, and less likely to be contaminated or biased by being collected for the evaluation purpose	Check existing information files and reports for several "generations" back; check data bases across horizontal and vertical layers of the organization (e.g., other departments and higher administrative levels)
Usefulness	Information which is timely and relevant to important audience questions	Evaluation information that cannot be used, or is not ready in time to be used, is not worth collecting	Make sure key stakeholders have been identified and their questions listed. Return to them for reactions to the information you plan to collect. Seek commitments from stakeholders to use information
Balance	Information that does not inordinately represent one point of view, value, perspective, etc. (e.g., collecting only *strengths* of a workshop)	Audiences realize that all aspects of the program were studied; program strengths aren't sabotaged when planning to meet identified needs	Make sure both advocates and critics are approached; use multiple and objective observers when possible
Cost effectiveness	Information that is worth the resources (dollars, people, time) spent to get it	Even useful information can cost too much to be fiscally or ethically defensible	Draft costs in terms of people, dollars, time. Forecast "costs" for prioritized evaluation questions and have these costs reviewed by important stakeholders

WHAT PROCEDURES SHOULD BE USED TO COLLECT INFORMATION?

Most often a number of procedures are useful for collecting information to answer a question. For instance, information to answer "How are students achieving?" might be collected by tests, observations of students, interviews with supervisors, or analyses of written assignments. There are multiple ways to collect information for most any question. And usually, the more measures you use, the more sure you can be of your results. This is especially true when whatever you are measuring (e.g., program, inservices, or trainees) is complex and made up of a number of variables, as one measure rarely captures the richness and variety of such evaluation "objects."

Selection of procedures is dependent upon resources. Information collection procedures must be practical; should you choose to use multiple procedures to collect information, considering time, cost, and interruptions to staff becomes even more important. Collection procedures, like information sources, must be selected with analysis and reporting in mind. That is, "Will this procedure produce information in a form that we have the capability to analyze and in a form our audiences will find credible?"

SOME QUANTITATIVE COLLECTION PROCEDURES AND INSTRUMENTS

Using these procedures results in numerical data. We call such data "convergent" in that phenomena (opinions, performance, behaviors) are "reduced" and put into categories that can be assigned a number. Then, these numbers can be summarized and otherwise manipulated.

Quantitative data collection procedures -

Procedure	What it Measures or Records	Example
Behavior Observation Checklist	Particular physical and verbal behaviors and actions	Record how frequently teachers use a new questioning technique
Interaction Analysis	Verbal behaviors and interactions	Observers code faculty classroom interactions.
Inventory Checklist	Tangible objects are checked or counted	School bulletin boards are checked for inservice related materials
Judgmental Ratings	Respondent's ratings of quality, effort, etc.	Experts rate the adequacy of the college's curriculum
Knowledge Tests	Knowledge and cognitive skills	Faculty are tested on knowledge of special education laws.

Opinion Survey	Opinions and attitudes	Superintendents are asked to rate their attitudes toward PL 94-142
Performance Tests and Analysis	Job-related and specific task behaviors	Principals are observed and rated on how they conduct an interview
Q-Sorts, Delphi	Perceived priorities	Parents prioritize teacher inservice needs
Self-Ratings	Respondents rate their own knowledge or abilities	Students rate how well they can administer different diagnostic devices
Survey Questionnaire	Demographic characteristics, self-reported variables	Teachers report how frequently they use certain resource center materials
Time Series Analysis	Data on selected variables are compared at several time points	Frequencies of key practicum behaviors of students are charted over the course of a new semester-long seminar

SOME QUALITATIVE COLLECTION PROCEDURES These procedures produce narrative information. (While narrative information can be converted into numerical categories, that would usually serve an antiethical purpose.) Qualitative procedures tend to capture broader and more open-ended perspectives about complex phenomena. These data are often harder to analyze and summarize.

Procedure	What it Measures, Records	Example
Wear and Tear Analysis	Apparent wear or accumulation on physical objects	Learning center materials are inventoried before and after a workshop to determine usage or removal.
Physical Evidence Analysis	Residues or other physical by-products are observed	Waste-basket contents are inventoried after workshop to see what material was thrown away
Case Studies	The experiences and characteristics of selected persons in a project	A few graduates from each degree program are visited at their jobs, and interviews conducted with their colleagues

SOME QUALITATIVE COLLECTION PROCEDURES (continued)		
Procedure	What it Measures, Records	Example
Interviews, Group or Individual	Person's responses and views	Department chair interviews students about course adequacy
Panels, Hearings	Opinions, ideas	A panel of teachers reviews the needs assessing survey data to give interpretations
Records Analysis	Records, files, receipts	Resource Center receipts are analyzed to detect trends before and after inservice
Logs	Own behavior and reactions are recorded narratively	Practicum students maintain a log of activities
Simulations, "In Baskets"	Persons' behaviors in simulated settings	Students are video-taped introducing a simulated inservice session
Sociograms	Preferences for friends, work and social relationships	An IEP committee pictures their inter-dependence for conducting meetings
Systems Analysis	Components and subcomponents and their functional inter-dependencies are defined	An evaluator interviews staff about program, depicts these perceptions in a systems analysis scheme
Advisory, Advocate Teams	The ideas and viewpoints of selected persons	Teams are convened to judge the merit of two competing inservice plans
Judicial Review	Evidence about activities is weighed and assessed	A "jury" reviews the data collected on a new practicum to decide if it should be repeated

SOME CONCERNS TO BEAR IN MIND WHEN DESIGNING INFORMATION COLLECTION PROCEDURES	Concern	For Instance . . .
	Availability	Make a list of data already available (records, reports, etc.) and see if you can use it to address evaluation questions. For example, a pre/post look at performance appraisal reports on trainees could indicate whether training is making an on-the-job difference.
	Need for Training Information Collectors	Trained information collectors usually collect better (more reliable) information. Interviewers, product raters, observers, etc. will do a better job if they know what to look for and how to tell if it's there.
	Pilot Testing	This is a fancy term for trying something out before you use it. Interviewers might try out a telephone interview with a few role-played participants to see whether and how well the interviewee notices and describes different training outcomes. Or, test a questionnaire on two groups of role-played trainees—one who loved the session, and another who hated it. The questionnaire group scores should be different.
	Interruption Potential	The more a procedure disrupts the daily flow of training life, the more likely it is to be unreliable—or even sabotaged. Try to be unobtrusive: An analysis of trash can contents can tell you something about whether trainees valued your materials—and is less disruptive than a questionnaire asking them to tell you if they valued them.
	Protocol Needs	Sometimes you can't collect (or shouldn't collect) information without first getting necessary permissions and clearances. Following traditional protocol is always a good idea: A letter from the employee's boss telling when and why you want to interview him or her gets you permission and makes cooperation a lot more likely. If you're not likely to be able to get needed clearance or permission, look for alternative information sources.
	Reactivity	You don't want *how* you measure something to change too drastically what you're after. A typical "laundry-list" questionnaire to survey training preferences can, for example, shape and re-prioritize a respondent's reaction; a simple interview question: "Tell me what you'd like" might get a very different response. Or, an observer's presence can suppress—or elicit—certain behaviors.
	Bias	Self-selected samples are often biased in ways that will contaminate conclusions. A follow-up questionnaire to trainees might elicit returns from extreme groups only. Or, a post-test administered only to those trainees who stayed until the very end of training may yield biased scores, since this sample of trainees may be more diligent, motivated, etc. Make sure the sample of what you'll measure is most likely to represent what you're after.
	Reliability	Consider how to get the most accurate information. When, for example, multiple observers, interviewers, or raters are used, *train* them to promote and check for consistency. Be sure that *when* or *where* you collect data isn't adversely affecting your data. Take time to make instruments readable, clear and error free.

SOME CONCERNS TO BEAR IN MIND WHEN DESIGNING INFORMATION COLLECTION PROCEDURES *(continued)*	Concern	For Instance . . .
	Validity	Will the collection procedure produce information that measures what you say you are measuring? Be able to support that the information you collect is, in fact, relevant to the evaluation questions you intend it for. Be sure that what you collect is a real indicator of the claims you make. "Graduates" of training might, for example, have knolwedge from your training; and/or they might *claim* to use it. Does that mean they *do* use it? Be sure, too, that your information collection procedure records what you want it to. A performance appraisal might, for example, record more about personality than behavior (what it supposedly measures).

CONSIDER INTERACTION EFFECTS

Remember that no collection procedure automatically meets, or violates, quality criteria. Reliability, cost effectiveness, validity, or ethics all depend upon the appropriate relationship of

the information source
with the
information collection procedure
considering the
evaluation question
given the
particular setting

This means that an excellent instrument with a reliability coefficient of .86 is still worthless if it is not investigating a relevant concern or if it is administered to an inappropriate group. In every evaluation situation, there will be tradeoffs in meeting criteria for sound information collection. That is why the important criteria should be determined at the beginning and reviewed throughout the evaluation.

HOW MUCH INFORMATION SHOULD YOU COLLECT?

Sampling is selecting a portion of a whole group taken to represent the whole group. The portion is known as the *sample*; the whole group is called the population. When you sample, you do so to learn something about a population without having to measure (interview, observe, etc.) all of the population.

Sampling is like a shortcut. It allows you to save time and money by selecting only a portion of all potential members of a population to provide information. Like any shortcut, sampling risks basing decisions on inadequate information. If you needed to choose a hotel for a convention, a tour of fifty guest rooms would provide a more complete rating than would a tour of five rooms. But, the five-room tour is quicker and easier, and you can make an estimate of the whole population (all the rooms) within a known degree of certainty.

Whenever you evaluate anything or any person you inevitably sample. That is, you don't collect information on *all* aspects of that thing or person. For instance, in evaluating whether a trainee should be certified, you would assess only a sample of competencies for each individual.

Often, it is wise to sample events, evaluees and respondents because you can generalize from your sample to the larger population, such as a course, a workshop, or a group. But you don't always want to sample among evaluees or respondents. If your purpose is to make diagnostic decisions about trainees, you have to evaluate a sampling of competencies from *each* trainee.

THE OPTIONS: DIFFERENT KINDS OF SAMPLING METHODS

There are two general kinds of sampling methods: random and purposive (called also objective and subjective). Random methods are used to produce samples that are, to a given level of probable certainty, free of biasing forces. They allow use of inferential statistics to generalize findings with calculable degrees of certainty. Purposive methods are used to produce samples that will represent particular points of view or particular groups in the judgment of those selecting the sample.

Here's a chart of some commonly employed sampling methods. Each is named and described, and a brief example of its use provided.

Some Sampling Techniques

Method	How it Works	Example
Random straight random sampling	One selects, via random method (such as a random numbers table), a predetermined portion of a population. The proportion of the population sampled determines the level of precision of the generalization to the larger population. The larger the sample, the more precise the generalization.	To determine the level of preparation of the average teacher, the SEA surveys a random sample of teachers accredited in the state.
quota sampling	The samples are drawn within certain population categories and can be made in proportion to the relative size of the category. A sample of parents, for example, could be drawn randomly from predetermined lists of upper income pupils, lower income pupils, Caucasians, blacks, Hispanic parents, or whatever other subpopulation categories were of interest. The quota sample ensures that the sample will include access to low-incidence subpopulations who would likely not be drawn in a straight random sample.	The university sends surveys to 5% of the graduates in each of several income and social categories to determine the perceived utility of the curriculum and its responsiveness to cultural differences.
Stratified samples	Samples are drawn for each of several "strata," such as freshmen, sophomores, juniors or seniors; or, teachers, administrators, and directors. Stratified samples are useful when you have more, or a different, interest in one particular stratum than another. You identify strata of greater interest, then take larger samples from them. Each stratum is considered a population.	The school district sends an inservice attitude survey to all of 15 principals, 50% of 40 administrators, and 10% of 1500 teachers.
matrix samples	This method samples both respondents from a defined population *and* items from an instrument. The notion here is that, when the respondent pool is sufficiently large and there are many instrument items, it is more efficient to have each respondent respond to only a certain subset of the items. If these item subsets are randomly generated, and respondents randomly drawn, generalization is possible to the entire population and the entire instrument. This method is particularly useful in broad-scale surveys or testing programs—but only, of course, where an individual's scores are not needed.	To determine whether a district-wide workshop impacted on knowledge of new state laws, 10% of all attendees were given tests. To keep tests brief, each person answered only 10 questions from the 50 items on the entire test.
Purposive key informants	This method of sampling individuals is employed to access those persons with the	Workshop staff conduct a de-brief

Some Sampling Techniques *(continued)*

Method	How it Works	Example
	most information about particular conditions or situations. Union representatives or de-facto leaders among teachers could be a prime source of teacher attitudes and opinions; community leaders, respected individuals, etc., could yield rich information on community issues and so forth.	with 6 participants to get their feedback. These 6 were selected because they emerged as small group leaders.
expert judges	This method involves sampling those persons with exceptional expertise about certain conditions or factors of interest. When information about best practices or recent advances is sought, an hour interview with an expert in the area can short-cut many hours of literature review and reading.	The university conducted case studies of employment of graduates who were deemed the most successful in the program to see if *their* preparation was sufficient, and to get their ideas for revision.
extreme groups	This intentionally seeks out conflicting or extreme viewpoints. Whereas the random methods aim to account for bias and converge on the average or typical case, the extreme group sample purposely ignores the middle ground or common viewpoint to learn about the atypical, extreme view. The known detractors of a program, be they small in number and inordinately biased, can offer rich clues as to a program's potential flaws—and even strengths.	Follow-up interviews are conducted with students who drop out of the program.
grapevine sampling	This entails a growing sample, where each successive sample member is determined by clues or explicit directions from the prior members. One might ask a principal, for instance, to be directed to the most voluble (or negative, or positive, or reticent, etc.) teacher in the school. That person would be interviewed then asked to recommend another person to the interviewer, and so forth, until the interviewer is satisfied that a sufficient sample has been obtained. Direction to the next case can be asked for explicitly or derived from each case's notes. The same method can be used in a survey questionnaire, much the same as a chain-letter operates.	In evaluating a technical assistance system, the evaluator interviewed first the teachers who got service. Then, went to the person who advised the teacher to use the service and also to the person who gave the service, using these contacts to get more contacts until repeats were encountered.

IMPORTANT
QUESTIONS TO
ADDRESS BEFORE
DETERMINING
WHETHER AND
HOW TO SAMPLE

Q: Should you use a sample?

A: Your most accurate alternative is always to get information from an entire population. But, this is also costly. Each additional sample member entails added costs of instrumentation, administration, analysis, and handling and storage.

Sampling can help with some typical sorts of problems. For example: an inservice coordinator received three telephone calls from irate teachers who just attended an inservice workshop, complaining of a poor instructor and disorganized session. The coordinator, before taking action (e.g., to change instructors) needs to decide whether these three teachers represent all who attended or whether they are a vociferous minority. A quick telephone call to a small, random sample of attendees could help determine this. Or, a few calls to some especially trusted attendees (a purposive sample) could also be used. In any case, the coordinator should also delve into the particular complaints from the vociferous three, for they are a "sample-of-opportunity" from which something of value can be learned; perhaps, for instance, they represent a small portion who are opposed to any inservice and thus their concerns need to be heard.

Q: What kind of sampling is most appropriate?

A: It happens often in training and personnel preparation that random samples are drawn when other—more purposive—sampling would be more useful. The best key to correct sampling is to reconsider why you are collecting information in the first place. What is it that you want to learn about, change, or report about?

For example, consider the typical case of sending a follow-up survey to graduates of a program or participants in an inservice. Usually, a random sample of attendees is drawn to receive the survey. But, this method assumes that you wish to make an inference (an estimate) about *all* attendees. Very often, however, the purpose is to make some judgments about the program (curriculum, workshop, etc.) itself, not about the typical or average attendee. Thus, it might make more sense to draw a sample of those whose judgments and opinion could mean the most or be most useful. This might be high-scoring graduates (or poor ones), or specially qualified attendees, persons with a lot of experience, etc.

The point is to choose a sampling method that will work best for your purpose. This means you have to be quite clear about your purpose. And, of course, you want to use a sampling method that suits your resources.

Q: What sampling unit should you use?

A: Sampling units are the basis on which you'll sample. Examples are:

People (e.g., teachers, trainers, parents, pupils)
Organizational units (e.g., schools, classes, districts, buildings)
Special groups (e.g., persons who received different sorts of experiences or treatments, users of different resources)

The sampling unit is very much related to the kinds of samples you intend to draw. It's thus dependent on your purposes for collecting information.

Q: How large a sample do you need?

A: The size of the sample you will draw will depend on four factors: (1) the amount of certainty you need, (2) the nature of the population, (3) how much money you have to spend, and (4) the nature of the information collection procedure.

▶ Certainty

Larger samples will give you greater certainty. For example:

A larger survey return on test population (e.g., 150 vs. 20) will increase the

IMPORTANT
QUESTIONS TO
ADDRESS BEFORE
DETERMINING
WHETHER AND
HOW TO SAMPLE
(continued)

certainty of estimates of population characteristics within fixed degrees of precision (e.g., ± 5%).

Most standard statistical texts (see references) contain tables that show you how large a sample is needed to achieve given levels of certainty.

A longer observation period or more periods, will enable you to record more, and more varied, behaviors.

A test or survey containing 100 items vs. 10 items will produce a more reliable estimate of the trait it measures.

The amount of certainty you need can be determined partially by projecting the consequences of a "wrong" (inaccurate, untrue) decision. If you're basing a major decision on data you're collecting—say whether to graduate a trainee, or refund a workshop—then you will want a lot of precision and certainty. If, on the other hand, you can live with a rough estimate, a smaller sample may do.

▶ How much variability is there in the population or trait about which you might make an estimate?

When variability is high, you need a larger sample. Some examples of variability are:

How many kinds of graduates complete a program?
How large a range of reactions to a training session might there have been?
How many different kinds of records might be in the files?
How many different behaviors constitute good (vs. bad) performance?

▶ Resources available

A larger sample will cost you more time and money. Along with greater certainty come greater costs. In all endeavors, there's a point of diminishing returns. You should consider whether the increase in certainty is worth the extra costs. And, consider, too, that a larger sample takes more time to access and handle data from: can you afford delay?

▶ Effectiveness of the information collection procedure

Not all procedures produce a 100% yield. If you expect: low return rates; inaccurate or partially complete records; partial completion of interviews, tests, observation; variably successful site visits; poorly attended meetings and hearings, etc; then you should think about increasing your sample size. The idea is to not just *try* for an adequate sample, but in fact *get* an adequate sample.

Q: Is your sample likely to be biased?
A: Yes. You will have some bias in any sample. The point is to anticipate and control it if possible; to consider and report it if not. Bias causes inaccuracy in estimates to a population. You might have a large enough sample to have good certainty, for example, but a bad (biased) sample can mean you draw an inaccurate decision despite high certainty. Some causes of bias in training programs are:

▶ Low response rates: Whenever you get less than 100% of your intended sample back, you run risks of response bias, more bias with lower returns. Those who actually respond might be significantly different from the population. To avoid low response:

Use smaller samples and spend your effort and money in more vigorous pursuit of the respondents.
Use a briefer instrument.
Pursue non-respondees.
Include a "reward" for response (money, a gift, a summary report, etc.). A teabag has been known to work: "Complete our survey, then have a cup of tea!"
Make return as easy as possible (stamped envelopes, self-mailers, etc.).

▶ Out-of-date population lists.

IMPORTANT
QUESTIONS TO
ADDRESS BEFORE
DETERMINING
WHETHER AND
HOW TO SAMPLE
(continued)

▶ Lack of complete data for some subgroups, such as poorly maintained records for handicapped and students.

▶ Use of the wrong sampling unit for the population you're interested in.

▶ Biased population listing, such as using the PTA roll for *all* parents.

CRITERIA TO AIM
FOR WHEN
SAMPLING

FREEDOM FROM UNWANTED BIAS

You need to be sure that some unplanned or unknown factor has not unduly biased the sample(s) you obtain. Some instances and examples of bias are:

lists and pools of names that are used to generate samples can be, themselves, biased. The classic example of this sampling error resulted in the famous 1932 headline, "Landon Beats Roosevelt." The pollsters took names from the phone book, which biased (1932) the sample to upper socio-economic strata.

the presence of an observer affects the samples of behavior that can be observed

some behaviors occur infrequently (e.g., managing violent pupil behavior) and wouldn't likely occur in a random sample

the timing of an information collection procedure is related to samples. Lesson plans sampled in September may be more conscientiously completed than those in March, for example. Or, behaviors in the morning may be different from the afternoon.

a directive from an authority to submit samples of lesson plans might influence respondents to submit their "best" work

a questionnaire mailed to parents in one school and carried home by pupils in another might reach different sorts of parents

EFFICIENCY

Samples should be no larger than what's necessary to obtain the desired level of certainty. Too much data is not only costing extra resources but places unnecessary demands on respondents and participants.

CHARACTERISTIC

Your sample should consider known incidence rates, distributions, and proportions in the population. When samples are drawn from larger populations to make inferences about certain characteristics or traits, you need to be sure that your sampling procedure accounts for what's known to be related to that trait. This often requires stratification. If, for example, you wished to sample district opinion on school programs, you would want to sample across socioeconomic levels, for these factors are known to be related to expectations and values about schooling. Or, your sampling procedure (purposive) would seek input from a spectrum of existing special interest groups.

REPLICABILITY

You should document the procedures by which you sample so that potential bias might be identified or so that others could repeat your procedures.

HOW WILL YOU SELECT OR DEVELOP INSTRUMENTS?

Instruments are the tangible forms which both elicit and record information you collect. There are many kinds of instruments: interview protocols, questionnaires, tests, checklists, observation records, etc.

Instruments have to be carefully chosen or designed. Sloppy or improper instrumentation can spoil an otherwise well planned information collection effort.

The tasks involved in instrumentation are deciding what you need, choosing to select or develop them, and developing if you have to.

COMMONLY USED INSTRUMENTS IN TYPICAL COLLECTION PROCEDURES

Surveys
Open-ended instruments
Forced-choice instruments

Interviews
Closed formats where questions and responses are read to respondent
Semi-open formats where questions are fixed, and interviewer transcribes interpretations of responses onto form
Open formats, where general guidelines are provided to interviewer; responses are transcribed in notes or on audio-tape

Observations
Open formats, where observer makes notes or general reactions, behaviors, etc. of subjects
Logs, where observer records own reactions and behaviors
Sign systems where specific behaviors are counted each time they occur to provide a record of certain behaviors that occur in a given time interval
Category systems, where behavior observed is classified in certain categories to produce a record of the kinds of behavior that have transpired in a given time interval

Tests
Multiple choice tests
Other forced-response formats; true-false, matching, etc.
Short answer, fill-in-the-blank
Essay tests

Inventories
Open-ended, where respondents make notes about certain objects; items as they find them
Checklist formats, where respondents check off—or count and enter numbers—next to listed items

Site visits, expert reviews, panel hearings
In these procedures, you can think of people *themselves* as "instruments." Kinds of "instruments" in these procedures might be:
Experts
Consumer representatives
Staff members
Public
Parents, etc.

GENERAL
SPECIFICATIONS
FOR AN
EVALUATION
INSTRUMENT

1. What **content** is needed?
   This relates directly to the variables you've decided on. The content of an instrument should be limited to and inclusive of these variables.

2. What **language** requirements exist?
   This can relate to the reading level of respondents, the kinds of examples and references to be used, avoidance of jargon or inclusion of definitions, foreign language translations, etc.

3. What **analysis** procedures will be used?
   If machine scoring or automatic coding is needed, the instrument must provide for these options. If sub-group analyses are projected, then demographic data must be included.

4. What **other special considerations** apply?
   This might include special versions for handicapped respondents, need for special directions, etc.
   In reviewing specifications, it's a good idea to construct a "blueprint" or list for each instrument you'll need. Also, you may want to get some special consultant help from your friendly local psychometrician at this point.

5. Determine how much **precision** is called for.
   Sometimes you plan to use data for relatively fine discrimination, such as ranking proposals for levels of funding or deciding how much remediation to provide different course participants. In other cases, less discriminating precision is needed, as in deciding whether a record meets completeness criteria or if participants are in favor of an evening or daytime workshop session. Don't be overly precise.
   Some variables distribute across a broad range of increments, such as clock-time spent in a learning module or the number of graduate courses completed. Others do not, and to measure them in precise increments lends an artificial degree of precision; examples of this are "participants rated satisfaction at 3.237 on a 10-point scale," or "3.7 participants completed the exercise."

6. Capacities of **intended** respondents.
   There is little to be gained, and reliability to be lost, when respondents and participants in information collection are asked to make discriminations beyond their abilities. Asking teachers in a questionnaire, for example, to list their undergraduate training courses would be less desirable than having someone analyze a sample of personnel files to get the same information.

7. **Suitability** for planned analysis
   Knowing what you'll do with data once they're collected helps decide how much precision to go for. If you think, for example, you'll want to see if amount of training is related to success on the job, you'll need relatively discriminating measures on each variable.
   Precision can be increased in a procedure by providing more detail and definition in instrument items and response guidelines and categories. Interviewers, for example, could read from a list of clearly defined uses of inservice outcomes, rather than ask for respondents' own interpretation.

GENERAL SPECIFICATIONS FOR AN EVALUATION INSTRUMENT *(continued)*

Or, proposal judges could rate each of 20 defined variables instead of making a global judgment.

Asking respondents (raters, observers, reviewers, etc.) for more objective vs. subjective responses can increase precision—but may limit richness and interpretation. Observers could, instead of rating teachers' "warmth and receptivity" count the instances of certain behaviors (e.g., verbal reinforcement, patting a child's head, smiling).

CHECKING TO SEE WHAT INSTRUMENTS ARE AVAILABLE

Before developing a new instrument, invest time in checking to see whether one already exists—even if it would need to be refined or adapted.

· friends and colleagues—ask them
· publishers of tests and materials
· catalogs (see references at end of chapter); especially helpful for training programs are the *ETC Instrument Catalog* and *Mirrors of Behavior*
· other projects and programs like yours
· libraries, resource centers, etc.

ASSESSING THE ADEQUACY OF INSTRUMENTS FOR YOUR PURPOSE

content: Do they contain what you need? Are variables appropriate? Is there irrelevant or missing content?
precision: Will they be precise enough, or *too* precise, for your needs?
availability: Can you get them? In time? Will copyright laws let you use them?
norms: When norms are used or provided, are the referent groups similar to those you'll use?
price: Can you afford them? Are they worth it?
technical accuracy: We'd recommend that you see the "Checklist" in the Appendix.

DEVELOPING YOUR OWN INSTRUMENT

1. List specifications for the instrument.

   content: what variables should it address?
   precision: how precisely and surely must it measure? What kinds of decisions will depend on the data produced?
   language requirements: will the instrument be read by 4th graders or Ph.D. candidates? handicapped persons? bilingual persons?
   analysis planned: machine scoring? special coding? analysis along with other instruments?
   demographic data needs: how much will the instrument need to record information about respondents themselves or the administration setting?

2. Clarify the *conceptual design/basis* for the instrument.

   An instrument shouldn't be a haphazard collection of items and directions. It needs a conceptual design—the "glue" that hangs it together. Some examples are:
   "Respondents will be asked to recollect their initial ability levels before the workshop, then rate their growth on each of the several workshop objectives"
   "The six typical behavior problems will be presented, and respondents will outline a proposed treatment strategy. Responses will be scored according to how well respondents incorporate Schwartzian theory"
   "The hidden observer will watch for, and list, behavior indicative of Schwartz's Syndrome"

DEVELOPING YOUR OWN INSTRUMENT
(continued)

"The questionnaire will list many resources, some of which the agency has disseminated. Then, it will ask people to check those they use most often"

3. *Block out* ("blueprint") the instrument
   Outline the major sections, where you'll want directions, how many items you want for each objective, etc.
4. Produce a *draft* of the instrument
5. Get the draft *reviewed*. Have it checked for:
   ease of reading and clarity
   content
   technical flaws (e.g., dual stems, overlapping response categories).
6. *Revise* the draft (Note: the more often you do this and Step 5, the better it will get)
7. *Try out* the instrument (see next sub-section) to be sure it has sufficient reliability and validity for your needs.
8. Revise again, and try-out again until:

ASSESS THE INSTRUMENT

Validity: The instrument provides truthful, useful and authentic information about what it measures or records

Reliability: The instrument measures and records accurately. (You want a minimum amount of error in the scores and information they produce.)

Non-reactivity: Instrument does not adversely change or otherwise affect what is measures and records. (Sometimes, some items on a test will give clues to correct answers on other items; questionnaire items may "key" a response; interview questions and phrasing may suppress certain information, etc.)

Appropriateness for responders and users: Language levels, examples, formats and item structures are suitable for the intended users.

Sufficient precision for intended analysis and usage; The instrument produces data in categories (e.g., scores, ratings) at least as fine as the finest discrimination you intend to make. (If, for instance, you wanted to sort users of resource services into four categories, you would need an item [or group of items] with at least four levels of response categories.)

Economy: The instrument is not too costly to select, develop, try-out, revise, aggregate, analyze and interpret. Nor is it too demanding of respondent's and user's time, patience and attention.

CHECKLIST FOR INSTRUMENTS

Introduction
☐ there is a clear statement of the instrument's purpose
☐ the respondent is told how information resulting from the instrument will be used

☐ those who will see the data are identified
☐ the respondent is told why s/he was selected to complete the instrument

Introduction

- ☐ the privacy of confidential information is insured
- ☐ the anonymity of the respondent is guaranteed (if appropriate)
- ☐ motivators for responding are supplied
- ☐ directions for returning the instrument are adequate (when, where, and how)

Item Stems

- ☐ the stem is relevant to the stated purpose of the instrument
- ☐ the stem focuses on one center (has one key verb)
- ☐ the wording of the stem is appropriate to the reading level of the respondents
- ☐ the possible response is not biased by the wording of the stem (giveaway hint for plural)
- ☐ "supply" items identify the appropriate unit of response
- ☐ each stem is independent of other stems
- ☐ the level of analysis necessary to respond to the stem is appropriate to the capabilities of the respondents

Directions

- ☐ directions are given when necessary for each section
- ☐ the language used is appropriate to the level of the respondents
- ☐ the directions are clear and complete
- ☐ an example item is provided (if necessary)

Directions

- ☐ directions are provided for responding to items which "do not apply"
- ☐ the respondent is told if other materials are needed to complete the instrument

Format

- ☐ individual items are appropriately spaced
- ☐ items are grouped in a logical order (by content, type, etc.)
- ☐ sufficient space exists for the desired response
- ☐ instrument is easy to read
- ☐ instrument is not too long
- ☐ instrument is "pleasing to the eye"

Responses

- ☐ response categories are unidimensional
- ☐ response categories are non-overlapping
- ☐ response categories are exhaustive
- ☐ response categories are relevant to the stems
- ☐ "not applicable," "I don't know," "no opinion" options are provided where appropriate
- ☐ a sufficient amount of space is left for supply responses
- ☐ space is provided for comments where appropriate
- ☐ a sufficient amount of space is left for supply responses
- ☐ space is provided for comments where appropriate
- ☐ guidelines are provided for comments

HOW DO YOU ESTABLISH THE VALIDITY AND RELIABILITY OF INSTRUMENTATION?

Validity and reliability are characteristics that must be present in your data collection efforts or you risk collecting information too inaccurate to be usable.

Validity refers to how truthful, genuine and authentic data are in representing what they purport to. To be valid is to make truthful claims; instruments must measure what they intend and claim to measure. Data produced by instruments must authentically represent the traits and phenomena you use them to represent.

Reliability relates to the accuracy of measures. The more error in a measure, the more unreliable it is. Reliability often means different things in different kinds of measures, but in general it represents the trustworthiness of data produced. We might know that a bath scale, for instance, is capable of producing valid indications of weight: the number of pounds is a valid measure of weight. But if the bath scales' indicator slips and is loose and its viewing glass is scratched and dirty, it is highly likely that any one weighing will produce an erroneous result. The scale is unreliable.

Reliability and validity are achieved through the careful design, try-out and revision of instruments and information collection procedures.

In thinking about how you can approach increasing the reliability and validity of your collection efforts, you should recognize and keep two facts "up front":

Neither reliability nor validity is a "one-time" phenomenon. You must be continually aware of them, working to increase them and deal with problems that arise throughout the life of an evaluation.

There is not on *a priori* level of minimum reliability or validity that can be set for your measures. The more you increase these characteristics, the more sure you can be of your results, and you can use them with more confidence.

In this section, we briefly characterize kinds of validity and reliability and present some general steps and considerations you can take to increase reliability and validity. Then, for each of five (5) commonly used quantitative instrument types, we present some techniques you can use to determine and increase reliability and validity.

KINDS OF VALIDITY AND RELIABILITY

Validity

Content Validity: does an instrument contain the right stuff? Are test items consistent with course content? Are behaviors listed related to diagnostic ability? Do rating items represent a meaningful range of criteria?

Concurrent Validity: does a measure produce results consistent with some other independent measure? e.g., do self-ratings of knowledge correlate with scores in a knowledge test?

Predictive Validity: this is the ability of a measure to faithfully predict some other future trait or measure; e.g., does score on the interview for admission predict success in the graduate program?

Construct Validity: this relates to the truthfulness of the theoretical construct underlying a measure and requires considerable research to establish and investigate. An example of construct validity inquiry would be research to determine if persons who achieve good scores on workshop objectives do, in fact, achieve good pupil learning results. Or, whether "ability to give positive reinforcement" is related to pupil learning.

Reliability

Stability, repeatability: a test or measure that provides consistent scores from instance to instance is reliable: stable over time. A content rating of a product, for instance, should not produce different scores depending on when and where the analysis takes place.

Inter-judge or rater agreement: a rating should reflect the characteristics of the object being rated, not vagaries and differences among users of the instrument (the judges). This kind of reliability is vastly improved by training of raters and judges.

Equivalency: this relates to the degree of consistency between two alternate forms of the "same" test or measure. If tests are equivalent (produce the same scores) then differences over time (e.g., after a workshop) can be inferred to be the result of instruction, not the result of having taken the test before.

Internal Consistency: this relates to how well a group of items or a measure "hangs together." It tells you how unidimensional the measure is— whether items are measuring one trait. Estimates of this kind of reliability can be made by checking the degree of correlation between split-halves of the test, or by other measures requiring only one administration of the test (see references).

Q: How do you get valid data?

A: Validity is not so much a characteristic intrinsic to some data. It's more related to how you *use* data. Self-ratings of knowledge are known, for example, to be quite an accurate estimation of actual knowledge. To use self-ratings in a certification program as a basis for grading, however, would likely be an invalid use. Use of self-ratings in a workshop, however, as a means for participants to select paths of study, would be far more valid.

Consider, then, how you'll use information. Will it provide a genuine and authentic measure of what you want to use it for? Might it be easily contaminated by another factor (as in the case of self-rating for certification)?

Q: How do you maximize the content validity on an instrument?

A: When constructing a test, rating scale, questionnaire, checklist or behavioral observation, you want to be sure that what you're measuring (the items on the form) are the right stuff. This is largely a judgment issue. Seek advice from colleagues, experts, literature and research. Ask:

GENERAL
QUESTIONS AND
CONSIDERATIONS
ABOUT VALIDITY
AND RELIABILITY
(continued)

does content reflect what's important in this workshop, course, program, etc.?

is there agreement that these variables are important?

does the literature, other programs, or research support these variables as being correct?

is there a logical connection between what you're measuring and what you need to know?

Q: How do you maintain validity?

A: Because validity is related to how data get *used*, you need to monitor and reflect on the uses of data you collect to avoid invalid applications. A department chair should not, for example, use grades assigned to students to compare faculty—or whose students are learning the most. Nor should an inservice coordinator base decisions of who in the district needs what training on preferences expressed from a volunteer survey.

An intended use could be quite valid; an actual use could be quite invalid. Monitoring usage of data, facilitating interpretation (See the "Reporting" chapter), and exploring meaning in data empirically and reflectively will increase validity and the utility of your evaluation.

Q: How do you design an instrument for reliability?

A: Reliability is related to error in measuring. An instrument that contains a number of errors (that is, it's unclear, vague, confusing and difficult to use) is bound to be unreliable. You can achieve needed levels of reliability very often by trying out an instrument and revising it based on feedback.

make sure directions are clear

be sure there's only one way to respond to and interpret an item

eliminate items with dual stems (e.g., "How useful and interesting was the workshop?"

Adherence to the criteria on the Instrument Checklist (pp. 98–99) will help you improve or assess reliability.

Q: Do you need to monitor data collection?

A: Yes. Instruments used differently in different situations will produce non-parallel, unreliable data. You need to be sure that data collection gets carried out the way it's intended and is consistent from instance to instance.

Q: Who should administer the instrument?

A: Train experts, judges and raters when you use rating instruments. Without training and adequate direction, raters are likely to apply varying criteria and to "see" different things. If you want to treat their data equivalently, then you need to train them. If you will use their judgments independently, then you'll need to know what rules they used, criteria they applied, their perspectives, etc. to reliably interpret their opinions.

Q: How can you increase the reliability of ratings?

A: Use more and more specific rating variables. For example, global judgments ("How did you like the workshop?") can easily be unreliable. To get more precision into your data, break the global concept into several subconcepts.

WAYS OF
ESTABLISHING
RELIABILITY
AND VALIDITY
FOR DIFFERENT
KINDS OF
INSTRUMENTS

HOLISTIC RATING SCALES

Holistic rating scales: where ratings on several items are added together to compute a total score.

Example

Student Diagnostic Test Administration Ability

		4	3	2	1	
☐ gives directions properly	excellent	( )	( )	( )	( )	poor

☐ gives directions properly   excellent ( ) ( ) ( ) ( ) poor
☐ checks comfort level
☐ repeats questions when necessary
☐ etc.

Total score = _____

Uses: The *total score* on the instrument (e.g., "Student's Diagnostic Ability") is used to rank student, grade performance, etc.

1. Reliability Concerns
   a. *Can different raters use it accurately?* Or, do results depend on who does the rating? To check this kind of reliability, have different raters rate the *same* behavior sample (e.g., a videotape), then compare scores. Train raters, then revise the instrument until scores are within acceptable limits. Make sure directions are clear and that rating scale "anchors" are clearly defined for each item.
   b. *Are the items reliable?* If all items are meant to rate the same general skill, they should be internally consistent, each correlating with the total score. Cronbach's "coefficient alpha" or one of the Kuder Richardson formulas should be used. If the instrument rates a varied set of skills, then you don't necessarily want high internal consistency. In this case, look for consistency over time, as in a repeated measure of the same subject.
2. Validity Concerns
   a. *Is the content meaningful?* Does it measure the "right" variables? This is a judgment call. Have a draft version of the instrument reviewed by experts in the area which you're rating.
   b. *Does the score represent the variables it's meant to measure?* You can test this empirically in several ways. One might be to have raters use the instrument on some videotape samples, some of which are known to show "good" behavior and some "bad." A valid rating should tell a good one from a bad one. Or, for example with a workshop rating scale, you might give the rating to two simulated "extreme" groups. Tell one group it was a great workshop and the other it was awful; scores should correlate with group membership.

SINGULAR ITEM RATING SCALES

Singular-Item Rating Scales: where an instrument contains several rating items (as on a workshop reaction survey), but each item is scored independently and you don't calculate a total score for each instrument.

Example

* Uses Schwartz question methods:
☐ always   ☐ frequently   ☐ seldom   ☐ never
* Can use a ratchet wrench:
With amazing grace ( )   ( )   ( )   ( ) Wretchedly

WAYS OF
ESTABLISHING
RELIABILITY
AND VALIDITY
FOR DIFFERENT
KINDS OF
INSTRUMENTS
(continued)

Uses: The total score is *never* computed. Rather, item scores are reported for diagnostic purposes, reporting progress, impact, etc.

1. Reliability Concerns
   a. *Do raters affect scores?* (see preceding instrument discussion of this question)
   b. *Is "halo effect" a factor?* Because the items are meant to rate different (independent) variables, you want to be sure that a person's score on some items doesn't influence their score on others. Your raters have to be able to see the differences among the items being rated. You can check for this by having raters rate a sample (e.g., a videotape) of someone *known* to vary on the different items. Correct halo effects by repositioning items, by careful writing of items and scales, and by training raters.
   c. *Is it consistent over time?* Check this by administering the rating to the same subject more than once when you *know* the variables rated haven't really changed. The item scores from different administrations should correlate highly.
2. Validity Concerns
   a. *Is the content valid?* Does the instrument assess the right set of variables? Again, this requires some expert judgment to be sure that what you've included on your instrument is defensible and fits your program.
   b. *Do items really measure the variables?* This requires some empirical testing, which could be extensive. Use of videotaped or other known good/bad samples can be used to see if items discriminate as intended.

BEHAVORIAL OBSERVATIONS

Behavioral Observation: where behaviors are observed then counted or categorized on a checklist type of instrument.

Example

* The teacher hyperventilated

☐ 3 or more times   ☐ 1–3 times   ☐ never   during the lesson

Uses: These instruments categorize particular verbal or other behaviors to be used diagnostically, record progress and growth, or assess changes as a result of training.

1. Reliability Concerns
   a. The main concern is to see whether observers can indeed see and accurately record the intended behaviors. Often, considerable training and instrument revision is needed to achieve tolerable limits of error. Careful definition and redefinition of items helps assure consistent usage.
   b. Another reliability concern is sampling. You need to be sure that the behaviors actually observed are representative of what you wish to make inferences about. If you wish to be able to draw conclusions about typical behaviors, then you must be sure what you observed was typical. Often multiple observations of the same subject are necessary.
2. Validity Concerns
   a. *Is the content valid?* There should be a rationale, based on research, expert judgment or other value bases, that the behaviors you will count are meaningful.
   b. *Can the instrument discriminate instances from non-instances of the behavior?* A useful procedure here is the extreme groups method, where you record behavior of two extremely different samples (e.g., a good diagnostician at work and a bad one). Your items, and your total score, should discriminate the two.

WAYS OF ESTABLISHING RELIABILITY AND VALIDITY FOR DIFFERENT KINDS OF INSTRUMENTS
(continued)

SURVEY INSTRUMENTS

Survey Questionnaire: where respondents are asked to classify and categorize their reactions, characteristics, etc.

Example

* Did you see the film *The Great Prune Robbery*? □ Yes   □ No
* Rate your feeling about prunes. Love them □   □   □   □ Hate them

Uses: These forms collect data on a broad range of variables, some of which are related to one another, and some not. Item scores are generally used to characterize traits of groups and sub-groups.

1. Reliability Concerns

   The major reliability concern is whether the instrument is stable over time. Is someone's response affected by when they completed the form? Would they respond the same way again? To check for stability, readminister the form to some respondents, then compare their responses. If item responses change—and what they're rating/responding to *hasn't* changed—you've got a reliability problem.

   Often, you can increase reliability by writing more items and/or by making items more specific. But be careful about length increases. A longer questionnaire will have a lower return/completion rate, and you'll trade greater reliability for bias.

2. Validity Concerns

   a. Expert judgment, prior research, etc. will help you determine whether you've included the right variables.

   b. Whether the form and items are valid for a particular use/group of respondents is a developmental issue. You should review draft versions with potential respondents and make appropriate changes.

   c. Whether the items measure what they intend to can be checked by comparing scores to some other, concurrent measure. Again, extreme groups—either real or simulated—can be used. Or, you can compare survey scores to some other kind of data known to be valid for the respondents.

KNOWLEDGE TESTS

Knowledge Test: where forced response items are grouped in an instrument to assess a particular knowledge (skill, competency, etc.) domain.

Example

* Check the behavior(s) below that is/are typical of a Schwartz Syndrome adult

   □ insults small mammals without provocation
   □ drinks from wrong side of glass
   □ believes septic tank can back up into refrigerator
   □ eats no vegetables except ketchup
   □ all of the above
   □ none of the above

WAYS OF
ESTABLISHING
RELIABILITY
AND VALIDITY
FOR DIFFERENT
KINDS OF
INSTRUMENTS
(continued)

Uses: Usually, total scores or scores on subtests are used diagnostically or to assess learning.

1. Reliability Concerns
   The most usual reliability concern is internal consistency: how well the items "hang together," and are they related to the other items. A split half or one of the other consistency measures listed in the references at the end of this chapter can be used. Adding more items and rewriting items (e.g., getting rid of ambiguous distractors, etc.) will enhance reliability. In general, reliability accrues to the carefully constructed test that is revised, revised again, then again.

2. Validity Concerns
   a. Is the content right? To determine this, you need expert judgment about the *scope* of the instrument; is it adequate for the domain you are testing? You also need a judgment about the *relevance* of the items to the tested domain. Again, expert judgment, prior research, and analysis of curriculum can be used. Revise the instrument drafts until you receive satisfactory judgments about scope and relevance.
   b. Does it measure validly?
      - try out your tests on known extreme groups. Test scores should correlate with group membership.
      - compare test scores against another, independent, criterion measure, such as expert judgments, other tests, ratings, etc.
      - correlate *item* scores with *total* scores. Items that don't discriminate (i.e., aren't related to total score) may be invalid.

CHECKLISTS AND INVENTORIES

Checklist: where tangible items or characteristics are observed, then counted, coded or classified (e.g., a content analysis checklist, an inventory of tangible goods).

Example
* How many times did teachers check out the film "Cattle Prods in the Classroom?" _____ times
* Does the *diagnostic* section make a specific reference to Schwartz Syndrome? _____yes _____no

Uses: These instruments are a lot like behavioral tallies, except they count and record characteristics of tangible items (e.g., the content of a report, or what's on a bulletin board).

1. Reliability Concerns
   a. Here (as in observation) you need to be sure that scores represent what got measured versus who did the measuring. Check this by comparing scores from different observers who observed the same thing. You can increase this reliability by training your checkers/observers and by carefully specifying items.
   b. When total scores are used (versus item-by-item reporting) you need to be sure that a score of "15," say, was arrived at in the same way by different observers. You need to have good internal consistency. Inter-item correlations should be high. When items are scored and reported independently, inter-item correlation is not an issue.

WAYS OF
ESTABLISHING
RELIABILITY
AND VALIDITY
FOR DIFFERENT
KINDS OF
INSTRUMENTS
(continued)

2. Validity Concerns
   a. Is the scope of items (characteristics) sufficient to represent the trait being assessed? This calls for expert judgments of drafts of the instrument.
   b. Are items relevant to the trait? Again, expert judgment can be used, research and theory could be referenced.
   c. Can observers in fact "see" the characteristics they're being asked to observe and check for? This requires careful item construction and specific phrasing and should be checked empirically.
   d. Does the checklist measure validly? Do scores represent the intended traits? An extreme groups method can be used, wherein checklist scores should discriminate instances from non-instances. A checklist to assess a report's adequacy, for example, could be tried out on a known complete report and a known incomplete report. Or, you could correlate the checklist score against some other independent measure of the object.

HOW CAN YOU PLAN THE INFORMATION COLLECTION EFFORT TO GET THE BEST INFORMATION AT THE LOWEST COST?

The information collection phase of evaluation is often its most costly activity. It is also the activity that produces the "meat" in the evaluation effort: information. The whole information collection effort should be carefully choreographed so that it will get you the most information at the lowest cost. You will want to make maximum use of each data collection instance, to save repeated demands on your resources and respondents.

From the economy standpoint, the ideal information collection plan would tap just one source. This hypothetical source would be so rich and accurate that it would adequately address all the questions of the evaluation. Unfortunately, this ideal source (an oracle, perhaps) does not exist, and one must consider many varied sources and procedures. But, the trick is to get the maximum mileage out of the sources you are going to access. For example, if you're going to be analyzing students' work for one purpose, are there other purposes the same analysis might serve?

The more sources of information (more perspectives) you get for one question, the more sure and whole your conclusions will be. Evaluation needs the richer understanding multiple sources can bring. The error or bias inherent in any single measure can be counterbalanced by using multiple perspectives and information collection procedures.

Information collectors should pay due respect to Mr. Murphy and his laws: what can go wrong, will. To get the data you've planned on, you need to watch what gets done. And, you must protect the vested public interest and trust by maintaining adequate ethical and moral safeguards. Collecting information is a complex process, and it relies on many steps being carried out adequately and often by different persons. Breakdowns in logistics can seriously harm the quality of data collected, or even render it unusable.

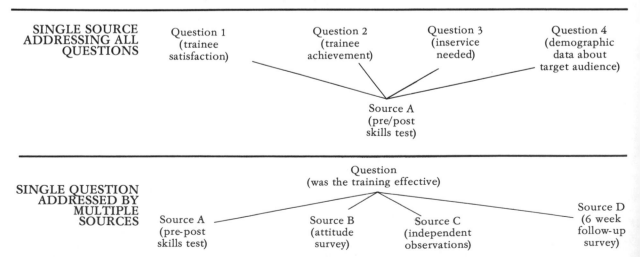

SINGLE SOURCE ADDRESSING ALL QUESTIONS

Question 1 (trainee satisfaction)   Question 2 (trainee achievement)   Question 3 (inservice needed)   Question 4 (demographic data about target audience)

Source A (pre/post skills test)

SINGLE QUESTION ADDRESSED BY MULTIPLE SOURCES

Question (was the training effective)

Source A (pre-post skills test)   Source B (attitude survey)   Source C (independent observations)   Source D (6 week follow-up survey)

MULTIPLE
MEASURES FOR
MULTIPLE
QUESTIONS

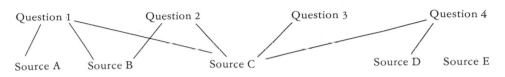

MULTIPLE
MEASURES
ANSWERING
MULTIPLE
QUESTIONS

EXAMPLE: A TRAINING WORKSHOP
Here some sources serve more than one question (like "Source C"). Also, each evaluation question is addressed by more than one source.

Here's the same multiple measures for multiple questions relationship pictured in a "matrix." *

Evaluation Questions

Information Collection Procedures	Knowledge Test	Behavioral Observation	Workshop Evaluation	Follow-Up Survey Questionnaire
Did they learn it	X			
Did they like it		X	X	X
Did they use what they learned		X		X
Did using what they learned make a difference		X	X	X
Was the training successful	X	X	X	X

* Frank Courts and Richard Quantz developed this very useful matrix format while working for the ETC project at the University of Virginia.

EXAMPLE: INFORMATION COLLECTION PLAN FOR A SCHOOL DISTRICT NEEDS
          ASSESSMENT

QUESTIONS

INFORMATION COLLECTION PROCEDURES	1. What are pupils attitudes toward handicapped classmates	2. What are the achievement deficits of handicapped pupils?	3. What problems do teachers face in mainstream classrooms	4. What current services do handicapped children receive	5. What problems do handicapped children encounter in mainstreamed classrooms?
A. Administer questionnaire to sample of pupils	X				X
B. Interview parents of handicapped pupils	X	X	X	X	X
C. Visit and observe a sample of mainstream classrooms	X		X		X
D. Analyze test scores from sample of handicapped pupils		X			
E. Interview sample of teachers	X	X	X	X	X
F. Analyze records of pupil personnel services office				X	

NOTICE

▶ Some data collection procedures (like B) do double duty (quintuple duty really).
▶ Multiple sources are provided for each question.

► Keep adding rows (more procedures) and moving "X's" around until you're satisfied you've optimally blended economy and multiple perspectives (see the Design Manual for more specific steps).

CONSTRUCT THE LOGISTICAL PLAN

Who will conduct the called for observations, ratings, etc. How likely are they to respond to various formats and procedures (e.g., interviews, questionnaires, self-report/observations measures)? Is their educational and experiential background such that special terminology is required to avoid ambiguity and elicit complete and accurate information? Is a special incentive required to insure full participation? Will they be willing to provide the information required? What biases or particular problems of the group should be considered in designing the procedure? Can they handle the job?

Just *when* are observations to be made, instruments delivered and picked up, etc.? The setting and timing of an information collection procedure must be carefully considered. Would teachers' perceptions of problems be characteristically different in the beginning of the year as opposed to the end of the year? Various legal, contract, or policy constraints must also be considered. Would the teachers' union cooperate with a survey or observations, and if so, under what conditions? Will you hand out instruments after a break? Before lunch?

Where will observations be made, interviews conducted, instruments administered? Special characteristics of the setting can influence data collected. An interview in *her* office might net different reactions, or be less controlled, than one in *yours*. A particular room or setting may contain clues and uses that will bias results.

What *timing, schedules*, are respondents and collectors to follow? The sequence or frequency of some information collection procedures can affect results. Essays graded first may be graded more harshly, final interviews in a busy schedule may be cursory, etc.

How are instruments, records, etc. to be returned? To whom? By when? A mailed survey, even though completed, may never get returned if it's a hassle to do so; participants in a rush to leave a workshop may not find someone to turn their rating forms to, etc.

It is a good idea to put your plan into writing, so it can be more easily checked over, monitored and adhered to. Gantt charts are especially useful, for they can show busy periods, overloads, slack times, etc.

See the following page for another example of a logistic planning form, called a "work plan." It shows when and how procedures will get carried out.

EVALUATION WORKPLAN

Instrument	Instrument Status	Evaluation Questions Addressed	Administration Schedule	Administrators	Respondents	Sample	Data Analysis Procedure	Report Available
1. Practicum Preference Form	Completed	B1	before practicum placement	self administered	Student	All students	Frequency, compare to site profile	4 weeks after practicum placement
2. Student Practicum Log Analysis Form	Completed	B1, B2, B3, E1	monthly	self administered	Evaluator	Logs from each student	Frequency of activities, mean time per activity area	End of semester
3. Student Self-Rating Form	Completed	C1, C2, C3, C4	weekly	self administered	Student	All students	Frequency trend over time	Monthly
4. Supervisor Rating Form	Completed	C1, C2, C3, C4	bi-weekly	self administered	Supervisor	All supervisors	Frequency trend over time	End of semester
5. Two step Graduate Questionnaire:	Completed	D1, D2, D3	annually	self administered	Graduates	All graduates	Frequency analysis, central tendency trend by years	End of year
6. Graduate Follow-up Questionnaire: Employers	Completed	D3	annually	self administered	Graduate employers	All; contingent on graduates'	Frequency analysis, central tendency trend	End of year
7. Site Profile Analysis Form	Completed	B1	end of semester	evaluator	Evaluator	One per site	Content analysis; compare to Student Preference	End of semester

Item	Status	Code	When administered		Administered by	Sample	Analysis	Reporting
8. Clinical Service Review Sheet	Completed	E1	annual	evaluator	Evaluator	Systematic Sample of Records	Frequency central tendency	End of year
9. Contact Record Analysis Form	Ready for field test	A1, A2, A3	end of semester	evaluator	Evaluator	Record for all students	Content analysis frequency, mean time	End of semester
10. Resource Center Usage Form	Completed	A5	end of semester	evaluator	Evaluator	New Materials	Frequency by materials categories	End of year
11. Drop Out Record Checklist	Completed	C4	annual	evaluator	Evaluator	All drop-out records	Content analysis	End of year
12. Module Feedback Form	Blueprint completed	A2, A3, A5	upon module completion	self administered	Students	All Students	Mean ratings	End of semester
13. Module Test Form	To be developed	A4, B1	upon module completion	self administered	Students	All Students	Mean ratings	End of semester
14. Diagnosis Analysis Checklist	Completed	C1, C2	end of practicum	evaluator	Evaluator	One per student	Content analysis frequency and rating scores	End of semester
15. Diagnosis Observation Sheet	To be developed	C1, C4	end of practicum	faculty	Faculty	One per student	Frequency by client type	End of semester
16. Lesson plan Analysis Sheet	Completed	C2, C3	end of practicum	evaluator	Evaluator	Random: 3 per student	Content analysis frequency, rating scores	End of semester
17. Classroom Observation Record	Blueprint Completed	C2, C3, C4	end of semester	faculty	Faculty	One per student	Frequency by client type	End of semester

MAINTAIN
QUALITY
CONTROL

Follow appropriate protocols, procedures and customs, and simple good manners.

Any information collection procedure makes demands on the time and attention of others. At best, failure to follow polite customs and protocols will earn you a bad reputation and cast the evaluation in a bad light; at worst, you may get bad, or no, data.

Get needed releases, permissions and clearances

In many cases, some information and data will simply not be available at all, unless certain permissions and releases are obtained. Some files and records, even persons, are not routinely accessible without prior arrangements. Or, you may obtain data but not be able to use or reference it because you don't have a needed release.

Monitor for consistency and good measurement practice

The more complex your procedures are, and the more they rely on others (e.g., a cadre of interviewers or document analysts), the more sure you need to be that everyone is playing by the same rules.

All aspects of the distribution, administration and return of instruments should be consistently carried out in all instances. If pupils in one school, for instance, did not receive test instructions while others did, their scores might likely be adversely affected. An interviewer who clarifies, repeats and rephrases questions will gather different responses than the interviewer who does not. In these cases, anomalies and differences in the data collection procedure can influence their results. Procedures must be designed so as to inhibit such anomalies, and monitored and reviewed to detect confounding anomalies when they occur.

Depart from your plan when you need to

There may be opportunities to gather unplanned for information. Don't let slavish adherence to a plan shut you off from other information. Likewise, don't stick to your plan if a need arises to vary. If, for instance, an interviewer has traveled 50 miles to meet with a superintendent but finds that some circumstance prohibits the superintendent's participation, it would probably be unwise to reject the offer to interview the assistant superintendent. The best laid plans are bound to need revision in the face of current events. Such revisions ought to be made when needed, but take care to document them when they occur and consider their potential consequences to the data collected.

Use appropriate coding, aggregation and reduction techniques (See next chapter: "Analyzing Information")

In many instances, data resulting from evaluation efforts will require reduction and aggregation just to be handled efficiently. In general, the larger the scope of information collection—the greater the number of completed instruments or forms—the more complex the aggregation and reduction scheme will have to be. On the other hand, it is critical to bear in mind that aggregation and reduction of *any* sort, while it can aid communication and interpretation, can remove meaning. For this reason, the less reduction, the better; the closer data are to their original, raw form, the richer they will be.

For example, a large-scale questionnaire survey requires careful planning to ensure that each form is returned, and pertinent data gleaned from it and prepared for analysis. Coding forms to record and portray each instrument's data need to be designed. The task of transferring data from completed instruments to a coding form is a simple clerical task, but one which if ill-planned or carried out lackadaisically can ruin the entire data collection effort. The aggregation and recording system must be accurate, so that the data are not changed by the aggregation process. The system must also be comprehensive, ensuring that all instrument items are recorded; in addition, extra information, such as date of receipt or other pertinent variables, may be included on the coding form. Finally, the aggregation system must be simple. Unnecessary complexity is likely to introduce error and contaminate the data needlessly.

Safeguard information with appropriate handling and filing procedures

Care must be taken to ensure that data and all reports based on it are responsibly handled, distributed and stored. Irresponsible or otherwise inadequate handling can do great harm to persons and their rights. Short of legal or ethical infringements, irresponsibility in the handling of data could do grave harm to future data collection efforts. We all live in a world of decreasing privacy and should do all we can to be attentive to persons' rights and feelings.

For all data collected, a record should be maintained and stored so that it might be retrieved, to verify or re-analyze it as may be necessary. Thus, an original set of survey forms should not be destroyed as soon as a frequency analysis is complete, for it may be useful at a later date to return to these raw data for verification or a new analysis.

HOW GOOD IS YOUR INFORMATION COLLECTION PLAN?	If you *had* the information you plan to collect for a given purpose/question, are you willing to defend the "answer?" If no, you need to plan to get more data. Are there additional existing sources of information you haven't included? Are there procedures planned whose payoff is so minimal they aren't worth the cost? Is the additional perspective or added certainty you get from an additional source worth the cost? Do you need, and can you use, the information you are planning to collect? Are logistic arrangements sufficient to carry out all steps of each procedure? Have safeguards and quality control checks been planned? Are responsibilities and assignments clearly defined? Are quality control checks being made to assure you that your plan is working? Are sufficient records being maintained to document activities occurring? Are human rights, customs and protocols being honored? Are data being protected from breaches of ethics and promises? Are data being organized, filed, and stored to maintain accessibility?

REFERENCES

Babbie, E.R. *Survey Research Methods.* Belmont, CA: Wadsworth, 1973.

Bruyn, S.T. *The Human Perspective in Sociology: The Methodology of Participant Observation.* Englewood Cliffs, N.J.: Prentice Hall, 1966.

Dalkey, N.C. *The Delphi Method: An Experimental Study of Group Opinion.* Santa Monica, CA: Rand Corporation, 1969.

Demaline, R.E. & Quinn, D.W. *Hints for Planning and Conducting a Survey and Bibliography of Survey Methods.* Kalamazoo, MI: Evaluation Center, Western Michigan University, 1979.

Ebel, R.L. *Measuring Educational Achievement.* Englewood Cliffs, N.J.: Prentice Hall, 1965.

Furst, N.J. *Systematic Classroom Observation.* In L. Deighten (Ed.), *Encyclopedia of Education.* New York: MacMillan, 1971.

Gronlund, N.E. *Constructing Achievement Tests.* Englewood Cliffs, N.J. Prentice Hall, 1968.

Guba, E.G. & Lincoln, Y.S. *Effective Evaluation: Improving the Usefulness of Evaluation Results Through Responsive and Naturalistic Approaches.* San Francisco: Jossey-Bass, 1981.

Patton, M.Q. *Qualitative Evaluation Methods.* Beverly Hills, CA: Sage, 1980.

Payne, S.L. *The Art of Asking Questions.* Princeton, N.J.: Princeton University Press, 1951.

Pennsylvania State Department of Education. *Suggested Methods for the Identification of Critical Goals.* Harrisburg, PA: Author, 1975.

Richardson, S., Dohrenwend, H.S., & Klein, D. *Interviewing: Its Forms and Functions.* New York: Basic Books, 1965.

Shaw, M.E. & Wright, J.M. *Scales for the Measurement of Attitudes.* New York: McGraw-Hill, 1967.

Sudman, S. *Applied Sampling.* New York: Academic Press, 1976.

Webb, E.J., Campbell, D.T., Schwartz, R.D. & Sechrest, L. *Unobtrusive Measures: Nonreactive Research in the Social Sciences.* Chicago: Rand McNally, 1966.

Analyzing and Interpreting Evaluation Information

WHAT IS IT

Analysis is the process of finding out what the information collected by the evaluation means. Analysis involves working with the data that have been collected to determine what conclusions these data support and how much support they provide for, or against, any conclusion. The purpose of analysis is to summarize from the data the messages it contains in order to bring this information to bear on tentative conclusions or decisions.

In most cases, analysis is done in stages. That is, the information is coded or organized so that some sense can be made of it (e.g., you put it in a frequency distribution, a percentage breakdown, or a set of lists). Once you "eyeball" your data using experience and common sense, you decide whether more analysis would be helpful and, if so, what kind. A more detailed analysis, while still preliminary, might entail using description (e.g., the average score, the high points on a response sheet, content analysis of how many times a topic was mentioned in an interview). Again, some interesting questions might emerge (e.g., "Persons in Friday's training session did better than those in Thursday's. Why?" or "Experienced teachers seem to be doing better in training than student teachers. Is the difference significant?") At this point, a secondary analysis using more sophisticated methods might be in order. For example, an inferential or correlational analysis might be done, external observers might be brought in to interview and observe, or a new data collection effort might be planned.

WHEN ANALYSIS DECISIONS ARE MADE

Early in the planning of an evaluation, some major analysis issues get decided. These early decisions are related to the purposes for the evaluation. For example, an evaluation to decide whether one training approach works better than another likely will find itself involved in some kind of comparative analysis, where the effects of training Strategy A are compared to information about the effects of Strategy B. On the other hand, an evaluation that will describe an innovative practicum might be more involved with qualitative analysis.

Later in the evaluation process when you decide on the kind of information to gather (test data, interviews, observations, etc.), the kinds of analysis to be performed are further narrowed and decided. And, you decide how to organize and store it when it is collected. Then, when information is finally collected—an interview round completed, a questionnaire returned, an observation report finished—analysis decisions are confronted again. Is it worth analyzing? What does it mean?

Analysis proceeds when data "come in" from information collection. First, data are organized and coded, then checked to see if they are complete and sound enough to warrant your time for analysis. Then, analysis for meaning begins and often cycles back through more information collection.

HOW WILL YOU HANDLE RETURNED DATA?

Data must be properly handled and stored in order to prepare it for analysis. This includes coding data (when called for), aggregating and organizing it, and storing it for safekeeping and ready access. The main idea is to organize data in ways that facilitate its use, and keep it from getting lost or forgotten.

Results of questionnaires, objective tests, checklists, observation records, and other quantitative methods used in training programs are readily and easily used if organized and coded. A coding system enables you to record the results of returned instruments on a single record. This code sheet can be scanned to get a "feel" for the data, and then data can be easily prepared for computer analysis.

There are two basic kinds of coding approaches you can use for quantitative data:

-numerical codes, where you break the narrative data down into smaller "pieces," for example, phrases, paragraphs, words, or sections, then assign numerals to each according to the rules of your coding scheme.

-literal codes, where narrative data are broken down and assigned to different literal categories, again according to the coding rules you establish.

EXAMPLE OF INTERVIEW DATA CODED NUMERICALLY

	Content Categories			
	Nature of Problem	Assistance Provided	Results of Assistance	Perceived Value
	Code # Category	Code # Category	Code # Category	Code # Category
	10. Instructional	20. Demonstration	30. Problem solved	40. Very positive
	11. Scheduling	21. Materials	31. Problem persists	41. Appreciative but qualified
	12. Diagnostic	22. Instructions	32. Problem improved	42. Ambivalent
	13. Behavioral	23. Referral to resource center	33. Problem deferred	43. Negative
	14. Administrative	24. Referral to other teacher	34. Other	44. Other
	15. Other	25. Other		

Normally, these categories could be drawn up only *after* narrative data were scrutinized. If categories were known and limited prior to inquiry, a questionnaire method would have been more efficient than interview.

When you code numerically, you are doing quantitative analysis of what used to be qualitative data. This might be useful, but it might also drastically sap your rich qualitative data of much of its meaning.

The codes above are strictly nominal (the numbers have no "value," they can't be added, subtracted, etc.)

Categories

A. Context of problem requiring assistance
B. Kind of assistance provided
C. Results of assistance provided
D. Attitude of recipient about assistance received

How the categories would be used to code:

1. The interview summary could be cut up into pieces (or certain phrases, sentences, etc., transcribed) then sorted into categories labeled A, B, C, or D.
   OR
2. The coder could read the interview notes, circling phrases, sentences, etc., and marking them with the appropriate A-D code.

Nominal codes can be used simply as organizers. That is, you categorize and file the qualitative information (or interview in this case) using a nominal code. But when you analyze the data for meaning, you return to the qualitative information using the labels only to retrieve the data you want.

1. Your department   _____
2. Your faculty rank   _____
3. How long have you been at Upstate U.?
   ☐ 0–3 years
   ☐ 4–10 years
   ☐ more than 10 years
4. Rate your agreement with the following comments:

Strongly Agree	Agree	Neutral/ Undecided	Disagree	Strongly Disagree
☐	☐	☐	☐	☐

Coding Scheme

Item 1 Column 1-2	Item 2 Column 3	Item 3 Column 4	Item 4 Column 5
00 = Blank	0 = Blank	0 = Blank	0 = Blank
01 = Accounting	1 = Instructor	1 = 0–3 years	1 = Strongly Agree
02 = Anthropology	2 = Assistant Professor	2 = 4–10 years	2 = Agree

EXAMPLE CODING SCHEME FOR PORTION OF A SURVEY QUESTIONNAIRE *(continued)*

Item 1 Column 1-2	Item 2 Column 3	Item 3 Column 4	Item 4 Column 5
03 = Art	3 = Associate Professor	3 = more than 10 years	3 = Neutral/Undecided
—			
—	4 = Professor		4 = Disagree
—	5 = Other		5 – Strongly Disagree
39 = Sociology			
40 = Special Ed.			
41 = Speech & language pathology			
42 = Other			

GUIDELINES FOR CODING & ORGANIZING DATA

1. *Use coding sparingly*
   Any coding you do transforms the data you have and potentially reduces the meaning. On the other hand, when you have a lot of data, coding is sometimes necessary for further analysis. In general, the larger the scope of the data collection effort, the more likely it is such procedures are necessary.

2. *Use the simplest coding scheme you can*
   Coding is like a second layer of data collection, and as such it can fall prey to reliability problems. If a coding scheme is complex and difficult, error is likely to be introduced. As a result, data will be made less reliable and useful.

3. *Carefully choose coding variables*
   You can code more than just the responses recorded on an instrument. Additional data may be useful for analysis. Some examples of additional coding variables are:

   When instrument was returned (e.g., early, late, serial, order)
   Who returned instrument (e.g., any demographic variables of interest)
   How instrument was returned (e.g., by mail, in person, by a friend, telephone response)
   Condition of instrument or other physical indicators (e.g., written on, dog-eared, crisp and clean, done in crayon)
   Whether respondent wrote *additional comments*, showed other signs of interest, care, etc.

4. *Train coders to accurately complete coding tasks*
   Normally, coding data is a simple clerical task. But, some training is probably in order. You don't want a bad job of coding to ruin an entire information collection effort.

5. *Design for coding*
   Incorporate coding into the instruments were possible. Design the instrument you use for the easiest possible coding.

GUIDELINES FOR CODING & ORGANIZING DATA
(continued)

6. *Keep records*
Maintain a record of each coding and processing step so that these steps can be retraced if necessary.

7. *Maintain ethics*
Safeguard your data from breaches of ethics, human rights, laws, privileges and commitments (anonymity, confidentiality) made or implied by the evaluation.

OPTIONAL CATEGORIES FOR ORGANIZING AND FILING DATA

Organized by:
information collection procedure: all the teacher interviews are filed together, all work samples, analyses, etc.
evaluation question
chronological sequence (first month's data, second round together)
source (all teacher data together, all trainer data together)
program element (all course data, all practicum data)

Stored within:
discs and magnetic tapes to be accessed by computer
folder systems in file cabinets
a rolodex system, using numerical or narrative filing
a cross-referencing card (or rolodex) file that references data by some of the categories listed above, such as program element, source, evaluation question, when collected, etc.

Example:
Assume that data are filed in folders, one for each information collection method (or some other basis). Each document, for example, an interview summary, could be assigned a code, say:

05-B-12-02-6

05 - in file folder #5
B - an interview
12 - Schwartz Elementary School
02 - prepared in Spring 81
6 - workshop participant

A code like this lets you locate data when it's needed, regroup it for different analyses, and get it back to the right folder.

ARE YOUR DATA WORTH ANALYZING?

Sometimes problems with data collection "spoil" some or even all of the data you've collected so that you might not want to take the trouble to analyze it. You should "clean" the data removing those bits (e.g., partially completed instruments) that you don't want to analyze. Inspection of the data you have on hand may indicate that more collection of information is needed. Or, it may indicate that you need to restructure your analysis procedures.

With quantitative data collection instruments (e.g., a test, a survey questionnaire), verification takes place when all the data are returned and coded. In qualitative inquiry methods, such as case studies or site visits, data collectors often analyze and check their notes and findings as they proceed, in order to optimize information collection opportunities.

	Problem	Example
PROBLEMS TO LOOK FOR WHEN VERIFYING DATA	1. incomplete response, or interrupted collection process	An interview with a superintendent gets cancelled part-way through; or, so many interruptions occur that the response is fragmented and inconsistent.
	2. coding errors; inconsistent coding	Two coders produce different results on the same instrument; code numbers are entered in wrong column on a form.
	3. respondents aren't a representative sample of the population	Only those who stayed until the end of a workshop completed the final rating form.
	4. low return rate of instruments, and/or a low response rate on items	Many of the surveys from the sample aren't returned and/or of the ones that were returned, many are incomplete.
	5. returned data which aren't from a representative sample of the population	Only parents who have handicapped children returned the questionnaire, even though they were sent to all parents in the district.
	6. administration and monitoring procedures which are not implemented as they were planned	Observations of some teachers occur one month after the workshop instead of three months as intended; some interviewers didn't explain questions.
	7. unusual responses; responses outside of the possible range	A classroom teacher who indicates that he/she serves 100 handicapped students per day.
	8. unlike responses on similar items by a respondent or like responses on opposite items	Respondent indicates a "high" rating on interest level of workshop and a "high" rating on how boring the workshop was.

PROBLEMS TO LOOK FOR WHEN VERIFYING DATA
(continued)

9. a series of like responses which seem to indicate that the respondent was not attending to individual items

The "middle" response (3) is circled for many items in a series of five-point rating scales, showing a particular pattern, on unrelated topics.

10. persons rating or observing the same thing classify it differently

In a behavioral observation, raters do not have uniform results because they are focusing on different aspects of the activity.

SOME VERIFICATION AND "CLEANING" PROCEDURES

"Eyeball" methods
scanning the code sheets can identify odd-ball responses, blank spaces, incorrect entries, etc.
incomplete interviews will be short
pages missing from forms
questions left blank

Spot-checks
arbitrarily select code sheets and compare against questionnaires
choose completed forms (e.g., tests) at random and check for accuracy and completeness

Audit
information collection procedures are retraced to ensure no breaches of good measurement practice invalidated data (e.g., a survey sent by mail in one district but carried home by pupils in another may not represent comparable samples. Or, failure to follow appropriate protocol or obtain needed releases may render data unusable.)

Group meetings of analyzers, interviewers
data collectors meet and discuss the procedures used
comparisons are made
problems that may have invalidated data emerge

Follow-up, repeated measures
persons interviewed are recontacted to elicit reactions to interview process
adherence to protocol is verified
unreliable information is identified

Ratings of accuracy, reliability
instruments (or interviewers) themselves ask respondents to rate the soundness of their own responses
respondents judge how thoroughly or reliably they could make responses. Example: "How accurate are your estimates of client load?"
☐ Extremely: based on good records
☐ Quite: based on memory
☐ Poor: I'm not very sure

GENERAL GUIDELINES FOR VERIFYING DATA

1. *The more complex the instrumentation and coding scheme* (e.g., a 12-page questionnaire), *the more likely there will be errors.*
2. *The larger the data collection effort, the more likely you'll obtain odd-ball information.* The tradeoff is that when there's a lot of data, a few bad items or messed up instruments will have less overall consequence.
3. *When precision demands are high—important decisions will ride on the data collected—you should do careful screening and cleaning of data.* Project proposals have not been funded because clerks mistotaled rater's point awards!
4. *If planned analysis procedures are extensive and expensive, then it becomes more important to spend time being sure you have data worth analyzing.*
5. *Set—and use—verification rules.* The verification step sometimes results in some data being discarded or analyzed separately; the purpose, after all, is to weed out bad data. You need "rules" to go by here. A survey analysis scheme may determine, for instance, that any instrument with less than 75% completion will be rejected from the sample. Or you may decide not to analyze further any interview data resulting from a session that lasted less than 10 minutes. Such rules are necessarily arbitrary and probably cannot be made until one has a notion of how the data actually look.
6. *Consider the possible biasing effects of verification rules.* As you decide not to use certain data, you run the risk of bias. Partially complete tests may represent slow readers; partially completed questionnaires may derive from a unique (e.g., negative, turned-off) sub-population; incomplete interviews may represent the busiest, most influential interviewees.
7. *Consider sub-analyses for weeded-out data.* Rather than discard potentially erroneous data, you may learn something useful from a separate analysis of it.
8. *Consider and deal with sampling effects.* You need to know if the samples you have are what you've planned on. Has some quirk in the information procedure given you a bad sample?

   a. Review the actual conduct of the data collection procedure looking for consistency and aberrations.
      - were instructions followed uniformly?
      - did collection occur under similar circumstances?
      - are returns especially low or unbalanced?
      - did raters or interviewers follow parallel procedures and rules?
   b. *Adjust analysis procedures where you suspect sampling problems.* You may be able to account for sampling errors if you determine the nature of differences in the samples you have.
      - compare the characteristics of your obtained sample to know what's known about the population.
      - determine the characteristics of the sample you in fact have. For example, in a low-return circumstance, see if those who did return survey forms represent a particular subgroup (e.g., recent graduates).
      - check a few non-respondents to determine how they differ from respondents.
   c. Collect more information; re-conduct the information procedure to procure a better sample.

SOME CRITERIA FOR VERIFICATION

1. All data collected should be verified, if only by a quick spot check.
2. Verification should not destroy or discard data that could represent a special opportunity (e.g., following up a low-return sample, determining why refusers refused).
3. Use consistent verification rules within each data set. Varying rules for same set of data (e.g., a set of questionnaires) could inordinately bias your analysis.
4. Document verification procedures, especially when data are rejected from analysis.
5. Increase verification attention as major decisions ride on results of analysis.

HOW WILL YOU ANALYZE THE INFORMATION?

The process of analysis is cyclical, and it works in a "Sherlock Holmes" fashion. Your initial data are beginning clues. You formulate hunches and tentative conclusions based on these clues, then work with your data (or collect more) to determine how well your hunches are substantiated or hold up. This leads you to more clues, then to more analysis and/or collection. As you move through these cycles, you learn and become more certain.

This section present procedures for guiding analysis and provides you with several examples of different kinds of analysis and considerations for assessing the sufficiency of the data and analyses you have completed.

GUIDELINES AND PROCEDURES FOR ANALYSIS

There are four (4) steps that you should consider in conducting analyses:
review the questions (or purposes) to be addressed by the evaluation
prepare descriptive analyses and frequency distributions (in quantitative data) for each set of data and display the results
prepare a summary of basic issues, trends, relationships and questions evident in the data
assess the available evidence in light of the issues and questions to be pursued.

1. *Review the questions to be addressed.*
   The evaluation questions that guided information collection were, of course, already identified before you got to this point. But now, they should be reviewed to help guide the analysis.

   a. Are the questions still appropriate in light of what's happened in the program and evaluation up to this point?
   b. Are there new questions that should be addressed?
   c. Are the questions sufficiently clear to guide analysis? Do you know what they mean?
   It is important that the evaluation clients and audiences be collaborated with and considered in this review.

2. *Prepare descriptive analyses.*
Descriptive analyses are meant to reduce the data into a briefer form so that its key features become more evident. The kind of analysis done depends on the kind of data you have gathered. In general, there are two kinds of descriptive analyses available:

a. Quantitative methods—included here are:
   1. descriptions of central tendencies, such as means, modes, medians
   2. descriptions of dispersion in the data, like range, standard deviations, variance
   3. frequency distributions, that show frequencies of response, numbers who chose certain options, etc.
   4. comparison of individual scores to group scores (percentile ranks, etc.)
b. Qualitative methods
   These methods are used to organize narrative information (like interview records, student essays, sample reports) into briefer narrative summaries that highlight key features of interest.* Again, what you use depends largely on the data you have. Some commonly used options are:
   1. checklist analysis, in which "yes-no" decisions are made as to whether a report contains certain information, a document has a key component, etc.
   2. content analysis, in which a document's characteristics and content are classified in different categories
   3. précis, summary analysis, in which narrative data are collapsed into briefer summaries

3. *Note basic issues, trends, relationships and questions.*
The point of this step is to decide what you have and what you want to do with it next. You review your preliminary analyses and determine what the data appear to be telling you.

Your options for completing this step range from a quick eyeball to more elaborate methods.

a. informal notation of hypotheses, questions, issues, etc. The least any evaluation should do is scan the preliminary analyses and make notes about what seems to be evident.
b. formal listing of hypotheses, issues, questions, etc. These listings, along with the preliminary analysis summaries, can be provided to several persons for their review and revision.
c. group reviews which can generate issues and questions or review and comment on those already listed.
d. formal hearing and panel reviews by key persons/experts.
e. preparation of working papers based on some major topics (e.g., the context, program description, effects). These papers would provide in-depth consideration of the preliminary analyses in light of the assigned topic.

---

* Often, you may decide not to reduce qualitative data in a descriptive summary, but to analyze it just like it is.

4. *Assess the available evidence.*

This is a "go-no-go" decision point. Considering the questions that the preliminary analysis stimulated, do you have what you need to perform more analysis? Do you need to recycle and collect more data?

Some decisions to make here are:

a. Are there issues, questions, hunches, etc. worth pursuing via further analyses? Are such questions sufficiently explicit that they can be used to guide further analyses?

b. Is there sufficient data to carry out the analyses needed to pursue the questions
- are samples of sufficient size?
- will missing data endanger conclusions?

c. Do the data you have available meet the requisite assumptions (e.g., homogeneity of variance, linearity) for the further analyses that are projected?

IMPORTANT PRINCIPLES AND CRITERIA TO GUIDE ANALYSIS	### Don't oversimplify.

Don't oversimplify.
Evaluation questions almost always relate to complex dynamic phenomena. The analytic procedure must be sensitive to such complexities and not reduce them for analytic convenience to an oversimplistic notion.

Account for differential effects and conditions.
You should avoid overall measures and analyses that assume an unrealistic uniformity. Program functions differ from location to location; participant needs, interactions and outcomes will differ by participant characteristics. Analyses should be conducted for different sub-groups or should account for sub-group differences.

Use multiple techniques.
Different analytic techniques employ different assumptions about the data. Where possible, multiple analyses based on different assumptions should be used.

Make sure assumptions of techniques to be used are met by the data you have.
A common violation in evaluation studies is to treat ordinal data (ratings, etc.) as if they were interval (data which can be added and averaged). Often, parametric statistics (t-tests, F-tests) are applied when their assumptions (e.g., that the group represents a "normal curve" or is homogenous) cannot

be met. Sometimes this is acceptable, for the violation doesn't make much difference (that is, the analysis technique is robust and can compensate for the faulty assumption). There are methods for estimating statistically the extent to which assumption-violations weaken results.

The rule is: be aware of the assumptions, and account for violations. *Just because an analysis operation is mathematically possible, doesn't mean it should be done.* Check with someone who has expertise in statistics for guidance when applying a statistic.

Use methods appropriate for audiences and purposes.

Analytic techniques should be chosen not to dazzle but to inform. Very often, the best, most communicative and convincing method will not be the most sophisticated. Choose one that will get the informing job done in the simplest, most direct way possible.

Use methods that are practical and affordable.

Do not plan collection efforts that require computers if you do not have ready computer access. Consider costs for expert judges, consultants, etc. Use resources available, such as graduate students, local expertise, libraries and computer centers.

Keep it simple.

Save the sophisticated and fancy techniques for journal articles and professional conferences. Most evaluation consumers are plain folks who need more to be informed than dazzled with analytic virtuosity.

Don't be overly rigorous.

The use of rigorous analytic methods intended for interval and ratio data allows the use of powerful statistic tools. When assumptions for such methods as covariant analysis or factor analysis can be met and the methods will yield needed information, use them. But, in transforming data to allow use of these powerful techniques, you should be careful that you haven't transformed the meaning of the data you have.

ANALYTIC
PROCEDURES
COMMONLY USED
IN TRAINING
PROGRAM
EVALUATION

There are two basic types of analytic procedures used in evaluation of training programs:

1. quantitative procedures for analyzing data consisting of numbers; and
2. qualitative procedures for analyzing primarily narrative data. Descriptions and examples of these procedures follow.

QUANTITATIVE PROCEDURES AND EXAMPLES

Here's a chart that lists three major kinds of quantitative analyses: *descriptive statistics, correlational analysis*, and *hypothesis testing*. The chart lists procedures

ANALYTIC
PROCEDURES
COMMONLY USED
IN TRAINING
PROGRAM
EVALUATION
(continued)

for each kind, showing the major sorts of questions they address and for which level of measurement data each is appropriate.

Following the chart is a description of each type and some example analyses.

Commonly Followed Analysis Methods for Some Kinds of Quantitative Data Typically Collected in Personnel Preparation Programs
(behavior observations, objective tests, rating scales, questionnaires)

Analysis Questions to be Addressed	Level of Measurement* (see notes below)		
	Nominal	Ordinal	Interval/Ratio
1. What do the scores "look like"? e.g., the distribution of answers to each of six multiple choice questions, the number of times participant questions were asked for each workshop unit	frequency distribution bar graph (histogram) line graph (frequency polygon)	frequency distribution bar graph (histogram) line graph (frequency polygon)	frequency distribution bar graph (histogram) line graph (frequency polygon)
2. What is the typical score; what represents the middle of the group? e.g., the topic most people want on the inservice agenda, the average number of years teachers have worked for the school	mode	mode median	mode median mean
3. How much do the scores "spread out"? e.g., the percentage of graduates getting jobs within six months, the high and low scores on the knowledge test	proportions percentages	range semi-interquartile range	range semi-interquartile range Standard Deviation
4. How does an individual score compare to the rest of the group? e.g., the rank of each state for number of federal projects awarded, the rank of each trainee on the supervisor rating		percentile rank	percentile rank standard scores
5. How do sets of scores change together? e.g., the relationship between amount of training received and number of supervisor citations	correlation (see correlation chart, p. 137)	correlation (see correlation chart, p. 137)	correlation see correlation chart, p. 137)

ANALYTIC
PROCEDURES
COMMONLY USED
IN TRAINING
PROGRAM
EVALUATION
(continued)

Commonly Followed Analysis Methods (continued)

Analysis Questions to be Addressed	Level of Measurement* (see notes below)		
	Nominal	Ordinal	Interval/Ratio
6. Are the sets of scores from different groups "really" different? e.g., the average performance rating of employees receiving training compared to those who were not trained	non-parametric tests, e.g., Chi-square	non-parametric tests e.g., median test para-metric tests e.g., when ratings thought of as interval data	parametric tests e.g., difference between mean (t-test), analysis of variance

*Measurement Scales
Nominal: categories, names
  Discrete: no underlying order; e.g., names of school buildings
  Continuous: underlying order; e.g., low, medium, high for parents' income levels
Ordinal: numerical categories with some underlying order, ranked according to that order; e.g., scoring
      1 to 5 for top five training priorities
Interval: numerical categories scaled according to the amount of the characteristic they possess, intervals
      are of equal value and zero is just another point on the scale; e.g., scores on PL 94-142
      knowledge test.
Ratio: same as Interval except that zero represents a complete absence of the characteristic being
      measured; e.g., this year's training budget.

Descriptive statistics

Frequency distribution

A frequency distribution is a collection of scores (usually raw scores) that have been arranged together in order from low to high values with the number of people (or other unit of interest) having each value presented. A frequency distribution is usually presented in a table listing the numbers of individuals with scores in each category or as a bar graph (histogram) or line graph (frequency polygon).

Mean, Median, and Mode

The mean, median, and mode are three different ways to describe the "central tendency" of a group of scores. The mean is obtained by adding together all of the values in a group of scores and dividing that sum by the total number of scores. The median is the score in a group of scores above which exactly half the score values are found and below which half are found. The mode is the value that occurs most often in a given group of scores. Much of the time, all of these ways to pick out a "typical" score will give you pretty close to the same answer. This is the case when the frequency distribution is nearly "normal" or forms a "bell-shaped curve."

But in skewed score distributions, these statistics can be quite different. For example, because a few people earn a lot of money in a city, the *mean* personal income might be high ($44,000); yet, half the people in the city might earn less than $20,000, the *median* income level.

Range and Standard Deviation

The range and standard deviation are two ways to describe the "dispersion" or spread of a group of scores. The range is the difference between the highest and lowest values in a group of scores. The standard deviation is the square root of the average of the squared deviations from the mean of the group. It is also the unit of measurement used to express "standard scores." A standard score is used to indicate the number of standard deviations a corresponding actual or "raw score" is above or below the mean. Scores that spread out a lot will have a high standard deviation and a broad range. Scores that cluster together (are much alike) will have a narrow range and a lower standard deviation.

Percentile rank and standard scores

Percentile rank and standard scores are two ways to describe how an individual score compares with the rest of the group. The rank is the percentage of cases which fall below a given individual score. A standard score is expressed in terms of standard deviation units above or below the mean of the group. The standard score scale depends on the numerical value assigned to the mean and to the standard deviation. For example, if the scale is set with the group mean (whatever it is) equal to 50, and the standard deviation (whatever it is) equal to 10, then an individual score (whatever it is) that falls half a standard deviation above the mean would receive a value of 55.

EXAMPLE #1   EXAMPLES OF DESCRIPTIVE STATISTICS

A large city school district was in the process of developing a one-day training workshop for its special education staff related to new requirements for planning and delivering services to students in special education. Since they planned to do the training in two groups anyway, they decided to randomly assign staff to the first or second session and then give a knowledge test to both groups after the first session to help decide if the training made a difference.

They administered a 75 point test to thirty people in each group, tabulated the results, summarized each group's performance, and compared the two. Here is a summary of what they found:

EXAMPLE #1
(continued)

Total Scores for Each Staff Person on Public Law (PL) 94-142 Test

	Without Training	With Training		Without Training	With Training		Without Training	With Training
1	15	29	11	22	20	21	14	33
2	19	49	12	24	34	22	20	45
3	21	48	13	49	28	23	30	35
4	27	35	14	46	35	24	32	39
5	35	53	15	52	42	25	34	36
6	47	39	16	44	43	26	42	48
7	46	23	17	64	46	27	40	63
8	38	74	18	61	47	28	38	57
9	33	72	19	55	40	29	54	56
10	67	50	20	54	54	30	56	65

SUMMARY OF DESCRIPTIVE STATISTICS ON KNOWLEDGE TEST

	Mean	Standard Deviation	Variance	Number
Without training	39.30	14.98	224.29	30
With training	44.60	13.36	178.39	30

	Median	Mode	Maximum	Minimum
Without training	39	38	67	14
With training	44	35	74	20

LINE GRAPH (FREQUENCY POLYGON) FOR KNOWLEDGE TEST

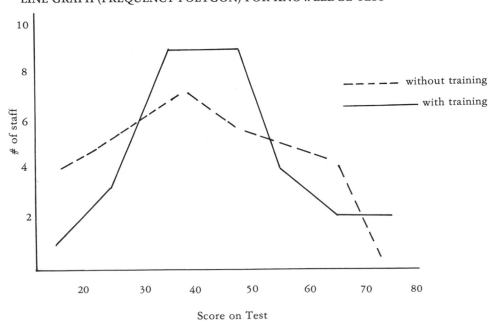

EXAMPLE #2   Here's another way of displaying similar information. In this case, the numbers (means, etc.) have been replaced by verbal statements representing a specific score category (like 0–2 = "low," 3–5 = "high"). The data shown are from a school survey.

	Respondents		
Variable	Regular Teachers	Special Education Teachers	Administrators
1. Self-rating knowledge on:			Note: response rate low
a. handicapping conditions	low	high	low
b. individualized instruction based on IEP	medium	high	low
c. resources/referrals	high	high	medium
2. Rating of knowledge by others:			
a. handicapping conditions	low	high	low
b. individualized instruction	low	high	low
c. resources/referrals	low	low	low
3. Problem ranking (highest 2)	inadequate planning time	inappropriate requests	too much paperwork
	getting enough help	too much paperwork	parent relations
(lowest 2)	knowledge of methods	knowledge of methods	knowledge of methods
	parent relations	access to resources	getting enough help
4. Knowledge test of District procedures for 94-142	low	high	medium/low
5. Training preferences	want release time	think classroom teachers need more theory	want release time dollars
	prefer in building	don't think selves need training	want involvement in training design
	less theory, more "skills"		

EXAMPLE #3   Here's another example of descriptive statistics used to portray the results of a checklist analysis of records maintained in a resource center.

Materials Re:	Total in % Available	Frequency of Use Sept.–Nov.	% of Total Usage	Increase/Decrease Over Last Year Same Quarter
Federal Regulations	15%	6	9%	1% increase
filmstrips		2		
articles		0		
handbooks for implementing		2		
etc.		0		
etc.		2		
Classroom & Behavior Management	40%	4	6%	2% decrease
texts		2		
problem diagnosis kits		0		
films		0		
intervention strategy pamphlets		1		
articles		0		
special technique handbooks		1		
etc.		0		
etc.		0		
Testing & Assessment	30%	27	41%	2% increase
reading		13		
mathematics		7		
career education		1		
values clarification		0		
etc.		6		
Classroom Methodology Packets	15%	29	44%	no change
Houzon-Furst Questioning		0		
SCI Sets		2		
Learning Center Packages		2		
etc.		15		
etc.		10		
	100%		100%	

Total Frequency = 67

Correlational analysis

Correlational analysis gives you an estimate of the size and direction of the linear relationship between two variables. It can usually be a number between −1 and +1. It *does not* provide an estimate of how likely it is that one variable *causes* changes in another. It is often used to a) describe relationships between variables more clearly, b) explore possible cause and effect relationships to be pursued later on, or c) supplement other evidence about how events seem to influence each other when a randomized experiment is not a reasonable alternative. Recommended types of correlation coefficients to use with different combinations of measurement scales are presented in the chart below.

Chart Showing Correlation Coefficient
Appropriate to Scales of Measurement for Variable X and Variable Y*

Scale of Measurement for Variable Y*	Scale of Measurement for Variable X			
	Discrete-Nominal	Continuous-Nominal	Ordinal	Interval/Ratio
Discrete-Nominal	1. a. *Phi (ϕ) b. Contingency Coefficient (C)	(5)	(8)	(10)
Continuous-Nominal	5. ** ↑	2. a. Tetrachoric b. multicell	(6)	(9)
Ordinal	8. Rank Biserial (r_{rb})	6. ** ←	3. a. *Spearman Rho (ρ) b. Kendall's Tau (τ)	(7)
Interval/Ratio	10. *Point Biserial (r_{pb})	9. Biserial (r_b)	7. ** ↑	4. Pearson (r)

* a special case of the Pearson r
** an undefined correlation coefficient, the preferred alternative is in the adjacent box indicated by the arrow

Chart adapted from G.V. Glass & J.C. Stanley, *Statistical Methods in Education and Psychology* (Englewood Cliffs, NJ: Prentice Hall, 1970), p. 158; and from D.E. Hinkle, W. Wiersma, & S.G. Jurs, *Applied Statistics for the Behavioral Sciences* (Chicago: Rand McNally, 1979), p. 96.

EXAMPLE OF CORRELATIONAL ANALYSIS

An agency has begun providing training to all its clerical employees to help them follow new legal client record requirements. In some agencies, nearly everyone has been trained, while in others, very few have been. In order to determine possible training impact, the agency analyzed data (already on hand) of errors in records and violations of record regulations leading to state reprimands (serious violations). Based on the correlation data shown below, they argued that the training didn't seem to affect overall error rates but was related to reducing serious violations.

Relationship Between Proportion of
Clerks Trained and Branch Office Error Rates

Proportion of Clerks Receiving Training	Average No. of All Errors*	Average No. of Serious Errors*
0– 20%	16	6
20– 40%	12	6
40– 60%	18	4
60– 80%	13	3
80–100%	15	1
Correlation Coef. =	−.07	−.97

* Monthly per-clerk rates

HYPOTHESIS TESTING

When you have information on two or more groups of people, like those who attended a workshop and those who did not, you can use that information to estimate whether those groups are "really" different. Hypothesis testing is a way of deciding whether differences found between groups are likely to be "true" differences or ones that could simply have come about by chance fluctuation in the data. Some characteristics of the groups that you would be most likely to compare include means, proportions, correlations, and variances (the standard deviation squared). The particular analysis you would use depends on a number of things, like the estimates you would like to test, the levels of measurement you have (e.g., names, ranks, intervals, ratios), and how you selected the groups you have information on (e.g., is information from one group independent of others).

EXAMPLE

After the large city school district (see Example #1 for Descriptive Statistics) put together their descriptive summaries, they performed a *t-test* to decide if the two groups (special education staff who attended a training workshop and those who did not) differed on the knowledge test. They also decided that they wanted to be 95% confident that any differences between the mean scores of the two groups were not due to chance. They computed the following "t" value and probability based on the information for the two groups.

	Number	Mean	Standard Deviation
Without training	30	39.30	14.98
With training	30	44.60	13.36

difference = 5.30   t = 1.45   probability = 0.15

They concluded that the 5.3 point difference between mean scores of the special education staff who did and did not attend the training workshop could have happened by chance alone. This finding, along with feedback from the first group of workshop participants, prompted the trainers to revise the workshop for the second group.

QUALITATIVE ANALYSIS METHODS

These are methods used to derive meaning from rich descriptive materials such as interview summaries, case studies, site visit reports, sets of records, and so forth. Such materials are usually primarily narrative (versus numerical).

As with quantitative analysis, there are many procedures and approaches available. And, there is a rich literature on the topic; see the chapter bibliography for some useful references. We have included here only a very brief and superficial sampling of the options, trying to relate these especially to the kinds of qualitative data that might be collected in a training program evaluation.

Qualitative analysis procedures differ from quantitative approaches in that they are not so mechanistic and prescriptive. The steps in computing an "F"-test are fixed and unvarying; there are no equally specific and predetermined steps for conducting a qualitative analysis. Rather, there are conceptual frameworks, cues and guidelines that an analyst may find helpful. But you will not find a cookbook.

The social phenomenon approach*

This approach provides six (6) units for inquiry and interpretation based on a continuum of levels of social phenomena, from the smallest level (an act) to the largest level (a complete setting). The next table describes these six levels and shows two kinds of analysis—static and phase—that can be used to guide inquiry into each level.

* This is borrowed loosely from John Lofland, *Analyzing Social Settings* (Wadsworth Publishing), Belmont, California, 1971.

Different Questions to Guide Inquiry

Defined by Levels of Social Phenomena and Kinds of Analysis

	Static Depiction of Phenomena	Depiction of Phases, Stages and Sequences
1. Acts: specific, brief action	What are acts comprised of? What categories do they represent? What labels can be assigned? What acts recur?	What led up to an act? What sequences occurred within a single act? What stages of acts recur?
2. Activities: action of a longer or continuing duration, especially by groups	What patterns and categories of activities exist? Are there characteristic types of activities, actors, and results?	Are there stages and phases that can be identified for all, or different kinds of, participants?
3. Meanings: the verbal signs of people involved that define and direct their action	What basic ideas do actors hold? What are norms and expectations? What explanations are given by participants?	What transformations in meaning occur? What changes in viewpoints, norms, expectations, etc. happen? Are there patterns or stages of change?
4. Participation: how people behave, react, etc. in a given setting	What kinds of persons (or personalities) are involved? What labels characterize participants? What levels and patterns of involvement exist?	Are there cycles or stages of participation?
5. Relationships: among several persons in a given time, in a given setting	What kinds of interactions and interrelationships are there? What hierarchies exist?	Do relationships move through stages and patterns of change?
6. Setting: the entire setting under study conceived of as a whole unit	What label or type characterizes a setting? What general types of settings can be discerned?	What stages or phases has the setting passed through? At what stage or phase is the setting now?

Example

A state department of education provided grants to several schools to conduct inservice training. As part of an evaluation effort to determine what kinds of benefits, changes, and impacts those grants had helped stimulate, they commissioned several case-studies to be conducted—one per site—by a graduate class from the local university. The case-study reports were then provided to readers (a few readers per case). The readers were asked to study the cases, guiding their analysis using the Activities, Participation, Relationship and Setting Categories from the preceding table. Then, they were asked to report their conclusions, citing the categories, as to what evidence supported or refuted the hypothesis that teachers and pupils had benefitted from the inservice.

Content analysis

Content analysis is a way of objectively and systematically identifying particular characteristics of documents, records, or any other kind of retrievable communication. Four major characteristics of content analysis include:

the process is carried out using specific rules and procedures;
it is systematic;
it aims toward generalizable conclusions;
analysis is of what is actually present, not an "interpretation."

Good classification categories should have the following characteristics:

they reflect the purposes of the study;
they should be exhaustive—cover all of the possibilities;
they should be mutually exclusive—have no or little overlap;
they should be independent—classification of one piece of information should not
    determine the classification of another;
they should reflect a single classification principle—e.g., classify only what is "in
    print."

Example

As part of an overall staff development program, a school district had established a technical assistance system to facilitate mainstreaming activities in the elementary schools. The Technical Assistance staff had the general impression that things were not going as smoothly as they could be, but they did not feel that they had a good handle on what was going on. As an initial step, they decided to interview a group of teachers in one building to get an idea of how the system was being used and what the teachers' attitudes were about it.

Following a semi-structured interview, key categories for summarizing comments were selected (some qualitative, some quantitative) and the relevant responses from each teacher were recorded. A section of this interview summary is in the next table. This analysis provided a manageable level of information for the technical assistance staff to use to start focusing on a variety of strengths and weaknesses of the system.

Example of Content Analysis (*continued*)

Interview Summaries

Interview	Background	Context of Problem	Categories	Results of Assistance	Summary: Attitudes toward T.A. System
			Assistance Requested/Provided		
7	Music tchr	Problems in providing music training for deaf student	Request help (materials, suggestions); Spec. Ed. tchr met w/music tchr and suggested materials emphasizing rhythm exercises	All of the children responded to the rhythm materials	Good system to have available.
8	4th grade tchr 23 students 2 handicapped children	Has child who is confined to a wheelchair—is always left out of activities during recess	Request training in recreational activities which don't require the use of the legs; P.E. tchr met w/classroom tchr leaving lots of ideas for recreational activities for small or large groups of children	Handicapped child suddenly seen as "special" by classmates because he knew games they didn't—they all wanted to learn	Tchr found that many of these activities could be done right in the classroom—and made good use of them on rainy days during recess time; has since shared many of the ideas w/other tchrs. Tchr had to buy own materials.

| 9 | 4th grade tchr 22 students 3 handicapped children | Recordkeeping seems inadequate | Request forms to simplify record-keeping; Building Team member discussed problems of recordkeeping w/tchr | Tchr decided he wasn't doing such a bad job of record-keeping after all | Tchr felt that no help was offered. |

Summary (in frequencies)

	Tchrs	Problem Type	Requests Made	Results of Assistance	Summary of Attitudes
(9 interviews)	(2) 1st grade	(1) reading	(4) materials	Negative = 4	(2) system is poor action taken, no help offered
	(3) 3rd grade	(3) behavior	(4) consultation	Positive = 7	
	(2) 4th grade	(1) motivation	(2) training		(3) materials difficult to access
	(1) 5th grade	(1) handwriting	(1) referral		
	(1) Spec. area	(1) music			(5) system is helpful
		(1) physical	Requests Provided		
		(2) recordkeeping	(5) materials		
			(2) direct contact w/child		
			(2) training		
			(4) consultation		

Records analysis

Qualitative analysis of records is distinguished from a quantitative analysis. A quantitative analysis might employ a checklist or aggregation form for gathering and summarizing, quantitatively, the numerical information from existing records. A qualitative approach would use a variety of techniques (e.g., content analysis, searching for clues and patterns, etc.) to pursue one or more questions, hunches, or tentative hypotheses. A useful approach for records analysis is called "tracking." Here, the evaluator forms one or more tentative hypotheses (e.g., "the teachers are using what they learned in the inservice"). The assumption is that when things happen, "tracks" are left. So, one searches for tangible evidence in a variety of records, looking for tracks that confirm, or disconfirm, the hypothesis.

Example

A district had been operating its resource center and teacher awareness program for several months. It wished to determine whether teachers had in fact made use of the center's resources in their school duties. Their working hypothesis was, " . . . Yes, there has been use!" Then, they projected what kinds of records and other tangible indicators would reflect such use, had there in fact been any.

They selected a small sample of teachers who had made several resource center visits and checked out materials. Then, from those teachers, they collected lesson plans, reports, faculty meeting minutes, principal's evaluation and classroom visit reports, and reports to parents. These materials were then intensively scrutinized, and evidence indicating usage of resource center materials was noted.

HOW WILL YOU INTERPRET THE RESULTS OF ANALYSES?

Interpretation is bringing meaning to the results of analysis; deciding on the significance and implications of what the data show. Interpretation involves making claims, such as: "The student can prepare an adequate lesson plan," or "Pat Jones is unable to interpret diagnostic data," or "The workshop helped teachers individualize instruction."

Interpretation of data also involves valuing and necessitates comparison of what the data show against some value, standard, expectation or other referent. Here are some sample results; *descriptive only* . . .

"Three site visitors felt that the workshop was a failure . . . "
Participants rated 'interest' at $\overline{X} = 3.2$ on a 1–5 scale"
"The teacher engaged in Schwartzian questioning techniques twice during the lesson"
"Participants achieved perfect (100%) scores on the post-test"
"No record contained a parent signature"

In the absence of referents, none of these data expositions has meaning beyond its descriptive function.

Now here are some possible *referents* . . .

the expertise (knowledge, experience, etc.) of site visitors
research on the expected and acceptable interest ratings of workshop participants
beliefs and values about proper teaching behaviors
previously established standards for performance (e.g., on tests)
laws and regulations

Comparing data against these referents allows interpretations (valuing). To continue, here are some example interpretations . . .

The workshop did not function as well as expected
Participants' interest was low and could explain poor performance
The teacher uses proper questioning technique
Participants met workshop knowledge objectives
Records are out of compliance with regard to parent signatures

POSSIBLE REFERENTS TO BE USED IN EVALUATING TRAINING	
	Expert judgments, opinions, viewpoints
	Staff expectations, arbitrary standards
	Public (democratic) viewpoints, e.g., as determined from a consensus or voting procedure
	Special interest viewpoints (e.g., a handicapped parents group)
	Research studies and reports (e.g., linking interest to learning)
	Institutional standards, guidelines
	Commonly accepted practice (e.g., adult learning theory)
	Regulations, laws (e.g., federal guidelines)
	Accreditation or licensing standards (e.g., AMA, NCATE, CEC, ASHA)
	Probabilities, rates of occurrence, predictable likelihoods
	Norms, expected scores, cutting scores

PROCEDURES FOR
JUDGING
FINDINGS

Statistical tests of significance
Consensus methods (Delphi, nominal group technique, Q-Sort, etc.)
Voting, democratic procedures
Discussions, meetings, reviews
Hearings, panel reviews
Debates
Jury trials
Individual opinions
Expert judgments

GUIDELINES FOR
INTERPRETING

1. *Deal with multiple and conflicting evidence*
   In evaluation, not everything and usually hardly anything lends itself to a summation process of interpretation where you can "add up" the scores from several data sources and arrive at a convenient single conclusion. One cannot, for example, rely on a formula such as "(2 × participant reaction) + (.07 trainer's perception) + (3 × work accomplished) = success of workshop."

   Our knowledge of many variables and the interrelationships among them is limited and prevents us from such manipulations. More often, we must rely on a holistic approach, wherein we react and judge based on a reaction to the whole of something as we consider data about its element parts. Or, we must interpret each element or part alone and report these, leaving holistic judgments to evaluation consumers. You cannot expect to provide consensus or resolution if there is none.

2. *Don't assume that statistical significance is the same as practical significance* or that lack of statistical significance has no practical significance.

3. *Beware of regression effect*
   Remember that a group selected for measured low performance on some variable will show improved measured performance as an artifact of measurement error. That is, error not showing up the first time in an extreme sample is likely to be caught the second time around.

4. *Look for confirmation and consistency with other sources of information*
   Often, single data sources will not, despite more analysis, yield more information that you can use. If, for example, workshop participants rated satisfaction high, check other bits of data before interpreting that they were satisfied. Did they stay for the whole session? What do instructors say? How did they behave while there?

   When you find obvious inconsistencies—e.g., participants said they liked the session, but no one came back after lunch—look for a third source, or yet more information.

5. *Know when to stop*
   Remember that you'll never be certain; any and all data are to some extent inconclusive. Some guidelines to know when to stop are:

   with quantitative data, you arrive at a level of certainty you're willing to defend
   with qualitative data, you encounter redundancy, or regularity
   remember: You never conclude analysis. You stop doing it.

6. *Consider and cite limitations of the analysis methods you use*
   There are limitations inherent in the analysis techniques you use and the assumptions necessary for their use.

   For example, a correlation coefficient does not account for all variance, and it does not merit causal inferences.

7. *Consider and cite limitations based on external phenomena and other data you have*
   No findings exist in a vacuum, and all must be interpreted against other data. For example, an interpretation might note that "Participants rated satisfaction low, yet all of them attended the optional sessions."

   Or, "Supervisors were satisfied with student performance, but student performance test scores were below criterion."

   Or, "Participants did not show a gain in knowledge, but they had just received notice of staff cutbacks and the interest in training was minimal."

8. *Audiences may, and often should, be involved in interpretation*
   This process sheds more light on what data mean and helps analyses be more responsive. In this way, interpretation overlaps with reporting. (See especially cases S-4 and L-1 for examples where audiences were asked to help interpret findings.) Should strong disagreements emerge regarding what data mean, consider appending a minority report.

CRITERIA FOR INTERPRETATION

1. Ensure that norms and referents are appropriate for the population or characteristic you are judging
2. Cite and provide rationale for particular referents used in interpretation
3. Formulate and explain interpretations in light of contextual and confirming, limiting, or disconfirming information
4. Use summations and holistic interpretation techniques appropriately
5. Cite limitations and clearly explain degrees of certainty warranted
6. Provide alternative explanations and interpretations where appropriate
7. Seek out and include "minority" opinions on opposing interpretations when appropriate

Reporting in Evaluation

The general purpose of reporting is to communicate information to interested audiences and to help them make use of information from the evaluation. Reporting is *not* a static, one-time event nor is it necessarily a product, such as a written report. Rather, reporting is an ongoing process that might include oral, visual, or written communication that commences before an evaluation begins and likely continues beyond its conclusion.

The content of reporting is not constrained to communicating the findings of evaluation. It includes communicating information about purposes, context, activities, results, and implications of programs and evaluations. It includes, too, communication among evaluation staff when more than one person is involved in an evaluation.

Reports are the only way some audiences have access to the evaluation. Sometimes the report can serve as the sole information base from which decision makers will work. This is especially true as time or distance elapses between the evaluation and the planned use for evaluation information. Reports, then, are extremely important. It is important that they are timely, open and frank, and as balanced as possible in their descriptions of strengths and weaknesses of what is being evaluated.

WHEN ARE REPORTING DECISIONS MADE?

The initial decisions for reporting are made as part of the overall evaluation plan. But you must expect to reconsider these decisions during the course of an evaluation effort. Special problems requiring reporting will crop up; opportunities and needs for special reporting will occur. Expect to vary from the original plan and to replan reporting as you go along.

WHO SHOULD GET AN EVALUATION REPORT?

Reports are written for people. The content of a report is determined by who will be using the information and why. The report format (whether it should be a written report, oral report, formal presentation or news release) is also determined by the audience—who needs to understand this information and how can you best present it for their understanding.

Your report audiences are the persons, groups, and agencies whose information needs and interests guided the evaluation or whose actions support the evaluation. They must be kept apprised of an evaluation's operation and results.

Audiences differ in the kinds of interests they have in an evaluation. Some will be decision makers; some will be reactors and providers of further information; some will be informees only. In all cases, audiences are defined by the "stake" they hold in an evaluation, or by what is being evaluated. In this respect, evaluation audiences and evaluation purposes are closely related.

GUIDELINES FOR IDENTIFYING REPORT AUDIENCES

Be comprehensive. You should take care not to ignore a particular audience. Return to the original purposes and audiences for the evaluation, and be sure your report plan accounts for each of the evaluation's audiences.

Differentiate audiences by purposes. Remember that when you report to someone you're doing it for a reason. It's good communication practice and certainly more efficient to make communications as specific and to-the-point as possible. Audiences should not "automatically" be everyone who has anything to do with a training preparation effort. Many times an evaluation will produce only one report (mistake #1) and then give it to anyone and everyone who has anything to do with the program (mistake #2). Deluging people with unwanted information can hurt the credibility and utility of the evaluation, and it is probably as bad as not giving an audience some information they should have received. Nearly as bad as leaving someone out is "junk-mailing" an audience. Choosing an audience carefully according to just what they need, then reporting to them in a timely, direct and appropriate manner, respects their needs, not to mention their time.

Attend to human rights, ethics, laws and guidelines. Review each intended report audience to ensure that, in providing information to that audience, you don't infringe on or violate the rights of another. Consider both the timing and editing of your report in advance. Who will be the last audience to review and edit? Who will decide when and how the report will be released? Evaluation reports usually become publicly accessible under freedom of information laws. Anonymity assurances, protocol, and other ethical considerations can be potentially violated and ought to be considered prior to reporting.

GUIDELINES FOR
IDENTIFYING
REPORT
AUDIENCES
(continued)

Reconsider audiences throughout the evaluation. Audiences for reports need to be reconsidered during and after an evaluation. Usually, an evaluation's original design is modified as evaluation work progresses and may require new audience considerations. Finally, when an evaluation has collected and interpreted information, you need to consider what audiences need to be involved in its further interpretation and who should receive what kinds of reports.

TYPES OF REPORT
AUDIENCES

· funders and supporters
· oversight agencies, advisory boards, licensing groups
· staff and consultants
· clients (students, trainees)
· administrators
· professional groups and organizations
· libraries, resource centers and clearing houses
· projects and programs similar to what you've evaluated
· the public
· others with a stake in the evaluation

ALTERNATIVE
PURPOSES FOR
EVALUATION
REPORTS

to demonstrate accountability: to show that objectives have been met, activities undertaken, resources expanded, and persons involved.

to convince: an advocacy argument providing evidence that activities have been effective in meeting objectives, or that worthwhile benefits have been achieved, or that a position or decision is justified.

to educate: enlightening audiences about how programs work, who they involve, why they are needed, what problems they face, what resolutions might be possible.

to explore and investigate: providing information that can help solve problems, shed light on successes and failures, and identify new directions.

to document: recording what has taken place for future use such as research and development.

to involve: attempting to draw uninvolved (or underinvolved) people and resources into activities.

to gain support: arguing for the worth and importance of activities, resources, outcomes, etc.

to promote understanding: providing information that can be used to interpret activities, problems, or outcomes in light of audiences' beliefs, knowledge, or values.

to promote public relations: demonstrating particular intentions, activities, and problems to enhance positive feelings.

decision making: providing information that can be used to design or revise programs and standards, direct staff development, redirect evaluation activities, rank order needs, or select alternatives.

Don't limit the purpose for reporting to decision making.
Recent research (Alkin, Daillak and White, 1979; Patton, 1978; Braskamp, Brown and Newman, 1980) reinforces the notion that evaluation can and does have impact beyond being "used" in decisions. It can reduce decision makers' uncertainty, make people more aware, reinforce policy, and create support, to name a few additional purposes. Further, this research shows that evaluation data can rarely be linked

directly to a decision. To limit reporting purposes to decision making is to drastically limit the potential ability of evaluation in personnel preparation.

CONSIDERING AUDIENCE NEEDS IN EVALUATIONS OF PERSONNEL OF TRAINING

Students (Trainees)

Report about progress and mastery for continued learning; through reporting, students also should be kept informed about program changes and the uses for their feedback.

Trainers, faculty, consultants, leaders

Report to these persons about their effectiveness, style, and results to improve their effectiveness, or report to them as a group or program unit for general staff development.

Staff

Program training staff need regular feedback on the program's progress and development and their own effectiveness. Internal evaluation reports can clarify issues and value conflicts, identify problems, and stimulate motivation and progress.

Public

Report about funding, program intentions, progress and results to enhance support, involvement, and awareness.

Funders

Most agencies or organizations require annual or other regular reports. These should concentrate on accountability, major impacts, and goal achievement.

Colleagues, other professionals, other organizations

Report in journals, newsletters and professional meetings to share your experience, successes and failures.

Disseminators

Report to agencies (your SEA, the National Diffusion Network (NDN), the Joint Dissemination and Review Panel (JDRP) and the National Inservice Network (NIN) at Indiana University, for example) and to journals to disseminate promising practices. Reports to them should concentrate on replicability information and proofs of accomplishments.

WHAT CONTENT SHOULD BE INCLUDED IN A REPORT?

Report content is simply what a report is about. Reports can be comprehensive, covering the setting, history, growth and achievements of a project. Or a report can be quite specific; for example, a report on why a problem emerged, how well a group of trainees performed a task, or what transpired at a meeting.

No matter what the purpose is for a report or who the report is for (or even how informal it is), it should be balanced, clear, and grammatically and technically sound. Each report, even if it is a memo, serves as a sample of the evaluation; biased, sloppy, or late reports have irrevocable and negative effects on key audiences.

TYPICAL KINDS OF REPORTS

Announcements and releases

These are brief, usually single-topic reports that highlight key decisions or aspects relating to a project or evaluation. Included would be information about evaluation designs, decisions to evaluate, purposes, staff, resources, schedules, etc.

Progress reports

These are reports on milestone accomplishments, major events, or significant achievements and activities that occur.

Interim and preliminary reports

These focus on predetermined time intervals (e.g., each quarter, semester) in the evaluation and report on the events and conclusions of that interval. They may include preliminary findings, modifications to plans, or progress toward goals. Some typical topics for interim reports are:

situation appraisals: How did the first workshop go; is the revised practicum installed; are we on schedule?
analyses of problems; Why was attendance low? Why are trainees unable to use new procedures?
assessments of quality: How good are the new workshop materials?
research conclusions: Did the new materials produce better impact? Has the revised workshop schedule raised attendance?
justifications: This is why the workshop has been revised to include consultation. These are the reasons for shortening the workshop.
updates: Schedule for interviews and training of field persons: the new plan for trainee follow-up.

Concluding reports

These are reports that occur at the end of an evaluation or program or at the end of a major period, such as the first year. Some usual kinds of concluding reports are:

main report: containing comprehensive information about evaluation purposes, objects, activities, findings and conclusions
executive summary: a précis of the main report, highlighting conclusions
popular report: a summary version, in simple language, of the main report
technical report: detailed information about information collection strategies, sampling, analysis procedures, data collection, etc.

TYPICAL KINDS OF REPORTS
(continued)

follow-up reports: (usually meetings, conferences, panels, or hearings) presentations containing interpretations, consequences, implications, and next steps concerning the results and conclusions of the evaluation

Internal reports

These are reports intended for internal use of the evaluation; they are "consumed" by the evaluation and enable it to move ahead. Questionnaire data, for instance, might be aggregated and displayed, then given to (reported to) a group for analysis and interpretation.

Internal reports might be produced any time by the evaluation and can be planned or spontaneous. Most often, the audience for internal reports is evaluation staff or helpers. Sometimes, reports are written only for the file. Some examples of internal evaluation reports can be found in the following examples.

PRELIMINARY PRESS OR ORGANIZATIONAL RELEASE TO ANNOUNCE AN EVALUATION

a. the reasons for, and purposes of, the coming study
b. the goals and objectives of the study
c. the groups and others involved
d. some of the crucial issues involved (e.g., the desegregation order, socio-economic variation among the schools)
e. the organization of the study (e.g., subgroups, task forces)
f. the variables to be investigated and the general information methods to be used
g. a time-line for the study, listing its major planned events and report schedule

---

MEMORANDUM REPORT TO KEY STAFF SENT PRIOR TO PRESS RELEASE

a. copy of drafted press release
b. a delineation of roles to be played by personnel
c. the duties and responsibilities of staff in supporting the study
d. the kinds of changes that might result—and would not result—from the study
e. request for reactions to press release

SUMMARY INTERIM REPORT

Introduction reviewing the major purposes, scope and goals of the study and delineating the audiences and content for the report
the general design
progress to date, noting what data were collected, what persons were involved, what reports had been made, and what problems (if any) had been encountered
next steps: this would outline the work that remained and show a plan for its accomplishment. Here, for example, a task force's filing system would be explained, their plans for preliminary analysis reviewed, and their sub-group organization and meeting schedule explained.

INTERIM DATA SUMMARIES

This report would be technical in nature and intended for use by groups in their preliminary analysis. The data summary would be organized by the major information collection procedures (e.g., tests, interviews, questionnaires, cumulative folder data) and would display the aggregated information in a form (reduced, if necessary, as with questionnaire data) amenable to analysis. This allows key audiences to anticipate findings.

MAIN CONCLUDING REPORT DISSEMINATED TO KEY AUDIENCES

I. Introduction
   A. Intent of document
   B. Audience(s) addressed
   C. Basic definitions (e.g., need, model training program, XYZ training approach)
   D. Limitations and caveats
   E. Overview of document
II. Basic information
   A. Background
   B. Group(s) involved
   C. Focus of the study (which schools, audiences, objects, etc.) - see *Focusing the Evaluation*
   D. Information collected
   E. Uses made of the information
III. Design of the study
   A. Objectives (evaluation questions)
   B. Logical structure and rationale
   C. Procedures
   D. Reports made (with brief summaries)
   E. Schedule - calendar of events
IV. Results
   A. Summary tables and displays of the data collected
V. Conclusions
   A. Interpretations and recommendations
VI. Evaluation of the study
   A. Summary assessment of its strengths and weaknesses, limitations
VII. Next steps
   A. What will happen next; programs to follow; further evaluation
VIII. Appendices

CONCLUDING TECHNICAL REPORT AVAILABLE UPON REQUEST

I. Introduction
   A. Primary intent
   B. Audience
   C. Basic definitions
   D. Limitations and caveats
II. Questions and information collected
   A. Enumeration (e.g., listing of the 4 major questions, the 10 variables, the information sources in each of the 6 sites)
   B. Comparison to objectives (a matrix showing how information collected was used to relate to the objectives of the study)
III. Sampling plan
   A. Definition of population (e.g., the 6 sites, levels assessed, contextual factors re: each site)
   B. Sampling specifications (numbers and types of samples drawn, numbers within each sample, such as how are variables assessed at each of the levels, the stratified random samples, etc.)
   C. Procedures (how each sample was drawn, by whom, when)
IV. Information collection plan
   A. Instruments and procedures (descriptions of tests administered, Delphi group constitution, site visit plans, etc.)
   B. Comparison to information needs (a matrix showing how instruments and procedures relate to particular needs assessment questions, *see Information Collection*)

CONCLUDING
TECHNICAL
REPORT
AVAILABLE UPON
REQUEST
(continued)

V. Information processing
  A. Screening and cleaning procedures (for each procedure, tell how data were verified and screened, noting recollection where it occurred)
  B. Aggregation and filing (description of how the data were reduced, filed and made ready for analysis)
VI. Preliminary analysis
  A. Preliminary analysis procedures (description of the subcommittees formed, concerns looked for, questions addressed, comparisons made among sites on attendance data, etc.)
  B. Preliminary analysis results (a description of each conclusion reached, e.g., the trends identified, issues defined)
VII. Needs analysis
  A. The questions addressed
  B. Procedures used (a description, for each information set, of how analysis was performed, e.g., a Delphi ranking of 10 variables, computation of school-scores for each variable. This would *include* new information collected.)
  C. Analysis results (displays - e.g., bar graphs, charts, and accompanying discussion of each major analytic procedure's results)
VIII. Appendices
  These would contain raw data summaries, the internal data reports, and other documents and reports that support the technical report and would be needed to replicate the analysis.

CONCLUDING
PRESS RELEASE

Study Team Recommends Staff Development
brief history of study and purposes
who was involved
what information was collected
results and conclusions
next steps
announcement of public report hearings

REPORT
MEETING(S) WITH
KEY GROUPS
(EXAMPLE
AGENDA)

I. Introduction by the superintendent: (a) purposes, scope and general design for the needs assessment; (b) major parties involved; and (c) overview of the agenda (15 min.)
II. Review of the assessment (30 min.) by the chair of the task force team (with overhead projector)
  A. The objectives of the study
  B. The procedures used (transparency: matrix of objectives and procedures)
  C. Results of analysis (transparencies of cumulative bar graphs, school comparisons, etc.)
  D. Conclusions of the study (overview of advocacy team procedures and convergence team conclusions
  E. Evaluation summary of limitations and caveats re: needs assessment
III. Questions for clarification: led by superintendent, task force team chair and evaluator; in which questions pertaining to clarification are raised by audience and answered by appropriate respondent (15 min.)

BREAK for Coffee and Rolls - (20 min.)

REPORT
MEETING(S) WITH
KEY GROUPS
(continued)

IV. Panel discussion (evaluator, task force chair, principals) (60 min.)

V. Evaluation: participants react to meeting, rate report, and note further questions and interests (5 min.)

VI. Closing (by superintendent) (5 min.)

HOW WILL REPORTS BE DELIVERED?

There are many more ways to skin the reporting cat than the traditional written report. The main message of this section is to consider alternative means and to choose them wisely. Also included in this section is one example of some effective visual display techniques.

OPTIONAL STRATEGIES FOR REPORTING

written documents: technical reports, interim progress reports, conference proceedings
media releases: press, TV, radio
meetings and small group discussions, presentations, luncheons
hearing, panel reviews, presentations to groups (e.g., PTA)
direct mail leaflets, pamphlets, newsletters
staged interviews of key participants with dissemination provision (e.g., "live" coverage, transcripts)
memoranda, letters
professional journals, publications
slide-tape, video, multi-media presentations, films
mock jury "trials," socio-dramas, theater
training sessions, workshops, conferences

GUIDELINES FOR CHOOSING ALTERNATIVE REPORTING STRATEGIES

Make use of multiple sensory channels (in written reports, use graphics: charts, tables, figures, displays)
Include provision for interaction and checking for comprehension (in written reports: use review questions, discussion summaries, etc.)
Be as simple as possible
Encourage audience participation (in written reports, this can be a tear-off response form)
Make optimal use of audio-visual display techniques
Incorporate varied displays
Gain the attention of the intended audience

USE CHARTS, GRAPHS, AND TABLES IN YOUR REPORT

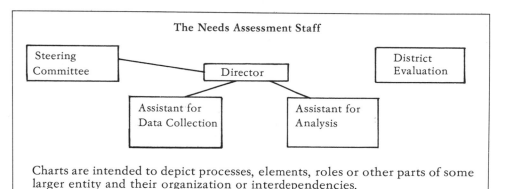

The Needs Assessment Staff

Steering Committee — Director — District Evaluation

Assistant for Data Collection — Assistant for Analysis

Charts are intended to depict processes, elements, roles or other parts of some larger entity and their organization or interdependencies.

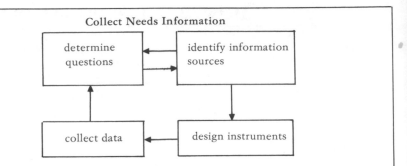

Collect Needs Information

The functions network is often used for program planning and analysis. It is used to show relationships of functions within a system. Arrows leading into a box indicate inputs to that function, and arrows leading out from a box indicate outputs of that function.

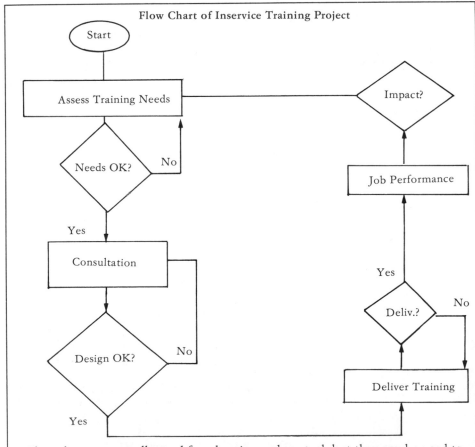

Flow Chart of Inservice Training Project

Flow charts are usually used for planning and control, but they can be used to report how a process works. Most flow charts make use of five symbols. An oval represents a starting and finishing place. Inputs and outputs are represented by parallelograms. An action is represented by a rectangle, and decisions are represented by diamond shapes. Arrows indicate direction of flow.

GRAPHS

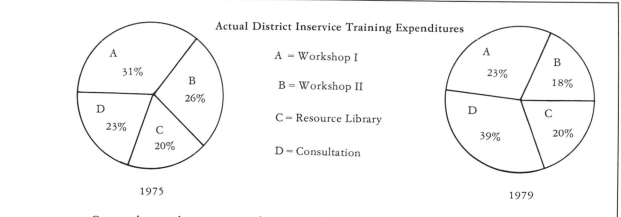

Actual District Inservice Training Expenditures

A = Workshop I

B = Workshop II

C = Resource Library

D = Consultation

1975

1979

One-scale graphs contain information about only one variable. The most common types of one-scale graphs are the pie or circle graphs, the bar graph, and the pictogram.

Pie or circle graph is the simplest of the one-scale graphs. It can show only parts of the whole (all parts must total 100% or 360°). Two or more circle graphs can be used to provide a comparison.

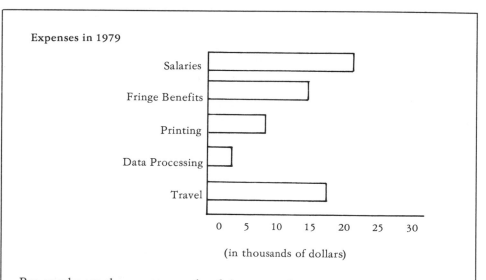

Expenses in 1979

(in thousands of dollars)

Bar graphs are the most versatile of the one-scale graphs. Relative size of the various categories of the single variable is indicated by the length of line or bar. Greater precision is possible with this than with the circle or area charts, and there is less chance for misinterpretation.

GRAPHS
(continued)

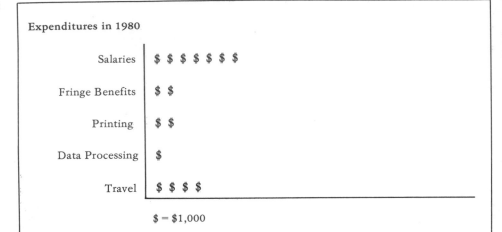

Expenditures in 1980

Salaries	$ $ $ $ $ $ $
Fringe Benefits	$ $
Printing	$ $
Data Processing	$
Travel	$ $ $ $

$ = $1,000

The pictogram is a modification of the bar graph. Rather than using a line to represent quantity, figures are used. This is often the most visually attractive graph, although it often sacrifices precision.

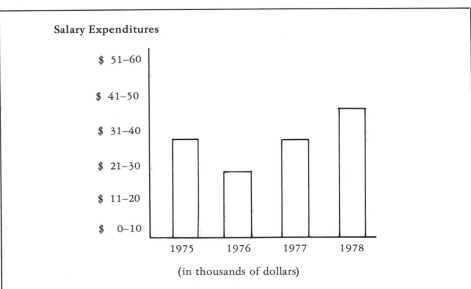

Salary Expenditures

(in thousands of dollars)

Two-scale graphs

The column graph contains two scales while the bar graph contains only one. Either graph can be horizontal or vertical, but usually the one-scale is better horizontal and the two-scale graph is better vertical.

GRAPHS
(continued)

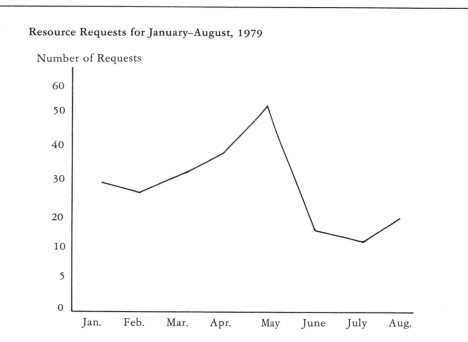

Resource Requests for January–August, 1979

More lines may be plotted on the line graph to provide information for additional comparisons. Be careful not to provide too much information; four or five lines are usually the maximum.

The line graph can be used to convey the same types of information as the column graph, but the line graph is better when there are several points which must be plotted or where there are small changes between the points.

TABLES   Tables present information, numerical or verbal, in rows or columns arranged so that relationships and trends can be readily identified. They may be quite simple, showing single variables, or quite complex, showing multiple variables and depicting several interrelationships.

Percentage of Workshop Participants
Who Achieved Objectives at 80% or Higher Level

	Objective 1 Diagnosis	Objective 2 Interpretation	Objective 3 Prescription	Objective 4 Evaluation
Workshop A	78%	93%	97%	100%
Workshop B	90%	94%	88%	73%
Workshop C	82%	80%	78%	75%
Workshop D	64%	53%	47%	68%

TABLES
(continued)

INCIDENCES of Crime in Schools (annual average)

		Minor	Major	Total
Socio-Economic Status of Schools	High	n = 73	n = 4	77
	Low	n = 81	n = 36	117
Total		154	40	194

The relationship apparent in the table above is that minor crime rates are about the same in "high" and "low" socio-economic schools, but major crime rates are dramatically higher in the "low" status schools.

CRITERIA AND GUIDELINES TO ASSESS REPORT FORMAT

Determine whether the chosen format(s) will meet the following criteria:

1. Comprehensible and engaging to audiences
2. Suitable for content (e.g., don't press release the results of a complex analysis of variance)
3. Useful for the purpose(s)

WHAT IS THE APPROPRIATE STYLE AND STRUCTURE FOR THE REPORT?

The medium is part of your message. That is, how a report is styled and structured can have a major impact on how it's received.

This section contains a listing of suggestions, research findings and guidelines that relate to incorporating appropriate styles and structures into reports, be they written, oral or some other format. This section also provides some examples of report structures (organization).

EXAMPLE ORGANIZATION FOR AN EVALUATION REPORT

I. **Précis, or abstract (written report only):** this enables a "nutshell" view of a report's content and lets a reader know if further reading is warranted.

II. **Table of contents (written report only) or other guide to organization:** this should clearly label portions of the report and indicate where they are and how to access them. In an oral report (meeting, etc.) an agenda can serve this function.

III. **Introduction:** this should relate the purpose of the report, its intended audience, its scope and coverage, including limitations, and how it is organized. Where selection among report parts is intended, the structure of such parts and decision rules for selection should be clearly provided. A preface, acknowledgments, or disclaimer section may also be called for in the introductory content. In an oral presentation, support this portion with a handout or audiovisual graphic.

IV. **Body of report:** this should contain whatever is "promised" in the introduction and be clearly organized around functional aspects related to the report's purpose. A report intending to explain the methods of a needs assessment might well be organized in a method-by-method presentation. Some other common organizing principles for report content are:

A. *Chronological*: arranging information by when it happened, series of events, stages, etc.

B. *Functional or conceptual stages*: arranging content by major functional steps, such as design stage, implementation, analysis, interpretation, etc.

C. *Purposes, goals or objectives*: organizing content by the particular goals, questions, or objectives of the study.

D. *Methods*: presenting content by each of the major procedures in the needs assessment, such as survey, research analysis, interviews, testing, etc.

E. *Conclusions, findings, results*: content can be organized according to each particular conclusion or result of the needs assessment.

F. *Organizational, administrative units*: content might be arranged by the unit, persons or groups who completed different parts of the study.

V. **Summary:** this section should briefly review and highlight the major aspects of the report, its conclusions, significance, etc. This content may also contain, where appropriate, devices for readers and audiences to check their understanding and interpretation of the report. A "Question and Answer" or discussion session can be added after this in an oral presentation.

VI. **Closing:** this should indicate implications for further related work or reporting and contain any content necessary for audiences to place the report in a proper context and perspective, relative both to what has gone before and what may, or should, next occur. This aspect of a report may also be used to provide or reiterate guidance to the audience as to how they might further understand, use, or benefit from the report.

KEY
CONSIDERATIONS
ABOUT CONTENT
WHEN PUTTING
THE REPORT
TOGETHER

Selection of Content

Content should be limited to what's needed to get the reporting job done or to meet the evaluation purpose(s). The ill consequences of including irrelevant content are far greater in a "live" reporting format than they are in a written report. An oral presentation, for example, allows little provision for the listener to pick and choose from a "table of contents" those bits of the report most suitable to his/her needs. Audiences exposed to irrelevant content are likely to tune out the entire report, often with more damaging consequences than if *no* report has been attempted.

Balanced Content

There are two or more sides to every story (probably more). Evaluation findings are rarely conclusive. Alternative explanations and interpretations are offered, along with the available evidence to support or refute them. Sometimes minority perspectives are appended. Evaluation should neither report only positive results if there are also negative results nor vice versa. This is not only ethical practice. The continuing power of evaluation as a force for change rests in its credibility and acceptance by involved persons. Biased, unbalanced reporting will destroy that power base.

Multiple Perspectives

Determine content from the audience's point of view. A report must be comprehensible and have meaning to the recipient audience. Content should be compatible with their point of view, experience and knowledge. Examples, for instance, must be within—and preferably in the forefront—of the audience's experience.

Direct and Simple Language

Keep it simple. Reports should not be overly complex, don't use references and language not readily understandable to intended audiences. Education, as most professions, has a regrettable tendency to use jargon and to use complex language and presentation in transmitting ideas. Evaluation should take extra care to use simple language, brief examples, and ordinary expressions and terminology.

Clarity

Be clear. Reports should be prepared and delivered so as not to introduce unnecessary ambiguity. Evaluation results often have multiple interpretations and are seldom precise and definite. Make sure your report does not add further ambiguity. Findings should be clearly and simply presented and, where appropriate, alternative interpretations clearly listed and explained. Opinions and other subjective expressions should be clearly defined as such.

Focus

Be direct. Reports should directly address the purposes for which they are intended. This means they should not ramble, or "beat around the bush,"

KEY
CONSIDERATIONS
ABOUT CONTENT
WHEN PUTTING
THE REPORT
TOGETHER
(continued)

but should in the sparest and briefest manner address their points. An audience's time is precious, demands upon it should be minimized. This often means eliminating content and providing only what is required for the consumer to receive and understand the intended communication.

Provide for Feedback

Provide for confirmation/feedback. Good communication requires that persons receiving messages be allowed to confirm their perceptions and understanding. Too often, as is true in interpersonal communications, messages received are quite different from messages sent, or intended to be sent. In reports where dialogue is available (as in presentations, oral reports, etc.), provision for questions and discussion can meet these needs. In written or other "one-way" reporting (as in a public media report), provisions should be made in the report for consumers to check their understanding and interpretation. There can be summaries, reviews, comprehension checks (e.g., a quiz) or other devices that enable the consumer to interact with the content of the report.

Overview

A general structure applies to virtually any report type or medium. Any report should be preceded by an overview—an introductory summary in which the reader is informed briefly as to what is coming. This guideline derives from principles of education and communication, In order for report receivers ("learners") to properly assimilate and comprehend a report's content, they require a cognitive organizer: the "whole picture" into which the communication to follow is intended to fit. This front-end overview is a courtesy to an audience, for it tells them what is coming and lets them choose to participate based on this information. More than courtesy, however, a nutshell overview makes good educational and communications sense.

Summarize

The report should close with a summary. This reminds readers (participants, etc.) of the report's main features and may suggest next steps or provide for interaction.

Guide

In journalism, an excellent guideline is offered to assist reports in their copy writing: "Tell them what you're going to tell them, then tell them, then tell them what you told them." This makes a good report structure also.

HOW CAN YOU HELP AUDIENCES INTERPRET AND USE YOUR REPORTS?

Recent research by Alkin (1978) indicates that evaluation reports have the most impact when reporting is construed as a "dialogue" between evaluators and the audiences. Reviewers of reports must interact with the report, rather than simply receive it in a one-way transmission.

SOME OPTIONS FOR INVOLVING AUDIENCES

1. Discuss the reports with key audience members.
2. Make oral presentations.
3. Submit a rough draft of a report to some audience members for an edit and critique.
4. Distribute preliminary summary reports.
5. Have audience members make reports, write reviews, conduct meetings, etc.
6. Conduct panel meetings, hearings, open forums, etc.
7. Incorporate reports into training workshops in which audience members are involved.
8. Present reports at professional associations and meetings.
9. Invite commentary and reaction through publishing report summaries in journals and newsletters.
10. Make yourself or others available to attend meetings where reports can, or may not, be used and discussed.
11. Commission reviews, partisan papers, or other critiques and commentaries by persons influential with key audiences.
12. Present reports at faculty meetings.
13. Conduct a "conference" around a report (e.g., invite past graduates, some employers, and other faculty to a one-day conference on your graduate follow-up).
14. Solicit questions, concerns and related issues (e.g., via mail back forms, 3×5 cards).

BALANCING AN EVALUATION REPORT

Evaluation reports, and especially those that are to be widely disseminated, should be balanced in their perspectives. The balance of a report (whether it is oral, written, or graphic displays) can be easily assessed by an audience. Forgotten perspectives or uneven emphases are inevitably spotted.

AREAS TO BALANCE	PITFALLS
AUDIENCE PERSPECTIVES	One audience has been over-represented or their perspective over-emphasized in a report.
RESOURCE ALLOCATION	One aspect of the evaluation (e.g., data analysis or front-end planning) receives a disproportionate amount of funds, time, personnel, and reporting space.

BALANCING AN EVALUATION REPORT *(continued)*	AREAS TO BALANCE	PITFALLS
	OBJECT DESCRIPTION	The strengths (or weaknesses) of the object become the focus of the evaluation—leaving audiences to search for what was bad (or good).
	ISSUES DISCUSSED	Discussions of one particularly "hot" issue begin to monopolize the evaluation and its formal and informal reports.
	STAFF INFLUENCE	One staff person (or small group of staff) begins to have increasingly greater responsibility for and influence on evaluation reporting—both formal and informal.

GUIDELINES AND CRITERIA FOR PROMOTING IMPACT

Know and understand your audience
relate findings to their problems and concerns
use examples familiar to them
speak their language (i.e., not over their heads, not beneath them)

Incorporate audience members into report activities where possible (e.g., as co-presenters, reactors, reviewers)

Provide minority viewpoints, alternative explanations, rationales, explanations

Provide references and ascribe sources to opinions, interpretations and judgments so that audiences can identify and weigh them

WHEN SHOULD REPORTS BE SCHEDULED?

Audiences have to get reports *on time* (e.g., to coincide with a decision point) or, in many cases, they might as well not get a particular report. The reporting schedule shows:

Who gets the report
What report
When, and
How (oral, written, summary)

   When you report to your intended audiences is not truly "optional." Your schedule is pretty well fixed by your purposes. If a purpose is, for example, to help administrators decide whether to continue a workshop series, they'll need your report just before they make the decision. But, you still need to consider how long before you should report, and how often (e.g., should you report in stages).

OPTIONAL STRATEGIES FOR SCHEDULING REPORTING

1. Determine report schedule by major audience decision/consideration events. This entails scheduling reports to coincide with or immediately precede events such as:
   · board meetings
   · formal reviews and hearings
   · internal decision sessions (e.g., staff meetings)
   · public hearings
   · elections and referendums
   · budget determination hearings or meetings
   · caucuses
   · etc.
2. Schedule by major events and stages in the "life" of the evaluation object, e.g.:
   · program design completion
   · completion of pilot workshops, trial classes, etc.
   · completion of phases
   · completion of project
3. Schedule according to commonly accepted time intervals, e.g.:
   · quarterly, semi-annual, bi-annual, annual, etc.
   · semesters, quarters
   · fiscal years
4. Schedule reports by major events in the course of the evaluation, e.g.:
   · completion of the evaluation design
   · draft of tentative purposes and criteria
   · completion of preliminary analysis
   · signing of evaluation contract
   · end-of-year report
5. Schedule opportunistically, e.g.:
   · major problems discovered

OPTIONAL STRATEGIES FOR SCHEDULING REPORTING
(continued)

· delays in schedule
· early success, rare occurrences
· unexpected findings
· ad-hoc meetings, councils, boards, etc.
6. Schedule incrementally, e.g.:
　· news release, followed by
　· draft report for edit and review, followed by
　· preliminary report, followed by
　· final report, followed by
　· hearings and public discussion of result

EXAMPLE OF A REPORT SCHEDULE

Here is an example of a report schedule for a school district needs assessment.

Event	Date/Frequency	Format	Nature/Scope of Content	Audience
1. Monthly Progress Updates	end of month	memorandum	work accomplished, projected; problems, revisions to design; important future events	program staff
2. Preliminary News Release	1st month of study	news story	purpose, budget, organization, schedule, staff involved	general public
3. Interim Media Report	near end of study—after all data collected	television interview w/ NA Director	progress, preliminary findings, next steps, possible consequences	general public
4. Quarterly Report	end of each quarter (90 days)	written report	progress, resources consumed, problems encountered, next step, revisions to plan	school board administration advisory committee
5. Final Report: Summary Revision	30 days after end of study	written report w/no appendices	review of study, present data, conclusions, interpretations, recommendations	school board advisory committee administration others
6. Final Report: Technical	90 days after end of study	written report w/appendices (instruments, etc.)	same as above, w/fuller data reports included	administration SEA
7. Final Report: Hearing	90 days after study	Panel review and public hearings w/ audio/visual presentation by NA Director	data summaries, conclusion summaries, recommendations, implications	general public school staff

GUIDELINES AND CRITERIA FOR ASSESSING REPORT SCHEDULES

Be timely: get information to audiences when they can best make use of it.

Don't be too early: In an effort to get reports on time, you can be too early, such that your reports are not important to audiences, will be forgotten, or otherwise dealt with superficially.

Be economical: reporting too frequently for the sake of "keeping in touch" could threaten the primacy of your more important reports. You don't want to generate so much background noise that your important signals get lost.

Be specific: schedule reports for particular audiences at particular times. You are often better off to divide a report into two events when two audiences have differing time demands.

Be flexible: revise your schedule and remain open to opportunities for ad-hoc reports.

Evaluate your schedule against your evaluation purposes, audience needs and resources. Check for:

sufficiency to meet purposes and audience needs
sufficiency to meet internal communication needs
compatibility with purposes of the evaluation
coincidence with other major supporting or possibly conflicting events
feasibility relative to your resources

CHECKLIST FOR REPORTS

Here's a checklist to guide and review the report function.

Identification of Purposes and Audiences

1. Review and clarify the *purposes* for the evaluation
2. Review and clarify the *audiences* for the evaluation
3. Identify report *purposes* and report *audiences*. Check to see that:

   purposes are realistic; e.g., can meet audience needs and purposes
   audiences account for all stakeholders in the program and its
      evaluation
      external mandates (e.g., funders)
      internal audiences (e.g., staff)
      public
      others
   purposes are comprehensive; will meet audiences' information needs and
      interests (e.g., decision making, garnering support, soliciting
      involvement)

Report Planning
1. *Content* planned for reports is consistent with (a) report purposes and (b) audience's information *needs, rights* and *interests*
2. *Types* of reports (e.g., interim, summary, technical) are consistent with:

program operations and phases
evaluation stages
audience information demands

3. *Formats* (e.g., written, media announcements, hearings, conferences, meetings) are consistent with:

   purposes for reporting
   audiences
   principles of multiple media, dynamism, interest and education

4. *Formats* provide for follow-up, interaction and confirmation of receipt and understanding

Conducting Reporting Events

1. Each report (written, oral, other) is:

   clear
   simple and concise
   comprehensive
   balanced (i.e., not negatively or positively biased)

2. Conclusions are justified with defensible information and evidence
3. Value perspectives and viewpoints are clarified
4. Feedback, clarification, discussion, exploration and confirmation occur where provided for
5. Audiences are provided opportunities to refute, explain and justify negative findings
6. Human rights and privacy are protected
7. Report activities follow sound educational designs (e.g., overviews and summaries are provided, support documents are included)

REFERENCES

Alkin, M.C., Daillak, R. & White, P. *Using Evaluations: Does Evaluation Make a Difference?* Beverly Hills: Sage, 1979.

Braskamp, L.A., Brown, R.D. & Newman, D.L. *Studying Evaluation Utilization Through Simulations.* Unpublished paper, University of Illinois at Urbana, Champaign and University of Nebraska-Lincoln, undated.

Flesch, R. *On Business Communication: How to Say What You Mean in Plain English.* New York: Harper & Row, 1972.

Hawkridge, D.G., Campeau, P.L. & Trickett, P.K. *Preparing Evaluation Reports: A Guide for Authors. AIR Monograph.* Pittsburgh: American Institutes for Research, 6, 1970.

Kearney, C.P. & Harper, R.J. The Politics of Reporting Results. In E.R. House (ed.), *School Evaluation: The Politics and Process.* Berkeley: McCutchan, 1973.

Lanham, R.A. *Revising Prose.* New York: Scribners, 1978.

Office of Program Evaluation and Research. *Handbook for Reporting and Using Test Results.* Sacramento, CA: Bureau of Publication Sales, California State Department of Education.

Patton, M.Q. *Utilization-Focused Evaluation.* Beverly Hills: Sage, 1978.

Popham, W.J. *Educational Evaluation.* Englewood Cliffs, N.J.: Prentice Hall, 1975.

Smith, D.M. & Smith, N.L. *Writing Effective Evaluation Reports.* Portland, OR: Northwest Regional Educational Laboratory, March, 1980.

Managing Evaluation

Managing an evaluation involves orchestrating or supervising the conduct of all evaluation functions—focusing, designing, information collection and analysis, reporting, and meta-evaluation.

Evaluation management is similar enough to the management of most systems that it can be judged according to some similar standards. Management of a department, program, or an evaluation, for example, should be efficient, equitable, and effective. It should not over-consume staff time, precious dollars and materials, and the goodwill of those it involves and affects.

While management of evaluation is important, if it is effective it can go almost unnoticed. Good evaluation management helps rather than hinders audiences, it shortens rather than lengthens the time necessary to run an evaluation, it reduces potentially controversial issues, and it serves well all those involved in an evaluation.

WHEN YOU MAKE MANAGEMENT DECISIONS
Management bridges all other evaluation functions. Management responsibilities begin before the evaluation is implemented, they run through the entire evaluation, and they are typically the last events to be concluded after the evaluation. While management activities permeate the evaluation process, the most efficient evaluation management is unobtrusive.

WHO WILL BE IN CHARGE OF THE EVALUATION?

An evaluation may falter or fail because the evaluator isn't competent or isn't perceived as being competent by others. This makes the selection of an evaluator crucial even though a number of practical and political constraints can effectively limit that selection. To provide the best possible leadership for evaluation, it is important to be aware of alternative means to staff evaluation and to identify the skills that are important to see an evaluation through successfully.

Whether there is one evaluator or a team, a part-time consultant or a full-time manager/evaluator, the responsibilities the evaluator will have must be defined. For example, will the evaluator:

· conceptualize the evaluation
· design the evaluation
· construct instruments
· collect the data
· analyze the data
· devise methods to code, store and access the data
· negotiate with the audiences
· prepare contracts
· write the reports
· deliver reports
· interpret and recommend
· manage and interact with personnel

These responsibilities will be based upon the evaluation design which, in turn, reflects the evaluation questions and the evaluation purpose generated by stakeholders. Based upon the complexity of the evaluation design, the job description or a list of responsibilities such as those listed above should be drawn up. This list of responsibilities will allow you to make decisions.

There are presently a number of national professional evaluation organizations including the *Evaluation Network*, the *Evaluation & Research Society* (ERS), and *Division H* of the *American Educational Research Association*. Additionally, there are state-wide branches of evaluation organizations, offices of planning and evaluation within school districts, evaluation centers at universities, and national and regional evaluation laboratories. In short, it is possible to hire persons who have studied program evaluation, who are members of evaluation organizations, who have been involved in a number of evaluations, and who have reports and recommendations to verify their competence.

Use of such professionals can be on a consulting basis for internally run evaluations or on a short-term, full-time basis for entire evaluations. Often the cost of one or two days' time from an experienced evaluator brought in at the design stage will save time and resources in the long run.

When persons with a complete set of evaluation skills are not available, an option is to train existing personnel so that they can do evaluation tasks.

One way to accomplish this is by providing inservice training for staff—either on-site training or training offered through workshops and course work elsewhere.

Whatever the strategy used to staff the evaluation, the criterion for success is the provision of an evaluator or an evaluation team that is seen as credible and is capable of competently running the evaluation. Even the most competent evaluator can be seen, for political or theoretical reasons, as inappropriate for some evaluation jobs. If the evaluation is to have any chance of being useful, it must be produced by persons with believable independence, political viability, and competence.

ALTERNATIVE MEANS TO STAFF EVALUATION

Staff vs. External

Person already on the staff		vs.	Individual hired from outside especially for evaluation work	
Pros	Cons		Pros	Cons
knows the organization has known reputation, status, credibility	bias because of conflict of interest in evaluating a program in which there is a personal investment		comes without preconceived notion about the program is seen as independent observer by staff	unfamiliar with known traditions, camps, and protocol, and might antagonize selection sometimes based only upon recommendation

Individual vs. Team

Individual solely responsible for the evaluation		vs.	Team including content and evaluation persons who, together, have necessary skills	
Pros	Cons		Pros	Cons
responsibilities for the evaluation clear	success or failure heavily dependent upon a single individual		diffusion of responsibilities composite of multiple skills & perspectives	time spent on team building, logistics, & political considerations expenses involved

ALTERNATIVE
MEANS TO STAFF
EVALUATION
(continued)

Full-time vs. Part-time

Individual or team with full-time evaluation responsibilities		vs.	Individual or team with part-time evaluation responsibilities	
Pros	Cons		Pros	Cons
organized & coherent evaluation	cost involved		multiple authorities can be brought in for short periods of time	brief visits don't allow for thorough study
timely & ongoing information	discourages participation in evaluation			expense & logistics involved in scheduling
independence of evaluator(s)	evaluator(s) seen as outsider		effective use of outside expertise	

Amateur vs. Professional

Person(s) with primary & major training in content area, no formal evaluation training or experience		vs.	Person(s) with primary & major training in evaluation	
Pros	Cons		Pros	Cons
knows content and object well	knowledge of object decreases evaluation objectivity		brings in experience & technical skills to run evaluation	outsider not acceptable to program staff; evaluation skills not valued
can "pick up" many evaluation skills through experience	limited evaluation competencies leads to few design options		provides multiple options through experience	bias toward a certain method prevents multiple options design

SKILL AREAS
CONSIDERED
NECESSARY FOR
AN EVALUATOR
OR AN
EVALUATION
TEAM

Keep in mind that evaluators must not only *be* competent, they must be *perceived* as competent. Conflict of interest or nonindependence may have more negative effects in the long run than missing skill areas (such as, computer know-how or statistical skills). While consultants can be brought in for technical assistance, no one can help an evaluator who is not perceived as trustworthy and credible.

Management skills
supervision
political savvy
professional ethics
communication (public relations) skills
interpersonal skills
systems analysis
contracting
budgeting
goal setting

SKILL AREAS CONSIDERED NECESSARY FOR AN EVALUATOR OR AN EVALUATION TEAM *(continued)*

Technical skills
instruments selection/development
test administration
statistical analysis
survey methods
observation techniques
psychometrics
experimental/quasi-experimental design
quality control of data
computer application
case-study methodology
cost analysis
report writing

Conceptual skills
ability to invent options
conceiving initial plans
categorizing and analyzing problems
ability to see and express relationships

Content expertise
working experience in area being evaluated
knowledge of major literature sources
understanding of important constructs in relevant field
familiar with experts in the field

SELECTING THE EVALUATOR

Is someone on the staff or in the immediate organization qualified to handle the job?

What kind of team might be put together from existing staff to achieve a composite of needed competencies?

Is there a professional evaluator who might be brought in on a part-time basis to provide consultation or do some of the technical tasks (e.g., designing an instrument, drawing a difficult sample)?

Is it possible to train some program staff to take on necessary responsibilities? Will they be credible to other staff?

If no one is available who is competent (or perceived as competent) to carry out the evaluation, should the evaluation be aborted?

EXAMPLE JOB DESCRIPTIONS

The person hired to do the evaluation will have the following responsibilities:
  a. Designing a major evaluation component for a $200,000 project
  b. Constructing instruments for the evaluation
  c. Analyzing and reporting data to audiences
  d. Managing evaluation budget and staff
1. Necessary competencies:
  a. Design skills (especially in the area of quasi-experimental or causal designs)
  b. Measurement expertise in designing instruments
  c. Statistical expertise in analyzing data; knowledge and experiences with computer programs preferable
  d. Past experience in handling budgets and managing other personnel

**EXAMPLE JOB
DESCRIPTIONS**
(continued)

The person hired to do the evaluation will have the following responsibilities:
a. Interviewing audiences to identify key evaluation questions related to curriculum revision
b. Designing an evaluation to answer key questions
c. Collecting ongoing information and reporting it to audiences
d. Managing the evaluation budget and staff

2. Necessary competencies:
   a. Interviewing and writing skills and sensitivity to multiple perspectives
   b. Design experience, especially in developing emergent designs
   c. Experience in synthesizing, sorting, and cataloging qualitative data (interviews, case studies) and reporting such data to multiple audiences
   d. Experience with managing budgets and coordinating staff

The project director will be responsible for evaluation tasks including:
a. Specifying evaluation questions and negotiating them with key audiences (e.g., chairperson, sponsor, trainees)
b. Determining information sources and drafting instruments to answer questions
c. Reporting results to key audiences in written form
d. Specifying a management plan for the evaluation activities

3. Preferred competencies:
   a. Experience with evaluation activities (training or actual evaluation experience)
   b. Background in drafting and analyzing surveys, attitudinal instruments, or interview data
   c. Credibility and interpersonal skills with fellow co-workers and trainees
   d. Ability to specify and maintain a management plan

**PROVIDING
SAFEGUARDS FOR
EVALUATOR
OBJECTIVITY**

1. Recruit or train staff with evaluation skills.
2. Bring in a "meta-evaluator" at certain phases such as design, analysis, or reporting.
3. Use an "independent" observer or multiple observers.
4. Plan at the outset for an ongoing or summative "audit."
5. Provide for public or staff reviews at various times throughout the evaluation.

(See also *Meta Evaluation*, the last chapter in the Sourcebook).

HOW SHOULD EVALUATION RESPONSIBILITIES BE FORMALIZED?

The evaluation agreement or contract specifies what will be done, how, when, and by whom. It is better if the contract or agreement is written before it becomes necessary to have it—usually after the evaluation has been focused and initial design decisions have been made. Even in the most informal of settings, it is smart to specify and document in advance the conditions that will guide these procedures and uses. The process of contracting provides an opportunity for the evaluator and stakeholders to review the services that will be provided by the evaluator and evaluation.

Remember that a management plan is not a legally binding contract and cannot be substituted for one. If you are unsure about the contents of a contract or what would constitute a breach of it, have it reviewed by an outsider or attorney.

CHECKLIST OF POSSIBLE ISSUES TO BE CONSIDERED IN AN EVALUATION CONTRACT OR AGREEMENT

1. Purpose of the evaluation
2. Major evaluation questions
3. Strategy for collecting information
   a. information sources
   b. sampling strategy or protocol to be used
   c. instruments/protocol
   d. schedule
4. Procedures that will be used to analyze the information
   a. the kind of information you will have (e.g., test scores, case studies, interviews, questionnaires)
   b. the appropriate ways to analyze it (e.g., content analysis, descriptive statistics, inferential statistics)
5. The reporting plan
   a. who will get reports
   b. what will the reports look like
   c. what is the reporting schedule
   d. how can people express reactions to the reports
6. Bias concerns
   a. what is likely to bias collection, analyses and reporting, and how will it be controlled
7. Client services
   a. what services are the client, program staff, or the housing organization providing to the evaluation (e.g., services, data, personnel, information, facilities, materials)
8. Timeline
   a. on what schedule will work be completed
*9. Revisions
   a. how, when and under what circumstances can the contract be amended or terminated

* Remember that it will probably be necessary to amend the contract or memorandum of agreement if the evaluation design is readjusted. Make sure that the agreement can be revised to accommodate changes, especially in a responsive evaluation that has an emerging design.

CHECKLIST
(continued)

10. Meta Evaluation
    a. who will be brought in to review evaluation progress and outcomes and at what points
11. Budget
    a. how will the evaluation be financed
    b. what amounts will be paid, at what point, for which tasks

---

USING A PROPOSAL FOR THE FORMAL AGREEMENT

1. The CONTRACTOR agrees to undertake, perform and complete the services more specifically described in "A Proposal for the Development and Implementation of an Educational Assessment Program," prepared jointly by the CONTRACTOR and SPONSOR and submitted on July 6, 1980, which Proposal is incorporated herein by reference.
2. The CONTRACTOR shall commence performance of this contract on the 6th day of July, 1981, and shall complete performance no later than the 31st day of December, 1982.
3. The SPONSOR agrees to pay the CONTRACTOR according to the following payment schedule:

December 1, 1980	$16,248.60
June 1, 1981	8,624.30
December 31, 1982	2,208.10

SAMPLE CONTRACT SPECIFYING RESPONSIBILITIES OF BOTH PARTIES IN THE EVALUATION

The Pokomo Heights School District, hereinafter referred to as the District, has requested technical research services for a curriculum study by Dakota University through its Service Center, hereinafter referred to as DU-SC. This agreement between the District and DU-SC specifies the responsibilities, schedule of events, costs, and payment schedule for the services. This agreement is in effect during the period of the project July 17, 1982, until January 31, 1982. It may be modified only by mutual agreement of the two parties.

In order to achieve the objectives of the research project, the District agrees to:

1. Meet with DU-SC staff to supply information about the capabilities, current practices, and constraints of the school system.
2. Collect documents as requested by DU-SC staff.
3. Specify needs to be addressed in the final technical report.
4. Identify criteria for evaluating plans for curriculum change.
5. Identify, and obtain the services of, people to serve on advocate and design teams.
6. Provide resource people for three advocate teams and one design team.
7. Provide for facilities, materials, duplication, and refreshments for advocate team and design team sessions.
8. Assist in data collection activities to support the work of advocate and design teams.
9. Provide secretarial support for three advocate teams and one design team.
10. Respond to any questions which DU-SC staff may have regarding this project.

SAMPLE
CONTRACT
SPECIFYING
RESPONSIBILITIES
OF BOTH PARTIES
IN THE
EVALUATION
(continued)

11. Submit a total payment of $59,605 for the services provided to the District by DU-SC upon completion of the project.

Dakota University Service Center agrees to:

1. Conduct an organizational meeting for the project between DU-SC and District staff.
2. Develop resource notebooks for advocate team use.
3. Develop a profile of students to be served by curriculum changes.
4. Coordinate project work with the District's Study Committee on Improving Student Achievement.
5. Identify promising strategies for curriculum change.
6. Design and implement an advocate team study.
7. Prepare a technical report for curriculum changes with operational details, budget, and special considerations.
8. Present a draft report to the District's administrative team.
9. Make revisions in the technical report as needed.

Signed on behalf of

Dakota University   Pokomo Heights School District

BUDGET

Personnel	$32,000
Fringe (25% of Personnel, excluding research assistants)	7,000
Travel and per diem	8,680
Materials and duplication	1,126
Communications	150
TOTAL DIRECT	$48,956
INDIRECT*	$10,649
TOTAL	$59,605

MEMORANDUM OF
AGREEMENT
BETWEEN A
PROJECT
DIRECTOR AND
EVALUATOR

October 12, 1979

Dr. Robert Brinkerhoff
The Evaluation Center
Western Michigan University
Kalamazoo, MI 49008

Dear Bob:

This letter is to confirm the various arrangements that Janet Tremain (of the University of Kansas) and I discussed with you by telephone on October 11 regarding three site visits that we would make on behalf of the Evaluation Training Consortium. We understand that the following conditions and stipulations will hold:

1. *Site selection.* You will select three project sites which we will visit for two days each. The projects should be chosen so as to be within reasonable travel distance of our two home bases: Lawrence, Kansas, and Bloomington, Indiana. Further, at least two of the sites should be representative of

MEMORANDUM OF
AGREEMENT
BETWEEN A
PROJECT
DIRECTOR AND
EVALUATOR
(continued)

sites at which you believe useful and constructive evaluation applications have been made. The third site may be either like the first two or chosen to represent sites at which little progress has been made in evaluation applications.

2. *Purpose of site visits.* Our inquiry at each site will be directed toward the following matters:

   a. Eliciting an adequate description of site activities primarily by asking various respondents what they believe, from their perspective, that we ought to know about their projects. These perspectives will be checked through document examination and actual site observation.

   b. Discovering what evaluation activities have taken place at the project site and determining what impact, if any, such evaluation has had on improving or refining the projects.

   c. Discovering what problems, if any, confront the project directors and/or evaluators in applying the results of evaluation studies. Their responses will furnish primary data for your task of designing a level III workshop.

   d. Discovering what residues exist at each site that are the result of participation in either a Level I and/or Level II workshop.

We shall of course not assert that whatever we discover at one or more of these sites holds for all sites or from some sub-set of them; our interest is not in what is happening universally but what *can* happen when conditions are right.

3. *Schedule.*

   a. *Advance materials.* Project directors should be asked to furnish copies of documents from their files in duplicate to both Dr. Tremain and me as much in advance of the actual site visit as possible. Such documents might include but not be limited to: project proposals, evaluation reports, reports to BEH, think pieces, mission statements, staffing documents, personnel vitas, and the like. We would like both current and existing historical versions of such documents to assess changes that may have occurred.

   b. *Site visits.* The following schedule of site visits and related analysis/reporting activity is proposed:

      1) Institution A .... November 29–30, 1979
      2) Preliminary analysis of Institution A data and development of interim report (probably oral) .... December 1, 1979
      3) Institution B: .... January 17–18, 1980
      4) Institution C: .... January 24–25, 1980
      5) Final analysis and reporting work session .... February 1–3, 1980*
      6) Final report .... February 15, 1980
      *Two of these three days.

---

* It is impossible at this time to be more definitive about just who will be interviewed. It seems likely that, in a University setting, such other interview subjects may include, say, the chairpersons of special, elementary, and secondary education; professors teaching special courses or new courses stimulated by 94-142 provisions or specific project activities; teachers and other program products that might be expected to have profited from project activities; project clientele such as administrators who hire teachers, special students exposed to them; and so on. Selections will be made in part after reading advance documents as in (a) above and partly on site as interviews unfold.

MEMORANDUM OF
AGREEMENT
BETWEEN A
PROJECT
DIRECTOR AND
EVALUATOR
(continued)

c. *Site activities*:
Day 1:

9:00–10:30	Interview with project director.
10:30–12:00	Interview with project evaluator.
12:00– 3:00	Reanalysis of documents based on inputs from first two interviews.
3:00– 5:00	Further interviews as unfolding information dictates.*

Day 2

9:00– 3:00	Further interviews as above.
3:00– 4:00	Development of staff feedback report.
4:00– 5:00	Staff debriefing and credibility check on our perceptions.

4. *Budget*. Note: except for honoraria all figures below are estimates. It is our expectation that this is a cost reimbursable proposal, so that our actual expenses will be reimbursed rather than being limited to the amounts shown. Of course should our expenses be less than the estimated amounts savings would accrue to ETC. We understand that since the ETC budget is not entirely firm you may wish to exercise the option of dropping one or all of the visits proposed. We expect the earliest possible notice from you in such a contingency.

a. *Honoraria*:

Howard Schmidt, 9 days @ $200/day..................	$ 1,800
Janet Tremain, 9 days @ $150/day....................	1,350

b. *Travel expenses*:

Travel to three sites, estimated @ $175, for two persons...	1,050
Travel from Lawrence to Bloomington (or vice-versa) for final analysis and report preparation, February 1–3, 1980...	175
Per diem, 14 person-days at sites plus 2 person-days for final analysis/reporting activity, 16 days @ $45/day ...	720
Local extras (e.g., mileage to airport, airport parking, taxis and limousines, etc., estimated at $30/trip/person (3 site trips × 2 persons plus trip for one person for final analysis)	210

c. *Clerical funds* (type and produce up to ten final reports).. | 150

d. Miscellaneous (site long distance calls, postage ,etc.).... | 100

TOTAL $ 5,555

It is our understanding that honoraria and expenses will be payable as services are provided and expenses are incurred. If there are aspects of this proposal which do not coincide with your understanding of our telephone conversation, will you please advise us at once?

We are excited about this task and look forward to working with you on it. We await your designation of the site for November 29–30 visit and receipt of advance documents from the project personnel.

Cordially,

Howard Schmidt
Professor of Education

HS:tl
cc: Janet Tremain

PITFALLS AFFECTING THE ADEQUACY OF AN EVALUATION AGREEMENT

1. Conflict with Overlapping Regulations
   failure to consider organizational guidelines
   union policies
   human rights guidelines & laws
   professional standards

2. Internal Inconsistencies
   budget, timeline & tasks aren't realistically integrated
   responsible personnel change throughout

3. Unrealistic Budget & Timeline
   budget is general, not tied to tasks, and is underestimated
   timeline is unrealistic & doesn't link tasks to a schedule

4. Failure to Negotiate Contract with Significant Audiences
   uncovering significant audiences who were not considered in the
      contract

5. Failure to Review
   contract initially responsive, but not amended when circumstances &
      goals changed
   contract not reviewed & hence inadvertently omitted facts

6. Failure to Indicate Report Responsibilities
   failure to indicate who is finally responsible for the evaluation report, its
      editing, and its release. Plans for the review, reaction & final release
      should be clear.

The final measure of an agreement's adequacy is the number of times
throughout the evaluation that conflicts arise that had to be resolved
without guidance from and outside the boundaries of the contract.

HOW MUCH SHOULD THE EVALUATION COST?

The budget for an evaluation is the plan for acquiring and using financial resources to conduct the evaluation. Budgeting, like contracting, provides another opportunity to review the evaluation design. Generally, an evaluation budget includes the following major categories:

1. Personnel (salaries and fringe benefits)
2. Consultants
3. Travel and per diem
4. Printing and shipping (postage)
5. Conferences and meetings
6. Data processing
7. Supplies and materials
8. Overhead (rent, utilities, telephone)

A rule of thumb is that an evaluation budget should be approximately 10% of the program or project budget. Like all rules of thumb, this is just a way of providing an estimate—a beginning point for you to figure. Evaluation also can be budgeted at only 5% of the budget or at 15–25%. There are good reasons for varying the budget percentage.

In general, the larger the percentage you budget, the more evaluation residue you should be expecting. Leftovers from a single-shot evaluation budget, for instance, might include a formalized information system, data bank, evaluation guidelines and workbooks, evaluation policies, trained staff, or even the plans for an office of evaluation. When a one-shot evaluation will serve short range and focused programmatic needs only, the budget probably should not extend over the 10% rule of thumb.

It's important that the expenses associated with various evaluation tasks be accurately estimated so you can plan for the needed resources. Of particular concern in costing out evaluation are: (1) the type of information collected; (2) the amount of information needed; (3) the location of information sources; (4) the timeline; and (5) the cost of personnel involved in collection, analysis, and reporting.

EXAMPLE 1–
PROJECTING THE
BALANCE FOR
THE END OF A
PROJECT YEAR

A cumulative report through the end of the second month for a 12 month project budget at $30,000*

A	B	C	D	E	F
Line Item	Total Budget	Total Expenses	Second Month Balance	Rate per Month	Projected Year End Balance
Salaries & Wages	18,000	3,800	14,200	1,900	(4,800)
Benefits	2,700	570	2,130	285	(720)
Consultants/ Expenses	5,500	300	5,200	150	3,700
Meeting Expenses	2,000	-0-	2,000	-0-	2,000
Duplicating/Printing	1,000	180	820	90	(80)
Office Supplies	300	250	50	125	(1,200)
Equipment	-0-	-0-	-0-	-0-	-0-
Communications	300	30	270	15	120
Audio-Visual	200	20	180	10	80
TOTAL	$30,000	$ 5,150	$24,850	$ 2,575	$(900)

A and B–Major categories and amounts of the line item budget for the project ($30,000)

C–Project director's accounting of his total expenses through the second month ($5,150)

D–Second Month Balance = Total Budget (B) less Expenses (C) = $24,850

E–Rate per month is the average amount being spent each month. To estimate this figure the director divided his 2-month total expenses (C) by two in order to determine the average amount being spent for one month. The total rate per month he averaged at $2,575.

F–To project the year end balance, the director multiplied his rate per month for each line item times 12 (12 months in his project year). Then he subtracted that projected amount from the total allocated for each line item (A). In the case of salaries and wages, for instance, this projected amount tells him that if he continues to spend at the same rate per month for 12 months, he will be in the red $4,800 at year's end. Parentheses indicate a minus or an amount which is in the red. In projecting budget amounts, most managers try to keep estimates of over-expenditures within 10%. This means that if a projected expenditure is over 10% action should be taken to bring it back in line. Notice, however, that when the project year end total is added, the director is anticipating a $900 over-expenditure.

* It is important to note that examples of budgets are included only to provide general information about budgeting and estimating costs. Time and economic changes quickly date sample budgets, and guidelines for estimating costs can change from institution to institution.

EXAMPLE 3
EVALUATION
COMPONENT FOR
A $216,000
PROGRAM

I. DIRECT COSTS $11,440.00
    A. *Personnel*
        Eric F. Schmidt, Ph.D. (23 days)
        Donald T. Trumper (14 days)
        Paul L. Simon (46 days)
        Donna T. Helbert (22 days)
        Eileen Feldt (28 days)
        Jane W. Newman (10 days)
        (in this budget, days as opposed to percentage of full
        responsibilities or FTE's are used. This is often the choice
        when many of the staff are not regularly on the payroll.
        See pp. 196 for corresponding management plan)
    B. *Fringe* (16% of salaries)   1,830.00
        (notice that the fringe or payroll deduction established by
        housing institution varies over time and across insti-
        tutions
    C. *Supplies*   4,345.00

        Keypunching $385.00
        Printing and duplicating (surveys,   1,750.00
            envelopes, cover letters and
            reports)
        Stamps and Postage   950.00
        Telephone   875.00
        Office Supplies   385.00
        (See Budget 2 for a breakdown of
        these items; keypunching is another
        item on which to seek competitive
        bids.)
    D. *Transportation and lodging for staff and consultants*   946.00
        (This item represents in-state mileage and per diem for
        meals. A subtotal without a breakdown, such as this one,
        invites investigation)
    E. *Computer Time*   2,750.00
        (This is an item for which you should seek competitive
        bids. It is an estimate affected by time, personnel, &
        deadline)
    F. *Consultants*   710.00
        5 days @ $100.00
        3 days @ 70.00
        (Consultant fees that vary usually indicate a formal
        educational training)
II. INDIRECT COSTS (8%)   1,762.00
III. TOTAL PRICE $23,783.00

TIPS FOR PROMOTING FISCAL ACCOUNTABILITY

1. maintain accurate financial records with public access
2. reflect comparison shopping or contract bidding for goods and services
3. reflect and document changes in the design or environment which bring about budgetary adjustments
4. account for dollars spent on evaluation objectives and tasks
5. systematically review the budget in light of evaluation progress
6. include fiscal information in interim and final reports for the public record

HOW SHOULD EVALUATION TASKS BE ORGANIZED AND SCHEDULED?

The management plan begins when the evaluator and stakeholders are ready to sit down and ask, "What must be done, when, and by whom?" The plan that emerges provides a breakdown of tasks and a timeline for all those involved in the evaluation. Keep in mind that a management plan is not a contract; it is not legally binding nor does it address ethical issues regarding responsibilities. Nor is the management plan an evaluation design; it does not determine the evaluation purpose and questions. In fact, it is guided by them.

The management plan charts the activities needed to implement the evaluation design and so provides a system for keeping track of progress. Most importantly, the management plan is a tool which encourages planning and forecasting and, depending upon the type of plan used, it can also demonstrate the relationship of tasks and the sequence of activities.

To put together a management plan for an evaluation, you need the following information:

1. specific activities that must be accomplished
2. when each activity needs to be done
3. who will be responsible for activities
4. how the activity will be accomplished
5. what resources are available to do the evaluation
6. the evaluation design or a general plan specifying what is to be done
7. update on design changes to revise and/or refine the management plan as time goes by

Additionally, it is important to specify who will be responsible for drafting, monitoring, and supervising the formalized management plan. Regardless of how many people are involved in an evaluation or its management, one person needs to be designated as ultimately responsible for the management plan. If that person is not also the evaluator, he or she needs to work closely with the evaluator.

PERT (PROGRAM EVALUATION & REVIEW TECHNIQUE)

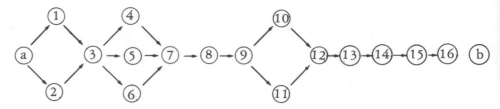

Activity or Procedure	Subgoal or Event
	a. Start scale development
1. Search literature for attitude scales	1. Complete search
2. Review attitude scaling procedures	2. Complete review
3. Select procedure to be used	3. Complete section
4. Construct scale items	4. Complete item construction
5. Assemble prototype scale	5. Complete scale assembly
6. Arrange field test of prototype scale	6. Complete arrangements
7. Field-test prototype scale	7. Complete field test
8. Score scale	8. Complete scoring
9. Item-analyze scale	9. ILLEGIBLE??
10. ILLEGIBLE??	

Pert is a set of time-related activities needed to accomplish an objective; it gives expected time for completing the work and probability for completing within that time. Many software programs at universities include PERT. They can be accessed easily and the PERT chart done efficiently from a computer terminal.

TIME/ACTIVITY ANALYSIS CHART

Time/Activity Analysis Chart

Activity	Personnel Responsible	Person Days	October 1 2 3 4	November 1 2 3 4	December 1 2 3 4
OBJECTIVE 1	Schmidt				
1. Develop research questions	Simon Trumper	14	├———┤		
2. Determine data collection procedures (includes development of instrumentation)	Simon Schmidt	15		├—————	———————┤
3. Develop analysis plan	Feldt Simon Schmidt	7			

**TIME/ACTIVITY
ANALYSIS CHART**
(continued)

Time/Activity Analysis Chart

Activity	Personnel Responsible	Person Days	October 1 2 3 4	November 1 2 3 4	December 1 2 3 4
4. Conduct study with appropriate respondents (develop sample)	Feldt Helbert	16		├———————┤	
5A. Collect data	Simon Helbert Trumper Feldt	38		├—————————	———————┤
B. Process data	Newman Helbert	13			├——┤
Objective 2: 6. Analyze all data	Schmidt Simon Feldt	21			
Objective 3: 7. Develop recom- mendations and produce final report	Schmidt Simon Trumper	19			

total = 143 days

The example above is a simple and easy way to break down evaluation tasks by objectives, person responsible, days allocated to task, and timeline for beginning, doing, and completing the task.

ACTIVITY CHART FROM MANAGING A PROJECT (EXCERPT)

The evaluator put this chart together initially by listing tasks on 3 × 5 cards and taping them to butcher paper. Only a portion of the chart is reproduced here.

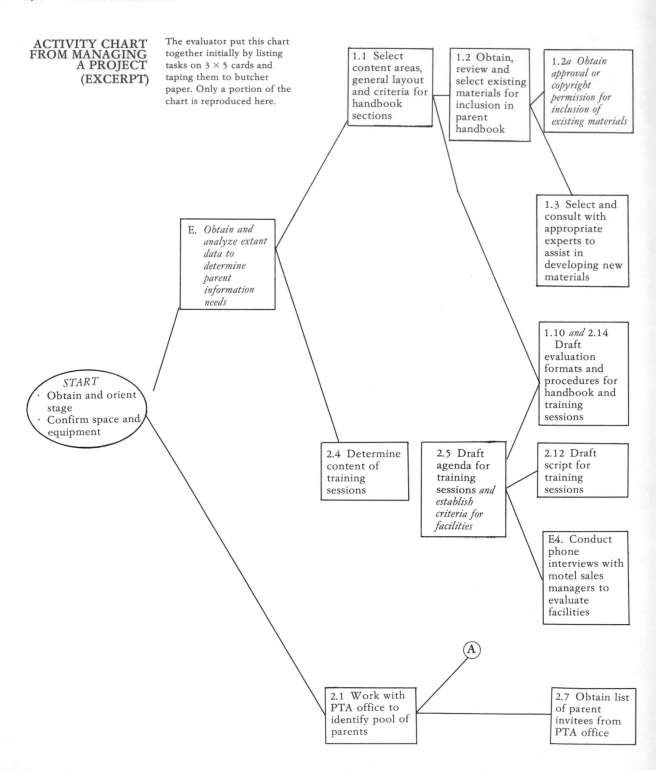

The Systems Network portrays each major management activity as an individual box. The arrows indicate what is needed to complete an activity and what the complete activity, in turn, feeds into. After the network is completed, activities can be linked to staff and timelines. This system is explained in the *Practitioner's Guide*, by Diane K. Yavorsky, Evaluation Research Center, University of Virginia, 1978.

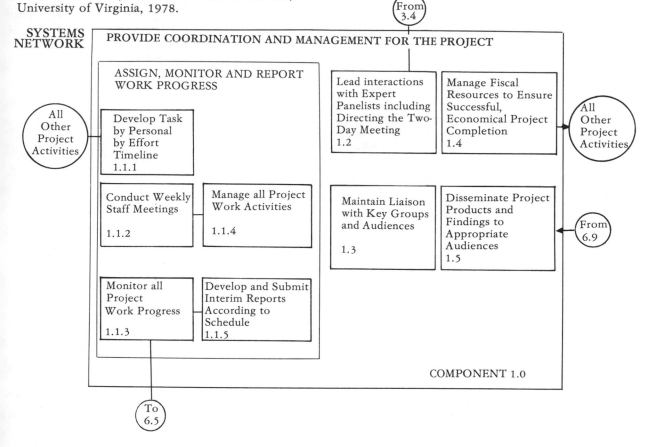

Activity by Staff Timeline

Activity Number	Primary Staff	Jan	Feb	Mar	Apr	May	Jun	Jul	Aug	Sep	Oct	Nov	Dec
1.1.1 Develop Timeline	Haladyna	⊢————⊣											
1.1.2 Conduct Staff Meetings	Staff		⊢————⊣		⊢————————⊣				⊢————⊣			⊢————⊣	
1.1.3 Monitor Progress	Haladyna	⊢————————————————————⊣											
1.1.4 Manage Activities	Haladyna	⊢————————————————————————————⊣											
1.1.5 Develop Interim Reports	Haladyna			X			X			X			

EXAMPLE OF A
MANAGEMENT
PLAN FOR AN
INSERVICE
EVALUATION
This example illustrates how a very small and limited evaluation effort can be documented by activity and deadline.

Management Plan

Steps	Person Responsible	When
PHASE I		
1. Analyze documents for pertinent information (e.g., district needs assessment, building and district policies and procedures)		Jan. 5–Feb. 1
develop analysis procedure	Joyce	
analyze documents	Joyce; teacher volunteers	
summarize	Joyce	
2. Analyze/interpret all findings	Joyce and Jane	Feb. 1–15
3. Prepare report for teachers and distribute	Joyce	Feb. 1–15
4. Conduct teachers' meeting	Joyce	March 15
5. Revise report as needed	Joyce and Jane	March 15–30
PHASE II		
1. Review literature on in-service programs	Joyce (with assistance from University consultant)	April 1–30
2. Review evaluations of past inservices in building	Joyce and former inservice coordinator	April 1–30
3. Identify and talk to experts from successful programs	Joyce and Jane	May 1–15
4. Develop design and list of criteria	Joyce and Jane	May 15–30
5. Review design		
identify reviewers	Jane	Sept. 1–20
contact reviewers	Jane	
conduct reviews	Joyce	
summarize findings	Joyce	
6. Review design, as needed	Joyce and Jane	Sept. 21–30
7. Prepare report for teachers	Joyce	Oct. 1–10

WHAT KINDS OF PROBLEMS CAN BE EXPECTED?

Evaluation literature and experience tells us that there are certain problems that can be counted upon when implementing evaluation. In this section we try to forecast some of these problems, provide information about how to monitor to prevent them from occurring, and propose strategies to use to intervene when they occur.

The key issue in monitoring the evaluation is making sure the design is still intact and, more importantly, that it is still relevant and appropriate. Don't adhere to an evaluation design that because of programmatic or situational changes is no longer meaningful. Review the design with stakeholders regularly to find out if revisions are necessary.

Set up a *review schedule* for the design (consider other people besides yourself that might be consulted)
Review the design in light of the management plan and budget
Make necessary changes, document them, and share them with key stakeholders

PROBLEMS TO ANTICIPATE IN EVALUATION

FUNCTION	AREA OF CONCERN	SOME PROBLEMS TO ANTICIPATE	SOLUTION STRATEGY
Evaluation Focus	1. Purpose	1.1 purpose becomes invalid 1.2 additional purpose emerges	1. · revise or add purpose or abort evaluation
	2. Evaluation questions	2.1 questions become invalid 2.2 more questions need to be added 2.3 questions need to be refined	2. · refine, add, delete evaluation questions and check congruence with purpose
	3. Audiences	3.1 audiences change 3.2 important audiences were overlooked 3.3 audiences react negatively	3. · add audiences initially overlooked · provide debriefing, open discussions, public information
	4. Setting	4.1 setting changes dramatically	4. · readjust purpose and design to setting or, if setting is too hostile, abort evaluation
	5. Object	5.1 object changes so that descriptions, design, and even purpose are not appropriate	5. · change the purpose and questions as appropriate, continue only if "changed object" still can and should be evaluated

FUNCTION	AREA OF CONCERN	SOME PROBLEMS TO ANTICIPATE	SOLUTION STRATEGY
The Evaluation Design	1. Evaluation approach	1.1 existing evaluation technique forced on problem 1.2 no personnel to run selected evaluation approach 1.3 disagreement about best evaluation approach	1. · provide alternative and competing designs · change design or bring in consultant · assess approach in light of program, purpose
	2. Design issues	2.1 inability to address all relevant design issues 2.2 design issues change 2.3 design will not provide valid information	2. · select and justify issues to be dealt with · monitor design issues and refine to meet needs · abort evaluation or redesign
	3. Design construction	3.1 design doesn't answer questions 3.2 design doesn't include practical or credible information collection	3. · abort or redesign · anticipate reporting, analysis, and information collection in the evaluation design and review
	4. Design quality	4.1 lack of agreement about the quality of the design 4.2 evaluators unable to implement	4. · select standards by which design will be assessed and apply bring in consultant (meta-evaluator) or change staff
The Collection and Plan Process	1. Information sources	1.1 existing sources aren't tapped 1.2 desired information not available 1.3 limited information available	1. · carefully review what already exists and attempt to use and not to duplicate · use multiple or alternative information sources
	2. Procedures	2.1 appropriate procedures limited 2.2 procedures impractical 2.3 procedures not trustworthy according to audiences	2. · review alternatives with experts · simplify if too costly · use procedures that are credible to audiences
	3. Information scope	3.1 too much information available 3.2 too little information available 3.3 much information isn't very reliable	3. · sample using relevant criteria · use multiple information sources (tests, people, documents)
	4. Instrumentation	4.1 no instruments available 4.2 a number of instruments available 4.3 instrument developed doesn't work	4. · construct after reviewing others · select according to predetermined criteria · pilot to prevent failure
	5. Reliability and validity	5.1 nothing known about validity or reliability 5.2 instrument or procedure has low or no validity or reliability 5.3 no one capable of assessing these criteria	5. · find out; pilot · scrap instrument or refine · have a consultant review

FUNCTION	AREA OF CONCERN	SOME PROBLEMS TO ANTICIPATE	SOLUTION STRATEGY
	6. Collection plan	6.1 plan is too costly in terms of time and money 6.2 plan is not documented	6. · document and access plan to prevent · include this in management plan and disseminate
The Analysis Plan	1. Returned data	1.1 data unreliable, missing, messy 1.2 data cannot be synthesized 1.3 data are bulky	1. · monitor and design to prevent · design so categories or sorting are determined in advance · store and safeguard using an access system
	2. Data worth	2.1 data don't answer evaluation questions 2.2 data aren't believable	2. · establish appropriate and credible evidence in advance
	3. Analysis procedure	3.1 difficulty understanding data and what they indicate	3. · try a number of dependable analyses · use graphs and aides to help audiences · justify appropriateness of analyses
	4. Interpretation	4.1 disagreement exists about what information "means"	4. · provide audience alternative perspectives in report · include minority opinions · interpret information in light of several value stances
The Reporting Strategy	1. Report purpose(s)	1.1 different audiences want different information 1.2 one report wouldn't be readable for everyone 1.3 information is too technical	1. · plan for and provide multiple reports · append technical material, clarify in graphs, provide lay person summaries
	2. Audiences	2.1 new audiences become interested 2.2 audiences confused about how to use report	2. · include new audiences in written or oral report schedule · prepare reports with audiences in mind
	3. Content	3.1 disagreement exists about what should be in report 3.2 client wants to delete material	3. · outline proposed areas to be included at outset; guarantee balance
	4. Delivery	4.1 audiences want reports at different times	4. · specify schedule in advance and follow it. Provide ongoing communications and updates
	5. Style and structure	5.1 multiple reports become necessary along the way 5.2 reports serve a number of purposes	5. · coordinate all reports through one person (team) · select best alternative report structures for sequential and multiple reports

FUNCTION	AREA OF CONCERN	SOME PROBLEMS TO ANTICIPATE	SOLUTION STRATEGY
	6. Interpretation	6.1 strong differences exist about what the evaluation means 6.2 evaluators' recommendations are not in agreement with key audience	6. · report different interpretations or append a minority report · seek consensus or report differing interpretations
	7. Schedule	7.1 evaluation reports not ready on time	7. · plan and document the schedule for report; plan backwards so report deadline is met
Evaluating the Evaluation	1. Why evaluate	1.1 credibility of evaluation questioned 1.2 quality of design, information collection or analysis is poor 1.3 evaluator needs guidance or competence questioned	1. · bring in credible outsiders for independent observation · anticipate stage of evaluation procedure that needs review · select consultant to provide ongoing assistance
	2. Who	2.1 decision as to whom should be brought in to assess evaluation	2. · plan for meta evaluation and provide alternative choices for key audiences to select from
	3. Criteria	3.1 by what criteria or standards should the evaluation be evaluated	3. · determine criteria at the outset and share them with others · plan the evaluation to meet criteria

STOP PROBLEMS BEFORE THEY OCCUR	Ensure minimal disruption to the program (e.g., humane interactions and appropriate use of program personnel/resources) Follow appropriate protocol (e.g., see and talk to supervisors first and then their staff) Use discretion in discussing the evaluation or program progress Respond to changes in the program or organization (crisis, changing goals) in light of the evaluation and not the program Oversee staff and/or evaluation responsibilities (monitor design, management plan, and budget) Absolutely adhere to final delivery date for the evaluation Be alert to political factions as they emerge and assess them in light of their influence on the evaluation Be full and frank in disclosures about the evaluation (when the evaluation is discussed, what is said should be such that it can be shared with all audiences) Involve critics and skeptics through discussions, memoranda, hearings, requests for minority opinions, etc. Consistently attend to key stakeholders and their views about the evaluation's progress and usefulness. (This will alert you to changes in purpose, questions, and object as well as refining your knowledge about "useful" information.)

REFERENCES

Anderson, S.B. & Ball, S. *The Profession and Practice of Program Evaluation.* San Francisco: Jossey-Bass, 1978.

Cook, Desmond L. *Educational Project Management.* Columbus, Ohio: Charles E. Merrill Publishing Co., 1971.

Joint Committee on Standards for Educational Evaluation. *Standards for Evaluation of Educational Programs, Projects & Materials.* New York: McGraw-Hill, 1981.

Scriven, Michael. Evaluation Bias and Its Control. *Occasional Paper Series*, No. 4, Evaluation Center, College of Education, Western Michigan University, Kalamazoo, Michigan, June, 1975.

Smith, Nick L. *Evaluation Contracting Checklist.* Northwest Regional Educational Laboratory, 300 S.W. Sixth Avenue, Portland, Oregon 97204.

Yavorsky, Diane K. *Discrepancy Evaluation: A Practitioner's Guide.* Evaluation Research Center, University of Virginia, 1978.

Meta-Evaluation

WHAT IT IS Just as you can evaluate a training project or a teacher training program, you can also evaluate your evaluations of those enterprises. In fact, if evaluators are going to "practice what they preach," this becomes mandatory. Meta-evaluation can often be done along with your "regular" evaluation activities to help make them better. It can also be done while you are evaluating or after you have finished the regular evaluation to give you and others an idea of how well things turned out.

Meta-evaluation (evaluating an evaluation) is based on the notion that evaluation ought to be a learning experience for all those involved in it, so that the evaluation can improve as it progresses and that future evaluations can be more successful. Meta-evaluation can serve many purposes. External meta-evaluation (e.g., using an expert evaluation consultant) can be used to certify and verify evaluation design, progress, and results for more certain and credible accountability. An internal evaluation report, for example, when accompanied by an external meta-evaluation report, will carry more authoritative credibility. Use of external meta-evaluation also provides an excellent basis on which to revise an evaluation design, its ongoing work, or evaluation reports. Or, if the evaluation's already concluded, a meta-evaluation can help you decide how seriously to take the results.

Less formal, internal meta-evaluation procedures are useful to revise an evaluation and also can help keep it on track. Likewise, meta-evaluation efforts help maintain commitment and involvement and raise the credibility and authority of the evaluation.

WHAT IT IS
(continued)
    Meta-evaluation efforts can range from an extensive verification and replication study, to a brief consultant visit, to a short staff meeting to check over a survey instrument. (In fact, you do meta-evaluation whenever you ponder and investigate your evaluation design and functions.)

WHEN YOU META-EVALUATE
You can and should bring in a meta-evaluator whenever the evaluator or evaluation needs assistance. This might be at the planning stage or at any point during the evaluation. Often meta-evaluation is used to assess the evaluation after its completion. In these cases, key audiences are able to assess how seriously they should take the evaluation results, and evaluators can consider how the next evaluation might be made better.*

---

* Dick Frisbie, Western Michigan University, was a primary contributor to this chapter and wrote several draft versions.

WHAT ARE SOME GOOD USES OF META-EVALUATION?

Since your evaluation may quickly become a rather complicated activity, it is helpful to think of its quality in terms of each of the functions we have presented in the previous chapters. That way, you can more easily zero in on a particular problem, if one area seems to be giving you more trouble than the others.

The grid below is used to present some uses to which you could put meta-evaluation in terms of the categories we have just discussed. What's important to remember is that it's never too soon or too late to question the soundness and the worth of any part of your evaluation. Furthermore, if you don't question its quality, rest assured that someone else probably will.

SOME META-EVALUATION PURPOSES	Focus of Meta-Evaluation		
Evaluation Functions	Evaluating Evaluation Plans	Evaluating Evaluation in Progress	Evaluating Evaluation after its Completion
Focusing Evaluation	to assess and help refine the evaluation purpose and questions, investigate setting and identify audiences	to determine whether selected questions and purposes are being pursued; to evaluate how worthwhile they are	to evaluate the soundness and worth of the evaluation purpose and the questions addressed
Designing Evaluation	to evaluate and refine design strategies or to provide information about options and aid in designing	to evaluate the effectiveness of the design being implemented; to help monitor or revise if necessary	to determine whether the evaluation design was sound, implemented properly, and useful for audience(s)
Collecting Information	to evaluate or help design or select instruments and collection strategy	to observe and evaluate the collection of information	to assess the quality and relevance of information collected and methods used to collect it
Analyzing Information	to guide primary evaluator in selecting possible analysis strategies and consider who will interpret and how	to evaluate the analysis process and how effectively data are being aggregated, sorted and analyzed	to evaluate the adequacy and the accuracy of analyses and the interpretations of analyses

**SOME META-
EVALUATION
PURPOSES**
(continued)

Focus of Meta-Evaluation

Evaluation Functions	Evaluating Evaluation Plans	Evaluating Evaluation in Progress	Evaluating Evaluation after its Completion
Reporting Information	to evaluate report strategy and suggest format, audiences to consider, and report contents	to read and evaluate report drafts, discuss alternative reports, refine technical or lay people reports	to evaluate the evaluation reports, their balance, timeliness, adequacy and ensuing use
Managing Evaluation	to evaluate and refine the management plan, budget, and contract	to evaluate how adequately the management plan is being monitored and the appropriateness of the contract and budget	to evaluate how well the evaluation was managed, and budgeted; to determine whether costs were reasonable and agreements upheld

**SOME TYPICAL
USES OF META-
EVALUATION IN
TRAINING
PROGRAM
EVALUATION***

Strategy for Meta-Evaluation

Have an external evaluation expert review the evaluation (its design, operation and findings), then write a summary meta-evaluation report for dissemination to key audiences.

Devote several (or even one) project staff meeting to a discussion of the evaluation's progress. Structure critical discussion around key criteria (e.g., utility, accuracy, propriety, feasibility).

Conduct reviews of all evaluation instruments with one or more of the following: measurement experts; staff members; potential respondents. Do this with analysis and other technical areas.

When It's Useful

Often, an internal evaluation may lack authority and credibility to outside audiences (e.g., a funding agent). The meta-evaluation can help increase the credibility of the evaluation. And, it helps the project staff weigh the significance of their findings.

When project staff are unfamiliar with evaluation, these meetings can do much to gain their greater understanding and commitment. Meetings like this help keep an evaluation on track and ensure greater flexibility and responsiveness when changes in the project occur rapidly.

"Home-made" instruments are notoriously susceptible to errors in content and structure. Reviews of instruments almost always result in revisions, and subsequently more reliable data.

---

* Most often, several of these are used in any one evaluation, and often in combinations not listed above.

SOME TYPICAL USES OF META-EVALUATION IN TRAINING PROGRAM EVALUATION*
(continued)

Strategy for Meta-Evaluation	When It's Useful
Have an expert review the evaluation design and prepare a report and/or conduct a summary discussion with evaluators and project staff. (See Case C-4 for an example.)	Evaluating an evaluation design before the evaluation is begun can help revise, verify and certify the design. The money spent on this will more than likely be recaptured in a better and more efficient evaluation.
Conduct panel reviews and hearings (e.g., at a conference) of your evaluation design, reports and findings. Disseminate your evaluation for critical reading and comment.	An especially important or otherwise significant evaluation ought to receive critical attention and dissemination.
Have an evaluation consultant work with you to review your plans and suggest revisions at several key points (e.g., design, data collection, interpretation, reporting).	When you do your own evaluation, an expert can help you make your work more effective, efficient and sound.

WHO SHOULD DO THE META-EVALUATION?

Even though the demands on evaluators are high, the demands on meta-evaluators are even higher. Not only should they be competent enough to *do* the original evaluation, but they also have to be able to tell if it was a good or bad one and be able to convince others that they know the difference. The types of staffing options mentioned in Managing Evaluation (pp. 177–178) are also available for meta-evaluation; but because of the additional expectations, some of the options will usually be preferred over others.

External meta-evaluators are usually preferred over insiders because they are likely to have more credibility to people outside of the project or organization. This is particularly important when you are concerned with an outsider's reaction to the evaluation. If you're doing the meta-evaluation mostly for people on the inside, having an external meta-evaluator (even if it's only someone from a different office of your own organization) also provides an excellent opportunity for you to get a fresh perspective, another point of view.

It is often preferable for a team to conduct the meta-evaluation, since it is difficult to get the necessary time and skills from a single individual. Of course, the more skilled the people are in relation to *all* of the content and evaluation areas, and the smaller your evaluation is, the fewer people you will need for the meta-evaluation.

If you're going for a fresh, outside perspective or for someone who has good credibility with outside audiences, it makes sense to have this kind of person around only for a short time. Have them do the job and be done with it. If you need them full time, maybe they should be running the evaluation outright.

Finally, if a choice *has* to be made between the two, we consider an expert in evaluation to be more crucial than an expert in the content area of interest. The reason for this is that meta-evaluation focuses on how good the *evaluation* is. If you don't have to choose between one or the other, you will do even better to include experts in both evaluation and content area.

Options	Reasons for Preference
Internal Meta-Evaluator(s) vs.	**CONS** bias (actual or perceived) because of conflict of interest in evaluating a program in which there is a personal investment
External Meta-Evaluator(s)	**PROS** comes without preconceived notion about the program is seen as independent observer by staff, outsiders

Options	Reasons for Preference
Individual Meta-Evaluation vs.	CONS success or failure heavily dependent upon a single individual
Team Meta-Evaluation	PROS composite of multiple skills and perspectives, especially regarding content area and evaluation expertise
Full-time Meta-Evaluator(s) vs.	CONS cost involved
Part-time Meta-Evaluator(s)	PROS multiple authorities can be brought in for short periods of time effective use of outside expertise
Content Expert vs.	PROS knows content and object well can "pick up" many evaluation skills through experience
Evaluation Expert	PROS brings in experience and technical skills to run evaluation provides multiple options through own background

WHAT CRITERIA SHOULD YOU USE TO EVALUATE THE EVALUATION?

If an evaluation is going to help improve a training program or be used to help decide if it should be continued, it's going to have to be a "good" evaluation. In order to decide what's good or bad about an evaluation you need a set of criteria or standards on which to base judgments. This is a different matter than deciding whether a program is good or bad. When you're looking at a training project, your evaluation question might be, "how can we tell if we have a good training project?" Your meta-evaluation question would then be, "How can we tell if we have a good evaluation of the training project?"

There are a number of sets of criteria and standards already available for judging evaluation. Some of them are listed below.

STANDARDS FOR
EVALUATIONS OF
EDUCATIONAL
PROGRAMS,
PROJECTS AND
MATERIALS

Standards for Evaluations of Educational Programs, Projects, and Materials is by the Joint Committee on Standards for Educational Evaluation. These *Standards* are organized into thirty standards and four domains of evaluation which address utility (evaluations should be useful and practical), feasibility (evaluations should be realistic and prudent), propriety (evaluations should be conducted legally and ethically), and accuracy (evaluations should be technically adequate). A listing of the *Standards* follows:

A *Utility Standards*

The Utility Standards are intended to ensure that an evaluation will serve the practical information needs of given audiences. These standards are:

A1 *Audience Identification*

Audiences involved in or affected by the evaluation should be identified, so that their needs can be addressed.

A2 *Evaluator Credibility*

The persons conducting the evaluation should be both trustworthy and competent to perform the evaluation, so that their findings achieve maximum credibility and acceptance.

A3 *Information Scope and Selection*

Information collected should be of such scope and selected in such ways as to address pertinent questions about the object of the evaluation and be responsive to the needs and interests of specified audiences.

A4 *Valuational Interpretation*

The perspectives, procedures, and rationale used to interpret the findings should be carefully described, so that the bases for value judgments are clear.

A5 *Report Clarity*

The evaluation report should describe the object being evaluated and its context and the purposes, procedures, and findings of the evaluation, so that the audiences will readily understand what was done, why it was done, what information was obtained, what conclusions were drawn, and what recommendations were made.

STANDARDS FOR
EVALUATIONS OF
EDUCATIONAL
PROGRAMS,
PROJECTS AND
MATERIALS
(continued)

A6 *Report Dissemination*

Evaluation findings should be disseminated to clients and other right-to-know audiences, so that they can assess and use the findings.

A7 *Report Timeliness*

Release of reports should be timely, so that audiences can best use the reported information.

A8 *Evaluation Impact*

Evaluations should be planned and conducted in ways that encourage follow-through by members of the audiences.

B *Feasibility Standards*

The Feasibility Standards are intended to ensure that an evaluation will be realistic, prudent, diplomatic, and frugal; they are:

B1 *Practical Procedures*

The evaluation procedures should be practical, so that disruption is kept to a minimum and that needed information can be obtained.

B2 *Political Viability*

The evaluation should be planned and conducted with anticipation of the different positions of various interest groups, so that their cooperation may be obtained and so that possible attempts by any of these groups to curtail evaluation operations or to bias or misapply the results can be averted or counteracted.

B3 *Cost Effectiveness*

The evaluation should produce information of sufficient value to justify the resources extended.

C *Propriety Standards*

The Propriety Standards are intended to ensure that an evaluation will be conducted legally, ethically, and with due regard for the welfare of those involved in the evaluation, as well as those affected by its results. These standards are:

C1 *Formal Obligation*

Obligations of the formal parties to an evaluation (what is to be done, how, by whom, when) should be agreed to in writing, so that these parties are obligated to adhere to all conditions of the agreement or formally to renegotiate it.

C2 *Conflict of Interest*

Conflict of interest, frequently unavoidable, should be dealt with openly and honestly, so that it does not compromise the evaluation processes and results.

C3 *Full and Frank Disclosure*

Oral and written evaluation reports should be open, direct, and honest in their disclosure of pertinent findings, including limitations of the evaluation.

C4 *Public's Right to Know*

The formal parties to an evaluation should respect and assure the public's right to know, within the limits of other related principles and statutes, such as those dealing with public safety and the right to privacy.

STANDARDS FOR
EVALUATIONS OF
EDUCATIONAL
PROGRAMS,
PROJECTS AND
MATERIALS
(continued)

C5 *Rights of Human Subjects*

Evaluations should be designed and conducted so that the rights and welfare of the human subjects are respected and protected.

C6 *Human Interactions*

Evaluators should respect human dignity and worth in their interactions with other persons associated with an evaluation.

C7 *Balanced Reporting*

The evaluation should be complete and fair in its presentation of strengths and weaknesses of the object under investigation, so that strengths can be built upon and problem areas addressed.

C8 *Fiscal Responsibility*

The evaluator's allocation and expenditure of resources should reflect sound accountability procedures and otherwise be prudent and ethically responsible.

D *Accuracy Standards*

The Accuracy Standards are intended to ensure that an evaluation will reveal and convey technically adequate information about the features of the object being studied that determine its worth or merit. These standards are:

D1 *Object Identification*

The object of the evaluation (program, project, material) should be sufficiently examined, so that the form(s) of the object being considered in the evaluation can be clearly identified.

D2 *Context Analysis*

The context in which the program, project, or material exists should be examined in enough detail, so that its likely influences on the object can be identified.

D3 *Described Purposes and Procedures*

The purposes and procedures of the evaluation should be monitored and described in enough detail, so that they can be identified and assessed.

D4 *Defensible Information Sources*

The sources of information should be described in enough detail, so that the adequacy of the information can be assessed.

D5 *Valid Measurement*

The information-gathering instruments and procedures should be chosen or developed and then implemented in ways that will assure that the interpretation arrived at is valid for the given use.

D6 *Reliable Measurement*

The information-gathering instruments and procedures should be chosen or developed and then implemented in ways that will assure that the information obtained is sufficiently reliable for the intended use.

D7 *Systematic Data Control*

The data collected, processed, and reported in an evaluation should be reviewed and corrected, so that the results of the evaluation will not be flawed.

STANDARDS FOR EVALUATIONS OF EDUCATIONAL PROGRAMS, PROJECTS AND MATERIALS
(continued)

D8 *Analysis of Quantitative Information*

Quantitative information in an evaluation should be appropriately and systematically analyzed to ensure supportable interpretations.

D9 *Analysis of Qualitative Information*

Qualitative information in an evaluation should be appropriately and systematically analyzed to ensure supportable interpretations.

D10 *Justified Conclusions*

The conclusions reached in an evaluation should be explicitly justified, so that the audiences can assess them.

D11 *Objective Reporting*

The evaluation procedures should provide safeguards to protect the evaluation findings and reports against distortion by the personal feelings and biases of any party to the evaluation.

EVALUATION RESEARCH SOCIETY (ERS) STANDARDS FOR PROGRAM EVALUATION

Based on the 1980 ERS Exposure Draft, fifty-five professional standards are divided into six categories.

Phases of Evaluation
1. Formulation and Negotiation (12)
2. Structure and Design (6)
3. Data Collection and Preparation (12)
4. Data Analysis and Interpretation (9)
5. Communication and Disclosure (10)
6. Utilization (6)

JOINT DISSEMINATION AND REVIEW PANEL CRITERIA

The purpose of JDRP is to review the evidence of effectiveness submitted for a wide variety of educational products and practices. Only those submissions approved by JDRP may in any way be endorsed by the Department of Education or disseminated as exemplary using Federal Education Division funds.

According to JDRP, an adequate evaluation must be interpretable and credible, in terms of both the project and its evaluation. This means that: (1) the existence of an apparent effect must be established; (2) there must be evidence that the effect occurred as a result of the intervention in question; (3) there must be evidence that it would not have occurred without the intervention. Six criteria have been established to help determine if an evaluation has established these points. They are:

Criterion 1: Did a change occur?
Criterion 2: Was the effect consistent enough and observed often enough to be statistically significant?
Criterion 3: Was the effect educationally significant?
Criterion 4: Can the intervention be implemented in another location with a reasonable expectation of comparable impact?
Criterion 5: How likely is it that the observed effects resulted from the intervention?
Criterion 6: Is the presented evidence believable and interpretable?

STANDARDS FOR
AUDITS OF
GOVERNMENTAL
ORGANIZATIONS,
PROGRAMS,
ACTIVITIES, AND
FUNCTIONS

These standards must be followed for audits when federal dollars are involved, and they are recommended for use by the Comptroller General for state and local audits. These standards are divided into three main elements for the expanded scope of auditing a government organization, program, activity, or function.

Scope of Audit Work Using the GAO Standards

1. *Financial and compliance*—determines (a) whether the financial statements of an audited entity present fairly the financial position and the results of financial operations in accordance with generally accepted accounting principles and (b) whether the entity has complied with laws and regulations that may have a material effect upon the financial statements.
2. *Economy and efficiency*—determines (a) whether the entity is managing and utilizing its resources (such as personnel, property, space) economically and efficiently, (b) the causes of inefficiencies or uneconomical practices, and (c) whether the entity has complied with laws and regulations concerning matters of economy and efficiency.
3. *Program results*—determines (a) whether the desired results or benefits established by the legislature or other authorizing body are being achieved and (b) whether the agency has considered alternatives that might yield desired results at a lower cost.

In determining the scope for a particular audit, responsible audit and entity officials should consider the needs of the potential users of audit findings.

U.S. OFFICE OF
SPECIAL
EDUCATION AND
REHABILITATION
SERVICES,
HANDICAPPED
PERSONNEL
PREPARATION
PROGRAM:
GUIDELINES FOR
DEVELOPING/
RATING THE
ADEQUACY OF
PROGRAM
EVALUATION
DESIGNS
INCLUDED WITH
FUNDING
PROPOSALS

These guidelines make up the specific criteria OSE uses to help select projects with sound evaluation designs. Here is a summary of the guidelines for the 1982 fiscal year (U.S. Department of Education, 1981).

Evaluation: Does the proposal describe an evaluation design which specifies:

1. An appropriate evaluation methodology used to judge the success of each project subcomponent?
2. The kinds of data to be collected for each subcomponent?
3. The criteria to be used to evaluate the result of the project?
4. Procedure for assessing the attainment of competence within the project?
5. A method to assess the contribution of project graduates
   a. toward meeting the needs of children INCLUDING the number of graduates prepared and placed by role;
   b. graduates' length of service; and
   c. graduates' proficiency as judged by employers?

U.S. OFFICE OF SPECIAL EDUCATION GUIDELINES
(continued)

6. A method for assessing the effectiveness and efficiency of project resource usage?
7. A method for assessing the impact of this project on related projects within the institution and the community?
8. At least annual evaluation of progress in achieving project objectives?
9. At least annual evaluation of the effect of the project on persons being served by the project, including any persons who are members of groups that have been traditionally underrepresented such as members of racial or ethnic minority groups and handicapped persons, etc.?

CONSIDERATIONS WHEN CHOOSING A SET OF STANDARDS

Since there are alternative sets of standards from which to choose, you will have to select those that are right for your purpose and context. Below are some issues you might consider when selecting a set of standards or criteria.

I. Content of the Standards
  A. Authority
    1. What were the bases for generating the standards? e.g.:
      a. problems emerging in the field
      b. professional objectives
      c. conventional practice
      d. natural laws
      e. theory of logical framework
    2. What level of authority do the standards carry? e.g.:
      a. postulates
      b. principles
      c. rules
      d. guidelines
      e. research
      f. concepts
      g. suggested procedures
    3. What was used to verify that the standards are responsible and consistent? e.g.:
      a. research findings
      b. conceptual theories
      c. conventional practices
      d. professional votes
    4. Have the boundaries for professional judgment within the standards been determined? e.g.:
      a. standards provide for professional judgment
      b. standards provide a basis for judgment
      c. standards provide a frame of reference to promote predictable judgment
      d. standards delineate areas for professional judgment
      e. standards establish limitations of professional judgment
  B. Scope
    1. Have the standards' scope of relevant applicability been specified? e.g., regarding:
      a. professional activities and products
      b. professionals
      c. clients
      d. contexts

2. Have limitations and areas to which the standards are *not* applicable been identified? e.g., regarding:
   a. legal and professional jurisdiction
   b. contextual and functional exceptions
3. Under what conditions has it been decided to revise the standards? e.g.:
   a. based upon relevant new research findings
   b. in response to regulatory intervention
   c. in response to societal changes
   d. as a result of a change in the state of the art
   e. in lieu of enforcement problems

C. Support Documents
   1. Are relevant support documents available? e.g.:
      a. interpretations
      b. quotes
      c. bibliographies
      d. policy papers
      e. research

D. Renewal Strategies
   1. Have strategies to update or revise the standards been established? e.g.:
      a. close interaction with constituents and other agencies
      b. extensive exposure to pronouncements before their release
      c. research before and after release
      d. systematic attempts to anticipate emerging problems
      e. post-enactment review
      f. ongoing or ad hoc revision process
      g. formal appeals system

II. Use of the Standards
   A. Role of the Standards
      1. How will the standards be used for self-regulation?
      2. How will the standards be used for educating audiences? e.g.:
         a. open board meetings
         b. due process procedures
         c. discussion memoranda
         d. public hearings
         e. public files
         f. newsletters and news bulletins
         g. speaking engagements
         h. instructional campaigns
      3. How will the standards be used to educate and train professionals? e.g.:
         a. accreditation
         b. licensure
         c. education
         d. continuing education
         e. training
   B. Promotion, Monitoring, and Enforcement of the Standards
      1. How will the standards be used to define admission and the right to continue practicing in the field?
      2. How will the standards be used to establish ethical behavior of professionals?
      3. How will the standards be used to define sound and substandard practices?
      4. How will the standards be used in developing quality control measures? e.g.:

        a. as a basis to establish internal quality control policies
        b. as a tool for peer reviews
        c. as a tool for analyses of substandard evaluations
        d. as a basis to review voluntarily submitted reports
        e. as a basis to issue certificates of compliance

    5. How will substandard performance be penalized within the profession? e.g.:
        a. letters of constructive criticism
        b. letters of censure
        c. acceptance of resignation
        d. suspension or expulsion

C. Legal Use of the Standards
    1. How will substandard performance be established and penalized within the legal system? e.g.:
        a. use of standards by state boards to revoke, suspend, or refuse to renew a license has been anticipated
        b. use of standards by federal agencies responsible for professional services that are funded by or affect the public has been anticipated
        c. use of standards by courts in litigation involving real or alleged substandard conduct has been anticipated

D. Monitoring or Controlling Use of the Standards
    1. How will use of the standards by public-sector agencies, general audiences, and courts be monitored and controlled? e.g.:
        a. level of specificity in language of standard statements and attestation reports has been considered in light of litigation
        b. analyses of relevant court rulings resulting from failure to adhere to professional standards have been considered
        c. use of court-appointed masters has been explored
        d. extension of "safe harbor" concept when using new methodologies has been explored
        e. avenues of discouragement of "nuisance" suits have been considered

HOW DO YOU APPLY A SET OF META-EVALUATION CRITERIA?

Once you have selected a *set* of meta-evaluation criteria, it is quite likely that you will need to adapt it in some way to better fit your particular situation. This can be accomplished by deciding how important each criterion is in relation to each other and by specifying indicators of compliance or quality for *each* criterion used.

At one extreme, you may say (or imply by default) that each criterion is just as important as every other one. On the other extreme, you may decide that every criterion is of different importance to you, and you might devise a scale to weight them accordingly. For a number of reasons, such as an inability to get consensus from the people involved or a tendency to clump groups of criteria, you will probably wind up with something in between the two extremes, usually some kind of ranking.

When you know which criteria are actually going to be applied, you can go on to specify how you will distinguish or measure compliance. This activity involves: 1) determining how precisely you will define compliance (for example, you may distinguish compliance at a dichotomous level, "met or not met"; you may rank order quality—"poor, so-so, good, great"; or you may use a scale with equal intervals—"On a scale of 1 to 10, I'd give it a 7."); 2) giving concrete descriptions of when an evaluation would be judged to be at a particular level of compliance; and 3) identifying the likely sources of information you will use as evidence of compliance.

As always, when you're involved in a valuing process, you need to consider who has something to gain or lose from the activity and determine how their perspectives should be represented. (Some perspectives that may be relevant to you have been listed in Chapter 4.) Also keep in mind under what conditions you intend to apply criteria. For instance, do they apply to *any* evaluation, or only evaluations of training and development projects, or only to your particular project? Do they apply to any *phase* of an evaluation, or only to evaluation designs?

Finally, to determine compliance indicators, you should consider the amount of information available, the level of precision needed, and the level of agreement possible.

If everybody agrees on how important the standards or criteria are and agrees on how clearly you can distinguish between them, coming to an agreement about the quality of an evaluation should not be much of a problem. On the other hand, if people cannot agree on what's important or how you can tell when you have a good evaluation, then you risk settling on the least common denominator, a watered down set of criteria on which everyone can agree. The following tables are used to summarize how you can adapt an existing set of meta-evaluation criteria for your own context.

WAYS TO ESTABLISH THE RELATIVE STANDING BETWEEN META-EVALUATION CRITERIA

All items are of equal standing (e.g., professional standards)

Items are ranked by key audiences (This technique is used in the American Psychological Association's testing standards)

    e.g., Use, Don't Use

        Priority A, Priority B, Priority C

        Essential, Useful, Supplemental, Not Needed

Items are weighted

    e.g., #1 = 20, #2 = 0, #3 = 30, #4 = 10, #5 = 30

        Category 1 = 100, Category 2 = 50, Category 3 = 25, Category 4 = 0

CONSIDERATIONS WHEN ESTABLISHING RELATIVE STANDINGS OF META-EVALUATION CRITERIA

Talk to the groups involved and explore their position for deciding what's important

    e.g., parents of deaf children wanting "Total Communication" vs. a funder who wants a randomized experimental design

    e.g., evaluation designs in proposals for innovative training projects

        evaluations of field placements for student teachers

        evaluations to decide which programs stay and which go

Determine the existing requirements for the evaluation

    e.g., since JDRP approval is desired, a premium is placed on demonstrating that any beneficial changes can be linked to the project itself

        it is known that the evaluation report *must* be completed by May 15, with specific recommendations, if the School Board is going to use it in deciding whether to fund the Teacher Center another year

Indicate the level of precision needed

    e.g. only general verbal feedback is desired on the first draft of an evaluation design

        since Grant funds are limited and the number of proposals is high, a two-stage cut will be made, first on general considerations related to the Grant purposes, second on relative rankings of project designs, evaluation designs, and budgets

Anticipate the level of agreement possible

    e.g., in the above parent/funder example, a conflict exists between the right to treatment and the generalizability of results

        everyone agrees that the evaluation should take no more than 2% of the project budget, so a "bare bones" approach is needed

---

SOME EXAMPLE INDICATIONS OF COMPLIANCE FOR DIFFERENT MEASUREMENT APPROACHES

KIND OF MEASUREMENT	DESCRIPTOR	INDICATOR	SOURCES OF INFORMATION
		"Report Timeliness" Standard	
Dichotomous	Met	The Model Training Program Final Report was delivered on time.	The report itself.
	Not Met	The Model Training Program Final Report was not delivered on time.	Recipients of the report.
		"Described Purposes and Procedures" Standard	
Ranking	Low	The purposes for evaluating the Model Training Program evaluation were ill-defined.	Evaluation design.
	Medium	General uses for the Model Training Program evaluation were described.	Preceeding needs assessment.
	High	A clear listing of the types of decisions to be made and when, which was to come out of the Model Training Program evaluation, had been identified.	Management plan.
		"Valuational Interpretation" Standard	
Weighting	Completely Unacceptable (−1.00)	No one directly involved in or affected by the evaluation of the Model Training program had input into deciding how the project would be judged.	Sources listed above.
	Minimally Acceptable (0.00)	The project staff cooperated with the evaluator to decide what makes a "good" Model Training Program	Key informants. News media reports
	Expected (+0.75)	A group of administrators, Model Training Program staff, faculty, and students got together to decide what makes a "good" Model Training Program.	
	Most Desirable (+1.00)	A group of people representing all major university, school and community groups jointly established the criteria to determine what makes a "good" Model Training Program.	

WHAT PROCEDURES ARE USED IN META-EVALUATION?

Up until now, we have presented some general uses of meta-evaluation, suggested what types of people should conduct a meta-evaluation, and offered a number of possible ways to develop meta-evaluation activities. For the most part, these ideas would help you primarily to focus your meta-evaluation. What comes next can be thought of just like any other evaluation. You are now going to have to carefully consider the various aspects of designing, collecting, analyzing, reporting and managing the meta-evaluation. If you want to use the *Sourcebook* as a guide, you will need to recycle through the chapters again, this time using your *evaluation* of the training project (or whatever) as the object of interest.

As your meta evaluation begins to take shape and you clarify some of the uses to which you intend to put it (e.g., evaluating evaluation plans, activities, or results), you will also have a better idea of what types of procedures would be most appropriate, such as hiring consultants, putting together a review panel, getting a funding continuation decision from your funder, and the like. The list below includes some of your options.

	Focus of the Meta-Evaluation		
	Formative Uses		Summative Uses
	Evaluating Evaluation Plans	Evaluating Evaluation in Progress	Evaluating Evaluation After Its Completion
Procedures for Doing the Meta-Evaluation	hire consultant, e.g., evaluator, measurement specialist, or content specialist	independent observers, e.g., meta-evaluator, evaluation team, review panel	review of final reports, e.g., send reports to evaluator, consultant, advisory group
	review panel, e.g., advisory group review of evaluation plans, e.g., design, contract management plan	review of progress reports, e.g., logs, interim reports, budget update, management plan, collection schedule	meta-evaluator, e.g., sponsors or funding agent, advisory panel, professional evaluator(s)

By attending to the advice and warnings about evaluation presented in this *Sourcebook*, we hope that you will be able to develop, conduct, and apply an evaluation of your training efforts which reflects sound and just practices in light of the current developmental state of the field of evaluation. At a minimum, we feel that this means that your evaluation should provide technically adequate information, which is realistically obtainable at a reasonable cost, for clearly useful purposes, which safeguard the rights and dignity of the people involved. If you can do this, you have done well.

For an example of a meta-evaluation, read Case C-4 in the *Casebook*. This case illustrates the use of the Joint Committee *Standards* to evaluate the evaluation design for a model training program at a university.

REFERENCES

American Psychological Association. *Standards for Educational and Psychological Tests and Manuals*. Washington, D.C.: APA, 1966.

Boros, O.K. *The Mental Measurements Yearbooks*. Highland Park, New Jersey: Gryphon Press, 1941–1965 (irregular).

Campbell, D.T., & Stanley, J.C. *Experimental and Quasi-Experimental Designs for Research*. Chicago: Rand McNally, 1966.

Comptroller General of the United States. *Standards for Audit of Governmental Organizations, Programs, Activities, and Functions*. Washington, D.C.: U.S. Government Printing Office, 1981.

Cook, T.D., & Campbell, D.T. *Quasi-Experimentation: Design and Analysis Issues for Field Settings*. Chicago: Rand McNally, 1979.

Evaluation Research Society. *Standards for Program Evaluation*. Exposure Draft, 1980.

Joint Committee on Standards for Educational Evaluation. *Standards for Evaluations of Educational Programs, Projects, and Materials*. New York: McGraw-Hill, 1981.

Tallmadse, G.K. *Joint Dissemination Review Panel Ideabook*. Washington, D.C.: U.S. Government Printing Office, 1977.

Ridings, J.M. *Standard Setting in Accounting and Auditing: Considerations for Education Evaluation*. Unpublished doctoral dissertation, Western Michigan University, 1980.

Stufflebeam, D.L. *Meta-Evaluation*. Occasional Paper Series, No. 3, The Evaluation Center, Western Michigan University, 1974.

U.S. Department of Education. *Application of Grants Under Handicapped Personnel Preparation Program*. Washington, D.C.: Author, 1981.

The Casebook

These cases are intended for public school, university, and state agency educators involved in teacher education and professional development related to special education. The purpose is to enable you to see how others have designed, conducted, and used program evaluation procedures as a regular part of their work. The people shown in the cases try, in the face of realistic obstacles, constraints and limitations to evaluate as well as they can while fulfilling their other very demanding responsibilities.

The *Casebook* contains twelve (12) "stories" about evaluation applications within particular personnel preparation programs. Some of these are about state agency (SEA) evaluation, some about public school (LEA) evaluation, and some about college and university (IHE) efforts. All are alike in that they portray evaluation being used to improve program efforts. The case examples are fictional accounts but are closely based on real programs and evaluation work.

There is a major tension in the cases. The very demanding process of carrying out educational responsibilities contends with the very demanding process of doing evaluation well. To put it another way, the tension is between the evaluation standards associated with feasibility and utility and the standards associated with technical adequacy.

The aim, in each case, is to do something educationally useful and to do the evaluation well enough so that any resulting educational decisions are based upon reasonably adequate data. The aim is achieved with differing degrees of success.

We will encourage you, through discussion questions attached to each case, to second guess the people involved. Did they give in too much to the immediate practical constraints? Did they override educational considerations too much in their efforts to do "good evaluation"? Did they override evaluation considerations too much in their efforts to get something done? Did they blunder badly? Did they perform brilliantly?

Good educators and good evaluators second guess their own decisions constructively—that's one way they get good and then get better. The people involved in the real work underlying the cases would no doubt do some things differently if they had it to do over; they learned from the experience. We hope that you will use the cases to learn from their experience.

It is not the aim of these materials to make you (or anyone else) an evaluator. As an educator, you already are an evaluator in the normal routine of doing your work. What you'll find in this book (and the companion *Design Manual* and *Sourcebook*) are materials meant to help you do evaluation more effectively and efficiently. And, as a result, your work should become more effective and valuable and help the program you assist to have greater effects.

HOW TO READ AND USE THE CASES

You will notice that marginal comments (brief questions) appear throughout the cases. These marginal notes point out the particular aspect of evaluation being dealt with at that point in the case. Each question is preceded and followed by one or more terms (e.g. "Focus", "Analysis"); these refer to headings and subheadings in the *Sourcebook*. The marginal notes are intended to help you understand what's happening "evaluation-wise" in the cases. The terms noted let you consult the *Sourcebook*; if you wish, for an additional perspective on that aspect of evaluation. Each case closes with a set of discussion questions and exercises. These can help you use the cases to teach others (or yourself) more about evaluation.

If you have more questions about how these materials are organized or how you might use them, please see the "User's Preface," which is a part of this materials package.

The Local School Case Examples

OVERVIEW BY ANN C. HALLAWELL

The case examples that follow illustrate evaluations of staff development programs in local and intermediate school districts. Each case is grounded in the experiences of the authors and the many persons to whom they spoke in educational institutions across the country. As a set, these cases describe a wide range of evaluation practices, activities, and considerations.

The first case (L1) describes the process for identifying staff development needs in a school building. The example further explores ways of meeting those needs. In the second case the evaluation of a one-time workshop is described. An inner city school district uses evaluation to solve problems in the operation of their resource center in case L3. Case L4 examines evaluation designed to assess staff development activities in light of benefits to children.

Each author has spent many hours gathering background information, drafting the cases, and submitting them to critical review. Additionally, there are others who have provided review and guidance for this section's development including Kathleen Byers, Wayne Welch, Jason Millman, Daniel Stufflebeam, James Sanders, Stanley Fagen, and Claudia White.

CASE L-1

AN ELEMENTARY SCHOOL PRINCIPAL ASKS: How Can We Determine What Inservice Training if any is Needed?

Terry Hluchyj

FOCUS—WHAT IS THE SETTING? (CONTEXT) Chestnut Hill Elementary School is one of the oldest in town. It is admired for its continued focus on traditional education emphasizing the basics while so many other buildings tend to follow fads. One reason for this traditional focus is the leadership of recent principals who believe that change ought to be slow and deliberate.

Jane Baer, who became the principal in the late seventies, follows that philosophical tradition. However, there were two concerns that led Jane to the conclusion that she needed to make some changes. One concern was the inservice program for staff. When the present program began, the student population was growing by leaps and bounds, as was the technology of teaching. Every month it seemed there was something new for the classroom—a new gadget, new audio-visual accessories, or new teaching approaches. The principal was under pressure from the state department and the regional center to provide opportunities for teachers to learn more about these innovations in the course of their work. At the same time the local teachers' union was becoming stronger and argued for (and won) some provisions in the contract for "inservice days."

FOCUS—WHAT SHOULD BE EVALUATED? (OBJECT) Over time, those "inservice days" became synonymous with a variety of lecture-type workshops. One was on stress management; another concerned an innovative reading program. While someone was always in charge of planning, it was difficult to determine whether there was any rhyme or reason to the choices. Usually, the sessions were one day long, involved an outside speaker giving a lecture with some time devoted to small group discussion. These workshops were usually organized at Chestnut Hill although occasionally the building would plan a joint session with others in the district.

FOCUS—WHY DOES EVALUATION APPEAR TO BE NEEDED? (NEEDS) Jane Baer sensed that the inservice program was in need of careful examination and probably some revisions. There were several reasons for this conclusion:

Teachers' groans were audible in every hallway just before and during the inservice days. While inservice may not have been a primary factor, it certainly was one contributor to what seemed to be increasingly poor morale over the past few years.

Although important issues (like individualizing instruction) were addressed, there was no apparent effect and things were rarely changed.

It was probably unrealistic to assume that a one-day quarterly lecture-type workshop could handle the variety of concerns that needed to be addressed.

The relationship between the building inservice program and the larger district staff development program was unclear.

Also related to the deficiencies, Jane thought, was the fact that teachers seemed to need direct help with problems in their classrooms. For example, the mandate to "mainstream" special education students had contributed a host of complications for teachers. Jane tried to help teachers with some of these problems through her quarterly visits and performance appraisals, but that didn't seem to be enough. Certainly, to some extent, teachers got help from each other, and from some of the inservice education activities, but these also seemed insufficient.

In sum, Jane thought that the poor state of the inservice program and the lack of support and guidance for individual teachers might be related.

Jane had some reservations about tackling a revision of the inservice program. Certainly there were some reasons to leave it alone. After all, it was an established routine and everyone knew what to expect. Why rock the boat?

Her conclusion was that the inservice boat was already rocked. Disgruntled teachers complained to her, to others in the school, and even to district administrators. It was just a matter of time before change might be directed, and fast changes could result in another poorly designed system. It was better to get a head start.

FOCUS—WHAT GOOD WOULD IT DO TO HAVE EVALUATION DATA? WOULD IT DO US ANY GOOD NOW? IN THE LONG RUN? (PURPOSES)

Jane decided to proceed systematically, using evaluation to help her plan the program. This would serve several important purposes, each increasing the likelihood for success:

It would allow her to make program decisions based on an assessment of past programs and future needs.
Evaluation could be used to gain support for and interest in the program by demonstrating that it was carefully and thoughtfully developed. Extra dollars from the district might even be justified.
Doing evaluation early in the planning effort would help her justify the worth of the plan. Later evaluation could build from those findings.

FOCUS—WHO MIGHT BE INTERESTED IN THE EVALUATION OR IN THE THINGS EVALUATED? (AUDIENCES)

Given these purposes, there were several evaluation audiences whose concerns should be addressed:

Audience 1. Teachers: Clearly, here is a key group affected by the evaluation. They would want to know about the inservice program, and how it was developed.
Audience 2. District administrators: The superintendent's office got pressure from two sources. One was the board of education, who seldom wanted to know about inservice education until problems were brought to their attention; then they demanded information right away.

The second source of pressure on the superintendent was parents. Like many others across the country, they complained about the poor quality of teaching in schools. The Superintendent saw inservice education as a way of improving teachers' skills. He made building principals responsible for inservice and demanded evidence that programs were worthwhile.
Audience 3. Jane and the person responsible for planning and conducting inservice next year would need information to help guide their planning. Also, to the extent that the evaluation generates support for the program, it will make their lives easier during the implementation of the plan.

A problem Jane faced was how to serve the needs of these varied audiences and maintain their involvement. She made a note to have them review the evaluation and work on parts of it.

WHO WILL DO THE EVALUATION?

DESIGN/MANAGEMENT— WHO SHOULD DO THE EVALUATING? (CREDIBILITY)

Jane wondered who might be the evaluator. Of course, she could do it herself, but that carried some risks. For one, teachers might misinterpret it as a part of the annual performance appraisal. Also, with her many other jobs, there was a danger of its being "back-burnered." Another option was to hire someone, but the superintendent would never approve that. A third option seemed to be the most likely choice: find someone in the building who could do it.

Joyce Fraser looked like a good choice for evaluator. Joyce was a tenured teacher who was generally well respected by the faculty. She was well organized, thorough, fair, and concerned about her teaching. She had a master's degree and had done some research requiring skills (e.g., instrument development, data analysis, and report writing) that would be helpful in the evaluation. Also, she used assessment techniques in her classroom that required similar skills and methods.

Joyce agreed to take the job. From her point of view, it was a good opportunity to get some relief from the mundane duties and to develop some administrative skills. Anyway, she was concerned about the quality of inservice education.

FOCUS—IS IT LIKELY TO BE POSSIBLE AND WORTH THE EFFORT? (UTILITY)

In spite of a need for the evaluation work, Jane knew it had pitfalls. Certainly, there was no precedent for program evaluation of this type in the building. The evaluations that did occur were done by district or state personnel and were directed toward measuring impact of specific programs like Title I. The kind of inservice evaluation Jane planned was quite different. It could be viewed as threatening by teachers who might think their efforts were critically reviewed. Also, evaluation could slow the planning work if it became burdensome, as could sometimes happen even in well-intended evaluation efforts. And, there were virtually no resources for staff, consultants, computer time, or other costs that a large-scale evaluation might entail.

DESIGN—HOW CAN WE DO IT SO THAT IT HAS A GOOD CHANCE OF WORKING? (AUDIENCE INVOLVEMENT; GENERAL STRATEGY)

In spite of these problems, Jane decided that the evaluation was important enough to warrant facing the risks, but she would take some precautions. For one, she would involve the teachers in the evaluation process and keep them informed of its progress and results. If they realized what the evaluation was intended to do, maybe it wouldn't be so disruptive.

Also, it was an advantage to have Joyce manage the evaluation because of her skills and good reputation among the teachers for being fair and thorough. That arrangement would also keep the evaluation out of the principal's office and lessen the likelihood that someone would think it was a form of teacher performance appraisals.

As another precaution, Jane knew that it would be important to monitor the evaluation to make sure it did not become unwieldy and create more problems than it solved.

Lastly, regarding resources, Jane knew she could get help from staff at the district office for planning and evaluation and from other teachers in the building if she needed them. As for other costs, such as paper and duplication, hopefully these would be minimal and the inservice budget could handle them.

GETTING STARTED WITH A PLAN

DESIGN/MANAGEMENT—WHAT HAS TO BE DONE TO DO THE EVALUATION? (TASKS/TIMELINESS)

During November, Jane and Joyce met to organize their work and establish a timeline. They agreed that they would begin right away and plan to have a new or revised inservice program in place by the following November. During that year, they would use the inservice time to work on the revisions. They also agreed that, in the long run, the evaluation should involve the assessment of the inservice program; but, since the program was currently undergoing revision, they decided that the evaluation should help them make decisions about what that program ought to be. In particular, it would help them with two major tasks:

Task 1: to understand their situation
Task 2: to design and assess a new inservice program

These evaluation tasks would probably entail more complex evaluation than they had first thought. Nevertheless, they took the attitude that this first evaluation effort was a start on a long-term project, so they would do what they could, realizing they would be operating within some strict limitations of time and resources.

PLANNING TASK 1

COLLECTION—WHAT INFORMATION DO WE NEED? (KINDS)

Their first task, understanding their situation better, was a potential lifetime activity. Having only a few months, they decided to narrow their focus to the three aspects of the setting that they believed would be most useful in their planning work:

problems, including circumstances in the classrooms or the building that hampered the teachers' ability to provide good instruction to students

strengths, including features of Chestnut Hill or the district that could be helpful in addressing these problems; and

constraints, including any factors that put limitations on or influenced solutions to those problems.

COLLECTION—WHERE CAN WE GET THE INFORMATION? (SOURCES)

Because they knew that each of them could easily generate some good ideas about these areas in fifteen minutes of thought and discussion, they didn't want to go overboard on fancy data collection. But they also didn't think they'd have much confidence in the list if they kept the procedure by which it was generated too narrow. This was a critical part of the evaluation. So they decided to improve their confidence by looking at some pertinent documents:

a recent district needs assessment report;
a list of objectives for the inservice developed by the teachers last year;
the building policies and procedures handbook;
the teachers' contract

COLLECTION—HOW CAN WE KEEP TRACK OF THE INFORMATION WE ARE GETTING? (PROCEDURES AND INTERPRETATION)

Joyce would keep a running list of problems, strengths, and constraints as they found them in the documents. That information would be combined with their own insights and personal experiences, resulting in a revised list that included a rationale for each inclusion. The next step would be for the teachers to confirm the findings and prioritize the problems.

ANALYSIS/INTERPRETATION—HOW CAN WE MAKE SENSE OF OUR FINDINGS? (INTERPRETATION)

Jane and Joyce realized that there was some risk involved in this final step. What if the teachers completely disagreed with the findings? There would not be much time left to collect more information, and the credibility of the inservice coordinator would be damaged. Nevertheless, they knew that it would be a mistake to make final judgments about this first phase of the evaluation by themselves. Having the teachers involved would probably contribute to better solutions, as well as increase their interest in and commitment to solving the problems.

REPORTING—HOW CAN WE KEEP PEOPLE INFORMED AND INVOLVED SO WE DON'T RUN INTO UNEXPECTED PROBLEMS? (DELIVERY/STYLE)

They decided that there were a few things they could do to minimize the risks. For one, they would watch out for confusion, misinformation or suspicion regarding the evaluation and try to head it off by involving teachers in planning the evaluation and by keeping them informed of the progress. Also, they would somehow try to test reactions to the findings before the meeting, particularly if they seemed surprising and controversial. And they would give teachers a written report—and be sure to document their conclusions with findings. If for some reason the teachers rejected the findings—and this seemed justified (e.g., because of some bias, etc., in the information collected)—they would set up a procedure for handling the information. Obviously, Jane and Joyce wouldn't revise the findings to suit the fancy of the teachers, but they also didn't think they would be such a confrontation if these other measures were taken.

PLANNING TASK 2

FOCUS—HOW CAN WE
ESTABLISH A GOOD
INSERVICE STRATEGY?
(QUESTION/PURPOSE)

The objective of the second task was to come up with a good inservice strategy—one that was likely to meet their needs. To do this they had to: (1) figure out what on earth was a good inservice strategy; (2) develop a design for their own inservice program; and (3) have that design reviewed with respect to criteria for good inservice practice.

DESIGN/COLLECTION—
WHERE CAN WE GET THE
INFORMATION? (SOURCES)

They decided that there were two ready sources of information about good inservice that could be used to develop a checklist to guide the design of their program and to evaluate it. One was literature on inservice education that would tell them what makes the good programs work. A second source was information about the previous inservice program at Chestnut Hill, which should tell about what's good and what's not so good. (Before changing the existing program, they wanted to be sure they understood the strengths and weaknesses of the existing program.)

ANALYSIS/
INTERPRETATION—WHAT
CRITERIA CAN WE USE TO
TELL US WHAT A GOOD
INSERVICE IS? (INTERPRET)

With a better idea about good inservice, they could design their own program. In addition, they could talk with experts from successful programs to learn about program design options. Then the design would be reviewed by people who were knowledgeable about program design options. Then the design would be reviewed by people who were knowledgeable about inservice, such as inservice coordinators from other buildings. To assess the design the reviewers would use a checklist consisting of the criteria Jane and Joyce developed (and any others they might want to add).

The two of them would revise the design in view of this feedback and prepare it for another round of reviews, this time by the teachers at Chestnut Hill. Any details that remained would be worked out then.

REPORTING—WHO NEEDS
TO SEE WHAT WE ARE
DOING AT THIS POINT?
(PURPOSES/DELIVERY)

Following the teachers' review, the plan could be revised and Joyce would prepare a report for teachers, district administrators, and others interested in the evaluation project and its results. The report would serve as documentation of the process. For the time being, one summary report seemed sufficient though Jane and Joyce recognized that multiple reports might be necessary to accomplish other purposes.

PUTTING IT ALL TOGETHER

MANAGEMENT PLAN/
REPORTING—HOW CAN WE
GET THE PLAN ON PAPER SO
WE AND OTHERS KNOW
WHAT WE ARE DOING?
(WHO, WHAT, WHEN)

With this outline of the evaluation tasks and some confidence in their feasibility, Joyce summarized the following: the information sources that would be used, how the information would be collected, what reports would be made, when all this would occur, and who would be responsible for each task. This evaluation plan was presented to the teachers during their meeting in early December.

The teachers were impressed by the plan. It seemed quite logical. Some even offered to help with the information collection, particularly by keeping track of ideas about what the inservice program ought to do and how it should be organized. One teacher who had been involved with the evaluation of previous inservice programs offered to help locate and review the reports of past inservice sessions.

MANAGEMENT PLAN

Task 1: Understanding the Setting
Objective: To develop criteria to guide program planning.

Steps	Person Responsible	When
1. Develop document analysis procedure	Joyce	Jan. 5–10
2. Analyze documents	Joyce and teacher volunteer (John Beaman)	Jan. 11–30
3. Analyze/interpret findings	Joyce and Jane	Feb. 1–15
4. Prepare report for teachers and distribute	Joyce	Feb. 1–15
5. Conduct teachers' meeting	Joyce	March 15
6. Revise report as needed	Joyce and Jane	March 15–30

Task 2: Designing the program
Objective: To design a program that is likely to work well

Steps	Person Responsible	When
1. Review literature on inservice programs	Joyce (with assistance from University consultant)	April 1–30
2. Review evaluations of past inservices	Joyce and former inservice coordinator	April 1–30
3. Identify and talk to experts from successful programs	Joyce and Jane	May 1–15

Steps	Person Responsible	When
4. Develop design and list of criteria	Joyce and Jane	May 15–30
5. Review design identify reviewers contact reviewers conduct reviews summarize findings	Joyce and Jane	Sept. 1–20
6. Revise design, as needed	Joyce and Jane	Sept. 21–30
7. Prepare report for teachers	Joyce	Oct. 1–10
8. Teacher review	Joyce	Oct. 15
9. Revise design, as needed	Joyce and Jane	Oct. 15–20
10. Prepare and distribute summary reports	Joyce	Oct. 20–31
11. Program implementation		Nov. 1

CARRYING OUT TASK 1

COLLECTION—HOW DO WE GET THE INFORMATION? (PROCEDURES/ INSTRUMENTS) To begin the information collection Joyce decided to tackle the *document analysis*. In order to organize the process, she set up a system for categorizing information pertinent to problems, strengths, and constraints using 3″ × 5″ cards. When she read about some policy or condition in the contract that could have implications for the staff development program, she made a note of it, its implication, and the document reference. For example:

STRENGTH

teacher consultant is available from the regional center up to one day per week.

REF: district manual of service and procedures

Implication: building may be able to make use of this person on regular basis. Note that arrangements must be made by principal, not individual teachers.

ANALYSIS/ INTERPRETATION—HOW CAN WE BE SURE THE INFORMATION ISN'T JUST ONE PERSON'S OPINION? (VERIFY, INTERPRET) Throughout this process, Joyce knew she would be making judgments—even in figuring out what parts of the documents were relevant to problems, strengths, and constraints, and certainly in deciding what their implications were for her work. As a check on the thoroughness and

accuracy of her judgments, she called on John Beaman, the fourth grade teacher who had volunteered to work on the evaluation. Both of them read the documents and followed the procedure Joyce outlined for analyzing them.

Wherever there were discrepancies between the judgments of these two raters, Joyce looked back at the materials on which the judgments were based and resolved the differences herself or asked Jane to do that. That procedure alerted her to some oversights.

By the end of this information collection process, Joyce had approximately 50 cards in her file. A few teachers followed through on their promise to help with this task by giving her some cards they had written based on their own observations. The analysis then began in detail.

Joyce began by sorting the information into three categories: "problems," "strengths" and "constraints." To bring some order to the piles, she identified major categories of findings, with points or elaborations under each. Also, she noted the frequency that each item was mentioned, to give her a rough measure of how salient or critical it was. For example, under "problem areas" she came up with three categories: "classroom management," "communication with special services staff," and "time management."

DESIGN—WHAT SHOULD WE DO IF WE FIND FLAWS IN THE EVALUATION DESIGN? (CRITERIA) After Joyce completed this procedure for all the information, she had a feeling that the findings were somewhat more sound than if she and Jane had simply made up a list when they began the project. But Joyce wasn't sure that they were sufficiently sound to guide their revision work. Some were vague, others conflicting. If her confidence was shaky, chances were good that others would feel the same way. After all, there was essentially only one information collection procedure used—document analysis—and that could have some biases, since it required that information be gleaned from rather formal documents. She got some good information from the document, but wanted to check it out or expand on it if she could.

With this reservation Joyce wanted to add a procedure to the evaluation plan—interviews of teachers (see figure 1). She decided that the plan could accommodate this change if she extended the analysis period from February 15 to March 12, which still allowed her to keep the teacher's review on March 15. She described this proposal to modify the design to the teachers at the next faculty meeting, since it represented a change in their agreement about how the evaluation would be conducted. Although there was some discussion about the importance of being sure the interviews wouldn't interfere with their free periods or lunchtime, the teachers thought that that change to the design was fine.

COLLECTION—HOW DO WE INTERVIEW THE TEACHERS SO THAT WE DON'T DISRUPT THINGS OR GET BIASED INFORMATION? (PROCEDURES/SAMPLES) The interviews took a while to complete, but also yielded very interesting information. The plan was to interview each of the twenty teachers individually or in small groups during their planning time over the course of three weeks.

When Joyce occasionally had to leave her classroom to conduct an interview, the principal would take over her class.

Although the interviews were intended to be "conversations" with the teachers, to learn what they thought about inservice and to get them involved in the planning effort, Joyce didn't want them to be haphazard or rambling. To keep the conversations fairly structured, without turning them into questionnaires, she wrote an interview schedule with major topics to be covered, followed by a series of probes. This schedule served as an outline for her, leaving room for deviations when discussion took off in an interesting direction. After the first few interviews, she revised the schedule by adding more probes.

TEACHER INTERVIEW SCHEDULE

Overview
Purpose of interview: To collect information from teacher that will help in planning the staff development program
Procedure: Ask questions, but leave room for additional comments. Will take about 30 minutes.
Information will be confidential; notes will not contain name of person interviewed.
Question areas
Past service: attendance
    strengths—what worked well, was useful, interesting, why
    weaknesses—what was poor, not useful, not interesting, why
    suggestions for changes—topics, format
Problems (note—interest in attending to teachers' classroom problems)
    identify persistent problems—interface with teaching
        describe frequency
                intensity
                duration
        describe attempted solutions
                when did they work, not work
        other problems: less frequent
                describe
Strengths: (note—interest in building on strengths)
    describe features of school/district which make it desirable to work here
    describe strengths that aren't being used
        e.g., personnel
                facilities
                local resources
    suggestions for using strengths better
Other: Comments about inservice programming in general, suggestions for next year's planning

Joyce gave some thought to taping the interviews, but decided that having complete information was not worth the effort of transcribing all those hours of tapes. Instead, she kept notes during the discussions, writing down topics and key comments, and elaborating on those notes immediately afterward. Thus, at the end of each interview, she had a few pages of notes which could be analyzed for

indications of problems, strengths, and constraints that could be noted on $3'' \times 5''$ cards.

Unlike the document analysis which was directed at locating fairly specific information, the interviews were open enough to collect a lot of information that seemed important but which might not specifically relate to problems, strengths, or constraints. So she wouldn't lose track of that information, Joyce made notes about it and kept them in a file of "miscellaneous but probably important information."

ANALYSIS/INTERPRETATION—HOW CAN WE MAKE SENSE OF WHAT WE GET FROM THE INTERVIEWS? (ANALYZE/INTERPRET) By the end of the interviews Joyce had added another 100 cards to her file. She sorted those, along with the set from the document analysis, and arrived at a list of problems, strengths, and constraints—each having a rationale and notes about how important it seemed to be based or how often it occurred or how much it was emphasized in the interviews.

Not all the findings were a surprise, but it was still worthwhile to list them with their rationale. The four primary problems were:

poor attitude of students,
large class size,
poor testing,
lack of direction in classroom activities.

As for strengths, among others she listed:

the comraderie among the staff,
their willingness to share ideas and seek help with problems from each other,
the resources available from the regional center

And under constraints she found, for example:

tight schedules,
a limited budget,
contract specifications for inservice education

REPORTING—HOW CAN WE REPORT THE RESULTS? (PURPOSES/CONTENT/DELIVERY) With the completion of this phase of the information collection and analysis, Joyce prepared for the teacher review. Such a review, Joyce thought, would be a good way of increasing the teachers' understanding of her work and an opportunity to discuss the findings as the basis for the next steps. In addition, she wanted the teachers to elaborate on the findings and prioritize the problems to be addressed.

To help prepare for the review, three days before the teachers' meeting in the middle of March, Joyce distributed a brief report of her findings to all teachers. In addition to the findings, the report contained a brief description of the information collection procedures so everyone would recall them and understand how the findings were derived.

For the first ten minutes of the meeting Joyce reviewed the report, explaining (again) the purpose of the evaluation and the results so far. For the next half hour, they discussed the findings, with Joyce directing them to some points that she wanted help with, particularly better understanding of the problems that had been identified and their importance.

Because no one else had analyzed all the information Joyce was concerned about whether her findings made sense, that is, whether they seemed to fit with others' perceptions. She and John had compared notes on the interviews and observations, but she wanted reactions to her emerging conclusions from the other teachers. While she hesitated to call this a formal validation of her findings, she and Jane decided that it was as close as they could get, given their time and resource constraints. Ideally, they would have had someone else, beyond what John had done, collecting independent information to compare to Joyce's findings. Maybe next year.

The review was a disappointment to both Jane and Joyce. After their hard work, they expected an enthusiastic reception—well, at least to be told they'd done a good job. But the reaction was apathetic, a ho-hum, so-what-else-is-new attitude. Nevertheless, the teachers did propose some helpful modifications: one of the problem categories—poor attitude of students—was subdivided into two areas, discipline and motivation, because the teachers thought they were each too important to be collapsed into one. Also, class size was eliminated from the list because the group decided that it would be nearly impossible to tackle, considering the constraints that would have to be overcome. Perhaps deluding themselves, Joyce and Jane took some encouragement from the lukewarm response. If attitudes about inservice were *this* bad, their work was certainly needed!

Having accomplished their first evaluation task, Joyce was ready to move to the next one, expecting that its results would elicit a stronger reaction from her colleagues. Meanwhile, Jane sent a memo to the superintendent describing their progress and next task.

CARRYING OUT TASK 2

FOCUS—IS INSERVICE REALLY WHAT WE NEED? (UTILITY)

With the problems, strengths, and constraints, Joyce's next step was to decide what strategies could be used to solve the problems, by capitalizing on the strengths, within the constraints she had identified. To a great extent, her responsibilities as inservice coordinator implied that the appropriate strategies in this case would be some kind of inservice education program. That outcome was known from the start, given Jane's intention to revise the inservice program. However, in discussion with Jane, the two of them decided that it would be inappropriate to try to force an inservice solution on problems that needed to be resolved in another way. Therefore, they added a step to the evaluation plan—they considered some options besides an inservice education program and outlined them with strengths and weaknesses next to each.

Use district library media center

Strength: detailed information is available
Weakness: presupposes recognition of specific problem areas; teachers must take initiative; no personal contact

Hire consultants from regional center or university
Strength: personal contact; makes use of local expertise
Weakness: teachers have had bad experiences in the past with paternalistic attitude of these consultants

Get materials from regional centers
Strength: good selection of materials that are too costly for building library
Weakness: difficult to access; lack of personalized service; demands teacher initiative

Jane and Joyce did not want to abandon their efforts to revise the building-level inservice education program—since that program was a necessary outcome of the evaluation and seemed like a good solution to the problems they identified in task 1. However, they thought these alternatives might provide some help. To explore this possibility further Jane took responsibility for finding out just what materials and people were available and what they would cost. Meanwhile, Joyce continued to work on the steps they'd outlined for task 2.

ANALYSIS/ INTERPRETATION—HOW CAN WE TELL IF THE NEW INSERVICE PROGRAM WE DESIGN IS ANY GOOD? (CRITERIA)

In the course of her reading, Joyce found a booklet on "Quality Practices in Inservice Education" produced in 1980 by a task force sponsored by the National Inservice Network.* The booklet contained a list of statements on what constitutes good practices in inservice education. The initial statements were based on a literature review and on a national survey and interviews of key individuals in inservice education. Those statements were modified, and then validated through a second survey. The result is a list of six major criteria: the first says that inservice education must be a system that's integrated into an institution; the second through fifth describe the characteristics of a good program—i.e., collaborative, needs-based, responsive to change, and accessible; and the sixth statement says that evaluation is an essential component. Under each of these statements are a number of more specific statements or guidelines for achieving a good program.

While Joyce thought there could be a variety of other ways of stating the criteria, she decided that the ones in the booklet were consistent with her notions of good inservice practice and had to be at least as good as a list she might develop in the next week!

COLLECTION—CAN WE USE EVALUATION DATA OR STRATEGIES WE'VE USED IN THE PAST? (KINDS OF DATA)

While this task was underway, Joyce also reviewed evaluations of past inservice programs in the building. Those evaluation reports were sketchy, based primarily on brief questionnaires to participants at the end of the workshop

* "Quality Practices in Inservice Education," Quality Practices Task Force, National Inservice Network, Indiana University, 1981.

sessions, and some observation notes by the former in-service coordinator. Originally, one purpose in completing this evaluation of the inservice program was to see whether the previous design could be used in solving the identified problems. However, after looking at the reports, Joyce was convinced that the previous inservice design was unlikely to work because it didn't make good use of the building strengths and didn't really seem to solve the problems for which it was intended (and those problems were similar to ones she and teachers had just ranked). However, it was possible that some elements of that design might still be appropriate. Working with the former coordinator, Joyce analyzed the reports to identify strengths and weaknesses of the previous inservice programs and looked back at her miscellaneous file of teacher remarks gathered from the interviews. To keep the procedure simple, she made a list of what seemed to work well or what participants liked, e.g., discussion about specific building problems and finding solutions to them; having written or self-produced materials that could be used later. She also noted what failed or what participants didn't like, e.g., lengthy lectures and lack of involvement in selecting topics. These points, too, could be instructive in her desk work if they served as guidelines or inspired ideas about ways to organize the new program.

Joyce was getting worried at that point because a perfect program had not emerged from her list of criteria or her critical review of the past inservice programs. She had hoped that, somehow, a solution would be obvious by that time.

COLLECTION—CAN WE BENEFIT FROM OTHERS EXPERIENCES? While waiting for inspiration, Joyce read about some innovative designs for inservice education programs, thinking that that broader term might guide her to look for ideas beyond the more narrow realm of lecture method workshops. The card catalog listing under inservice education and an ERIC search turned up a number of recent books and articles. As she read, she kept in mind the other information she had collected (the criteria for good programs, the evaluations of past inservice programs, the problems, strengths and constraints), and weighed the design possibilities against them until she found one that seemed to fit well. The design that seemed to fit best was a "consultation" or "staff team" program, as described, for example, in a monograph developed by the National Inservice Network, "School-based Staff Support Teams: A Blueprint for Action."* While the specific operation of such a program could vary, it was generally characterized by a team of teachers and others, usually four to seven, who represented a variety of positions including classroom teachers, administrators, and special services personnel. This team would meet regularly, every two or three weeks, to discuss and help solve problems for the building as a whole or problems that individual teachers brought to the team. The primary advantage of this

program is that it was a continuous system, rather than a periodical educational event like a workshop. Also, it made good use of the talents of teachers in the building and facilitated their working together to share skills.

To learn more about this kind of program Joyce talked with a few people who had written papers about their experiences implementing consultation programs in their own buildings. In this further research, she particularly wanted to find out what the preconditions for establishing this program were, how team members were selected, and what their specific responsibilities were.

During May, with this information and what she knew about her own building and the district's requirements for the inservice program, she drafted a design for a similar program and prepared for its review. Jane then got involved to help brainstorm ideas about the specific features of the design and to tell Joyce what she thought about the other strategies for solving the problems—using the district library media center, getting materials from the regional services center, and hiring consultants.

REPORTING—WHAT DO PEOPLE THINK OF OUR WORK UP TO THIS POINT? (PURPOSES) The first review of the evaluation work that Fall was done by inservice coordinators in other buildings and some district administrators. They read the design description and the findings from task 1. Then they completed the checklist of criteria based on the "Quality Practices" booklet, adding any criteria they thought were important (see table 1).

A week later Jane and Joyce met with the reviewers to discuss their reactions and to elaborate on their ratings of the program. These discussions proved to be helpful, particularly when reviewers needed more information to make the required judgments and when they had a lot to say, but little patience in writing it.

REPORTING—HOW CAN WE GET USEFUL REACTIONS FROM PEOPLE ABOUT WHAT WE'VE DONE? (STYLE/USE) Following the reviews—at the end of September—Jane and Joyce revised the design and prepared for the teachers' meeting. Like the reviewers, the teachers received a description of the program, a rationale for it, and the checklist of criteria a week before the meeting. In that way this information could serve as preparation for the meeting and as an information update on Joyce's progress since June. Wanting to be sure the teachers had enough time to be involved in this stage of the work, Jane and Joyce decided to devote a half-day to the teacher review and discussion.

A week before the meeting, Jane got wind of some grumblings about the meeting. A few teachers who heard about the evaluation findings and program plans were skeptical about them. Based on what they'd heard, there were some serious problems with the design—particularly its feasibility, considering how much time the team would apparently have to spend working with individual teachers.

Jane decided to head off what could have become unproductive bickering at the teachers' review meeting by inviting any dissenters to write a brief paper titled "Why the Program Won't Work." These could be distributed a few

* Stokes, Shari (ed.), "School-Based Staff Support Teams: A Blueprint for Action," Building Based Teams Task Force, National Inservice Network, Indiana University, 1981.

TABLE 1. Excerpt of Checklist for Evaluating Chestnut Hill Proposed Inservice Education Program

	HOW WELL IS THE CRITERION MET?			
	VERY	MODERATELY	NOT AT ALL	DON'T KNOW
1. Procedures exist to assure adequate faculty resources. Comment:	☐	☐	☐	☐
2. The program is well integrated with the organization. Comment:	☐	☐	☐	☐
3. Participants in the program will have a voice in decisions about it. Comment:	☐	☐	☐	☐
4. The program design is derived primarily from a set of assessed needs of students, personnel, and the school as a whole. Comment:	☐	☐	☐	☐
5. Etc.				

days before the meeting so everyone could see in writing some major pros and cons of the plan. They could then be a basis for discussing the evaluation findings and the program plan.

The meeting began with Joyce's summary of the program design, followed by two dissenting papers which argued that the program wouldn't work for several reasons: for one—it would take too much time; for another—teachers wouldn't want to expose their classroom difficulties to the whole school by reporting them to the team. As the presentations offered fuel for the debate which followed, Joyce and Jane wondered whether apathy didn't have some attractive features. But it wasn't a disaster. It turned out that overall, most teachers agreed that the design was sound, although they had some concerns about the specific operation. For example, who would serve on the teams first, when would meetings take place, would information discussed by teams be a part of the personnel evaluation? Jane and Joyce had answers to many of these questions based on what they thought was appropriate for their building and on what they learned from model programs using this approach to inservice education. However, some answers had to be worked out or were revised during the meeting. By the end of the meeting, the teachers gave their endorsement to the plan. Nevertheless, wrinkles remained in the plan and could only be ironed out through the course of the program's operation, and that meant more evaluation to assess how well the program was being implemented, what problems arose, and how appropriately it was used.

REPORTING—HOW CAN WE KEEP KEY PEOPLE INFORMED? Before implementing that program, Joyce wrote reports on the evaluation findings so far for several other audiences. One report was a several-page description of the inservice program plan for those who reviewed the design a month earlier. Another report went to the superintendent. It contained a brief summary of both tasks 1 and 2—the steps and the findings. Since the superintendent had to approve any changes in the program, Jane was particularly concerned that he know why they made the changes by showing him that they had a solid grounding.

Two weeks after he received the report, Jane met with him to discuss the details and answer any questions. After ten minutes he knew that he liked the program. His only question was whether it would last for long, considering the high investment of time it would take. But that could be tested easily enough. Anyway, Jane was obviously enthusiastic enough about it to give it a good try.

The conversation turned then to the board of education and how to let those members know about the program. After all, considerable work was done to arrive at the plan—and all with the expenditure of few resources. The board would like that. Maybe they'd do a presentation at a board meeting in a few months when they could also report on the progress of the program. Wider dissemination of information about the program through the local newspaper was another possibility. The education reporter recently confessed his boredom with the usual finance and teacher lay-off articles. This might be an interesting change—for both the school district and the newspaper.

* * * * *

DISCUSSION QUESTIONS AND TOPICS

1. If you know "typical practices"—how does what Jane did in using evaluation compare with what other good school principals would do in a similar situation?

2. What new information emerged through the evaluation activities i.e., what did Jane learn that she didn't already know?

3. Suppose someone were to contend that the evaluation effort was a waste of time—that they didn't learn anything important. What arguments can you put forth against that contention? (Hint: Consider both what they

learned and the value of documenting or disconfirming what they already believed.)

4. What are some good ideas for doing evaluation and/or for designing inservices that you can dig out of the case? (Hint: Consider the value of involving the teachers, identifying quality practices, and of specific techniques for interviewing, analyzing documents, etc.)

5. What are two or three reasons why it was a good idea for Joyce to keep everyone informed about what she was doing?

6. What recommendations would you make—based upon your knowledge and experience and what you've learned from the case—to Jane or Joyce and others in similar positions about how to "determine what inservice training, if any, is needed?" (Hint: Make your recommendations in the form of a list of guidelines.)

SUGGESTIONS FOR STIMULATING DISCUSSIONS ABOUT THE CASE

1. Organize a debate between two persons or subgroups around question 3. Resolved: This case demonstrates the value of assessing the needs for inservice training.

2. Have one person or subgroup make a brief presentation on "good educational practices shown in the case" and another person or subgroup present on "good evaluation practices shown in the case."

3. Have one person or subgroup make a brief presentation on "what Jane or Joyce should have done to improve the technical adequacy of the evaluation." Have another person or subgroup present on "what Jane or Joyce should have done to improve the usefulness of the evaluation." Then have a discussion about the feasibility of the suggestions presented. (Hint: Ask the presenters not to be constrained by feasibility considerations but to be more freewheeling or idealistic or textbookish in their recommendations.)

4. Identify one or two turning points or major decision points in the case. Then have people prepare to take on the role of key persons in the case and role play a discussion they might have.

5. Prepare, then discuss and critique the case from several value perspectives. The discussion could take the form of a role play, each person representing a particular value perspective or bias. (e.g., "It ought to be economical and get results!" "It ought to serve the needs of children!" "It ought to involve everybody concerned?" "It ought to reflect standard educational practices." "It ought to be comparable to what the best schools do!" "It ought to be methodologically sound!" "I don't care how marvelous your intentions are, don't confuse needs with results—and I want to hear about results!" "It ought to be consistent with the latest educational and psychological research!")

APPLICATION EXERCISES

1. If you have the *Sourcebook*, read some of the material in the *Sourcebook* indicated by the asides. Then suggest alternative things people in the case might have done at several points in the case. Or suggest a whole new approach they might have taken.

2. Using the case as a model (and foil) and your suggested alternatives as guides, design an evaluation for a situation or problem similar to that shown in the case.

3. Using Chapter 7 of the *Sourcebook* as a guide, do a meta-evaluation and critique of the case (and/or your evaluation design).

4. Use the *Design Manual* to develop an improved evaluation design for the case.

5. Use the *Design Manual* to develop an evaluation design for a situation or problem similar to the one described in the case.

CASE L-2:

A SPECIAL EDUCATION STAFF MEMBER ASKS: How can I design, operate, and evaluate a workshop?

Dale Brethower

FOCUS—WHAT IS THE SETTING? (CONTEXT)   The Midvale School District serves approximately 12,000 students in three high schools, six junior high schools, and twenty-three elementary schools. The community has some light industry and borders on a large city where many of the residents work. Community support of and involvement in education is in no way remarkable, although a number of families have moved into the district hoping it would provide a better education for their children than could the city schools.

FOCUS—WHO IS CONCERNED? (AUDIENCE)   Mainstreaming had become a hot topic in the district.

1. The local group of parents of special education children wanted to be sure that the children weren't shunted off to the side in special classes and weren't dumped into the mainstream without proper support.

2. The parent and teachers' association was supportive of the special education parents and wanted to be sure that regular classes weren't disrupted by the presence of special education students and weren't weakened by diversion of funds to special education.

3. The teachers' union wanted to be sure that teachers were not required to do extra work or work with more difficult students without receiving support services.

4. Candidates for the school board took stands on or tried to evade the issues associated with mainstreaming.

5. Administrators worried about the budgetary implications of successfully assuring that students were properly placed in least restrictive environments. They also worried about the legal implications of failing to do that.

6. School psychologists, special education staff, and other professionals gave well attended talks and inservice sessions on the maintaining of "least restrictive environments."
7. Surveys done in the district usually contained items related to mainstreaming; responses indicating that strong and conflicting opinions were common.
8. Mainstreaming was a frequent item of shop talk. It was rumored that: (a) regular education teachers had filed grievances over mainstreaming; (b) parents had filed law suits; and (c) a high percentage of mainstreamed students made little or no progress in regular classrooms. (The first rumor was true although grievances were rare. The second was false although law suits had been threatened. The third was not verifiable since no one had compiled such data.)

FOCUS—WHAT IS MY DIRECTIVE? WHAT HAS SOMEBODY DECIDED NEEDS TO BE DONE? (PURPOSE/ QUESTIONS) The school administration, with support from teachers' union leaders, had decided that there should be some inservice training on mainstreaming. Jan Caldwel, a member of the special education staff who worked out of the administrative offices, was assigned responsibility for developing the workshop in late September. Jan, who had taught in one of the six junior high schools before going into special education, asked what the workshop should accomplish and how much time and money she could spend on it. "It's your job to find out!" she was told. "Figure out what has to be done and then give me a cost estimate. We'll see if there's money available to do it. Don't be extravagant, but ask for what you need." She was also told that the workshop should be conducted by the end of November.

DESIGN-HOW CAN I GET SOME INFORMATION IN A HURRY? (ALTERNATIVES) Working without a clear charge as to what she was to do, without a budget, with other demands on her time, and in a climate where there was a perceived need to get something going in a hurry, Jan developed a set of objectives for the workshop (see figure 1). Her notion was that the best needs assessment strategy she could use under the circumstances, was what her former husband had called test marketing: "Try to sell it and see if anyone will buy it!"

---

1. To provide teachers with information about characteristics of several types of mainstreamed students
2. To expose teachers to a variety of teaching methods appropriate for use with regular special education students.
3. To provide teachers with guidance and opportunity to prepare instructional materials and procedures for use by mainstreamed students
4. To enable teachers to develop positive attitudes toward special education students and the mainstreaming process

---

Figure 1: First Draft Objectives for Mainstreaming Workshop

---

1. Icebreaker—Chat briefly with each person about his/her work and concerns about mainstreaming.
2. Transition—Comment somewhat as follows: "It appears to me that you'd be a good person to help me with a mainstreaming workshop I've been asked to develop. I'm trying to figure out just what it should accomplish. What do you think needs to be done to facilitate mainstreaming?" (Ask follow-up questions based upon the responses.)
3. Transition—"That's very helpful." "I hadn't thought about some of the issues you raised." (or "Your thinking seems to be consistent with some of my ideas.") "Now, would you look at this rough draft of workshop objectives? I'd like to improve them, so feel free to criticize and to suggest other objectives."
4. Closing—"Thank you. This has been very useful to me. As I understand it, you would like to see..." (summarize viewpoints and clarify as needed.) "Thank you, again. Would you like me to keep you informed about the progress of the workshop?"

Figure 2: Structure of Objectives Review Interviews

COLLECTION—WHO SHOULD I TALK TO AND HOW SHALL I GET THE INFORMATION? (SAMPLE/ PROCEDURES) She then sought out several people (some were friends and teachers whose opinions she valued, others were key figures in the district, e.g., an outspoken school board member, a couple of principals, the teachers' union president, a school psychologist). She interviewed them, showing them the objectives and getting comments. Her natural interviewing style is depicted in figure 2 as an interview protocol.

ANALYSIS/ INTERPRETATION—ARE THERE ANY KEY ISSUES OR PATTERNS IN THE INTERVIEW RESULTS? She uncovered many general concerns. The teachers' union president, the school psychologist, and one of the principals were each emphatic about the point that a one-shot workshop wasn't going to solve the mainstreaming problem. Information, teaching methods and materials, and positive attitudes were all commendable, but not enough. There were social problems to contend with: children (as well as adults) respond to people who are different as if there is something wrong. A tension results which all too often leads to ridicule, teasing, and ostracism. "The social integration problem is much larger and more complex than making tape recordings for blind students!"

There were also criticisms of the objectives themselves. One principal, a reader of books on behavioral objectives, had a field day with "To provide teachers with information..." and "To expose..." Two people (the school board member and one of Jan's friends) complained that it was all focused on doing things to *teachers*. None of the objectives said anything direct and tangible about what the workshop would do for children. Objective 3 "... prepare instructional materials and procedures for use by mainstreamed students" came close but not close enough.

The purpose of the workshop is to provide teachers with knowledge, techniques, attitudes, and preparation time sufficient to enable them to:

a. ease the entry and assure the acceptance of qualified special education students into regular classrooms.
b. prepare and use instructional materials and procedures that are effective with mainstreamed students, and
c. use the entry of special education students as an opportunity to enhance the learning environments for regular education students.

Figure 3: Current Objectives for Mainstreaming Workshop

REPORTING—WHAT SHOULD I DO WITH THE RESULTS? WHAT'S THE BEST WAY OF USING AND TELLING OTHERS ABOUT WHAT I'VE FOUND? (PURPOSES/AUDIENCE)

Jan was both discouraged and pleased by the results of the interviewing process. She was pleased with what she had learned and discouraged by the difficulty of designing a workshop that could actually make an impact on the problems in mainstreaming. She pressed on, revising the objectives based on the information she gathered during the interviews.

The revised workshop objectives are shown in figure 3.

She sent copies of the revised objectives to numerous persons (including leaders of parents' groups and presidents of student councils in schools that had them) asking for comments. Comments ranged from, "It's about time!" to "Vague!" and "Impossible! How are you going to do that?" The changes suggested were more editorial than substantive and she felt she was on the right track.

She went through a similar procedure (on a smaller scale) to design the workshop. Her first design was drafted by mid-October. It became obvious that rushing to run the workshop before Thanksgiving or between Thanksgiving and Christmas was a bad idea. The new target date became "sometime in Winter or Spring."

FOCUS—HOW CAN I FIND OUT HOW TO DESIGN AN INSERVICE THAT WILL BE RESPONSIVE TO WHAT I'VE LEARNED? (PURPOSE)

It had become clear to Caldwel, as she considered the variety of issues people had raised, that the mainstreaming workshop wouldn't be successful if it were a side show effort. Somehow she had to insure that it enhanced rather than disrupted the broad mainstream of education and that it not lose its focus on the special legal issues and educational problems relevant to developmentally delayed students. Somehow she had to insure that it connected with other efforts and other projects going on in the district, without losing its special mission or being engulfed in something else.

DESIGN/COLLECTION—HOW CAN I FIND OUT HOW OTHERS HAVE DEALT WITH THESE PROBLEMS? (ALTERNATIVES)

She talked with people from other districts to see how they were handling such problems. (She made a few telephone calls, but most investigation came during found opportunities while doing other work.)

She decided her strategy would be to start a mainstreaming workshop and to encourage linking the workshop to other projects and concerns as time went on. She reasoned that there were always going to be new students to be integrated into the system, and new instructional procedures to be developed or integrated into teaching practices. Even if the perceived need (for help on mainstreaming) evaporated there would be an ongoing need for mechanisms to integrate new or different students, teachers, and materials into an effective educational experience.

INTERPRETATION/ REPORTING—HOW CAN I SHOW MOST CLEARLY WHAT I'VE FOUND AND WHAT I PLAN TO DO WITH THE INFORMATION?

Consequently, the second draft of the workshop design had features to accommodate both current and changing needs. It also modeled much of what it taught. The design included:

Airing teacher concerns
Developing individualized objectives with the teachers and for the teachers in each workshop
Using instructional modules
Allowing time for the production of instructional materials and plans to be used back in teachers' classrooms
A follow-up component

Jan received general agreement with the goals and design of the workshop; however, due to time and budget constraints, the full design could not be implemented. "I wish we could but . . ." was the reply to her initial budget, which asked for $5,000 for materials preparation funds and another $5,000 in expenses, mostly for paying substitute teachers to allow the workshop to run for three days during school hours. (The union president liked that idea.)

A compromise was reached. Jan could offer a three-session, 4 p.m. to 6 p.m. workshop (plus dinner paid by the district) if she could beg, borrow, and "adapt" materials and get fifteen teachers to sign up for it. If the workshop was a success, then she and one other person could have two weeks in August to prepare for a workshop to be run in the fall involving one full day (paid) plus follow-up. If that worked, there might be a chance to expand it into what she had originally proposed. (The union president, having taken the position that *all* inservice training should be done on school time, opposed the workshop. Jan persuaded him to limit the opposition to a memo gently advising teachers not to participate. If the memo had any effect, she planned to call several teacher friends and persuade enough of them to sign up to enable the workshop to run; however, that turned out not to be necessary.)

FOCUS—HOW CAN I BE SURE THAT PEOPLE KNOW HOW EFFECTIVE THE WORKSHOP IS? WHO HAS TO BE CONVINCED? (PURPOSE/ AUDIENCE)

Jan sensed that more evaluation work would be in order. Converting the workshop next fall from a brief workshop run after school to a regular and more intensive workshop run during school hours would require a commitment of funds. Even though she was pretty sure her immediate boss would be inclined to support it based solely upon her recommendation, she was sure he'd need more powerful ammunition than her say so. Besides, he'd said to her recently, "Jan, if I gave you everything you asked for, you'd soon have my entire budget and a lot of enemies!" Jan wanted to be sure that the decision of whether or not to continue development was based on reliable information.

Jan called one of her former instructors, Professor Stegman, to check out some of her ideas about how to get that information. After describing the background and workshop objectives she told him that she wanted to do two things: First, get enough evidence to determine whether the workshop was effective enough to continue; and second, determine how to improve the workshop by improving the effectiveness of what was there, deleting anything not needed, and finding out what else was needed. Part of the conversation went something like this:

DESIGN—HOW CAN I GET THE DATA PEOPLE WILL NEED IN ORDER TO DECIDE WHETHER THE WORKSHOP IS WORTH CONTINUING? (ALTERNATIVES)

PROFESSOR: There are several ways you could achieve these evaluation purposes. What have you thought of so far?

JAN: I don't know. I suppose I could do some post-testing or questionnaires or something. Somebody said I should do an attitude survey.

PROFESSOR: Is an attitude survey going to tell you if the workshop is effective enough to continue or how to make it better?

JAN: It would tell me something, but I need more than that.

PROFESSOR: That's what I thought. Now, what kind of data can you get easily?

JAN: I don't understand what you're asking.

PROFESSOR: I'm asking about sources of information. For example, how could you tell what materials the teachers make in the workshop?

JAN: That's easy! I could just look?

PROFESSOR: And having looked, you could write down what you saw. That's one source of information. Now, how could you tell if they used those materials?

JAN: I could go look, I guess. But I don't really have time to go running all over the district all the time.

PROFESSOR: What else could you do . . . call them? Have them send you reports?

JAN: I suppose. But that sounds like a lot of work.

PROFESSOR: Look—we'll never get anywhere if you keep doing "yes-buts."

JAN: Yes, but I've got to be realistic.

PROFESSOR: Okay—now I'll do a "yes-but" to you. Yes—it's got to be realistic. *But* let's get some ideas out before we start shooting 'em down. First—get out the ideas. Then—get realistic. Okay?

JAN: Okay. But we've still . . .

PROFESSOR: . . . got to be realistic! I understand. Now then—can you use a camera? So you could take pictures of teachers using workshop generated materials in their classrooms?

JAN: I suppose I could borrow one.

PROFESSOR: Good. Now we've got surveys, post-tests, lists of materials, as well as inspection of work samples, classroom visits, and pictures. What else?

WHAT DATA DO I NEED AND HOW CAN I GET THEM? (KINDS/PROCEDURE)

The conversation went on like that, exploring possible sources of information to respond to Jan's evaluation questions. They talked about whether answering those questions would satisfy the various people whose support Jan needed to keep the workshop going. They talked about whether the data would help Jan figure out how to improve the workshop. These were the major results of the conversation:

1. They decided that pre- and post-testing would make it possible to tell if the material had been learned by these motivated teachers.
2. The results of an individual planning exercise at the beginning of the workshop would enable them to determine if the workshop had exercises and materials relevant to the individually identified needs. It would also generate information relevant to what else was needed for later workshops or for other projects.
3. Keeping records of the instructional materials and plans developed in the workshop would provide concrete examples of what practical steps teachers take to aid the mainstreaming process.
4. Follow-up visits to classrooms would help determine if teachers were using the materials and implementing the plans. (Jan didn't have time to make special visits, but she often had other business in the schools and could visit the classrooms then.) She planned to take pictures of materials in use, bulletin board progress displays, etc., to show what she saw.
5. Jan planned to hold a (Dutch treat) class reunion luncheon about a month after the workshop and find out how things were going and how participants felt about the workshop and its impact.
6. Professor Stegman suggested keeping track of Media Center materials used by the teachers after the workshop to see if there were changes in the amount and patterns of material they used. (On good terms with the manager of the Media Center, Jan thought she could arrange that with a phone call.)
7. The Professor recommended that the materials and plans generated during the workshop be designed to include pre- and post-testing or other assessment wherever possible so that it would be possible for the teachers, at least, to determine if they were effective.

The Professor suggested an evaluation planning format and volunteered to review the plan Jan developed. He also suggested that she make use of some evaluation checklists, referring to a couple of books she might find useful.

ANALYSIS/ INTERPRETATION—WILL I BE ABLE TO INTERPRET THE DATA ONCE I GET THEM?

Two drafts later, she had the following evaluation design. She sent a copy to the professor, and followed up with a call to discuss it.

Evaluation Worksheet: *Workshop Impact*

Questions	Data Sources and Collection	Analysis
Do the teachers learn specific facts about (a) specific disabilities (b) mainstreaming philosophy and legality and (c) school policy and practices?	Pre- and post-testing	Test results analyzed by item and by participant. Percent correct answers to each item reported.
Do the teachers develop plans and materials consistent with facts, policies, practices, etc.?	Completed materials reviewed by peers in the workshop aided by evaluation checklists.	Percent of criteria met reported by type of material and by participant. Percent of times each criterion is met also tabulated in an item analysis format.
	Completed materials and plans described by numbers and types of children to be impacted and by listing of the instructional objectives or problems dealt with.	Numbers and types of children to be involved tabulated.
Do the teachers implement the plans and use the materials?	Follow-up observations and Dutch Treat lunch	Percent of plans implemented and materials used. Number and types of children affected.
		Results of summaries, e.g., percent of objectives attained.
	Materials usage data collected from the Media Center to determine if usage had increased	Patterns examined to see if teachers select more and/or better materials.
	Materials and plans made by teachers subsequent to the workshop evaluated by the checklist.	Comparisons between materials made during workshop and after workshop.
	Pictures taken in classrooms showing students at work using materials produced in the workshop, relevant bulletin board display (e.g., progress displays of mainstreaming-related items), etc., to provide a visual record of "artifacts" generated by the workshop.	Pictures to be shown or presented with narrative. (This material will also be used in the workshop itself as an overview of what others have done.) Viewers will be asked, "Can you tell which children are benefitting from the mainstreaming experience?"
How do the participants feel about the workshop content, process, and impact?	Dutch Treat lunch	Identify major issues and/or concerns

When Jan called Professor Stegman to talk about the evaluation design, they had a conversation that went something like this:

JAN: What do you think of the evaluation design now?

PROFESSOR: It's a fine effort under the circumstances. You've really come a long way from your initial idea about using an attitude questionnaire! You did a pretty good job with evaluating the impact, too. You have a check on immediate outcomes—you'll be able to tell if they learn the material. You also have a check on whether they continue to use what they learn and what they produce in the workshop.

JAN: Well, thank you! Do you have any other comments?

PROFESSOR: Yes, I'd still like to try to find out if the workshop has any positive effect on kids.

JAN: I'm not sure what more you want. Isn't it enough to show that the workshop graduates help special education kids get accepted by their classmates, provide them with proper instructional materials, and use better materials with regular education kids?

PROFESSOR: Maybe. But what do you mean by "get accepted," "proper materials," and "better materials"?

JAN: That's all laid out. The criteria called for in the evaluation design will get spelled out, and we'll have data to show how well the criteria are achieved.

PROFESSOR: Oh yes. I'd forgotten what good use you make of work sample analysis.

JAN: Work sample analysis—what's that?

PROFESSOR: You do a lot of evaluation by analyzing work samples. You look at samples of the work teachers do in the workshop and at samples of work they do later. I think you'll even look at children's work samples to see if instruction objectives are met.

JAN: Oh sure. I always do that. I just didn't make a big deal out of it.

PROFESSOR: It can be a very good evaluation technique.

JAN: Of course! It's something teachers do all the time.

PROFESSOR: You are right. They do it. But you have to be careful. If your criteria don't result in better student learning, you can totally miss the boat.

JAN: Don't worry. We won't say the materials are better if they just keep the kids busy and out of trouble making mud pies or something!

FOCUS/INTERPRETATION-AM I GOING TO GET THE DATA I NEED TO EVALUATE THE REAL PURPOSE OF THE WORKSHOP? (PURPOSE/QUESTIONS/INTERPRETATION) PROFESSOR: That's reassuring. But if you keep on running this workshop for a while, let me urge you to put more evaluation emphasis on benefits to children. There has to be a limit on what you do during the developmental period of the workshop, but later on I'd press you a lot harder on the issue.

JAN: Oh. Could I bring up another issue?

PROFESSOR: Sure.

FOCUS-IF I DO ALL THAT WILL THE INFORMATION I GET BE WORTH THE EFFORT? (UTILITY) JAN: I still don't like the idea of pre- and post-tests. It'll cause me a lot of extra preparation time to make the tests, and it'll consume valuable workshop time.

PROFESSOR: You are absolutely right. Why not build the testing right into the design, right into the instructional process of the workshop?

JAN: Oh yes. I seem to recall something about that in the instructional design course I took.

PROFESSOR: Maybe you should dust off your notes.

After the conversation Jan did indeed dust off her notes and referred to her old instructional design textbook. She then did the following things:

1. She set aside, as best she could, her own preconceptions of what "they need to know" and made up a criterion test. (The criterion test asked directly what teachers needed to do to be in compliance with relevant policies, law, and instructional practice rather than sampling their knowledge of laws and policies.)
2. She used the criterion test as a diagnostic test for use in individualizing the workshop to match individual needs of teachers. (She planned to develop alternate items for using the test as a post-test, but didn't get that done in time for the first workshop. Due to the open-ended nature of the items, that didn't invalidate the post-test.)
3. She decided to administer and score the post-test during the workshop, recording the results in an item analysis format. Frequently missed items (should they occur)

would be used to form remedial groups. Teachers who missed items would engage in remedial work, then verbally demonstrate mastery. (She had thought it a good idea to teach formative evaluation of student performance in the workshop, and this provided an experiential learning demonstration.)
4. She began to believe something the professor had said: "A well-designed workshop is easy to evaluate." She began to wonder if the other half of his statement wasn't true also: "If a workshop is hard to evaluate, it's not well-designed!"

INTERPRETATION—HOW CAN I TELL WHETHER WHAT THE TEACHERS PRODUCE IS ANY GOOD? (CRITERIA) The hardest work in implementing the design was developing the checklists for evaluating the materials teachers prepared and classroom procedures they implemented as a result of the workshop. She located some checklists and statements of criteria. She wasn't quite satisfied with them and wasn't sure the teachers would accept them, so she decided to incorporate the problem into the workshop. As the introduction to exercises on the design of materials (and other exercises on the design of classroom procedures) she would present a couple of sample checklists for evaluating those materials. Teachers would be asked to (a) modify the lists according to their own beliefs about criteria of "goodness" and (b) add to the lists to emphasize special items for mainstreamed students. And, it occurred to Jan that the teachers were likely to accept, understand, and use criteria they had a hand in generating.

The results of the evaluation were reported interactively. Some of the pictures of materials in use were put on a bulletin board display near Jan's office in the administration building. An adjacent bulletin board displayed the list of materials developed and procedures that had been implemented. She arranged to be standing near the bulletin boards occasionally when key individuals came down the hall. It was only natural for her to strike up a conversation about the bulletin boards and the workshop!

REPORTING—HOW CAN I SHOW PEOPLE THE RESULTS EASILY AND IN A USEFUL WAY? (CONTENT/DELIVERY) Six weeks after the workshop the evaluation data were summarized in a two-page memo sent to the administrative committee who reviewed Jan's proposal for further development of the workshop. The data showed that all of the teachers met the learning objectives and prepared materials successfully in the workshop. Thirteen of fifteen teachers used the materials in their classrooms. (One teacher entered the hospital and one family moved so that the mainstreamed child left the classroom.) Eight teachers had evidence of successful use of the materials and five reported undocumented successes. Six teachers had developed additional materials and five others said they intended to do so in the future. And so on. The data showed that the teachers had liked the workshop, used what they had learned, and that children's educational experiences seemed to have been affected for the better.

The data also indicated some problem areas and Jan's

proposal showed how she planned to modify the workshop to improve it.

She arranged to follow the memo with an appearance before the administrative committee to discuss the evaluation and the proposal for further development. The proposal was approved; however, Jan was urged to check with other districts in the area to find out what they were doing and, perhaps, combine forces in some way to reduce costs.

* * * * *

DISCUSSION QUESTIONS AND TOPICS

1. Do you believe that the information described in the beginning of the case justified the conclusion that a workshop on mainstreaming was needed? Or did it just suggest that "something" needed to be done, e.g., establish a better public relations program?
2. Do you think Jan interviewed the right people about her "first draft" objectives? Did she overlook any important group?
3. What do you think of her "Here's what I plan to do— What do you think of it?" evaluation strategy? Is it likely to get useful information? Do you think she is running too great a risk of biasing the information she gets toward "That's nice, Jan!" rather than critical comments? If so, what might she do to counteract the bias? (Hint: Consider who she asks and review her interview protocol before answering.)
4. If you had been Jan, would you have decided to use evaluation to help justify the expansion of the workshop? (Or would you have taken a more political approach? Or would you just have gone on to run the workshop, hoping others would somehow make a wise decision?)
5. The professor helped Jan identify some inexpensive and easy-to-obtain sources of data—can you think of other information they could have gotten?
6. Do you think Jan and the professor gave up too easily on getting child change data? Or do you agree that doing so might have been premature or too costly?
7. What do you think of Jan's tactic of asking teachers, as part of the workshop, to develop evaluation checklists for the materials they were planning to use in their classrooms? What are some potential advantages of having the teachers develop their own checklists? What are some of the disadvantages or risks?

SUGGESTIONS FOR STIMULATING DISCUSSIONS

1. Ask a small group to imagine that they are the administrative committee that has to decide whether or not to continue and expand the workshop. They should discuss the matter, make a decision, and write a memo to Jan (copy to her boss) stating the decision and their reasons for it. (Alternatively, the memo could ask for specific additional items of information to help them make their decision.)
2. Arrange for someone to do a brief presentation on "Good evaluation practices shown in the case."
3. Arrange for someone to do a brief presentation on "Good educational practices shown in the case."
4. Arrange for someone to do a brief presentation on "Suggestions for improving the adequacy and usefulness of the evaluation."
5. Arrange a debate: Resolved: Well designed workshops will be easy to evaluate.
6. Identify one or two turning points or major decision points in the case. Then have people prepare to take on the role of key persons in the case and role play a discussion they might have.
7. Prepare, then discuss and criticize the case from several value perspectives. The discussion could take the form of a role play, each person representing a particular value perspective or bias (e.g., "It ought to be economical and get results!" "It ought to serve the needs of children!" "It ought to reflect standard educational practices." "It ought to be comparable to what the best schools do!" "It ought to be methodically sound!" "I don't care how marvelous your intentions are, don't confuse needs with results—and I want to hear about results!" "It ought to be consistent with the latest educational and psychological research!")

APPLICATION EXERCISES

1. Read some of the material in the *Sourcebook* indicated by the asides. Then suggest alternative things people in the case might have done at several points in the case. Or suggest a whole new approach they might have taken.
2. Using the case as a model (and foil) and your suggested alternatives as guides, design an evaluation for a situation or problem similar to that shown in the case.
3. Using Chapter 7 of the *Sourcebook* as a guide, do a meta-evaluation and critique of the case (and/or your evaluation design).
4. Use the *Design Manual* to develop an improved evaluation design for the case.
5. Use the *Design Manual* to develop an evaluation design for a situation or problem similar to the one described in the case.

CASE L-3:

THE STAFF OF A RESOURCE CENTER ASKS: How Can We Find Out Why Our Learning Center Isn't Working As Well As We'd Like?

Ann L. Hallawell

FOCUS—WHAT IS THE SETTING? (CONTEXT)   Last year the Superintendent and the School Board of the Inner City School District (ICSD) established as one of their three-year goals the improvement of services to exceptional children. Federal, state, and local resources were expected to diminish over this three-year period. The superintendent and the board agreed that effective staff development, reaching all regular and special teachers, was an essential step toward reaching their goals; and they were prepared to commit additional monies in support of this goal, even in the face of federal cuts.

FOCUS—WHAT WILL BE EVALUATED? (OBJECT) One component of the broad scale staff development program that was undertaken in the district was a learning center for teachers. The learning center was established in an empty classroom of an elementary building centrally located among the district's 56 school buildings. It was implemented as a means of meeting the individual needs of ICSD teachers who work with special ed students. The teachers in the district had often complained of the difficulties they experienced while working with these kids in regular classrooms. A survey conducted by the district indicated that teachers could benefit from such a center where they could receive training for working with new materials, strategies for working with kids, and help from a consultant on an individual basis for problems that they were having. The superintendent and the school board for the ICSD agreed to financially support the learning center for two years.

Dorothy Weber, one of the codirectors of the learning center is providing an orientation for two teachers who are at the learning center for the first time.

"This is where we keep our samples of newly published materials and books that we've been given for preview. They can be checked out if you'd like to take any of them home with you. And over here are our reading and math skills boxes. We have activities, worksheets, etc., for all skill levels with competency materials at the end of each level. These materials for reading and math are all teacher-made here in the district, and you're welcome to photocopy them. We'd be delighted to display any materials that you'd like to share with other teachers, too, so feel free to bring things in to us whenever you like. We're always looking for new ideas."

"One of the teachers in my building was here last week," one of the visiting teachers began, *"He came back to school with 30 old pressure gauges. His kids are using them in the robots they're building, and they love them."*

"Those were given to us by the water purification plant. We're given all kinds of things that are seemingly useless. Sometimes we're given new things, too, like the movie theater gave us 500 popcorn boxes. Teachers have been using them for all kinds of things, and for all of the kids in their classrooms, not just the special ed kids. So you see, we have things for you to read, to take, to make. We'd be glad to provide you with instruction for using anything you see here. There's a laminating machine in the back that you should feel free to use, and our brochure will give you information about our hours, special classes, and the like. Please spend as much time here as you like. I'm here to help you in any way that I can."

FOCUS—WHAT NEEDS TO BE IMPROVED? (PURPOSE) As the orientation ended, a familiar face appeared in the doorway.

"Well, Charlie, Hi!" Dorothy was truly glad to see Charlie White, the district staff development coordinator. He was an advocate of the learning center and dropped in frequently to see how things were going.

"Dorothy, Fran, how's it going?"

"Actually, Charlie, things are a bit slow around here." Fran began.

"Too slow for our liking, anyway." Dorothy added, "We're glad you're here. We'd like to talk to you about it. Can you stay for a bit?"

"Sure, in fact, I'm here because there are some things that I need to discuss with the two of you."

Charlie had been receiving some complaints about the learning center through his contacts with the building level staff development representatives. The complaints ranged from the materials being oriented toward elementary use only to complaints that the center's hours weren't convenient.

Dorothy and Fran reported to Charlie that not many people had been using the center. Certain individuals were "regulars" but there were some schools in the district where none of the teachers had ever come to visit the center. Occasionally there would be a spurt of heavy use but those times were infrequent (between Thanksgiving and Christmas a large number of teachers stopped by looking for holiday ideas). Fran also reported that she was frustrated when she was unable to provide teachers with as much help as they were asking for—she felt as though she needed a consultant to turn to herself. Fran, Dorothy and Charlie were all committed to making the learning center work. They felt that the concept itself had great potential, it just wasn't being used to its capacity.

From their own observations and from the complaints that Charlie had received, they formulated a plan to get information about the "why's" and the "what-to-do-about's" the following problems:

a. Not enough teachers were making an initial visit to the center.
b. Not enough teachers were making return visits to the center.
c. Procedures for the center's operation were, perhaps, not appropriate.
d. The curricular contents of the center, were perhaps, not sufficient.

FOCUS/COLLECTION—WHAT DO WE NEED TO KNOW? HOW CAN WE GET THE INFORMATION? (QUESTIONS, KIND OF INFORMATION, PROCEDURES) They began to discuss and list the kinds of information that would lead them to methods of solving these problems and ways to get that information. They outlined the plan in table 1.

DESIGN—CAN WE GET THE INFORMATION READILY? (COMPONENTS/ APPROPRIATENESS) As a set, the information collection procedures looked as though they would be easy to implement. Most

Table 1. Plan for Resource Center

PROBLEM	QUESTIONS TO ANSWER	INFORMATION COLLECTION PROCEDURES
A. Not enough teachers were making an initial visit to the center	—how was the center being publicized? —what methods of publicity seemed to be most effective?	—examination of publicity procedures and procedures that were available within the district —survey of teachers, "Have you heard about the center? How did you hear? Would you use? Why or why not?"
B. Not enough teachers who did come were making return visits to the center	—what were the characteristics of "successful" use of the center? —what were the characteristics of "unsuccessful" use of the center?	—interviews of one-time users and repeat users —analysis of feedback forms completed by users —analysis of information from suggestion box —examination of attendance records, look for patterns (school representation, etc.)
C. Procedures for the center's operation were, perhaps, inappropriate	—what were the center's operating procedures? —what operating procedures were used by "successful" materials centers in other districts and/or topical areas	—examination of the center's policies and procedures —interview one-time users and repeat users to determine appropriateness/convenience of center's procedures —interview directors of materials centers in other districts to describe their operating procedures
D. The curricular contents of the center were, perhaps, insufficient	—what was the curricular breakdown of the center's contents? —what was the grade level breakdown of the center's contents?	—content analysis of the center's materials —examination of procedures for solicitation of donated materials (look for balance/or lack of)

of them required examination of already existing information (attendance records from the center, policy and procedure review). Fran, Dorothy and Charlie would have to "go out" to collect minimal information. For most procedures, they already had the information they wanted or it was right at their fingertips (the content analysis of the center's materials, for example). There would be some surveying/interviewing work to be done, but they didn't anticipate that it would be a lengthy nor a time-consuming process. Fran, Dorothy and Charlie began to outline a time/ task chart to gather this information.

COLLECTION—WHAT WORKSHEETS, QUESTIONNAIRES. ETC. DO WE NEED? (PROCEDURES/ INSTRUMENTS)

Charlie felt that he could design a questionnaire that would address problem a, b and c. The questionnaire would begin with a "Have you heard of?" kind of question and branch out depending on the teacher's response. If the teacher had not heard of the center, that would be the end; if he/she had, the questionnaire would attempt to find out through what means the teacher had heard, what sort of impact hearing had had on the teacher, and whether or not the teacher had ever been to the learning center. If the teacher had never

been to the center, a set of questions would be posed to find out why (was it because the times were inconvenient?) If the teacher had been to the learning center, how many times would be asked, as well as whether he/she plan to go back. What did the teacher like and dislike about the center? Charlie planned for the questionnaire to end with open space for the teachers to write in their own suggestions for improving the services of the center. Although this questionnaire description that Charlie posed sounded long to both Fran and Dorothy, he assured them that he could design a branching questionnaire that would not be too lengthy. The trio realized that a questionnaire like this that addressed all of these areas would be time efficient, since there seemed to be no need to conduct interviews of one-time and repeat users.

MANAGEMENT—WHO DOES WHAT WHEN? (ORGANIZATION OF TASKS)

Charlie also took on the responsibility of outlining both the center's and the district's publicity procedures/options since that could be done for the most part from outside the physical boundaries of the center. Fran and Dorothy split up the remaining tasks. They decided that they would be able to get one of their parent volunteers to gather the solicitation/donation of materials information.

Their discussion closed with the time/task breakdown chart shown in table 2.

COLLECTION—HOW CAN WE BE SURE THE QUESTIONNAIRE WORKS BEFORE WE SEND IT TO EVERYONE? By the time two weeks had passed the evaluation work was well underway. As Charlie worked through the process of developing the questionnaire, he tried it out periodically on a few teachers to work out the bugs. That process was helpful to him in assuring that the questions were written properly and that the directions were easy to follow. When Charlie felt comfortable with the questionnaire's content and format, he sent copies through the ICSD mail system to every tenth teacher as their names appeared in the ICSD staff directory. He had attached to each questionnaire a cover letter indicating that the information would be used to improve the services/operation of the learning center. He also provided directions for returning the completed questionnaires to his office through the ICSD mail by February 16. Also in the cover letter he assured the teachers that their responses would be seen only by himself and the co-directors of the learning center. He wanted the teachers to be candid and to feel confident that neither their building principals nor other administrators would see their responses.

ANALYSIS/ INTERPRETATION—HOW CAN WE PULL THE INFORMATION TOGETHER TO SEE WHAT WE HAVE? For Charlie's other task he had developed a list of all publicity procedures that were commonly used in the ICSD, then used it as a checklist to indicate which of the procedures had been used by the learning center (see table 3).

Charlie wanted to save this checklist information to use a comparison with the questionnaire results on how the teachers had heard about the learning center.

Dorothy had examined all of the feedback forms that users had turned in since the center had opened. Some users had been compulsive about completing a form each time they came, others had not. The form itself contained three open ended questions followed by a space for comments:

what did you do while you were here?
was it useful?
do you expect to use it in your classroom?

Dorothy was able to sort the responses to the first question into categories that paralleled the functions of the learning center:

receive training with materials
learn strategies for working with students
receive help with an individual problem

What Dorothy found was that most teachers (who completed the feedback forms) came to the learning center for group activities rather than individual help. Most teachers thought their experiences were useful and expected to use what they had learned in their classrooms

Table 2. Time/Task Breakdown Chart

PROCEDURE	PERSON RESPONSIBLE	TIMELINE
1. Survey of teachers	Charlie	Feb 2–Feb 27
2. Outline of publicity procedures and options	Charlie	Feb 2–Feb 13
3. Analysis of feedback forms	Dorothy	Feb 2–Feb 6
4. Analysis of suggestions box info	Dorothy	Feb 9–Feb 13
5. Analysis of attendance record	Fran	Feb 2–Feb 6
6. Outline of Center procedures	Fran	Feb 9–Feb 13
7. Content analysis of materials	Fran & Dorothy	Feb 2–Feb 20
8. Outline of materials donation/solicitation process	Parent volunteer	by Feb 20
9. Review of other "successful" materials centers' procedures	Dorothy	by Feb 27

Table 3. Checklists of Procedures

TYPES OF AVAILABLE PUBLICITY	HOW/WHEN USED BY LEARNING CENTER
Bulletin board display in central office	last September
TV	
Radio	
Open meetings	
Presentations to groups (PTA, etc.)	
Leaflets	sent brochures to each building mentioned in staff development newsletter
Newsletters	
Memos	
Publications	
Multi-media presentations	
School board presentations	
Training sessions	
Announcements for staff members	
Announcements in paychecks	

(whether they actually did or not Dorothy had no way of knowing). Many teachers who had come for individual help had written in their comments.

The suggestion box, over the months, had collected only a few slips of paper, and Dorothy felt those were not crucial to improving the operations/services of the learning center. They contained comments like, "It would be nice if coffee were available," and "It's too hot in here." But, Fran disagreed. She felt those comments, although few, were important to consider. She felt that anything they could do to make the learning center a more pleasant environment would be to their advantage.

Analysis of the learning center's attendance records showed that of the 263 teachers that had come to the center, 74% had made at least one return visit, 35% had been to the center more than five times. It seemed to Fran that if more teachers were encouraged, or enticed, to visit just once many of them would would come back again on their own.

FOCUS—JUST WHAT PARTS OF THE LEARNING CENTER DO WE NEED TO LOOK AT? (OBJECT)

After examining the attendance records, Fran moved on to the procedures under which the center operated (see table 4).

Functions:

1. Provide training for teachers to work with materials
2. Provide teachers with strategies for working with special needs students
3. Provide consultation to teachers

Functions 1 and 2 are regularly scheduled activities as well as being offered by request

Function 3 is available on request

Functions 1 to 3 are available on a group or individual basis

Fran and Dorothy worked together to produce an inventory of the center's contents. Table 5 shows an estimate (in percentages) of their materials by curriculum and grade level range.

The learning center had only one volunteer while this information was being collected. He agreed to outline the process used to obtain recyclable materials for the center. The next day he handed Fran the following description:

Solicit donations Spread need by word of mouth to store owners, industry workers, etc. Ask PTA members to help spread word.

Pick-up When someone calls in with a donation make arrangements to go pick them up (within a week)

Maintain contact Send a thank you letter to anyone that makes a donation asking them to keep us in mind when they have other things.

Dorothy spent part of the next day on the telephone talking with the directors of three other materials centers.

Table 4. Procedures under which the Center Operates

PROCEDURE	SPECIFICS
Hours	10 am–5 pm M, T, TH 12 pm–5 pm W 9 am–5 pm F
Staff	2 teacher consultants 1 teacher aide parent volunteers (1–3 per semester)
Contents	text books student materials recyclable materials consumable supplies (paper, etc.) records, tapes laminating supplies

One was primarily an educational media center in a large down-state district; one was the teachers' resource center at a private college in the state capital; and one was the special education clearinghouse operating in the largest urban district in-state. Common knowledge recognized all three as outstanding, but Dorothy had called the State Department of Education just to confirm her notions.

ANALYSIS/ INTERPRETATION—WHAT DID WE LEARN BY COLLECTING ALL THIS INFORMATION?

Charlie began to receive the completed questionnaires. Quickly he sent a memorandum to each of the expected respondents reminding them to return the questionnaires to him as soon as possible. By March 3 he had 67% of the questionnaires back, and he began tabulating the frequencies of response.

The responses Charlie had tabulated from the returned questionnaires indicated that over 83% of the respondents had heard of the learning center.

Table 5. Estimate of Materials in Resource Center by Curriculum and Grade Level Range

Curriculum Area	Grade Range				
	1–3	4–6	7–9	10–12	Total
Reading	21	7	2		30%
Math	16	12	2		30%
Science	1	5	10	4	20%
Social Studies		2	4		6%
Health	2			1	3%
Career Awareness	1	2	2		5%
Physical Ed.	1				1%
Music	1				1%
Art	1	2			3%
Other	1				1%
Total	45%	30%	20%	5%	100%

"Well, that doesn't surprise me," Frank remarked. "Your outline of our publicity procedure shows we've sent our brochures to every school in the district."

"But, that certainly raises some other questions," Charlie began. "If we're doing such a good job with publicity, why haven't more teachers been here?"

The questionnaire showed that even though the respondents had heard of the learning center, many had no interest in checking it out for themselves. They just weren't interested. Respondents who had been to the center were enthusiastic about their visits, were satisfied with the help/ services they'd received there, and had definite plans of returning.

"Getting the word out doesn't seem to be our biggest downfall, as we'd expected," Dorothy commented. "We've got a pretty high percentage of teachers who come for a second time once they've been here to see what we have to offer."

"There's something funny about that, though," Fran added.

"The outlines of the center's procedures and the process for soliciting materials don't seem to tell us anything we didn't already know," Charlie raised his eyebrows.

"And," Fran added, "We can see by the content analysis of our stock that the secondary teachers' complaints about the scarcity of materials suitable for their use is valid. But,

look at this," Fran points to a section of the results from the feedback forms, "Elementary teachers are also saying that we don't have relevant materials. I don't understand that. We stock lots of elementary materials in the basics."

From her sometimes rambling inquiries with the other materials centers, Dorothy had learned that these three centers operated somewhat differently. Their open hours were shifted toward the evenings, staying open until 6:00 p.m usually. One stayed open until 9:00 p.m. on Mondays and reported lots of business then. Materials check-out policies differed, and all three reported more service offered in custom, center-staff developed materials.

"It seems to me," Dorothy began, "that what we've learned from all of this is that there's a lot more we need to learn."

REPORTING—HOW CAN WE SUMMARIZE, FOR OURSELVES, WHAT WE'VE LEARNED AND WHAT WE SHOULD DO NEXT?

As they waded through the results of their efforts, they kept in mind their original objective of responding to the four problems they had identified. They interpreted the meanings of the data as best they could and attempted to determine their significance as they outline recommendations for solving the four problems (see table 6).

Their decision to collect more information seemed an

Table 6. Recommendations for Solving Resource Center Problems

PROBLEM	INFORMATION SOURCE	RESPONSE/RECOMMENDED ACTION
A. Not enough teachers were making an initial visit to the center	Outline of publicity procedures/ options Questionnaire	Most teachers are aware of the center's existence, but there seems to be a lack of interest. Further information is needed to determine why lack of interest exists.
B. Not enough teachers who did come were making return visits to the center	Attendance records Feedback forms Questionnaire	This does not seem to be a problem. The revisit rate is actually very high. (The initial visit rate is the one that is low)
C. Procedures for the center's operation were, perhaps, inappropriate	Outline of center's procedures Questionnaire Suggestion box Outline of donation/solicitation procedure Discussion with other centers	Procedures seem ok on the surface, but this may have something to do with the low initial attendance. Hours may be changed and services modified, but further information is needed to determine the best local operations.
D. The curricular contents of the center were, perhaps, insufficient	Content analysis of center's materials Feedback forms	Materials are not sufficient for the upper grade levels. Develop procedures for obtaining more materials from publishers, teachers, etc. Also, even though materials seem sufficient for elementary grades teachers have indicated otherwise. Further information is needed to determine why they feel this way.

obvious one to them. Just how to do that became the issue.

"Another questionnaire might do the trick," Charlie offered.

"Maybe, Charlie." Dorothy presented her own feelings on the subject. "But the questionnaire we used before has done little except to raise more questions that we don't have the answers to."

FOCUS—WHAT ELSE DO WE NEED TO KNOW TO SOLVE THE PROBLEMS WE STARTED WITH? (QUESTIONS)

"I think Dorothy might be right," Fran began. "What I'd really like to do is talk to some people about these questions we still can't answer. I'd like to ask the teachers who've never been here why and what kinds of things we could do to encourage them."

"That's it!" Dorothy's excitement became apparent. "Talking to people to get firsthand, from-the-horse's-mouth, as it were, information. I think it's a great idea. I'd like to talk to the elementary teachers who think we don't have materials—I could explain to them that we really do."

"Hold on a minute." Charlie presented a danger signal. "If you're talking about interviewing people to get information, I'll go along with that; but let's not get defensive about what we've got, what we do with it, or anything else like that. If there are teachers who think we don't have enough materials, there must be a reason for that. Let's find out why. We can't treat the illness until it's been diagnosed properly."

COLLECTION—HOW SHOULD WE GET THE INFORMATION?

Dorothy, seeing Charlie's point backed down. "Guess you're right about the posture we should or shouldn't take in these interviews, so let's do them the right way, but let's do them" (see table 7).

With this plan laid out they began making contacts and scheduling interviews. They also outlined the kinds of questions they would ask leaving enough flexibility to respond to circumstances as they arose during the interviews.

Those three weeks passed quickly for Fran, Dorothy and Charlie. They took turns visiting the district, all the while gaining more insight to respond to the original four problems they'd identified at the center.

ANALYSIS/ INTERPRETATION—WHAT DID WE LEARN FROM THIS NEW INFORMATION?

During the interviewing process, Fran, Dorothy and Charlie had each kept notes in their own styles. When all of the interviews had been completed, they sorted the responses they had gathered into like categories. Five of the categories contained substantially more responses than the others:

a. comments/complaints about the materials
b. perceptions of what the learning center is from those who've not been there
c. principals' attitude descriptions of their teachers who frequent the center

Table 7. Persons to Interview about Resource Center

PERSON(S) TO INTERVIEW	WHY/RATIONALE	PERSON RESPONSIBLE	HOW/METHOD USED
Teachers from building where no one has ever been to the learning center	find out why they've never come	Fran	group interview at one of their teachers' meetings
Questionnaire respondents who said they'd heard of the learning center but had never come	find out why interest/ motivation is so low	Dorothy	telephone interviews
Principals from buildings where there are a number of repeat users	find out if those teachers are self-motivated or if there is encouragement from the principal	Charlie	personal interviews or phone interviews
Teachers in the center right after they've finished a group presentation	find out why they came, if they were satisfied with what the center had to offer and why/ why not	Dorothy	group interview held at the center
Teachers who reported on questionnaire that there are insufficient materials for elementary grades	find out if they just had trouble locating them or what they wanted that they couldn't find	Fran	telephone interviews

d. principals' attitudes toward the center
e. comments/complaints about the ease of using the learning center

"Now do we have enough information to respond to our four problems?" queried Fran, sounding a bit impatient.

"Those interviews were interesting all right, but they were really a lot of tiring work.

"Putting all of the interview information into a common set of topics wasn't easy either," Charlie added. "But we did it because we really wanted to know the answer. I think we'll find that it's been worth it."

"I hope you're right, Charlie," Fran responded. "Now let's see what we've got here."

REPORTING—HOW CAN WE SUMMARIZE WHAT WE'VE LEARNED AND WHAT WE SHOULD DO NEXT? WHO ELSE SHOULD BE INFORMED? They spent three hours looking at all of the information they had gathered. They discussed their meanings, the significance of each and what effect they would or could potentially have on the learning center. Using this information to address their original four problems they developed recommendations to help alleviate the problems and jotted down notes about who would be responsible for which recommendations and when (see table 8).

"I think you two should begin right away to schedule demonstrations of our services in the schools," Charlie suggested.

"I'm sure we could get ourselves on the agendas of some of the regularly scheduled teachers' meetings so that we wouldn't be an extra burden." Dorothy's enthusiasm was building. "By taking our services to them for a demonstration we can do some real face-to-face selling of our center, build interest, and hopefully improve our attendance."

"Great idea!" Fran agreed. "At the same time we can try to get more materials in other than the basic subject areas for our elementary teachers. We've already begun to collect more things for secondary use based upon the results of the original questionnaire."

"But there's still one problem area that we haven't addressed," Charlie reminded them. "I'm not sure what we can do about the complaints from the outlying schools that we're too far away for them."

"We're smack dab in the middle of the district. What more can we do?" asked Fran.

"Maybe nothing, at least just yet," was Charlie's response.

As they talked, they decided to develop a plan over the next couple of months for providing the center's services to the outlying schools. Perhaps a mobile unit, perhaps weekly visits to the schools on a rotating basis—that would mean closing the center one day a week. They weren't sure what their plan would be yet—they would keep thinking. In the meantime, if they could boost interest in the center enough in those outlying schools, maybe the teachers would be sufficiently curious about the center to make the drive into town. They'd have to wait and see.

Table 8. Recommendations to Solve Resource Center Problems

PROBLEM	RECOMMENDED ACTION	IMPLEMENTATION OF RECOMMENDED ACTION	
		WHEN	WHO
Not enough teachers were making an initial visit to the center	Schedule demonstrations of the learning center's services right in the schools.	Begin scheduling one demonstration per week immediately	Dorothy
Not enough teachers were making an additional visit to the center	Improve environment at the learning center by making available coffee and tea, and by monitoring the thermostat.	Immediately	Fran
Procedures for the center's operation were, perhaps, insufficient	Shift center hours into the evening except on Fridays. Develop a plan for making the learning center more easily available to outlying schools.	Bi-weekly meetings to discuss options	Fran, Dorothy, Charlie, Representatives from outlying schools
The curricular contents of the center were, perhaps, insufficient	Collect materials in support subject areas at elementary grade levels. Continue to collect materials at secondary grade levels in all subject areas.	Personal contacts during building demonstrations. Contacts with publishers should be ongoing.	Fran, Dorothy

The trio shared their findings with building principals as they scheduled visits, and teachers as they held demonstrations in the outlying schools.

Charlie, Fran and Dorothy could see that this process of evaluating the learning center was not over. In fact, it appeared to be a system for gathering information that would be useful for making subtle changes in their program on an ongoing basis as warranted. They could sense that this process would help them grow and adapt to changing needs in the future years.

* * * * *

DISCUSSION QUESTIONS AND TOPICS

1. What do you think of the list of four problems the learning center staff began with? Are they too narrowly focused? Or are they about right to guide a useful and feasible small scale evaluation effort?
2. What do you think of the evaluation questions they asked about each problem area? (Try adding one or two evaluation questions for each problem and notice how the new questions might change the evaluation. And notice whether you believe your questions would have been better questions.)
3. Some school based evaluators caution against overuse of questionnaires arguing that if you send out questionnaires freely for every little evaluation problem you bury people's willingness to fill them out carefully under an avalanche of badly constructed questionnaires. In view of that caution, the data they actually received, and possibilities for getting similar information in other ways, do you believe using the questionnaire was a good idea?
4. Look at the recommendations the staff came up with. Do they appear reasonable and justified by the data?
5. Notice that much of the evaluation work went into "describing the object" i.e. describing the learning center, how it operated, what services it offered, and what materials it had. Do you think of that as a waste of time, writing down what they already know? Do you think of it as something they should have done already as part of operating and managing the center? Were you surprised that it was a major part of the work?
6. Notice that two of the evaluation questions weren't answered in any obvious way. (What were the characteristics of successful use of the center? What were the characteristics of unsuccessful use of the center.) Why do you suppose they weren't answered?
7. Describing the characteristics of "successful" and "unsuccessful" cases can be a very simple and powerful evaluation tactic. Given the purposes for the evaluation, do you believe the (probably unconscious) decision to not pursue the questions was a good one? Do you think that they should pursue those questions later, perhaps for some other purpose?

SUGGESTIONS FOR STIMULATING DISCUSSIONS ABOUT THE CASE

1. Organize a debate. Resolved: The evaluation practices shown in the case should be incorporated into the ongoing routine for managing the center. (Hint: The affirmative side might suggest ways for further advertising, needs assessment, and follow-up data collection could be combined with normal service activities. The negative side might argue that stopping to take a critical/evaluative look from a fresh perspective is too valuable to risk being lost by co-opting evaluation into data-based management.)
2. Arrange for someone to do a brief representation on "good evaluation practices" shown in the case. (Hint: Emphasize the orderly process from problem to question to data collection and interpretation to recommend action.)
3. Arrange for someone to do a brief presentation on "hidden value perspectives" in the case. (Hint: Consider the lack of questioning of the need for the center. Consider also the recommendation for providing coffee and tea—a relevant debate topic would be: Resolved: School funds should not be expended to encourage and model for our children the ingestion of drugs or other harmful substances.)
4. Identify one or two turning points or major decision points in the case. Then have people prepare to take on the role of key persons in the case and role play a discussion they might have.
5. Prepare, then discuss and criticize the case from several value perspectives. The discussion could take the form of a role play, each person representing a particular value perspective or bias (e.g., "It ought to be economical and get results?" "It ought to serve the needs of children!" "It ought to reflect standard educational practices." "It ought to be comparable to what the best schools do!" "It ought to be methodologically sound!" "I don't care how marvelous your intentions are, don't confuse needs with results—and I want to hear about results!" "It ought to be consistent with the latest educational and psychological research!")

APPLICATION EXERCISES

1. Read some of the material in the *Sourcebook* indicated by the asides. Then suggest alternative things people in the case might have done at several points in the case. Or suggest a whole new approach they might have taken.
2. Using the case as a model (and foil) and your suggested alternatives as guides, design an evaluation for a situation or problem similar to that shown in the case.
3. Using Chapter 7 of the *Sourcebook* as a guide, do a meta-evaluation and critique of the case (and/or your evaluation design).
4. Use the *Design Manual* to develop an improved evaluation design for the case.
5. Use the *Design Manual* to develop an evaluation design for a situation or problem similar to the one described in the case.

CASE L-4

PROJECT STAFF MEMBERS (AND A SUPER-INTENDENT) ASK: How can we tell if our developmentally impaired/multiply handicapped students are making educational progress? Is our project for computer assisted management of IEPs helping?

Dale Brethower

FOCUS—WHAT IS THE SETTING? (CONTEXT) The Oakview Intermediate School District provides a variety of educational services to ten local school districts. One of those services is Project Proof. Funded by federal, state and local sources and based at the District's Westwood Center for developmentally impaired and multiply handicapped persons, Project Proof evolved from efforts of a consortium and educational leaders from several districts who wanted to develop a comprehensive set of curricular objectives for severely and multiply handicapped children.

THE ADMINISTRATOR'S POINT OF VIEW

FOCUS—WHAT WILL BE EVALUATED? (OBJECT) The Assistant Superintendent for Special Education, Orville Johnson, was very interested in Project Proof, hoping it would help him with two major problems he faced in ensuring the adequacy of special education services:

The first problem was complaints from teachers that they were asked to do the impossible. They had to be lawyers, diplomats, caretakers, materials designers, teachers, record keepers, report writers, team players, assertive leaders and dynamic models while good naturedly taking time away from their own families for inservice training to get prepared to do even more. Balancing these demands was a fundamental problem for all personnel. Project Proof could contribute at least a partial solution by helping teachers with the painstaking endeavors of identifying objectives for each child's IEP and providing instruction tailored to those objectives.

FOCUS—WHAT ARE THE MAJOR EVALUATION QUESTIONS THE SUPERINTENDENT HAS? (QUESTIONS) The second problem was Orville's difficulty in getting answers to three apparently simple questions:

where is each child in terms of educational achievement, goals and progress?
how effective is each classroom?
how effective is each program or school?

HOW IT WORKED

FOCUS—WHAT ARE THE MAJOR PARTS OF PROJECT PROOF? (OBJECT) Project Proof consisted of seven major components (see table 1).

Table 1. Seven Major Components of Project Proof

COMPONENT	PURPOSE
The Project Proof (as a whole)	To provide a system teachers can use to improve efficiency of the individual educational planning process, the quality of the plans and the measured educational growth of the children.
Computer services	To provide time efficient services for composing IEP's and monitoring achievement of individual students and sets of students.
The Objectives catalog	To be a resource in which (trained) teachers can efficiently locate objectives appropriate to the curriculum and to the individual.
Workshop	To provide teachers with knowledge, skills, and techniques sufficient to use the objectives system efficiently and accurately.
Administrative support	To provide teachers with the logistical support, tools and materials necessary to use the objectives system efficiently and accurately.
Cumulative process report: individuals	To display information regarding current status (past achievements, current objectives, dates of achievement) of individuals in a clear, readable and easily updated form.
On-Site coordinator's training meetings	To provide a vehicle whereby the coordinators from each district can be trained so solve problems encountered in each district, use and disseminate new techniques, etc., and improve the overall functioning of the system.

FOCUS—WHAT PARTS OF THE PROJECT HAVE BEEN EVALUATED? (OBJECT) During the first few years of operation, the project staff concentrated on several activities under the leadership of the Director, Cynthia Fairchild. One was to establish the objectives catalog. First, objectives were written for each of several different content areas and organized within these content areas to make them more useful, accessible, and comprehensible. Each objective that went into the computer-assisted system was evaluated by teachers and other professionals as to specificity, clarity, and face validity. Second, different ways of getting information into and out of the computer were tried and cumbersome methods discarded. Input and output formats were revised and simplified to increase ease and utility while reducing errors. Third, workshops were designed and delivered to train teachers at different sites to use the system.

The staff viewed Project Proof as a system. The computer services and objectives catalog were intended to be resources for teachers; the workshop provided training for using the resources; and the administrative support and monitoring components were essential for keeping people working together, maintaining team spirit and keeping the project on track. A deficiency in any one component could be due to deficiencies in other components. For example, if graduates of the workshop didn't use the objectives system efficiently and accurately, it might be attributable to lack of administrative support, poor coordination or inadequacies in one part or another of the objectives system itself.

FOCUS—HOW COULD PROJECT PROOF CONTRIBUTE TO ANSWERING THE MAJOR EVALUATION QUESTIONS? HOW COULD IT HELP IN MONITORING STUDENT PROGRESS AND IN EVALUATING EDUCATIONAL PROGRAMS? (UTILITY)

Because it was comprehensive, the project held great promise as an educational and evaluation tool. It could enable people in participating districts to evaluate many of their inservice programs and educational projects in terms of child change data. On the other hand, if teachers weren't given the training and support necessary to use it, the system would become a costly white elephant for the district and an albatross for Cynthia, her immediate boss (Mike Williams, principal of Westwood Development Center), and Orville Johnson.

THE WORKSHOP IS DEFINED AS A CRITICAL COMPONENT

FOCUS—WHY WAS THE TRAINING WORKSHOP CONSIDERED AN IMPORTANT PART OF THE PROJECT? (OBJECT)

In spite of the high importance of each component and their close relationship to each other, Cynthia treated the workshop as a particularly critical component because it was the teachers' primary introduction to the system. She believed that if teachers perceived the computer objectives system as worthwhile, they'd want to get to work on using it; on the other hand, if the teachers thought the objectives system was a bunch of foolishness dreamed up by a deranged data processing person in cahoots with an administrator, they would not use it. The workshop activities were designed to involve teachers in activities they would consider worthwhile.

FOCUS—HOW WAS THE WORKSHOP DESIGNED TO MEET TEACHER'S NEEDS? (QUESTIONS)

Day #1

I. Orientation to Catalogue of Objectives

Process: Catalogue described using overhead transparencies organized around teacher questions (e.g., "How can I decide what social skills to teach?")

Outcome/Product: Answer to "Will it help me do things I believe are worth doing?" Teachers encouraged to ask questions focusing on one or more children.

II. Setting Curriculum Priorities

Process: Teachers given a model notebook showing how the objectives were grouped to match the classroom organization and curricular priorities in Westwood Developmental Center. Working with the two workshop leaders, the teachers set up a similar notebook for their school.

Outcome/Product: Partial answer to "Will this system work for our school and our priorities?" A working draft of an operational statement of curriculum priorities for the school.

III. Computer Assitance

Process: Teachers shown how to get the computer to type out the objectives they selected for their students and classes.

Outcomes/Product: Partial answer to "Will this system help me do things I believe are worth doing?" Sample computer input forms filled out relevant to selected objectives and curriculum priorities.

IV. Assessment Procedures

Process: Teachers shown how to make use of the assessment suggestions to each objective they select.

Outcome/Product: Further answer to "Will this system help me do things I believe are worth doing?" Specific techniques devised for assessing current status of individual children relevant to objectives selected.

V. Next Steps

Process: Teachers, calendars in hand, planned *who* had to do *what* by *when*.

Outcomes/Products: Further answer to "Will this system work for our school and our priorities." Specific action plans for obtaining materials, doing assessment, etc., to get the job done and be ready for the second day of the workshop, usually two to six weeks later.

Day #2

I. Data Input, Errors, and Output

Process: Teachers shown computer outputs from material they submitted, shown samples of coding errors made and how they were corrected to produce the output.

Outcome/Product: Usable outputs.

II. Class Achievement Status Reports

Process: Teachers reviewed their printouts. Leader discussed how to use the status reports as part of their classroom record-keeping system.

Outcome/Product: Partial answer to "Will it help me do things I believe are worth doing?"

III. IEP Process Overview

Process: Overhead transparencies described how objectives system is used in the IEP development process: Sample IEP forms shown for a variety of different students.

Outcomes/Products: Further answer to "Will it help me do things I believe are worth doing?" Issues raised about the IEP planning process.

IV. Review of Curricular Priorities/Deciding IEP Issues

Process: Teachers modified or reaffirmed earlier curricular priorities. Workshop leaders reviewed IEP issues casting them in terms of specific actions (e.g., Which staff should select which objectives for which students? How many objectives should be specified for each student? Should objectives be set high, challenging, or low, to be easily attainable?) Teachers decided which actions to take, at least for the time being.

Outcomes/Products: Mutually accepted curricular priorities. Mutually accepted strategies for dealing with IEP issues.

V. Completing a Possible IEP Form

Process: Teachers worked to produce an IEP for one student from each program or classroom in the school.

Outcome/Products: Further answers to teacher questions about utility and value of objectives system. "Model" IEP's for other students. Reaffirmation or modification of accepted strategies for dealing with IEP issues.

VI. Completing Possible IEP's for all Students

Process: Using models and strategies previously generated, the teachers completed possible IEP forms for their other students. (Workshop leaders assisted, cheered, commiserated, helped them find objectives in the catalogue, etc.)

Outcomes/Products: Fatigue, further answers to questions and a demonstration that possible IEP's could be generated quickly. Possible IEP's for (nearly) all the children.

VII. Next Steps

Process: A calendar for the year presented with due dates, etc., for using the objectives system during the remainder of the year. Teachers add to it their own calendars for doing further refinement of the possible IEP's, etc.

Outcomes/Products: Action plans and calendars.

There was follow-up by telephone and letter and occasional visits. A major part of follow-up, by design and in practice, came from coordinator meetings held five times per year. The meetings were problem-solving sessions, planning sessions, mutual support/sharing sessions, as well as training sessions. Coordinators learned about new developments, changes in formats and techniques, new ways of assessing, how problems have been solved by others, etc.

EVALUATING THE WORKSHOP

Cynthia and her assistant, Elton Garfield, who collaborated with her on the workshop, wanted to be sure it was designed and run properly. That's why evaluation became a part of their development and administrative work—to the degree possible. Ideally, they knew they should have evaluated each step of their instructional design procedure. For example, prior to devising the instructional procedures for the workshop, they should have tested to see whether their assumptions about the teachers' initial knowledge, skill, and attitudes were correct. However, they were dealing with an area where they both had considerable experience and were working on a tight budget and time line. Consequently, they adopted an assessment strategy they had often used as teachers (and recommended in the workshop), "Start your assessment with your best judgment about where the student is; supplement your judgment as much as you can and assess as you go."

COLLECTION—HOW COULD THEY COLLECT INFORMATION TO DETERMINE WHETHER THE WORKSHOP DESIGN WAS WORKING? (PROCEDURE)

They viewed the first workshops as a vehicle for evaluating their workshop design assumptions as well as training sessions for teachers. The first workshops were evaluated with considerable care but little public documentation. When Elton was presenting, Cynthia could be observing reactions and making notes for revision and vice versa. After each workshop session, they got together to compare notes, share impressions, and plan revisions for the next iteration of the workshop. Also, the two to six weeks between the two days of the workshop allowed Cynthia and Elton to prepare materials or tactics for dealing with unexpected problems.

The workshop design provided the opportunity for teachers to demonstrate acquisition of new skills, thereby enabling Cynthia and Elton to see whether each part of the workshop was working as it should and whether teachers were learning the material. But, as time went on, Cynthia and Elton were not satisfied with this level of evaluation. By the time that they were making only minor workshop revisions they felt that an evaluation of educational impact should become a more important part of their evaluation.

THEY TRY TO FOCUS THEIR EVALUATION

FOCUS—WHAT SHOULD WE BE TRYING TO FIND OUT ABOUT HOW WELL THE WORKSHOP WORKS? (QUESTIONS) Cynthia and Elton had a lengthy discussion about the focus of the impact evaluation. (A small part of that discussion follows.)

ELTON: The main thing we have to show is that the teachers who come out of our workshop do a better job in their classrooms.

CYNTHIA: I'm sure you're right, but it's not that simple. The whole project is about helping teachers' efforts. But if things aren't getting better in the classroom, we couldn't be sure the workshop is at fault. A lot of things could go wrong.

ELTON: Yes, I know. We've had problems in the past with the computer printouts. Some of the old formats were really cumbersome! It was almost impossible for anyone to use them.

CYNTHIA: That's part of what I mean about it being complicated to evaluate the impact of the workshop. The workshop has to be good but so do the objectives catalog, the formats, the computer services, and the on-site coordinators. Not only that, but the teachers have to have the support of their principals.

ELTON: That's true. If we weren't getting results it might take a very careful evaluation to pinpoint the cause. But if we're getting results, we know that all those factors are working reasonably well.

CYNTHIA: That's a good point. But I think we should tighten up the workshop evaluation a little bit. What we've done so far has been useful, but it wouldn't be very convincing to anyone who hasn't seen it operate. I'll talk to Louise Mandler over in the Administrative Services Offices to see what ideas she has.

FOCUS—HOW BROAD OR HOW NARROW SHOULD BE THE FOCUS OF THE EVALUATION? (PURPOSE/ QUESTIONS) A few days later Cynthia called Elton in to discuss the evaluation worksheets that she, with Louise's help, had used to draft an evaluation design for the impact of the workshop. Louise had pointed out that they could use the workshop evaluation to begin an evaluation of the total project by specifying outcome goals for the workshop, then see if the goals were met.

ELTON: So, the first thing we do is state our goals. The goal I want to meet is having the young people in Westwood Center make better educational progress as a result of the workshop!

CYNTHIA: That's too broad. Remember when we specified purposes for the project as a whole? The immediate goal of the whole project was to "provide a system teachers can use to improve efficiency of the individual educational planning process."

ELTON: You must have that memorized!

CYNTHIA: I do. Someone's always asking me.

ELTON: But I don't remember it that way. Wasn't there something about making the IEP's better and having people learn more?

CYNTHIA: Yes, those things are in there too. To evaluate the whole purpose we'd have to show that IEP's get better and that students make better progress. But to evaluate each component we just have to show whether the component does what it's supposed to. For example, the workshop is supposed to "provide teachers with knowledge, skills and techniques sufficient to use the objectives system efficiently and accurately."

ELTON: All right. I see the logic. We just look to see if each component is meeting its benchmark objective. For now. But sometime we have to see if the whole project is helping students make better progress.

CYNTHIA: Exactly! If the system works we'll have a data source for doing a lot more evaluation using child change data. Now can we look at the evaluation worksheets I've done?

ELTON: Sure. Let's look at immediate outcomes (see table 2).

DESIGN—WILL OUR EVALUATION DESIGN GIVE US THE INFORMATION WE NEED? (CRITERIA FOR JUDGING DESIGNS) ELTON: I like the emphasis you've given to looking at the things teachers do in the workshop.

CYNTHIA: Good. By using the criterion checklists I think we can find out during the workshop whether things are working or whether we need to do a remedial session right on the spot.

ELTON: It also shows us where we have to revise next time. We can use the products as examples for our next group, too. But, Cynthia, what are you getting at with the last question: "Do the teachers believe the material will be useful and valuable?"

CYNTHIA: Two things. One is whether we've "made a sale." Are they sold on the system enough to try it? If not, we've really goofed. The second thing I wanted to get was data to help us plan the follow-up. I'd have items on the questionnaire on what obstacles they think they'll run into and what positive effects they hope for.

ELTON: I like that. We should use some open-ended questions, too. We could have them fill that out as a lead-in to the last action planning session.

CYNTHIA: That's a good idea. That would get us right into that session. We could deal right then and there with obstacles people see and we could identify those who are just saying nice things but don't really expect to do anything.

DESIGN—HOW CAN WE GET DATA TO DOCUMENT AND SHOW OTHERS WHAT WE ARE DOING? (CRITERIA) ELTON: Speaking of saying nice things, I don't see any questions about how the teachers like the workshop. I thought all evaluators were supposed to get data about that.

CYNTHIA: Not necessarily. I did ask if teachers believe what they learn will be useful. But the workshop is about

Table 2. Workshop Evaluation Worksheet: Immediate Outcome

EVALUATION QUESTIONS	DATA SOURCES AND COLLECTION	ANALYSIS
Do teachers learn the material? SUBQUESTIONS: Do teachers learn the material presented in each segment of the workshop? e.g., Do teachers organize the objectives to match curricula in their schools?	Examination of the products done in each segment of the workshop. Workshop leader notes on student questions, requests for assistance, etc.	Assess products according to criterion checklists, identify strengths, deficiencies or errors—note where in the workshop they occur. Workshop leaders predict responses, compare with tabulations of questionnaire data.
Do teachers produce IEP's exemplifying a realistic match between child and curriculum and having variety/comprehensiveness, specificity, etc.?	Workshop leader impressions of teacher belief in utility, augmented by items on teacher questionnaires. (Questionnaire items tailored to each segment administered at the end of each day.)	
Do the teachers believe the material will be useful and valuable?		

educational tools and techniques, not whether teachers like learning the tools!

ELTON: That's true, but I'd rather run it so teachers like it rather than hate it.

CYNTHIA: So would I, but we'll know whether they like it or hate it without a questionnaire.

ELTON: But a questionnaire would *document* it. Remember, we need to show others.

CYNTHIA: Well . . . maybe. I suppose that if there's more general dissatisfaction than we think, we need to know. And if there's not, it would be nice to find out. Still, it seems like it would take more time and effort than its worth for us or the teachers.

ELTON: I'll go with that. But let's not avoid evaluation questions because we're afraid they'll turn up negative information.

CYNTHIA: Certainly. I've always found it useful to look hard for information about what's not working very well. If it's not working, I want to find out about it and fix it. Anyway, it's a useful evaluation tactic.

ELTON: What do you mean?

DESIGN—HOW CAN WE CONTROL OUR OWN BIASES? (CRITERIA)

CYNTHIA: We're biased in favor of the workshop. We need to counteract that bias or any evaluation we do won't be very credible.

ELTON: Going after negative information helps to control positive bias, that's for sure!

CYNTHIA: Yes, it gives a better balance. That's another reason for talking to Louise about our evaluation. She's an outsider as far as this project is concerned. That independent perspective will make our evaluation more credible, especially if we ever need it to defend the success of our work.

ELTON: Good, let's go on to the worksheet on "Use of Material Learned" (see table 3).

CYNTHIA: Since you are the coordinator for Westwood, what do you think about interviewing the coordinators and reviewing their logs?

ELTON: It's important. I've already been keeping a log of problems we run into. I have to, just to keep myself organized: But before you add "reviews of coordinator logs" to the worksheet, we'd better check to see if others have been keeping theirs.

CYNTHIA: Let's put some time on the next coordinator meeting agenda to help them get going with their logs. From what I've seen, it's really helped you keep on top of things. The fact that it would help in evaluation is a bonus.

DESIGN—HOW CAN WE CONTROL FOR BIASES IN OUR ASSESSMENT INSTRUMENTS? (CRITERIA)

ELTON: I think I can tell you the main problem the coordinators are having. Teachers keep checking out the assessment materials we've made for some of the objectives. They won't give them back either, because they build teaching exercises around them!

CYNTHIA: But then we can't use them for assessment!

ELTON: I know, but I'm beginning to think the assessment techniques we devise probably aren't any good if the teachers don't take 'em for instructional purposes. If teachers don't think they assess anything important, they won't want them.

Table 3. Workshop Evaluation Worksheet: *Use of Material Learned*

EVALUATION QUESTIONS	DATA SOURCES AND COLLECTION	ANALYSIS
Do teachers use what they learn in the workshop? SUBQUESTIONS		
Which of the possible "computer assistances" do they use?	Computer center work orders reviewed monthly	Tabulation, by use and by user
What errors do they make in requesting assistance?	Error codes on computer printouts	Tabulation by error code and by user.
What problems do they encounter in using what they learned?	Interviews/discussions with coordinators at each school. Logs of telephone calls and examination of minutes and agendas	Listing of types and frequencies of problems. Estimated costs of problems compared to estimated costs of solutions.

CYNTHIA: Perhaps we should come up with at least two sets of assessment devices for all our objectives: one for teaching and one for assessment.

ELTON: And if no one takes the teaching set, we should throw it out and make a new one!

CYNTHIA: I suppose that's right. We *are* trying to make an impact on instruction. Every time someone makes teaching exercises out of assessment devices, it has a very direct and explicit impact!

ELTON: It sure does, but I notice you don't have anything about that on your third worksheet (see table 4). You don't ask about changes in instructional materials.

DESIGN—ARE WE GETTING ENOUGH INFORMATION? (CRITERIA)

CYNTHIA: No. I thought we ought to evaluate the quality of the IEP's and try to get some student-achievement data. If we had IEP quality and student achievement plus teacher perceptions about how efficient the system is and how well it works, I thought that would be enough.

ELTON: But I thought you were arguing that analysis of IEP's and student achievement should be part of evaluating the project as a whole, not part of the workshop evaluation.

to do. I'd like to get some of that kind of data as soon as we can.

ELTON: Is there any reason we couldn't try to answer an evaluation question about how much change there has been in the instructional materials teachers use?

CYNTHIA: No. It might be hard to get good data, though since we didn't do any preassessment of what materials the teachers use. That would have been expensive and nobody thought of it.

Table 4. Workshop Evaluation Worksheet: *Impact/Value of Using Material*

EVALUATION QUESTIONS	DATA SOURCES AND COLLECTION	ANALYSIS
Does using what was learned have a beneficial impact?		
SUBQUESTIONS		
Are the IEPs developed good ones	Samples of IEPs from schools in which teachers have been trained.	Plans evaluated by judges according to criteria of clarity, appropriateness, etc.
Do the children demonstrate better achievement?	Longitudinal analyses of student records for schools; (a) before using the system, (b) during the first year of use, and (c) during later years.	Trends in the number and variety of objectives selected, monitored, and achieved. Reported by disability types, classes, schools, etc.
Do the teachers believe they (a) get better results or (b) get the job done more efficiently?	Annual teacher survey regarding efficiency, effectiveness, ease, value, etc.	Survey questions tabulated by response frequencies. Year to year trends noted.

DESIGN—IS IT FEASIBLE TO
GET THE DATA WE WANT?
(CRITERIA)

ELTON: We could build more preassessment of materials use into the workshop. Or maybe on-site coordinators could easily do that for us. Or we could have each teacher bring in some IEP's. Then we could see if the IEP's they do in the workshop are better!

CYNTHIA: We tried that for a while in the earlier days of the project, but the teachers objected to it. They felt we were trying to show how bad they were. We thought they'd be pleased to see the progress, but it didn't work out that way.

ELTON: I hadn't heard about that. Maybe we could do something like we did for the parenting workshop.

CYNTHIA: You mean where we had parents work in groups to define the changes they wanted to see in the ways they interacted with their children?

ELTON: Yes. It was easy to evaluate the impact of that workshop. We just looked to see how many of the parents got the changes they wanted.

CYNTHIA: It wasn't as simple as you make it sound. Several of the parents got their "results" by deciding that the things that were bugging them weren't so bad after all.

ELTON: That was a positive result! Some of the parents had very unrealistic notions of what to expect from their kids.

CYNTHIA: They sure did. But let's get back to evaluating our objectives workshop.

ELTON: I don't know about you, but that is what I've been talking about. Why don't we use evaluation techniques like the ones we used with parents for this workshop?

CYNTHIA: How can we do that?

DESIGN—WOULD THE DATA
WE ARE GETTING SHOW A
SUCCESS IF THERE WAS
ONE? (CRITERIA)

ELTON: I'm not sure. I just know that some of the teachers who go through the workshop really get it and do some really fine work, and some teachers don't really do all that much. They go through the motions and use the computer, but I can't see that they do a very good job implementing the IEP's.

CYNTHIA: Maybe that's a clue. I'll bet that some teachers right here in Westwood work a lot more closely with you than others do.

ELTON: That's true. Some I just see for the routine things—giving them the printouts and stuff. But others really keep after me for help.

CYNTHIA: Then why don't we take a closer look at those you work with a lot. Let's see if they are accomplishing more than the other teachers.

ELTON: That wouldn't work. Some don't ask for help because they've got it together. Others ask for help because they are desperate. I'm afraid some of those I'm working with are doing the worst!

CYNTHIA: Well then, what if you and the other on-site coordinators just identified some teachers we'd call "success cases." You know, teachers who, for whatever reason, are doing things the way we think they ought to.

ELTON: What would that tell us?

DESIGN—WOULD THE
INFORMATION HELP US
FIND OUT HOW TO RUN
THE WORKSHOP BETTER?
WOULD IT HELP US
IMPROVE? (CRITERIA)

CYNTHIA: If the success cases are doing a lot of good things it would show us the potential. It would show more of what could be done with the system.

ELTON: We'd have to be careful how we selected the success cases, and it wouldn't tell us how the typical workshop graduate performs.

CYNTHIA: No, but it would tell us more about how things work when they are working right. Then we could keep working to get the "typical" cases to be more like the "success cases."

ELTON: I like it. It sure would give us something to shoot for in running the workshop! It's a way of setting high standards for ourselves.

CYNTHIA: Right. I'm excited about this idea because it's something we can use. We can learn something from it.

Elton and Cynthia worked together for another hour and produced the Revised Evaluation Worksheet (see table 5).

EVALUATION FINDINGS SPUR NEW CONCERNS

ANALYSIS/
INTERPRETATION—WHAT,
IF ANYTHING, DID THE
SUCCESS CASES HAVE IN
COMMON?

Elton found that working on the "success cases" was a particularly challenging part of the evaluation. It turned out that the successful teachers at Westwood had six common characteristics:

they completed the workshop at least two years ago;

they began making changes in their instructional materials and practices soon after completing the workshop, but it took considerable time for those changes to be noteworthy;

they did a lot of sharing and borrowing from one another;

they believed they were getting good results and enjoyed teaching;

they could identify two or more students who were making more rapid progress. (Computer printouts confirmed these perceptions—although the preworkshop records were rather poor.)

they wrote IEP's that were more specific, clear, and varied.

REPORTING—HOW COULD
THEY MAKE USE OF WHAT
THEY LEARNED FROM THE
EVALUATION?

Based on their experience at Westwood Cynthia and Elton thought they could specify criteria for identifying recent workshop graduates who were on their way to becoming success cases. They planned to have the on-site coordinators keep track of their interactions with the

Table 5. Revised Evaluation Worksheet: Impact/Value of Using Material

EVALUATION QUESTIONS	DATA SOURCES AND COLLECTION	ANALYSIS
Does using what was learned have a beneficial impact? When the workshop works, what beneficial impacts does it have on kids?		
SUBQUESTIONS:	"Success Case" Methodology	
Are the IEPs developed good ones?	1. Identify workshop graduates at Westwood (and other sites where aid of the site coordinator can be enlisted) who, in the coordinator's judgment, are making best use of the objectives system.	1. Describe teacher credentials background, etc. to answer "Are they exceptional in ways other than being success cases?" Describe criteria for selecting them as a success case. "How did they differ from other graduates in use of this objectives system?"
Do the children demonstrate better achievement?		
What ripple effects does it have in terms of development of instructional material, assessment devices, etc.?	2. Observe and interview teachers and describe what they do differently with respect to individual children.	2. Compare previous IEP's with post workshop IEP's according to clarity, variety, etc. Compare previous instructional procedures with current procedures. Compare, if possible, previous academic progress of child with current progress.
What problems are encountered? How are they dealt with?	3. Observe and interview teachers and describe problems and solutions.	3. Describe instances of solutions being used by other teachers and/or with other children.
Do the teachers believe they (a) get better results or (b) get the job done more efficiently?	4. Interview teachers regarding their beliefs about results and efficiency.	4. Report specific statements about results and efficiency. Report on "evidence" teachers cite in support of results.

teachers so that the growth in use of "new" instructional techniques (stimulated by Project Proof, IEP's and services) could be monitored at all the sites. They figured out how to do that easily by focusing on "success children," i.e., those for whom new instructional activities were being undertaken.

Elton had all sorts of ideas for a "focus on success" campaign: the best gains for each child would be highlighted and celebrated; "terrific techniques of the week" would be shared among teachers; other (less corny) tactics would also be used to focus on student progress. Cynthia cautioned him that he might be going beyond making the evaluation methodology constructively reactive; he might be making it into something that should be considered a treatment in itself. That would make it even *harder* to evaluate the impact of the workshop per se. After further discussion, they decided to consider the "success student" monitoring part of the workshop follow-up, therefore, not a separate treatment. Cynthia talked with Louise about the matter and then made sure the monitoring was instituted in such a way that, if anyone queried her about it, she could point out that it was instituted as part of a time series design

so that they could tell if it made a substantial impact on its own.

As Cynthia and Elton began to collect their evaluation data, they realized that the workshop was changing. When the teacher/participants began using IEP's developed in the workshop, they discovered they needed help with easy-to-use, practical, inexpensive, quick assessment techniques that could also be used as instructional devices.

As a matter of fact, Cynthia and Elton discovered that the majority of the workshop time was now devoted not to developing IEP's but to developing instructional techniques to help attain the planned objectives.

Elton was delighted to see the pattern emerge. He knew that if Project Proof was really effective, it ought to make an impact on the teaching techniques teachers want! They could see what's working and what wasn't. Teachers kept asking, and Elton and Cynthia kept providing, and it was changing things!

REPORTING—WHAT
PROBLEMS OR RESULTS
STOOD OUT THAT OTHERS
SHOULD KNOW ABOUT?
But Cynthia was worried. Her charge had been to implement Project Proof as a planning and monitoring system. The workshop was supposed to teach teachers how to use the system. Clearly, part of the "using the system" was developing good IEP's. Clearly, good IEP's required good assessment and good teaching techniques. She considered Project Proof to be a kind of spearhead for educational improvement, providing an essential feedback mechanism for teachers and administrators alike. Nevertheless, the drift of workshop activity into instructional improvement raised territorial and coordination problems. Should the workshop be part of special education inservice? Fred Morgan, coordinator of special ed inservice, had already expressed some concern about the workshop, wanting to "bring it under my wing" as he put it. Should some of the assessment and some of the instructional techniques be made more generally available to other teachers? Joanna Flynn, coordinator of regular ed inservice, often wondered "if all those things special ed is hoarding shouldn't be available to everyone, especially with mainstreaming and all."

In short, the current emphasis of the workshop was such that the territorial and coordination problems needed to be dealt with. The project was beginning to make a noticeable impact. It had been Cynthia's experience that when a project began to have an impact it created organizational stresses and resistances. That's why Cynthia was not surprised to hear that Orville was about to initiate an overall evaluation of Project Proof.

THE EVALUATION GOES FORMAL

FOCUS—WHAT FURTHER
EVALUATION SHOULD BE
DONE? WHO WANTS MORE
INFORMATION? (PURPOSE/
AUDIENCE)
The reasons for the evaluation were not crystal clear to everyone involved. The timing coincided with the maturing of the project, to be sure; but it also coincided with a nationwide economic recession and a political climate in which the flow of federal money into the special education coffers was being disturbed.

Orville called Cynthia to tell her "We've been running Project Proof over three years now. I think it's time we did a comprehensive evaluation of the project, don't you?" Cynthia tried to tell him about the evaluation work she and Elton had been doing, but he didn't seem to see any connection between their work and his questions.

The evaluation design development was assigned to Louise Mandler. Constrained by a small budget, and predisposed by her training, Louise developed the evaluation design around the major listed objectives of the project.

FOCUS—WHAT IS THE
MAJOR EVALUATION
QUESTION? (QUESTIONS)
The basic evaluation question was: "Has the project done what it set out to do?" At first glance, evaluation of Project Proof appeared to be a very simple matter.

1. Were curricular objectives for students developed? Yes. Over 6,000 objectives now existed!
2. Were there computer assisted procedures for making the objectives accessible to teachers? Yes. Teachers from cooperating districts sent in forms and got back objectives.
3. Were there computer-assisted procedures for keeping track of objectives students achieved? Yes. Teachers got printouts on individual students and on various groups of students.
4. Did procedures for using the system help to produce IEP's? Yes. IEP's were produced in each of the workshops and afterwards, by teachers from each of the schools using the system.
5. Were teachers in participating districts able to use the system? Yes. Eleven other districts used it, and per child costs to all but the two smallest districts were quite low.

Documentation to support these answers could be obtained in a ten-minute visit to Cynthia's office. The materials were there to see on shelves and in cabinets. The participating districts were shown on a map and on "user calendars" on the wall. Files on each district showed the extent to which each district used the system. Computer printouts showed objectives for IEP's cumulative progress records, etc.

FOCUS—WHAT ARE THE
SUBQUESTIONS? HOW CAN
WE MEASURE QUALITY?
(QUESTIONS)
At a second glance, however, evaluating whether the project was doing what it had set out to do was a very complex matter. The question of quality needed to be addressed. The project had set out to produce a tool. It had done that, and the tool was being used. But was using it doing any good?

FOCUS—WHO IS
CONCERNED ABOUT THE
PROJECT? (AUDIENCE)
Their workshop evaluation data suggested that it was, but Cynthia and Louise did some additional brainstorming and speculating about the various decision makers and others who had a stake or an interest in the success of the project. They also made a list of some of the possible evaluation questions. After several meetings and some discussions with a few of the stakeholders, they were able to complete an audience/decision worksheet (see table 6).

Cynthia and Louise could see that serious problems were on the way. It became clear to them that the new evaluation questions could keep them busy collecting and analyzing information for a long time. Feasibility was a potential problem.

Their solution was to draft an evaluation design so they could see just what they were headed for. To avoid getting carried away with the task, they limited their effort to a three-hour meeting.

FOCUS—WHAT ARE WE
REALLY TRYING TO FIND
OUT, ANYWAY? (PURPOSE)
Just as they suspected they could easily come up with more than enough evaluation work for themselves. But if they couldn't do a complete and comprehensive evaluation, what parts of an

Table 6. Audience/Decision Worksheet

MAJOR EVALUATION QUESTION:
DOES IT DO ANY GOOD TO USE
THE SYSTEM?

SUBQUESTIONS	AUDIENCE/DECISION MAKERS	AUDIENCE/DECISIONS RELEVANT TO ANSWERS
Does it save time or money?	1. Educational leaders Administrators	1.1 Whether or not to use the project services and/or financially support them.
Do teachers who use it get better results than they did before? Do children progress more rapidly? Do children learn a richer curriculum?	2. Teachers	2.1 Whether or not to organize more of their instructional efforts around the system.
Does the school system have some other way of measuring educational growth? Are there other systems?	3. Parents	3.1 Whether to cooperate with, ignore, try to change, or sue the school district (or move to another school district).
What are the advantages of this system compared to other systems? What are the disadvantages? Are other systems better?	4. Taxpayers	4.1 Whether or not to support the school district, vote for millages, etc.
Are other systems less costly? What would it cost to make this system better or change to a better system?	5. Legislators	5.1 Whether or not schools are efficiently providing quality service and therefore deserve more (or less) funding. .2 Whether or not to initiate and vote for particular regulatory practices.
	6. Students	6.1 Whether or not it's worth it to try to learn.

Table 7. Project Evaluation Design Worksheet

MAJOR EVALUATION QUESTION:
IS USE OF THE SYSTEM EFFICIENT?

SPECIFIC QUESTIONS	DATA SOURCES AND COLLECTION	ANALYSIS
How much work is it? Do the teachers like to do it? Can the work be done on school time? Is it complex or mystifying or unpleasant?	Teacher/Coordinator Survey	Survey questions tabulated by response frequencies.
Are there many delays? Is the computer turnaround time short enough? Are errors made that slow things down? Are the errors preventable?	Teacher/Coordinator Survey Project records Error Print-out records	Survey questions relevant to perceptions of delays and frequency and seriousness or errors tabulated by response frequencies. Projects records analysis by tables showing frequencies and types of errors and delays.

"incomplete, but feasible" evaluation should they do? They needed to know more about how the information would be used. Although Orville had not been particularly helpful in answering their questions so far, they decided to try again.

With the draft in hand they met with Orville to find out what questions were his priorities, what resources were available to do the evaluation, and when it had to be done. After an hour of conversation, they had marked up their design draft, and crossed things off until they had one they could use (see tables 7, 8, and 9). The parts that Orville was most concerned about (and willing to provide resources for) would be handled first. The rest would become part of the project's ongoing evaluation that Cynthia and Louise were doing. Considering that the workshop evaluation had begun to address some similar impact questions, it was a natural progression to collect good longitudinal data on student performance. They made an appointment to work on proposals to get funds for this second phase from the statement department of education, the federal government or a foundation.

FOCUS—HOW CAN WE BE SURE WE AGREE ON WHAT THE EVALUATION WILL DO AND WHAT IT WON'T DO? (PURPOSE)

To formalize the agreement, Cynthia and Louise sent Orville a copy of the design worksheets and an outline of the report they would write for him in six months.

I. Introduction (one page containing the purposes of Project Proof and the purposes of the evaluation)
II. Overview of the objectives of the project (one page, written by Cynthia)
III. Evaluation conclusions (four pages written by Louise)
   A. What teachers thought of the project
   B. What unbiased judges thought of the IEP's developed by those using the computer system of objectives.
   C. The costs of the service to Oakview and to participating districts.
IV. The evaluation design: what was done and why (A two-page description of the evaluation methodology written by Louise)
V. Data summaries (A result section showing the graphs and tables and calling attention to the data used to support the conclusions)
VI. Questions we can and can't answer (Five pages written by Louise and Cynthia describing the answered evaluation questions, listing unanswered questions, and summarizing why the unanswered questions were not answered).

Table 8. Project Evaluation Design Worksheet

MAJOR EVALUATION QUESTION:
ARE THE IEPS PRODUCED USING
THE SYSTEM OF GOOD QUALITY?

SPECIFIC QUESTIONS	DATA SOURCES AND COLLECTION	ANALYSIS
Are they appropriate for the students? Do they cover the range of performances needed? Are there important aspects of the curriculum not covered by the objectives? Do they specify important performances?	Samples of IEPs obtained and analyzed from newly trained schools and from schools trained earlier. Samples of IEPs generated in the same schools prior to training. Samples of IEPs from schools currently not using the system but matched to be otherwise similar. Some would be users of other systems.	Judges not connected with any of the schools would be hired to evaluate the IEPs according to; (a) designated criteria of clarity, appropriateness, etc., and (b) any set of additional criteria established by the judges.
Are the objectives clear and specific? Are they easy to understand? If two people (e.g., parent and a teacher) read them do they agree about what they mean? Can they be used to guide instruction?		Comparisons of ratings made to determine if; (a) newly trained schools differed from older schools, (b) trained schools differed from schools using other systems and from schools not using a system and (c) trained schools were better after training than before.
Do they relate to specific needs of children?	Teacher/Coordinator Survey	Teacher/Coordinator survey items tabulated by response frequencies

Table 9. Project Evaluation Design Worksheet

MAJOR EVALUATION QUESTION: CAN THE SYSTEM OF OBJECTIVES BE USED TO MEASURE EDUCATIONAL GROWTH OF THE CHILDREN?		
QUESTION	DATA SOURCES AND COLLECTION	ANALYSIS

Do teachers who use it get better results than they did before?
    Do children progress more rapidly?
    Do children learn a richer curriculum?
 	
Does it save time or money?
	Project budget information
	Budgets for use of other systems
		Survey items tabulated showing frequencies.
		Budget analyses reporting per child, per district and per year costs.

MANAGEMENT—AND HOW CAN WE GET THE WORK DONE IN AN ORDERLY WAY? They then set out to write a schedule and assign responsibilities for doing the evaluation. Above all, they wanted to be sure the evaluation was done carefully and efficiently, particularly since they were limiting its scope. This phase would serve as a base for ongoing evaluation, and they wanted a good foundation.

* * * * *

DISCUSSION QUESTIONS AND TOPICS

1. How is Project Proof intended to help the participating schools in their efforts to evaluate educational progress of individual children? How might it help with the three "simple" evaluation questions about educational achievement?

2. Notice the difficulties involved in defining the scope of the evaluation. The evaluators have to decide which evaluation questions are relevant to their limited scope (evaluate the workshop) and which are relevant to a wider scope (evaluate the project). The problem is similar to the problem one would have in evaluating a workshop on classroom discipline as a part of a general effort to improve discipline in a school. Can you give other examples of the problem? Do you see why the problem is likely to be commonplace for workshops dealing with important educational topics as contrasted with tangential topics?

3. What are several instances which illustrates how formative evaluation was built into the project through the way the project was operated? (Hint: Be sure to notice how evaluation was used to design the workshop and how evaluation was built into the workshop process.) What are several examples, from your personal experience of use of similar ongoing, often unformalized, evaluation techniques?

4. What were at least three things Cynthia and Elton did to deal with (and compensate for) their own biases.

5. What were two or three instances of using preexisting data and evaluation of available documents in the evaluation?

6. Do you agree that teachers' tendency to use test items as instructional activities is evidence of a positive outcome? What problems does this use pose for evaluation?

7. What were two uses of "success case" methodology in the case? What can be learned from a study of success cases? What does the study of success cases *not* tell you (unless all the cases are success cases)?

8. How could success case methodology be used early in the development of a workshop, course, or curriculum?

9. Examine the worksheets near the end of the case. Select one or two items abandoned as not feasible. See if you can construct an argument that they are so important that some other aspect of the evaluation should be sacrificed, if necessary, so that those evaluation data could be obtained.

10. What are several ways in which Cynthia and Elton built an ongoing needs assessment into the project?

SUGGESTIONS FOR STIMULATING DISCUSSIONS ABOUT THE CASE

1. Organize a debate. Resolved: Cynthia and Elton should have done the total project evaluation before beginning their evaluation of the workshop. (Hint for the affirmative: Argue that because the workshop *can't* be successful unless other parts of the project are successful, evaluating the workshop first is premature. Hint for the negative: Consider arguing that the total project evaluation would not be feasible initially and that evaluation data are needed as the project evolves.

2. Arrange for someone to do a brief presentation on "good evaluation practices" shown in the case.

3. Arrange for someone to do a brief presentation on the importance of object description in the case.

4. Arrange for someone to do a brief presentation on "good educational practices" shown in the case.

5. Set up a role playing session in which Cynthia and Elton, along with Louise Madler, meet with Orville Johnson to consider his request for an overall project evaluation.

6. Prepare, then discuss and criticize the case from several value perspectives. The discussion could take the form of a role play, each person representing a particular value perspective or bias (e.g., "It ought to be economical and get results!" "It ought to serve the needs of children!" "It ought to reflect standard educational practices." "It ought to be comparable to what the best schools do!" "It ought to be methodologically sound!" "I don't care how marvelous your intensions are, don't confuse needs with results—and I want to hear about results!" "It ought to be consistent with the latest educational and psychological research!")

APPLICATION EXERCISES

1. Read some of the material in the *Sourcebook* indicated by the asides. Then—suggest alternative things people in the case might have done at several points in the case. Or suggest a whole new approach they might have taken.

2. Using the case as a model (and foil) and your suggested alternatives as guides, design an evaluation for a situation or problem similar to that shown in the case.

3. Using Chapter 7 of the *Sourcebook* as a guide, do a meta-evaluation and critique of the case (and/or your evaluation design).

4. Use the *Design Manual* to develop an improved evaluation design for the case.

5. Use the *Design Manual* to develop an evaluation design for a situation or problem similar to one described in the case.

The State Agency Case Examples

OVERVIEW BY ROBERT OLSEN

The four cases which follow in this section were developed specifically with State Department of Education, Regional Resource Center, Intermediate Educational Units, or other similar educational practices in realistic settings, operating in conditions similar to those of the primary audience. However, the purpose is to be illustrative, not definitive. The characters in these cases were faced with difficult decisions and limited resources. They often have to accept compromise and occasionally do not exercise the best option available. But they learn from these detours, as hopefully we all do.

The cases treat different topics and have different settings. The Winnemucca State Department of Education in the heartland of America wrestles with the complexities of planning and conducting a needs assessment for their comprehensive staff development efforts. A whimsical 23rd century state department of education sets about examining its procedures to call and assess proposals for delivery programs. The problems in evaluating staff development activities are explored in an anonymous state education agency. A special, legislatively mandated commission in the State of Confusion examines a number of issues involved when staff development related services are provided by paid contractors. Each case attempts to present its informative points in entertaining fashion.

To develop these cases we attempted to learn from a broad sampling of today's educational agency people what problems in evaluating staff development issues most plagued them. The cases were written from this background information and have been submitted to an in-depth review by both educational evaluators and by staff from educational agencies. The authors gratefully acknowledge Charlie McCormick, Wayne Welch, Jay Millman, Dan Stufflebeam, Jim Sanders, and Bud Paulson.

If these cases instruct or illuminate the work entailed in evaluation, we can attribute much of our success to the patience of those many persons with whom we have spoken at some point in the development of these materials.

CASE S-1

EVALUATION CONSULTANTS ASK: How can we meet a state commission's information demands?

Robert M. Olsen, Joan Shaughnessy and Gary Dennerline

FOCUS—WHERE IS THE EVALUATION WORK TO BE DONE? (CONTEXT)

In Chaos, the State capital of Confusion, the legislature had recently established the Commission on Educational and Related Training Situations (CERTS). The legislative mandate instructed CERTS to engage in fact finding and develop recommendations and possible legislation regarding all staff development activities which utilized public funds. The commission was politically separate from, and given charge to review, public education, higher education, the county intermediate education service districts, and the State's Department of Education (DOE).

FOCUS—WHAT WAS THE COMMISSION SET UP TO DO? (PURPOSE)

Their charge was to develop a cost-effective and accountable system for monitoring and directing these activities. The seven-member commission was to have a staff of three—the executive secretary, also selected by the governor, a research assistant and a secretary. The commission was given nine months to investigate expenditures related to staff development and to report its findings and recommendations to the House Select Committee on Educational Expenditures.

MANAGEMENT—WHO WILL BE RESPONSIBLE FOR DOING THE WORK? (FORMALIZING RESPONSIBILITY)

Tilly Tidy was selected by an interview committee, approved by the governor's appointment secretary, and named Executive Secretary to the CERTS. Mrs. Tidy had taken a one-year leave of absence from her position as Assistant Superintendent of the Northern Nil County Intermediate Educational Service District where she was in charge of special services. An organized, robust, congenial woman, she had made a quick climb up the educational administrative structure following a brief stint as a teacher of EMR children. Tilly was compulsive and very thorough; a good worker, if not very dynamic.

Tilly's first task was to hire a research assistant to work with her. From the 86 applicants for the position, Tilly finally selected a young doctoral candidate from Paragon University, Constance Kooling. Now in the process of completing her dissertation (A Monte Carlo Analysis of the Long-Range Effects of Evaluation Findings in Studies Employing the Solomon Four Design), Constance had gone directly into the doctoral program from her undergraduate work. Tilly felt that Constance's educational expertise and familiarity with the classic and emerging evaluation methodologies would be very useful in serving the commission's needs.

COLLECTING—WHAT DATA CAN WE HAVE READY FOR THE COMMISSION'S FIRST MEETING? (INFORMATION NEEDED)

Tilly and Constance worked feverishly in the remaining week before the first commission meeting gathering information about the level, extent and breadth of educational and related training within the State. Most of this introductory information was collected from the state inservice needs assessment and a review of the DOE's fiscal records. The information was intended only as an introductory background for the commissioners. Tilly had little idea what to expect from this first session.

FOCUS—WHO IS ON THE COMMISSION? WHAT AX DOES EACH HAVE TO GRIND? (AUDIENCE)

The first committee meeting was an important one for Tilly. Although she knew two of the commission members from her former work, she needed to get to know the others. Dr. Learned Mann, the commission Chair, sat at the head of the table. Mann, the Chair of the Education Department at Paragon University, a Columbia Ph.D. and postdoctoral fellow at Oxford, was generally regarded as the guiding educational leader in the State. A forceful man in his middle 40's, Chairman of the National NAACP Educational Committee, he was rumored to be next in line for the higher education chancellor's position. He prided himself on his thorough and cautious approach to change.

Across from Mann was the slightly overweight and rumpled Ole Timer, Superintendent of the Central Turmoil Unified School District. Nearing retirement, Ole was still as energetic about education as when he began his climb through the teacher, coach, counselor, vice-principal, principal and assistant superintendent ladder that had brought him to the leadership of a conservative middle-sized district in the State. Conservative and very traditional in his views about good educational practice, Ole didn't particularly like these kinds of committee groups, preferring to be at work within his own district on pressing issues. Ole was talking to Fred Cashdollar, owner of the Turnpike Trucking Company and a self-made prominent small businessman in the State. Fred was known for his tough fiscal positions with programs that couldn't prove their worth. The hardline member of his own local school board, he was regarded favorably by Ole. The two were already on their way to becoming fast friends.

Next to Dr. Mann sat a small and quiet woman, Mary Committee, President of the mid-State regional PTA congress, chair of the New Democratic Women's Caucus, social coordinator for the Legal Aid Auxiliary and a former kindergarten aide. Mary had already taken out her manila folder and note pad in preparation for the meeting.

Just closing her Gucci attaché case next to Mary sat Sue Striver. Sue had taken a position with the public relations division of the Whole State Bank after completing her MBA degree and one year of law at Stanford. Clearly upward bound, she seemed coolly pragmatic.

Across from Sue was the slight, wiry figure of Manuel Jose Garcia Fernandez, State Vice-President of the United Teachers of Confusion. He believed fiercely that education should not be abused and had no time for slackers. Presently the coordinator of the Title I program in the Bedlam County District, Manuel was glad to be on this commission because he saw a real opportunity to deal with the inequalities in educational offerings for minority students.

Just as 3:30 p.m. arrived, so did Ziggy Efftest, an independent educational evaluator and President of the United School Associates consulting firm. Ziggy always looked a little disheveled and was usually rushing to or from some meeting. His professional life seemed reflected in his appearance.

MEETING #1

With the group all assembled, Dr. Learned Mann called the first meeting to order and had each member briefly introduced themselves.

Following the introductions, Dr. Mann described the nature and extent of the legislative mandate which had brought them all together. He offered some thoughts about the current political and social climate and their relationship to this work. Clearly he saw the recommendation which the commission would develop as important pieces to guide future policy decisions within the State. Dr. Mann then introduced Tilly and Constance and asked them to hand out the background information which they had prepared.

Tilly prefaced the brief collection of information with an apology for its rough form and content explaining the frantic pace of the first month's schedule. The information should allow the members to familiarize themselves with the current status of training in the State and build a long-range plan for their evaluation and development of recommendations to the next legislature

FOCUS—HOW WILL THE COMMISSION INTERPRET IT'S CHARGE? HOW WILL THE PURPOSE OF INDIVIDUAL COMMISSION MEMBERS INTERACT WITH THE COMMISSION'S CHARGE TO PRODUCE THE "REAL" AGENDA? (PURPOSE)

During her comments, some of the members were already thumbing through the assembled narrative and tabular information.

Ole Timer remarked that this would be helpful, but in his experience, the great majority of training services provided to teachers were of little real value. Mary Committee asked what he meant. Ole admitted that, while he had no concrete evidence, his staff often commented that the majority of outside consultants and trainers were apt to spout too much theory and not give enough practical, real work-related assistance. Teachers simply could not use what was presented back in the classroom.

Fred Cashdollar interrupted. He was more worried, he said, about the budgetary figures. Nearly $800,000, by his estimate, of the figures for the various categories were being contracted with outside consultants for services related to educational and related training. If Ole was right, then why were they spending all of this money? Furthermore, why hire outsiders to do the work that was the mandate of the DOE staff? What did the DOE staff do anyway?

Sue Striver leaned forward. She could understand the large figures for training and technical assistance which were reported, but what about the monies for evaluation and dissemination. Certainly evaluation was part of the responsibility of the people running these publicly supported activities; and wasn't the State Library doing its job? Teachers and others should be sharing good ideas as a part of their professional interaction, she thought.

Ziggy quickly cleared his throat. It was essential, he said, to have evaluations contracted externally from the project and its personnel in order to ensure that the findings were unbiased and accurate. These monies were absolutely necessary "if we were going to have any accurate evaluation of educational services," Ziggy proclaimed.

Mary Committee returned to Sue's point. Well, what about this dissemination then? Why couldn't networks be developed within the DOE to spread the word around about different activities and developments? She noted that her Democratic Women's Caucus had an effective and thorough telephone tree system that always kept them informed. They didn't have to hire outsiders to do their work. Manuel agreed. "A lot of those newsletters to teachers get thrown away immediately. This dissemination is just intellectual junk mail!"

The room exploded with members all talking at once.

Dr. Mann wielded the gavel and brought the group back to some quiet and order. He reminded the group that there were still many agenda items left, and this was the first, introductory session. He suggested that the discussion could be continued next meeting when they would begin drafting the mission statement and timelines for the commission's work.

FOCUS—WHAT'S THE FIRST THING THE COMMISSION WANTS TO KNOW ABOUT? (QUESTIONS)

Fred Cashdollar, with a brief aside about the speed of public agencies, said he for one, would like more specific information for the next meeting. "If I summarize correctly, there are some pretty serious questions about the amounts spent for contracts related to staff development. This dissemination is especially hard to follow. I think we need to look pretty closely at this."

Still wanting to move along with the agenda, Learned Mann asked if Fred wanted to make that request in the form of a motion. Fred did, and Ole Timer seconded the motion. Tilly, knowing that she and Constance were going to have to do the work, asked if the commission could clarify its request. Dr. Mann replied that further discussion would not be appropriate and directed the commission staff to prepare for the next meeting a report addressing the question: "Are dissemination services necessary?"

The group rather quickly worked its way through the rest of the agenda items, the travel reimbursement forms were handed out, and Dr. Mann adjourned the meeting in time to meet with the press assigned to cover the proceedings.

DESIGN—HOW CAN WE GET ANY DECENT DATA IN THE TIME AVAILABLE? (APPROPRIATE PROCEDURES)

The next day Tilly arrived at her office with a heavy heart. How was she going to collect data which would prove the need for dissemination services in the next three weeks? She would need to have the report prepared at least a week before the next meeting, so that it could be typed, printed and distributed. Tilly would have been prepared to answer the question of whether contracting was being handled appropriately by the DOE, but now the commission was questioning the need for a service at all. Tilly knew this question must be resolved before the group could look at the particulars about the dissemination contracts.

FOCUS—JUST WHAT DISSEMINATION SERVICES ARE OFFERED? (OBJECT)

Tilly had determined that the dissemination services provided were in four areas:

1. Production of cassette tapes describing educational material done by several audio-visual centers;
2. Compilation, preparation and binding of instructional materials into comprehensive documents;
3. Preparation, printing and mailing of newsletters and bulletins describing information available or services provided related to staff development; and
4. Services provided by the "Skills on Wheels" mobile unit which visited workshops, conferences, IEU's, etc.

COLLECTING—HOW CAN WE DO THE BEST WE CAN IN THE TIME AVAILABLE? (EFFICIENCY)

As part of her report on the status of dissemination contracts, Tilly planned to collect direct-use data on how many of the cassettes and bound documents were checked out during the year, on the number of newsletters mailed, and on how many staff visited the Skills on Wheels Van, but she knew that this information would not be sufficient to answer the Commission's question. Tilly and Constance began by brainstorming some possible additional procedures for data collection. They could collect testimony from the users of the services, asking them to verify the need for this service. Tilly was uncertain, though, if the Commission would accept testimony from a few select individuals.

She wondered if more "objective" information would be better? Constance suggested visiting districts to determine if dissemination actually did have an impact on classroom activities. Tilly shook her head. They couldn't collect onsite data like that in three weeks!

They finally agreed it was feasible to collect three kinds of data to address three different issues embedded in the Commission's question, "Is it necessary to provide dissemination services?" First, they would see if a need for dissemination was identifiable in the existing data collected in the State's annual Staff Survey; a part of the DOE needs assessment conducted each spring. This survey of a sampling of teachers asked staff to indicate how accessible information was on (1) instructional materials and (2) innovative programs. By reviewing the answers to these questions, they would know if staff in the schools reported a need for access to additional information. Curiously, Constance had found that this information had never been examined or analyzed.

Secondly, Tilly felt that Manuel's comment about the newsletter deserved a response. She wanted to document any benefits which could be attributed to the frequent mailing of notices. To begin addressing this question, Tilly had to examine what benefits the services were designed to provide. By interviewing the DOE agencies who contracted for the dissemination service, Tilly discovered that most of the funds were used for special "flash bulletins" alerting staff about upcoming staff development events. For example, the SEA was paying printing companies to send out notices to teachers in a specific region of the State whenever the Skills on Wheels van was going to be in the area. The purpose of this bulletin was to increase the use of the Skills on Wheels. One such flash bulletin had just been mailed to alert the teachers in Shambles County that the van would be parked for two days at the IEU, starting on the upcoming inservice day. Then the van would be driving across the State to Turmoil County. Another bulletin announcing the van's availability for one day in Turmoil was due to go out later that week. If Tilly stopped the bulletin to teachers in Turmoil, she could determine if this had any negative effect on the number of staff visiting the Skills on Wheels van. Although she finally had to ask the Superintendent, she succeeded in having the second mailing stopped. She would ask the Skills on Wheels personnel for their sign-in sheets and also ask van users in both Turmoil and Shambles to answer a brief questionnaire asking how they had learned that the van would be in the area that day. By comparing the overall attendance in Shambles with the attendance in Turmoil, Tilly felt she would get some perspective on whether the bulletin was helpful in advertising the van's whereabouts.

ANALYZING/ INTERPRETING—COULD WE INTERPRET THE DATA IF WE COLLECTED THEM? (ANALYSIS)

Constance was quick to point out that those two regions of the State were not equal in terms of the number of staff who would be in the vicinity of the van and who had the opportunity to visit it, or the number of hours the van would be open for service. They could not alter the demographics of the counties nor the van's hours, but they could look at average hourly attendance in the regions compared both to (1) the number of staff who used the van in past visits and (2) the total number of staff in districts within 50 miles of the van's location. Constance would use this information to test whether or not attendance had dropped off in Turmoil when the flash bulletin had not been sent.

Tilly would collect the questionnaires given to the van visitors and count how many were using the van because they had been notified via the flash bulletin. Constance thought this part of the evaluation was particularly weak because too many situational factors were unaccounted for which would affect attendance.

FOCUS—WHAT WOULD HAPPEN IF . . .? (QUESTION)

Tilly and Constance also planned to collect a third kind of data which would answer the question, "What would occur if this service were *not* available?" Tilly felt that if she could show some of the hardships and costs incurred if the staff did not have access to dissemination services, she would be able to comment on the relative need for these services. She and Constance designed a "what-if" exercise for a sample of dissemination users. The sample would include users of the cassette tapes, the bound documents, the newsletters and the Skills on Wheels van. On this exercise users would describe alternatives to dissemination services and the time, effort and money likely expended if this service were terminated (Table 1).

COLLECTING—CAN WE GET A DECENT SAMPLE OF USERS? (SAMPLES)

This sounded good on paper, but Constance was concerned about selecting a scientific sample of users and collecting data in a standardized administration procedure. Tilly argued that they would be forced to select a sample of convenience and assume that the sample was unbiased. They randomly selected one day each of the dissemination services would be used to have a sample of users complete the what-if exercise. For example, on next Tuesday, a day chosen at random, Constance would stay with the Skills on Wheels van asking each third user to complete the exercise. Constance wanted to randomly sample the users of the cassette tapes and documents by choosing the name of every tenth staff member who checked out those materials and calling them to get their answers on the what-if exercise.

In the time allotted, Constance was able to get only 16 users to complete the exercise. When she brought these back to Tilly, they were able to extrapolate quite a bit of information from this sample. From the responses they determined that the contracted services saved these 16 staff members around $900 in staff time and money, including phone calls, travel, etc. Estimating the cost of the users' time from their staff position, Tilly determined that, on the average, dissemination services saved about $56 of staff time and direct costs per user. The dissemination contracts served around 1,625 staff members per year. At the average savings of $56 for these 1,625 users, the dissemination services prevented $91,000 of expenses from being incurred. The average annual expenditure on dissemination contracts had in the past three years been around $65,000. Her report for the following meeting would show how the contracted services provided not only a service that was convenient, but also cost effective.

Meeting #2

REPORTING—HOW SHALL WE TELL THE COMMISSION WHAT WE'VE FOUND? (CONTENT)

Tilly arrived confident that her report would shed some light on the dissemination services contracts. In addition to descriptions of the contracts, she had a table documenting the needs for dissemination as described by respondents on the needs assessment questionnaire, and she also had an estimate of the staff hours which would be used to gather information if dissemination services were not available. She had prepared an overhead slide which compared the present expenditure in dollars for dissemination with the estimated cost figures derived from the "What if" exercise.

Her report also verified the limited impact of the flash bulletin mail-out approach. She was going to recommend that the utility of all newsletters, etc., be examined further by the DOE before they renewed any contracts in this area. She felt the Commission members would agree with these recommendations.

Tilly presented her report and was gratified when Mary Committee indicated that the findings had for her "shed quite a bit of light on this dissemination issue." In general, most of the members seemed satisfied with her report.

Ole Timer asked if there were anecdotal reports from teachers about the Skills on Wheels program. He was genuinely disappointed to learn that no extensive personal statements were taken.

Ziggy asked Tilly to review briefly the computations used to arrive at the figures for the "probable savings."

Tilly replied that they had just multiplied average figures by the total number of appropriate personnel. Ziggy explained carefully, and very politely, that there may have been better ways to compute these estimates. The net effect, he suggested, was that these figures were probably overstated. He did not doubt that there were real savings though.

Dr. Mann asked if the group would like to adopt the report and recommendations in Tilly's report.

Fred Cashdollar moved to accept Tilly's report. Sue Striver seconded the motion and suggested the report be incorporated into the Commission's Final Report. Dr. Mann felt it might be a little premature to begin determining the contents of the Final Report since the Commission still did not have a well-developed plan of inquiry.

The Commission then voted 5-2 (Dr. Mann and Ziggy Efftest in the minority) to accept the report and include its

Table 1. "What If" Exercise for Staff Using Dissemination Services

Directions to Users: Your answers will be as complete as possible if you can envision the steps you would go through to acquire any information needed. Your response to the first three questions will give us background information to enable us to estimate the costs incurred. In completing Questions 4, 5 and 6 in this exercise, you are being asked to hypothesize or imagine what would occur if dissemination services were not available.

1. What is your present position? _____

2. How long have you held this type of position? _____

3. Which method of dissemination about staff development has been your major source of information?

   ☐ Cassette Tapes

   ☐ Bound Document

   ☐ Newsletter

   ☐ Skills on Wheels Van

4. Suppose that this source of information was not available and so you were unable to get access to information needed from the source. Is there another source you could have accessed to get the same information? Such as: (Check all that apply)

   ☐ State Library   ☐ Supervisor/Administrator

   ☐ University Library   ☐ Magazines, Journals

   ☐ Colleague   ☐ Subject Area Expert

   ☐ Professional Consultant   ☐ DOE/IEU Personnel

   ☐ Other (please describe) _____

   _____

5. If you have checked more than one in the question above, which would be the source you would be most likely to turn to?

   Preferred Source: _____

6. Now please estimate what it would cost you in time and resources to secure the same information from your preferred source. List these estimates below:

	Time Which Would Be Spent (In minutes)	Be Spent
A. Phone calls to source	_____	_____
B. Travel to source	_____	_____
C. Research at source	_____	_____
D. Meeting or contact with source	_____	_____

major points and recommendations in the Final Report.

Mary Committee then suggested that the funds allocated for dissemination which would be reduced as a result of these recommendations be shifted to other necessary activities. Sue Striver concurred.

FOCUS—WHAT ELSE STANDS OUT AS AN ISSUE? (POTENTIAL UTILITY)

"Look," Fred argued, "at these incredible sums of money being spent on consultations and contracts. We have some idea from this first report that not all of these services are necessary or well-performed. Just how can we tell if these firms or consultants are good ones? How are these contractees selected anyway?"

Ziggy explained, for some of the other Commission members less experienced with education bureaucracies, that consultants were often used when technical expertise was lacking, or already used to its maximum.

This whole notion of consultants was somewhat new to Mary Committee, and she asked in what area related to staff development they were most often used.

Ole Timer snorted. What really bothered him was the way consultants were often hired to provide the technical assistance he felt was the work of DOE or IEU personnel.

Manuel Fernandez had had occasion to work frequently with technical assistance consultants in his position with the Bedlam County District, but he noted that he seldom worked with any minority consultants. He was more than a little concerned about this, since many of the teachers in his County were minority staff. Just how were these people selected anyway, he wanted to know, echoing Fred's question?

Ziggy noted that consultants were often hired because of their previous experience in the field and even past work with the contractor. Often these consultants, particularly providers of technical assistance, were not required to go through the bidding process.

Sue Striver was surprised. She wanted to know then if there was no competition in the awarding these contracts. Dr. Mann explained that technical consultants were a highly specialized group who usually had extensive experience in their field.

Mary, again just trying to learn as much as she could, asked if there were any reports on these technical assistance contracts so that she might get some idea of the magnitude of the issue. Tilly regretfully indicated that, to her knowledge, there were no recent reports which described the numbers, or selection processes involved, or the costs of these consultants.

Sue Striver immediately requested that Tilly and Constance develop a complete report on the processes used to select these consultants.

While the question was clear to Tilly, she was concerned about the possible scope of this work. She explained that the task was very broad and should be narrowed. Ole Timer, who felt that the primary offender was the DOE, suggested that the report be restricted to DOE contracts written for technical assistance services. Manuel Fernandez asked that the staff look specifically at the state of minority contracting to determine whether any biases existed. Tilly was to report to them in two months, since their next meeting would involve a joint session with the legislative Select Committee on Educational Direction.

DESIGN—WHAT'S A GOOD APPROACH TO DEALING WITH THE NEW EVALUATION QUESTIONS? (COMPONENTS)

As she entered the office the next day, Constance apologized for having been ill and asked how the Commission had received the report on dissemination. Tilly told her what had happened and then assigned the job of analyzing DOE contracts to Constance.

Tilly continued by saying that at least this time the question was specific, the data source was identified, and they had two months to complete the report. Constance asked if it would be all right to consult with her graduate advisor, Dr. Nitpick, to help design the evaluation. With Tilly's permission Constance contacted Dr. Nitpick and explained the task. They agreed to meet early the following week.

When Constance arrived Dr. Nitpick had already outlined the steps he felt Constance needed to follow. He felt that additional clarification was needed for the definition of technical assistance and suggested that Constance:

1. define the question,
2. identify the intended audience and their concerns,
3. identify the best data source(s) related to the question,
4. establish the comparison standard for valuing decisions,
5. identify the most desirable data collection technique(s),
6. develop the necessary data collection instrument(s),
7. collect the required information,
8. select and complete the appropriate data analysis(es), and
9. report the findings to the various audiences.

Constance recognized the list as a basic ordering of some, but not all, of the key steps in good program evaluation. This time they would have a respectable, if not "flashy", evaluation.

FOCUS—JUST WHAT ARE WE EVALUATING, ANYWAY? (OBJECT)

Looking at the Commission's questions she thought that "technical assistance" was not fully defined and needed additional clarification. Checking with the DOE, Constance learned that they categorized contracts as being for: (1) direct training, (2) program evaluation, (3) dissemination of information, and (4) technical assistance. Since the other areas listed were reasonably clear, she identified technical assistance as any service that did not fall into the other three categories.

The primary audience for the finding was, of course, the Commission. Others, though, such as DOE persons, IEU persons and even some of the technical assistance staff, were also possible users of the findings, so reporting styles and formats should also be useful to them too.

COLLECTING—WHERE CAN WE GET THE INFORMATION WE NEED? (COLLECTION PROCEDURES)

Constance planned to collect information from both contractors and contractees and to use multiple data sources to help verify her findings. The next step was to identify the technique for collecting the data. The CERTS office was only a few blocks from the State DOE, and she could schedule frequent visits with DOE staff. She decided to develop an interview guide to structure her discussions with the staff. Later she would ask to review old Personal Services Contracts to collect and code the information available in them.

Constance spent about a week interviewing staff at the State DOE about their past contracting with consultants, particularly those related to providing technical assistance. She kept careful records of the costs of the contracts, their duration, the nature of the services provided, any special notes about the contract (such as situational constraints, etc.), and any information about the contractor. Very little surprising information was learned from the interviews. She was particularly interested in the "sole-source" contracts in which a particular person or firm was the only one with whom discussions were held prior to developing the contract.

When Constance reviewed her interview notes she saw that they lacked much detail about the sole-source issue, and she had little information about the minority issue which Manuel had raised. She could remember some comments from the staff, but she couldn't find them in her notes. She knew she couldn't treat these "remembrances" as solid information. Dr. Nitpick had been emphatic about this issue in class. "If it involves information collection via interview or observation, and it isn't written down in your notes, it didn't happen!"

Maybe the records analysis of the contracts on file in the DOE would help document this better. she also needed to learn from this analysis (1) when, and under what circumstances, sole-source contracts were used, (2) the agency person's knowledge about the contractor, (3) what prerequisite experience and/or skills the sole-source contractors had had with the group(s) to be served through the contract, (5) the extent to which the contracted-for skill existed within the DOE or another State agency, (6) about any prescreening of potential contractors invited/allowed to bid for jobs, (7) the process by which requests for proposals (RFP's) were developed, (8) any information describing client satisfaction, and (9) any information describing minority status. Armed wth the Commission's mandate she arranged a visit with the Assistant Superintendent of Public Instruction and secured his cooperation in providing her access to all of the information she might want.

Constance spent the rest of the week searching for files and then sifting arduously through them. She learned that the "cooperation" which she had gained really meant that no one would get in her way; it did not mean that anyone would go out of their way to be helpful. She also learned that the secretaries were the real keys to the information, because they readily could tell her where to look.

ANALYZING/ INTERPRETING—HOW CAN WE SUMMARIZE THE INFORMATION COLLECTED? (ANALYSIS)

The next week she began her analysis. After reviewing the range of comments and information for each question, she developed her coding scales and then completed her tabulations. She wrote one summary statement about each area, carefully limiting herself to not more than 50 words per statement.

What she found was that the DOE had pretty specific procedures for most of the technical assistance. Their internal policy required that if staff in a State or local agency were capable, and had the unassigned time, they were to provide the needed technical assistance.

What was unclear were the criteria used for selecting the successful applicant when competitive bidding was employed. Usually a committee of some kind was involved, but beyond that there was surprisingly little information justifying the selection. The DOE regularly disposed of the unsuccessful bids, so Constance was at a dead end.

There were some inconsistencies in the bidder listings. According to the information shown, a few large, powerful firms were almost always included, while smaller firms were included or excluded with no discernible logic. She also learned that only four minority contractors were selected for technical assistance contracts awarded competitively.

Her information summary clearly indicated that minority contractors did much better when sole-source contracts were the focus. The selections were always heavily supported with descriptions of previous work either in the field generally or specifically for the agency unit in question.

Sole-source contracts depended a good deal on the relationship between the contractor and the agency person(s) involved and were significantly more likely to please the agency person than were competitively awarded contracts. Constance knew that often the sole-source contracts involved ideas which had actually been developed by the consultations and "sold" to the agency. She noted that there did not seem to be any practical difference in costs between the sole-source and the competitive proposals. She did find an area of possible conflict of interest, or even abuse, when she noted the number of former DOE and other State agency staff who received multiple contracts to provide services augmenting those which DOE staff were to deliver.

REPORTING—ARE THERE SOME USEFUL RECOMMENDATIONS THAT CAN BE MADE? (PURPOSE)

Constance wrote her report and included some recommendations regarding: the establishing prior criteria for selection in competitive bidding; developing uniform notification lists with clear administrative procedures for placing new names on the list or taking old ones off; justifying sole-source contracting over competitive bidding; justifying the individual contractor as the sole-source; and awarding of multiple or consecutive sole-source contracts. She also included data summaries regarding the demographics of time, duration, costs, etc., including a breakdown of the ethnic information about the contractors.

She handed the report to Tilly for her review and editing.

MEETING #3

After quite a bit of discussion about the joint meeting with the legislative committee, Tilly distributed Constance's report. Manuel asked for some clarification about the minority contracting figures, but there was little further discussion of the report. The report was accepted unanimously, and Dr. Mann complimented Constance on a fine, thorough report.

ANALYZING/
INTERPRETING—WHAT ARE
THE REAL CRITERIA (I.E.
THE ONES COMMISSION
MEMBERS USE) FOR
INTERPRETING THE
RESULTS?
(INTERPRETATION
CRITERIA)
Fred Cashdollar echoed, "A very informative report." But he continued, "I'll tell you one thing I have never understood. We have these evaluation consultants come in from time to time, you know, the ones usually from the University, and I tell you, it's beyond me what they've done while they're on the job. It all seems pretty mystical how they get their information, except when they give tests. I understand that."

Ole passed the coffee pot to Fred and voiced the same feelings. He'd taken care of that by doing away with his district evaluation unit. Ole laughed aloud. He had even had a conversation with a fellow one time who was going to evaluate a reading program they were trying, and this fellow had not wanted to talk with any of the program folks, look at the materials directly or even review the program's goals. He just wanted to "see what had happened." Goal-free evaluation, he'd called it. Well, Ole assured the commission, he'd set that fellow straight and promptly gotten two graduate students who have reviewed the goals and given some tests to the kids and questionnaires to the teachers involved.

Ziggy, a twinkle in his eye, wanted to know how Ole's graduate "evaluators" had developed the questions on the tests or those on the questionnaires? How had they determined who would be tested or surveyed? What kinds of analyses had they performed? What kinds of options had they reviewed and not selected? Had they been timely and organized in their work?

Ole blustered, "Lookit. They got the job done. I knew it was a good program, and their data supported that. We still use it. All my evaluation staff had done were mystical things that they would never explain in plain language, and it was impossible to tell when they were working or not. They always had a lot of planning time, and all I could see was a lot of reading and talking to people. We weren't paying them to talk or read; we were paying them to evaluate!"

Mary leaned forward and spoke in rather an uncharacteristically firm tone. "It was essential," she remarked, "that evaluators have time to get to know the contexts of the situation and the program being evaluated. There were many diverse evaluation strategies which could be employed successfully in the same situation, and one was often selected as much for political reasons as technical ones. Even this fellow with the goal-free notion who did not want any constraints and could not begin by describing his methodology would have observable work, but these plans did not come ready-packaged like some sandwich from a vending machine.

There was a long pause in the room. Sue asked Mary where she had developed these notions, and Mary explained that she had been doing some reading on evaluation, since she had figured that that was really what the commission was up to. Ziggy suppressed his grin.

Manuel asked if there were normally systems used to monitor the work progress and quality of these contracted efforts before they were completed? Or, was the product the measure of success? He would be worried if there were not some way that this work was supervised to ensure that it was being done and was being done well.

Dr. Mann asked if anyone would like to summarize this discussion.

Sue Striver moved to have the staff examine the extent of the work effort, and quality, which contractors were devoting to their tasks.

DESIGN—WHAT'S A GOOD
APPROACH TO DEALING
WITH THE NEW QUESTIONS
RAISED BY THE
COMMISSION?
(COMPONENTS)
The next morning Tilly and Constance talked with the assistant fiscal officer in the DOE and learned that there were no procedures used to monitor contractors' job performance. He explained that determining acceptance of the work and authorizing final payment was solely the responsibility of the DOE employee initiating the work. There did not seem to be any history of monitoring work in progress. What they could learn suggested that where it happened, it was done very informally and was not well documented.

Tilly was sure that the commission would be displeased to learn that there did not seem to be any existing information about their question, and she doubted they would be able to collect any appropriate information in the very short time available. Constance suggested that before the next Commission meeting they could develop and perhaps test a set of procedures which the group seemed to be after. Perhaps the Commission would include such a model as a recommendation in their final reporting.

Tilly liked the idea and told Constance to take the lead for this responsibility. She agreed and set off immediately for the library. In one of Constance's last graduate seminars there had been some discussion about a new set of standards for educational evaluations. She thought that these might provide her with a good place to start her search about the ways in which progress might be evaluated.

Constance knew that these standards were developed for evaluations and not contract monitoring, but they seemed fair and applicable. She thought that five of them could be particularly helpful. She decided that the ways in which contractors dealt with others, especially subjects, could be evaluated during the work. With a description of the planned procedures, the contractor's past skill level might possibly be examined. Information could also be gotten which would examine the validity and reliability of the planned methodologies. These should also be sensitive to the constraints in the real world. The approach should cause the least disruption and provide the best outcomes. And she knew from her own experience and from the comments in the last Commission meeting that timely reporting to those involved often helped remediate, or avoid, a past mistake.

She listed these five variables:

1. sensitivity in human interactions,
2. descriptions of purposes and procedures,
3. using valid and reliable methodologies, and
4. attending to practical procedures (such as disruption, etc.)
5. timely reporting.

Next she laid out a matrix and started listing the ways in which someone might be able to collect this information. The evaluation proposal and design should contain enough information about reporting and procedures so that what was expected could be described and compared with what actually occurred. Constance was pleased about that. So many of the evaluation questions which the Commission members had asked had no apparent, or data-based, expectations involved. Members always seemed to have some hidden, internal standard which they would apply. The other three would have to be set against a more subjectively defined standard.

She was a little troubled that she had made no provision to monitor the fiscal expenditures of the contractor in order to insure that adequate funds existed to complete the work. She almost did not add the fiscal variable to the grid, but then decided she should. While she did not personally think that was that important or informative, she knew that Fred Cashdollar and Ole Timer would be pleased to see it included. Good evaluation, she knew, was getting information which the decision-makers prized. Table 2 contains Constance's completed grid.

FOCUS—WHO IS THE INFORMATION BEING COLLECTED FOR? (AUDIENCE)

Constance knew that the primary audience for this kind of an evaluation would be administrative, or even legislative. This helped her think through the evaluation again and begin working through the information selection and collection techniques issues.

COLLECTING—HOW COULD THE INFORMATION BE OBTAINED? (SAMPLES)

Constance felt that the only legitimate source of information about the sensitivity in human interactions would be those persons, if any, who in fact interacted directly with the contractor. It would be nice to observe the contractor with the people. She recognized that this would seldom be appropriate and possible. Where possible, later interviews from a sample of these people should provide both valid and reliable information. She would later develop an interview guide to include as a reference for this question.

ANALYZING/INTERPRETING—HOW COULD WE ANALYZE THE INFORMATION IF WE HAD IT? (INTERPRETATION CRITERIA)

Constance knew that inexperienced people would have to trust the contractor to use appropriate procedures. Other experts could be asked but this could lead to winless fights about which of two strategies were the best. What was really important, she decided, was to know if the procedure did not work. It would be difficult to do this during the contract, though, and it would cost a lot to pay a qualified "expert" to audit the work. She wondered if the description of planned procedures from the proposal could be used as evidence of their inappropriateness. Expert reviewers could examine these descriptions as a part of the proposal reading.

Similarly experts could look at the strengths of the selected methodologies and the potential for disruption and other practicality aspects. It would also be possible to have a program person keep a complaint log about the various problems encountered while the contractor was working.

The participants could be asked directly about the degree to which they felt the contractor had disrupted or interfered with the routine. Constance knew that this approach could have some negative potential for the contractor. Particularly with evaluations, program people can become

Table 2. Options for Collecting Information

Monitoring Variables	Information					
	Ask the subjects	External expert review	Ask the participants (hosts)	Keep a complaint log	Log contacts with contractee	Get periodical reporting
Sensitivity in Human Interactions	X					
Procedures Description		X				
Validity and Reliability of the Methodology		X				
Procedures Practicality		X	X			
Timely Reporting						
Fiscal Status						

resentful and angry, especially if they are insecure with the activities or the reporting. This source of monitoring information would have to be used sparingly, and the recommendations Constance would develop would carry a warning describing situational characteristics where participants, or subjects, should not be asked directly about the contractor.

DESIGN—HOW CAN I TELL IF MY PROPOSED EVALUATION DESIGN IS ANY GOOD? (CRITERIA)

She thought about this issue for some time and finally asked Dr. Nitpick to review the plan for her. He could have some of his students in the graduate evaluation seminar review and critique it. This would give her a chance to assess the guide and the instrumentation.

REPORTING—HOW CAN I TELL IF THE CONSULTANTS' REPORTS ARE TIMELY? (WHEN)

Constance was still unclear about how to go about collecting information about the timeliness of reporting. She was sure that this variable should not be so narrowly construed as to be solely concerned with the *final* reporting. No, Constance, thought, it should reflect the importance of interim reporting, updating to keep the people informed. She personally felt that this kind of update/reporting should be called for and scheduled in the contracts, but she knew that that would mean changing a lot of the contracts, and necessary resources would be diverted by the contractor into the reporting activities and away from the main work if the requirements became too stringent. Perhaps a controlled log could be used in which an entry would be made after each contact with the contractor. The log would ask for certain kinds of information at each entry as well as encouraging more frequent descriptive narrative entries.

She developed a rough draft of this guide to include in the reporting to the commission (see table 3).

This left only the problem of establishing some guide for monitoring and reporting the fiscal status. Constance personally did not think that the fiscal monitoring was all that necessary, and she would recommend in her report that this be developed to better match the situational requirements of each contract.

REPORTING—AND HOW CAN I PRESENT MY REPORT TO THE COMMISSION? (PURPOSE)

She pulled all of her notes together and developed a draft report of suggested procedures to monitor evaluation contracting. It occurred to her that with very little, if any, modifications this would do to help with monitoring almost any contracted service the DOE, or a similar agency, might require.

MEETING #4

Dr. Mann had a difficult time keeping the group focused through the early agenda items. The State Senate's Ways and Means Committee had been dealing with an important bill and most of the group was preoccupied. He was still trying to get them to develop some type of systematic plan to evaluate the educational and related training in the State. Most of what had been done so far was of value, but he was

---

Table 3. Contractor Contact Log

Date ___ / / ___

Contact via: ☐ In Person   ☐ Mail   ☐Telephone
Initiated By: ☐ Contractee   ☐ Contractor

Approximate Length of Contact in Hours:
Mark One: 0   1/4   1/2   3/4
Mark One: 0   1   2   4 or More

Descriptors of the Contact (Check as many as apply):
☐ Informational · Contractor→Agency
☐ Informational · Agency→Contractor
☐ Planning
☐ Progress/Status Update
☐ Unclear
☐ Clarifying

Topic(s) _____
_____
_____
_____

Describe Any Decisions/Plans Made:
_____
_____
_____
_____
_____

---

concerned that it would be difficult to pull all of this together for final reporting to the legislature.

He called for the report regarding the monitoring of evaluation contractors and was mildly surprised when Constance rather than Tilly presented this report. She described her work, including a thorough rationale for what she had done. This, exclaimed Manuel Fernandez, was just what was needed. Agencies could make good use of Constance's work. Fred Cashdollar and Ole Timer were disappointed that there was no real reporting, but both liked the work which Constance had done. Ziggy Efftest thought the approach rather simple-minded and was convinced that there wasn't the need to formalize these recommendations.

After the members had reviewed Constance's report, they were ready to address any new concerns. Dr. Mann asked if any new issues needed to be considerd. Long-range planning for the Commission's final report was his suggestion.

FOCUS—IS THERE ANY WAY TO TELL WHETHER THE CONTRACTORS ARE PRODUCING GOOD RESULTS? (POTENTIAL UTILITY)

Fred Cashdollar instead voiced his anxiety about an issue which, he felt, the Commission had failed to consider. "These consultants are really just operators of small businesses trying to undercut each other, with each of them trying to do each job the quickest, cheapest way possible. How does the DOE staff check up on these contractors to insure they are getting what they paid for? Constance's approach is a step in the right direction, but it wouldn't insure a decent product or service."

This was a sensitive area for Ziggy Efftest, and he voiced his feelings that the effectiveness of a contractor was situation-specific and the details of contract fulfillment should be left up to the discretion of the DOE.

Sue Striver joined in support of Fred, indicating that she felt the Commission was expected to "stick its nose into DOE business if it needed to!"

Dr. Mann turned to Tilly, "Well, what can you tell us about DOE efforts to evaluate the outcomes of the contract?" Tilly admitted that she was not aware of any such systematic efforts.

"Well, then," Fred remarked, "I think we need to know if the DOE has been pleased with the outcomes of all of this contracted work. If we are spending this much money, are the agencies getting something useful out of?" He suggested that the Commission staff develop an evaluation form, rating the performance of all contractors. Ole Timer concurred, saying he'd like to see the State keep public records assessing contractors' products or services so "we won't be buying pigs in a poke in the future." Dr. Mann recommended that a sample of recently completed contracts be assessed to give the commission some data about how an evaluation procedure like this might look.

The commission concurred and voted to have Tilly develop a performance rating form, use the form with a sample of contracts and bring the results to the next meeting.

COLLECTING—IS THERE A WAY TO GET THE INFORMATION THE COMMISSION WANTS? (INSTRUMENTS) Tilly and Constance arranged a meeting with several DOE staff who frequently contracted with outside consultants or businesses.

The DOE staff was convinced that each of their contracts was unique, and no single form could be designed which would be useful.

Tilly had a sense that DOE staff were resisting any potential mandate to evaluate the contracts they wrote. She also realized that she would need their help to design an evaluation procedure which would be workable. Tilly asked them to try to describe what kind of information about contractors is needed, what information about work performance or products is needed, and how this information should be summarized to help them review contractors in the future. She suggested too that they need not limit their thinking exclusively to rating forms; there were other evaluation approaches to use.

COLLECTING—WHAT ARE SOME ALTERNATIVE WAYS OF GETTING THE INFORMATION? (COLLECTION PROCEDURES) One DOE staff member recommended that contractors be required to keep detailed records of completion of each assignment. These records could be collected and analyzed. Another suggested interviewing a sample of staff served in order to evaluate the results of the contract. Both of these suggestions were rejected as impractical.

Together they arrived at the following procedures:

1. Contractors would be alerted that all products or services rendered would be rated on a three-point scale ranging from excellent to poor on three criteria: quality of outcome, timeliness of completion, responsiveness to DOE needs. If more than one product or service were delivered as a result of the contract, each product or service would be rated.

2. Ratings should be completed within two weeks of the contractor's delivery of each product or service.

3. Ratings should be shared with the contracting individual or agency with explanations of any problem areas.

4. Contractors who were dissatisfied with their ratings would be encouraged to ask for a second rater and/or to file an addendum documenting extenuating circumstances and/or other problems affecting performance.

COLLECTING—DO THE PROCEDURES WE'VE SELECTED GET US THE INFORMATION NEEDED? (RELIABILITY AND VALIDITY) Tilly was now ready to try out the procedures and the instrument with a sample of recently completed contracts. She realized that the procedure must work equally well with contracts for delivery of products and with those for direct services.

Since she knew two dissemination contracts had just been concluded, she asked three DOE staff who had worked closely with the printer and audio tape recording studio to rate their newly delivered products. Constance suggested that she also have the quality of the products rated by others in the DOE who were not familiar with these contracts. They discovered that different staff members were likely to give different ratings. While there was pretty good agreement on the quality variable, there was some discrepancy for the other two variables, especially for contractor responsiveness. Constance noted that the three DOE raters had different levels of involvement with the contractor; thus their basis for judgments was different. Second, there was always some problem with what terms like excellent, fair, etc., meant to different people. Tilly decided to add a question asking about the frequency of contact with the contractor. This would help the users to immediately examine one possible reason for different ratings, if they occurred.

Tilly then selected a sample of service contracts. She asked two different groups of three DOE staff to use the format and then explain any help which the form provided. As she observed them working their way through the form, and then spoke with them, she discovered that they were having a difficult time differentiating among the three variables. Constance suggested bringing the two DOE groups together to see if the language introducing the tasks might be improved, making the instruction and task clear.

At the meeting of the two groups, Tilly was surprised to learn that trying out these forms had evidently been a catalyst in starting staff discussions about the merits and shortcomings of various services or products delivered. Both groups had spent some time after the exercise reviewing the contracts in question.

Tilly pulled together the data from the developmental tests of the form and her notes from the interviews with the participants and drafted a brief report.

MEETING #5

Tilly's report at this meeting documented the procedures and rating form developed by the DOE staff. She also shared with the Commission the sample ratings which the groups had generated. Cashdollar was proud that his recommendation had resulted in a developed product. Ziggy doubted to himself that any of this would ever work into general operating practice.

Sue Striver leaned forward. "Listen, what still keeps gnawing at me is, if any of this work will have any lasting effect? Contractors are monitored, we can see if the immediate outcomes are useful, but does the system change? Does it keep improving itself?"

Ole Timer looked around the now suddenly quiet room. "Well, I can tell you one thing," he said, "one of the least useful services we contract for in terms of what happens in the future is evaluation. We have had a couple of evaluation reports done in our district, but all they were ever good for was to convince the Feds or the State DOE that we really deserve the money we were getting for the program. Finally, I saw the nonsense of this and fired the whole damn evaluation unit. I saved $51,000 that year. And I'll tell you," he intoned, "we haven't missed them at all." Ziggy reminded Ole that he had already told the members about eliminating his evaluation unit.

Was it really possible, Fred asked, to save that amount of money by eliminating evaluations? He was definitely interested in pursuing this area further.

Mary Committee's eyes were now wide open. "You mean," she said, "this evaluation isn't of any use to you school people? Why I remember the nice young evaluator who called and interviewed me on the telephone. He asked so many thoughtful questions about those nasty, immoral library materials, why, we just had such a pleasant conversation; we must have talked for an hour and a half."

Ziggy Efftest was clearly on the defensive. "Now wait a minute, wait a minute. Don't go steamrolling past this issue. These evaluations are often reported to school boards, and they are well received. These reports help local decision makers wrestle with, and solve, all kinds of policy issues."

"Yes, these reports do often have an impact on policy, even when the reports themselves are badly done," challenged Manuel Jose Garcia Fernandez. "They are used to decide policy, all right, particularly when someone wants some evidence to support what they already believe. I move that we have Tilly *thoroughly* examine this question of the impact of evaluation on policy."

Mary Committee seconded the motion, which passed unanimously, and with no further discussion.

Tilly was already very busy handling the growing routine of the commission and preparing a presentation for the upcoming Statewide Inservice Day. So Tilly told Constance that she could begin work on the last evaluation issue raised by the commission. Constance was ecstatic! This was an issue of real importance. She retreated to her office and began work.

She felt fairly comfortable about the question itself. It was clear to her that the commission wanted to evaluate the impacts which contracted evaluations had on policy decisions, chiefly in the local school districts. She decided that she should look at the impacts on the local, county and State levels to learn if there were different kinds or levels of impacts. Constance was a believer in asking carefully worded questions of those involved. Basically she felt people prefer to talk truthfully about things that affect them. She planned to randomly select school people to interview via telephone about their perceptions of evaluation impact. She listed the various groups which might have slightly differing perceptions and from which she would sample. Local board of education members, school administrators and officers from local teachers' unions would all be included. She didn't feel that contacting parents or students would add anything to this inquiry.

Constance knew also that people's memories, however well intentioned, often omitted important information or misconstrued facts just slightly. To back up her interview information, she decided to collect board minutes from each of the schools and agencies represented in the interview sample. These minutes would report little by way of the discussion and rationales for decisions but would provide firm evidence of actions taken.

Constance developed her sample after categorizing the districts in the State and the position titles in the three populations. Then she finalized the interview guide and went home for a quiet evening.

The *Daily Discrepancy*, Chaos' award winning newspaper, that night carried notices of three school board meetings scheduled for later that week in surrounding towns. Constance read with excitement that the Disjunction Township board meeting planned to discuss the evaluation of a homework experiment in the intermediate grades. If there were other districts which were meeting and where evaluations would be presented, maybe she could attend these meetings and do some ethnographic work, recording what she saw and heard. Her reporting could also include impressions and brief speculations as they occurred to her.

The next morning she asked Olene Awfiss, their secretary, to look for districts within 75 miles of Chaos which were having board of education meetings within the next 10 days and where evaluation reports were to be discussed.

Olene found four such districts. Constance immediately began planning visits to these meetings. Since the board meetings were at night, she would be able to finish her interviews on about the schedule she had targeted.

She took home some materials on ethnographic work by Rist and Guba to refamiliarize herself with the concepts.

Constance attended all the sessions in the four different towns. At each meeting she sat where she had a good view of all the board members and of the person presenting the evaluation information. After each meeting, she returned home and dictated from her notes all of the information she could. It was all very hard, time-consuming work, but she wanted to do it right. Her hand seemed perpetually cramped, and she was up late driving and dictating.

When all of the reports were concluded, she began reading through them to develop the variables and codings. She also noted particular points which seemed to hold in common across the situations or which were in stark contrast with others. This all took her four working days.

MEETING #6

REPORTING—WHAT SHOULD I TELL THE COMMISSION? (CONTENT)

Constance was asked to summarize the report. She reported the major findings indicated that evaluation reporting to boards of education at the local, county, or even State level had little major, direct impact on the policy decisions which were made. The evaluation results were usually cited at length by proponents of the view which the report tended to support. The methodology, and thus the findings, were refuted by those who took the opposite side.

Ziggy noted that there were few, if any, evaluation studies which had been done which could not be successfully challenged on methodological issues. The world was not a laboratory, and what with the regulations and restrictions on information, etc., the reports did an admirable job. It was his feeling that the era of the big evaluation, or research, study was long past. The real use of evaluation studies, he said, lay in their abilities to point toward areas in need of further clarification and to augment and support positions on issues which were often decided as much, if not more, for political or other reasons.

He noted that recent looks at evaluation concluded that there were real, though subtle, impacts. More often evaluation was valued to *identify* possible problem areas than to *judge* impact; to *orient* people to possible problems than to *establish* solutions; to *point* to alternate goals than to *measure* those originally described. Evaluation also had a much better chance of being used when evaluators did some advance work with the clients to overcome the threat and skepticism of new, evaluation information; when reporting forms were familiar for the recipients and delivered to coincide with a related, pending decision; when school management generally operated with a cooperative, shared decision-making approach; and especially when the objects were new programs; when smaller procedural changes were recommended; or when the issue was not strongly politicized. During his explanation, delivered in a quieter and more even voice than was characteristic, Ziggy cited frequently Alkin, Patton, Thompson, King and others.

Far from being ready to give up the ship, though, Ziggy felt that building some evaluation information into educators at all levels and thus improving their regard for information, and hopefully then impacting the many subtle ways in which evaluations augment decisions, was the way to go.

Dr. Learned Mann spoke in the quiet room, commending Constance for the rigor and quality of her work and stating simply that the text of Ziggy's remarks would be taken from the meeting tapes and added as a summary section of their final report. Dr. Mann entertained a motion to accept the report. It was so moved and seconded and carried unanimously.

He then reminded the Commission that there was only one month remaining in their appointment. They would need a subcommittee to develop the outline for the final reporting. At the next meeting...

* * * * *

DISCUSSION QUESTIONS AND TOPICS

1. What were three or four of the major biases or value orientations represented by Commission members? Are these value orientations reasonably common for commissions, school boards, and advisory groups?

2. What were some of the advantages and disadvantages of having the several value orientations represented?

3. What were several of the things that Constance and Tilly attempted to evaluate?

4. What are several rather ingenious evaluation techniques that Constance and Tilly used?

5. Do you believe Tilly should have interviewed Commission members more (and more carefully) than she did in order to get greater clarity about the questions they were asking? What would have been some of the advantages of doing that?

6. Tilly set out to prove the need for the dissemination services, a natural and probably unnoticed bias. Do you believe her evaluation was balanced or biased toward proving the need? What are your reasons?

7. Why was it important for Tilly and Constance to make considerable use of available information and analysis of existing documents? What are some advantages of doing that—even when there is more time and money?

8. What was good about Tilly's attempt to answer the question "What would it cost if the dissemination services weren't available?"

9. In several instances, Constance tried to record what was said in interviews and in meetings. Then she analyzed her notes by trying to decide on the important categories of opinions and issues expressed and, finally, tabulated frequencies and types of comments to get a more quantitative perception. What are some of the advantages of this procedure? Do you think there are

situations where the categories should be decided in advance of the interviews? Why?

10. What were several instances in which the evaluation effort, while not providing answers, clarified issues? Do you think that was a valuable thing to have done?

SUGGESTIONS FOR STIMULATING DISCUSSIONS ABOUT THE CASE

1. Arrange a role playing session in which Ole and Ziggy argue about whether outside evaluation efforts are worth doing or whether, as Ole believes, they contribute considerably to cost and not much to benefit.

2. After the Ole/Ziggy role playing session has gone on for about five minutes, have Cashdollar begin to take part. (Observers should write down, beforehand, the position they expect him to take.) After the role play, call on observers to determine the range and accuracy of their predictions and then discuss whether the observers believe the role was played authentically—those believing it was not can be given an opportunity to take the role and attempt to play it as they believe it should be played.

3. Select one of the following topics and organize a debate:
   Resolved: The evaluators performed ingeniously and commendably within the time and resource constraints.
   Resolved: The evaluators should have refused to work under the constraints imposed upon them rather than providing the Commission with such flawed evaluation data.

4. Do a role playing session in which Tilly presents the cost savings on the dissemination services. Fred Cashdollar and one other Commission member should be played.

5. Role play the final meeting of the Commission. Persons playing each Commission member should prepare one policy recommendation he or she would like the Commission to adopt. Determine which of the policies get adopted. After the "meeting" have Constance lead an analysis of the policy recommendations to determine which appear predictable from knowledge of the Commissioner's value positions and which were subtly or strongly influenced by the evaluation.

APPLICATION EXERCISES

1. Read some of the material in the *Sourcebook* indicated by the asides. Then suggest alternative things people in the case might have done at several points in the case. Or suggest a whole new approach they might have taken.

2. Using the case as a model (and foil) and your suggested alternatives as guides, design an evaluation for a situation or problem similar to that shown in the case.

3. Using Chapter 7 of the *Sourcebook* as guide, do a meta-evaluation and critique of the case (and/or your evaluation design).

4. Use the *Design Manual* to develop an improved evaluation design for the case.

5. Use the *Design Manual* to develop an evaluation design for a situation or problem similar to the one described in the case.

CASE S-2

A PROGRAM MANAGER (FROM A STRANGE LAND) ASKS: Now that funds are cut, how can I review proposals without alienating applicants or legislators?

Robert J. Siewert

THE SETTING

FOCUS—WHEN, WHERE, OR WHAT IS THE SETTING? (CONTEXT) In the confusion following another legislative session, a state department of education in the 23rd century began taking stock. What new directives needed attention, what financial changes were needed, what policies had become inoperative? The Chief had much to occupy his mind.

"Gather my section leaders," he intoned, "I need reports."

Deep within the agency, a section leader emerged from the vertical riser and walked through the corridors toward a small, landscaped cubicle. A battle-armored program knight, a warrior attached to 1210, a section of some size and power, sat despondently, head in hands. The leader's eyes fell upon the forlorn figure as he rounded the sound resistant partition to enter the cubicle.

"Hans, why so low?" the leader asked softly. "We may not have won all the battles during the session," he said, "but we cut our losses, and we have survived."

FOCUS—WHAT IS HAPPENING TO MAKE EVALUATION IMPORTANT? (CONTEXT) Hans raised his head slowly. "My program took a direct hit, sir." He glanced at the ceiling where the agency speaker dully droned musak. "My policies are in a shambles and program funds have been cut!" Hans looked sadly at the stack of communiques from the local project directors who counted on support from his program.

"Well, assess your situation, Hans, and write me a memo," the section leader replied (see figure 1). "The Chief wants a complete update on our status, and I am tied up with new directives. The Chief and all of the outstation supervisors are coming unbonded about all the new requirements, and I am going to need a particle barrier to survive. Do the best you can, Hans. Why don't you call that friend of yours, Yodle, and get some help." The leader looked furtively in both directions, darted into the corridor and disappeared.

Memo

TO: Section Leader 94-142
FROM: Program 1210
RE: Assessment of Last Session Changes

The following occurred during the last session:

1. Program policies were changed from a minimum standards approach to granting projects on a competitive basis.
2. Funds were cut in half.
3. A directive was passed for destruction of the program unless defensive evaluation steps are taken.

Assessment:

1. The agency must use some new method for evaluating proposals from the projects. Decisions will have to be made about their relative value. The agency must be ready to defend against accusations when some projects don't get the funds they want.
2. With only one-half the funds, fewer projects can be supported even if grant amounts are reduced.
3. We must prove the worth of our projects or face a "destruct" vote next session; defensive evaluation is important. No funds were given to the sub-section for the evaluation, so the projects will have to collect information even though they get fewer funds. The program has always given the projects power over their own destiny, and directing them to do this evaluation will probably cause unrest. We must be careful to carry out this directive in a cooperative, rather than a dictatorial way, and hopefully, avoid a rebellion.
4. To survive the next session, the defensive evaluation must be a complete one. The agency will need to develop an all-inclusive plan to monitor the projects, the program's own operations, and report findings in a coherent fashion.

I await your reply.

FIGURE 1.

THE SITUATION

FOCUS—WHAT SHOULD BE EVALUATED? (OBJECT) Hans had come to the agency a green recruit from a distant substation the previous year to operate a new, handsomely funded program established by the legislature. No structure had been developed before he came, and he had barely enough time to patch together guidelines for making grants before the program had started.

The guidelines asked the substations to describe the types of services they proposed to provide. The proposals were general, wordy, and often confusing. Most often they contained philosophical purposes, vague goals, and little else. But, because funds were sufficient to give every proposal the amount requested, none was turned down.

Even before this legislative session, Hans had known that the way proposals were selected for funding needed changing. He had observed confused program staff and less than acceptable services when he had visited each of the programs during the year.

Now, with the changes in the program adopted by the legislature, he had little time to work out all of the changes needed. And the legislature was demanding an evaluation report on the program. They wanted to know that the

FOCUS—WHO WANTS THE EVALUATION REPORT? (AUDIENCE) projects funded were successful— and specifically the value of the services the projects conducted.

In a dark mood Hans began to write an assessment of the impact of the legislature's actions on his program (figure 2).

The labyrinthine corridors of Ivory Tower had always been confusing to Hans. He was sure even a Minotaur would need a string to find his way. But Yodle seldom left the Hobbitish environs of his cubicle, and Hans wound his way through the ancient and decrepit catacomb in search of his friend.

"Come in, Hans," Yodle piped.

DESIGN—HOW SHOULD THE EVALUATION BE DONE? (APPROPRIATE DESIGN) Yodle was Ivory Tower's resident expert on evaluation of all sorts. Hans had often come to him for counsel, and had contracted with him for evaluation work. During that time, Hans and Yodle had formed a friendship—of rather a father/son type, since Yodle was at least 10 times Hans' age.

Yodle, unlike many of the others on Ivory Tower, kept in close touch with the realities of state agency and substation work. Because of this, Hans trusted Yodle's suggestions and recommendations as being practical, as well as theoretically interesting. Yodle's genius was in his ability to combine the theoretical and practical into the workable. The fact that

MEMO

TO: Hans, Program 1210
FROM: The Chief
RE: Damage Assessment

Memo received and understood. The agency holds the program in high regard. Good luck.

FIGURE 2

Yodle resembled a Persian cat with a goat's torso had never really bothered Hans.

"I don't mean to interrupt you," Hans said as he inched into the opening. "How did you know I was here?"

"Sometimes you depress me, Hans," Yodle murmured and turned back to his desk piled with mysterious charts and diagrams. Hans removed a mass of papers and books from a questionable-looking chair and sat down.

"I knew you would come and why," Yodle looked sharply at him. "A lot of good those rundown generalities and testimonials did protecting your program in the last legislative session, hrumph!" Yodle snorted disparagingly as he slowly rose into the air and began to rotate clockwise. "You might as well have used a light sabre without extra Duracells," he croaked gleefully.

Before Hans could open his mouth to say anything, Yodle propped his hooves on the desk. He shook his head and said, "Let's get to the point here, boy."

Yodle whirled into the air, floating upside-down rapidly around the room, streaming curly, long fur behind him. "Since you can't articulate your concerns, I'll do it for you," Yodle began.

DESIGN—HOW CAN WE BE SURE THE EVALUATION GETS US THE INFORMATION WE NEED? (APPROPRIATE DESIGN) "First, how will you award funds to projects when your appropriation is cut in half, and the project directors are barely able to make ends meet now? Second, how will you treat their requests for funds on a competitive basis instead of judging them on minimum criteria? Already the project directors are muttering that favoritism and biases will creep into these decisions. Third, how can you evaluate the effect of the projects and your whole program to avoid its destruction at the next session? And fourth," Yodle looked menacingly at Hans, "How can you do all this with fewer funds yourself?" Yodle snapped, "What do you propose to *do*, boy?"

I was hoping you would help me use 'The Wisdom'," Hans said.

Yodle made a face and bounced into his chair. Hans always wanted to tap "The Wisdom," that force of logic which drove all good projects. Maybe in time he would learn.

"Listen, the outstation supervisors insist on their local control," Yodle said. "Besides, the project directors are going to be responsible for much of the evaluation you need. You will need to win their support."

FOCUS—WHAT QUESTIONS NEED TO BE ANSWERED FIRST? (QUESTIONS) Yodle continued. "You need information, Hans. One, has there been any bias in awarding funds in the past; if any, what kind? Two, how have these requests for funds been used in the past by the agency and by the projects? Three, how have you decided on the projects to get funds and how much did it cost you to decide? Four, how have you evaluated the effects and operations of the projects?"

Hans opened his mouth to reply.

"And," Yodle continued, "there must be concerns other than these among project directors, your supervisors, and the general public out in the substations. You need to identify these, too, or you'll wind up in an uncomfortable situation when you make your legislative report."

Hans opened his mouth again . . .

"Not now, boy. I've got another appointment. The Wisdom *is* in you. Now try to get *it*, and the lead out. Put your thoughts together, get your facts straight, and come back in three revolutions." Yodle waved him out the portal.

FACT FINDING

COLLECTING—WHAT CAN I FIND OUT FROM THE INFORMATION I HAVE IN HAND? (INFORMATION NEEDED) Hans sat at his desk surrounded by files of computer data cubes. One contained all of the requests for funds from projects for the past cycle. In another were the projects' final reports on their accomplishments. In a third were reports he had written after visiting the projects, and in a fourth the forms rating the project requests when they were reviewed. In front of him on his desk were computer printouts on the amount of funding each project had used during the past cycle. The task was to decide what further information he needed and if it could be teased from the files.

Hans began by listing questions. The first, how to award credits to projects when only half the funding was available, was a policy question. But this was also interconnected with a second question, how to award funds to projects on a competitive basis in a bias-free way. The answer to one would, to a great extent, determine the answer to the other. Hans was unsure whether the present scoring process used by readers prioritized the proposals in any way or whether biases of proposal readers entered into the scoring.

FOCUS—WHAT CAN I FIND OUT ABOUT HOW WELL PROPOSALS ARE REVIEWED NOW? (OBJECT) Hans could think of only one way to find out about the proposal reading process. He had to analyze the scores given by readers to proposals in the last cycle. He scanned the data cube with the proposal score summaries. Each proposal had been read by a panel of three readers. Each reader had given the proposal a total score, based on ratings of subsections such as rationale, objectives, budget etc. In addition, each reader had given the proposal a "fund"/"do not fund" rating. Since Hans had had funds for all proposals which the panels had agreed were "fundable," no further analysis of points had ever been done.

ANALYZING/ INTERPRETING—HOW CAN I ORGANIZE THE INFORMATION I HAVE SO THAT I CAN TELL WHAT'S BEEN HAPPENING? (ANALYSIS) Hans began by adding up the total scores of the readers for each proposal, and then he arranged them in rank order from the most points awarded to the least points. The new policy question would be to decide how far down the list to go in funding projects.

The answer appeared easy until Hans added the reader panels' "fund"/"do not fund" decisions to the list. He immediately recognized trouble. Several top-rated proposals had at least one "do not fund" vote and one proposal

Table 1. Scores of Readers for Proposals

Project	Points	Fund	Do Not Fund
Antares III	292	3 yes	0 no
Betelgeuse I	230	3 yes	0 no
Alpha Centauri VI	207	2 yes	1 no
Neptune Station	169	3 yes	0 no
Greater Magellanic	152	1 yes	2 no
Funicular Depot	116	1 yes	2 no
Group 7	110	3 yes	0 no
Battle Star	99	1 yes	2 no
Sector III	85	0 yes	3 no
Intimidation Station	74	1 yes	2 no

	Rationale (10)	Problem (15)	Objectives (15)	Method (25)	Evaluation (15)	Budget (20)
ANTARES III (292)						
Reader 1	10	15	13	25	15	18
Reader 2	10	15	14	25	15	17
Reader 3	10	15	15	25	15	20
FUNICULAR DEPOT (116)						
Reader 1	3	7	7	10	8	10
Reader 2	0	3	2	5	0	9
Reader 3	5	7	10	18	8	4
INTIMIDATION STATION (74)						
Reader 1	5	4	5	4	2	5
Reader 2	3	5	5	6	2	3
Reader 3	5	6	4	5	2	3

near the bottom according to awarded points had all three "fund" votes (see table 1). Hans was unsure. He decided to discuss these discrepancies between scores and funding recommendations with Yodle and he turned to the problem of bias.

FOCUS—WHAT IF I FIND OUT SOMETHING BAD? (POTENTIAL UTILITY) As Hans prepared to figure out a way of collecting information, a thought occurred to him. What if he did find bias and it was due to the readers rather than the way the proposals were read? Hans shuddered. He had used his advisory committee for readers during the last cycle. They were appointed by the Chief, and political considerations were certainly a factor! If he found evidence that reader selection was involved, he would have an additional, political problem to deal with. With some trepidation Hans attacked the fact-finding task.

ANALYZING/ INTERPRETING—HOW CAN I FIND OUT IF THERE WAS READER BIAS? (ANALYSIS) He thought of several approaches to learn if bias had entered into the proposal reading process. The most straightforward would be to ask the readers. Though subjective, their comments might be useful in finding a solution if one was needed. He could also prepare a statistical analysis of the score sheets. By plotting the

projects receiving funds, he could see if any regional bias were indicated. With a sigh of resignation, Hans started all three tasks.

First, he began by plotting the scores for each project, reader by reader. The reader scores for projects at the head of the list and the bottom of the list were consistent, but for a number of projects in the middle, large discrepancies between the scores were evident. In these cases, interrater reliability was questionable—and this had a direct bearing on the total scores. The inconsistent "fund"/"do not fund" recommendations could be partially explained by this discrepancy. Hans knew that there were statistical tests for this interrater reliability which would estimate its severity, and Yodle could do them in his head. But for this review it was painfully clear that the readers had some real differences in their assessments. Knowing the significance level of the problem wouldn't help Hans with a solution, he decided.

There was one quick test that occurred to Hans. He took the scores each reader had given to all proposals they had read and averaged them. He then combined these averages to get an average for each three-member panel. The results were shocking (see table 2).

Had the proposals been judged competitively last year, it appeared that decisions would have depended more on which of the four panels did the reading than the specifics of

Table 2. Averages for Panel Members

Panel Members	Reader's Average Score	Panel's Average Score
Clark Kennt	96.2	
Lois Layne	74.8	80.43
Jimminy Olsen	70.3	
Major Concerns	32.5	
General Quarters	48.2	41.13
Corporal Offense	42.7	
James Kirt	87.2	
Dr. Bones	51.6	71.06
Dr. Smock	74.4	
Prince S. Lea	83.4	
Okie Pen Canopy	78.7	81.33
Duke Wingwalker	81.9	

Table 3. Questions and Probable Information Sources.

QUESTION	PROBABLE SOURCE OF INFORMATION
1. What measurable changes have the projects accomplished with their clients?	1. Project Reports
2. What serendipitous effects have the projects had— unplanned yet important?	2. Project Reports/ Program Monitoring Visits
3. Have the projects' operations been cost efficient?	3. Project Budgets/ Reports
4. Have the projects been operated according to standards of the state education agency and the legislature?	4. Program Monitoring Visits
5. Has the program delivered sufficient and appropriate support services to the projects?	5. Project Directors, the Outstation Personnel
6. Has the program office managed resources in a cost-efficient way?	6. Program Budgets; Project Reports
7. What are the unmet needs and in what ways can the program serve them?	7. Project Directors; Other Outstation Personnel; Clients

the writing. Hans also noted the variations within the panels. Some readers had average scores much higher or lower than their panel average. He now had pretty good evidence that a bias did exist, though he could not attribute it yet.

Second, Hans plotted the projects on a large map. He knew what he would find but wanted to actually see it visually—the projects tended to cluster around heavily populated stars, where the strongest outstation supervisors were. "Oh, damn!" he muttered.

Hans set about developing the points he would probe in the Vidphone (a combination auditory and visual receiver/ sender, data storage bank, and programmatic computer) interviews of his readers. He came up with three parts concentrated on getting the readers' input on improving the review process and answering the question of which method should be used to select projects for funding.

FOCUS—WHAT MIGHT BE A CAUSE AND/OR CURE FOR THE BIAS PROBLEM? (QUESTION) The first part would see if bias might be attributed to the way readers were picked, the scoring guides, the panel discussions, or including the "fund"/"do not fund" decision? The second part asked the readers directly to suggest process improvements and the third part asked their opinions or methods to select those projects to receive funds and to apportion the available dollars.

Hans set this draft of questions aside for the time being, feeling that he may add to it later. Right now, he wanted to tackle program evaluation. Several evaluation issues emerged in his thoughts, and he rapidly listed them and probable information sources as they occurred to him (see table 3).

Hans reviewed the list, leaned back in his chair and thought about the task ahead of him. It was becoming overwhelming.

The wall in front of him began to blur as if he were

crossing his eyes. With a discernible pop, Yodle emerged from the wall and sat down on Hans' daily timer.

COLLECTING—WHAT INFORMATION DO I NEED AND WHERE MIGHT I FIND IT? (INFORMATION NEEDED) "Look, Hans, you are drifting into hyperspace. If you are going to get anywhere, you'll need to limit your efforts to the realistic. Pick the questions that you have direct responsibility for and focus on those." Yodle stood and walked purposefully toward the wall. "Get on with it, Hans. I'll expect you in my office next revolution." A snapping sound filled the room, and Yodle disappeared through the partition.

Hans returned to his work, and looked over the list of questions he had written down. Numbers 4 through 7 were ones he was responsible for and also had practically accessible sources of information. Number 4, the compliance issue, seemed like a relatively simple task, since he had already used a method for monitoring the projects

Table 4. Have the projects been operated according to standards and the projects' intended activities?

DIMENSIONS

Information Source	A Assess whether all standards are evaluted during monitoring	B Analyze scoring process for inclusion of all standards	C Analyze whether the projects' proposal intents are being accomplished	D Determine if the monitoring was useful to the projects	E Determine if the monitoring reports were useful in summarizing across all projects
Survey Directors				X	
Survey Readers		X			
Analysis of Monitoring Guide	X		X		
Analysis of Monitoring Reports	X				X
Analysis of the Proposals			X		
Analysis of Project Budgets		X			
Analysis of Proposal Scoring Worksheets			X		
Analysis of Project Reports					

through onsite visits. He wrote this question on a separate piece of paper and listed its various dimensions across the top of the page (table 4). The first three dimensions were fairly obvious, though he had not thought of the proposal scoring process as a means of evaluation before now. The fourth and fifth dimensions he added for his own purposes. He wanted to know if the proposal scoring and project monitoring processes had any value to the projects, and whether the reports he wrote after monitoring the projects could be aggregated and summarized.

COLLECTING—HOW CAN I GET THE INFORMATION WITHOUT WASTING A LOT OF TIME, MONEY, OR GOOD WILL? (EFFICIENCY) Down the left side of his paper, Hans listed the various methods he could use to collect the information he needed for each dimension. Since he would be surveying the project directors anyway, he would add to it to collect information on the dimensions he had listed, making the overall job a bit easier. He was glad he had not yet initiated the Vidphone reader survey—it looked like he might need to add to it. He had the monitoring guide—a list of questions he asked when he visited a project, the budget for monitoring, and the written reports from his monitoring visits, all of which he could

analyze. He cross-hatched the dimensions and methods on his paper and put checks in the boxes where each dimension called for a particular method of collecting the information he needed. He could identify at least two sources of information for each dimension—except for the last one.

COLLECTING—HOW CAN I SURVEY THE PROPOSAL READERS TO GET THEIR OPINIONS? (INSTRUMENTS) He decided to start with the second dimension which required surveying the readers. He added several questions to his reader survey asking whether all standards had been considered during the scoring of the proposals, and if not, which had been left out. He asked also that the readers make suggestions for improvements in the process.

When he turned to the other method, analyzing the scoring worksheet, he realized that he had just deactivated two winged bipeds with one laser cannon shot! He was already having this analysis done by the readers. "I think I'm getting the knack of this," he thought happily. By developing the grid, he had been able to see where a particular collection method could serve more than one function. This would save him time and energy—and reduce duplicate effort. With renewed energy he looked at his grid for other combinations where he could develop more than one type of information using a single method.

He quickly determined that, while the project directors were indicating whether monitoring was useful for them, he could also ask them to critique the monitoring guide, commenting on whether the information requested in it would adequately represent their progress toward the intents and purposes they had set out in their proposals.

Hans worked late into the night, designing specifications for each of the analysis tasks, analyzing the materials, and summarizing the information.

FOCUS—HOW CAN I CUT THE COSTS OF EVALUATING PROPOSALS? WHERE ARE THE BIGGEST EXPENSES? (QUESTIONS)

The next morning Hans began work on the sixth question, the one focusing on his program expenditures. He needed to determine the efficiency of his present expenditures in order to find ways to reduce them in the future.

Hans pulled his paper toward him and began to list where his expenditures were:

1. personal travel and per diem = $1,200 (this paid for his anti-matter fuel, food and lodging costs during the year);
2. office maintenance–$1,000 (Vidphone, reproduction, terminal service cost for the year);
3. directors' meetings–$900 (two general meetings of all the project directors, one at the beginning and one at the end of the year);
4. monitoring costs = $2,000 (this paid for the travel and per diem costs for the monitoring visits, to which he usually invited at least two other people to accompany him, which gave him observers in addition to himself to check his evaluation against);
5. proposal review = $2,500 (travel and per diem for the readers for three revolutions during which they read, graded and recommended proposals for funding).

As he reviewed his expenses, it became apparent that reductions would have to be made in the costs of monitoring proposal reading—his two largest expenditures. Perhaps some saving could be made in the directors' meeting expenses also. But outside of these, the fixed costs involving his own travel and office expenses would probably continue to increase slightly in the future. Changes would need to be made in how proposals were processed and how monitoring was accomplished.

Hans fed the survey of proposal readers and the survey of project directors he had prepared the day before into the Vidphone. It would contact each of the respondents, explain the survey, record their responses, and summarize the information for him.

ANALYZING/ INTERPRETING—WHAT CONCLUSION CAN WE DRAW FROM WHAT WE KNOW AT THIS POINT? (INTERPRETATION CRITERIA)

Hans always got lost trying to find Yodle's room. But he stubbornly continued his way through the ill-lighted corridors.

"Well, boy, what did you come up with?"

Hans nearly lost his balance as he jerked about to see where the voice had come from. Yodle was leisurely floating directly above him.

Yodle entered his cubicle, closely followed by a somewhat shaken Hans. "Sit down and tell me what you have found."

Hans sat, collected his thoughts and notes and began to describe what he had accomplished. "I think I have enough information to make the decisions," he said, "but I need help coordinating changes in how the program operates. Everything is interrelated, and I haven't had time to sort out all the combinations yet."

"Let's get on with it then," Yodle chimed, and settled down in his chair.

The concern Hans first shared was his information on the reader scoring system. "I reviewed how the readers awarded scores to the projects' proposals, and found that, when using total scores, the proposals spread out considerably in a rank order. It looks like the review system I have now will work on a competitive basis, which the new policies dictate."

Hans took a deep breath and forged ahead. "But it isn't that simple. We can keep the general design for proposal reviews, but we do have problems with bias. That was the second concern, remember?"

"I took different tacks in evaluating bias, analyzing individual reader scores, comparing them with other reader's scores and looking at recommendations to fund or not to fund. I found that there were large discrepancies between scores among the readers on a given proposal." Hans handed Yodle the chart he had drawn of the scores.

Yodle interrupted, "What seems to cause the discrepancies?"

Hans shifted uneasily in his chair. "I suppose that a reader could have preconceived notions about a given proposal—doesn't agree with the basic concepts, doesn't like the project personnel, something like that. Or, the readers as a group may not agree what value (number of points) to assign various aspects of the proposal. The interesting point, though, is that the discrepancies were greatest for proposals in the middle of the rank order, and the discrepancies are frequent enough that they could change the rank order. I don't think there was real disagreement about the value of the points among the readers or the discrepancies would have been more frequent throughout the rank order. Also fund/do not fund recommendations from the readers did not correlate well with the rank order of the proposals."

"This fund/do not fund issue, you think that is strange?" Yodle interrupted.

"Well, it just doesn't seem to match up with the points that are awarded, either by the individual reader or when the proposals are rank ordered. Honestly, I just don't understand it."

ANALYZING/ INTERPRETING—WHAT IS THE MOST IMPORTANT CRITERION OF ALL THAT READERS USE IN EVALUATING PROPOSALS? (INTERPRETATION CRITERIA)

"Perhaps, Hans, the readers aren't using exactly the same criteria for the total points as they are for the fund/do not fund recommendation. Maybe," Yodle paused and leaned back with that impish twinkle, "those points relate to only a part of the criteria you think are being applied to the proposals.

"Tell me, Hans, what is it, what component is so important that, no matter how good the rest of the proposal is, you would not allow funding if this *one* component was, as you might say, stinko?"

"Client Services!" Hans screamed and almost jumped clear of his seat. "Of course, no matter how good the rest of the proposal was, the delivery of services to the clients described by the project would have to be of a certain caliber to warrant funding. It's more than just numbers too," he repeated, "there are real quality issues in the design and delivery of these services. Of course!"

"Good. It might seem that your readers are attending to this deep-seated, and actually quite good concern, that the project be able to meet its primary responsibility." Yodle turned to his desk, picked up an obviously ancient document, and faced Hans again. "The venerable Scriven Scrolls of the 20th century describe this as the assessment of 'salient features.' All programs, like the ones you fund have certain activities which are the key features. Now, how to turn this to an advantage?" Yodle looked at Hans and waited.

REPORTING—HOW CAN WE USE WHAT WE'VE LEARNED? (USE)

"No ideas, Hans?" Yodle asked after awhile. "Well, if this service delivery component is the critical one, then why not have it scored first? If the project doesn't get a minimum number of points there, you know *both* that your readers are apt to recommend 'do not fund' and that it is unlikely that the proposal will get enough funds to put it at the top of the list no matter how well the supporting components are done. The first is the

ANALYZING/ INTERPRETING—HOW CAN WE DO FURTHER ANALYSIS TO SEE IF OUR CONCLUSION IS SUPPORTED? (ANALYSIS)

most important. What you want to do is to test statistically the relationship of the fund/do not fund recommendation with the scores for the various components to see if anything else pops up. Save yourself some time and start with the service delivery component. Get over to the evaluation unit and ask your contact there to try a point-biserial correlation. He will explain it to you."

"There are other problems," Hans continued. "I also plotted the funded proposals on a tri-dimension map." Hans entered the recall code in Yodle's terminal and the map with small red arrows appeared. "You can see that the projects cluster around the more metropolitan sectors, very few in the remote, isolated sectors."

"Yes, yes," Yodle said. "A common phenomenon in your agency," he said with some contempt in his tone.

REPORTING—WHAT ELSE HAVE WE LEARNED? HOW CAN WE USE SOME OF THE SUGGESTIONS MADE BY PEOPLE WE SURVEYED? (USE)

"I asked the readers their opinion as to whether there is bias, and if so, how it developed," Hans continued. "They have seen the same data I've been describing, and they unanimously agree that bias does enter into the process."

Hans flushed. "But they don't think any of the reasons I listed were the cause."

Yodle laughed. "Ah, the best laid plans of quadrupeds and featherless bipeds! I've warned you to be careful about how you construct a survey so that you don't unintentionally dictate the results by the way you ask questions. You are just lucky your readers are intelligent, outspoken people! So what did they say was the problem?"

"They think that too much pressure is put on a reader when he or she is reading a proposal from their own local area. Consciously or unconsciously the reader gives more credence to a project which he or she knows personally."

"That is all?" asked Yodle.

"Well, no, they also made several suggestions. First, some means should be used to assign readers proposals which do not pose a conflict of interest. Second, the scoring sheets can be made more specific by describing the criteria for point awards more clearly. Third, some way to allow readers to compare their scores for a proposal and change them if they wish should be used."

"There is some potential here," Yodle said. "So what are the alternatives you pose?"

Hans thought for a moment. "For the first problem, I could select new readers who are from areas where no proposals were submitted. But I would have to wait until after I knew which projects submitted proposals, causing a scheduling problem. The best idea would be to find a way not to give proposals to readers where conflicts might exist."

Yodle turned to his terminal. "Perhaps a simple matrix," he said. "One axis is the readers, the other axis is the projects' proposals. We can determine possible conflicts and mark out the intersection of the conflicting reader and proposal. We can then use the matrix to control the random distribution of proposals among the theoretically unbiased readers. This will help to address your problem of the differences in panels' average scores.

Yodle turned back to Hans. "Now how about a way to allow the readers to see others' scores and modify their own?"

"Up till now, we have had the three-person panels discuss each of the proposals among themselves. You have just told me that the panel approach might not have been such a good practice. And now I'm expecting double the number of proposals so the panel work will become inefficient and more costly. Readers will have too many proposals to discuss each in depth."

Hans thought for a moment. "If I could somehow work it so that each reader could review how the other readers scored a proposal, that would allow him or her or it to rethink their scoring. That may help solve the problem of discrepancies among readers on a given proposal, or at least legitimize the discrepancies as honest differences of opinion."

"Have you ever heard of the Delphi techniques?" Yodle asked.

Hans shook his head no.

"They do in principle, exactly what you are suggesting, Hans." Yodle turned again to his terminal. He quickly punched in a program. "Tell me what components and criteria the readers use to score the proposals." Hans listed the different areas in which points were awarded. "What about criteria?" Yodle asked.

Hans blushed. He knew what was coming since he had spent several hours analyzing the score sheets. "Well . . ."

"You don't give the readers any criteria for scoring, do you? Humph," Yodle admonished. "You did analyze the score sheets, didn't you?"

Yes, and I guess the scoring guidelines were not specific enough to assure that there was consistent assessment from proposal to proposal," Hans replied.

REPORTING—HOW CAN WE REDESIGN OUR PROCEDURES TO PREVENT SOME OF THE PROBLEMS WE'VE DISCOVERED? (USE)

"O.K.," Yodle said. "At least you know where you need to focus some attention. After we are done today, rewrite your scoring sheets. Be sure that you give specific guidelines in each of the areas where points are awarded. Review the standards you have and be sure every one is included in the guidelines. Now, back to the Delphi. We'll allow each reader to see how the other readers scored a proposal, give them a chance to reconsider their own scores and change them if he or she wishes."

"It would have to be anonymous though, wouldn't it?" Hans suggested.

"Naturally, boy. You do finally seem to be catching on! If it weren't anonymous, the personal relationships among the readers might influence their view of the scores. We have the readers enter their scores into the terminal using a code rather than names. The readers can call up the results, see how other readers scored each component of the proposal, be signaled if any of their own scores are notably different from the other, review his or her own scores and change them if he or she wishes."

"An expanded Delphi could go on and on in this cyclical fashion until the extremists have all been moved toward the center. But that's not our purpose here, Hans. You're not after a forced consensus on the scores. You do want to give your readers a chance to know how they stand with regard to the others so that they can rethink some positions."

Hans was caught up. "That means that the panels wouldn't need to discuss proposals where agreement on points was close. Only those proposals where discrepancies among readers persist would a panel need to be convened. That would cut down on panel discussion time or maybe even eliminate it!"

"That will help," Yodle cautioned, "but you had better establish some clear guidelines for what is a major discrepancy. The guidelines can be developed with some fairly clean statistics. Go see old Buck Rodgers in the Agency's Evaluation Unit. He can work that out for you."

"Now, what is next?" Yodle said.

ANALYZING/ INTERPRETING—HOW WELL HAVE I BEEN DOING IN MONITORING THE PROGRAMS THAT WE'VE FUNDED? (ANALYSIS)

"Program evaluation," Hans replied, and handed the chart to Yodle. "I listed the major evaluation questions, I think, on this grid and looked at ways to collect information."

"Looks like we've just handled B on the chart. For the others I did some data collection. I analyzed the monitoring reports I wrote last time and found little consistency among them. I had reported findings, but in no uniform way, so summarizing the findings will be very difficult. In some reports I made reference to the standards, and in others I didn't, so they are not very helpful."

ANALYZING/ INTERPRETING—WHAT WORKED AND WHAT DIDN'T? (INTERPRETATION CRITERIA)

"I then turned to the guide I had used for monitoring." Hans gave Yodle a copy of the guide. Again, I included questions about some standards but not all. The questions about whether the project is achieving its original intents seems to be appropriate, however. In fact, my monitoring reports deal with this aspect pretty well. I compared my reports to the original project proposals, and I did include comments in the reports about the projects' progress according to their intentions. This is a pretty closed view of monitoring and evaluation and those ancient Scriven Scrolls you gave me did point out that we should include inquiries about serendipitous outcomes in our evaluations. In fact, he'd go further, but I am not quite prepared for that." Hans paused briefly to look for Yodle's reaction to his obvious research work. No reaction.

Hans took a breath. "I surveyed the project directors, asking them how useful the monitoring reports were and in what ways they had been used. I got mixed reviews. Most thought the monitoring was or could be useful. It helped them look at their programs—a hard thing to do when you are in the midst of the daily hubbub of running a project. Most also thought the visit could be better organized, and they wished they could get the written reports faster."

"Was there some delay?" Yodle asked.

"Well, yes, Yodle." Hans appeared defensive. "I visited each project—it took several weeks. Then I came back to my office and wrote the reports—several weeks more. It was just time consuming."

"All right, all right." Yodle was becoming impatient. "Let me see if I can summarize all this.

1. Your monitoring of project compliance is inconsistent both in how you review the projects when you visit them, and in your report back to them.
2. Because of the inconsistency, you will have a difficult time summarizing your findings across the projects.
3. Your reports do seem to accurately reflect the projects' progress toward their intended outcomes, as does the monitoring guide.
4. The project directors think the visits are useful in that it helps them step back and look critically at their project activities. But they also thought it could be better organized, and that the report should be received by them in a shorter period of time."

REPORTING—HOW CAN WE REDESIGN OUR PROCEDURES TO PREVENT SOME OF THE PROBLEMS WE'VE DISCOVERED? (USE)

"So what does all this tell you," he asked Hans.

"I think I need to do a couple of things," Hans replied, hoping he could keep it all straight. "One, I need to rewrite the monitoring guide to include all the standards, as I am going to do to the proposal scoring sheets, and . . ."

Hans paused. "Hey! Why can't I combine the two—use one guide to both score proposals and guide my observations during onsite monitoring?"

Yodle's eyes seemed to twinkle. "Go on," he said.

"That should solve the report problem, too. I'll put in a checklist for all of the standards, then include the questions related to the intents of the specific proposal/project. When I write the report, I will comment on both. I will have a document, too, rather than having to depend on my memory and sketchy notes."

"What about the time problem," Yodle prompted.

"Well, I could leave a copy of the checklist and my notes with the project director when I leave, and explain what my report would contain. They would get the information immediately. The report would just formalize the verbal report and the checklist."

"You don't seem to need my help on this one," Yodle noted. "Now what about this fourth concern?"

Hans had been dreading this moment. All of the solutions that he and Yodle had discussed so far had not helped with his budget problems. "My major expenses are in proposal reviews and in monitoring," he said. "I don't know what to do to cut the expenses."

"What kind of expenses are they?" Yodle asked.

Hans gave him a copy of the breakdown.

"O.K., per diem first, travel expenses second, and everything else third for proposal review; your travel expenses for monitoring. What could you do about these?" Yodle asked.

Hans began to open his mouth to plead ignorance, but shut it again. He thought for a moment. "If the readers won't be meeting in a group to score the proposals the first time through, there is no reason to bring them together. I could send them the proposals by mail, have them do the scoring and enter the scores in their own terminals. If my estimate is right, discrepancies will occur in only about a third of the proposals. They would need to meet for group discussions for only one day instead of three. That would cut the per diem expenses by two thirds, overall maybe by half!"

"That is a good start," agreed Yodle. "But you could also use electronic mail to enable discussion of the difficult proposals. Anonymous comments could be supplied to each reader to be weighed in reconsidering their own judgment. In fact, you'll know this works if there are just a couple of cases where the majority is persuaded to change scores by an observant, thoughtful, minority scorer."

"Look, I'm trying to cut costs and save time. Do you know what electronic mail costs?" pleaded Hans.

"As well as I know what it costs in time and travel to set up one of your meetings," Yodle shot back. "Meetings require everyone to be in one place at one time. Neither of these is really needed for a 'meeting of the minds.' Anyway, think about it. Now how about monitoring?"

"I could try a couple of things," Hans said. "One, I could spend less time at each project site, but I don't get to the projects often and the time is important for discussions about other things, like budgets, staffing, instructional strategies, etc. Second, I could have the project directors do a self-evaluation before I arrived. This would cut down on

the time spent strictly in monitoring. They would have collected necessary documents, filled out the checklist, and have answers ready for the monitoring questions. I could cut down the overall time spent on monitoring and still have time for other discussions. Three, I could monitor projects on a rotating basis, have the projects do a self-evaluation and send it and supporting documents to me. I could review these and pick out those I think I need to visit to gain further information."

Hans thought for a moment. "I think I like the third plan best. I can cut the monitoring expenses in direct proportion to the reduced number of projects I visit. I can still write reports on the information the projects send me—the ones I don't visit. I think that is the best alternative, Yodle."

Yodle looked up. His eyes were drooping—he had been asleep. "I knew you could do it, Hans. You are not the asteroid-brain everybody says." Yodle got up and walked toward the door. "Now go do your work and be back here in three revolutions. I want to work on the rest of your questions."

Hans walked out feeling pleased with himself. "Maybe the program will survive after all," he thought. He returned to his office and drafted an update memo to the Chief. He felt the Chief would be pleased with his success.

Hans had just finished keying the memo (see table 5) to the Chief when there was a loud pop behind him. Yodle floated into view as Hans swiveled in his chair.

"You seem very pleased with yourself," Yodle taunted mildly.

DESIGN—CAN WE REDESIGN OUR APPROACH TO FUNDING PROPOSALS AND MONITORING PROGRAMS SO THAT WE ARE AHEAD OF THINGS RATHER THAN SCRAMBLING TO KEEP UP? (APPROPRIATE DESIGN)

Hans was a little annoyed, and surprised at Yodle's visit and the tone in his voice. "I am pleased with how things have worked out. Is there something wrong with that?" Hans said cautiously.

"No, that's fine, as far as it goes, but what happens now?" asked Yodle.

Hans crossed his legs and leaned back. "Well, you know, coping with this threat has made me all the more confident that I can cope with the next one, as well."

"Then there certainly will be a 'next one.'"

"What do you mean by that?"

Yodle explained patiently, "What you have accomplished so far has been reactive rather than proactive, an effort to avoid things you do not want rather than to achieve something you do want. Mentally you are facing the wrong way to make progress. As the prophet Ackoff said three centuries ago:

'One who walks into the future facing the past
  has no control over where he is going!'"

Hans was troubled. "What do you think I should be doing then?"

"It's really quite simple. You've been concerned with proposals, projects and evaluations. Your job is to identify good projects as they happen, help them happen, then tell people what happened."

"Isn't that what I'm doing?" Hans asked.

Table 5

MEMO

Revolution Dated 138.5

TO: Section Leader 94–142
FROM: Program 1210, Hans
RE: Progress to date

Following are my decisions and program changes implemented in order to meet legislative directives.

1. Proposal Review
   New readers will be included in future cycles selected so that conflict of interest will be minimized.
   A system for assigning proposals to readers will be used to further minimize conflict of interest—a two-dimensional matrix of readers and proposals will be used to randomly assign proposals but control conflict of interest.
   A more definitive set of criteria for awarding points to proposals are now being developed to bring consistency to scoring among readers.
   A key features preliminary reading of proposals will be used to eliminate poor proposals early in the process, thereby saving time and costs.
   A modified Delphi process will be used to eliminate interreader discrepancies on scoring for any single proposal.
2. Program Evaluation
   A common evaluation format will be used to both evaluate proposals and conduct onsite reviews. This will bring consistency to both, and aid in bettering the onsite evaluations and the SEA's ability to summarize results across projects.
   An evaluation design has been started which clarifies evaluation responsibilities of the SEA and the projects.
   The evaluation of compliance of projects with minimum standards has been included in both the proposal review process and monitoring.
3. Summary
   The above changes and planned changes will allow the program to award funds to projects on a competitive basis with little susceptibility to accusations of bias. By changing the grant review process and monitoring process, program expenditures for these activities can be reduced significantly. Common changes in both monitoring and project review processes will enhance consistency, the ability to report data across projects, and increase the value of the data collected.

I will report further work in the next few revolutions.

"You have made a good start," Yodle responded patiently. "Your efforts to improve reliability and eliminate bias in reviewing proposals will make it possible to examine the relationship between proposal quality and later measures of project quality. Consistent predictions are good. Consistently *good* predictions would be even better. Your new evaluation procedures will allow you to document and tell the story of your projects. It is good to have *documentably good* projects. As you improve and clarify your criteria for "good" projects, as you get better at picking really "good" projects for funding, and as you get better at giving helpful feedback to projects to make the good even better, you'll find that more and more you *will* be documenting good projects, for all to see. When that happens you'll stop even thinking about 'destruct' threats from the legislature, and they won't be thinking about sending such messages, either."

"Thanks, Yodle," Hans said humbly. "You've given me a lot to think about."

Yodle floated to the partition and disappeared through it leaving Hans to his work.

* * * * *

DISCUSSION QUESTIONS AND TOPICS

1. How strange is the setting? That is, are the people similar to those in 20th century state departments of education? Are the problems similar to 20th century problems?
2. Do you believe that a funding crisis represents a good opportunity for doing evaluation? Why or why not?
3. What were some of the major findings of the evaluation? Do you believe that enough was learned to enable Hans to design a significantly improved funding review and program monitoring system?
4. Do you believe the funding review and monitoring system designed will protect "local control" adequately?
5. Why was it a good idea for Hans to begin the analysis with information that was easily accessible to him? What risk is involved in doing that?
6. What do you think of Hans' list of seven program evaluation questions? Do they seem specific enough so that you understand what data could be used to answer them? What evaluation questions should be added? (Try to add at least three.)
7. If, due to practical constraints, Hans could answer only three questions from his list of seven (and your list of three) which questions do you believe he should focus on?
8. How was the "planning grid" (shown in Fig. 1) useful to Hans in managing his evaluation efficiently?
9. What were several useful or clever evaluation techniques Hans used?
10. How important were Yodle's suggestions about clarifying criteria for scoring proposals and for observing projects?

SUGGESTIONS FOR STIMULATING DISCUSSIONS

1. Arrange a debate. Resolved: Yodle is *really* strange if he thinks that legislators in the 23rd century would stop making "destruct" threats just because programs were demonstrably good.
2. Have one person or group specify the main features of the improved design for reviewing and monitoring.
3. Have a person, or group, challenge the design from the perspective of a local educational agency.
4. Have a person or group challenge the design from the perspective of SEA evaluators.
5. Arrange a debate. Resolved: State monitoring of local projects is fatally flawed by the State's natural desire to show positive results of the projects they fund.

APPLICATION EXERCISES

1. Read some of the material in the *Sourcebook* indicated by the asides. Then suggest alternative things people in the case might have done at several points in the case. Or suggest a whole new approach they might have taken.
2. Using the case as a model (and foil) and your suggested alternatives as guides, design an evaluation for a situation or problem similar to that shown in the case.
3. Using Chapter 7 of the *Sourcebook* as a guide, do a meta-evaluation and critique of the case (and/or your evaluation design).
4. Use the *Design Manual* to develop an improved evaluation design for the case.
5. Use the *Design Manual* to develop an evaluation design for a situation or problem similar to the one described in the case.

CASE S-3:

A STATE SPECIAL EDUCATION CO-ORDINATOR ASKS: How can we find out if the staff development activities we've been funding are doing what they are supposed to do?

Joan Shaughnessy and Kenneth R. Olsen

FOCUS—WHAT IS THE SETTING FOR THE EVALUATION EFFORT? (CONTEXT)   After five months working for the State Education Agency (SEA), Ned Novice had begun to feel comfortable in his position as the Coordinator of Inservice Training for the Division of Special Education (DSE). He had come to the DSE from one of the large local district special education

departments. Ned was in his early thirties and with his wavy hair, deep tan and careful attention to clothes, looked like he had stepped out of the pages of *Gentleman's Quarterly*.

Ned had gotten a good handle on the working of the SEA from frequent lunches, and a couple of more relaxed dinners, with Sue Savvy, a colleague in the DSE. Ned profited from Sue's grasp of Division history. In her five years there, since starting as a graduate intern, the attractive specialist for hearing impaired had carefully studied the Division's subtle workings. Sue told Ned that Gloria Goal, his predecessor, had done a decent job developing Division objectives for staff development, had rarely left her office to visit training sites around the state and because of this lack of visibility and lack of responsiveness to the legislature's House Subcommittee on Education had gently been "moved out" a year ago. Ned felt he couldn't do a good job reviewing and approving proposals for state funding of staff development without establishing a strong working relationship with the regional and local education agencies (LEA's). Ned was also eager to start on-site visits.

THE TASK

FOCUS—WHAT PROBLEMS ARE WE FACING? (PURPOSE)   Tuesday morning Dr. B.G. Gruff, the Director of the Division of Special Education, called Ned into his office. Ned was pretty apprehensive. No one in the Division liked to be summoned to "the old man's" office. Gruff, a man of few words, told Ned that the DSE would be trimming down next year's budget for staff development and training. Novice's new assignment was to collect information the Division would need to make fair choices in the coming months. Dr. Gruff warned Ned that the DSE must ensure that all "reductions in services were spread equally, and no specific region or interest group would be hit with the brunt of the cutbacks." Training efforts which were provided with state dollars must reflect exemplary practices so criteria needed to be established to identify model inservice activities. Ned felt overwhelmed, and very alone, when Gruff dismissed him. All Division staff would be asked to help Ned in his efforts, but that responsibility for coordination was Ned's.

Ned left the meeting uncertain about where he should begin. He was to have a plan of attack developed for a staff meeting the following Monday. The DSE needed answers before the departmental/policy/budget meetings taking place in five months. He turned to the evaluation component of last year's DSE personnel development plan, hoping to find some guidance. In the past each trainer conducting an inservice was required to file a report, but there apparently was no way to judge the value of the activities against each other, since each inservice activity was viewed as a unique effort responding to a specific personnel need. Now Ned was being asked to look at the inservice activities as a programmatic effort rather than a series of unrelated events. And then there was the exemplary practices issue! How would he assess the effectiveness of the inservices? Where should he begin?

FOCUS—WHO IS MOST
CLOSELY INVOLVED?
(AUDIENCE)

Ned found several handbooks which suggested that evaluation should begin with a list of questions to be answered. But Ned was concerned about single-handedly designing an evaluation. He was afraid he would be caught in the middle. Probably his best strategy would be to get staff agreement now on the important issues in evaluation and in defining exemplary inservice efforts. What they wanted to consider would guide the data collection for the evaluation.

Ned laid out a plan of action.

DESIGN—WHAT GENERAL
STRATEGY SHALL I USE?
(ALTERNATIVES)

First, he'd ask the Division staff members to *identify the key issues which would be helpful* (a) in evaluating the DSE program of inservice activities, and (b) in identifying exemplary inservice practices.

Next, for each issue identified at the meeting he'd *generate sample evaluation questions*. The Division staff would help select which of these questions should be tackled during the coming months. Ned knew this was where other potential audiences outside of the DSE could be involved in the development of evaluation questions.

Then once the evaluation questions were identified, the next work would be to *determine what types of evidence were needed* to answer the questions. Here he would be working under time and budget restraints in selecting what types of evidence were feasible to collect.

After that he'd *design an evaluation plan* for each question by determining (a) what procedures could be used to collect the evidence, (b) what instruments should be designed or identified to collect valid data, (c) how the data collected could be analyzed, (d) how this information would be reviewed to assess the "value" of the findings, and (e) how the analysis could best be reported to the groups needing the data, so they might use the results to plan for the coming year's RFP or criteria for funding.

And finally, for each question, he'd *implement the five steps in the evaluation plan*, i.e., *procedures, instrument development or identification, analysis, valuing, and reporting*. This meant that several mini-evaluations would be conducted in the next few months, and Ned would be responsible to develop the appropriate timelines and to divvy up the responsibilities where possible. For economy's sake, Ned would also need to check if there were any overlap where two types of information could be collected simultaneously.

THE STAFF MEETING TO DISCUSS ISSUES. Ned didn't like the way the staff meeting began. Dr. Gruff explained that

DESIGN—HOW CAN I GET
PEOPLE CONSTRUCTIVELY
INVOLVED? (ALTERNATIVES)

there would be cutbacks in training, and then abruptly turned to Ned and sat back in his chair. Ned gulped!

He began by admitting his own hesitancy to design an evaluation plan without the input of Division staff. He wanted to have the staff (a) define their own perceptions about what was desirable in a staff development program in special education, and (b) describe what considerations they would use to select the exemplary inservices which would be maintained despite budget cuts. Perhaps they could begin by suggesting issues in the definition of a "good" statewide staff development program.

A long silence ensued. Finally Sue Savvy asked if Ned were talking about an issue like the balance of the staff development offerings in all regions of the state. Babs Battleaxe, a Division fixture for many years, objected. Balance might seem important to legislators, but it was really a surface issue she felt. If the staff development program was under attack, the DSE would need evidence of the practical effectiveness of their inservice efforts. They'd have to prove that inservice changes what happens in the classroom.

Ned smiled. Both of these issues were good ones. Yes, they could look at both balance and practical effectiveness in their evaluation of staff development. Ken Koncern quietly explained that he felt good staff development activities were ones which avoided any misinformation. Inservice trainers needed to be current about SEA and federal regulations. Dennis Document, the DSE representative on the SEA needs assessment committee, commented that a good inservice program is one which addresses the needs of the educators in the state. Ned added that he felt effective instructional approaches were a vital component in inservice efforts. He had been to several workshops recently where "half the participants were cat-napping!"

With this list of issues in hand Ned explained how he'd now generate some sample evaluation questions and get staff input again. But first he wanted to know how much of a commitment to data collection the Division would be willing to make. Dr. Gruff leaned forward. He said he'd been convinced for some time the staff's efforts had been hampered by the SEA's lack of a vision for the Division. Gruff was gratified by the discussion and felt that an evaluation of the type described by Ned could serve several purposes. Evaluation information would be useful to (1) make cutback decisions about next year's funding of proposals, (2) to design better training packages, (3) develop grant proposals, and (4) insure that offered inservices were in keeping with the new State and Federal guidelines being adopted.

Ned was elated! The meeting adjourned, and Ned and Sue celebrated over dinner.

FOCUS—WHAT EVALUATION
QUESTIONS SHOULD WE
ADDRESS IN ORDER TO
DEAL WITH THE LIST OF
ISSUES THE STAFF HAS
IDENTIFIED? (QUESTIONS)

The next day they met to list some evaluation questions. While not exhaustive, it helped define the issues raised. Along with the list (see table 1), they drafted a memo to the SEA Division staff asking them to:

1. Indicate if the answers to each question would be useful (a) in their jobs, and/or (b) for Division planning;
2. Write their comments and reactions on the margin of the list; and
3. Return the list to Ned, and he'd prepare a summary of their reactions for the next staff meeting in two weeks.

COLLECTING—HOW CAN WE
FIND OUT IF THESE ARE
THE RIGHT QUESTIONS?
(INFORMATION NEEDED)

Before the list of questions was finalized, Sue argued that other groups who are potential users of the data on staff development activities should also be involved. Ned agreed, knowing that if additional audiences were involved in planning the evaluation, there was a greater likelihood that the reports would have the desired impact. Sue arranged for Senator Downstate, Chairman of the Educational Subcommittee to review the list over lunch. This way Sue and Ned got an idea of his Committee's interests and need for information.

Using all these responses, Sue and Ned drafted a final list of five evaluation questions:

1. Are staff development offerings funded by the Division balanced?
2. Do the SEA-funded staff development activities meet the needs of special educators in the State?
3. Are the training methods being used in inservice activities effective and appropriate in light of the goals of the staff development activity?

4. Is the content selected for inclusion in staff development activities consistent with State and Federal policies and regulations?
5. Are participants in certain staff development activities more likely to apply their newly acquired knowledge and skill on the job than those in other activities?

Ned submitted this list to Dr. Gruff for his approval and requested that he be permitted to draw upon the capabilities of four DSE staff members in designing and executing an evaluation for each question.

FIRST QUESTION: ARE STAFF DEVELOPMENT OFFERINGS FUNDED BY THE SEA BALANCED?

DEVELOPING PROCEDURES. Ned was unsure how to begin. The subcommittee would be making their recommendations to the legislative body in 6 weeks so quick

Table 1. List of Sample Evaluation Questions for Each Issue Raised

Issue	Questions	Check if Answer is Useful		
		In Your Job	In DSE Planning	Comments and Reactions
Balance of Staff Development Offerings	1. What geographic areas of the state are served by present training opportunities? 2. What type of staff (i.e., regular classroom teachers, special education teachers, support personnel) are being served? 3. What grade levels are served: K–3, 4–6, etc.			
Needs of Educators Being Addressed	1. Is there adequate information about the needs of educators in the state? 2. Are training opportunities diverse enough to meet these needs? 3. Do SEA-funded activities meet the needs of special educators in the state?			
Effective Instructional Methods	1. Are the teaching methods used appropriate and effective? 2. Are the instructional methods responsive to participants' needs? 3. Are the participants able to get involved in the activities?			
Accuracy of Information Presented by Trainers	1. Is the content covered in these efforts consistent with the State and Federal laws, regulations or Board policies? 2. Do trainers keep themselves current on regulations, etc.? If so, how? If not, how can this be encouraged?			
Effectiveness of Staff Development in Changing On-the-Job Educator Performance	1. Do participants change their attitudes on the job? 2. Do participants apply their knowledge and/or skills learned in their work settings? 3. Are certain staff development activities more likely than others to promote participant use of skills?			

COLLECTING—HOW CAN WE FURTHER REFINE THE QUESTIONS SO THAT WE CAN BE CLEARER ABOUT WHAT DATA WE'LL NEED TO COLLECT? (INFORMATION NEEDED)

reporting was a must. Sue argued that they should first limit their definition of balance to two topics raised by Senator Downstate, geographic distribution of the inservice participants, and distribution of participants across professional roles. Pressure on these topics was always applied by legislators from the rural sectors and by the state's teacher association, who wanted assurances that all groups of teachers were being served equally in the state.

COLLECTING—WHERE CAN WE GET SOME OF THE DATA WE NEED? (COLLECTION PROCEDURES)

For starters, they would need information about, (1) the type of position held by inservice participants, (2) the region of the state where they were employed, and (3) the distribution of population and the number of classroom teachers, administrators, education support staff, etc., in the different regions of the state. Ned began by reviewing SEA printouts on personnel classification. They oriented him to the type of statewide data available. He wanted to be sure he collected comparable information on inservice participants.

DEVELOPING INSTRUMENTS. Ned made a list (see table 2) of all inservice activities funded by the Division, descriptions of the participants and the content covered. Using the

COLLECTING—HOW CAN WE GET THE DATA? (INSTRUMENTS)

final reports, he filled in as many of the columns as possible. He circulated the partially completed list to the other DSE staff asking them to provide him with leads on missing data. Ned was disappointed to find that for some inservices, the information needed was woefully incomplete. For example, in half of the workshops, no specific information about the number of contact hours was described in the final report. Ned was glad then that the list included trainer names, phone numbers, addresses and/or affiliations. He instructed his secretary to contact each trainer. Also, there was no information about professional position and geographical region of the 500 participants at the summer workshop. Ned couldn't exclude information about these summer participants, neither could he take the time to call or write all 500 persons. To speed up the process, Ned showed a DSE research assistant how to select a random sample of 10% of the participants. The research assistant then contacted the participant's school and asked the secretary what the participant's position was at the time of the inservice (many had since changed roles). From their addresses, the assistant was able to determine which area of the state the participants represented. Now Ned could use extrapolation to approximate the composition of the entire group of summer participants.

ANALYZING THE DATA. Meanwhile, Ned had prepared a summary of the educational personnel population in the state.

ANALYSIS/INTERPRETATION—CAN WE ANSWER OUR EVALUATION QUESTION ABOUT BALANCE OF STAFF DEVELOPMENT OFFERINGS FROM THE DATA WE'VE COLLECTED? (INTERPRETATION CRITERIA)

He and Sue sat down over lunch to examine the figures. They were both surprised that regular K–6 teachers were receiving twice as many hours of special education inservice as teachers at grades 7–12. The data also confirmed that staff in Good and Plenty Counties (the population centers of the state) were receiving more contact hours of special education inservice than other regions of the state combined.

ASSESSING THE VALUE OF FINDINGS. What did the findings mean? What should their recommendations be? Perhaps there should be an equalization of hours of inservices offered at elementary (K–6) and secondary (7–12) levels, but what if elementary teachers needed more inservice to better work with special education students in their rooms?

ANALYSIS/INTERPRETATION—CAN WE USE THE DATA TO DIG OUT AN ANSWER TO A QUESTION WE HADN'T THOUGHT OF? (ANALYSIS)

Ned reported to Gruff who reviewed their results superficially and then asked if they had collected data on costs of the inservice hours offered around the state. For example, he said while more hours were available to Good and Plenty educators, it was considerably cheaper to run workshops right here in Capitol City.

Ned realized that he had neglected looking at dollars spent for each group. He translated the hourly data collected into cost of inservice so he could report the information to the legislative committee both ways.

REPORTING THE RESULTS. Ned shared his information about the hours of inservice and dollars spent for each County and for each category of educational staff with the

REPORTING—WHAT SHOULD WE RECOMMEND, BASED UPON THESE DATA? (PURPOSE)

DSE staff. Together they worked out these recommendations: (1) inservice trainers should collect data describing the educational groups and counties served; (2) several inservice activities aimed at elementary teachers could be eliminated in the following year; and (3) inservices offered in Good and Plenty Counties could be reduced. A complete report was forwarded to Senator Downstate for distribution to the Legislative Subcommittee.

SECOND QUESTION: DO THE SEA-FUNDED STAFF DEVELOPMENT ACTIVITIES MEET THE NEEDS OF SPECIAL EDUCATORS IN THE STATE?

FOCUS—DO STAFF DEVELOPMENT ACTIVITIES MEET REAL NEEDS? (QUESTION)

Dennis Document was familiar with the needs assessment so he was the logical candidate to help answer this question. Dennis, the quietest of the DSE staff, had earned respect as a knowledgeable if methodical worker.

Table 2. Information Needed to Describe Participants Served in SEA-Funded Staff Development

Name of Each SEA-Funded Inservice Activity	Trainer Name (Include present phone no., address and/or affiliation)	Content Covered	Number of Participant Contact Hours	Participants (Classify Using List* Below)			
				Professional Role (List all positions represented and No. of each at session)	N	*County* (List all counties represented and No. of participants from each)	N
New Technology in Special Education	Martha Mumble 911-555-4321	Innovations in instructional technology	12	Media Specialists	21	Groan and Moan Counties	7
						Grimace and Grumble Counties	14
Teacher Stress in Regular Classrooms	Karl Complaint 020-555-2424	Time management; communication skills	5	Elementary Teachers	32	Good and Plenty Counties	
				Junior High Teachers	18		62
				District Administrators	12		
Etc.							

* Professional Role classification:

Regular Classroom Teachers (list by building level):
  Elementary
  Junior High or Middle School
  Senior High

Special Education Teachers

Special Education Directors/Coordinators

Teacher Aides

Support Personnel:
  Media Specialists
  Librarians
  Guidance Counselors
  Health Personnel
  Psychologists
  Social Workers
  Physical Educators
  Audiologists
  Physical Therapists

Building Administrators

Regional Administrators

District Administrators

Non-instructional Staff

Other:
  Volunteers
  Parents

DEVELOPING PROCEDURES. Ned arrived at the first meeting with Dennis full of suggestions. How about doing follow-up interviews with a sample of participants after the

COLLECTING—WHAT DATA DO WE NEED IN ORDER TO FIND OUT IF ACTIVITIES MEET NEEDS (INFORMATION NEEDED)

inservices? Or maybe use a pre-post questionnaire to collect information about staff needs at all inservice activities?

Dennis shook his head. Data on staff needs were already collected each year in the annual needs assessment and were summarized and consolidated each year to serve as a guideline for the annual update of Division priorities. Dennis suggested that the priorities themselves serve as the starting point for the evaluation.

COLLECTING—HOW CAN WE GET THE DATA? (COLLECTION PROCEDURES)

DEVELOPING INSTRUMENTS.

First they matched the priorities to the workshop

offerings. For each priority (listed in table 3) Dennis noted workshops addressing that particular need.

It looked as if priority needs were being addressed disproportionately. For example, six workshops were funded for art, music, and PE teachers, but only one for principals to help them learn about chairing IEP meetings. Division workshops varied widely in the number of educators served, and there were unequal numbers of educators statewide in each of these priority need categories. The SEA Certificate Division could give the state totals in each category. So Dennis determined the total number of staff served by the inservice in each "need" category. Completing the remaining columns in Table 3 showed him that 10% of the state's Physical Education, Art and Music teachers received training, but only 2% of the principals were served.

Dennis wanted further evidence that this year's inservice activites were addressed to needs. Maybe the SCE could compare this year's needs assessment data to the data collected next year. Then if the needs changed it would

Table 3. Review of Inservice Activities

Need Category	Number of Inservice Activities	Total Number of Staff Served	State Totals from SEA Certification Division	Percent of Total Served in State
State Priorities				
1. Regular educators for unprovided competencies	11	640	21,300	3%
2. Updating special educators	7	140	3,500	4%
3. Train preschool and kindergarten teachers in identifying handicapped children	4	200	980	22%
4. Train principals to chair IEP meetings	1	34	1,700	2%
Part D Application				
A. Train art, music, and PE teachers to accommodate handicapped	6	180	1,800	10%
B. Vocational education counseling	4	120	1,200	8%
C. Skills for preschool teachers to participate in team	1	24	980	3%
D. Clinical speech therapy	3	78	710	11%
E. Other _____				

have an indication that the old needs were being met, although many factors other than staff development opportunities could contribute to change in stated needs. Since the needs assessment form was being revised comparisons would be difficult.

Dennis considered a mail survey asking participants if their needs were met but remembered most of their mail surveys had low return rates. Maybe they could grab inservice participants as they completed training. Of course the participants were not necessarily representative of the state's population, but their input could tell the DSE staff how well the inservices were meeting their needs.

Dennis constructed a questionnaire by selecting several questions from the needs assessment survey and adding an open-ended section to ask what needs were still unaddressed. DSE staff members distributed this questionnaire to a sample of participants at each of the workshops they attended during the next month.

ANALYZING THE DATA. At the end of the month, Dennis contrasted the need for training of those surveyed in the

ANALYSIS/ INTERPRETATION—WHAT SENSE CAN WE MAKE OUT OF THE DATA? (ANALYSIS)

annual needs assessment with the participant perceptions of their own need after training. He reported to the DSE staff that unlike the educators surveyed the previous year, inservice participants did not report a strong need for training.

ASSESSING THE VALUE OF FINDINGS. These findings on staff-stated needs did not create the stir in the DSE which Dennis had hoped for. The only comment was made by

Fred Fussbudget, who wise-cracked that if he'd been the one who'd been sitting through one of those inservices, he wouldn't be itching to sign up for another so soon either.

There was staff interest in Dennis' table showing the percent of total staff being served by inservice activities. Babs felt these percentages were low and could provide excellent backup for the argument that inservice funds should not be cut.

REPORTING OF RESULTS. Babs encouraged Dennis to enter the data collected on percent of staff served on the

REPORTING—WHO SHOULD SEE THE DATA AND/OR OUR RECOMMENDATIONS? (AUDIENCE)

Division word processor so it could be easily retrieved for future requests for funding.

Dennis also wanted to pass his findings on to the Evaluation Division, who were immersed in revising the needs assessment instrument. They were particularly interested in reading the comments written in on the open-ended section. Dennis' recommendations to the Division were:

1. Future applicants for funds should be required to specify in their proposal which priority need(s) will be addressed during the inservice.
2. Inservices with extraneous goals, i.e., those not specified in the DSE priorities, should be earmarked for elimination.
3. Final decisions on funding should be based upon information about the number of personnel receiving training in each need category.

THIRD QUESTION: ARE APPROPRIATE AND EFFECTIVE INSTRUCTIONAL METHODS BEING USED IN STAFF DEVELOPMENT ACTIVITIES?

FOCUS—ARE THE INSTRUCTIONAL METHODS (USED IN THE INSERVICES) ANY GOOD? (QUESTION)
Now that he and Dennis had finished their involvement with the second question, Ned would be able to attack the issue of Instructional Methodology. But he wondered what type of evidence would be valid to evaluate the instructional methods being used in the inservices?

No one on the staff had ever had the time to keep tabs on instructional approaches used in inservices so it was impossible to know if the "right" approach was being used. Even the goals of the inservices were often pretty vague.

DESIGN—HOW CAN WE GO ABOUT FINDING OUT WHAT INSTRUCTIONAL METHODS ARE USED? (APPROPRIATE PROCEDURES)
Ned was stymied, so he turned to Dr. Fixit, a faculty member in the Educational Policy Program at Solution University, for help. Dr. Fixit suggested they begin by collecting data to describe the instructional methods used. Ned's idea was to send out questionnaires to all trainers asking them to list what they would be doing at the upcoming workshops (i.e., lecture, lead discussions, etc.) Dr. Fixit cautioned that trainers just might be a biased information source. Observers could better record the instructional approaches being used during an inservice session. She showed Ned some sample observational instrument and suggested that a research assistant be hired to attend workshops and record the instructional process. Ned nixed that. He knew Dr. Gruff would not approve of such an expenditure.

Well, if Ned's budget were restricted he could limit his evaluation effort to a different group of inservices each year rather than tackle the entire set. Ned liked Dr. Fixit's suggestion for a cyclical evaluation to be spread over the next few years. Of course only some data would be defensible and accurate. Dr. Gruff also approved of cyclical evaluation with the condition that they justify the selection of the first inservices to be examined. Together they decided that inservice activities to be reviewed should be:

COLLECTING—WHAT INFORMATION SHOULD WE TRY TO GET FIRST? (INFORMATION NEEDED)
1. Those which are repeated year after year and influence a large number of participants. This yielded four types of workshops listed in the first column on table 4.
2. On a topic in which staff needs for training had remained consistent (i.e., had not diminished on the annual needs assessment).
3. Those which had been often criticized for using ineffective procedures or having unstimulating presentations.
4. Ones in which a variety of training techniques were used.

Ned used the remaining three columns in table 4 to determine which inservice activities should have their training methods evaluated. In each of the boxes he recorded whether the group did or did not meet each criterion.

The only inservices meeting all the criteria was a group for regular classroom teachers which presented strategies for working with mainstreamed students. These sessions were in high demand, frequently criticized and used a variety of instructional techniques. Eighteen workshops of this type were offered to almost 900 teachers each year. The 18 training activities represented a variety of instructional approaches, and the DSE staff didn't know which approaches were effective and which weren't.

DEVELOPING INSTRUMENTS. Ned returned to Dr. Fixit to hammer out the details for evaluating these workshops with

COLLECTING—HOW CAN WE GET IT? (COLLECTION PROCEDURES)
her. Together they designed a simple observational instrument upon which one could record how much time in each inservice was spent using each of several instructional approaches (such as listening to oral presentations, practicing skills, developing materials for own use). Next they outlined the procedures for data collection. At each of the 18 inservices, the DSE staff member monitoring the training activity would randomly select three observers to record the training approaches which were used during the workshop itself.

Dr. Fixit recommended that the observational instrument be tested for observer agreement (i.e., reliability). Ned asked three participants to complete the instrument at an inservice held later that week. When he and Dr. Fixit compared the participants' estimates, they found that all three estimated about the same amount of time was being spent in each of the instructional approaches.

Ned was still uneasy about the plan they had outlined. Yes, he wanted to know more about the instructional approaches being used at the inservice activities, but he was uncertain how to analyze and use the collected data. Dr. Fixit suggested that they leave these descriptive data untouched until they collected some evidence about workshop usefulness. How could they get information

COLLECTING—AND WHAT DO WE DO IF WE CAN'T AFFORD TO GO AFTER SOME OF THE INFORMATION WE NEED? (COLLECTION PROCEDURES)
about utility from participants? The best method of collecting data would be an on-site visit to check if teachers were actually applying what was learned during the inservice. There was little chance of that happening! These participants were spread around the state, and visiting even a sample of participants from the 18 workshops would be an impossible task. Ned felt he'd have to contact participants by phone or mail two or three months after they had returned to their classrooms. This meant he would need names and addresses of each participant so he could contact them later on in the year.

Dr. Fixit wasn't pleased with this approach. There were so many problems with validity of the data and the possibility of a low return rate. But she helped Ned construct a self-report measure which was easy to complete, hoping this, perhaps, would help increase the number returned.

Table 4. Criteria for Determining Which Inservice Activities to Evaluate

Criteria 1 & 2	Criterion 3	Criterion 4	Criterion 5
List Group of Workshops Repeated Year After Year, Influencing Great Numbers of Participants	Staff Needs Remain Constant on Needs Assessment	Frequently Criticized as Ineffective	Variety of Instructional Techniques Used
1. Construction of Instructional Materials (includes Make It and Take It Workshops)	YES High Need	NO Criticisms	NO Same Approach
2. Special Education and the Law	NO Diminished Need Perceived	YES Criticized	Yes A Variety
3. Teaching Strategies for Instructing Mainstreamed Students	YES High Need	YES Criticized	YES A Variety
4. IEP Preparation	NO Diminished Need Perceived	NO Criticisms	YES A Variety

At first, Ned wasn't sure whether he should allow the participants to remain anonymous. After some discussion, he and Dr. Fixit decided to assign each participant a code number so they could trace the response back to the participant's name and could, if needed, contact the respondents to collect additional or more specific information about the utility of the inservice activity. Although Ned would code the questionnaire forms, he'd guarantee the respondents confidentiality.

All that teachers were asked to do was to circle three numbers, indicating the workshop's usefulness, fold and staple the sheet, and mail it back. Ned planned to mail out this questionnaire three months after each of the 18 workshops ended and conduct one follow-up of non-respondents.

Ned designed the data collection operation so the work could be managed by clerical assistants. They would mail out the questionnaires and follow-ups, and summarize returned data by calculating the average scores for questions one and two. The frequency of responses in each category would be tallied for the third question.

ANALYZING THE DATA. The data collection proceeded smoothly. Three weeks before the spring meeting data had

ANALYSIS/ INTERPRETATION—ARE THERE ANY DIFFERENCES IN INSTRUCTIONAL METHODS BETWEEN THE HIGHEST RATED AND LOWEST RATED INSERVICES? (INTERPRETATION CRITERIA)

been collected on 11 of the 18 inservice activities. From these 11, Ned selected the three with the highest utility ratings and the three with the lowest, and then pulled out the data collected on the observational instrument for these six inservices. First, he looked at the instructional techniques used in the three highly rated workshops. All three of these spent 50% or more of the inservice time with participants actively engaged and using interactive instructional techniques, i.e., permitting participants to practice skills, to role play, etc. The three inservices with low ratings included long periods when participants were passively listening to the trainer or watching films. For example, in one low-rated workshop participants said they spent almost half of the workshop time with two slide presentations. Ned's preliminary hypothesis was that useful inservices involved participants.

Ned had to get more specifics. Using his codes he located and contacted a sample of participants who had rated inservice utility highly. He asked them to describe the portion of the inservices which had helped them in their classroom. These phone interviews permitted Ned to round out his sense of workshop utility and its relationship to inservice instructional methods.

ASSESSING THE VALUE OF FINDINGS. After completing data analysis, Ned informally shared the results of this

REPORTING—WHAT DO WE DO WITH THE RESULTS? (PURPOSE)

evaluation with the DSE staff. Of course Fussbudget discounted Ned's conclusions. Weren't they based upon a review of only one group of inservice activities? This was not a comprehensive evaluation of all the SEA-supported inservices. Ned was relieved when Babs defended the findings. She felt Ned's data gave the DSE staff an indication of which inservices were most valuable. In the future they should encourage inservices providing in-depth, hands-on training for participants.

REPORTING THE RESULTS. When all data on training methods and inservice utility were summarized, he sent the results out to all trainers in the state for their information. In the cover letter which went with this report, he invited their comments and reactions to the findings. He was surprised at their response. The trainers felt left out. They wanted to know why they had not been given a chance for input before their inservices had been evaluated. Maybe next year Ned could get the trainers to participate in the preparation for evaluation. Trainer insights into instructional practices could only strengthen this evaluation component for the Division. In addition, their involvement might smooth relationships between the various trainers and the DSE.

FOURTH QUESTION: IS THE CONTENT SELECTED FOR INCLUSION IN STAFF DEVELOPMENT ACTIVITIES CONSISTENT WITH STATE AND FEDERAL POLICIES AND REGULATIONS?

FOCUS—DO THEY TEACH THE RIGHT THINGS IN THE INSERVICES? (QUESTIONS) Ken Koncern had been the impetus behind including this issue in the evaluation effort and was asked to take the initiative in addressing this question. Ken began by visiting the DSE monitoring unit. Monitoring team members had complained that some LEA staff, who were not in compliance with a requirement, reported that they were just doing what they had been told in a workshop. For example, one of the teachers visited claimed she was told that she could "temporarily place" children suspected of having emotional handicaps while diagnostic evaluation was being collected. The DSE staff had to point out that the state regulation had been revised in 1980, and diagnostic placements were no longer legal.

DEVELOPING PROCEDURES. Ken was a sympathetic listener, and the staff welcomed the chance to discuss potentially problematic areas:

1. Untrained IHE faculty could be inaccurately interpreting laws and regulations during these workshops; and/or
2. Information was occasionally being presented from other states which included concepts and policies inappropriate for this state.

FOCUS—IS THE MISINFORMATION PROBLEM SERIOUS ENOUGH SO THAT WE NEED TO TAKE ACTION? (PURPOSE) If the spread of misinformation was pervasive, the monitoring team recommended that the DSE stop it by regulating choices of consultants and materials or by extensive training of IHE personnel. If the problem was only spotty, action would only be needed in specific cases.

DESIGN—WHAT DATA CAN WE GET WITHOUT UPSETTING PEOPLE UNNECESSARILY? (APPROPRIATE PROCEDURES) Some DSE staff were concerned that Ken not do anything which would further alienate the faculty in the various state colleges and the university. Any data collection would have to be very tactful. Ned also felt that too many questionnaires or phone surveys were being used with workshop participants.

Ken racked his brain for a procedure that would allow him to determine the amount and frequency of discrepancies between the content of workshops on the one hand, and laws, regulations and policies on the other. He considered testing the trainers' knowledge of recent state and federal mandates in an interview. He realized this would be too demeaning. Maybe a panel of LEA workshop coordinators and IHE faculty who had served as consultants could review the problem. That would have the potential for creating bad feelings.

DESIGN—CAN WE IDENTIFY SEVERAL DIFFERENT KINDS OF DATA WHICH TAKEN TOGETHER WILL BE WHAT WE NEED (CRITERIA FOR JUDGING DESIGN) When he was really stumped, he met with Ned and Sue to get some fresh ideas. Sue remembered the Division's file of complaints and questions which came from LEA's throughout the year. Maybe they could analyze its contents. Together they checked the file and found that most questions were very nebulous. Even the clear ones could not be attributed to workshop discrepancies. They could follow-up specific complaints, but it would take lots of time and the information collected about these selected incidents would probably be unreliable.

Sue always did her best thinking over lunch, so they adjourned to the cafeteria. There they hit upon two procedures that just might work. Ken would examine workshop handouts and materials for incidents of misrepresentation; Ned would determine if the current group of inservices included incidents of discrepancies.

INSTRUMENTATION AND ANALYSIS OF WORKSHOP MATERIALS. For last year's workshops, Ken would begin by collecting a sample of materials, handouts and presentation

COLLECTING—ONCE WE'VE IDENTIFIED IT, HOW CAN WE COLLECT IT? (COLLECTION PROCEDURES) papers. He randomly selected one-fifth of the 50 workshops and then called these 10 LEA workshop coordinators to request copies of the materials used. He had limited the number of workshops sampled, so he could afford to spend the time to track down all the materials. He made additional phone calls to other participants and searched until he had 90% of the materials used at the workshops.

ANALYSIS/ INTERPRETATION—AND ANALYZE THE RESULTS? (ANALYSIS) He used the state monitoring categories to create a simple form to tally instances of discrepancies (table 5). He tried it on two sets of workshop handouts, made minor changes and then totaled the number of "direct" and "interpretive" discrepancies for each item. He defined interpretive discrepancies as procedures which would be illegal if interpreted incorrectly. An average frequency of discrepancies per workshop was computed so that a single workshop with bad materials couldn't bias the overall results.

INSTRUMENTATION AND ANALYSIS OF CURRENT WORKSHOPS. Ned decided to use inservice observers to get a more up-to-date picture of discrepancies. He asked SEA staff attending inservices to note frequencies of discrepancies for each presenter and each handout on a

Table 5. Form for Reviewing Workshop Materials

Requirement Categories	Number of Discrepancies	
	Direct	Interpretive
1. Child Find		
2. Confidentiality		
3. Parent Involvement		
4. Participation in Regular Education		
5. Use of Funds/Non-supplanting		
6. Non-public schools		
7. IEP:		
a. Team		
b. Timelines		
c. Procedures		
8. Notice, Approval and Other Procedural Safeguards		
9. Non-discrimination		
10. Related Services		
11. Categorical Requirements		
a. LD		
b. MH		
c. PH		
d. EH		
e. HI		
f. VI		
g. OHI		
h. SPH		
TOTAL		

form (see table 5). Ned analyzed data from these observations in the same way as Ken had in his materials review.

ASSESSING THE VALUE OF FINDINGS. They were surprised and pleased to find that the average number of discrepancies found in workshop materials was less than one direct discrepancy per workshop and fewer than three interpretive discrepancies per workshop. The monitoring tallies showed that less than 5% of the LEA staff interviewed reported any discrepancies at all. Finally, the current year's workshop observers recorded only one presenter making statements obviously at odds with state and federal requirements. All three of them agreed these discrepancies were within acceptable limits.

REPORTING THE RESULTS. Ken prepared an oral presentation for the DSE staff. His conclusions were that the problem was not as great as had been feared, and no broad-scale policy revisions were necessary. He did recommend that a small task force be formed to establish criteria and guidelines for LEA's to use in selecting consultants and materials for their workshops.

FIFTH QUESTION: ARE PARTICIPANTS IN CERTAIN STAFF DEVELOPMENT ACTIVITIES MORE LIKELY TO APPLY THEIR NEWLY ACQUIRED KNOWLEDGE AND SKILLS ON THE JOB THAN THOSE IN OTHER ACTIVITIES?

FOCUS—ARE SOME INSERVICES MORE LIKELY TO PRODUCE ON-THE-JOB RESULTS THAN OTHERS? (QUESTION)

The DSE was originally interested in identifying effective inservice activities, but before they could begin an ad hoc committee was appointed by the legislature to investigate SEA expenditures. Babs Battleaxe was called to testify and was berated for the DSE's

FOCUS—WHO WANTS TO KNOW ABOUT THE UTILITY OF THE INSERVICES? (AUDIENCE)

failure to document the utility of certain workshops. Superintendent Assault was most critical of the DSE-funded "Make It and Take It" workshops. These were designed to train educators to construct their own instructional materials. Assault argued these workshops were just a bonus for teachers. They were getting extra money to do what was already their job!

Another committee member, Dr. Dubious, warned Babs that he was critical of staff survey data to verify workshop success. After all teachers would "bite the hand that feeds them" and tell the truth about the usefulness of an inservice!

The committee directed Babs (1) to report whether or not participants were using the workshop training, and also (2) to determine whether materials construction inservices, like the Make It and Take It workshops, produced high quality instructional materials. Her findings were to be reported in one month.

DEVELOPING PROCEDURES TO ASSESS USE OF WORK-SHOP TRAINING. Babs talked over these directives with Ned. It was clear they couldn't rely upon survey or

DESIGN—WHAT DO WE DO IF THEY WON'T LET US GET BY WITH A QUICK AND DIRTY EVALUATION AND IF WE DON'T HAVE THE MONEY FOR ANYTHING ELSE? (APPROPRIATE PROCEDURES)

interview data with teacher respondents to collect evidence, yet, with limited time and resources, they couldn't use onsite observations, either.

Ned suggested hiring an outside evaluator to observe the classrooms of inservice participants. But that would be costly and after classrooms were visited, how could they determine if workshop attendance had any effect? No pre-workshop information about these classrooms was available.

Evidence had to be collected in the workplace itself, where any changes reported by staff could be verified. But who could do the job? Ned remembered that the regional special education coordinators spent a great deal of time at school sites. How could they solicit their help?

Babs wanted to give an onsite checklist for data collection to the coordinators at the meeting. Ned agreed that a checklist would be a useful instrument, but why not let the regional coordinators help develop it since the coordinators would be using the checklist they needed to help design a form they were comfortable with? They couldn't pressure the coordinators to do the data collecting but would have to convince them of the need for onsite data collection. A regional coordinator meeting was already scheduled for the next week at Lakeside Retreat; Ned and Sue volunteered to attend. They planned to stay on for the weekend and relax.

DEVELOPING INSTRUMENT TO ASSESS USE OF WORK-SHOP TRAINING. At the meeting the coordinators were uninterested in helping with the onsite data collection until

COLLECTING—WHAT INFORMATION DO WE REALLY NEED? (INFORMATION NEEDED)

Ella Enthusiasm of the Southeast region suggested that perhaps they could use the data both for Ned's purposes and in their own evaluation of regional inservices.

The coordinators spent some time discussing what kind of instrument would be useful. Ella took the lead in the discussion and the group agreed that they must know (1) if participants have any observable or tangible outcomes which resulted from their training, and (2) what kinds of

changes resulted, i.e., numbers served, forms used (such as IEP's), communication strategies (new approaches to IEP monitoring or increased number of meetings with parents), instructional materials, classroom environment (bulletin boards, seating arrangements), etc. Also they needed some rating on the extent of changes made. The rating could be as straightforward and subjective as a designation of whether changes made were major or minor. It might not be an acceptable approach in a measurement textbook but it would help describe what had happened after the inservice. First they all talked over what constituted a major or minor change.

After some discussion, the coordinators developed a simple form (see table 6) to record data from their onsite visits. Since the group had no time for a field test, they knew there might be some problems with this form. If any serious problems developed with the use of the checklist, the coordinators agreed to contact Ned.

Near the end of the meeting, Sue distributed lists of recent participants in SEA-funded staff development activities. These lists were now being regularly prepared for each region as a result of the recommendations made about balance of staff development offering (Question 1). The coordinators selected five of these participants whose sites they would be visiting in the next two weeks. They would spend 5–10 minutes with each of these five participants asking for evidence of job changes.

Before the meeting adjourned, Sue expressed a concern to the group. The coordinators were going to have a free choice in selecting teachers to visit. That was a problem. The legislative committee could argue the data had been collected from a biased sample. She encouraged the coordinators to draw a random sample of teachers in their region from the list and to visit those sampled whenever possible. If a chosen teacher could not be visited, the coordinators could randomly select the name of another teacher as a replacement.

ANALYZING THE DATA ON USE OF WORKSHOP TRAINING. At the end of two and one-half weeks, Ned had received 43 of the onsite inventory checklists in the mail.

ANALYSIS/ INTERPRETATION—CAN WE TELL IF THE INSERVICES HAD ANY ON-THE-JOB IMPACT? (ANALYSIS)

He hurriedly tallied up the number of responses and tabled the results for the committee's report.

The summarized results were for the most part impressive. Eighty-eight percent of the teachers visited were able to show evidence of changes made which they attributed to their participation in the workshop. Sixty-three percent of these changes were rated as minor. Most changes noted by the teachers were in the areas of newly developed management forms or instructional materials.

REPORTING THE RESULTS. Ned was so relieved to have that report turned over to Babs, he forgot his promise to the regional coordinators. They wanted to have the results to review at their next monthly meeting. Hurriedly he

Table 6. Onsite Inventory Checklist

Participant Name _____   School Building _____
Participant Position _____   Workshop _____

Instructions for Coordinators: Begin by asking participant
   Has anything about your job changed as a result of your participation in the SEA Workshop _____?
(Use workshop description)

    Yes ☐ If yes, ask: No ☐ If no:

Do you have anything which is evidence of the changes   Probe further by asking if each category on the list
made? (Describe evidence shown in one or more of the   below has changed (i.e., Have *forms* you've used
categories below)   changed, etc.?)

Categories of Evidence

	Rate each change using your own judgment		
Numbers Served: How changed? _____ _____	☐ Major	☐ Minor	☐ Unable to say
Forms: How changed? _____ _____	☐ Major	☐ Minor	☐ Unable to say
Communication Strategies: How changed? _____ _____	☐ Major	☐ Minor	☐ Unable to say
Instructional Materials: How changed? _____ _____	☐ Major	☐ Minor	☐ Unable to say
Class Environment: How changed? _____ _____	☐ Major	☐ Minor	☐ Unable to say
Costs: How changed? _____ _____	☐ Major	☐ Minor	☐ Unable to say
Speed: How changed? _____ _____	☐ Major	☐ Minor	☐ Unable to say
Other: How changed? _____ _____	☐ Major	☐ Minor	☐ Unable to say

prepared a data summary for them. When they saw the results the coordinators were interested in using the checklist for regional inservice evaluation.

DEVELOPING PROCEDURES: EVALUATION OF MATERIALS CONSTRUCTION WORKSHOPS. Meanwhile, Babs was tackling the evaluation of the "Make It and Take It" workshops. She contacted Superintendent Assault to ask him to clarify his concerns, and he again cautioned her against the use of surveys, questionnaires, or even self-observation. Given the constraints, Babs decided instead to collect and review samples of some of the instructional materials developed at these workshops. For comparison, she would also collect teacher-made classroom materials not specifically developed at a workshop. Reviewers would rate both and compare the teacher-made materials developed at "Make It and Take It" with those developed outside the workshop. To insure impartiality, the reviewers would not be informed which of the materials were developed at workshops and which were not.

FOCUS—BUT WHAT ABOUT THOSE "MAKE IT AND TAKE IT" WORKSHOPS ARMSTRONG WAS UPSET ABOUT? (QUESTION)

Sampling from the list of participants at the Make It and Take It workshops, Babs phoned 10 participants and asked each for a copy of the materials developed at the workshop. Teacher-made materials were harder to come by. Babs drew a sample of 10 teachers from participants at other SEA workshops. She phoned these teachers and also asked for copies of any instructional materials the teachers had developed for their own classroom use. Less than one-third of these teachers had self-developed materials. It took 33 phone calls to locate nine teachers with independently constructed materials.

DEVELOPING INSTRUMENTS: EVALUATION OF MATERIALS CONSTRUCTION WORKSHOPS. Each of the three "expert" reviewers was asked to rate the materials on the following criteria:

ANALYSIS/
INTERPRETATION—WHAT
CRITERIA DO WE USE TO
JUDGE QUALITY OF
MATERIALS?
(INTERPRETATION
CRITERIA)

1. importance of content covered;
2. organization of materials;
3. opportunity for student to learn using various modes;
4. provision of practice opportunities for student;
5. sequencing of instructional activities;
6. appropriateness of difficulty; and
7. motivational capability.

ANALYZING THE DATA: EVALUATION OF MATERIALS CONSTRUCTION WORKSHOPS. When ratings were completed Babs used a t-test to compare the average ratings of the Make It and Take It materials with the average rating of the other materials. Make It and Take It materials were rated more positively on organization, sequencing of activities and motivational potential. Independently constructed materials were more highly rated on providing practice opportunities for students.

REPORTING THE RESULTS. Babs began her report to the committee with an argument for the Make It and Take It

REPORTING—THE
WORKSHOPS SEEM OK BUT
CAN WE RECOMMEND SOME
IMPROVEMENTS? (PURPOSE)

workshops. Almost all of the participants constructed high quality materials. Most non-participating teachers didn't construct classroom materials. The committee agreed to recommend continuation of these workshops but wanted the Make It and Take It trainers to promote materials in which students practiced skills. They were also satisfied with Ned's report on usefulness of workshop training.

EPILOGUE

At the division budget meeting, Gruff acknowledged that the year's evaluation effort had been a success. There would be continued support for the great majority of DSE inservice activities. Only 7 inservice activities needed to be eliminated. Gruff summarized the findings for each evaluation question and explained his decision (see table 7).

FOCUS—WERE THERE ANY
REAL BENEFITS OF THE
EVALUATION EFFORT?
(POTENTIAL UTILITY)

After the meeting, Sue Savvy was the first to congratulate Ned. The evaluation effort had been a success! Ned was

Table 7. Outline of Evaluation Activities

Evaluation Question	Findings	Decision Rules Established for Cutbacks	No. of Inservice Activities Effected
Are offerings of staff development activities balanced?	Elementary teachers received more inservice than secondary teachers	Workshops given for elementary teachers should be among the first to be cut	4 eliminated
Do activities meet the needs of educators?	Not all priority needs were being served adequately	Several workshops in areas where high percent of staff already are being served should be eliminated	3 eliminated
Are appropriate and effective training methods being used?	Activities which engage participants more actively were viewed as most useful	The number of workshops which allow attending staff to remain passive should be reduced	2 eliminated; format change recommended for all workshops
Is the content in the staff development activities consistent with state and federal regulations?	Few instances of discrepancy were identified	No change in policy	None
Are some activities more likely than others to result in staff applying knowledge and skill?	Staff do apply knowledge

Make It and Take It workshops produced high quality materials | Legislative committee recommended that support for workshops be continued. It also recommended that materials construction workshops be maintained | Funding of workshops was cut only 6.5%

11 Make It and Take It workshops kept |

more guarded in his reaction. Sure, Dr. Gruff said he had relied on the evaluation findings, but when he read the list of which inservice activities had been kept, he knew there had been other factors at work. Dr. Gruff had not axed the workshops offered by one of the friends of the Superintendent of Public Instruction, although he was one of the trainers who avoided hands-on activities for participants. And one of Babs' pet workshops for deaf educators was still funded, even though it was not offered in answer to any of the DSE priority needs.

Sue shook her head; Ned was never satisfied. Over lunch she reviewed the year's accomplishments with him.

The success of the year lay in more than just Gruff's politically motivated decisions. For example, the DSE now had in place a better system of information collection and data retention. There were better lists of inservice participants and their positions and data were filed on the word processor for future reference. Ned had pioneered new data collecting procedures too, like the cyclical evaluation of workshops and the use of regional coordinators to collect onsite data for the DSE. The DSE had saved the Make It and Take It workshops and also had greater confidence that training activities were not conveying inaccuracies about state and federal regulations.

By the time lunch was finished Ned felt a little more like celebrating.

* * * * *

DISCUSSION QUESTIONS AND TOPICS

1. The evaluation work shown in the case didn't completely fulfill one of its purposes—that of identifying exemplary practices in order to identify model inservice activities. How, if you were Ned, would you support your argument to Dr. Goff that you had made reasonable progress in that direction?
2. Why was it a good idea for Ned to enlist the aid of the rest of the DSE staff early in the project? What are some things that happened as a result that probably wouldn't have happened otherwise? What are some things that *didn't* happen that probably would have happened otherwise?
3. Do you think the list of issues the staff came up with was a good list? Why? What other issues might have been listed?
4. Do you think the informal reporting of interim results was sufficient? Do you think there should have been more formal reporting, e.g. to the legislature committee?

5. Several times Ned made "feasibility compromises" by not going after the best data for answering questions. Do you think he compromised too much? If so, what suggestions do you have for something else he could have done?
6. What do you consider to be some of the most ingenious tactics (for doing good evaluation) demonstrated in the case?

SUGGESTIONS FOR STIMULATING DISCUSSIONS ABOUT THE CASE

1. Organize a role playing session in which Babs Barker and Ned present the overall results of the evaluation work to Dr. Goff, Superintendent Armstrong, and Dr. Thomas.
2. Organize a role playing session in which Sue Knowles and Ned confront Dr. Goff on his tendency to allow political considerations to override recommendations based upon evaluation data. (Suggestion: Knowles can mediate a bit by suggesting that part of the problem was a failure of the evaluation to identify all the key audiences and issues relevant to the evaluation.)
3. Organize a debate. Resolved: The evaluation shown in the case, while ingenious, was not very useful.
4. Have a role playing session in which the members of the legislature's committee discuss with a few members of the legislature, the question "What criteria should be used to evaluate the effectiveness of staff development programs in the state?"
5. Have a group assume the role of an advisory committee. What advice would you give Ned regarding evaluation of staff development in the coming months?

APPLICATION EXERCISES

1. Read some of the material in the *Sourcebook* indicated by the asides. Then suggest alternative things people in the case might have done at several points in the case. Or suggest a whole new approach they might have taken.
2. Using the case as a model (and foil) and your suggested alternatives as guides, design an evaluation for a situation or problem similar to that shown in the case.
3. Using Chapter 7 of the *Sourcebook* as guide, do a meta-evaluation and critique of the case (and/or your evaluation design).
4. Use the *Design Manual* to develop an improved evaluation design for the case.
5. Use the *Design Manual* to develop an evaluation design for a situation or problem similar to the one described in the case.

The College and University Case Examples

Overview by Jeri Ridings Nowakowski

The five cases that follow were developed with institutions of higher education in mind. The cases have been grounded by actual evaluations with settings, conditions, and constraints that should be recognizable if not typical. As is true of the other cases in the *Casebook*, these cases are meant to be illustrative and are not meant to serve as a definitive model. In each case, contextual events play an important role in determining evaluation options. The decisions made often are not optional, but reflect the tradeoffs and compromises that characterize evaluation practice in any setting.

Each of the five cases focuses on different aspects of personnel preparation evaluation. Dr. Powers teaches in a special education department; she develops an exceptionally thoughtful course evaluation. The evaluation designed for an innovative model training program that must prove its effectiveness is assessed using a set of professional standards. Project management, consistently a concern of small-budget projects housed in universities, is effectively guided by systematic evaluation. And, finally, two curricula in two special education departments are evaluated; both evaluations provide information for planning, revising, and assessing the effectiveness of curricula.

To develop these cases, we turned to the field. First, we learned about common evaluation problems from a sample of institutions of higher education. Then we turned to specific sites and selected special education faculty members, department chairpersons, and administrators to tell us about specific evaluations. Persons with evaluation expertise and experience worked with these special educators to help organize, explore, and refine the evaluation story. Finally, these stories were modified or edited to serve instructional purposes. The end result, then, is a set of cases that have been written and reviewed by persons closely involved in real evaluations, but these cases have been revised and elaborated to provide specific evaluation lessons.

CASE C-1

A SPECIAL EDUCATION DEPARTMENT ASKS: How can we revise our curriculum to meet new and very different teacher certification requirements?

A. Edward Blackhurst

| FOCUS—WHAT IS THE SETTING IN WHICH THE EVALUATION IS TO BE DONE? (CONTEXT) | The Department of Special Education at Normal State University (NSU) is one of |

eight departments in the College of Education. It was made a separate department when Dean Tidings was hired in 1968. The Chairperson of the Department is Dr. Champion, who has been at NSU since 1966 and was elected Chairperson in 1974. Professor Champion has the full support of Dean Tidings and is proud of the fact that she has been able to recruit a highly competent and committed group of faculty members over the years.

The department offers programs from undergraduate study through the doctorate. At the undergraduate level, programs have been designed to prepare teachers for state certification in the areas of the educable mentally retarded, emotionally disturbed, trainable mentally handicapped, and communication disorders. Masters level programs provide specialization and advanced study in these areas plus the severely/profoundly handicapped. Post masters programs prepare people for positions in colleges and universities or for administrative posts in public schools.

There are 22 full and part-time faculty members in the academic program. There are approximately 300 undergraduate students, 175 full-time and part-time masters students, and 15 doctoral students. The department also operates an educational assessment clinic as a service to the community and is fully accredited by the National Council for Accreditation of Teacher Education (NCATE) and the regional accrediting body.

DECISION TO REVISE THE CURRICULUM

| FOCUS—WHAT'S HAPPENING TO BRING ABOUT A NEED FOR EVALUATION? (CONTEXT) | Faculty members at NSU in the areas of the educable mentally retarded, emotionally disturbed, and learning |

disabled had become increasingly dissatisfied with the practice of labeling handicapped children and educating teachers in categorical areas. As long as the state continued to certify teachers in categorical areas, there had been little that could be done about it.

Dr. Champion worked with legislative committees in the early 70's to study the issue of teacher certification. During the 1978 session of the State Legislature, and largely through Dr. Champions's efforts, legislation to authorize noncategorical special education teacher certification was introduced. After two years of intensive committee work, new certification standards were adopted that called for the elimination of separate certification for the educable mentally retarded, emotionally disturbed, and learning disabilities. These were to be replaced by a single certification in learning and behavior disorders.

The work had just begun. New certification guidelines meant that all colleges and universities must revise their old categorical teacher certification programs and develop a new curriculum responsive to the learning and behavior disorders certification requirements.

FOCUS—WHO IS GOING TO BE INVOLVED? (AUDIENCE)   Chairperson Champion appointed a six-person planning committee to revise the existing categorical programs to meet the requirements of the new noncategorical certification program. Professor Belfrey was appointed chair of the committee. The six members were:

1. Professor Tower coordinated the program in learning disabilities and was considered an expert in educational diagnosis. He taught courses in the characteristics of learning disabilities, diagnosis of learning disabilities, and remediation of learning disabilities.
2. Professor Belfrey taught similar courses in the area of emotionally disturbed and coordinated the program in that area.
3. Professor Stein was responsible for the program in educable mentally retarded and taught characteristics and methods courses in that area.
4. Ms. Dale supervised students preparing to work with the learning disabled and emotionally disturbed.
5. Mr. Menton supervised students in the educable mentally retarded.

6. Ms. Feldmeer was assigned part-time to the program. She taught the introductory special education course that was a prerequisite to the content courses in the different areas.

Although members of the curriculum revision committee had been involved in the development and revision of their own courses, none of them had ever been involved with a curriculum revision effort of this magnitude. Consequently, they were faced with the very troublesome question: "How should we proceed?" Professor Belfrey believed that it would be most efficient and productive if the committee approached their charge in a systematic fashion.

FOCUS—WHAT ARE WE DOING? (OBJECT)   With the help of his graduate assistant, Hal Gosling, he surveyed the literature relative to large-scale curriculum revision in higher education. They came up with a competency-based model for curriculum development that they thought would meet their needs (Blackhurst, 1974, 1977, 1979; Blackhurst, McLoughlin & Price, 1977). This model is shown in figure 1.

The first element deals with the development of a mission, assumptions, philosophy, and rationale for the training program. The single-headed arrows indicate the sequence of program development activities. The model is

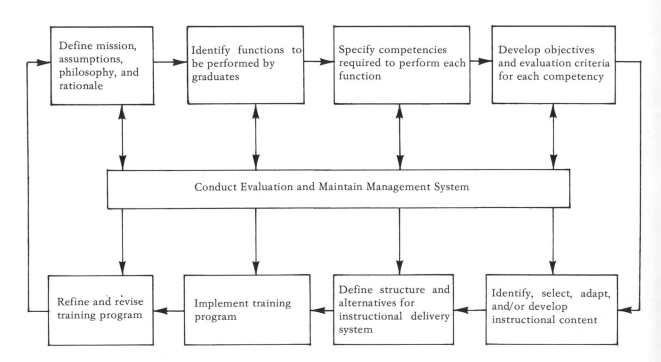

FIGURE 1. Curriculum Development Model

flexible and dynamic, rather than linear. Formative evaluation, central to the process, permits program development revisions at any point.

The curriculum committee liked the model and saw that consideration of the factors involved in each element would force them to look at the entire curriculum. By following the sequence specified, they would be able to approach their task in a systematic fashion.

THE DECISION TO EVALUATE

FOCUS—WHY IS EVALUATION NEEDED? (PURPOSE)

One of the factors becoming a way of life at NSU was the demand for accountability from citizens' and legislative committees. These translated into requests for data and documentation of program effectiveness by the various levels of the university administration. Chairperson Champion secretly prided herself on the fact that the Department of Special Education was more diligent than most other departments in the collection, use, and dissemination of such data. She could support her department more effectively when she had data to support her arguments. Consequently, she very specifically charged the Curriculum Development Committee to incorporate evaluation into their efforts. Champion indicated that the ultimate purpose of the evaluation would be to determine the effectiveness of the curriculum that was developed. Primarily, she was interested in whether the curriculum adequately prepared the students and whether they were effective teachers after they were graduated. However, a second purpose was to evaluate the adequacy of the curriculum revision process. She knew there would be future curriculum changes and wanted to know about the process that was designed by the committee. Was it workable? Could it be improved for future curriculum revision?

THE EVALUATOR

DESIGN—WHO SHOULD BE THE EVALUATOR?

Although Professor Belfrey was chairing the Curriculum Revision Committee, Champion elected to appoint one of the other members of the committee to develop and coordinate the evaluation plan. She chose Professor Tower for several reasons. First, he had a minor in educational research and was one of the best researchers in the department. Second, he was tenured and could be counted upon to proceed in areas where untenured faculty may have been reluctant to tread for fear of stepping on someone's toes and thus possibly jeopardizing chances for promotion. Tower had also attended three evaluation workshops that had been designed and offered by the Evaluation Training Consortium to special education departmental personnel throughout the country. All factors considered, he seemed to be the best internal person for the job. And, at this point, Champion felt an external evaluator was neither feasible nor desirable. She felt she needed someone trustworthy who would be on site throughout the revision process.

AUDIENCES

FOCUS—WHO HAS A STRONG INTEREST IN THE EVALUATION EFFORT? (AUDIENCE)

Professor Tower and Champion met to discuss the evaluation effort. They paid particular attention at first to the identification of audiences for evaluation reports and the needs that these audiences might have to insure that useful information would be collected for the different audiences. Tower's primary audiences were the curriculum development committee and Champion. These were the people who would be making direct decisions about the curriculum and its revision.

Dr. Champion pointed out that another audience was the faculty in the Department of Special Education. She was concerned that faculty were not paying sufficient attention to the evaluation of their own efforts; and, she believed that reports of the evaluation efforts of the curriculum revision committee would promote interest and serve a staff development function. She also realized that if faculty felt information about the curriculum revision or its evaluation was being kept from them, they would be justifiably indignant.

Champion was a primary evaluation audience for a number of reasons. She needed data to assist decision making about program needs and allocation of resources. She also used such data as ammunition in the fight for scarce college resources. She was required to provide evaluation data to the certification agency; and, finally, evaluation data were mandatory for inclusion in the annual proposal that she wrote for federal funds to support the program.

Together, Tower and Champion consulted briefly with Dean Tidings about the evaluation and his data needs. Since the last NCATE accreditation visit had resulted in a major admonition to attend more diligently to the evaluation of College of Education programs (special education came out all right but many programs didn't), the Dean offered his support. In fact, he indicated that he wanted to follow the process closely to see if it might have applicability throughout the college. The Dean also alluded to the fact that he could always use positive findings and simple demographic data to justify his budget requests with the central university administration. In turn, the President of NSU needed data to support his biennial budget used in the five-year plans that were updated every two years.

It became very apparent to Champion and Tower that what was originally seen as an evaluation geared specifically to curriculum revision might have very broad potential impact. Even the Council on Public Higher Education, which made decisions about college and university programs throughout the state, might also be a recipient of appropriate data channeled to them by the president. Tower made note of audiences and the possible uses of information; he would have to keep both in mind as he designed the evaluation plan. In some cases, he might expend some minor extra efforts to obtain additional information for the different audiences that he and Champion had identified.

COSTS

DESIGN—HOW CAN WE PAY FOR THE EVALUATION WORK? Chairperson Champion was initially worried by the costs of the evaluation effort. There were no college or extramural funds allocated for evaluation efforts. It would be necessary to "bootleg" the resources for the evaluation. She went back to the dean to solicit his support and asked that Professor Tower be given a one-course release time to design and coordinate the evaluation effort. The Dean agreed but urged that the evaluation be coordinated wherever possible with the ongoing evaluation efforts already being conducted by the Office of Institutional Research. As it turned out, Tower was able to work well with this unit. By suggesting a few modifications in procedures they were developing, he could obtain data useful to his evaluation plan, as in the college-wide evaluation of courses and teaching procedures developed by them.

Champion decided that costs of typing, printing, mailing, and telephone would simply be absorbed into the departmental budget. Computer time was arranged through the allocation of "computer dollars" that all programs could get from the University Computer Center. Finally, she anticipated that she would have to deal with unforseen expenses during the evaluation. She asked Professor Tower to forewarn her about upcoming costs so that she could have lead time to try to find the resources that would be necessary.

TOWER BEGINS THE EVALUATION DESIGN

FOCUS—WHAT ASPECTS OF THE PROCESS ARE WE EVALUATING? (OBJECT) Tower organized his initial evaluation effort around the elements of the curriculum development model. By structuring the evaluation components within and around the steps in the curriculum model, he could meet the "outcome" and "process" purposes specified by Champion for the evaluation. He would also be able to provide ongoing data that would be useful in guiding curriculum development. Using the curriculum development model, Tower proceeded to spell out the evaluation concerns.

FOCUS—WHAT ARE OUR MAJOR EVALUATION QUESTIONS? (QUESTIONS) The list of evaluation concerns and questions were circulated to the faculty and to Chairperson Champion and Dean Tidings for their review and reaction. Most importantly, the list became a working document for the Curriculum Development Committee. This is Tower's statement of concerns and questions. It contains a description of each major evaluation concern, a brief rationale for its inclusion in the evaluation study, and the evaluation question or questions associated with each area of concern.

Tower's (draft) list of Evaluation Questions

1. *Mission and Philosophy*

   The mission for the revised curriculum is critical to its development as it will serve as the conceptual and philosophical underpinning for all other activities. If the mission is unclear or if there is uncertainty or disagreement about it, any program stemming from the mission will be difficult to implement and decisions required later in the program will be difficult to make. Furthermore, if the mission statement is inappropriate or inaccurate, a curriculum derived from it will be invalid. The major evaluation questions related to this concern are:

   Is the mission statement worthwhile?
   Does it give adequate direction for program developmental activities?

2. *Functions of Graduates*

   To define the areas in which curricula must be developed, it is necessary to define the general functions that graduates of the program must be able to perform. General guidance for identifying these functions is available in the state certification guidelines; however, faculty believe that these are inadequate and have generated a set of training functions that they believe are more representative of the roles that teachers of children with learning and behavior disorders are required to assume. It is important to estimate the appropriateness.

   How adequately are the general training functions defined for this program?

3. *Competency Validity*

   Some indication concerning the competencies for the program are available in the state certification guidelines. Since these are minimal competencies, faculty have elected to expand upon this list through literature review and judgment of the curriculum committee. The question related to this concern is as follows:

   How valid are the competencies for teaching children with learning and behavior disorders?

4. *Objectives and Evaluation Criteria*

   Objectives for the program will be derived from the competencies specified. In addition, evaluation criteria will be established for the purposes of determining whether the objectives were met. This listing will also serve as the basis for the structure of the various courses in the program. It is important to determine that these are accurate and appropriate.

   Do the objectives reflect the competencies?
   Are the evaluation criteria appropriate for the objectives?

5. *Content Selection and Development*

   Because new objectives will be included in the curriculum, it will be necessary to select or develop new instructional materials, textbooks, and other curricula content.

   How effective are the materials that are selected and developed for the curriculum?

TO: Special Education Department Faculty
FROM: Curriculum Development Committee:
Professor Belfrey, Chairperson
Professor Tower, Evaluator
RE: Draft of Plans for Curriculum Revision to be
Reviewed During Next Faculty Meeting

MAJOR TASKS	PROPOSED STRATEGY	EXISTING INFORMATION	(TOWER'S) KEY EVALUATION QUESTION(S)
1. Define mission, assumptions, philosophy and rationale	1) Specify criteria for mission. 2) Define and justify mission 3) Review of mission by department & advisory board	1) Present mission statement 2) Two guiding assumptions formulized by department: a) decision to address education through a competency-based program b) the legal and ethical mandate to move to non-categorical program	Is the mission statement worthwhile and does it give adequate direction for program development activities?
2. Identify functions to be performed by graduate	1) Identify general functions on which there is consensus 2) Have functions reviewed by stakeholders in the field	1) An existing department statement regarding the general functions that teachers of children with learning and behavior disorders must perform	Are the general training functions that are defined for the program adequate?
3. Specify competencies required to perform each function	1) Review existing competencies identified by department 2) Sort into functional areas identified in step 2 3) Devise a strategy to generate and validate a more complete list of competencies	1) A listing of generic competencies provided by a task force two years before	Are identified competencies valid and adequate for teaching children with learning and behavior disorders?
4. Develop objective and evaluation for each competency	1) Specify objectives (cognitive, affective, performance, consequential, psychomotor) for competencies in functional areas 2) Identify evidence or outcomes that might be used to assess achievement	1) Efforts in a few methods courses to operationalize functions into objectives 2) Existing syllabi with objectives identified	Do the objectives operationalize the competencies and are the evaluation criteria appropriate for the objectives?
5. Identify, select, or develop instructional content for program	1) Determine the adequacy of present materials for new programming 2) Find or develop appropriate materials 3) Monitor their adequacy in classroom settings	1) Course rationales for existing materials 2) Isolated evaluation questions on many course evaluations with student responses to materials rated	How effective and appropriate are materials that are selected and developed for the curriculum?
6. Determine the structure for the instructional delivery system	1) After competencies, objectives and content have been determined, consider structures for presenting 2) Develop "modules" (practicum, lecture, auto-	1) Present delivery structure and rationale for each module's use 2) Prototype or pilot	How effective is the structure of the program in the delivery of the instructional content?

FIGURE 2. Memo from Champion to Faculty

(figure continued)

MAJOR TASKS	PROPOSED STRATEGY	EXISTING INFORMATION	(TOWER'S) KEY EVALUATION QUESTION(S)
	instructional, etc) appropriate to competencies, learning activities, content, and resources 3) Monitor for balance in delivery structure		
7. Implement the program	1) Monitor faculty implementing program 2) Monitor students' acquisition of competencies 3) Monitor graduates' ability to implement concept	1) Intact review system for NCATE 2) Testing 3) Follow-up questionnaires to graduates (return about 20)	Is the program being implemented as planned? Does the plan still seem to be sound?
8. Monitor and revise curriculum revision process as needed	1) Document and monitor the entire revision process to provide formative evaluation and later prototype 2) Review Tower's on-going reports	None	How effective is the curriculum revision process?

FIGURE 2 *(continued)*

6. *Program Structure*

It is anticipated that an entirely new curriculum with new courses, new practical, and new clinical experiences will be provided for the students. Some courses will include auto-instructional modules, others will be traditional lecture-type courses, while still others will use simulation.

How effective is the structure of the program in the delivery of the instructional content?

7. *Program Implementation*

None of the new curriculum can make a difference, of course, if it doesn't get implemented. And, its final "proof" is in how well it really works.

Are faculty effective in the implementation of the new program? Do students acquire the competencies that are taught in the program? Are the graduates of the program able to implement the concepts that they were taught?

8. *Curriculum Revision Process*

Although data related to the curriculum revision process will be obtained through the systematic evaluation conducted in the previous seven areas, there is a need to review the entire sequence and procedures that were used as per the charge of the chairperson.

How effective was the cirriculum revision process?

COORDINATING THE PROGRAM AND EVALUATION EFFORTS

DESIGN—HOW CAN WE DO THE EVALUATION SO THAT IT HAS A GOOD CHANCE TO MAKE A BENEFICIAL IMPACT? (AUDIENCE INVOLVEMENT/ COMPONENTS)

While Tower had been progressively focusing evaluation needs, Professor Belfrey and the Curriculum Development Committee were outlining issues and tasks in the curriculum development model. Champion, after reviewing both Tower and Belfrey's reports, decided that a first draft of issues and procedures, along with Tower's evaluation questions, should be shared with the faculty as a whole. Though Champion believed that it took individuals or small task forces to drive major projects, she wanted and needed the support of her faculty. Her memo to the faculty is shown in figure 2.

DESIGN—WHY DOES THE FACULTY ACCEPT THE DESIGN? (A QUESTION NOT ANSWERED—CRITERIA FOR JUDGING DESIGNS)

The memo was raised at the next faculty meeting. After a surprisingly short period of the expected hollering, hemming, and hawing a motion was made to "accept" the curriculum tasks as outlined. With approval gained from the faculty, Champion personally shared this memorandum with the Dean. Tower and Belfrey and the rest of the Curriculum Development Committee began to flesh out their initial plans. From this point on, Tower would work closely with the committee so that he could provide information to them, monitor and evaluate the effectiveness of the actual revision process, and eventually provide summative information about outcomes.

THE EVALUATION DESIGN

Tower ended up planning the evaluation for each element in the curriculum model as the committee dealt with that element (an emerging design). He did not, in fact, plan the whole evaluation at the outset (a preordinate design). However, in order to help guide the reader through Tower's evaluation activities over the next three years, we have provided a blueprint of the evaluation as it would have looked at the end of the three years (a retrospective design).

EVALUATING THE MISSION

ANALYSIS/
INTERPRETATION—HOW
WOULD WE KNOW IF OUR
MISSION STATEMENT WERE
ANY GOOD?
(INTERPRETATION
CRITERIA)

To guide the development of the mission and its evaluation, Tower worked with the curriculum committee to specify criteria for the mission statement. The following criteria that emerged from their dis-

cussions were:

a. The mission should specify the *context* within which the program will operate and identify the major forces to which the program should respond.
b. The mission should specify the major *responsibilities* of the learning and behavior disorders program which the program faculty have accepted, with respect to each of the agencies or groups with which it interacts.
c. The mission should include a *specification of goals* for the program. These are broad, general statements under which specific objectives and subsequent priorities can be subsumed.
d. The mission should include statements of *administrative objectives*. These will: (1) reflect the commonalities that this program of learning and behavior disorders has with similar programs in other colleges and universities; (2) identify the uniqueness of this program; (3) be specific enough to form the basis for programmatic decision making; (4) be broad enough to subsume the activities of the faculty within the program; (5) provide sufficient flexibility to permit program modifications and growth; and (6) include both product and process objectives to provide a specification of procedures faculty would use in meeting their obligations.
e. The mission should be judged by representatives from all relevant audiences as ethical and valuable.

With these criteria in mind, Professor Tower began working with Professor Belfrey to develop procedures necessary to evaluate the mission.

NOMINAL GROUP TECHNIQUE

FOCUS—WHAT QUESTIONS
DO WE HAVE TO ANSWER
ABOUT THE CURRICULUM
SO WE KNOW WHAT WE
ARE TRYING TO DO—AND
WHAT ARE WE TRYING TO
EVALUATE? (OBJECT)

A number of philosophical issues needed to be resolved before the faculty could synthesize a mission statement. The identification and resolution of issues was the first important step in the actual revision process. Tower kept a log of the issues; he noted, for instance, the questions with which the faculty initially dealt.

1. How does our department define learning and behavior disorders? Should an attempt be made to define these? Should we simply focus on a functional analysis of children's problems?
2. Are there differences between children diagnosed as learning disordered and those diagnosed as behavior disordered? If so, what are these? What are the similarities between these groups?
3. What are the implications of the answers to questions 1 and 2 for teacher preparation?
4. What are the differences in expectation for persons who are being prepared at different degree levels?
5. As severity of disability increases, do differences between these two groups become more apparent? If so, what implications does this have for the training programs?
6. What is our position on the resource room vs. the special class (or other alternatives) for service delivery to children?
7. If our program is to be competency-based, what characteristics should it have (e.g., How should competencies be stated? Will the program be modularized? Should a standard format for curriculum design be adopted?)
8. What role do field experiences and practica have in our program?
9. How can personnal be prepared to be flexible enough to adapt to new or different special education service delivery models that may emerge in the schools?
10. If philosophical differences cannot be resolved, how can the program be developed to accommodate to differences?

FOCUS—WHAT ARE OUR
BASIC ASSUMPTIONS?
(QUESTIONS)

After initial issues had been identified and discussed over several consecutive faculty meetings, the Nominal Group Technique was used to facilitate discussion about the elements in the mission. Faculty were asked to write one-sentence descriptions of the assumptions underlying the program. In round-robin fashion, each faculty member was asked to list one assumption until all assumptions had been specified. At that point,

COLLECTING—HOW CAN WE
FIND OUT WHAT EACH OF
US THINKS ABOUT OUR
MISSION? (COLLECTION
PROCEDURES)

discussion ensued about each point until everyone had agreed that they understood each statement. The faculty selected five major assump-

SUMMARY OF EVALUATION EVENTS DURING THE NEXT THREE-YEAR PERIOD

	KEY QUESTION	FORMATIVE EVALUATION	SUMMATIVE EVALUATION	TIME LINE
1. Defining philosophy and mission	Is the mission statement worthwhile and does it give adequate direction for guiding the program?	1) Monitoring of Nominal Group Technique by Tower 2) Adherence to criteria specified for mission content	1) Evaluation of mission Field Advisory Board 2) Outcome data from graduates	Sept-Dec, 1978 Jan. 1981
2. Delineating major functions students must master	Are the general training functions that are defined for the program adequate?	1) Monitoring of input and process used by faculty to establish functions 2) Function optionaire	2) Validation and approval of Field Advisory Board	Jan-Feb, 1979
3. Specifying competencies required for each function	Are identified competencies valid and adequate for teaching children with learning and behavior disorders?	1) Assessment of existing competencies 2) Aggregation of competencies through Critical Incident Technique	1) Approval of competencies by department faculty	April 1979
4. Developing supporting objectives & evaluation criteria for competencies	Do the objectives operationalize the competencies and are the evaluation criteria appropriate for the objectives?	1) Monitoring of process to negotiate and approve objectives 2) Support to faculty in establishing evaluation criteria	1) Voting of department for final approval	Apr-Sept, 1980
5. Identifying, selecting, or adopting instructional content	How effective and appropriate are materials that are selected and developed for curriculum?	1) Monitoring group process to negotiate content 2) Instructional Materials Analysis Form	1) Isolated questions on graduate follow-up and end-of-course evaluation forms	Apr-Dec, 1980
6. Determining Program Structure	How effective is the structure of the program in the delivery of instructional content?	1) Design of new program based upon previous steps 2) Questionnaire to existing students	1) Items on the questionnaire to existing students 2) Graduate's follow-up evaluations	Apr-Dec 1980
7. Implementing the Program	Is the program being implemented as planned? Does the plan still seem to be sound?	1) Evaluation of faculty teaching through Instructor Assessment Instruments 2) Content analysis of Practicum Evaluation Forms to revise course 3) Follow-up student questionnaires 4) SOS tapes from graduates	1) Employer evaluation of NSU graduates	Jan 1981
8. Evaluating the Revision Process	How effective is the curriculum revision process?	1) Tower's log of the whole process 2) Multiple reports throughout evaluation	1) Faculty questionnaire 2) Impact and further case of evaluation reports	Sept 1978-Jan 1981 and still going

tions from the list of nearly 30 that had been generated. The results of this balloting were placed on the board for discussion. Following this, for each of the assumptions that was picked by the majority of faculty, a list of implications for the curriculum was generated. As was done earlier, votes also were taken on the appropriateness of the implications.

The information thus generated was collated by Professor Belfrey, who synthesized the information and drafted a mission statement that described the purposes of the training program, the assumptions that would serve as its foundation, and the general philosophy that would be used to guide curriculum revision efforts, and other statements that related to the criteria that had been established.

Field Validation

COLLECTING—HOW CAN WE FIND OUT IF KEY PEOPLE AGREE WITH US? (COLLECTION PROCEDURES/ SAMPLES)

The criteria generated by the curriculum revision committee stipulated that there should be input from the relevant audiences in the field for the curriculum revision efforts in general and the mission statement in particular. In this way, the committee believed that the resulting product would be one that would be responsive to the needs of the field and also be reality based. Consequently, a Field Advisory Board was established. This was made up of three teachers of children with learning and behavior disorders, an administrator of a school program for such children, a member of the Association for Children with Learning Disabilities and the Council for Exceptional Children, an educational diagnostician, and two parents of children with learning and behavior disorders.

REPORTING—ONCE WE'VE GOTTEN THEIR INPUTS CAN WE MODIFY OR CLARIFY OUR MISSION STATEMENT SO THAT IT'S ACCEPTABLE? (PURPOSE)

The mission statement produced by the faculty was presented to the Field Advisory Board. During their first meeting, the board outlined issues that they felt were relevant, but not included. Faculty members responded during their next meeting to the field board's questions. Through this negotiation, ultimately the board unanimously voted approval of the mission statement. It was, they felt, responsive to the criteria established by the Curriculum Development Committee, comprehensive and appropriate in its focus, and worthwhile for developing a sound program to develop productive special education teachers.

In summary then, the evaluation of the first question (Is the mission statement worthwhile and does it provide adequate direction?) yielded some useful benefits. Since the answer to the question was in the affirmative, faculty were reinforced for their efforts and felt that they were headed in the right direction. They also had a mandate from significant people in the field who would be consumers of the graduates. This was an encouraging sign. Some secondary benefits that were not anticipated from the evaluation emerged; the discussion of general issues had uncovered some internal conflicts over appropriate curriculum direction that might have undermined future activities had they not been identified and dealt with. Professor Tower was

pleased with the results of this first activity and he and Belfrey moved to the next programmatic and evaluation concerns.

Evaluating the General Training Functions

FOCUS—WHAT FUNCTIONS DO WE BELIEVE ARE NECESSARY TO FULFILL THE MISSION? (QUESTIONS)

After developing a mutually satisfying mission statement, faculty had to turn their attention to the task of defining functions they believed that the graduates of their program should be able to perform. To do so, the Curriculum Development Committee, along with Tower, identified the following issues for faculty resolution:

1. Are the functions performed by teachers of children with learning disorders the same as those required for children diagnosed as behavior disordered? If so, what are these?
2. Are the functions different? If so, how are they different?
3. Do functions differ according to type of setting in which the children are educated (e.g., resource room, special class, intinerant)? If so, what are the differences?
4. Do functions differ according to age of the children or their grade placement? If so, how do they differ?

In addition they listed 23 general functions (derived from existing research and a survey of other departments' functions) that they considered important. While faculty could add or delete functions, they were at least provided with a beginning slate to which they could react.

FUNCTION OPINIONNAIRE

COLLECTING—HOW CAN WE FIND OUT IF KEY PEOPLE AGREE WITH US?

To help select functions, Tower designed an opinionnaire for rating their appropriateness. He kept the opinionnaire relatively simple. The 23 functions were listed, and the faculty were asked simply to rate each by circling the number 1 if they felt it was inappropriate, 2 if it was somewhat appropriate, or 3 if it was very appropriate. Opportunities were also provided to suggest other functions or to modify those functions that were included in the opinionnaire. After the responses were tabulated, Tower convened the Field Advisory Board to review the data and to reach consensus on the functions that they believed should be included in the curriculum.

ANALYSIS/ INTERPRETATION—WHAT SENSE CAN WE MAKE OUT OF THE DATA WE'VE GOTTEN? (ANALYSIS/ INTERPRETATION CRITERIA)

As a result of the faculty ratings and subsequent discussions with the advisory board, 13 of the 23 functions were discarded, while the 10 functions viewed as most appropriate became the framework for the curriculum.

The ten functions selected were:

1. Assessment of learner behavior
2. Design and implementation of instructional programs
3. Selection and utilization of instructional materials

4. Management of the learning environment
5. Provision for the unique needs of children with sensory and physical impairments
6. Implementation of resource teacher programs
7. Implementation of due process standards
8. Effective working with parents
9. Maintenance of student records
10. Demonstration of appropriate professional characteristics

Thus ended Tower's inquiry into the second evaluation concern. Of course, the true test of the functions selected would come later in the assessment of graduates training in the selected areas.

EVALUATING THE VALIDITY OF COMPETENCIES

FOCUS—WHAT COMPETENCIES ARE NEEDED TO CARRY OUT THE TEN FUNCTIONS WE'VE IDENTIFIED? (QUESTION)

As with most university faculties that base their curricula on competencies, the great concern of the Curriculum Committee was focused on whether the competencies identified were valid. The literature on competency-based teacher education was ripe with criticisms and concerns about competency specification, and calls for efforts to validate the competencies—an admittedly difficult task.

DESIGN—HOW CAN WE GET THE INFORMATION WE NEED TO RESOLVE COMPETING NOTIONS ABOUT COMPETENCIES? (APPROPRIATE PROCEDURES)

Tower was convinced that there was merit in looking at effective and ineffective teaching practices as a means of arriving at a list of competencies that had at least a measure of face validity. He reasoned that competencies effective in teaching were valid and should be incorporated into the curriculum.

Fortunately, Professor Tower had a doctoral student, Steve Sloan, who was at the point of making a decision about a potential dissertation topic. Sloan expressed interest in this topic and began to investigate the possibilities. After some library research, he focused on the "Critical Incident Technique" as a method that could be used in the identification of the competencies that Tower was looking for.

In the Critical Incident Technique, observers record teaching behaviors that are either effective or ineffective in meeting some general aim. They describe the antecedents that lead to the behavior, the actual behavior that occurred, and the consequences of the behavior that lead them to believe that it was either effective or ineffective. The only a priori assumptions that are made in the application of this technique is that effective and ineffective behaviors are occurring and that these can be identified and reported. There are no preconceived notions about what should or should not be occurring in the setting under observation. The criterion used to determine effectiveness is some perceived positive effect on the target of the behavior. Because the technique permits reports of past behaviors it lends itself to the collection of a great deal of data. This is

also a potential weakness, however, since the reports rely upon the respondents' memories.

Doctoral candidate Sloan believed that he could use this method to identify effective and ineffective behaviors of teachers of children with learning and behavior disorders. Subsequently, he developed a proposal that was accepted by his committee and proceeded to conduct his investigation. Using a sample of some 200 teachers of children with learning and behavior disorders and their supervisors, he collected three reports from each describing behavior that they had either observed in other teachers or had encountered in their own teaching efforts.

COLLECTING—WHAT DEVICE CAN WE USE TO COLLECT THE DATA? (INSTRUMENTS)

The form for collecting "effective" incidents is illustrated in figure 3 and includes a sample of one of the teacher's responses.

ANALYSIS/ INTERPRETATION—HOW CAN ALL THOSE INCIDENTS BE USED TO GENERATE COMPETENCIES?

This critical incident in teaching was then translated into the following competency statement: "Teachers of children with learning and behavior disorders should be able to select and use appropriate teaching machines and audio-visual aids in their classrooms." Ineffective incidents were translated into positive competency statements during the incident analysis phase of the study.

A total of 510 incidents were collected from the respondents, of which 300 were reports of effective behavior and 210 were reports of ineffective behavior. After redundancies were eliminated, the statements consisted of some 66 different competencies that were grouped into the ten different functional areas identified in the preceding stage.

Think of a recent time that you observed yourself, or another teacher of children with learning and behavior disorders do something that you felt was an extremely effective teaching act. Tell exactly what was done and what happened.

What specific circumstances led up to this situation? Jim, 5 years behind in reading, balked at the study of flash cards containing sight words, claiming that it was "baby stuff."
Exactly what did you or the other person do? I obtained a tachistoscope and used it to flash the same words at Jim at high speed.
What resulted that made you feel that this was an example of good teaching? Jim attended to the task because he thought it was a game. He learned his sight words.

FIGURE 3. Form for collecting effective incidents

```
FUNCTION:  Implement Resource Teacher
           Programs
COMPETENCY: Participate in school-wide planning
           for mainstreaming activities
    TASKS: Work with principal to develop
           administrative   arrangements   for
           effective transition to mainstreaming

           Negotiate with school staff for place
           ment and grouping of students

           Participate in orientation program for
           regular and special students

           Develop strategies to facilitate the
           transition of the special student into
           the regular class
```

FIGURE 4. Formats for functional areas

These were formatted as illustrated in figure 4. (Note also the "task" statements. These tasks eventually became course objectives.)

The competency statements generated through this study were viewed by Professor Tower and his curriculum committee as having a greater degree of validity than the lists of competencies generated by other departments or solely the opinions of faculty members.

There were some problems. Competencies were not identified in all areas that logic dictated were important (e.g., working with parents, interacting with other professionals). In addition, because the study relied upon retrospective reports, there was always the question of accuracy and the amount of bias that could have crept into the investigation.

ANALYSIS/ INTERPRETATION—WE ARE SATISFIED FOR THE MOMENT BUT HOW COULD WE BECOME MORE SURE OF THE COMPETENCIES? (CRITERIA)

Yet the faculty were reasonably sure, thanks to the study, that the majority of competencies included in the program are valid for teachers of children with learning and behavior disorders. As Champion put it, "We at least feel that we have a more valid set of competencies than had we simply generated a competency list as a result of discussion among ourselves and through literature reviews. Our competencies are based in part upon data that related them to effective teaching procedures."

Tower intended to do further follow-up on the validation of competencies by studying the graduates that had been produced under the new curriculum. Sloan's dissertation proposed that a checklist, based on the adopted competencies, be used to guide observations of graduates. The follow-up study could explore which competencies they were using and which they didn't use. And it could look for competencies "missed" by the program. But that would be another story and one that would have to wait.

EVALUATING THE OBJECTIVES AND EVALUATION CRITERIA

FOCUS—NOW THAT WE HAVE THE COMPETENCIES REASONABLY WELL IN HAND—WHAT NEXT?

Belfrey and the curriculum committee recommended that the various faculty members who would be involved in the different competency areas be assigned the responsibility of conducting further task analyses of the competencies. They were in fact the best group to determine whether the tasks associated with the presentation and acquisition of a given competency were included. And, faculty were to develop evaluation criteria for each of the tasks in working sessions guided by Tower.

The evaluation questions associated with the objectives and evaluation criteria were: (1) Do the objectives reflect the competencies; and (2) Are the evaluation criteria appropriate for the objectives?"

COLLECTING—HOW CAN WE DETERMINE IF WE ARE IN AGREEMENT ABOUT OBJECTIVES AND CRITERIA?

Professor Tower recommended a form of consensus building. After each of the faculty members had completed their individual work, all of the faculty who would be teaching in the new program would be called together for a series of meetings about the objectives and evaluation criteria. For each competency statement and its associated tasks, faculty would be asked whether they understood the statements that had been generated. Following this, they would be asked whether they agreed with the statements. Revisions were to be made in the statements until consensus had been reached. A similar process was to be pursued with the evaluation criteria that had been developed with Tower's assistance. Omissions would also be identified at this time.

ANALYSIS/ INTERPRETATION—OUR CRITERION IS THAT WE ACHIEVE CONSENSUS—BUT DO OTHERS AGREE WITH US?

Professor Tower proposed that an 80% level of agreement be selected as the criterion for consensus. It was then his intent to bring the findings to the Field Advisory Board. But Chairperson Champion couldn't afford to reimburse the advisory board members for their time and expenses; consequently, this aspect of the evaluation process had to be cancelled. At least, Tower acknowledged, the faculty had reached consensus that the objectives and evaluation criteria were appropriate.

Even though this phase of the evaluation didn't produce the hard data Tower wanted, it had generated much discussion among faculty and served to clarify a number of misconceptions. It gave direction for course development, and everyone involved gained an understanding of the objectives of the program, what was to be taught, and how objectives were to be evaluated. This would have significant implications for the efforts of individual faculty members in the design of the procedures for their areas of teaching responsibility.

Instructional Materials Analysis Form

Directions: 1. Read or use the enclosed instructional materials and respond to each of the items below by circling the appropriate number.
2. Use the line next to each item to provide any comments by way of explanation or to suggest needed changes or improvements, if such appear to be warranted.

1. Amount of information
   1   2   3   4   5   _____
   too little   appropriate   too much

2. Sequence of information
   inappropriate 1 2 3 4 5 appropriate _____

3. Clarity of presentation
   confusing 1 2 3 4 5 clear _____

4. Level of language is:
   inappropriate 1 2 3 4 5 appropriate _____

5. Difficulty level
   1   2   3   4   5   _____
   too easy   about right   too hard

6. Terminology and technical terms
   undefined 1 2 3 4 5 well-defined _____

7. Writing style
   1   2   3   4   5   _____
   too informal   about right   too formal

8. Examples are
   confusing 1 2 3 4 5 clear _____

9. Number of examples
   not enough 1 2 3 4 5 too many _____

10. Figures, graphs or other visual-aids are
    Inappropriate 1 2 3 4 5 appropriate _____

FIGURE 5. Instructional Materials Analysis Form

Upon completion of this task, the curriculum committee also reached decisions about the way that the courses would be structured, and who would be assigned for the design of the various courses and practicum experiences.

EVALUATING CONTENT SELECTION AND DEVELOPMENT

FOCUS—HOW CAN WE TELL IF THE COURSES AND INSTRUCTIONAL ACTIVITIES ARE CONSISTENT WITH OUR MISSION, OBJECTIVES, AND CRITERIA? (QUESTION)

As faculty members began designing specific courses and other instructional activities, they selected the various texts and instructional materials that would be used. In some cases, it was necessary to develop new materials. All of these materials were examined by the entire program faculty. Agreement was reached only after considerable discussion and argument about appropriate placement and sequencing of some of the content.

One major problem stemmed from the paucity of materials specifically designed for cross-categorical use. Other issues (noted in Tower's log) needing resolution included the following:

1. Since most texts are "categorical," should students be required to study all of those (e.g., characteristics texts) that are relevant?

2. Should categorical content be presented separately and then integrated, or should content be integrated as the program progresses?

3. How much emphasis should be placed upon content that some authors have indicated as specific to a given category?

4. What relative priority should be given to content concerning social, academic, or language behaviors (and others)?

5. Should more emphasis be placed upon certain problem

areas, such as reading, that are quite common in the target population?

6. What criteria should be used for selecting content?
7. Should the use of all categorical terminology be discouraged? What are the alternatives?
8. How can content such as career education be integrated into the curriculum?

COLLECTING—WHAT DATA DO WE NEED IN ADDITION TO OUR OWN EXPERT JUDGMENT? (INFORMATION NEEDED) Given the agreement among faculty, there appeared to be face validity for the content finally selected and developed. However, Tower felt that there should be further investigation of its relevance. Tower and Belfrey decided to obtain data from the students about their perceptions of the appropriateness of the content selected for the various courses. Of particular interest were instructional materials that were either selected or developed for the courses. Consequently, Tower developed a brief, 10-item instructional materials analysis form that faculty used to obtain student feedback. This form is shown in figure 5.

FOCUS—HOW CAN WE USE THE INFORMATION WE ARE GETTING? (POTENTIAL UTILITY) Results of the various analyses performed using the instructional materials analysis form would provide valuable feedback. In fact, it became clear after one or two uses that its usefulness was greatest for instructor-developed materials. That is, students provided many useful items that resulted in the revision of the instructional materials. The forms were less useful for commercially developed materials because these were protected by copyright and could not be easily modified. Poorly rated commercial materials were generally eliminated from the program. This evaluation procedure was an ongoing one, as more materials development and selection was pursued.

EVALUATING THE PROGRAM STRUCTURE

FOCUS—DOES THE NEW CURRICULUM APPEAR TO BE DIFFERENT IN IMPORTANT WAYS FROM THE OLD CURRICULUM? (OBJECT) The structure of the program that finally evolved was very different from the old categorical programs, as can be seen in figure 6.

Before		After	
The three categorical programs		The single non-categorical program	
EDUCABLE MENTALLY RETARDED		**LEARNING AND BEHAVIOR DISORDERS**	
EDS 375	Introduction to Education of Exceptional Children	EDS 250	Introduction to Special Education
EDS 530	Characteristics of the Mentally Retarded	EDS 510	Early Childhood Education of the Handicapped
EDS 526	Education of the Mentally Retarded	EDS 511	Speech and Language Development
EDS 577	Survey of Speech Pathology	EDS 512	Language Disorders
EDS 358	Practicum in Special Education	EDS 513	Protecting the Human Rights of the Handicapped
EDS 359	Student Teaching	EDs 514	Special Education Learning Environments
LEARNING DISABILITIES		EDS 515	Career Education for the Handicapped
EDS 375	Introduction to Education of Exceptional Children	EDS 516	Behavioral Management of Exceptional Children
EDS 525	Characteristics of Children with Learning Disabilities	EDS 517	Prosthetics for Handicapped Children
EDS 527	Education of Children with Learning Disabilities	EDS 518	Working with Parents of Exceptional Children
EDS 358	Practicum in Special Education	EDS 528	Educational Assessment of the Mildly Handicapped
EDS 359	Student Teaching	EDS 529	Educational Programming for the Mildly Handicapped
EMOTIONALLY DISTURBED		EDS 317	Introduction to the use of Media
EDS 375	Introduction to Education of Exceptional Children	EDS 358	Field Experiences in Special Education
EDS 570	Characteristics of Emotionally Disturbed	EDS 359	Student Teaching in Learning Behavior Disorders
EDS 571	Education of Emotionally Disturbed		
PSY 533	Abnormal Psychology		
EDS 612	Practicum in Emotionally Disturbed		

FIGURE 6. Comparison of the Categorical and Noncategorical Programs

FOCUS—HOW EFFECTIVE IS THE NEW STRUCTURE IN DELIVERING THE NEW CONTENT? (QUESTION) The three categorical programs were quite similar in their approach, with typical introductory, characteristics, and methods courses followed by practica and student teaching. The new noncategorical program was much wider in scope and covered the ten identified functions, some of which were not included in the old programs. It should be noted that students also took the entire elementary certification sequence, so they had considerable grounding in traditional elementary teaching techniques.

The big evaluation question now was: "How effective is the structure of the program in the delivery of the instructional content?" Professor Tower and the other members of the curriculum committee discussed many issues related to this question; deciding finally that the best source of information for this question was the students who had gone through the program.

GRADUATING STUDENT QUESTIONNAIRE

COLLECTING—HOW CAN WE GET STUDENT PERCEPTIONS? (INSTRUMENTS) Professor Tower designed a questionnaire to be used with students who were about to graduate (see figure 7). He aimed for an objective measure of the students' perceptions of the relevance of the various courses and also asked for subjective judgments and comments relative to each course. Dimensions included on the questionnaire were:

quality of instruction and advising
adequacy of entire preparatory program
adequacy and quality of the practicum
confidence in own preparation
perceived redundancy in program elements

The first administration of the questionnaire yielded a one hundred percent return rate, thanks to a careful distribution and collection procedure. Questionnaires were distributed by the practicum supervisors during the last visit to evaluate their students' teaching. The questionnaires were given to the students, and they were told that they must return them when they submitted their final practicum log. They were informed that the awarding of their student teaching grade would be contingent upon submission of the questionnaire. To avoid likely bias, questionnaires were submitted in sealed envelopes and kept anonymous.

ANALYSIS/ INTERPRETATION—AND ONCE WE GET THE DATA WHAT CAN WE DO WITH THEM? (ANALYSIS) After the data were collected, responses were tabulated and percentages computed for each response category. Open-ended responses were tabulated and grouped into logical categories for interpretation.

REPORTING—TO WHOM DO WE SHOW THE RESULTS (AND HOW DO WE GET THE RESULTS TO INFLUENCE DECISIONS?) (AUDIENCE) Professor Belfrey and the curriculum committee breathed a sigh of relief, since the data were relatively favorable. A brief report was circulated to the entire faculty which specified the results of the evalua-

tion and a list of modifications suggested by the data. Fortunately, no single course was really blasted by the students. Had this been the case, Chairperson Champion was prepared to work with individual faculty members rather than sharing very negative data about a specific faculty member among other faculty colleagues.

The data revealed several areas of redundancy among courses. Faculty elected to eliminate some of the redundance; but decided to leave other redundancies in. For example, "basic principles of classroom management techniques" were discovered to be presented in three different courses. This redundancy was eliminated. In three other courses, however, there was information related to the preparation of individualized educational programs (IEP's). Faculty believed that this redundancy was helpful in reinforcing this important concept and providing additional practice for the students.

Students stated that they believed that the general quality of the program, its courses and practica, was satisfactory. though they believed that there were insufficient practica. In attempting to examine and possibly rectify this perceived deficiency, however, faculty found that that there was no immediate way to increase the amount of field placements because the cooperating school district was overflowing with practicum placements. As a result, faculty moved to develop some simulations and micro-teaching activities in place of additional practica.

A major finding of the evaluation was that there was considerable overlap between the introductory special education course and the course on mainstreaming that was required for all students who were preparing to be teachers. Armed with this information, Champion approached Dean Tidings about the possibility of exempting special education students from the mainstreaming course. Much to the chagrin of the special education personnel, the dean rejected this recommendation. He had expended considerable energies in getting college-wide acceptance of this course as part of another federal grant. It was his position that special education teachers and regular education teachers were already too separated. He was also of the opinion that negative attitudes among faculty members toward special education would be reinforced if the college did not require this course of the special education majors. As a result, a few modifications were made in the special education introductory course. A major compromise was that special education students would be given the opportunity to test out of the course. This opportunity was also made available to regular education majors.

This particular evaluation effort and the attempt to take some positive steps with school officials and administrators brought some disappointments. Tower and the faculty learned that logistic details and political considerations sometimes militate against implementing program revisions that appear to be warranted by evaluation data. Faculty were heartened, however, to see that students were, in general, pleased with the quality of the program and the individual courses. And, they were willing to make the specific revisions based upon the student feedback. This evaluation process was continued each semester as a way of monitoring changes made in the program.

1. For each course, indicate whether it overlapped with any other course in either elementary or special education by placing the course number in the appropriate blank. If there was no overlap, put an X in the appropriate blank.

2. Provide your reaction to each course by circling the number that best reflects your opinion according to the following key:

   0 = did not take the course
   1 = the pits! delete this course from the program
   2 = could be OK, but needs major revisions
   3 = adequate course—minor revisions needed
   4 = above average course—do not change
   5 = really super course—couldn't teach without it

3. In the space marked comments, make any suggestions for change that you believe would strengthen the course. Also, if there is anything that is particularly strong about the course, please note it here.

4. Answer the questions at the end of the course listing.

COURSES	RATING	COMMENTS
EDS 250 Introduction to Special Education _____no overlap overlapped with_____	0 1 2 3 4 5	
EDS 510 Early Childhood Education of the Handicapped _____no overlap overlapped with_____	0 1 2 3 4 5	
EDS 511 Speech and Language Development _____no overlap overlapped with_____	0 1 2 3 4 5	
EDS 512 Language Disorders I _____no overlap overlapped with_____	0 1 2 3 4 5	

1. In general, how would you rate the quality of teaching that you received in the special education program?
   _____lousy   _____mediocre   _____O.K.   _____pretty good   _____super

2. Do you believe that you are prepared to teach in your area of interest?
   _____no   _____unsure   _____yes

3. How would you rate the quality of the advising that you received during your program?
   _____lousy   _____mediocre   _____O.K.   _____pretty good   _____super

4. What is your reaction to the *quantity* of the practicum and field experiences that you had?
   _____not enough   _____about right   _____too much

5. What is your reaction to the *quality* of the practicum and field experiences that you had?
   _____lousy   _____mediocre   _____O.K.   _____pretty good   _____super

6. In the space below (and on the back of this page if you need more room) list any recommendations that you would make that would help us to improve the preparation programs of future special education students. Please comment specifically on what should be done about the overlap between EDP 203 and the special education survey course.

FIGURE 7. Excerpt from Graduating Student Questionnaire

EVALUATING PROGRAM IMPLEMENTATION

FOCUS—WHAT ELSE DO WE NEED TO KNOW ABOUT PROGRAM IMPLEMENTATION? (QUESTIONS) Several evaluation questions were formulated for the area of program implementation and several techniques to collect data were designed.

Evaluation of Faculty Teaching.

COLLECTING—ARE THERE INEXPENSIVE WAYS OF GETTING SOME OF THE DATA WE NEED? (COLLECTION PROCEDURES) The first question asked was: "Are faculty effective in the implementation of instructional content?" Earlier, Professor Tower had developed a relationship with the NSU Office of Institutional Research, charged with the collection of data on a university-wide basis. One of the current charges was to design a system for evaluating faculty teaching. Tower was instrumental in getting several items included in the instrument that this office designed, so that it was possible to have a single instrument serve the university and the needs of his department's curriculum revision effort. Thus, potential redundancy was reduced, to say nothing of the repetitious collection and analysis of data. In fact, data analyses for this aspect of the evaluation were conducted by the Office of Institutional Research; thus, lifting a burden on the resources of the department.

An excerpt from the evaluation instrument is shown in figure 8. It was designed to permit optical scoring and computer analysis of responses for each class. Space was provided on the forms to obtain open-ended responses to the following questions:

What do you feel were the strong points of this course that should be retained?
What do you feel were the weak points of this course that should be changed?
In what ways or areas has this course helped you?

In response to Tower's prompting, space was also provided on the form for up to 15 optical scan responses to questions that were not part of the standard form. Thus, questions idiosyncratic to a particular course could be asked.

REPORTING—WHO SEES THE DATA? HOW ARE POTENTIALLY EMBARRASSING, NEGATIVE RESULTS DEALT WITH? (PURPOSE/AUDIENCE) In each class, a student was designated to pick up the completed forms and take them to the Office of Institutional Research. The handwritten responses to the open-ended questions were then typed (in order not to give clues as to the student respondent due to the instructor's knowledge of the student's handwriting), and the forms were taken to the computing center where the data were summarized. Printouts of means, standard deviations, and ranges for each item, along with an itemized analysis were made available to the faculty along with the typed subjective comments. These data were channeled to the faculty through the department chair, who also received a summary print-out for the department as a whole.

Because of the poentially sensitive nature of these data, Chairperson Champion dealt with individual cases, and Tower was given access to the summary data for the department as a whole. While students regarded faculty teaching performances in a positive fashion, several individual problem areas were dealt with by Champion in consultation with the appropriate faculty members.

Practicum Evaluation Records

COLLECTING—HOW CAN WE GET THE DATA WE NEED TO FIND OUT IF THE STUDENTS ARE "PUTTING IT ALL TOGETHER" BY THE END OF THEIR PRACTICA? (INSTRUMENTS) A second question asked about program implementation was: "Do students acquire the competencies taught in the program?" As students were in route, competency checks were naturally made in each class as a part of grading. There was a need, however, to perform a summative evaluation of student performance that would reflect a synthesis of the various competencies.

A "practicum evaluation form" was already in use by both the university faculty who supervised student teaching and the cooperating teachers in whose classes the student teachers worked. This form, shown in figure 9, was based upon the competencies that were originally identified.

Although each student was evaluated several times using this instrument, little was done with it except to file the necessary copies in the various student files. Professor Tower believed that these forms could provide valuable data relative to the evaluation question concerning the attainment of program competencies. Consequently, he performed an analysis of these records in order to determine their implications for program evaluation.

In general, Tower found that the students were achieving the competencies as evaluated by the university faculty and cooperating teachers. He did find a number of areas in which problems were identified. Of the first 165 reports that he examined, the following rank order list of problems encountered by student teachers emerged:

1. Using preventative discipline
2. Reading instruction difficulties
3. Using clinical teaching techniques
4. Dealing effectively with educationally relevant characteristics
5. Evaluating the effectiveness of IEP's
6. Problems in teacher-student interactions
7. Selecting appropriate mathematics materials
8. Planning for academic instruction
9. Using effective verbal and non-verbal communication
10. Establishing behavioral skills
11. Developing language skills
12. Implementing resource teaching programs

This information was given to Belfrey, and appropriate modifications were made in course content to provide additional emphasis to these areas of difficulty.

Follow-up Questionnaires. Because it may be one thing to exhibit competencies in the controlled environment of the student teaching placement and quite another to imple-

SECTION A: INSTRUCTOR ASSESSMENT

Respond to each item in terms of the extent to which it describes your instructor:

(1) Not at all descriptive
(2) Descriptive to a small extent
(3) Descriptive to a moderate extent
(4) Descriptive to a large extent
(5) Descriptive to an extremely large extent

THE INSTRUCTOR:

1. ① ② ③ ④ ⑤ Has command of the subject.
2. ① ② ③ ④ ⑤ Is open to other viewpoints and contrasts these effectively.
3. ① ② ③ ④ ⑤ Discusses current developments.
4. ① ② ③ ④ ⑤ Relates topics to other areas of knowledge.
5. ① ② ③ ④ ⑤ Makes the subject clear.
6. ① ② ③ ④ ⑤ Acts in a professional manner.
7. ① ② ③ ④ ⑤ States objectives.
8. ① ② ③ ④ ⑤ Accomplishes course objectives.
9. ① ② ③ ④ ⑤ Summarizes major points.
10. ① ② ③ ④ ⑤ Presents material in an organized manner.
11. ① ② ③ ④ ⑤ Uses examples or illustrations to help clarify material.
12. ① ② ③ ④ ⑤ Gives examination questions which are reasonable and fair.
13. ① ② ③ ④ ⑤ Is well prepared for each class.
14. ① ② ③ ④ ⑤ Emphasizes important subject content.
15. ① ② ③ ④ ⑤ Is enthusiastic about the subject.
16. ① ② ③ ④ ⑤ Considers individual students' needs.
17. ① ② ③ ④ ⑤ Is sensitive to class responses.
18. ① ② ③ ④ ⑤ Encourages student participation.
19. ① ② ③ ④ ⑤ Stimulates students to intellectual effort beyond that required by most courses.
20. ① ② ③ ④ ⑤ Aids students to develop creative capacities.
21. ① ② ③ ④ ⑤ Welcomes questions and discussions.
22. ① ② ③ ④ ⑤ Is readily available for consultation with students.
23. ① ② ③ ④ ⑤ Makes the course exciting.
24. ① ② ③ ④ ⑤ Lectures.
25. ① ② ③ ④ ⑤ Class discussions.
26. ① ② ③ ④ ⑤ Laboratory experiences
27. ① ② ③ ④ ⑤ Textbook(s)
28. ① ② ③ ④ ⑤ Supplemental readings.
29. ① ② ③ ④ ⑤ Out-of-class assignments.
30. ① ② ③ ④ ⑤ Examinations.
31. ① ② ③ ④ ⑤ Organization of course activities.

32. ① ② ③ ④ ⑤ Your initial enthusiasm for this course.
33. ① ② ③ ④ ⑤ The level of effort you put into this course.
34. ① ② ③ ④ ⑤ The level of difficulty of the coursework.
35. ① ② ③ ④ ⑤ The amount of required coursework.

36. ① ② ③ ④ ⑤ Rate the overall value of this course.

1. ① ② ③ ④ ⑤
2. ① ② ③ ④ ⑤
3. ① ② ③ ④ ⑤
4. ① ② ③ ④ ⑤
5. ① ② ③ ④ ⑤
6. ① ② ③ ④ ⑤
7. ① ② ③ ④ ⑤
8. ① ② ③ ④ ⑤
9. ① ② ③ ④ ⑤
10. ① ② ③ ④ ⑤
11. ① ② ③ ④ ⑤
12. ① ② ③ ④ ⑤
13. ① ② ③ ④ ⑤
14. ① ② ③ ④ ⑤
15. ① ② ③ ④ ⑤

OPTIONAL QUESTIONS

37. Was the class size appropriate for the teaching method?
○ NO, CLASS TOO SMALL ○ NO, CLASS TOO LARGE ○ YES, USUALLY
38. Rate the pace of instruction in this course:
○ VERY SLOW ○ SLOW ○ ABOUT RIGHT ○ FAST ○ VERY FAST

FIGURE 8. Excerpt from Student Evaluation of Teaching Form

DESCRIPTIVE COMPETENCIES	PERFORMANCE EVALUATION	COMMENTS

Upon completion of this practicum, the student teacher will demonstrate the ability to:

2.1 Extrapolate educationally relevant data from formal and informal assessment instruments.   ONA 0 1 2 3

2.2 Identify and state long-term educational goals and short-term behavioral objectives for each student.   ONA 0 1 2 3

2.3 Perform task analyses.   ONA 0 1 2 3

2.4 Organize teaching objectives following a consistent sequential development of skills for each instructional area.   ONA 0 1 2 3

2.5 Design instructional programs that match the objectives for each student.   ONA 0 1 2 3

2.6 Implement instructional programs designed to achieve previously indentified objectives.   ONA 0 1 2 3

2.7 Utilize instructional procedures appropriate to the learning task in terms of conditions needed for successful achievement, materials, motivation and methods.   ONA 0 1 2 3

2.8 Individualize instruction for students.   ONA 0 1 2 3

Notes about this instrument:
(1) Response key:

ONA - Opportunity not available for the student to demonstrate competency
    0 - Not yet competent
    1 - Marginal performance, definitely in need of improvement
    2 - Competent
    3 - Outstanding performance

(2) The space for comments was reserved for notations that would be used to verify that rating and/or provide suggestions for remedial activities.

FIGURE 9. Excerpt from Practicum Evaluation Form

ment one's own classroom program, this evaluation question was "Are the graduates of the program able to implement the concepts that they were taught?" Several data collection procedures were implemented to arrive at a response to this question.

The first procedure was to design a study that would follow-up graduates of the program. This was a relatively standard procedure designed to obtain feedback from graduates about the relevance of their training for their current job situation, whether there was any course work superfluous to their needs, and whether there was content that should have been covered, yet was not. An excerpt from this questionnaire is shown in figure 10.

Provide your answer according to the following key:
1 = Strongly Disagree
2 = Disagree
3 = Agree
4 = Strongly Agree

ANALYSIS/ INTERPRETATION—CAN WE USE THE DATA TO FIND OUT WHAT PARTS OF THE CURRICULUM NEED TO BE CHANGED?

Tower found that graduates believed that they had received good instruction and preparation in many areas, such as how to teach reading, science, social learning, physical education; classroom management; testing and measurement and the interpretation of educational assessments; general teaching skills; program evaluation; use of media and materials; and parent support services. On the other hand, graduates felt weak in developing scope and sequence of instruction, concept development, drill, setting long-term objectives, maintenance of student records, using supportive services, legal implications of teaching, screening students, and translating test results into objectives.

Graduates also reported that completely new instruction was needed in the areas of teaching language, writing, spelling, use of prosthetics, early childhood education and career education.

		CIRCLE ONE			
a.	Training received at NSU was relevant to my job.	1	2	3	4
b.	My performance is at least comparable to my colleagues who graduated from other colleges and universities.	1	2	3	4
c.	Coursework that I had at NSU was beneficial to me.	1	2	3	4
d.	Practicum experiences at NSU were relevant to my current job	1	2	3	4

What aspects of the NSU program were particularly beneficial in your job? _____

What experiences at NSU did you have that were irrelevant to your job? _____

In what ways could your training at NSU have been improved? _____

FIGURE 10. Excerpt from Graduate Follow-up Questionnaire

As a result, course content was revised to reflect the reported needs of the program graduates. It was of particular interest to note that there was virtually no area of curriculum that graduates suggested should be eliminated.

A second questionnaire related to this evaluation question was designed for response by employers of the graduates. An excerpt of this is illustrated in figure 11. Because of the implied consent provision of the human subjects clearance process within the university, it was necessary to send the questionnaires to the graduates, who then were given the option of either returning them or giving them to their employer for completion and return to Professor Tower. This procedure undoubtedly led to some bias, as the best teachers would probably have no qualms about having their performance evaluated; while those who were marginal would have a tendency not to forward the question-

Using the rating scale below, please rate the preparation of this NSU graduate:

o = unable to judge
1 = not prepared
2 = poorly prepared
3 = adequately prepared
4 = very well prepared

		CIRCLE ONE				
a.	Relevance of training to current job	0	1	2	3	4
b.	Performance as compared to graduates of other colleges or universities	0	1	2	3	4
c.	Performance as compared to others with the same position and experience	0	1	2	3	4
d.	Knowledge base for job	0	1	2	3	4
e.	Performance skills for job	0	1	2	3	4
f.	Interpersonal and communication skills	0	1	2	3	4
g.	Professional qualities	0	1	2	3	4

NSU Graduates appear to be strong in _____

NSU Graduates appear to be weak in _____

NSU's training program could help my employees by including or focusing on _____

FIGURE 11. Excerpt from Employer's Follow-up Questionnaire

naire to their employer. Unfortunately, there was no easy way to gauge or counter this bias.

Tower found that employers tend to rate NSU graduates as "adequately to very well" prepared, and he was able to glean some useful information from the open-ended responses. Employers tended to indicate that NSU graduates were particularly well-prepared in the areas of behavior management techniques, diagnostic-prescriptive procedures for teaching reading, use of multi-media materials, and how to set up a classroom.

On the other hand, the employers felt that they were less than adequately prepared on how to deal with administration and regular classroom teachers, how to teach without adequate instructional materials, techniques in teaching mathematics, and how to deal effectively with older handicapped students and those with more severe emotional problems. These data were reported to the faculty and, through Belfrey, modifications were made to bolster instruction in the areas mentioned.

MORE FOLLOW-UP DATA: THE HELP LINE

COLLECTING—HOW CAN WE GET SOME MORE INFORMATION ON THE KINDS OF PROBLEMS GRADUATES ENCOUNTER? As a pilot study, the first group of students to graduate from the program were given an audio cassette as a "graduation present." They were told that they could record any concerns, comments, or requests for help on these "SOS Tapes" and send them to a designated faculty member in the Department. This faculty member would either record a response or contact the student directly to provide assistance for the problem. This technique was used by only a few students. But those who used it reported that they thought it was useful in helping them to get over their first-year teaching jitters. And, the types of problems reported were helpful in interpreting the other data collected on survey forms.

Although some of the problems could be dealt with in the curriculum, others (e.g., misplacement) could only be dealt with on the basis of providing moral support and giving students some helpful tips.

EVALUATING THE CURRICULUM REVISION PROCESS

FOCUS—HOW CAN WE TELL IF OUR CURRICULUM REVISION PROCESS WAS EFFECTIVE? (QUESTION) The final question of interest was: "How effective was the curriculum revision process?" The process used was systematic and required considerable time and effort, and had done the job. Chairperson Champion wondered about revisions needed in the revision method and whether it had implications for other curriculum efforts. A structured interview was designed to ask involved faculty the following questions:

What was your role in the curriculum revision process?
How effective was the process?
What problems did you encounter?
What were the benefits of the approach that you used?
How would you change the process for further curriculum revision efforts?

COLLECTING—HOW CAN WE FIND OUT WHAT THE FACULTY THINK ABOUT THE PROCESS? Champion found that, in general, faculty were satisfied with the process that was used. As might be expected, the biggest problem encountered was that of the time involved for implementation. Faculty thought that their efforts were appropriate, that they were moving forward in appropriate ways, and that the results of their efforts were personally gratifying in that a high-quality program emerged. However, several faculty reported that considerable time was being expended over and beyond their regular duties. Most wanted partial release time to perform such efforts if future revisions were needed. They felt, however, that the time problem was primarily due to the fact that the total curriculum was being revised. They believed that smaller revision efforts could be performed without release time.

REPORTING—WHO MIGHT BENEFIT FROM KNOWING ABOUT THE CURRICULUM REVISION PROCESS? Tower kept a log of the entire revision and evaluation process. This process study turned out to be a gold mine for other departments on campus when a university program review system was constructed the last year of the revision. While their evaluation was not exemplary in every fashion, it had been comprehensive and enjoyed high faculty involvement throughout. It helped the department in a number of ways and put them ahead of the game in the program review system.

CONCLUSIONS

Although limited resources prevented a more detailed and sophisticated evaluation (e.g., questions related to whether students with learning and behavior disorders learned as a result of the efforts of graduates of the program could not be answered), Chairperson Champion, Professors Tower and Belfrey, and Dean Tidings were satisfied with the results of the evaluation and the resultant curriculum. The evaluation reports became immensely useful in responding to the various audiences that were described in the evaluation plan. Most importantly, however, the data that were collected seemed to support the contention of faculty that students were obtaining a quality education and that graduates of the program were adequately performing their teaching responsibilities.

REFERENCES

Blackhurst, A.E., Some practical considerations in implementing competency-based special education training programs. In J.J. Creamer and J.T. Gilmore (Eds.), *Design for competence-based education in special education.* Syracuse: Division of Special Education and Rehabilitation, Syracuse University, 1974

Blackhurst, A.E., Competency-based special education personnel preparation. In R.D. Kneedler and S.G. Tarver (Eds.), *Changing perspectives in special education.* Columbus: Charles Merrill, 1977.

Blackhurst, A.E., Curriculum planning as an element of quality control in special education personnel preparation. *Teacher Education and Special Education,* 1979, *2,* 39–41.

Blackhurst, A.E., McLoughlin, J.A., and Price, L.M., Issues in the development of programs to prepare teachers of children with learning and behavior disorders. *Behavior Disorders,* 1977, 2, 157–168.

* * * * *

DISCUSSION QUESTIONS AND TOPICS

1. The case revolves around a model used to coordinate and guide a curriculum revision process. An alternative model would have been simply to describe requirements of noncategorical teacher certification to the faculty, then let each modify the courses he or she teaches (consulting with colleagues as necessary). What are the advantages and disadvantages of each model?

2. After having identified the apparent advantages and disadvantages of each model, consider this question: What is the potential value or usefulness of attempting to evaluate a curriculum revision model?

3. The evaluation of the revision model appeared to be relegated to secondary importance in the case. The primary effort was to get the curriculum revised. In what ways did use of the model help in revising the curriculum?

4. In what ways was the model's emphasis on evaluation helpful in getting the revision done? In what ways did the emphasis on evaluation seem to hinder or at least add cost to the process? On the whole, do you believe the evaluation benefits exceeded the evaluation costs?

5. Much of the case revolves around design evaluation: What is our mission: What are our objectives? Are our planned courses and materials consistent with mission and objectives? The major strategy for answering such questions was, first to *describe* (write the mission, specify objectives and competencies, assemble teaching materials). Having described the objects of evaluation, the next step was to get expert opinions about the objects described. Who were the major experts whose opinions were influential? In what sense is that a very biased sample of expert opinion? In what ways did that biased sample help the effort in terms of involvement of key audiences, gaining acceptance of the revisions, and generally aiding the feasibility and utility of the effort? In what ways does that biased sample limit the value or credibility of the evaluation?

6. When it came to generating the mission statement, Tower got agreement upon evaluation criteria first before making attempts to draft the mission statement. In what way is that a very good evaluation tactic? In what ways is it a very good educational practice and team building or consensus building practice?

7. Tower used the tactic of first let's agree on criteria, then let's see how our work measures up to our criteria successfully in getting an accepted mission statement. Why do you suppose he didn't continue to use that tactic for later phases of the evaluation? Do you think, if he tried harder, that it would have been feasible to continue to use the tactic? Would that have been desirable?

8. Notice that figure 2 lays out the overall plans for the curriculum revision and that the overall plan was shared and discussed with faculty early in the process. Why was that an important step?

9. Had you been Champion or Tower, would the apparently easy acceptance of the overall plan by the faculty reassured you or worried you? Why?

10. The doctoral dissertation on competencies added strength to the curriculum revision. What were some strengths and weaknesses of that study? (Hint: Consider the large number and specificity of critical incidents. Consider also the sample of persons who produced the incidents. Consider also the procedures for transforming the incidents into competencies.)

11. Consider the overall utility of the evaluation. What educational decisions were relatively easy to influence? What education decisions were relatively hard to influence?

12. The evaluation was formative throughout most of the case. What were some of the attempts at summative evaluation? Do you think that the formative evaluation emphasis was appropriate? Why?

SUGGESTIONS FOR STIMULATING DISCUSSIONS

1. Arrange a debate. Resolved: The decision to forego outside critiques and validations (because of lack of funds to pay an advisory board) resulted in a fatal flaw in the evaluation.

2. Have a role playing session in which Tower argues that funds for outside validation are essential, Champion argues that they are highly desirable, and Tidings argues that the outside validation is probably unnecessary and certainly premature.

3. Arrange a debate. Resolved: Consensus of faculty is a dangerous substitute for establishing evaluation criteria and collecting data as a foundation for decision making. (Suggestion: The affirmative might argue that relying on consensus is too readily flawed by political processes and that criteria and data of good evaluation are needed to offset purely political processes. The negative might argue that consensus is the ultimate criterion for acceptance of evaluation results, so it makes sense to go for consensus rather than wasting time in academia disputes about criteria.)

4. Identify one or two turning points or major decision points in the case. Then have people prepare to take on the role of key persons in the case and role play a discussion they might have.

5. Prepare, then discuss and critique the case from several value perspectives. The discussion could take the form of a role play, with each person representing a particular value perspective or bias. (e.g., "It ought to be economical and get results?" "It ought to serve the needs of the children!" "It ought to involve everybody concerned!" "It ought to reflect standard educational practices!" "It ought to be comparable to what the best schools do!" "It ought to be methodologically sound!" "I don't care how marvelous your intentions are, don't confuse needs with results—and I want to hear about results!" "It ought to be consistent with the latest educational and psychological research!")

APPLICATION EXERCISES

1. In the *Sourcebook*—Read some of the material in the *Sourcebook* indicated by the asides. Then suggest alternative things people in the case might have done at several points in the case. Or suggest a whole new approach they might have taken.
2. Using the case as a model (and foil) and your suggested alternatives as guides, design an evaluation for a situation or problem similar to that shown in the case.
3. Using Chapter 7 of the *Sourcebook* as a guide, do a meta-evaluation and critique of the case (and/or your evaluation design).
4. Use the *Design Manual* to develop an improved evaluation design for the case.
5. Use the *Design Manual* to develop an evaluation design for a situation or problem similar to the one described in the case.

CASE C-2

THE DIRECTOR OF A SMALL TRAINING PROJECT ASKS: How can I use evaluation techniques to help in managing the project?

Ken Olsen

FOCUS—WHAT IS THE PROJECT? (OBJECT) Dr. Martin "Marty" Munez had just been notified by the State Protection and Advocacy Office that his $30,000 training project had been funded. The project's purpose was to increase the awareness and knowledge of parents of developmentally disabled and/or severely handicapped children regarding their educational rights. Specifically, the project was to prepare parents to serve as advocates for themselves and their children, using two main strategies: (1) develop a comprehensive handbook for parents on the rights of developmentally disabled people and the advocacy process, and (2) conduct four training sessions for parents on their rights and the advocacy process.

Marty was happy about the grant. Not only was project work a nice break from regular faculty routine, but it was a chance to expand his competency repertoire—and his vita. He was confident of his ability to run a project and felt the needed resources were there.

FOCUS—HOW CAN I MANAGE THE PROJECT SO THAT IT IS LIKELY TO HAVE A GOOD IMPACT? (PURPOSE) Evaluation wasn't a problem, either. Marty was a good researcher, and he'd been to a workshop on outcome evaluation. He'd be able, without much trouble, to measure and report on his project's impact. What concerned him more was making sure the project would in fact have some impact

he'd be proud of and also that it would not eat up too much of his time. Marty had 25% release time to direct the project, but knew the job could take much more real time than that. A few years earlier, Marty had codirected a project much like this new one. Neither he nor his partner had really given the project much management attention. It was, they thought, well designed and should have pretty much run itself. But, things slipped and they got behind, and a part-time job quickly became a full-time hassle. Marty was determined that things would go better this time.

Marty decided he'd use evaluation procedures throughout his project to try to keep things on schedule and to make the changes he'd inevitably need to make. His three graduate assistants called him to task on this. Evaluation, they respectfully noted, wasn't "real" if it didn't assess the worth of the training project: did it make a difference? Marty agreed with them, and assured them their evaluation would investigate the impact question. But he also knew he'd get nothing from the impact evaluation to help him out along the way.

DESIGN—HOW CAN I EVALUATE THE MANAGEMENT OF A PROJECT THAT HASN'T REALLY GOTTEN OFF THE GROUND YET? (ALTERNATIVES) Bart Hanson, Marty's lunchtime racquetball partner and the university's resident evaluation expert, assured him he was on the right track. He noted that many evaluators focused only on what can be called outcome evaluation and didn't develop procedures to increase the chances for a successful outcome. He suggested that Marty start by evaluating his plan as it was written in the proposal. From the review he would be better able to focus his evaluation.

Bart suggested Marty take another look at his proposal to get a better handle on what he most needed to evaluate. He told Marty how to develop an activity chart that would

COLLECTING—WHAT ARE THE MAJOR PROJECT ACTIVITIES I HAVE TO MANAGE? (INFORMATION NEEDED) highlight the key dependencies among the many planned project functions. Then, Marty could use the chart to plan his evaluation.

Here's how Marty developed his activity chart (shown in figure 1 in its final form).

1. He obtained some 3 × 5 cards, tape, black magic marker and some butcher paper.
2. He transferred all of the tasks from his proposal to individual 3 × 5 cards.
3. He arranged the cards on the butcher paper to represent an appropriate sequence and to represent contingencies.
4. He checked his arrangement for additional tasks and added cards as necessary.
5. He taped the cards to the paper and drew lines representig the relationships.

ANALYSIS INTERPRETATION—ARE THE ACTIVITIES LISTED COMPLETE AND FEASIBLE (I.E. CAN I REALLY DO ALL THAT AND, IF I DO, WILL IT BE ENOUGH?)? (INTERPRETATION CRITERIA) At first, Marty worked with his activity chart in draft form. As he looked at the draft, Marty realized that his plan had not been as ready as he thought. Some of his timelines were off because it would be impossible to have sufficient staff to accomplish all activities in the time allotted. He found that he had to add some steps, e.g., 1.2a, a step obtaining approval or copyright permission to use existing materials in his handbook, and 1.4a and 2.13a, steps for compilation and product revision. And, he found that he could be more efficient by joining steps from the two different strategies. For example, when he was to work with the Protection and Advocacy Office to identify a pool of parents to be invited to the training sessions, he could select from that same pool of parents a few individuals to review the draft handbook.

REPORTING—HOW CAN I KEEP MYSELF AND OTHERS AWARE OF WHAT I'VE LEARNED FROM THIS EVALUATION? (PURPOSE/USE) The activity chart represented a form of evaluation that had already helped him revise his plan. It let him know, for instance, that there was a need for more staff support in the beginning of the project than toward the end. So, he arranged to have three half-time graduate assistants for the first semester (Larry, Lyn and Luther) and only one for the second semester (Larry). He assigned himself and his assistants to the tasks on the chart by putting their initials in various boxes. They overviewed their responsibilities and estimated start and end dates for each task. They then were ready to outline their evaluation questions.

ANALYZING THE ACTIVITY CHART TO FOCUS THE EVALUATION

FOCUS—WHO REALLY NEEDS THE EVALUATION DATA I'LL COLLECT? (AUDIENCE) Marty and his assistants began their evaluation design work by assuming that they—the staff—were the primary evaluation audience. They wanted their evaluation to tell them how things were going and where they needed to

FOCUS—WHAT SPECIFIC EVALUATION QUESTIONS DO WE HAVE? (AUDIENCE) more closely control or revise the project. They then listed evaluation questions they thought were important in each of these categories:

1.0 Are We Ready?

1.1 How valid are the needs of parents for information on their rights?
1.2 Is our parent handbook adequate to meet parent needs?
1.3 Are our training plan and materials adequate to meet parent needs?
1.4 Is our training staff sufficiently prepared?
1.5 Are our facility arrangements adequate?

2.0 Are We Implementing According to Plan?

2.1 Are we meeting our timelines?
2.2 Is the Protestation and Advocacy Office Office satisfied with our progress?
2.3 Are we consuming our fiscal resources at an appropriate rate?
2.4 Are we attracting an appropriate population?

2.5 Are we implementing our training activities adequately?

2.5.1 Are we using our facilities adequately?
2.5.2 Is our time allocation to different training activities appropriate?
2.5.3 Are we using our materials appropriately?
2.5.4 Are we using our training staff appropriately?
2.5.5 Are the participants satisfied with their involvement?

3.0 Are We Making A Difference?

3.1 Are we causing any changes in the advocacy activities of parents?
3.2 Are we causing any changes in the ways parents perceive themselves?
3.3 Are we creating any ripple effects in terms of additional training or products?
3.4 Are we causing any unexpected positive or negative effects?

Right away, Marty could see they had more questions than they could reasonably pursue. He reviewed the list to see which were most important and which ones needed the most attention in an internal evaluation. He was safely able, he felt, to delete three questions:

Question 1.1: Parent Needs: Marty had already done a considerable needs assessment in preparing his proposal. He had reviewed literature, and had analyzed records of school site visits conducted by the state division of special education. In their planned review of the handbook, they could ask parents to reaffirm these needs and look for omissions.

Question 1.5: Facility Arrangements: As an experienced trainer, Marty knew that bad arrangements could ruin an otherwise well-planned workshop. But, Larry had recently been to a workshop on how to plan workshops and had shown Marty a book he'd read by Davis and McCallon, *Conducting and Evaluating Workshops.* Given this, and work already done, Marty decided not to pursue this question further.

Question 2.2: Protection and Advocacy Office Satisfaction: No doubt, satisfaction was a key issue. But Marty met with this office each month and felt the communication lines here were already in place. There was no doubt he'd hear, and hear in time, if problems cropped up. This question really didn't need more evaluation than was already in place.

DESIGNING THE EVALUATION SYSTEM

DESIGN—WHAT DOES AN EVALUATION SYSTEM HAVE TO DO FOR ME AS PROJECT DIRECTOR? (CRITERIA FOR JUDGING DESIGNS) Next, Marty sat down and wrote himself some notes about what criteria the evaluation system must meet to help him better manage his project. When he was done his list looked like this:

1. It must help me make decisions as a project director.

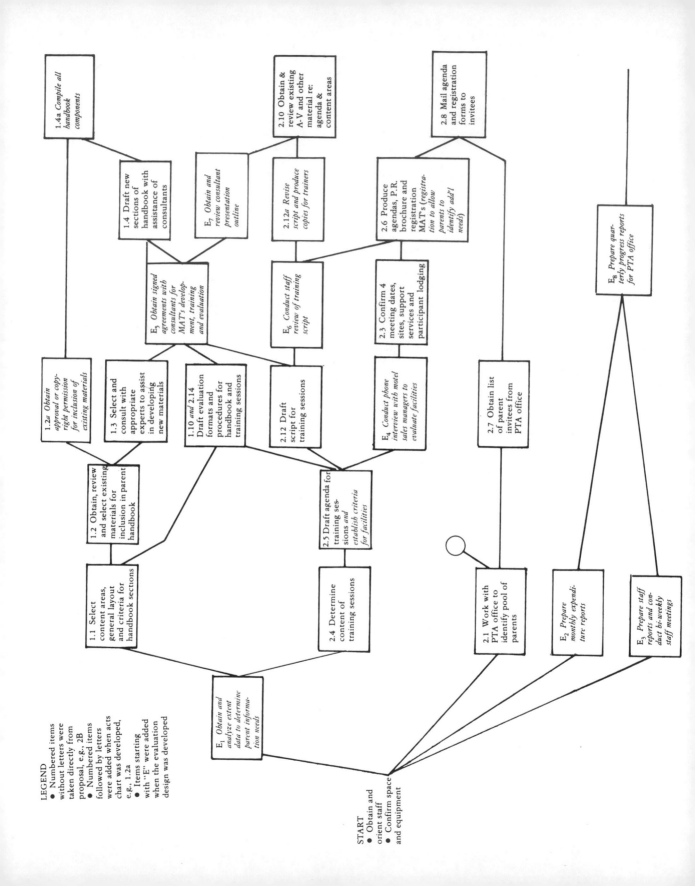

LEGEND
• Numbered items without letters were taken directly from proposal, e.g., 2B
• Numbered items followed by letters were added when acts chart was developed, e.g., 1.2a
• Items starting with "E" were added when the evaluation design was developed

START
• Obtain and orient staff
• Confirm space and equipment

E_1 Obtain and analyze extent data to determine parent information needs

1.1 Select content areas, general layout and criteria for handbook sections

1.2 Obtain, review and select existing materials for inclusion in parent handbook

1.2a Obtain approval or copyright permission for inclusion of existing materials

1.3 Select and consult with appropriate experts to assist in developing new materials

1.4 Draft new sections of handbook with assistance of consultants

1.4a Compile all handbook components

E_5 Obtain signed agreements with consultants for MAT's development, training and evaluation

1.10 and 2.14 Draft evaluation formats and procedures for handbook and training sessions

2.4 Determine content of training sessions

2.5 Draft agenda for training sessions and establish criteria for facilities

2.12 Draft script for training sessions

2.12a Revise script and produce copies for trainers

E_6 Conduct staff review of training script

E_7 Obtain and review consultant presentation outline

2.10 Obtain & review existing A-V and other material re: agenda & content areas

E_4 Conduct phone interview with motel sales managers to evaluate facilities

2.3 Confirm 4 meeting dates, sites, support services and participant lodging

2.6 Produce agendas, P.R. brochure and registration MAT's (registration to allow parents to identify add'l needs)

2.7 Obtain list of parent invitees from PTA office

2.8 Mail agenda and registration forms to invitees

2.1 Work with PTA office to identify pool of parents

E_2 Prepare monthly expenditure reports

E_3 Prepare staff reports and conduct bi-weekly staff meetings

E_8 Prepare quarterly progress reports for PTA office

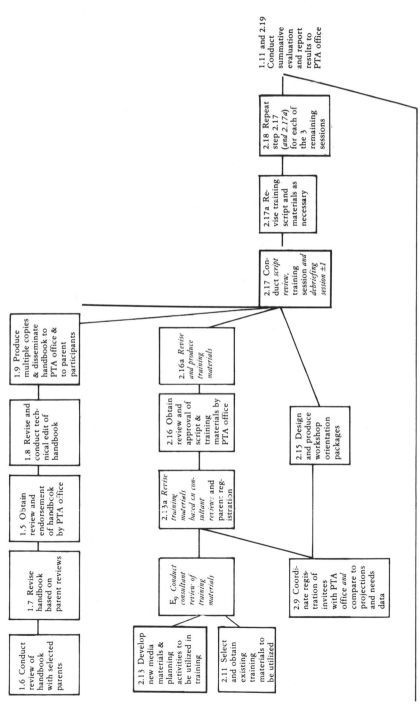

FIGURE 1: Activity Chart of Marty's Project, Showing Project Functions & Dependencies

2. It can't take much time or money and should use existing data and sources wherever possible.
3. I don't want to bother the parents or the Protection and Advocacy Office.
4. Information has to come to me in time for me to do something about it.
5. My evaluation steps must fit into my general activity framework.

DESIGN—CAN WE DESIGN SOME EVALUATION PROCEDURES THAT MEET OUR CRITERIA? (APPROPRIATE PROCEDURES)

Marty and his assistants began brainstorming techniques to deal with their evaluation questions. Techniques that did not meet Marty's criteria were thrown out. When they were done, they had developed the chart in figure 2.

Before they were through, they added the procedural evaluation steps to the activity chart (see shaded items in figure 1) so that Marty could monitor his evaluation activities just as he monitored his program activities. In doing so, he found that he could tie some of his evaluation procedures together. For example, the graduate assistants' weekly handwritten summaries of their activities could be timed to give him sufficient information to prepare quarterly reports for the Protection and Advocacy Office. Also, training script review sessions before each workshop would help him judge the readiness of trainers as well as allow him to use the Protection and Advocacy Office staff and consultants to evaluate the training plan.

After reviewing the entire picture, he was satisfied that the plan met his criteria. Of course, there was more he could do. But, all-in-all, he felt the evaluation plan would give him the information he needed to make program adjustments at the time they were needed. He was confident that his strategy of "using data to plan for impact" rather than waiting to evaluate for impact was the best use of his scarce evaluation dollars.

EVALUATING PREPARATION

ANALYSIS-INTERPRETATION—HOW COULD WE TELL IF THE PARENT'S HANDBOOK IS READY TO USE? (INTERPRETATION CRITERIA)

Under the general question "Are we ready to implement?" Marty and his graduate assistants had posed several specific questions. The first dealt with the parent handbook, a key step in their project.

Lyn used the list of parent needs already identified to select content areas for the parent handbook, so she felt that the outline matched the needs data very closely. But that was no guarantee, Marty patiently explained, that it was therefore "adequate to meet parent needs" as their evaluation question asked. They would need to incorporate several review steps as the handbook developed.

Establishing Criteria. Lyn's outline was reviewed at the next staff meeting. As a group, staff recommended inclusion of a glossary of terms and an index organized by specific parent questions they had identified in their document analyses. They also suggested that all materials in the handbook be written at a fourth or fifth grade reading level and that maximum use be made of pictures and other graphics. Lyn made notes regarding these criteria and drafted a review form which she would later pilot with a selected group of parents and with the Protection and Advocacy Office.

Lyn asked Marty to help her identify consultants who could write technical or special topic sections of the handbook. Larry was far enough along in developing his training plan that the three of them outlined their joint needs for consultants. Lyn asked each consultant to submit a draft for preliminary review. While she was waiting for the drafts to arrive, she began making arrangements for a review by a few parents.

PARENT REVIEWS. Lyn obtained from Luther the names of three parents who had helped the Protection and Advocacy

COLLECTING—WHO SHOULD WE HAVE CRITIQUE EARLY DRAFTS OF THE HANDBOOK? (SAMPLES)

Office review earlier products. She called each and asked if they would help her. When they agreed, she arranged to pay for them for their review time. As the drafts arrived, she compiled and copied them together with a copy of the

COLLECTING—HOW CAN WE ASSURE THAT PEOPLE WILL REVIEW THE DRAFTS CAREFULLY AND TELL US WHAT THEY THINK ABOUT THEM? (COLLECTION PROCEDURES)

questions she wanted to ask the parents. She sent each parent a copy of the draft handbook and her criteria. Because she wanted an in-depth review but didn't want them to have to write out their responses, she told the parents she would call them in a week to discuss their reactions.

Using the criteria as an interview guide, Lyn called each parent reviewer and discussed the following:

Topics—Are critical areas of concern addressed?
Coverage (each topic)—Is there enough detail? Is there too much detail?
Readability—Is the level of language O.K.? Is it clearly written?
Format/Layout—Is the order O.K.? Do the pictures and charts help?

RESULTS. Two of the parents said they were disappointed that the handbook did not contain at least a general description of the roles of the Protection and Advocacy Office and the Division of Special Education. All three felt the handbook used too much jargon. They also wanted a separation of procedures for referral and evaluation from those for placement. They said that the various due process forms in the text were helpful but that placement within the text interrupted their reading and made it difficult to maintain a flow of ideas.

USE OF PARENT REVIEW DATA. Lyn brought her notes to staff meeting at which time they agreed on a table of

ANALYSIS/INTERPRETATION—HOW WELL DO THE MATERIALS SATISFY THE CRITERIA WE ESTABLISHED FOR THEM? (ANALYSIS)

contents. Marty then drafted summary overviews of the roles of the Protection and Advocacy Office and the Division of Special Education

EVALUATION QUESTIONS	DATA SOURCES	EVALUATION PROCEDURE(S)
1.0 ARE WE READY?		
1.1 Is our parent handbook adequate to meet parent needs?	P & A Office Staff Parents	Conduct staff review of handbook outline. Ask workshop consultants and P & A Office to review handbook.
1.2 Are our training plan and materials adequate to meet parent needs?	Consultants P & A Office Staff reports	Conduct staff review of training script. Obtain professional judgments by consultants and P & A Office.
1.3 Is our training staff sufficiently prepared?	Training script Agreements with consultants Outlining of consultant's presentation	Conduct joint review of workshop script. Obtain signature of consultant on agreement.
2.0 ARE WE IMPLEMENTING ACCORDING TO PLAN?		
2.1 Are we meeting our timelines?	Staff reports Activity Chart	Collect staff reports and conduct weekly staff meetings according to Activity Chart
2.2 Are we consuming our fiscal resources at an appropraite rate?	Monthly University account records	Compute expenditure rate per month in each line item and project for entire year. Compare to proposed budget.
2.3 Are we attracting the appropriate population?	Consultants P & A Participants Key informants (parent participants) Staff Parent participants	Conduct and document script review and de-briefing sessions before and after each training session. Utilize exit evaluation questionnaire.
3.0 ARE WE MAKING A DIFFERENCE?		
3.1 Are we causing any changes in the advocacy activities of parents?	Parent participants P & A Office	Exit evaluation questionnaire. Conduct and document three month follow-up through phone interviews.
3.2 Are we causing any changes in the ways parents perceive themselves?	Sample of parents	
3.3 Are we creating any ripple effects in terms of additional training or products?		
3.4 Are we causing any unexpected positive or negative effects?		

FIGURE 2. Evaluation Design

while Lyn went back to the consultants with her specific concerns on their units and to review the final table of contents. When he received their reactions, these were incorporated in their revisions of the final drafts.

PROTECTION AND ADVOCACY REVIEW. The Protection and Advocacy Office had been kept apprised of each step in the development of the handbook. Therefore, by the time the final draft was prepared and sent to the Protection and Advocacy Office for approval, there was little question about Protection and Advocacy endorsement. When Ms. Strike asked why an overview of the Division of Special Education was necessary, Marty simply explained the

REPORTING—HOW CAN WE KEEP PEOPLE INFORMED ABOUT WHAT WE ARE DOING SO THAT THERE AREN'T LIKELY TO BE ANY RUDE SURPRISES WHEN THE MANUAL IS COMPLETE? (PURPOSES/USE)

request made by parent reviewers for information clarifying the roles of the two agencies. She and her staff recommended some minor editorial changes, which were subsequently made, and the product was sent for typesetting and printing.

EVALUATING TRAINING PLAN AND MATERIALS IS NEXT

COLLECTING—JUST WHAT IS OUR TRAINING PLAN? (INFORMATION NEEDED)

While Lyn was working on the parent handbook, Larry and Marty developed the training plan and support materials. Their first activity involved drafting an agenda, which would serve as the basis for their training script, help establish criteria for the type of facility needed, and would help them select training consultants (see figure 3).

STAFF SCRIPT REVIEW. Larry took this draft agenda and sketched a script, a portion of which is provided in figure 4. Copies were provided to Marty and the other two graduate assistants, and a review session was set up. Lyn and Luther were asked to review the script from the perspective of a parent and consultant respectively. Marty reviewed the scripts from his own perspective and that of a Protection and Advocacy Office staff participant.

ANALYSIS/ INTERPRETATION—CAN WE ANTICIPATE THE REACTIONS OF PARTICULAR TRAINING AUDIENCES? (INTERPRETATION CRITERIA)

USE OF STAFF REVIEW. When the staff script review was complete, they each felt they had simulated the workshop and worked out major bugs. They used this experience to discuss and select consultants who would fit into their training structure. Marty called the parent and lawyer selected and asked them if they would be available. Marty also arranged to discuss the revised script and agenda with Ms. Strike at her next opportunity.

TRAINING MATERIAL REVIEWS. After a formal agreement was made with the consultants (see figure 5) they were sent the agenda and asked to recommend simulation or audio-visual materials. Larry gathered and screened the materials for appropriateness to parents. He rated each in terms of the language, graphics, and how well it addressed the objectives of increasing awareness and knowledge regarding advocacy roles. He also judged length and format for ease of use. Marty and Larry went over Larry's ratings and notes. Generally, they found that the materials didn't address the participants' needs very well, primarily because they were oriented toward teachers and used too much jargon.

COLLECTING—HOW CAN WE IDENTIFY MATERIALS THAT MIGHT BE SUITABLE TO USE AS PART OF OUR TRAINING? (SAMPLES)

ANALYSIS/ INTERPRETATION—DO THE POTENTIAL MATERIALS SATISFY OUR CRITERIA? (ANALYSIS)

DAY 1

9:00 AM	WELCOME & INTRODUCTION
	Welcome—Ms. Strike
	Introduction/Purpose—M. Munez
	Warm-up—L. Lavorini
9:45 AM	BREAK
10:00 AM	OVERVIEW OF LAWS REGARDING THE DEVELOPMENTALLY DISABLED
	Presentation by M. Munez and L. Lavorini
11:30 AM	LUNCH
1:00 PM	EDUCATIONALLY RELATED ASSESSMENTS
	Presentation by M. Munez
2:00 PM	BREAK
2:15 PM	TESTING SIMULATION ACTIVITY
	Led by L. Lavorini
3:30 PM	GROUP DISCUSSION OF SIMULATION
	Led by L. Lavorini
4:30 PM	ADJOURN UNTIL DAY 2

DAY 2

9:00 AM	THE PARENT'S ROLE IN THE IEP PROCESS
	Presentation by consultant parent
9:45 AM	BREAK
10:00 AM	GROUP ROLE PLAYING OF IEP CONFERENCE
11:30 AM	LUNCH
1:00 PM	DUE PROCESS & APPEALS PROCEDURES
	Presentation by consultant lawyer
2:00 PM	BREAK
2:15 PM	SIMULATION OF HEARING
	Led by L. Lavorini
4:15 PM	CLOSING STATEMENT AND EVALUATION
	M. Munez

FIGURE 3. Agenda

WHEN	AGENDA ITEM	WHO/WHAT
Night before Day 1 6:00 PM	—	Marty: Lead script review by explaining roles, lead discussion Larry: Distribute scripts All: Revise scripts as appropriate
Day 1 8:00 AM	—	Larry: 1. Check on room set-ups 　　　2. Get A-V equipment 　　　3. Check on late arrivals Marty: Meet Ms. Strike for breakfast and review presentations All: Mingle and get to know parent participants.
9:00 AM	Welcome	Marty: Introduce Ms. Strike Ms. Strike: Overview background, needs, Protection and Advocacy role, welcome 　　participants Larry: Check that coffee will be ready at 9:45
9:20 AM	Introduction	Marty: 1. Introduce purpose as increasing knowledge for role as advocates 　　　2. Outline agenda 　　　3. Open for questions 　　　4. Briefly describe contents of handbook 　　　5. Check that all participants received a copy Larry: Set-up warm-up exercise
9:35 AM	Warm-up	Larry: Lead group through finding correct name tags and introducing each other Marty: Set-up screen and overhead projector

FIGURE 4. Portion of Script

FURTHER TRAINING MATERIAL REVIEWS. Larry began adapting simulation materials for the testing session, the IEP conference and the hearing from some of the better materials available. When he was done, he sent the IEP conference simulation to the consultant parent and the simulated hearing to the lawyer. He asked Marty to review the testing simulation. He provided them the same criteria he had used in his screening. Their reviews helped modify the final packages. Marty took these packages to the Protection and Advocacy Office for review and approval. He discussed with Ms. Strike how they had been developed and reviewed, the concerns raised by the reviewers and what he and Larry had done to correct any problems. Ms. Strike endorsed the simulations and the final script after a few small changes. Marty then directed Larry to begin mass production.

ANALYSIS/ INTERPRETATION—DO THE REVISED MATERIALS SATISFY OUR CRITERIA?

REPORTING—IS THE PROJECT SPONSOR SATISFIED WITH THE TRAINING PLAN? (PURPOSE)

EVALUATING STAFF READINESS

FOCUS—ARE THE PEOPLE WHO'LL DO THE TRAINING SUFFICIENTLY PREPARED? (QUESTION)

By the time the staff script review was completed and the simulation materials were developed and reviewed, Marty was fairly certain that he and Larry were well prepared for the training sessions. He didn't want any surprises from his consultants or from Ms. Strike, however. He remembered his painful experience in the previous project when a consultant showed up only five minutes before his presentation, gave his talk with references to "your administrative responsibilities" when the audience consisted of teacher aides, and left before anyone could ask him any questions. Marty wanted to evaluate the readiness of all who would present at the workshops. To answer the evaluation question, "Is our training staff sufficiently prepared?" he would use a three-pronged approach.

CONSULTANT AGREEMENT. The first approach was to develop an agreement with each consultant which specified roles and responsibilities. A signed agreement would indicate that the consultants were aware of project expectations. Lyn and Larry got together and outlined what their expectations would be of each consultant and what support the project would give each. Marty then drafted an agreement according to the following outline:

ANALYSIS/ INTERPRETATION—HOW COULD WE TELL IF THEY ARE "SUFFICIENTLY PREPARED?" WHAT'S THAT MEAN? (INTERPRETATION CRITERIA)

Overview of Project Purpose

Consultant Roles, Procedures and Timelines
Handbook
Materials reviews
Script review sessions
Presentation
Availability
Debriefing sessions and evaluation
Documentation

Project Roles, Responsibilities and Timelines
Support services, e.g., typing, phone, supplies
Timelines
Reimbursement and honoraria

Signatures

FIGURE 5. Outline of Consultant Agreement

As the agreements were discussed with the consultants, the consultants asked further role clarification questions. When they signed, Marty was certain they understood how they were to participate in project activities.

Presentation Outline Review. The consultant agreements called for the consultants to submit a draft of their

COLLECTING—WHAT DOCUMENTS DO WE NEED FROM THE TRAINING STAFF SO WE CAN CHECK ON HOW WELL PREPARED THEY ARE? (COLLECTION PROCEDURE)

presentation outline several weeks prior to the training session. Marty was interested in their emphasis on specific topics and wanted to see if they intended to address the audience needs his staff had identified. And, requiring the consultants to submit an outline might cause them to better prepare for their presentation. The same criteria were used in evaluating the presentation outlines as Larry had used in screening training materials. Comments to the consultants included discussions about potential changes and points of emphasis. Together the consultants and Marty refined and developed a new outline.

As a last minute check of both the script and the staff, Marty conducted a script review the night before each day of each training session. The review followed the same format as the staff review except that each person represented himself.

READINESS SUMMARY

Marty gained confidence as he proceeded with his workshop preparations. He felt he had done an adequate job of defining parent needs; and the staff, parent and Protection and Advocacy reviews of the parent handbook seemed to have lead to a manual targeted on parent needs. The

extensive script and training material reviews by staff and consultants had definitely improved those training components. The consultant agreements and script reviews had assured him that his training staff was ready. Finally, he was fairly confident that the four motels they had selected were ready to accommodate the workshops. He was ready to move into his next stage of evaluation: monitoring progress.

MANAGEMENT—HOW ARE WE GOING? ARE WE ON SCHEDULE? HOW DO WE USE WHAT WE'VE GENERATED SO FAR TO MANAGE THE REST OF THE WORK? (TASKS/SCHEDULES)

Marty placed a big copy of his activity chart on his office wall. As activities were completed he colored the boxes in or checked them off. The agenda for each of his weekly staff meetings was based on uncompleted boxes on his activity chart. Marty added standard agenda items to deal with such issues as equipment, space, support staff and finances. On the Friday before the first and third Mondays, each of the graduate assistants plus Marty submitted a handwritten report such as that in figure 6 on activities to which they had been assigned. Each report was brief and casual but recorded the status of the activity.

Figure 7 is an example of a list of staff assignments resulting from a staff meeting. Before the next meeting Marty distributed the staff assignment list for the staff to cross off items which had been completed so they weren't carried over to the next staff meeting. Marty found that by using these procedures he was able to keep his meeting short and targeted on issues. Marty also found that the staff reports provided an historical record or audit trail of project progress.

REPORTING—WHAT SHOULD WE DO IF THE QUARTERLY PROGRESS REPORTS DON'T GIVE US THE CHECKPOINTS WE NEED? (WHEN)

By the time the first month had ended, Marty knew that quarterly reports called for on his proposal would be insufficient for maintaining awareness of the Protectifon and Advocacy Office. If he waited until after the third month to have a review session with the Protection and Advocacy Office, he would be too far down the road in his workshop and handbook planning to make necessary modifications. He decided to prepare two-page monthly reports. These reports would follow pretty much the same format as the reports he received from his graduate assistants but would collapse all information under two reports, one for the handbook and one for the training workshops. He arranged to have meetings with Ms. Strike. Marty also used these meetings with Ms. Strike to review the various products, agendas, and choices of consultants and participants.

RESULTS. As a result of this ongoing process of updates and problem resolution, Marty found that his problems were resolved before they became issues. He also found that he was able to get Protection and Advocacy Office concurrance with his plans before implementation. A side benefit was that these monthly meetings made Marty aware of new initiatives planned and conducted by the Protection and Advocacy Office. For example, during one of their monthly

2.3   Confirm Dates & Sites - Luther

Status: I called the Hideaway Inn at Levinsboro and placed tentative reservations on a block of 40 rooms for October 16 & 17. They have a large meeting room that can be divided in four sections for small group activity.

Question: Manager wants a deposit. How do we handle that?

Next: Marty: (Handle deposit)
      Luther: Meet with Larry on —
              to set up meeting rooms.
      Luther: Call Hideaway Inn with results

FIGURE 6. Sample Handwritten Staff Report

STAFF ASSIGNMENTS			DATE ASSIGNED	DATE DUE
Marty:	1.	Meet with B. Strike on agenda	6/20	6/27
	2.	Check with V. Vaikunta on procedure for putting deposit on hotel rooms & let Luther know his response	6/27	6/29
Luther:	1.	Meet with Larry 10:00 AM to set-up meeting room layout.	6/24	6/27
	2.	Call Hideaway Inn with meeting room layout.	6/27	6/29
	3.	Arrange facilities for session #3	6/20	7/5
	4.	Send multiple copies of brochure to Lenin Co. parent's coalition	6/20	7/5
Larry:	1.	Meet with Luther 10:00 AM on mtg room set-ups	6/24	6/27
	2.	Call Dr. Grevey to get signed consultant form back	6/27	6/29
Lyn:	1.	Call Mrs. Molten to rush handbook review.	6/27	7/5

FIGURE 7. Sample Staff Assignment List

meetings, Ms. Strike described a parent training project which was being conducted by another university across the state. Marty was able to make contact with that project director and together they planned the workshop for that region.

MONITORING FINANCES

MANAGEMENT—HOW CAN I KEEP TRACK OF COSTS? (BUDGET)   Marty wanted to make certain that he was on target with his fiscal expenditures. When the project was designed, Marty knew he could not afford a bookkeeper so he had his secretary, Mary, keep all fiscal records. At the end of each month her records were reconciled with University Research Accounts, the fiscal agent for the University. Around the fifteenth of each month University Research Accounts gave Marty a printout on his project for the previous month. Marty decided that Mary could help him monitor his finances using the University Research Accounts reports even though they were fifteen days late.

PROCEDURES. As soon as Marty's project was funded, University Research Accounts set up an account number and established a budget by line item according to the budget in Marty's proposal. Around the fifteenth of the month, the fiscal report arrived from University Research Accounts for the previous month. This report provided expenditures and balances by line item. Marty instructed Mary to add all encumbered items through the end of the month to bring the line items in the expenditure report up to date. She then computed new balances. As demonstrated in figure 8, Mary then computed the following:

Rate of expenditures per month = total expenditures + number of months

Projected year-end balance = budget − (rate per month × 12)

Mary gave this handwritten sheet to Marty as soon as it was completed each month. She tried to have it to him by the third Monday staff meeting so he could discuss any necessary fiscal measures with his graduate assistants.

USE OF RESULTS. Marty was able to stay on top of his expenditures through this system. As he received reports from Mary, he analyzed them in terms of upcoming events and costs. When the report in figure 8 arrived, he was neither alarmed about nor especially comfortable with his fiscal status. He knew that the projected deficits in salaries and benefits reflected the fact that Lyn and Luther were hired full time for the first semester but not during the second semester. The wages, salaries and benefits would balance out by the end of the year. He also knew his consultants/expenses balance was high only because the workshops hadn't started. He had paid only two consultants for work on the parent handbook and no parent participant expenses had been incurred. The same was true for his meeting expenses. Marty was a little concerned about his rate of expenditures on duplicating and printing, however, since the workshop materials hadn't been printed yet. The office supplies rate didn't concern him because he had stocked up enough in the first two months to carry him almost the entire year. He also knew his communications (phone and postage) would increase as the project became more involved in workshops. All in all, he was fairly satisfied with his fiscal status. But he directed his staff to cut back on the number of copies of draft materials to hold down duplicating costs.

SOME OF THE TRAINING ACTIVITIES ARE REVIEWED

FOCUS—ARE WE LIKELY TO GET THE RIGHT PEOPLE TO ATTEND THE WORKSHOP? (QUESTIONS)   Marty knew the project would fail if they didn't attract the population intended as participants in their workshops, or if actual attendees had different needs from those pro-

---

Cumulative Report Through the End of the Second Month

LINE ITEM	BUDGET	URA EXPENSES	TOTAL ENCUMBR.	SECOND MONTH BALANCE	RATE PER MONTH	PROJECTED YR. END BALANCE
Salaries & Wages	18,000	3,800	3,800	14,200	1,900	(4,800)
Benefits	2,700	570	570	2,130	285	720
Consultants/Expenses	5,500	100	300	5,200	150	3,700
Meeting Expenses	2,000	–0–	–0–	2,000	–0–	2,000
Duplicating/Printing	1,000	120	180	820	90	(80)
Office Supplies	300	150	250	50	125	(1,200)
Equipment	–0–	–0–	–0–	–0–	–0–	–0–
Communications	300	30	30	270	15	120
Audio-Visual	200	–0–	20	180	10	80
TOTAL	$30,000	$4,740	$5,150	$24,850	$2,575	(900)

FIGURE 8. Sample Fiscal Report

jected. He assigned Luther to begin making group registrations and to gather some further needs information. Marty's intent was to compare the group registration and the new needs data with the needs they had identified earlier. Any discrepancies could be addressed in last-minute planning for the training sessions.

PROCEDURES. Luther made arrangements with each hotel to turn in a group registration. This allowed the project staff to be aware of how many people would be attending and also to gather some additional participant information. Luther prepared a form for participant registration as in figure 9.

COLLECTING—HOW CAN WE MONITOR WHO IS REGISTERING? (COLLECTION PROCEDURES)

RESULTS. Marty and his staff had estimated that approximately forty persons would be registering for each workshop. When the first set of 47 registrations arrived, Marty and Luther felt they were right on target. They analyzed the data on handicaps and found that approximately one-half of the registrants were parents of learning disabled children. Therefore, Marty asked each consultant to include at least one example during his or her presentation related directly to children with learning disabilities. Marty also decided to emphasize related services in the presentations since eighty percent of the registrants listed problems that dealt with related services. Another problem that was commonly raised by the registrants was that of solving problems with local school districts without getting into adversarial relationships. Approximately twenty-five percent of the respondents listed some statement that dealt with this issue. Therefore, Marty decided to ask the social worker who wrote a section of the handbook to make a presentation at each workshop regarding positive problem solving. The script was changed accordingly.

ANALYSIS/ INTERPRETATION—IF WE KNOW WHO IS ATTENDING, HOW CAN THAT HELP US IN FILLING IN THE DESIGN OF THE WORKSHOP? (ANALYSIS)

MONITORING TRAINING

FOCUS—"ARE WE IMPLEMENTING OUR TRAINING ACTIVITIES ADEQUATELY?" (QUESTIONS)

By the time they began implementing the training activities, Lyn and Luther were no longer with the project. Marty and Larry were left to answer evaluation question 2.5, "Are we implementing our training activites adequately?" and its five subquestions:

2.5.1 Are we using our facilities adequately?
2.5.2 Is our time allocation to different training activities appropriate?
2.5.3 Are we using our materials appropriately?
2.5.4 Are we using our training staff appropriately?
2.5.5 Are the participants satisfied with their involvement?

PROCEDURES. Larry and Marty agreed that the participants themselves were the best source of data to answer these questions. So, Larry suggested they give a questionnaire to each parent at the end of the workshop. A nice, neat rating scale would be easy to tabulate and analyze he argued.

COLLECTING—HOW CAN WE GET INFORMATION THAT WILL BE REALLY USEFUL TO US IN IMPROVING THE WORKSHOPS? (COLLECTION PROCEDURES)

But Marty had other ideas. In his many years of experience, he rarely found these ubiquitous rating scales to be much good. Sure, they produced numerical data that looked good in a report. But they didn't provide the richer information you needed to actually figure out what was good, or bad, or how you might make changes.

A BETTER PLAN. For each workshop Larry worked with Marty and the Protection and Advocacy staff to select three parent participants to serve as key informants. The key informants were to serve as communication links between staff and participants. In addition, Protection and Advocacy staff members and the consultants were asked to meet with Larry and Marty for script reviews and for debriefing sessions. On the first night before the workshop, Marty and Larry met with the key informants, the Protection and Advocacy staff members, and the consultants to review the script. Larry asked each person to pay special attention during breaks and free time to comments made by parents regarding the progress of the workshops. He asked them to focus on the use of resources, satisfaction with accommodations, and sequence and timing of the workshop. Marty and Larry planned to spend time with parents during breaks and to eat lunch with parents rather than with the Protection and Advocacy Office staff or with consultants. That evening the group got together for their first debriefing session. Marty led the discussion and Larry documented comments made by the various participants. Topics were as follows:

Accommodations
Breaks
Clarity of purpose
Sequence and timing
Content adequacy
Resource materials
Use of resource people
Participant satisfaction

To obtain evaluation data from all participants to help interpret results Larry prepared a brief exit evaluation questionnaire, seen in figure 10.

RESULTS. At the first debriefing session it became apparent that the participants had been uncomfortable during the first part of the morning session. Many had arrived late and during the break indicated how hungry and tired they were. Marty and Larry arranged to have coffee and donuts available at 8:30 the next morning, and they moved their discussion activities to earlier in the day (for later

ANALYSIS/ INTERPRETATION—DID WE GET ANY INFORMATION THAT GIVES US SOME CLUES ABOUT HOW TO MAKE IT WORK BETTER? (ANALYSIS)

Yes, please register me for the Protection and Advocacy training session on October 16–17 at Levinsboro:

NAME: _____   ADDRESS: _____

PHONE: _____   _____

Reserve room for me the nights of:

    OCTOBER 15 _____   I will arrive:
    OCTOBER 16 _____   BEFORE 6 _____
    OCTOBER 17 _____   AFTER 6 _____

I would like the following assistance:

  _____ None necessary   _____ Assistance to and from room
  _____ Large print materials   _____ Interpreter (Deaf)
  _____ Braille materials   _____ Someone to read for me
  _____ 1st floor room   _____ Interpreter (_____)
                                                        Language

  _____ Other (Please specify) _____

My child(ren) have the following handicap(s):

  _____ Retardation   _____ Hearing Impairment/Deaf
  _____ Learning Disability   _____ Vision Impairment/Blind
  _____ Emotional Disturbance   _____ Other Health Impairment
  _____ Orthopedic Impairment   _____ Severe/Profound Handicap

Some of the problems I have had in getting appropriate services for my child are as follows:

I am especially interested in information on the following:

  _____ 1. What I can do to help my child's educational program.
  _____ 2. What I have a right to expect from the schools.
  _____ 3. What comprises "educational assessments".
  _____ 4. What comprises "related services".
  _____ 5. Under what conditions my child is eligible for services.
  _____ 6. What procedures the schools are supposed to follow.
  _____ 7. Where I can go if I think my child needs more services.
  _____ 8. Definitions of terms.
  _____ 9. Other (Specify):

FIGURE 9. Participant Registration Form

FIGURE 10. Satisfaction Questions included
in Exit Questionnaire

1. My reactions to the workshop

	Not at all Satisfied				Completely Satisfied
a. Overall	1	2	3	4	5
b. Accommodations	1	2	3	4	5

Comments:

c. Procedures Used	1	2	3	4	5

Comments:

d. Information Presented	1	2	3	4	5

Comments:

e. Resource Materials	1	2	3	4	5

Comments:

f. Resource Persons	1	2	3	4	5

Comments:

2. I would ☐ would not ☐ recommend this workshop to other parents.

---

sessions) in order to open people up and to reduce boredom. They also changed seating arrangements during the afternoon sessions to reduce any communication barriers. Marty found that the debriefing sessions allowed him to make changes in the workshop before little problems became big ones. He also found that having a face-to-face discussion with some of the participants at the time that they were experiencing the workshop provided him information that he would not have obtained through the questionnaire. The questionnaire data provided only quantitative information that he could use to report to the Protection and Advocacy Office but that was not particularly helpful to him in designing later workshops except as it helped confirm the narrative information.

EVALUATING IMPACT

FOCUS—DOES THE WORKSHOP HAVE A POSITIVE AND LASTING IMPACT ON PARENTS? (QUESTION)

Marty had suggested in his proposal that the state provide him funds to hire an external evaluator to measure his project's impact. An external person could provide a more credible, independent and bias-free report than could Marty. The state agreed that credibility and lack of bias were important, but didn't give him any money for an evaluator. Instead, they directed him to collect some impact data on his own, doing what he could to ensure its credibility.

With minimal resources available, and also quite frankly, because there was little use Marty himself could make of final impact data, he decided on a relatively meager impact evaluation. While fairly simple and cheap, it was designed to get at the general question, "Has the project made a difference to parents?"

COLLECTING—SINCE I DON'T HAVE THE TIME OR MONEY TO GET THE DATA I REALLY NEED, WHAT SEMI-APPROPRIATE QUICK AND DIRTY DATA CAN I GET? (COLLECTION PROCEDURES)

Marty decided on a two-step approach that would use participants as the sole data source. First, he decided to have participants project the possible use and value of the workshop to them. Then, he would use these projections as the basis for a follow-up telephone call. The projections would help focus his follow-up inquiry and also help parents think through the question of in fact using what they'd learned.

PROCEDURES. Larry drafted a tentative set of questionnaire items that could be appended to the end-of-workshop questionnaire they'd already decided to use. He field-tested

COLLECTING—HOW CAN I BE SURE THAT MY QUICK AND DIRTY DATA ARE COMPETENTLY COLLECTED? (INSTRUMENTS)

his draft with some fellow students, asking them to "role-play" participants. This led to revisions, then Larry put together the items shown in figure 11. Larry and Marty decided that they would not try to keep evaluations anonymous but instead would assure participant confidentiality. They assigned code numbers for each participant and prepared a cover sheet on the evaluation form with the participant's name. The participant was told to tear off the front sheet before completing the form. At the end of the workshop all forms were collected and additional forms and a stamped, self-addressed envelope were sent to those who failed to complete the form before leaving. After each workshop, results were tallied and all comments were transferred to a master list. A cumulative tally was also prepared, and Larry also reported frequencies under each item. At the end of the year, the cumulative data were reported in a summary submitted to the Protection and Advocacy Office.

RESULTS. Neither Marty nor Larry had intended to rely solely on the impact data for making decisions about the remaining workshops. They were cautious in their interpretations because so much of the information was speculative. They usually found, however, that the "best," "worst" and "recommendations" sections confirmed what the workshop debriefing sessions had already determined. They were both pleased that the participants predicted great changes once they returned home. Marty especially looked forward to his three month follow-ups for verification.

THREE MONTH FOLLOW-UP

COLLECTING—HOW CAN I GET THE MOST OUT OF THE TELEPHONE FOLLOW-UPS? (SAMPLE/INSTRUMENTS)

Marty and Larry knew that the exit questionnaire was too limited in scope. Wanting to see if any change had actually

---

P & A Workshop Evaluation

Directions

Please tear off cover sheet and throw it away. All responses will be kept confidential and no names will be associated with individual comments. To ensure that you are not bothered with follow-ups once you have submitted your evaluation, you have been assigned this unique code number <u>xxx</u>.

Please complete this form and return it in the box provided or mail to: Larry Lavorini
                 University Station

1. This workshop was designed to provide information to help you effectively assert yourself to serve as an advocate for yourself and your child(ren). To what extent was this accomplished?

				Almost Completely
Very Little				Achieved
1	2	3	4	5

Comments:

2. To what extent do you think this workshop will change *your* advocacy activities?

Very Little				Very Great
Change				Change
1	2	3	4	5

Comments:

---

3. To what extent do you think this workshop will change or has changed your perception of your role as a parent or guardian?

Very Little				Very Great
Change				Change
1	2	3	4	5

Comments:

4. With how many people do you think you might share information from this workshop?

_____ 0–1 persons

_____ 2–5 persons

_____ 6–20 persons

_____ 21+ persons

Comments:

5. What was best about this workshop?

6. What was worst about this workshop?

7. What recommendations do you have to improve it?

FIGURE 11. Impact Questions on Exit Questionnaire

occurred, they decided to interview a sample of participants. They decided that three months was about long enough for some impact to occur. In addition to the three questions posed through the exit questionnaire they decided to ask also, "Are there any unexpected positive or negative effects?"

PROCEDURES. Larry drafted a structured interview format, with branching questions leading to other questions (see figure 12). Then an argument over a sampling ensured.

Marty proposed a small sample of participants who would be selected based on their responses to the questionnaire. This would allow them to answer the question, "When the workshop 'works' (i.e. parents want to make changes), how well does it work?"

Larry argued for a random sample. He felt they needed to demonstrate how much the workshop had impacted all who

attended. The only way to generalize to all participants was a random sample.

A compromise seemed best. They drew a random sample, then noted—from the exit questionnaires—just how much change participants expected. This would let them see whether parents who projected utility experienced greater utility, or whether the workshop worked regardless of expectation.

Three months after the second workshop, he and Marty drew a random sample of the 111 parents who had participated in those two workshops. They used the registration forms that Luther had collected and that contained phone numbers and addresses for their population. Marty hired Lyn and Luther to conduct the follow-ups to reduce bias. They called each parent in the sample and asked the questions in figure 12. They also called the Protection and Advocacy Office representatives from the two regions

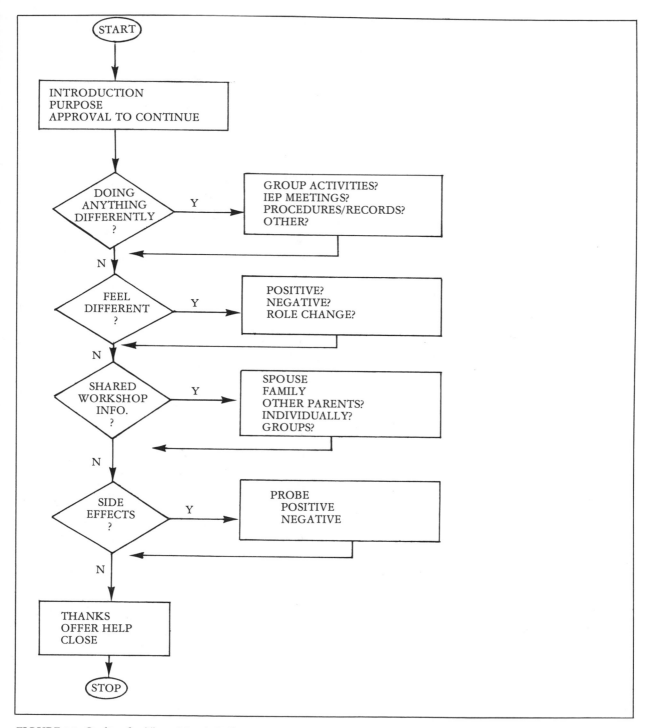

FIGURE 12. Outline for Three-Month Follow-up Interviews

in which the workshops were held and asked parallel questions.

RESULTS FROM PARENTS. Lyn and Luther were able to locate 18 of the 20 parents. Of the 18, only 6 could identify specific advocacy activities they had undertaken differently

ANALYSIS/ INTERPRETATION—WHAT DID WE LEARN FROM THE INTERVIEWS? (ANALYSIS)

as a result of the workshop. There seemed to be no relationship between what they projected and what they actually did. Only 2 had done anything but share the information with their spouses. Even though they couldn't name specific things they did differently, 17 out of 18 said that they felt more positive about themselves when they participated in IEP meetings. A common side effect reported by the parents was the establishment of an informal communication and problem solving network. The parents made friends at the workshop with others who had similar problems and subsequently used the participant list and phone numbers to get in touch with each other.

RESULTS FROM PROTECTION AND ADVOCACY STAFF. The two Protection and Advocacy office regional representatives reported several incidents of changed behavior that they felt were attributable to the workshop. They had

COLLECTING—WHAT OTHER INFORMATION IS AVAILABLE RELEVANT TO IMPACT? (COLLECTION PROCEDURES)

experienced a reduced number of general questions to the Protection and Advocacy Office and an increased specificity in the types of questions related to topics presented at the workshop. No workshop parents had contacted Protection and Advocacy Office for direct intervention with school districts; however, they were aware of several parents who had undertaken informal negotiations with school districts themselves and were apparently having success within the system. The Protection and Advocacy regional representatives had been asked on several occasions by nonworkshop parents when the next series of parent training sessions would take place. The Protection and Advocacy regional representatives found that these parents had heard good things about the workshops from parents who had attended. The Protection and Advocacy staff also reported a side benefit of increased communication between themselves and Division of Special Education staff regarding hearing procedures.

USE OF RESULTS. Larry compiled this information into a narrative report and gave it to Marty. Marty was especially pleased with the results reported by the Protection and

ANALYSIS/ INTERPRETATION—WHAT CAN WE TELL FROM SUCH INFORMAL OBSERVATIONS? (ANALYSIS)

Advocacy staff but knew that since they had funded the project, they would be hoping for such impact and therefore might have presented some biased information. He would have liked to have taken the time to follow-up on the parents' hint that things were happening differently in IEP meetings by calling principals, but he felt that it wasn't cost efficient to do so and would take too many clearances. He was satisfied that he had accomplished his goals, and he decided to look back over

what he had done and what he might have managed differently.

EPILOGUE

FOCUS—I WONDER WAS ALL THIS EFFORT WORTH IT? (POTENTIAL UTILITY)

As he was about to put together the final quarterly report, Marty pulled out his staff reports and evaluation summaries. He decided to look back at the evaluation procedures he had used and make some notes for future reference. He wanted to make sure he capitalized on the successes and avoided the failures in any future projects.

ACTIVITY CHART

ANALYSIS/ INTERPRETATION—WHAT DID I LEARN FROM EACH PART OF THE EVALUATION?

A major success in planning; it had helped him evaluate his plan and create necessary relationships. (Next time he would develop an activity chart *prior* to submitting his proposal.)

PARENT HANDBOOK REVIEWS

Having parents review the handbook was an essential step in anchoring the content in reality. In retrospect, a form might have been as helpful for the parents as was the interview conducted by Lyn, but he couldn't be sure. Lyn had been so enthusiastic about her results. Maybe there was something added from the face-to-face dialogue.

TRAINING SCRIPT REVIEW

The initial walk-through of a script prior to finalizing it served as a field test and simulation which allowed necessary debugging. Sequence and timing flaws had been pointed out through group discussions.

CONSULTANT CONTRACTS

While Marty had been afraid that consultants would resent the specificity in their agreement forms, on the contrary, they were pleased to have their roles outlined in advance. They also had expressed appreciation for participating in the script review session so that they knew how the entire training package went together.

WEEKLY REPORTS AND STAFF MEETINGS

Next to the activity chart, the weekly reports and staff meetings appeared to be the most effective in helping staff to stay on task. The colored boxes on the activity chart gave Marty a sense of satisfaction and a visual picture of his status at every step. All three graduate assistants had said that writing the weekly reports was not much of a burden but actually helped them plan their activities and avoid omissions. They also felt that it have given them an opportunity to ventilate concerns on a timely basis.

FISCAL REPORTS

Reports provided by Mary on a monthly basis had given Marty sufficient information to make fiscal adjustments throughout the year. If he had a bigger project, he would have liked to have tracked his expenditures by strategy and assigned costs to individual workshops to know where his expenditures actually were incurred. Even for the smaller project he would have liked to have had his data more rapidly, especially toward the end of the project year. During the last two months he had become overly conservative and ended up with a balance which had to be returned to the Protection and Advocacy Office. In the future, his goal would be to have information that would allow him to come out with a zero balance.

PARENT REGISTRATION

Marty was especially pleased with the impact that the parent registration procedures had on last minute preparation. He would continue to gather parent registration information in any future training endeavors.

EXIT QUESTIONNAIRE

Marty was the least satisfied with his exit questionnaire procedure. He felt he had simply collected that information to satisfy someone else and the information was not particularly helpful to him in making decisions. He reviewed the exit questionnaires and realized that he had asked very general questions. He had done this purposely so the questionnaire did not become too long. In the future, he would either have to ask more detailed questions or not plan on getting much help from the questionnaires. He decided that he would use a brief form simply to allow his participants a chance to express themselves as needed. He would use other forms only if required by his funding agent.

DEBRIEFING SESSIONS

In contrast to the exit questionnaire, Marty was pleased with the debriefing sessions. He thought the use of key-informant procedure was especially helpful. Information from these debriefing sessions came to him at a time when he could still make adjustments in the workshop. He would continue to use this procedure in future workshops.

THREE MONTH FOLLOW-UP

Marty was ambivalent about the use of the three month follow-up interviews. The information he and Larry obtained through these interviews was interesting, but it tended to frustrate him. If he had been on a longer term project, such a follow-up system would be helpful in planning future endeavors; but because his project was over he wasn't able to do much about his results.

SUMMARY

Marty had made major improvements over the way that he had codirected his previous project. He and his graduate assistants had spent a good deal of time on evaluation activities, but since these activities were so integrally connected with managing the project, he never felt that he was wasting anyone's time. He looked at whether or not the staff and materials were ready for implementation, he monitored the project's progress and he assessed whether or not they had made a difference. In summary, he had achieved his goal of planning for impact instead of waiting to evaluate to see whether or not impact had occurred.

* * * * *

DISCUSSION QUESTIONS AND TOPICS

1. This case illustrates blending evaluation into the procedures for accomplishing and managing the work of the project. What do you see as some of the potential advantages of such a blend? What are some of the potential disadvantages?
2. Marty began by assuming that he and his staff were the primary audience for the evaluation (since it focused on how to manage the project rather than on outcome evaluation). In view of the way the project actually developed, do you think their assumption was correct? If not, who were the other significant audiences? (Suggestion: Notice who received report of and/or was affected by the evaluation. And go over the list of evaluation questions, noting other persons or groups who would be interested in the answer.)
3. What questions, if any, would you suggest adding (or deleting) from the list of evaluation questions?
4. Much of the actual evaluation work in the case went into describing particular parts of the project. What were several of the things described (e.g., activities, outlines): How did those descriptions help in the evaluation work? How did they help in doing the project work itself? (Suggestion: Consider the staff training benefits as well as the direct production and communication benefits.)
5. What did you think of the key informant tactic of workshop evaluation? What are some of the benefits? What are some potential disadvantages or risks?

SUGGESTIONS FOR STIMULATING DISCUSSIONS ABOUT THE CASE

1. Organize a debate. Resolved: Blending evaluation and project management destroys the credibility of the evaluation effort.
2. Have a person or subgroup make a short presentation on "useful educational and/or useful evaluation techniques shown in the case." (Suggestion: Be sure to consider the value of specifying criteria early in the process as was done in producing and reviewing the parents manual.)
3. Have a person or subgroup make a short presentation to support this argument: The case makes a valuable point by showing that evaluation of design and implementation of a project can increase the probability that the project will have a positive impact. Have another person or subgroup make a short presentation arguing that the case doesn't show that at all because there was precious little data—and that's not very credible—showing any real impact. The case really shows one more example of neglecting impact evaluation behind a smokescreen of other activity. After the presentations, discuss and attempt to resolve the conflicting positions.

APPLICATION EXERCISES

1. Read some of the material in the *Sourcebook* indicated by the asides. Then suggest alternative things people in the case might have done at several points in the case. Or suggest a whole new approach they might have taken.
2. Using the case as a model (and foil) and your suggested alternatives as guides, design an evaluation for a situation or problem similar to that shown in the case.
3. Using Chapter 7 of the *Sourcebook* as a guide, do a meta-evaluation and critique of the case (and/or your evaluation design).
4. Use the *Design Manual* to develop an improved evaluation design for the case.
5. Use the *Design Manual* to develop an evaluation design for a situation or problem similar to the one described in the case.

CASE C-3

AN ASSISTANT PROFESSOR OF SPECIAL EDUCATION ASKS: How can I get the information I need to improve my foundations course?

Dale Brethower

THE SETTING

FOCUS—WHAT IS THE SETTING WITHIN WHICH THE EVALUATION WILL BE DONE? (CONTEXT)

The College of Education, one of the oldest colleges at State University, is neither the largest nor the most prestigious. Individual faculty members in the college are well respected on the 16,000 student campus. A few have genuine national reputations.

The dean, aware of enrollment-related demographic patterns, is concerned with the future. Convinced that there will continue to be a strong demand for pre-service, continuing, and in-service education and training but convinced that "business as usual" will not prepare the college to meet the demand, the Dean is very interested in encouraging appropriate changes in the   offerings and organization of the college.

FOCUS—WHAT TRENDS OR VALUES ARE RELEVANT? (CRITERIA)

The Dean has been making more and more references to the importance of research by

faculty. Full professors with few publications are secretly glad they've already attained the rank. Assistant and associate professors worry about the new handwriting that's appearing on the wall; however, they believe they are fairly safe when it comes to talk about excellence in teaching because the talk is ordinarily about as well documented as the talk about the emperor's new clothes.

The dean, in private conversations with faculty, claims that supply and demand factors make it possible to demand more of faculty: more research, more community and university involvement, and more documentation of teaching effectiveness.

THE SPECIAL EDUCATION DEPARTMENT

The Department of Special Education has eight members, five of whom are tenured. Their M.A. program has a solid reputation in the state and has been growing in numbers and, some say, in quality as well. The normal teaching load is three courses per term, and faculty are expected to do research, serve on university committees, and be active in schools in the community.

FOCUS—WHAT ARE SOME POSSIBLE REASONS FOR EVALUATING? (PURPOSE)

The Chairperson and two other tenured faculty hold a very pragmatic view about the evaluation of teaching and the evaluation of special ed courses: "Since modeling is demonstrably effective, we had better practice what we preach; if we want to be sure our graduates can produce specific knowledge, skill and affective instructional outcomes, we had better be sure we are producing specific outcomes in our courses!" (The other tenured faculty provide no overt support for that viewpoint.)

ASSISTANT PROFESSOR POWERS AND SPECIAL ED 534

Professor Powers had taught secondary school English before getting an M.A. in Special Education. She then worked as a special education teacher for several years while earning a Ph.D. in Education. She has taught several different graduate and undergraduate special ed courses. Students consider her to be humanistically oriented. Her colleagues aren't sure whether that is because of or in spite of her emphasis upon competency based instruction.

FOCUS—WHAT WILL BE EVALUATED? (OBJECT)

Dr. Powers teaches Special Ed 534, Psychological Foundations of Instructional Design, as part of her regular course load. The course was originally intended to cover the psychological foundations of individualized instruction as a general prerequisite to a series of specialized short courses on teaching methods for specific populations; however, shortly before Powers was assigned to teach SE 534 the short courses were dropped as a result of follow-up information. (Employers said that graduates just couldn't design instruction for the range of students typically encountered in special education classrooms. Instructors of the short courses alleged that students were lacking, on entry, any useable knowledge of psychological foundations.) Conse-

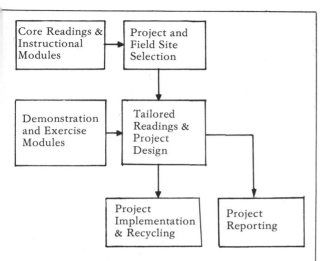

FIGURE 1. SE 534, Psychological Foundations of Instructional Design

quently, Powers redesigned SE 534 to incorporate practice applications as shown in figure 1.

Dr. Powers designed the course to serve the wide variety of students who were required to take it. Some, she had discovered, had ten to fifteen years' teaching experience; others had none. Some had an extensive background in the relevant psychological foundations; others had apparently forgotten or elected to disbelieve whatever they had learned previously. When students selected a project and site (usually a classroom in one of the local schools), she required them to submit a rough draft project design based upon the core readings and lectures and a design format she provided. The draft served as a diagnostic for tailoring both the students' individual reading lists and the subsequent in-class demonstrations and exercises.

FOCUS—WILL EVALUATING DO ANY GOOD? WHAT DO WE ALREADY KNOW AND WHAT MIGHT IT BE USEFUL TO KNOW? (OBJECT) Dr. Powers has taught Special Ed 534 several times. Each time it has gone more smoothly. Students seem to enjoy the course and rate it quite positively on a not very well constructed course evaluation questionnaire. (She uses it because it is available and has local norms.)

Dr. Powers is reasonably satisfied with the course and the improvements she has made based upon the evaluation she has done.

1. Student responses to a questionnaire item about quality of the course as a whole have moved from the 4th to the 2nd decile on local norms.
2. She routinely asks students about 1/3 and 2/3 of the way through the course to turn in notes listing three things they like and three things they dislike about the course. The notes are useful in picking up hints about what is

and isn't working; she has made several changes based on them.
3. It seems to her that the quality of student work is getting better.
4. Students are obviously working harder now than they had the first time she taught the course, but they complain less about the work load.
5. She infers that the students now perceive greater value in what they are learning. (Questionnaire results are consistent with that impression.)
6. Some of the "best" and most experienced students have volunteered the information that what they learn in the course is more valuable to them than anything they've learned in their last several education courses.
7. Another common comment is that it is refreshing to have a professor who does things the way she says they should be done.
8. Colleagues who come in as guest speakers commonly remark about how lucky she is to have such highly motivated students. (She doesn't tell them that the students hadn't been that "highly motivated" the first time she taught the course.)
9. She has asked colleagues what they think should be taught in the course and has made some changes based on their suggestions.

THE DECISION TO EVALUATE

FOCUS—WHAT DOES SHE WANT TO EVALUATE? (PURPOSE) As is the case with most faculty, Dr. Powers has a lot of information about how well the course is working; nevertheless, she has several reasons for wanting to do more systematic evaluation.

1. Parts of the course aren't working as well as she wants them to. She isn't sure whether she needs to: (a) add more material to give them a better conceptual foundation; (b) delete material because the total amount is too much to master; (c) provide more practice exercises; (d) provide for more give-and-take discussions to bring out issues that aren't surfacing; (e) add field trips so the students can see a broader range of application; or (f) something else.
2. The course is working well enough so that she wants to "advertise" it better. The kinds of students she wants to attract aren't likely to respond well to vacuous hoopla.
3. She has other courses that she wants to improve. If she develops better evaluation procedures in Special Ed 534, they could also be used in the other courses.
4. She wants to do better evaluation as part of modeling. She often tells students that getting good feedback is as essential to the successful special ed teacher as giving good feedback.
5. She wants to have better documentation of teaching when she is considered for promotion. Whether it will help or not she doesn't know, but at least she'll feel better about it.
6. She believes that better course evaluation is good for the long-run health of the department and would improve the quality of the educational experience for students.

She wants to put her house in order and provide a working model for her colleagues should they, for whatever reason, want to do more evaluation.

It was clear to Dr. Powers that her major reasons for evaluating were personal: she wanted to get clearer evidence of how well the course was working so she could improve whatever needed improving and so that she, students, and interested colleagues would know what was working well. She wanted to assure that she was offering a good course and serving as a responsible role model for students and colleagues alike.

FOCUS—WHO IS REALLY CONCERNED? (AUDIENCE)

GENERAL COURSE EVALUATION QUESTIONS

FOCUS—WHAT ARE THE GENERAL EVALUATION QUESTIONS? (QUESTIONS)

Her general purposes clarified, Dr. Powers turned to considering the evaluation questions she wanted to answer. It seemed only fair to apply the evaluation logic she used in the course to the course. For example, she evaluated the students' designs for instructional projects; therefore, she would evaluate the design of her "instructional project," SE 534. She also evaluated student work according to how well they implemented their designs, dealt with unexpected problems, and modified their approaches based upon what they learned as they worked. Similarly, student projects were evaluated according to results: Did the special education students they worked with demonstrate gains? Did they learn? As she told her students, "If your students don't learn, then you and I have both flunked in SE 534!" (When students and colleagues asked how she handled giving grades in that case, she had a ready answer: "Simple. If I approve the design and the SE 534 student implements it well, then I chalk up a failure for me and the student gets a good grade. If the student can't come up with a design I'll approve or if the student doesn't implement the design well, then the student gets a low grade and I try to figure out what went wrong.")

Thus her basic evaluation questions were straightforward:

Is the course well designed?
Is it well implemented?
Does it produce desireable outcomes? (e.g., Do the students learn enough to produce projects? Are the projects implemented well? Do the children benefit from the instruction by SE 534 students?)

QUESTIONS ABOUT DESIGN OF SE 534

FOCUS—WHAT DO THE GENERAL QUESTIONS MEAN? (QUESTIONS)

Dr. Powers' next step was to break the broad question, "Is the course well designed?" into a set of subquestions. The first, "What is the design of

SE 534?" she answered by drawing the flow chart description. The next questions were inspired by a set of design criteria she used in evaluating project designs that her students produced:

"A well designed project should
a. be directed toward worthwhile outcomes, and
b. use instructional procedures consistent with
   (1) the desired outcomes,
   (2) the relevant learning processes, and
   (3) good educational practice."

Her second design evaluation question, therefore, was, "Is the course design directed toward worthwhile outcomes?" That question could be answered, she thought, by a combination of empirical data ("Do successful teachers do the things taught in SE 534 more effectively than unsuccessful teachers?"), a literature search ("Is the value of the objectives supported by a body of relevant research?"), and expert opinion ("Are the stated objectives judged valuable by qualified and experienced professionals?")

Her third, fourth and fifth design evaluation questions were, "Are instructional procedures consistent with the desired outcomes?" "Are the instructional procedures consistent with the relevant learning process?" and "Are the instructional procedures consistent with good educational practices?"

After reflecting about it briefly, Dr. Powers decided not to go further to evaluate the worth of her objectives. (She believed that if student projects were successful in teaching special education children, that would be enough to support the worth of the objectives. Besides, she had already discussed the objectives with several of her colleagues who agreed with her about the importance of the objectives. She had also already begun including research support for particular objectives within the relevant instructional modules.)

COLLECTION—WHAT DATA ARE NEEDED TO ANSWER THE EVALUATION QUESTIONS? (INFORMATION NEEDED)

She then filled out the worksheets shown in figure 2 to help her think through her remaining three evaluation questions about the design of her course.

ANALYSIS-INTERPRETATION—HOW COULD THE DATA BE ANALYZED IF THEY WERE COLLECTED? WHAT CRITERIA MIGHT BE USED TO JUDGE THEM?

She used the completed worksheets to help her make several decisions about the design evaluation.

1. *Consistency of instructional procedures with desired outcomes.* She decided to deal with the question of the matchup between objectives and instructional activities as part of evaluating the *delivery* of her course rather than as part of evaluating the *design*. Or, to put it another way, she decided to pay special attention to that aspect of the design, collecting relevant data when she taught the course. The decision was partly a matter of expediency since she knew what data she'd collect and could do so comfortably; however, the major reason for deciding not

EVALUATION QUESTION	DATA SOURCES AND COLLECTION	ANALYSIS
Are instructional procedures consistent with the desired outcomes?		
SUBQUESTIONS		
Are the instructional procedures likely to produce unintended or undesired outcomes such as drops, sycophancy, conflicts within the course, or conflicts with other parts of the curriculum?	Review of course materials (syllabus, reading lists, etc.) by: a. two instructional design experts, and b. two colleagues (While reviewing the materials to answer the subquestions and make any comments they choose, the reviewers could ask the instructor questions.)	Unedited report of review comments. Possibly a tabulation of reviewer comments.
Can each instructional activity be related in specific ways to one or more objectives?		
Can each specific objective be related in specific ways to one or more instructional activities?	(Alternatively, Dr. Powers could provide a design document showing what she believes the relationships are and the reviewers would provide consensual validation or disagreement with her analysis.)	
Are instructional procedures consistent with the relevant learning processes?		
SUBQUESTIONS		
Are procedures relevant to cognitive domain objectives consistent with principles and research findings relevant to cognitive learning?	Colleagues would be asked to review the syllabus, reading lists, project guides, exercise guides, and study guides for the course and comment on adequacy of the procedures for helping to achieve cognitive, affective, and psychomotor objectives.	Unedited report of colleagues' comments.
Are procedures relevant to affective domain objectives consistent with principles and research relevant to affective learning?	Review paper/Rationale paper written by the instructor. Critiques of the paper sought from persons who have published educationally related research in each of the three areas.	Unedited report of reviewers' comments
Are procedures relevant to psychomotor domain objectives consistent with principles and research relevant to psychomotor learning?	An evaluator checklist would be developed as part of the paper, revised based upon critiques, then applied to the course design by two colleagues. The checklist would be applied to the course as a whole and to each unit.	Observer reliabilities Strengths and weaknesses recorded (for each unit) and available for validation against data on effectiveness of the units.
Are cognitive, affective, and psychomotor learning experiences properly integrated?		
Are instructional procedures consistent with good instructional practice?		

FIGURE 2. Evaluation Worksheet: *Course Design*

(continued)

Question	Data Sources and Collection	Analysis
SUBQUESTIONS Are procedures consistent with University policies and procedures? Are instructional procedures used which are importantly different from procedures commonly used at the University. Are the requirements reasonable in terms of demands upon student time, grading standards, etc.? Does the design call for reasonable amounts of instructor time, instructional support services, etc.?	Review of Syllabus by Department Chairperson, University Ombudsman, and representative of Student Affairs office. Reviewer's Form developed to ask specifically about grading practices, attendance policies, provisions for make-up of missed work, etc. (Student course evaluation questionnaire plus student self-report data from previous terms made available to reviewers.)	Unedited report of reviewer's comments.

FIGURE 2 *(continued)*

to have colleagues and instructional design experts review the course materials was a credibility problem. After informal inquiries among her colleagues she decided that there weren't instructional design experts, either local or national, whose opinions would be given much weight.

2. *Consistency of procedures and research on learning.* In order to evaluate the design adequacy from the perspective of research on learning (and/or teaching) Dr. Powers drafted evaluation checklists for cognitive, affective, and psychomotor learning. She planned to ask two or three colleagues to review the course materials and make whatever comments they wished, offering them the checklists to let them know the design considerations she was most interested in. The department chairperson suggested that instead of writing a review/rationale for the educational procedures for her course that she write the rationale as part of a proposal to develop and validate the checklist for use as an evaluation instrument. (She was undecided about whether or not to do that.)

3. *Consistency of procedures and educational practices.* She planned to have the department chairperson, etc., review the general educational procedures.

QUESTIONS ABOUT IMPLEMENTATION OF SE 534

DESIGN—IS IT FEASIBLE TO GET THE DATA? (APPROPRIATENESS)

Dr. Powers' first thoughts about determining how well the course was being run revolved around the design flow chart shown in fig. 1. She did a one-person brainstorming exercise and generated many questions, some of which follow:

Is it possible to obtain field sites? Do the core modules prepare students to select an appropriate project? Are the demonstration and exercise modules properly tailored to project needs? Are the designs implementable? Are other exercises needed to provide students with the skills to implement? Do the designs and the techniques of implementation generate the information needed for adequate reports? How much

recycling is necessary? What percentage of the reports show beneficial effects on the special education children?

FOCUS—WHAT PARTS OF THE COURSE SHOULD I BE MOST CONCERNED WITH? (OBJECT/PURPOSE)

This brainstorming session seemed useful, but she felt she needed some orderly way of organizing and prioritizing the questions she needed to answer. Looking at the flow chart again, she noticed that to do a complete evaluation of the big box, (the whole course) she needed to evaluate the little boxes (the major parts) and each instructional module within some of the little boxes. She was beginning to feel

FOCUS—WHAT ARE MY QUESTIONS ABOUT HOW THE COURSE IS RUN? (QUESTIONS)

overwhelmed by all the possibilities for meaningful evaluation questions she could not ask. After some struggling she decided there were three main questions for evaluating delivery:

1. Are logistics well managed? (There was a lot to keep track of in this design and she'd gotten badly bogged down in logistical problems the first time she taught the course.)
2. Are the teaching functions well performed? (She knew that how she treated students made a difference.)
3. Are the unit objectives met? (It was important for her to know if each box was working properly and if each instructional module was working properly.)

COLLECTION—WHAT INFORMATION IS NEEDED AND HOW SHALL I GET IT?

The worksheets shown in figure 3 show how she organized her queries around those three questions.

EVALUATION QUESTIONS ABOUT OUTCOMES

FOCUS—WHAT DO I WANT TO KNOW ABOUT OUTCOMES?

Dr. Powers considers it important to "teach for transfer" and has an unusually high number of transfer and application exercises built into her instructional units. Some of these provide opportunities to collect both use and usefulness data during the course and after it has been completed. For example, students in the course nearly always arrange to do their major projects in classrooms of local teachers, many of whom are friends or acquaintances of either Dr. Powers or of the students. (Some of these friends and acquaintances are also Dr. Powers' former students, providing an opportunity to observe what the former students are now doing with what they learned in the course. While such observations do not satisfy assumptions for random sampling methodologies, they provide an opportunity to demonstrate that some students effectively use what is being taught in the course. This attests to the potential worth of attaining the objectives.)

COLLECTION/ INTERPRETATION—HOW CAN I GET THE INFORMATION? HOW CAN I INTERPRET IT ONCE I GET IT?

Although she had already decided not to do further "social validation" of the course objectives, she wanted to know if students considered the objectives to be worthwhile and if the students believed that the objectives were attained. The worksheet in figure 4 describes the thinking she went through. She hoped that students would perceive the objectives as reasonably worthwhile at the outset. She also hoped that students would value the objectives even more by the end of the course and that they would perceive themselves as having gained significantly in knowledge and skills related to the objectives. Consequently, she set up the skills project sheet (shown in figure 4) and a values profile sheet (which used the same format).

She also noticed that those outcomes defined in terms of content learning were measured by the tests or application exercises at the end of each unit or module in the course. There was a progression or cumulative effect as students moved through the course which provided data on retention of earlier material. Since many of the modules had application components and since the major project was (nearly always) conducted "in the field," she had reasonably good immediate transfer and utility data. (She also thought about doing some longer term follow-up work to supplement her contact file system—described on the worksheet; however, she was already feeling a little exhausted by the amount of energy she was putting into operating and evaluating the course, so she put that idea in a "things to do later file" that was overflowing in her bottom desk drawer.)

USING THE EVALUATION DATA

REPORTING—HOW CAN I USE WHAT I LEARN FROM THE EVALUATION? (PURPOSE/USE)

Dr. Powers insists that evaluation efforts are basically aids to judgment; she has considerable confidence in her judgment and doesn't believe it needs a whole lot of aid. She gets a lot of information by reading papers, grading tests, seeing how students react to what she says in class, talking with students during office hours, and doing occasional "quick and dirty evaluations" (e.g., taking five minutes at the end of a class period to have students write comments

about the lesson or course, interviewing a student who seems not to be trying, interviewing a student who seems to be trying but not making it, asking a colleague what he hears about her course). Nevertheless, she had reached two general conclusions.

The first conclusion was that she could do a much better job of running and improving the course if she focused her attention on individual units. The global evaluations and impressions were important—she needed to know how the course was going in general; however, she needed more specific information to know what she needed to do to improve it. (That was one of the reasons she tended to set up her courses as sets of instructional modules and one of the reasons she advocated the same practice when she taught instructional methods.)

The second conclusion was that she really did need to collect, analyze, and display the data more carefully to identify trouble spots more precisely and to demonstrate more clearly to others that the course really was effective. The more careful evaluation proved to be useful to her. The item analyses of tests were an important source of data, even though so many of them were short answer and essay tests. In order to assure reliability of grading and to pinpoint strengths and weaknesses, she used criterion checklists as answer keys. She also tabulated, separately, the scores for questions at the application, analysis, synthesis, and evaluation levels of Bloom's taxonomy, cognitive domain. (Memory and comprehension levels were tested using multiple choice and other so-called objective test items.)

Some of the units (and tests associated with them) were developed so students used the checklists to grade their own exams. (She planned also to have them record the results on an item analysis worksheet but hadn't gotten around to that yet.) The procedure enabled her to administer, grade, and hold a debriefing discussion all during the same period. (After the discussion, students sometimes point out grading errors they had made; Dr. Powers also quality control checks by glancing over each paper and by careful blind grading of some papers.)

Dr. Powers made similar uses of evaluation checklists for evaluating student papers and other products and for doing observations of student performances (e.g., role-plays of presentation of lessons, providing verbal comments to children).

These item analyses enabled Dr. Powers to determine readily whether students learned particular concepts and skills and whether they retained or transferred the learnings in later parts of the course. They also enabled her to provide necessary remediation in the short run and to make specific revisions of materials, assignments, and exercises to reduce or eliminate specific deficiencies. For example, if an item was consistently missed by her best and brightest students, she looked to the instructional materials; if an item was missed by students who had skipped the relevant class or assignment, she looked to the motivational techniques; if some students consistently missed synthesis or evaluation level items, she recommended outside work, using instructional material designed to teach students how to prepare for and approach such test items.

Question	Data Sources and Collection	Analysis
Are the logistics well managed? SUBQUESTIONS Are there systematic procedures for: (a) scheduling facilities (b) advertising the course (c) preparing, producing, and/or ordering materials (d) scheduling media, etc. (e) scheduling out-of-class meetings, etc. (f) prompt return of student work (g) managing production of tests, surveys, etc. (h) managing student records (i) etc. Are the procedures efficient, accurate, and effective?	Examine records, calendars, etc. Since procedures include recording of actions taken, use them as a data source. Look especially to see if there are adequate lead times so as to avoid last minute rush, changes of plans, etc. Establish a "Problems Encountered" list for self, assistant, and students to use to record any logistical problems.	Rating of each procedure as to efficiency, accuracy and effectiveness. For each procedure— list of any problems that occurred and impact, if any, on operation of the course. Rate severity of each "Problem Encountered" on a scale of 1–5. Maintain a graph showing number and average severity of problems, updating the graph once per month.
Are the teaching functions well performed? SUBQUESTIONS Are class sessions well run? Are assignments well presented? Are students responded to properly? Do students receive constuctive information about their performance? Are instructional unit objectives usefully related to course objectives? Are instructional unit activities usefully related to unit objectives? Is it clear what studying procedures, tasks, and activities are required in order to meet unit objectives?	Criterion checklist developed for each function. Student volunteers from the class (selected by posting a sign-up sheet listing times, items to be evaluated, etc.) complete the checklists. Questionnaires administered twice during and once at the end of the course. Questions constructed to get students' perceptions of some of the items covered by checklists. Also "open ended" questions administered at same time: What are three things (about how the course is run) that you find most helpful? Least helpful?	Percentage of items checked off as accomplished. (Some items on the schedule require more than one evaluator, allowing computations of observor reliabilities, also *all* visitors to the class fill out checklists providing added reliability checks.) Tabulations of questionnaire responses; correlations between checklist responses and questionnaire responses. Listing and tabulation of responses to open-ended questions.
Are unit objectives met?	Use one or more of the techniques listed below for each unit.	Appropriate to:

SUBQUESTIONS

Do they like it?

Like—*Observations*, e.g. of smiles, procrastination, late work, complaints, time on task, work through breaks, after class discussions, electing to do optional activities, responsiveness in discussions.
Structured questions, e.g. questionnaires, interviews, rating scales, sentence completion, controlled association, checks on what's in the rumor mill.
Permanent products, e.g. student logs, marginal comments, judgment of positive or negative tone in written work, later course selections, solicited and unsolicited letters.

Like—for general liking *and* for measurement of affective objectives rely on muliple sources of data with emphasis on observational. Analyze student questions asked by taxonomic level.

Do they learn it?

Learn—*Observations*, e.g. listening to accuracy in student discussions, student questions asked, responsiveness in discussions.
Structural questions, e.g. Tests, quizzes, interviews, individual or group oral exams, structure "probe" questions in class.
Permanent products, e.g. papers, project reports, accuracy of notes taken in class, written work done en route, incorporation in later written work. (Use criterion checklists for self-evaluation and use the weighted checklists for purposes of grading.)

Learn—Item analysis of test items and other testing devices. Data broken down by taxonomic level of test item and objective.

Do they use it?

Use—Collect data relevant to subsequent use (of what was learned in the unit) in doing later units, the major project, etc.
Observations, e.g. listening/watching to determine if students use the material in discussions, if they ask questions or run into difficulties that show they aren't using earlier material.
Structured questions, e.g. ask "probe" questions in class, use review questions and "compare new with old" questions and "compare new with old" questions on tests, use questions requiring use of "old" to do "new."
Permanent products, e.g. later papers, the major project, etc.

Record number of observed failure-to-use, search for patterns.

Item analyses of "retention" tests and criterion checklists for permanent products.

Does it help?

Help—Use data, etc., that were collected to evaluate *Use*. Also—administer questionnaire items to get student perception of the value of particular items of learning, e.g., Has it been/do you think it will be useful?

Examine item analyses for deficiencies in items relevant to cumulative learning.

Tabulate student opinion data.

FIGURE 3. Evaluation Worksheet: *Course Delivery*

Evaluation Questions	*Data Sources and Collection*	*Analysis*
Are the outcomes considered valuable?	(Note: Dr. Powers had already done a minimal "consensual validation" relevant to the course design re. "Do colleagues perceive the objectives as worthy?" She also built evidence of research support into the content.)	(No further analysis planned.)
SUBQUESTIONS		
Do students consider the objectives valuable?	Pre and post questionnaire in which students rate the value of attaining the knowledge, skills, and attitudes specified by the objectives.	Descriptive statistics on before, after and change. (See Profile below)
Do the students perceive significant improvement in their knowledge and skill?	Pre and post questionnaire in which students rate their competence level in specific areas relevant to major course objectives (e.g., Ability to establish worthwhile learning objectives tailored to demonstrated needs of a special education students, ability to interact with others to facilitate educational planning, ability to establish procedures for motivating individual students).	Collect pre-questionnaires immediately. Return them after post-questionnaires are completed and have students plot results on a Personal Skills Profile Sheet: 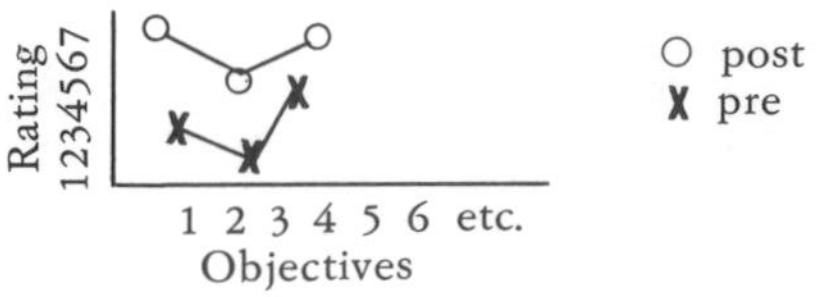 Summarize by a Class Profile of Median Ratings for each objective.
Are there outcomes other than those stated in the objectives?	Questionnaire item: List three desirable and three undesirable outcomes, learnings, or by-products of the course.	Listing of responses. Judgments by two colleagues as to the importance of each item listed.
Are the course objectives met?		
SUBQUESTIONS		
Do students like the course?	Data collected from unit evaluations supplemented by global questionnaire items, "rumor" notes, etc.	

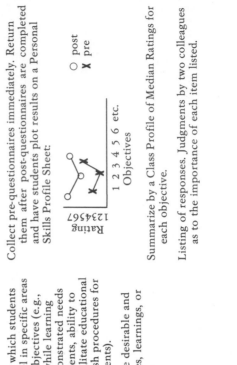

Do they achieve the objectives?	Assessed primarily as part of unit evaluations and compiled for course as a whole. Emphasize observational data for psychomotor and for affective objectives. Emphasize test data for measuring cognitive objectives. Use questionnaire data as supplementary evidence.	Data from sample test questions, etc., recorded in tabular form, organized by objective and taxonomic level of assessment device.
Do they use what they learn?	Some of the instructional units have "application options" built in that enable some of the students to apply what they are learning. Also, three of the units result in the design of procedures that could be used later. Self-addressed post cards are stapled to their work when it is returned, asking them to return the cards when they use the procedures (or use procedures modeled after them.) A card file maintained on former students: When subsequent contacts with students occur, a card is started or updated. These contacts (chance or otherwise) afford opportunities to interview students about if, when, how, and how well they use things they'd learned in the course.	Descriptive statistics—e.g., percentage of students electing application options, percentage returning post cards, percentage of students with whom there is post-course contact, etc.
Does using it help?	The major projects have built in evaluations of effectiveness. (Additional data obtained in conjunction with assessment of use.) Interviews with other instructors whose courses utilize similar or the same knowledge, etc., to determine whether students who've completed the course do well or poorly in the relevant parts of other courses. Possibly follow-up survey items done in conjunction with follow-up studies on program graduates.	Summary statistics on effectiveness of projects, using the guidelines or checklists from project guidelines and the (approved) project proposals to define effectiveness criteria.

FIGURE 4. Evaluation Worksheet: *Course Outcomes*

351

REPORTING THE DATA

REPORTING—HOW CAN I
USE THE EVALUATION
DATA TO HELP STUDENTS?
(AUDIENCE/USE)

Dr. Powers found that the within course evaluation work facilitated course operation.

1. Setting up procedures to evaluate the logistics disclosed some logistical problems which were immediately corrected.
2. Using the criterion checklists relevant to teaching functions seemed to make planning for the daily class sessions faster.
3. It also produced more day-to-day consistency, enabling Dr. Powers (and the students) to make the daily transition from outside concerns to concentration on the business at hand more easily.
4. The quicker turn-around time for grading some of the essay exams, plus the immediate discussions had positive motivational effects (students reported) and reduced the need for remedial activities.
5. She believed that her conferences with students were also more productive. She displayed the item analyses on a bulletin board in her office and referred to them when talking with students. Students who missed things that most students did correctly seemed less inclined to blame "confusing materials"; Dr. Powers found herself even less inclined than usual to attribute causation to "careless students" when looking at items missed by several students.
6. Building in more explicit research support for the value of what they were learning probably contributed to better performance on and liking for two of the units. (The units hadn't been modified in any other way; however, the improvement could have been an interaction effect of other changes or a chance result of prior preparation and ability of this particular group of students.)
7. The amount of time she spends grading student work was reduced while the specificity of evaluation comments and suggestions for improvement increased. (The time savings on grading compensated for some but not all of the extra time it took to do the more systematic evaluation.)

Thus, the evaluation data were used as they were being collected by the two "audiences" Dr. Powers was most concerned with: herself and the students in the course. She also found that it was easier to "advertise" the course. When students occasionally stopped by wondering whether to take it as an elective, she pointed to tabulations of student perceptions of the course ("Do students like it?") and to the scores on unit tests ("Do they learn it?"). By showing some of the evaluation checklists for student products and for essay exams, she could quickly and precisely show what knowledge and skills students acquire. A student expecting to become a "regular ed" middle school teacher could then decide whether he or she thought the material would be worth learning. ("One of these days" Dr. Powers plans to develop a display for one of the bulletin boards in the hallway, showing sample units and summaries of the evaluation data.)

REPORTING—HOW SHALL I
TELL OTHERS ABOUT THE
RESULTS?

She has had other small successes in using the evaluation information she keeps posted on the bulletin board in her office. For example, a colleague (from another department), upon hearing her course described, chided her for taking a "cold, mechanistic approach." He grudgingly walked down the hall with her to look at the student evaluation data and some sample essays written in response to synthesis level questions. He left having seen, as he put it, that precise feedback could still be effective even if delivered mechanistically.

Dr. Powers was much less sure of the value of her more formal attempts at reporting the evaluation results. No one had asked her for an evaluation report, so there was no great clamoring to see the results. Nevertheless, she wrote a five-page summary report, gave a copy to the department chairperson (appended to her annual service report), presented a ten-minute summary to the departmental curriculum committee (and gave copies of the report to the committee members), and used material from the report as part of her dossier that went to the college promotions committee.

The data in the promotion dossier were used for documentation of service as well as documentation of teaching. She could report that students from the course provided direct services to twenty-three special education children during the term, that each of the service interventions was evaluated in terms of educational results with the children, and that the results were positive in eighteen instances and negative in none. (These data also supported the notion that her students were learning worthwhile and applicable skills.)

Using the evaluation report in these ways was satisfying in terms of Dr. Powers' own professional standards. The impact of the reports on those receiving them was generally positive according to the rumors she heard. The curriculum committee said laudatory things about her report, but were not moved to immediately initiate further evaluation efforts. The chairperson acknowledge the report, commenting that he wished others would follow her example. The information leaked from the promotions committee was that, as usual, they spent most of their time arguing grand issues; however, her evaluation of the course had been referred to once or twice in the context of making invidious comparisons to documentation of teaching effectiveness for other faculty. Dr. Powers considered the evaluation effort to have paid off handsomely in terms of improving her course and documenting its effectiveness. She planned to continue refining and extending her evaluation efforts, sure that she was getting short-term benefits from doing it and hoping that the long-term benefits would be there too.

* * * * *

DISCUSSION QUESTIONS AND TOPICS

1. Dr. Powers, in evaluting SE 534, did not raise the question of whether or not the course should be taught

at all. Do you believe that was a serious oversight? Or do you think that question is more appropriate to deal with as part of a more sweeping curriculum evaluation?

2. Dr. Powers also did little to evaluate her course objectives. What evidence did she already have and/or collect during the evaluation that is relevant to establishing the value of the objectives? Do you think that under the circumstances, that was enough? Or should she have done something more?

3. How did previous informal evaluation work she had done contribute to Dr. Powers' efforts to evaluate the course?

4. Considering her major purposes or reasons for evaluating, do you believe that Dr. Powers would be likely to overemphasize any positive results and neglect or underplay negative results? How would that defeat some of her major purposes?

5. Regardless of whether or not it would defeat her purposes, there would be a human tendency to seek out the positives. Considering that and considering the evaluation procedures she actually used, would you consider her course evaluation results to be credible?

6. What do you think of the general criteria she used to evaluate her design (consistency with common educational practices, the literature on learning, and the characteristic of the desired outcomes)? Would you recommend other or additional critera?

7. What did the evaluations of student learning that were part of the course contribute to the evaluation of the course? (Consider measurement of immediate mastery, transfer to "the field," and utility in the field.)

SUGGESTIONS FOR STIMULATING DISCUSSIONS ABOUT THE CASE

1. Arrange a debate. Resolved: This case is fatally flawed due the potential for bias inherent in self-evaluations.

2. Have a person or group make a presentation listing specific instances in which doing the evaluation leads to establishing good instructional practices. (List both changes due to the results of the evaluation and checklists to evaluate student products.)

3. Have one person or group make a list of "good instructional practices or devices" shown in the case. Have another person or group make a list of "good evaluation techniques or devices" shown in the case. Compare the lists.

4. Have a person or group present a series of suggestions for improving the quality of the evaluation. Have another person or group discuss the feasibility and probable utility of the suggestions.

5. Arrange a debate. Resolved: All this evaluation is pointless unless Dr. Powers can show that the things her students are learning benefit the children her students are teaching.

APPLICATION EXERCISES

1. Read some of the material in the *Sourcebook* indicated by the asides. Then suggest alternative things people in the case might have done at several points in the case. Or suggest a whole new approach they might have taken.

2. Using the case as a model (and foil) and your suggested alternatives as guides, design an evaluation for a situation or problem similar to that shown in the case.

3. Using Chapter 7 of the *Sourcebook* as guide, do a meta-evaluation and critique of the case (and/or your evaluation design).

4. Use the *Design Manual* to develop an improved evaluation design for the case.

5. Use the *Design Manual* to develop an evaluation design for a situation or problem similar to the one described in the case.

CASE C-4

AN INTERNAL EVALUATOR FOR A DEAN'S GRANT PROJECT ASKS: How can I tell whether my evaluation design is good enough to use?

Pat Kennedy

Dick Frisbie

Herb Prehm

Mainstreaming, intending to provide handicapped students with a more equal education and more "normal" social contact, has had many implications for the education of regular elementary and secondary classroom teachers. For example, Dean's Grants were made available in 1974 to colleges of education from the Bureau of Education for the Handicapped (now the Office of Special Education) in response to the mainstreaming mandate. The grants were intended to help prepare regular elementary and secondary teachers for the challenges of mainstreaming. This involved revising preservice training programs to include knowledge and skills in accommodating the special needs of handicapped children.

FOCUS—WHAT IS THE SETTING IN WHICH THE EVALUATION WILL BE DONE? (CONTEXT) This case focuses on the first year of a Dean's Grant Project at a medium-large univesity in the southwest. The first year of their three-year grant is for faculty development and program planning. The second and third years are for program implementation and institutionalization. The Departments of Special, Secondary, and Elementary Education collaborated on the grant proposal and will collaborate on faculty development and program planning efforts. Project directorship is shared by the dean of the college of education and an associate professor in the college, with the Dean serving a key advisory role.

FOCUS—WHO ARE THE PEOPLE WHO HAVE AN INTEREST IN THE EVALUATION? (AUDIENCE) The full-time project director coordinates the work of a learning cluster (one tenured faculty member each from the Departments of Special, Elementary, and Secondary Education), a part-time assistant coordinator, a secretary, and two graduate assistants. Two school districts near the University, which have mainstreaming programs in progress, provide sites for field experiences for faculty and students.

The Dean provides important administrative feedback for all project activities. He does not meet with the staff on a regular basis, but rather consults with them periodically on policy-related project decisions. Department heads for Special, Elementary, and Secondary Education serve on the Dean's Grant Advisory Committee and provide release time to their faculty to teach and do project-related development work. The Special Education Department provides technical assistance to elementary and secondary faculty who want to teach mainstream education principles in their classes.

The relationship between Special Education and Elementary and Secondary Education might best be described as "collaborative competition". Generally, departmental faculty maintain cordial working relationships; however, competition between departments occurs in relation to resource acquisition, student recruitment, and program orientation. While all three departments are committed to the preparation of high quality teachers, the departments differ in their view of what are the best approaches for doing so and what content their programs should emphasize. Competition is also fostered by common misperceptions of the skills of faculty in departments outside one's own. In short, sharing expertise and resources to better prepare regular teachers to handle handicapped children is a new and challenging game in many respects for all involved.

MANAGEMENT—WHO WILL DO THE EVALUATION? Pat is the full-time director for the Dean's Grant. She has planned and will implement the evaluation. Evaluation and research aren't new to her, although she would probably not label herself as an experienced evaluator. She does know that evaluating the project you run brings problems.

FOCUS—WHAT IS THE REASON FOR DOING THE EVALUATION? (PURPOSE) Since approval of the program by outsiders (including the Joint Dissemination and Review Panel) is an important goal, she's interested in establishing an evaluation design that is judged credible at the outset. To this end, she chose a set of criteria to use in judging the design and sought a professional with some expertise in evaluation to help her evaluate the evaluation design. The criteria she chose are the Joint Committee *Standards for Evaluations of Educational Programs, Projects, and Materials* published in 1981 by McGraw Hill. She picked them because a number of professional organizations with which she is affiliated were involved in their development. However, since the standards are new, she has no prototype to follow.

DESIGN—WHAT EVALUATION CRITERIA WILL BE USED? (CRITERIA)

Steve, Pat's consultant ($150 day $\times$ 2 days) has been recommended to her by several colleagues; she has also read some articles he has written on evaluation in special education. For both of them, this is a first attempt at applying these standards although Steve has used them as a reference book in a course he teaches on program evaluation.

FOCUS—WHAT WILL BE EVALUATED? (OBJECT) In their first meeting (one hour), they agreed to organize the meta-evaluation into three parts: assessment of the design; monitoring the implementation of the design; and assessing the final reports and their uses. Steve's role will be to work with Pat directly on conducting the design assessment and then help her plan the next two parts. If they later agree to have Steve participate in those planned activities, it will require additional consulting time.

Pat and Steve are having their second meeting today (two hours before lunch and two hours after lunch) to review the evaluation design. They agreed that Steve would read the proposal for the Dean's Grant and come to the meeting

FOCUS—WHAT ARE THE EVALUATION QUESTIONS, DATA SOURCES, AND METHODS EMPHASIZED IN THE EVALUATION DESIGN THAT IS TO BE EVALUATED? (OBJECT) with a "discussion guide" to help review the evaluation design. Steve has pulled the following pages from the proposal, which provides a general overview of the evaluation design (Table 1).

THE MORNING

DESIGN—HOW CAN WE USE THE *STANDARDS* TO EVALUATE THE EVALUATION DESIGN? (APPROPRIATE PROCEDURES) We join Pat and Steve as Steve is explaining his homework and suggestions for the work ahead, "To start with, I should probably tell you some of my biases about doing an evaluation. Even when you have a set of criteria, like the *Standards,* it's still important to consider each of them individually. You should think about how important they are in relation to each other for your particular situation, and find a way to set them apart from each other, or to group them if you don't think they're all equally important. You also have to have a working understanding of the meaning of a standard or a criterion, with what precision it should be measured, what will serve as evidence that evaluation quality is present, and where you could reasonably expect to find information sources to provide evidence.

"Once you've done all this groundwork, you can collect and organize the evidence for and against meeting a criterion, or one of the *Standards* in this case. After that, you are in a position to make an overall judgment about how

Table 1. Evaluation Questions, Data Source and Collection Method by Objective

OBJECTIVES	EVALUATION QUESTIONS	DATA SOURCE	METHOD OF COLLECTING
1.0 Resource support			
1.1. Establish advisory structures *–Dean's Council *–Interdisciplinary teacher Education Advisory Committee *–PRIME Advisory Board	Have the groups been established? Are the groups performing their advisory functions? Do groups contribute to Project planning decisions? Do groups review Project programs & products? Do groups contribute to resource pool?	3 advisory groups	Survey members Analysis of minutes and other records.
1.2. Info-services *–materials center –responses to info requests	Has a materials center been established? Is it used? By whom? How often? What is quality & extent of resource collection? Are requests for information processed quickly and efficiently?	IRL collection Project files	Review IRL records Review files on infor. requests.
1.3. Consultants and resource persons	Does project make effective use of local and outside consultants for conferences, training workshops, planning input, program development, etc?	Meeting agendas* Training agendas. Project documentation records	Review agendas
1.4. Develop learning resources *–select –adapt –develop	Have appropriate materials been selected, adapted, and developed to assist faculty in mainstreaming implementation in their courses? Are the materials effective? To what extent are the materials used? By whom? How often?	Project files Faculty members	Review materials Survey faculty
2.0 C.O.E. FACULTY *–awareness –knowledge –application/implementation –attitudes	Is there a change in each of these areas from beginning to end of Project?	C.O.E. faculty	Pretest—Fall '80* Posttest—Spring '83
2.1. Disseminate info –advocate *–use established channels *–newsletter & p.r.	Was info. disseminated to faculty? Were appropriate chanels used to reach greatest number of faculty? Did staff act as project advocates? Was a newsletter published?	Project files C.O.E. faculty	Review documentation files. Analyze dissemination efforts. Survey faculty.
2.2. Implement faculty development activities –conferences –colloquia –discussion groups –learning resource teams –collaborative research teams	Were development activities implemented? Were they effective in providing faculty with new skills and ideas? Were the objectives of each activity attained? Were resource teams established? What was the extent of participation in development activities? Are faculty from different departments conducting mainstreaming research?	Project files C.O.E. faculty C.O.E. students	Review agendas of each activity* Brief evaluation form for each activity* Review mainstream content on course syllabi Student course evaluations. Publication of research on mainstreaming

(Continued)

355

Table (*continued*)

OBJECTIVES	EVALUATION QUESTIONS	DATA SOURCE	METHOD OF COLLECTING
			Student performance on mainstreaming competenices test Fall '80 Spring '82 Spring '83
2.3. Clinical & field experiences –on-site –contact w/handicapped on campus	Were faculty provided with clinical & field opportunities? What was the extent of faculty participation? How effective were field experiences?	C.O.E. faculty	Faculty survey & interviews Teacher surveys
3.0 Establish Learning Cluster Teams (faculty & students) 3.1. Faculty teams *–select members *–team building and organizational development training –field-based practica –Learning Resource Teams –Collaborative reseach awards	Were faculty members selected for Learning Cluster Teams? Was training provided in team building & organizational development? Were training objectives achieved? Did Learning Cluster faculty have field-based experiences? Were incentives provided for conducting collaborative research? What was degree of faculty participation? Did team select plan for model program?	Project files C.O.E. faculty	Faculty survey & interviews Brief evaluation form for training activities Expert review of model program
3.2. Student teams –provide info. –orient to PRIME –counsel & advise –select students for model program	Did project succeed in reaching large number of potential student team members? Were students adequately informed about project goals & model program? Were 60 students selected for model program by May '81?	C.O.E. students	Student interviews Checklist for academic and personal profile Pretest mainstreaming competencies of Learning Cluster students, Fall '81

Objective / Evaluation Questions	Data Sources	Methods / Instruments
4.0 Implement Learning Cluster (model program)		
What are entering competencies in mainstreaming of students selected for model program? What is academic & personal profile of 60 students?		
4.1. Program development Was 2-year model program developed incorporating the 10 areas of mainstream capabilities? What are specific program objectives? Is program attractive to students?	Project files Faculty members of Learning Cluster Experts in field. Students	Program review by local & outside experts Program review by students.
4.2. Program implementation Was 2-year model program implemented? Were program objectives achieved? How do students in Learning Cluster compare to: 1) C.O.E. students prior to Dean's Grant 2) C.O.E. students who received some integration of mainstreaming content in core courses	Regular C.O.E. & Learning Cluster students Teachers in field who worked with Learning Cluster students C.O.E. faculty	Performance & attitudes of 3 groups of C.O.E. students in mainstreaming Student interviews Teacher interviews and/or survey Faculty interviews and/or survey Follow-up study of success of model program students

*Completed or in progress

well your evaluation is meeting the standard and, finally, start making some changes to improve the design or implementation of the evaluation. If it's already over, you have a good sense of how seriously you should take the findings."

"Well," Pat responded, "that sounds like a helluva lot of work to me."

Steve laughed, "Oh, it is, and sometimes it's impossible or unreasonable to do it all; but you'll find it becomes routine rather fast, and I guarantee you it will help provide a better and more defensible design.

COLLECTING—HOW CAN WE PUT TOGETHER INFORMATION WE HAVE RELEVANT TO EACH STANDARD? (INSTRUMENTS) "Let me show you what I've done. This is a chart I ·put together to summarize what I see as the basic strengths and weaknesses of your evaluation design for the Model Training Program in terms of the *Standards,*" (see Table 2).

"What I'd like to do this morning is talk about the design by focusing on the *Standard's* functional table of contents for that activity. Since I also like to think of five standards as representing what I call 'core' concerns, areas that you need to keep in mind throughout just about any evaluation, I'd like to discuss them too. All but one of these are already listed in the functional table of contents under design, so we can just cover them first; then we'll discuss the rest of the standards listed under that area. Once we've discussed those standards, that would probably be a good time to break for lunch.

"When we return, we can cover the rest of the standards, just to make sure that we haven't completely overlooked some important issues. When we've covered all 30, we can talk about any tradeoffs we'll have to make and settle on a list of recommendations to change the design. We can finish by talking about your next steps."

ANALYZING AND INTERPRETING—HOW CAN WE MAKE SENSE OUT OF THE INFORMATION WE COLLECT RELEVANT TO EACH STANDARD? (INTERPRETATION CRITERIA) "That sounds fine to me, Steve, but before we start, I'd also like to know a little bit more about how you expect to go through all those steps you mentioned in the beginning." Pat continued, "I can see how you've gotten at some of them, like distinguishing among standards by grouping them into concern areas, but what about the rest?"

A1. AUDIENCE IDENTIFICATION. Audiences involved in or directed by the evaluation should be identified, so that their needs can be addressed.

ANALYZING AND INTERPRETING—HOW DOES THE "AUDIENCE IDENTIFICATION" STANDARD RELATE TO OUR EVALUATION DESIGN? (ANALYSIS) "The Audience Identification standard," explained Steve, "asks that an evaluator, or a project director serving as evaluator, identify all persons and agencies affected by the evaluation. These audiences should then be ranked and asked to rank their own

information needs. Knowing this, you can plan to collect and report data to meet their needs.

"The obvious audiences are paying for the project or will make decisions about its continuation. However, less obvious audiences, stakeholders, can get lost or treated as an after-thought. When these audiences are identified at the project's conclusion nothing can be done to collect information to meet their special needs," Steve said.

Pat glanced at her evaluation design. "The obvious audiences," she replied, "are personnel participating from college of education departments. In the college, project evaluation data will most likely be used to make curricular changes to incorporate mainstreaming education content into required programs of study.

"Of course, at the federal level, the funding agency must be apprised of program effectiveness. This information may be used to guide funding of similar projects. Also, results of Dean's Grant evaluations could be pooled to influence federal policy-making regarding mainstreaming education.

"I think those are the main audiences I need to address. I hope to publish some data-based research from the project. Do I consider researchers to be an audience?" she asked.

"All right," Steve began, "I think some of them are relatively easy to deal with and others are not. I think the way you start to get a good understanding of the criteria we're working with is to READ the *Standards* and summarize what you think they are trying to say in your own words. We'll do that for each standard as we go along. The sources of our information will also be pretty straightforwad for us today. We're going to use the grant proposal and your personal knowledge about things.

"The rest of it is another story. The *Standard* is not really designed to specify LEVELS of quality, as such, or to make judgments about HOW MUCH of the standard has been met; but the overviews, guidelines, pitfalls and caveats do provide us with several indicators of quality, good and bad. It's going to be up to us to keep these indicators in mind and pull everything together to make our own judgments about quality. We won't be able to say 'met' or 'not met,' or give the design 7 out of 10 points on Audience Identification; but we should be able to make some meaningful conclusions and recommendations about the design by the time we're done."

"O.K., Steve. That sounds reasonable."

"Great, let's start on the design concerns by going over the core concerns first."

CORE CONCERNS

ANALYZING AND INTERPRETING—WHAT ARE THE MOST IMPORTANT STANDARDS RELEVANT TO OUR EVALUATION DESIGN? (ANALYSIS) Steve began their meta-evaluation of the Model Training Program evaluation design. "The core concerns are, in my opinion, the backbone of a sound evaluation. The five standards I've included address who is involved, why and how it's being conducted, what's actually being evaluated, it's unique setting, and the values that are in operation. Let's start by talking about who's involved."

Table 2
Discussion Guide: Strengths and Weaknesses of the Model Training Program Evaluation Design
Prepared by: Steve
Date: Last Week

	STANDARD	STRENGTHS	WEAKNESSES
A1	Audience Identification	Major audiences identified. Basic information needs identified.	Range of secondary audiences not well identified, & probably too narrow. Ranking of all audiences & their relative information needs not well identified.
A2	Evaluator Credibility	Have hired external evaluator for 3-phase meta-evaluation. Using set of meta-evaluation criteria developed by professional peers. Evaluator has research & evaluation experience.	Evaluator is not totally independent. Faculty from other departments may be biased against evaluator due to existing interdepartmental policies.
A3	Information Scope and Selection	General scope looks good, considering potential for changing information needs over course of program.	Few existing information sources listed. "Triangulation" of information for some questions may be weak.
A4	Valuational Interpretation	A number of bases for judging the program have been identified.	The relative standing of different bases is ambiguous & procedures for making tradeoffs unclear.
A5	Report Clarity	Guidelines for report content & readability have been developed— objectives focused, nontechnical, lots of visuals, audience-specific & executive summaries	By focusing reports on program objectives, some flexibility is lost on areas like the management plan, reporting schedule, analysis strategies, and impact plans may not be adequately addressed.
A6	Report Dissemination	Major recipients of reports have been identified. Content & presentation method have been tailored to different groups.	Diversity and number of reports may be logistically unwieldy.
A7	Report Timeliness	Basic timetable has been established.	Timetable may be more for convenience of evaluator than timeliness needs of audiences. Timetable should be verified with audiences.
A8	Evaluation Impact	Dean is personally committed to goals of program. Program has many similarities with work of College Improvement Team. Graduate follow-up planned.	Reports plans don't call for systematic recommendations for actions. Follow-up with other key audiences not systematically planned.
B1	Practical Procedures	Review of documents, questionnaires, & observation checklists appear practical. Test scores should be credible.	First three procedures may not be credible. Obtaining test scores may be impractical.
B2	Political Viability	Inter-departmental political actions have been anticipated. Avenues for resolving possible conflicts are established.	Possible political actions of employing schools, unions, and accrediting associations have not been taken into account.
B3	Cost Effectiveness	Financial & time costs of evaluation are usually piggybacked on other project activities.	Actual costs in time & money for evaluation will probably be higher than anticipated.
C1	Formal Obligation	Most of the activities & responsibilities have at least been generally identified in the proposal & management plan.	No formal agreement between evaluator & dean has been established.
C2	Conflict of Interest	Potential conflicts of Learning Cluster Faculty, Dean, non-participating faculty, and evaluator identified along with viable safeguards.	Identifying possible sources of conflict may lull evaluator into thinking they will not, in fact, occur.

Table 2 *(continued)*
Discussion Guide: Strengths and Weaknesses of the Model Training Program Evaluation Design
Prepared by: Steve
Date: Last Week

	STANDARD	STRENGTHS	WEAKNESSES
C3	Full and Frank Disclosure	No reason to believe pertinent, available information may be unduly withheld.	Information based on peripheral faculty & students is sketchy but may be relevant to basic findings—nondisclosure by omission. Guidelines for withholding information not spelled out.
C4	Public's Right to Know	Members of several right-to-know audiences on program's advisory committee.	Handicapped students themselves are not on advisory committee. Guidelines for withholding information are not spelled out.
C5	Rights of Human Subjects	University has strict guidelines for human research. No individual data will be reported.	Procedures for insuring security of individual data unclear.
C6	Human Interactions	Evaluator aware of possible sensitivity of various participants. No reason to believe they will be treated improperly.	
C7	Balanced Reporting	Various opportunities to measure both strengths & weaknesses of the program. Drafts of interim & final reports will be reviewed & changes recommended by major audience representatives.	Decisions on including minority reports rests with evaluator. May also be potential conflict of interest.
C8	Fiscal Responsibility		No distinct evaluation budget. Cost-accounting procedures for the evaluation unclear.
D1	Object Identification	Good description of what program is *intended* to do. Some likely side effects have been identified.	Programs long term, large, & new. Describing what it actually becomes will be extremely difficult.
D2	Context Analysis	Importance of attending to peripheral faculty, relevant Federal actions, & unforeseen University events acknowledged.	Variety of possible important contextual factors & sources of such information a bit narrow.
D3	Described Purposes and Procedures	Project objectives operationalized in terms of evaluation questions, date sources, methods of data collection, & sources of evaluation criteria.	Formative evaluation, summative evaluation, and demonstration of effect roles of study not clearly distinguished. Evaluation criteria & analysis methods not clearly specified.
D4	Defensible Information Sources	Range of sources identified seems appropriate.	Several information sources are labeled, rather than described (or how subjects will be selected).
D5	Valid Measurement	Good start on competencies faculty & students would like students to be tested on.	Most instruments will be new & are untested regarding whether they measure what is intended. The diversity of measures for complex constructs like "competency" and "appropriate materials" may be too narrow.
D6	Reliable Measurement	Many measures, like "Are advisory groups formed?" or "Was newsletter published?" ask relatively clear-cut, yes/no questions.	Most other instruments are new & have no reliability information. Insufficient plans to test reliability of instruments.

Table 2 (*continued*)
Discussion Guide: Strengths and Weaknesses of the Model Training Program Evaluation Design
Prepared by: Steve
Date: Last Week

	STANDARD	STRENGTHS	WEAKNESSES
D7	Systematic Data Control	Evaluator has experience in large-scale longitudinal study. Data entry & calculations will be verified.	A large number of people will be recording and maintaining data.
D8	Analysis of Qualitative Information		Very little description of specific procedures to be employed.
D9	Analysis of Qualitative Information		Very little description of specific procedures to be employed.
D10	Justified Conclusions	Reporting format allows for main issues to be addressed, as well as "robustness" of conclusions.	Overall design does not allow for strong causal claims. Any such conclusions must be highly qualified.
D11	Objective Reporting	Good participation regarding input to reports.	Control over final form of reports not clear.

ANALYZING AND INTERPRETING—IS OUR EVALUATION DESIGN RESPONSIVE TO SPECIFIC NEEDS OF THE VARIOUS AUDIENCES? (ANALYSIS)

"Sure, as long as you make plans in advance to collect the data you need. I'd like to say more about that later on. Can you rank order the audiences in terms of obtaining formative and summative data reports?" Steve asked.

"Yes," Pat replied, "the formative data wouldn't interest the Feds. They require summative discrepancy evaluation organized around project objective. That way they can determine the extent to which the project has done what it promised to do with its funds.

"The college would benefit from formative reports to improve the program over time and to replicate the project's model program after funding ends. With that information, they can institutionalize the project, instead of losing it."

Steve nodded, "Can you think of audiences with special interests that might be affected by the program now or down the road, say in three or four years?"

Pat thought a moment. "Sure—parents of handicapped children have strong feelings about experiences and skills our teachers should have. They're a vocal special interest group. I could include them on our advisory committee. Then I can plan to answer their questions through the evaluation."

"Good, but be careful not to imply that your project or the evaluation is going to address all their needs. Help them develop realistic expectations about the project and the evaluation."

"Good point, Steve, I don't know if this is relevant here, but with the move away from the federal support of individual projects to state block grants, it seems like the State might be an audience. You know, to get state block grant money projects will have to be marketable. Since no one knows yet what form state data will need to be in, I could focus reports of project effectiveness to help us compete for limited resources."

"Sounds good. And another reason for being able to demonstrate project effectiveness is as a hedge against declining enrollments.

"I suppose that one purpose of this standard is to remind directors planning evaluations to anticipate where more than one version of evaluation results should be written so they're useful to each audience. However, it seems to me that the same evaluation report can be submitted to multiple audiences *if* you've accommodated their needs in a readable report.

"The most important point is not to overlook any important audience, especially when you're drafting evaluation questions," he concluded.

"Well," Pat said, "I think I'll add the parent group to the Advisory Board and have them review the evaluation questions now and at a couple of other points when some information is coming in. I'll add "review by stakeholders" to my management plan to remind myself. Still, the Dean and OSE have to be primary audiences and, in addition to them, the three departments implementing the program. I have to take care of their needs first."

D3. DESCRIBED PURPOSES AND PROCEDURES. The purposes and procedures of the evaluation should be monitored and described in enough detail, so that they can be identified and assessed.

ANALYZING AND INTERPRETING—HOW DOES THE "DESCRIBED PURPOSES AND PROCEDURES" STANDARD RELATE TO OUR EVALUATION DESIGN? (ANALYSIS)

"This standard is really talking about two basically different things," Steve began. "In fact, I think they're different enough to be two different standards. The purposes of an evaluation include its objectives and its intended uses. The procedures are how you collect, organize, analyze, and report information. The purposes and procedures should be clear enough that people can agree or disagree on whether that's what they should be. Sometimes it's helpful to get an outsider's opinion on what he or she thinks these things actually are, and it's also helpful to review them more than once, like at the beginning, middle, and end of an evaluation. When the purposes and procedures of an evaluation are clear, it's much easier for people to judge how good it is, reproduce it, or pick up some helpful hints from it. In fact, the main reason you and I are talking today is to make sure this evaluation has the appropriate purposes and procedures."

Steve scrutinized Exhibit 1. These tables summarize your plan. I see they're organized by objective. Each objective is operationalized in terms of evaluation questions and data sources. Records of how the plan 'works' will be kept in the project's documentation file."

"Yes. The plan will be modified if project objectives change, which I don't anticipate, or as parts of the plan are found to be unworkable. Changes in the plan will be reported in interim reports and in the final evaluation reports."

"Here's a copy of the task sheet which the staff keeps that tells them and me which objective they're working on, for how long, and for what purpose. It leaves an audit trail of the procedures," she added.

ANALYZING AND INTERPRETING—ARE WE SURE OUR KEY AUDIENCES AGREE WITH THE PURPOSES? (ANALYSIS) "You've noted that the evaluation is serving both formative and summative purposes. Do you think the Advisory Council and the Learning Cluster understand that these are different?" Steve asked.

"Good question. Maybe I should go over that at both the Council and Cluster meetings next week. The major purpose for most of us during the next two years is formative . . . but I know the Dean and our funding agents are interested in the summative purpose. It would probably be wise to make sure we all understand each other," Pat concluded.

ANALYZING AND INTERPRETING—DOES IT LOOK LIKE WE CAN FULFILL ALL OUR EVALUATION PURPOSES WITH THE PROCEDURES WE'VE DECIDED UPON? (ANALYSIS) "There's something else, Pat." Steve said. "I understand that you're focusing on formative evaluation at the beginning and shifting to summative evaluation at the end, but there's also a third purpose that I see cropping up here and there—demonstration of effect. Going for JDRP approval and talking about research activities makes me worry that you might be spreading yourself a bit too thin. I wonder how much the Dean and other people expect the evaluation to show 'hard core' effects of the program."

"When you put it that way, I can see how some other people might get the wrong idea, even though I think it's pretty clear. I should probably check that out next week, too."

"So do I, Pat. Considering how little money you have to work with, you obviously can't serve all three purposes very well. If push comes to shove, I'd recommend that the JDRP approval be the first to go, but that's up to you and your folks."

D1. OBJECT IDENTIFICATION. The object of the evaluation (program, project, material) should be sufficiently examined, so that the form(s) of the object's being considered in the evaluation can be clearly identified.

ANALYZING AND INTERPRETING—HOW DOES THE "OBJECT IDENTIFICATION" STANDARD RELATE TO OUR EVALUATION DESIGN? (ANALYSIS) Steve continued, "The object of the evaluation is whatever it is you want to study. Obviously, if you don't know what it is you're evaluating, you're not going to do a very good job at it. An important point to remember, though, is that what you're studying probably isn't going to stay the same over time, so you can't just describe what it's supposed to be or what it is initially and then think you're finished. Having this description makes it much easier to interpret your findings at a given point in time and could also be helpful in other evaluations of the 'same' thing later on. So what, exactly, is this program supposed to be doing, Pat?"

"Seven things. These are the objectives:

1. develop a comprehensive system of resource support;
2. implement faculty development activities designed to enhance knowledge of the intent and application of PL 94-142 and to facilitate active participation by faculty in mainstream activities;
3. identify and build teams of faculty and students who will participate in Learning Cluster Teams;
4. develop and implement the teacher preparation program based on the Learning Cluster concept;
5. document the change process;
6. assess and evaluate the impact of the change process;
7. disseminate project information and products."

ANALYZING AND INTERPRETING—DOES OUR EVALUATION DESIGN RELATE CLEARLY TO ALL OF THE CRITICAL COMPONENTS OF THE DEAN'S GRANT PROJECT? ARE THOSE COMPONENTS CLEARLY IDENTIFIED? (ANALYSIS) "The major program goal is the graduation of students who have competencies in mainstream education because they participated in this project's model program. The basic format for their training will be Learning Clusters. Learning Clusters are teams of 20–30 students and four faculty from regular and special education. The Learning Cluster becomes a team that receives intensive training related to mainstreaming, the concept of infusion, group process, team-building, and collaborative research and development with special education. They will deal with students who are recruited into the program.

"During the second project year, the model teacher preparation program based on a cross-disciplinary integrated model, which infuses or integrates mainstream education principles, will be implemented with college of education juniors and faculty who have worked intensively with Dean's Grant staff. Also, faculty development activities continue, as in Year One, with all other college of education faculty in order to infuse appropriate knowledge, skills and attitudes into the regular education curriculum. Extensive field-based experiences in mainstream classrooms continues for students and faculty alike."

"I don't think I need to tell you that linking project activities and outcomes is going to be hard as dispersed as programmatic efforts are," Steve interrupted.

ANALYZING AND INTERPRETING—IS OUR EVALUATION DESIGN SENSITIVE TO CHANGES THAT OCCUR IN THE CURRICULUM AS A RESULT OF THE DEAN'S GRANT? (ANALYSIS) "True. But, you know, that's not my primary concern. Making the program work is important, and I want the evaluation information to help me do that. If it provides causal implications I suppose that's wonderful."

"How much changing is likely to occur?" he asked. "Possibly a good deal—we've already had quite a few changes. That's why I'm keeping the project log," she answered.

"Who is involved; how are you getting personnel to cover these areas?"

"The departments are obliged to give us some personnel as a state cost share. I plan to ask for the people I know who can do the job for us. I will also ask the Cluster people to ask the designated faculty in their departments. They are friends and will perhaps do us the favor of teaching in the model program (coordinating with us in the program will be more time-consuming than their ususal independent teaching assignments)."

REPORTING—WHAT HAS OUR ANALYSIS SHOWN US ABOUT HOW WE SHOULD BE CAREFUL ABOUT AS WE IMPLEMENT THE EVALUATION DESIGN? (USE) Pat continued, "I will pay an honorarium to key faculty we ask to participate in the infusion. Later all faculty will be expected to infuse mainstream information into all of their courses as a matter of their regular responsibilities."

"What side effects do you anticipate?" Steve asked.

"I suspect that once the key faculty alter course content in important, basic courses, other faculty will make similar adjustments to keep pace. Also, once a faculty member has infused mainstream content into one course, I suspect he or she will infuse in other courses. I'll check out this hypothesis by reviewing syllabi of all courses taught in elementary and secondary, not just the courses we are looking at in the project.

"Another side effect I anticipate," Pat said, "is that students will begin requesting information and experience with handicapped pupils as part of all programs once it becomes common knowledge that handicapped students are being mainstreamed into virtually all regular education classes. I also expect that our model program students will feel elite because they are getting special attention. I hope they will tolerate our evaluation efforts in return."

"Is it also possible that they will feel overworked because besides completing the regular program requirements, they will also learn mainstreaming information? Learning is always work," Steve said.

"Quite possibly. We will have to build in other incentives and team-building activities to keep them in the program. Although some attrition is to be expected, we plan to keep the same group of students throughout the two years."

"Pat," Steve concluded, "it's going to be important that you put together a good description of this program so everyone knows what you're evaluating. Its slippery—and that quicksilver characteristic of a program that changes focus each year and changes personnel can lead to real evaluation problems. My suggestion is to document and review constantly."

D2. CONTEXT ANALYSIS. The context in which the program, project, or material exists should be examined in enough detail, so that its likely influences on the object can be identified.

ANALYZING AND INTERPRETING—HOW DOES THE "CONTEXT ANALYSIS" STANDARD RELATE TO OUR EVALUATION DESIGN? (ANALYSIS) Moving right along, Steve summarized the next standard, "The context of an evaluation can include any number of things that are not directly a part of the object, including geography, time, politics, legislation, professional activities, staff characteristics, economics, weather, and on and on. It's not only important to be aware of these things to temper your conclusions and recommendations, but they're also crucial at the beginning when you're designing the thing and carrying the evaluation out. When you understand an evaluation's context, you'll have a good idea about how far you can generalize your findings. If you plan on disseminating what's being evaluated, later on, it's also a good idea to demonstrate that the different contexts are probably compatible.

"Let's start with the political context of the program. What's the relationship of the Special Education Department to Elementary and Secondary Education?"

"The relationship among the three departments is typical of most colleges where the three departments co-exist. The relationship between Elementary and Special Education is closer, programmatically, than is the relationship between Special and Secondary Education. This is due to the fact that about 50 percent of the students in both departments pursue dual majors and because most of the Special

ANALYZING AND INTERPRETING—ARE THE PERCEIVED BENEFITS OF THE DEAN'S GRANT PROJECT GREAT ENOUGH TO OVERCOME THE PERCEIVED THREATS? (ANALYSIS) Education graduates acquire elementary level special education teaching positions. I would characterize the relationship among Special Education and Elementary and Secondary Education as 'collaborative competition'."

"What do you see as the bonuses for the Special Education Department in participating in a project to prepare regular-ed teachers?" asked Steve.

"Potential bonuses include increased efficiency, in a period of declining resources, in the preparation of undergraduate teacher education majors. Another would be the opportunity to work cooperatively and share skills with faculty from outside departments. Also there is the opportunity to assist in significantly strengthening the quality of undergraduate teacher preparation. Plus there is the assurance that handicapped students will have teachers who have the skills necessary for effectively teaching handicapped pupils."

"While we're at it I might as well run through potential concerns that are being created through the Grant. There is a fear regarding faculty roles and responsibilities should the Dean's Grant result in the reorganization of the undergraduate teacher preparation program. I think this concern centers on the loss of program visibility and autonomy."

"You mean," Steve interrupted, "if the program *works* it could threaten some faculty members?"

"Yes," Pat continued, "the infusion of Special Education content into the Elementary/Secondary curriculum has raised some issues. Will the infusion create the illusion of competence in program graduates? The Special Education faculty are not sure that the infusion will provide sufficient preparation opportunities for students enrolled in, for example, Secondary English Education, to acquire Special Education competence. There is decreased accountability regarding whether or not content was taught when it is infused rather than presented in a self-contained course. I guess this concern encompasses conceptualizing the reorganization of the undergraduate teacher preparation program as a 'watering down' of the current Special Education course offerings."

"Can you deal with these concerns?" Steve asked.

ANALYZING AND INTERPRETING—IS THE EVALUATION DESIGN LIKELY TO BE AN IMPORTANT FACTOR IN DEALING WITH CONTEXT PROBLEMS? (ANALYSIS)

"Well, I'm aware of the bonuses and concerns, and I hope to work constantly to promote the bonuses. I have an excellent working relationship with the Chair of Special Education—we communicate well. The Dean also works well with the Chair and neither one of them would do anything to jeopardize or compromise the Special Ed Department which draws a heavy student enrollment. All I can do is keep on top of possible conflicts so that maybe they can be avoided or minimized."

Steve said, "Isn't the context at the federal level influx, particularly with the possibility of the State block grant?"

"It certainly is," Pat replied. "The context at the federal level is uncertain as administrative changes affect funding and the security of many sponsored projects. In addition, PL 94-142, the law on which the Dean's Grant is based, is a controversial one and has caused much disagreement among educators at all levels. Staff will be made aware of changes in any political, social or economic conditions that may have implications for mainstream education."

"It's also important in reports for audiences to know whether a project's success or failure was due to impoverished economic conditions, a divisive relationship between departments, enthusiasm or resistance, or the program itself," Steve added.

"How are you reporting the changes in context in the university over the three years?" he asked.

REPORTING—WHAT HAS OUR ANALYSIS SHOWN ABOUT HOW WE SHOULD DEAL WITH CONTEXT VARIABLES DURING THE EVALUATION? (USE)

"The assistant director is keeping a log of unusual events that affect the program or its evaluations. It's not much, just a diary that requires an entry every week. And, our three-year plan calls for us to review the evaluation questions regularly to see if, among other things, the context has changed enough that we ought to change the program and what we're asking about it" Pat concluded.

"I'm really not sure if that's enough," Steve remarked. "I'm worried that you could miss some pretty important contextual events. Maybe you or someone else should also keep a log, along with news clippings, articles, flyers, or other tidbits that you can get a hold of."

"O.K., I'll try to work something out with a news hound or two."

A4. VALUATIONAL INTERPRETATION. The perspectives, procedures, and rationale used to interpret the findings should be carefully described, so that the bases for value judgments are clear.

ANALYZING AND INTERPRETING—HOW DOES THE "VALUATIONAL INTERPRETATION" STANDARD RELATE TO OUR EVALUATION DESIGN? (ANALYSIS)

Steve said, "This standard asks how you're going to interpret the information you collect. Who decides if it's a good program and how do they decide . . . based on what criteria?"

"Maybe we could use some unobtrusive indicators of worth," Pat offered tentatively. "If our model program is good, it will be endorsed by the participating departments after the project terminates and students will enroll in it. If it cannot compete with the other programs already in place, the program must not be as good as the others."

"The Darwinian notion of survival of the fittest assumes that only worthy and useful programs survive," Steve said with a smile. "That's debatable. And a program that survives isn't necessarily worthwhile. Maybe it just means they're good at surviving, but not necessarily at what they're supposed to do."

"Maybe I could identify characteristics of a worthwhile program at the outset based on input from stakeholders. Then I could objectively rate our product against a predetermined standard," Pat offered.

"That would work for the final results of the model program," Steve said, "but how can you rate the project's impact on that success or failure?"

"By examining course syllabi, observations, faculty post-tests after inservices, etc. I could determine the extent to which course instructors had incorporated mainstream education principles into the regular course content," Pat replied.

ANALYZING AND INTERPRETING—WILL THE EVALUATION DESIGN ENABLE US TO DETERMINE WHETHER THE PROJECT'S MEETING ITS OBJECTIVES? (ANALYSIS)

"I'm forgetting the obvious," Pat laughed. "Our evaluation questions are built around the program's objectives. Answers to those questions will tell us whether the program did what it intended to do. So, 1) we'll interpret by judging the program in light of its own objectives, and 2) we'll investigate whether the program is responsible for meeting, or not meeting, the objectives."

"What about the real outcome—the students or, better put, the new teachers," asked Steve, "how do you judge whether they're better or not?"

ANALYZING AND INTERPRETING—WILL THE EVALUATION DESIGN ENABLE US TO SEE IF OUR CURRICULUM IS TEACHING MATERIAL THAT PROFESSIONAL EDUCATORS BELIEVE IS VALUABLE? (ANALYSIS)

"We've really worked on this one. First we did a needs assessment. We questioned faculty members across elementary, secondary and special education about competencies they thought were important to mainstreaming, how students and faculty should get them, when, etc.

"Then we sent questionnaires to 526 elementary, secondary, and special education majors who were student teaching in Fall 1980. These students were our own as well as some from competing state universities. We specifically asked them five questions related to the skills the faculty seemed to think they need and were getting."

1. How knowledgeable are you about the application of PL 94-142, the mainstreaming mandate?
2. Have you written, or have you helped to write, any I.E.P.'s during your student teaching?
3. Have you adapted any instructional materials or methods to special needs of exceptional students during your student teaching?
4. Do you feel your A.S.U. classes prepared you to deal with exceptional students who are mainstreamed into a regular classroom?
5. Are you aware of your school's plan (where you are student teaching) to implement mainstreaming? If yes, how did you become aware of the plan?

"To double check, we gave students a list of 25 specific competencies and asked them to note where they needed help. The results allowed us to come up with a list of competencies that faculty and student teachers think are important. Those competencies have become a part of the Program curriculum, and I am using pre-post competency tests to gather data about whether they've been attained.

"Let's talk about that competency test again under the Valid Measurement standard. Did you also say you were trying to prove effectiveness to funders and for JDRP approval?"

"Uh huh," nodded Pat.

ANALYZING AND INTERPRETING—WILL THE EVALUATION DESIGN ENABLE US TO SEE IF THE CURRICULUM IS ECONOMICALLY SOUND? (ANALYSIS)

"That seems like two additional sets of criteria we should include as important in interpreting results. How about the Dean, is he likely to use a set of criteria of his own to judge the program?" asked Steve.

"No. He'll use the better-informed-teachers standard and the program objectives. I imagine, though, if we show gain in competencies, but not remarkable gain, he'll look closely

Results of Faculty Questionnaire Regarding Competencies for Mainstreaming

ELEM.	SEC.	SPEC.	
			1. Ten areas of mainstreaming competencies have been identified by existing Deans' Grants. We are responsible for disseminating information and offering faculty development activities in each of the following ten areas. Please check the three areas you think are most important in preparing teachers for mainstreaming.
33	6	23	curriculum K-12
22	50	23	teaching basic skills
67	33	62	classroom management
16	28	23	professional communication
39	56	23	teacher-parent-student relationships
33	56	0	student-student relationships
11	6	23	exceptional conditions
61	56	85	individualized teaching
5	12	0	professional values
			other (Please specify) _____
			2. How would you prefer to receive information about these competency areas which could be incorporated into your courses? (Please rank from 1-4 in order of your preference.)
1	1	4	through faculty workshops covering each of the areas
2	2	1	through the services of an instructional consultant who would work with me on a one-to-one basis
4	3	2	through access to an extensive mainstreaming resource library
3	4	3	through a regular project newsletter
			other

at costs—both dollars and the problems of coordinating three departments." Pat concluded.

"You might," Steve added, "add some cost criteria so you can report dollar differences for this program."

"I don't lack for criteria to use." Pat laughed.

"Nobody does," Steve added, "it's not being clear at the outset about which ones you're to use and why that creates the problems."

REMAINING DESIGN CONCERNS

"The rest of the design concerns," Steve said, "round out what's included in the functional table of contents of the

Standards. They include some additional issues of utility, feasibility, and propriety, but most of them are part of the accuracy standards—to ensure that the design is technically adequate."

ANALYZING AND INTERPRETING—WHAT SHOULD WE DO IF WE CAN'T BE SURE RIGHT NOW OF THE ADEQUACY OF OUR INFORMATION SOURCES? (ANALYSIS)

"Our information collection techniques are cheap—they have to be. But we cover a comprehensive set of sources and questions. I suppose I'll have to review again after I see if this information is thin and lacks credibility. How about if I put a review of scope and selection into the management plan?" asked Pat.

"Fine, that would fit in well with reviewing the purposes again. If they choose, formative and summative purposes, I think the scope looks good. If anything, I'd scrutinize to see whether some of this information might be used to answer a number of questions. Also, few existing information sources are listed, like demographic data and past evaluations. You might inventory that kind of information just to make sure you're using everything that's available to you."

"Check," grinned Pat, "first, I find out what I need to know; second, I explore existing information; and, third, see if I can use the same sources to answer a number of evaluation questions."

A3. INFORMATION SCOPE AND SELECTION. Information collected should be of such scope and selected in such ways as to address pertinent questions about the object of the evaluation and be responsive to the needs and interests of specified audiences.

ANALYZING AND INTERPRETING—HOW DOES THE "INFORMATION SCOPE AND SELECTION" STANDARD RELATE TO OUR EVALUATION DESIGN? (ANALYSIS)

Steve studied the data Pat proposed to collect. "The trick here is to have the appropriate scope of information; that is, information collected must be important to most significant audiences. The information must be relevant to decision makers, to program objectives, and to evaluation questions posed throughout the evaluation. When the information is put together, it should support a judgment of worth and merit about this model training program.

"Sometimes audiences don't know what to ask for, so without an external evaluator, there will be more pressure on you to ask the right questions. That means trying not to overlook harmful side effects, or cost-benefit, or responsiveness to societal needs.

"Well, you can see the information that will be gathered under the columns 'Data Source' and 'Method of Collecting' in the design summary. Frankly, I don't know if it's too much or too little at this point. We've concentrated on ongoing reviews of documents, observation of training, and short questionnaires to get useful formative evaluation so we can improve the project. That will provide a look at implementation for funders, though they'll probably be more interested in the results of the competency tests we're giving to students."

B1. PRACTICAL PROCEDURES. The evaluation procedures should be practical, so that disruption is kept to a minimum, and that needed information can be obtained.

ANALYZING AND INTERPRETING—HOW DOES THE "PRACTICAL PROCEDURES" STANDARD RELATE TO OUR EVALUATION DESIGN? (ANALYSIS)

"The heart of this standard is that you should use procedures that are minimally disruptive, possible to do and realistic, given your limitations of time, money, staff, participants, and information. If you don't watch out for this, you might wind up planning something that's sound but unworkable, and that's not going to help out anybody.

"As I look at your budget summary," Steve said, "I notice that there really is no money allocated specifically for research or evaluation."

"That's right," Pat replied. "Most of our money goes for salaries within the college for faculty to work on the model program and infusion plans and work with the students. While no one anticipated evaluation cost in the proposal, the Dean has given me descretion to spend. That's why I had to keep the evaluation practical, in terms of money and time," Pat continued. "I do the obvious: evaluation forms are distributed at the completion of a workshop or faculty development activity. Students are polled regarding their attitude toward what we do, and so forth. One criticism I have of the evaluation design is that it's not only practical, its safe and unambitious."

"There is one area where you do collect 'unsafe' effectiveness data; if not unsafe, at least unpredictable," Steve said with a smile.

"The competency test?"

"Yes. Tell me about the tests."

"I don't have a particular test in mind. I'm still searching the literature and writing to other project directors to see what kind of teacher competency tests have been developed. If I don't find an appropriate test, I'll develop one from the competencies used to teach the model project courses. Or maybe I'll develop a test from competencies identified as those the faculty says they expect our graduating teachers to have, coupled with mainstream education competencies, if they were not included."

Steve studied the evalution design. "You plan to administer this competency test to model project students when they enter the program and when they graduate?"

"Yes. I'll also do the same testing on a random sample of students in the regular preservice teacher program."

"And you expect what?"

"I expect that our model project students will do better at least on the competencies related to mainstreaming."

"They probably will. The idea of a competency test is good, but not having a developed test in hand is a weakness. The time and effort it takes to develop a sound and valid competency test are going to be extremely high. In other words, among other things, the test won't be very practical."

"So what are my alternatives?"

"Well, some alternatives to using a competency test might include instructor ratings, self ratings, analysis of work products, or follow-up interviews."

C7. BALANCED REPORTING. The evaluation should be complete and fair in its presentation of strengths and weaknesses of the object under investigation, so that strengths can be built upon and problem areas addressed.

ANALYZING AND INTERPRETING—HOW DOES THE "BALANCED REPORTING" STANDARD RELATE TO OUR EVALUATION DESIGN? (ANALYSIS)

Before Steve could open his mouth, Pat began to summarize the standard. "Balanced reporting means making sure that all sides to an issue are fairly and honestly presented. This is important in and of itself, but presenting both strengths and weaknesses of a program in a report has other advantages, too. For instance, identified strengths may be used to help bolster identified weaknesses. On the other hand, efforts to remedy some weaknesses may inadvertently dilute an unidentified strength, so it's important to go for balance."

"What are you doing in terms of assessing both negative and positive aspects of the project?" Steve asked.

"The attitude surveys at the end of workshops, colloquia, and activities will assess the participants' reported changes in attitudes, skills, and knowledge plus report what they liked or didn't like in the format and content. Syllabi of courses will reveal the nature and extent of infused mainstream content. The pretest to posttest change on the competency test will assess development of mainstreaming competencies in model program students. When model program students are compared to regular education students not in the model program the efficacy of the model program will be determined. I'll report all collected data and emphasize both strengths and weaknesses of the project."

Pat summarized, "What you're saying to me, I think, is that the evaluation procedures I've outlined, such as the reviews of documents, questionnaires, and observation checklists, are practical if not totally credible. On the other hand, the test scores that might really provide the credible data for some audiences are going to be timely and costly to produce."

ANALYZING AND INTERPRETING—ISN'T ZERO COST A LITTLE LOW TO EXPECT TO GET VERY MUCH OF A BENEFIT FROM OUR EVALUATION DESIGN? (ANALYSIS)

"Well, Pat, I think you've tried to be practical on a budget that is no budget at all, and you're smart to use multiple measures to compensate for the quality of information. I also think the pre-post test is a good idea and well worth some of your time and budget. Keep searching for an existing instrument and consider a symposium or sack-lunch seminar to discuss a constructed test. There might be volunteer help available." Steve offered.

"I'm going to try to do it. Frankly I think it's not practical to avoid student achievement." she concluded.

D4. DEFENSIBLE INFORMATION SOURCES. The sources of information should be described in enough detail, so that the adequacy of the information can be assessed.

ANALYZING AND INTERPRETING—HOW DOES THE "DEFENSIBLE

"This standard," Steve began, "has to do with more than just

INFORMATION SOURCES" STANDARD RELATE TO OUR EVALUATION DESIGN? (ANALYSIS)

naming the sources of your information. It also addresses the detailed characteristics of those sources. You should relay any pertinent demographic characteristics the sources do or should have, the rules and procedures for selecting sources, exactly how information was collected, and information about attrition of your sources. You should also stay in tune to existing sources of information. If you don't describe your sources well, the evaluation could lose credibility when it's otherwise sound, or mislead people to think judgments are based on sound information when they're not."

Pat said, "A variety of information will be used during the evaluation, as you can see in Exhibit 1. Two different groups of students will be involved in the data collection effort. One group consists of students who are training to be teachers but who are not in the model teacher education program. The other consists of the students who go through the two-year program. The first group will be selected for data gathering by a random selection process. Since the second group is small (we can realistically expect to recruit 20 to 40 students), the entire group will be used.

"I plan to use the same system of collection of facullty data: a random sample of college faculty who are not directly involved with the model teacher education program will be selected, while all faculty teaching courses in the model program will be sources."

"What if you get some minority opinions . . . for instance, conflict about the meaning of information collected on the part of one of your departments or one of your advisory board members?" he pursued.

"I plan to send a draft of the interim and final reports to all principal audiences for review. I'll correct factual errors and attach minority opinions where there is strong disagreement.

"The important thing about balancing the report, I think, is to give interested parties an honest look at what did and didn't work. So, even if the model program isn't a complete success, we learn something from the experience."

"It's good that you're having people review drafts of reports," Steve commented, "but you could strengthen this area even more by developing a simple grievance procedure for people who don't like what you've included or left out. I think this is particularly important, considering you're both program coordinator and evaluator."

D5. VALID MEASUREMENT. The information-gathering instruments and procedures should be chosen or developed and then implemented in ways that will assure that the interpretation arrived at is valid for the given use.

ANALYZING AND INTERPRETING—HOW DOES THE "VALID MEASUREMENT" STANDARD REALTE TO OUR EVALUATION DESIGN? (ANALYSIS)

Steve moved on to the Valid Measurement standard, "I think this is one of the more important and difficult standards to meet. It's also very difficult to figure out how well you've adhered to it or what should be done to make things

Table 3
Summary of the Conclusions and Recommendations for the Model Training Program Evaluation Design
Prepared by: Pat and Steve
Date: Today

	STANDARD	CONCLUSIONS	RECOMMENDATIONS (*PRIORITY)
A1	Audience Identification	Major audiences & their most importanat information needs have been identified. However, other stakeholders may have been neglected.	*Add handicapped student, parent, union, state, & accrediting association representatives to Advisory Board. *Add review by stakeholders to management plan. *Rank all audiences & information needs.
A2	Evaluator Credibility	Evaluator appears to be sufficiently trustworthy & competent to conduct or coordinate evaluation activities. Opportunity to review evaluator's activity available.	Be prepared to acknowledge & respond to questions of evaluator credibility.
A3	Information Scope and Selection	Adequacy of information scope & selection is unclear.	Review current scope & selection based on above ranking of information needs. Use existing sources & triangulation whenever possible if scope & selection are determined to be inadequate.
A4	Valuational Interpretation	Criteria for judgments based primarily on whether objectives are being or have been met. Not adequate for sound causal statements.	Add criteria for judging costs of program to strengthen summative evaluation. Point out weaknesses in claiming cause.
A5	Report Clarity	Objectives—focused report format is strong on purposes & findings but may be weak in other areas.	Include summaries of actual collection procedures, timetables, analyses, 7 follow-up activities.
A6	Report Dissemination	Distribution of reports to right-to-know audiences is adequate but is logistically difficult.	Develop complete specifications & timetable for all reports to audiences as specified below.
A7	Report Timeliness	Timing or reports may be more for convenience of Feds and evaluator than other audiences.	Discuss report specifications with recipient representatives. Decide on specifications e.g. Relevant audiences, major decisions, information needed, data needed, presentation style, length, # of copies, person responsible.
A8	Evaluation Impact	Good initial support from leaders to support impact, but more should be done to promote actions based on evaluation.	*Be sure to include specific recommendations for specific audiences in reports. Allow for follow-up sessions with recipients of recommendations.
B1	Practical Procedures	While individual procedures may be either weak in practicality or credibility, overall mix should be adequate.	Consider alternatives to competency test, like instructor ratings, self-ratings, analysis of work products & follow-up interviews.
B2	Political Viability	Most obvious political relationships have been anticipated, but potentially influential stakeholders have been overlooked.	See recommendations for A1 Audience Identification.
B3	Cost Effectiveness	Piggybacking evaluation on other budgeted activities may make it impossible to estimate cost effectiveness.	*Document actual or estimated costs of evaluation in time, money, resources, lost opportunities, conflicts, etc., as well as perceived benefits of *evaluation.*
C1	Formal Obligation	Although grant proposal outlines most of the tasks & responsibilities of the program, the Dean/evaluator agreement is too loose.	Draft memorandum of agreement between Dean & evaluator using proposal as major framework. Specify or refer to: objectives of evaluation; questions; data collection plan; analysis plan, reporting plan, especially editorial control; bias control, non-evaluator responsibilities; timeliness, contract amendment & terminating rules, and budget.

368

	Standard	Assessment	Recommendation
C2	Conflict of Interest	Evaluator has vested interest in success of program but has allowed for outside checks and balances.	Follow plans for public and expert review of procedures, data, reports and so on.
C3	Full and Frank Disclosure	Sufficient safeguards in place to expect fundamental compliance with this standard.	Be sure to present limitations of evaluation along with any findings.
C4	Public's Right to Know	Although several stakeholders have input to evaluation, procedures for withholding information are ambiguous.	Specify editorial guidelines & criteria for withholding information in memorandum of agreement.
C5	Rights of Human Subjects	Rights of human subjects appear to be adequately protected, but would benefit from recommendation.	Specify procedure for insuring security of individual data in memorandum of agreement.
C6	Human Interactions	Expect acceptable compliance with this standard.	Keep an eye out for stepped on toes, real or imagined.
C7	Balanced Reporting	Several opportunities to find & report favorable & unfavorable findings of the evaluation.	Develop mechanism to appeal minority opinions the evaluator, or any editors listed in memorandum of agreement, chose not to include in reports.
C8	Fiscal Responsibility	Costs of evaluation may be too easily "buried" in costs of program.	At least estimate portions of program budget to be used for evaluation. Establish accounting procedures for evaluation expenditures.
D1	Object Identification	The program is well planned but will be inherently elusive to describe in practice.	*Be particularly alert to describing characteristics of the program which were not part of the design through logs, critical incident reports, issue papers, etc.
D2	Context Analysis	Identified contextual factors appear relevant, but selection is too narrow.	Log or collect accounts of social, educational, legislative, political, economic & natural events that may affect the nature of the project.
D3	Described Purposes and Procedures	Three distinct purposes of evaluation will dilute resources too thin if priorities are not clarified or additional resources obtained.	*Review formative, summative, & demonstrative of effect purposes of evaluation with major stakeholders. *Redirect resources to primary purposes or pursue additional support.
D4	Defensible Information Sources	Information sources are not described in detail sufficient enough to judge their adequacy.	*Go beyond labeling information sources. Describe how sources are to be selected & their characteristics. Be prepared to describe any changes that occur over the period of collection.
D5	Valid Measurement	Validity of instruments has not been demonstrated & design does not adequately address the issue.	*Clarify & operationalize meaning of concepts besides student teacher competency. Be sure multiple measures of these concepts are made.
D6	Reliable Measurement	Reliability of most measures has not been adequately demonstrated or planned for in grant proposal.	*Develop procedures to demonstrate inter-rater reliability on content analysis & observational measures & internal consistency & test-retest for the competency test.
D7	Systematic Data Control	Data generated by people other than evaluator may be "sloppy." Procedures beyond that are probably adequate.	Provide relevant training to collectors & processors of data.
D8	Analysis of Quantitative Information	Description of quantitative analysis too sketchy in design.	*Embellish description of quantitative analysis for subsequent review.
D9	Analysis of Qualitative Information	Description of qualitative analysis too sketchy in design.	*Embellish description of quantitative analysis for subsequent review.
D10	Justified Conclusions	Several of the previous issues cloud the level of compliance with this standard.	*Resolve other priority recommendations. Have mainstream experts review conclusions in final report.
D11	Objective Reporting	With exception of editorial control question, safeguards on objectivity appear to be adequate.	Settle editorial control with memorandum of agreement. Establish report content grievance procedure.

369

better. Some things that are suggested in the standard to accomplish this validation are having detailed descriptions of what you WANT to measure, analyzing what your instruments DO measure, describing how measurements will be administered, scored, and interpreted for your evaluation, providing qualitative and quantitative evidence about whether your measurements are justified, and making an overall judgment about the validity of your measurements.

"So, to begin with, to assess the validity of the measurement procedures you plan to execute," Steve said, "it would be good to have a detailed description of what you are intending to measure."

"Whenever possible," Pat responded, "we've tried to come up with multiple criterion measures in both the achievement and attitude domains to hedge against false gains or false losses, hoping for better validity."

"During the first and second project years, most evaluation tasks will be formative in nature and generally process-oriented. Exhibit 1 indicates how project documentation and products will be used as the basis for this process evaluation. Do you have any questions about the major criteria for measuring the success of the first four program objectives?"

| ANALYZING AND INTERPRETING—HAVE WE DESCRIBED OUR MEASUREMENT PROCEDURES WELL ENOUGH TO ASSESS THEIR ADEQUACY? (ANALYSIS) | "The criteria are open to interpretation variations. One of the biggest validity issues you're likely to run into," Steve added, "is the validity of the competency test you intend to find or develop. You'll |

also have to work at getting a commitment from the Cluster members and departments regarding what they intend to teach and in fact are teaching. You've got a good start on 'which competencies' but I think that's an area you should monitor," he concluded.

"What I'm worried about is that you don't have a competency test in hand, and the design also mentions things like 'appropriate materials' and 'effective field experiences.' All of these things are very abstract and dependent on the valuational interpretations we discussed earlier. I think you and your audiences need to clarify what you mean by these other terms and terms like them, sort of like how you did with the competencies, and make sure how you actually measure them gets at what you want. Then be sure to keep track of everything you've done so that you and others can decide how valid these measurements are."

"All right," Pat answered. "I knew this one was going to be tough. I think that just by doing some of the other things we've discussed already, our validity is going to be a lot better.

"My project files will contain an objective-by-objective record of all project activities. This record will provide process information and can be used to determine whether the project is on-task and whether staff efforts are related to accomplishing ojectives. Data will be collected through a variety of methods including written surveys, checklists, assessment of competencies, review of files and records, and interviews."

| ANALYZING AND INTERPRETING—HAVE WE DESCRIBED OUR SOURCES WELL ENOUGH TO BE SURE THEY ARE ADEQUATE? (ANALYSIS) | "I don't have any problems with the sources of information you've identified," Steve replied, "but I do have some problems with the depth of description in the grant pro- |

posal. I think what you've done is label them without describing them."

"I suppose you're right," Pat answered, "but I think that was the proper level for the proposal. We left a lot of things out that we could have included."

"I can go along with that, Pat, but now I think it's time to get more specific so that you and other people can really judge the adequacy of your sources and make any changes that need to be made before it's too late."

"O.K."

One way to get at a sort of concurrent validity on project-developed instruments," Pat added, "is to obtain independent confirmation of activities from participants. An example of this is the recordkeeping system. Upon completion of any key activity, project staff members complete an 'Activity Report Form'. One of my graduate students will file the form sequentially by objective. Concurrent validity is attained by independent consensus among the staff involved. Also, this system will allow easy access to process information related to each project sub-objective. Review of documentation files will reveal areas in which procedures need to be revised to be more efficient or effective."

"Boy, am I glad that's done!" gasped Steve. "That should tide you over for a while."

"It had better," Pat retorted. "I wouldn't be too heartbroken if I didn't see your cute little face around here for a week or two, no offense. Why don't I take all this stuff and start working on some revisions with the Dean and a few other folks? I really don't know if we can handle them all, but I'll make sure to do the best I can with the ones that we've listed as most important. Let's meet again in about two weeks. I'll try to get as much settled as possible so we can do a quick review of the revised design and then start working on how to monitor implementation of the design and assessing the final reports and their uses."

"Great, but next time, I'll pick the restaurant!"

THE AFTERNOON

| REPORTING—WHAT CAN WE SAY, NOW, ABOUT OUR EVALUATION DESIGN? (PURPOSE) | After lunch, Pat and Steve continued their discussion by covering the standards that remained. This time, they |

went straight down the list, leaving out the ones they had discussed in the morning. Steve or Pat summarized a standard and then they discussed the strengths and weaknesses of the evaluation design pretty much as Steve had summarized them in in table 2. They also discussed how well they thought the standard had been met and what might be done to improve the design in light of this. Then they began to discuss tradeoffs in the evaluation. We join them again as Steve begins the discussion.

"The way I see it, I think we can cover most of the tradeoffs under one broad issue with three major components. What we have here is an evaluation which MAY be conducted for three basic purposes—formative, summative, and demonstration of effect. We also have a number of design concerns which are directly related to the types and quality of information needed to serve these different purposes—which are not always the same, and may even be incompatible at times. Finally, and as always, there are not enough resources available to do everything that everybody wants well. As a result, priorities are going to have to be set, and tradeoffs are going to have to be made."

"That sounds like a pretty good summary, Steve, but I think we already HAVE set priorities and made tradeoffs."

"So do I. I'm just saying that I think there's more to be done."

"Fine. I can go along with that. So what now?"

REPORTING—WHAT SPECIFIC RECOMMENDATIONS DO WE HAVE? (USE) Pat and Steve agreed to review their notes together to develop a list of the day's conclusions and recommendations about the evaluation design. They also starred the recommendations that seemed to be the most important to them (see table 3 for the final product). They then finished the day with this exchange.

* * * * *

DISCUSSION TOPICS

1. There was considerable discussion of the Audience Identification Standard in the case. What are several reasons the standard is important, not only in this case, but in other situations as well? What are several other standards or aspects of evaluation that relate closely to (and are somewhat dependent upon) audience identification?

2. Another very important Standard was the Object Identification Standard. How was the standard important to the case? What are several other standards or aspects of evaluation that relate closely to (and are somewhat dependent upon) object identification?

3. What was the "object" being evaluated by Pat's evaluation design? What was the "object" Pat and Steve were evaluating? What were some of the problems with object identification that Pat's evaluation design had to deal with? What were some similar problems Pat and Steve had in evaluating her evaluation design?

4. Why was the Context Analysis Standard important to Pat's evaluation design? Do you think Pat's and Steve's recommendations relevant to the Context Analysis Standard were good ones? Do you have additional recommendations?

5. Pat and Steve made recommendations relevant to all 30 standards. Review their recommendations and decide which five are probably the most important ones.

6. What do you think of their recommendation about the competency test (B1)? What other ways might they get at the question of whether the program students acquire the competencies?

7. What do you consider to be the strongest and weakest parts of Pat's evaluation design? (State reasons.)

SUGGESTIONS FOR STIMULATING DISCUSSIONS

1. Arrange for a debate—Resolved:
   Evaluating the evaluation design was worth the effort.
2. Arrange for a debate—Resolved:
   The evaluation of the Dean's Grant would be but a "straw in the wind" in the face of the context variables that would really influence decisions.
3. Arrange for a presentation on "Useful educational practices" described in the case.
4. Arrange for a presentation on "Useful evaluation practices" described in the case.

APPLICATION EXERCISES

1. Read some of the material in the *Sourcebook* indicated by the asides. Then suggest alternative things people in the case might have done at several points in the case. Or suggest a whole new approach they might have taken.
2. Using the case as a model (and foil) and your suggested alternatives as guides, design an evaluation for a situation or problem similar to that shown in the case.
3. Using Chapter 7 of the *Sourcebook* as a guide, do a meta-evaluation and critique of the case (and/or your evaluation design).
4. Use the *Design Manual* to develop an improved evaluation design for the case.
5. Use the *Design Manual* to develop an evaluation design for a situation or problem similar to the one described in the case.

CASE C5:

A DEPARTMENT OF SPECIAL EDUCATION CHAIRPERSON ASKS: How can we use evaluation data to refocus the department's curriculum?

Yvonna S. Lincoln
Edward Meyen

INTRODUCTION

FOCUS—WHAT IS THE SETTING FOR THE EVALUATION? (CONTEXT) This is the story of a massive curricular evaluation and revision project at a major midwestern state university. The story line concerns that effort, which was conducted over a three-year period.

Four other large efforts, begun at roughly the same time, are important to the curriculum evaluation and revision project not only because they *helped to create a new mind set among faculty* regarding planning, evaluation and change, but also because they *contributed data to the curriculum revision* project. The four projects are described because they had an impact on the curriculum evaluation and revision process.

FOCUS—WHAT IS HAPPENING THAT INFLUENCES HOW WE'LL DO THE EVALUATION. (CONTEXT)

PROJECT 1: The supply and demand data management system

In 1974 the Bureau of Education for the Handicapped (now the Office of Special Education) issued a policy paper on manpower planning. States were required to establish cooperative manpower planning projects and institutions of higher education were required to report data on students in training. The absence of accurate data on students in training made it difficult to meet the data requirements of federal grant applications and to answer the critics on the number of teachers being trained.

In response to this need, the department designed and field tested a student management system. The first inventory form was 16 pages in length and proved to be too time consuming for students and too costly to process for the department. Three drafts later, it became a one-page form returned to students after their initial enrollment; students then checked responses from the previous semester and made corrections. The Student Data Management System serves two functions. It provides information to the department for internal planning and data to districts about the upcoming supply of teachers.

PROJECT 2: Evaluating faculty performance

The university offered an evaluation service which involved a student opinionnaire administered at the end of each semester and the reporting of results on the basis of peer norms. The university also required each faculty member to file an annual report consisting primarily of a vita update. Faculty members were required to provide evidence of evaluation of their teaching as part of the promotion and tenure process.

The special education faculty delegated the evaluation responsibility to the chairperson who designed a working form and a set of procedures (see table 1). The evaluation process, reviewed by faculty, allows faculty members to present to the chairperson their aspirations, an analysis of their strengths and weaknesses, and suggestions for the department. The chairperson, in turn, is able to use the report for reinforcement, decisions on new directions, advisement on professional development, and as a method for monitoring the talent base of the department.

PROJECT 3: *The Development of Support Services* in the department helped facilitate research and development efforts on the part of faculty and students. Because all grants and contracts were centrally monitored by the department, it was possible to analyze the amount of funds being spent by projects and the department for purchasing services on a piecemeal basis. A decision was made to establish specific services or functions within the department and amortize the costs across the projects and the department on a use basis. User fees were determined, and when proposals were being planned, the need for support services was identified and budgeted accordingly.

PROJECT 4: *The Research Management Project* came about as faculty members became more involved in seeking external support for research and training projects. They were often not experienced in budgeting nor interested in the process, and since there was a high turnover among project secretaries, faculty members were frequently encountering problems with the university bureaucracy. The Research Management Project represented a movement to centralize control of proposal development and budget monitoring to accomplish more effective management of department research and teaching time.

Program announcements and RFPs channeled through the central office are distributed to faculty members with appropriate interests. Support staff become familiar with the requirements of the funding agency while the faculty members reach decisions on whether to respond to the competition. When a decision is made to respond the support staff is ready to begin work on the budget with the faculty member(s). Support staff now are experienced in writing budget justifications and are knowledgeable about fringe benefits, purchase agreements, personnel policies, and affirmative action. If funded, support staff participate in negotiations and set up books for the project.

This information and support system serves as a backdrop to the Curriculum Evaluation and Revision Project. It is to that project we now turn. The department evaluated and completely updated an entire curriculum doing so in eleven staged phases.

THE DEPARTMENT

FOCUS—HOW DOES THE DEPARTMENT OPERATE? (CONTEXT)

Evaluation was an integral (versus an identifiable but separate) part of an evolving planning process. While enrollment in the School of Education has been declining, in special education it has continued to grow. There is a moratorium on new courses and programs. Faculty members are being asked to meet more stringent promotion and tenure requirements. Federal support of special education teachers has been shifting in priority, with potential reductions an on-going threat. The department offers training in most areas of exceptionality. Faculty members are officed in two primary sites; both locations offer laboratory classes for children, a small instructional materials center, faculty offices, and instructional classrooms. The chairperson's time is divided between the two sites on a need basis.

The beliefs, motivations, and administrative style of the chairperson has greatly influenced the operation of this department. Four basic principles reflect the beliefs of this particular chairperson. They can be described as follows:

Table 1 Student Data Management System

Date Reviewed
By Student:

Name: Soc Sec #:

Street: Student ID:

Cty/St/Sp: Degree
                                                   Working on: BA   MS   EdS   EdD   PhD   non
Ac/tel home:
        work: Expected
                                                   Grad Date:
    ____ Kansas resident:
                                                   Hrs Enrolled:

Adviser: cmps1   cmps2   cmps3   cmps4   cmps5   cmps6
                                                   Lawr.   Linw.   MedC.

Career Objective (circle up to 5):

A Spec Ed class   F Diagnostic   K Adapt. PE   P Univ. Research
B Reg Class   G Media/Mat Spec   L School Psych   Q Univ. Teach Ed
C Resource Teach   H Speech/Lang   M Spc Ed Admin   R Univ. Admin
D Consul Teach   I Audiologist   N Reg Ed Admin   S Prof Non-Ed
E Itin Teach   J Work Coord.   O Researcher   T Other

Current Certifications (Circle as appropriate):

A Pre-School   C Elem/Primary   E Elem/Inter   G Sec (Jr. Hi.)
B Sec (High)   D Kans. Cert.   F In Cert. Prog.

Area Emphasis (Circle up to 5):   Future Degree Plans:

A LD   F Vision Imp   K ECE-H   ____ MS   ____ EdS
B EMR   G Hear. Imp   L Voc/Career   ____ PhD   ____ EdD
C TMR   H Autism   M Speech   ____ Non-Degree
D ED   I Sev/Hul H   N Sch Psych
E Phys H   J Gifted   O Admin

Current Employment: P Interrel
                                                   Q Non-Decl
    ____ Employed full time   R Other
    ____ Part Time
                                                   (If University Position:)
    ____ Hours/week
    ____ Related to Special Ed?   ____ Pgm Assist   ____ Instructor
                                                        ____ T Assist   ____ Res Assist
                                                        ____ Proj Staff   ____ Clerical
                                                        ____ Assist Inst   ____ T Assoc
                                                                             ____ Trainee

The Department wants to help employers find qualified special educators. Do we have your permission to send copies of this page to prospective employers? Yes ____ No ____

373

Belief 1: The collective allegiance of the faculty should be *to* the department.

Belief 2: Circumstances must be created which allow faculty members to teach and do research from strengths.

Belief 3: Program effectiveness (as measured by the quality of the graduates produced) is primarily the consequence of a responsive curriculum, effectively implemented. Thus, from an evaluation perspective, all questions relate in some manner to the curriculum, the heart of any training program.

Belief 4: Evaluation is best applied as an integral part of an operational planning process. This is in contrast to an evaluation system externally applied by an evaluation specialist, committee, or even the chairperson. In other words, the administration of a training program involves bringing an evaluation attitude to all decision making.

FOCUS—HOW DO WE KNOW THERE'S A NEED FOR EVALUATION? (POTENTIAL UTILITY) — The initiation of planning and evaluation was to some degree choreographed by the chairperson, who introduced concerns during monthly faculty meetings and annual retreats. In an attempt to increase awareness on the part of faculty members for the need to examine the curriculum the chairperson methodically presented issue-laden questions to the faculty. For example, topics included: the possibility of eliminating separate characteristic courses and moving toward generic courses; offering courses based on roles; and, offering an Educational Specialist's degree. There were discussions about the negative implications of further piecemeal planning. Noncategorical special education teacher training and competency based teacher training, for instance, had both crept into the departmental curriculum without the benefit of systematic planning. The principles later to be included in PL94-142 were well known, and their implementation seemed imminent. By 1974 the faculty, with the chairperson's help, were sensitive to the need for planned changes. They also understood that a major investment of effort would be required on their part to carry out the revision process successfully. The chairperson felt this level of sensitivity and commitment, or "evaluation readiness", was necessary to begin any revision project.

BASIC EVALUATION QUESTIONS

FOCUS—WHAT ARE THE MAJOR THINGS WE WANT TO FIND OUT BY DOING THE EVALUATION? (PURPOSES) — The questions which guided the curriculum revision process evolved from a broad question articulated by the faculty at their Spring retreat: "As a faculty how do we want to be perceived by our colleagues in the university and in general?" Using this perspective a number of questions surfaced.

"What kinds of students do we want to attract and what do we have to offer them?

Given we can attract students of our preference what will be their expectations?

Do we prepare our graduates for existing roles or do we try to initiate changes by preparing personnel to perform functions which school districts have not institutionalized into roles?

As faculty members what do we do best and what are our omissions in terms of talent?

How do we strengthen and maintain the interrelatedness of our research and training mission?

If we elect to make changes in our program what skills are required on our part as faculty and what data do we need to systematically evaluate our present programs and make the necessary changes?"

(Interview Notes, May 15, 1981, chairperson)

A central issue for the department was maintaining current program and professional commitment while at the same time investing in the revision and evaluation process.

The most difficult part of the process was to avoid a pattern of evaluation questions evolving which were parallel in form but specific to each categorical area of the handicapped, (e.g., mental retardation, learning disabilities, emotional disturbance).

FOCUS—WHAT THINGS DO WE NEED TO FIND OUT? (QUESTIONS) — Rather than rely on study groups to generate the basic evaluation questions that would guide the curriculum revision, they were generated in a group. This was done to allow everyone to interact and seek agreement on the basic questions. These questions later served as the basis for the revision model which was employed.

GENERIC EVALUATION QUESTIONS FOR CURRICULUM REVISION

1. What sources of information are available to aid in making decisions about the general roles for which our graduates should be prepared in the future?
2. What elements of our existing curriculum will apply to the future and should be further developed?
3. How do we analyze potential content in an organized and efficient manner?
4. Should the delivery of curriculum include a core of experiences for our students in the Special Education teacher education program?
5. How do we insure that the curriculum content and experiences are appropriate to graduates once they are employed?
6. What configuration of courses, practica, and related experiences will be necessary to implement the revised curriculum?
7. Would standards for assessing performance as well as levels of successful achievement be established as part of the curriculum/revision process, or left to the discretion of individual faculty members during implementation?

8. What implications will the curriculum revision have on the post-master's degree program and the undergraduate electives? (No undergraduate program is offered by the department.)

9. How do we meet the College requirements for organizing curriculum change that tends to be course oriented?

DESIGN—WHAT GENERAL STRATEGY SHOULD WE USE IN DOING THE EVALUATION? (ALTERNATIVES)

In addition to the evaluation questions, the faculty and chairperson made some *Evaluation/Planning Decisions* that were to guide the revision project.

1. Students were to be provided an opportunity to participate in the evaluation/revision process with advanced graduate students given an opportunity to engage in all dimensions of the project. Other professionals, through review panels, would be invited to respond to proposed curricular revisions. In this way, stakeholding audiences could be involved in the evaluation.

2. Emphasis was to be placed on creating written documentation, or "tracks", in the form of papers, minutes, and reports to insure communication with faculty members being housed at different sites. Coordination would rely on the sharing of written information which documented planning, data collection and evaluation activities.

3. All faculty were to participate and, when feasible, those faculty members assuming major leadership roles were to be provided a reduced teaching load with others assuming a share of their teaching responsibilities.

4. During the curriculum evaluation/revision particular attention was to be given to the post-masters program. Thus the "target" of the evaluation and revision project was very clearly specified through faculty consensus.

The decision to initiate the curriculum evaluation/revision project was formally made during the 1974 Spring retreat, but it was not until Spring of 1975 that Phase I of an 11-phase project would begin. During the 1974–1975 school year two position papers were written on roles and skills required by future graduates of the program. These papers served as a basis for faculty discussions about goals. During this same year an ad hoc committee clarified the roles faculty would play; identified audiences who should be incorporated into the phased evaluation; and recommended that the effort be run by a Curriculum Coordination Committee. The ad hoc group drafted prototype forms for documentation and recommended that timelines should be determined as stages *developed*. While the curriculum revision/evaluation would emerge—that is, would not be fully designed in advance—nevertheless, due dates were to be set for the various task force reports. Faculty members serving on the various task forces would have to meet those due dates, since missing them meant other faculty could not

review findings, assess data, and be prepared to make decisions at the retreats and department meetings.

THE EVALUATION TEAM BEGINS

MANAGEMENT—WHO ASSUMES RESPONSIBILITY FOR CARRYING OUT THE EVALUATION? (STAFFING OPTIONS)

The Curriculum Coordination Committee functioned as the senior evaluator and contractor on an evaluation team. Under the direction of the Curriculum Coordination Committee a needs assessment was carried out. A major need identified was that of responding to new Federal programmatic thrusts for special education programs and funding; in short, the department had to accommodate new ways of thinking about the content of curriculum. Generally, they found that content could be broadly grouped into categories called: characteristics (of handicapping conditions), assessment, remediation and management. The Committee turned to their own students as "indicators"; specifically, they analyzed the roles recent graduates were filling. Here data from the

FOCUS—WHAT ARE RECENT GRADUATES DOING? (QUESTIONS)

Student Management System were fed into the evaluation effort, since they provided the faculty with actual, field-based data on what teachers in special education *were actually doing,* rather than answering the question, "What were they supposed to be doing?"

FOCUS—WHAT CURRICULAR MANDATES MUST BE CONSIDERED? (CONTEXT)

Based on this needs exploration, the evaluation and revision process began, focusing initially on the revision of curriculum to conform to emergent demands on special education teachers and emergent roles which were being identified at the Federal and local level. They did not focus on the specific handicapping conditions; this represented a large break from tradition in the training of special educators. In fact, this break from tradition provided a genuine constraint, since faculty were accustomed to thinking in terms of a curriculum organized around specific handicaps, although the language of PL 94-142 had already somewhat altered their thinking. In the consensual process for setting goals a forthright commitment was made by the department to begin thinking in terms of new generic competencies and roles.

OPERATIONALIZING THE COMMITMENT TO CHANGE

MANAGEMENT—WHO IS TO FOCUS ON EACH MAJOR ASPECT OF THE REVISION/ EVALUATION PROCESS? (FORMALIZING RESPONSIBILITY)

The curriculum evaluation/revision was essentially a team effort. The senior team, the Curriculum Coordination Committee, assigned responsibilities to two sets of faculty teams. To revise the actual curriculum, the first set of faculty teams was organized around the new content thrusts: *characteristics* of handicapped, *assessment* and diagnosis, *remediation* and prescription, and *management* of resources. To plan and evaluate content delivery questions, there was a set of three other teams that dealt with materials, communication, and role specifics. These two sets of teams were labeled Cycle 1 and Cycle 2.

Alongside these curriculum specification teams, there would be eventually five other teams: Curriculum Structure Teams, which considered organizational structures for the delivery of course offerings, and considered instructional options (e.g., didactic, clinical, module, computer assisted); a Program Standard Team, which recommended curriculum review guidelines and standards for grading practices; an Instructional Resource Team, which reviewed existing instructional resources and recommended priorities for acquisition of resources and guidelines for their use; and Consumer Validation Teams, about which more will be said later.

REPORTING—HOW DO WE KEEP TRACK OF WHAT OTHER TEAMS ARE DOING? (CONTEXT) All teams at all stages reported back to the faculty at large by using a single form, the Curriculum Planning Project Monitoring Form, figure 1. The curriculum specification teams (Cycle 1 and 2) also disseminated forms that specified the content recommended for the four major areas (characteristics, assessment, remediation, and management) by levels of instruction (early childhood, elementary, secondary, and post-secondary) and by handicap (emotionally disturbed, learning disabled, etc.).

MANAGEMENT—HOW ARE THE TASKS DEFINED FOR THE SEVERAL TEAMS? (TASKS/SCHEDULES) Figure 2 captures the content specification process. The four "clusters" had been identified in the first retreat, and "competencies" and "competency components" were to be developed by the Cycle 1 teams. To some extent, this was a

---

less difficult task than it appeared, for two reasons: faculty members already knew more about curriculum development than they thought they did, and the content specification model literally forced a breakdown to be made if for no other reason than to fill in the blanks. The same held true for the content delivery (Cycle 2) phase. The content specifications needed to include generic as well as area specific content using the three level specification process.

While the specification process for competencies parallels the process frequently employed in competency based teacher education projects, the intent was not to present CBTE as the only option. The stating of general competencies and related objectives was used because of its value in curriculum development and evaluation of on-going programs. The intent was to argue for a systematic procedure for detailing the curriculum by looking at "needs" which were expressed in the form of generic competencies that newer practitioners of special education were thought to need. Those needs were expressed by curricular objectives which, in turn, translated into specific courses with content and objectives outlined. The approach suggested met the needs of the department in terms of outlining the new curriculum.

STAGING OF THE CURRICULUM EVALUATION AND REVISION PROCESS

MANAGEMENT—WHAT IS THE TIME FRAME AND WHAT ARE THE ACTIVITIES, I.E., WHO DOES WHAT AND WHEN? (TASKS/SCHEDULE) This particular project took over three years to complete. The phases are outlined in figure 3. The basic evaluation questions are reflected in the topics of the eleven different phases. Although the process operated on a continuum there was a division of tasks which is worth noting, Phases I through V were carried out without much attention being given to how the new curriculum might be delivered. The delivery questions were intentionally avoided until substantial progress had been made on the content specification questions.

In Phase I when Department Position Papers were needed the entire department, acting in teams, produced papers which both specified new and emergent roles for special education personnel as perceived by the faculty and

FOCUS—WHAT DO WE NEED TO FIND OUT? (QUESTIONS) analyzed the existing courses. Evaluation questions in Phase I included:

1. What roles are students in the field being asked to perform?
2. Are these roles significantly different from those being performed in the past? In what ways? What agency or agencies were responsible for the conception of these roles?
3. What are we currently providing, in terms of core courses? Does it speak to new and emergent roles? If not, what skills and competencies does it impact?

COLLECTING—WHAT DATA ARE AVAILABLE TO HELP ANSWER THE QUESTIONS? (COLLECTION PROCEDURES) The first two questions were answered with a data base that included on-site visits to school systems, current litera-

---

Date:

Team: Materials Attached

Members Present: _____ Yes
                            _____ No

Major Activities (may attach)

Topics Discussed:

Agenda and Tasks-Next Session:

Date of Next Meeting:

Resources Needed from Curriculum Coordinating Committee:

FIGURE 1. Curriculum Planning Project Monitoring Form

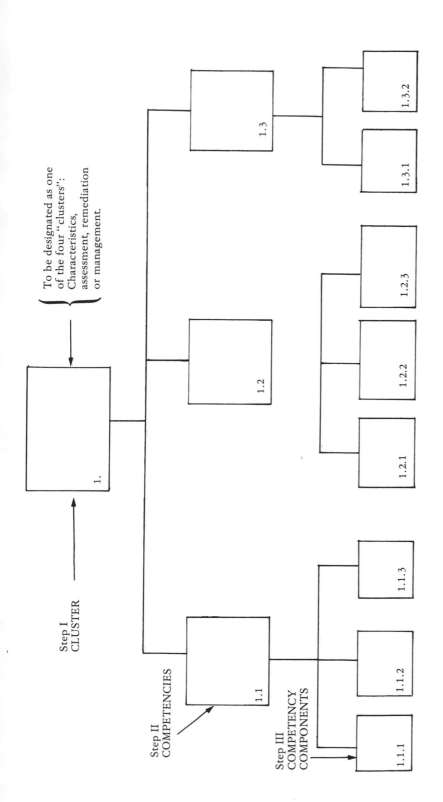

FIGURE 2. Specification Model

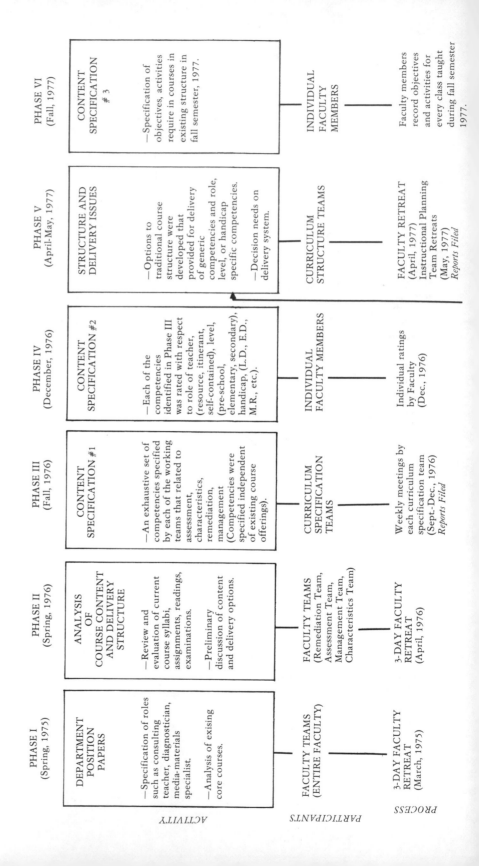

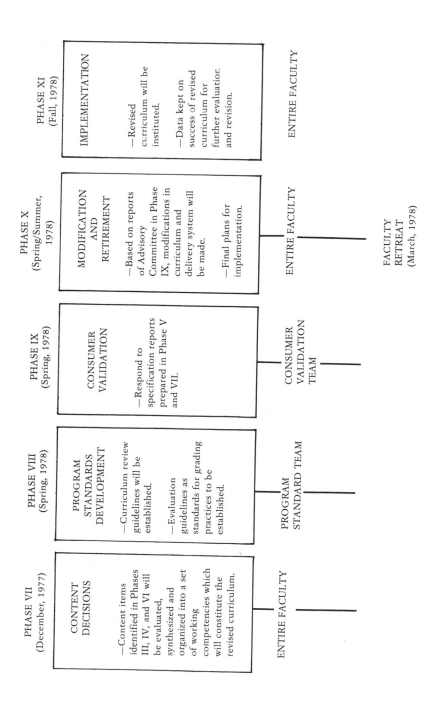

FIGURE 3. Curriculum Revision and Development Project 1975–Present

ture reviews, the Student Management Information System, information generated by other states and other special education personnel training programs, data from the Bureau of Education for the Handicapped, and national data relative to roles new special education resource personnel were being asked to fulfill.

Literature on past roles was compared with literature which was current, and analyses were made of expected directions that service in school districts might take. The literature which interpreted PL 94-142 was analyzed to make certain that new "clusters" of roles were not overlooked.

Site visits to schools, both in the state and beyond its borders, were conducted in order to interview special education teachers about actual job responsibilities. All these sets of data were analyzed, synthesized, and interpreted by a task force which began to look both at roles and at the competencies needed to adequately perform those roles.

ANALYSIS/ INTERPRETING—WHAT DID WE FIND OUT DURING THIS PHASE? (ANALYSIS) As a result of this initial study, the department determined that it was on target with its goal of revision toward the four "cluster" areas—characteristics, assessment, remediation and management—and defined a set of roles toward which they would move the preparation program. Those roles included, but were not limited to, consulting teacher, diagnostician, media-materials specialist, itinerant teachers, resource room teachers, self-contained classroom teachers, and "mainstream-directed" classroom teachers. Further, those roles were defined by level: pre-school, elementary, secondary, etc.

When the specification of appropriate clusters and roles was completed, the department, in the words of the chairman, "laid the notion of emergent roles and possible competencies against the current practice", and in a discrepancy mode, attempted to determine where the program as it stood failed to train new teachers appropriately. The third question, "Are we preparing teachers for those new and emerging roles", then became, "How can we cover the ball park?" This question was to be asked again in Phase III, when the specification of competencies had begun.

FOCUS—WHAT DO WE NEED TO CONSIDER NOW? (QUESTIONS) Phase II, one year later, was initiated as teams of faculty began work on an analysis of both current course content (all courses) and the course delivery structure. The faculty, under the leadership of the chairperson, began to examine options for course content, delivery, and ways in which delivery of content might relate to the four areas—remediation, assessment, management, and characteristics. During a three-day retreat, the four teams addressed the following planning and evaluation questions:

1. What kinds of courses do we now offer? Are they focused too sharply on specific handicaps to the detriment of newer thrusts?

2. In what ways do the current course syllabi reflect the newest literature and thrusts, and in what ways do they not?

3. How might content and delivery options be altered so as to reflect a focus on skills (remediation, assessment, management, and characteristics) rather than on traditional handicap typing?

COLLECTING—HOW CAN WE GET THE DATA WE NEED? (COLLECTION PROCEDURES) The process which was used to answer these questions was rather simple. Course syllabi for each course taught in the department were gathered up. Where faculty did not prepare formal syllabi, they were asked to create them based on content covered in the course, textbooks assigned, activities in which students were asked to engage (e.g., preparation if IEPs, clinical observations), and products which were required of students.

ANALYZING/ INTERPRETING—HOW CAN WE ANALYZE COURSE SYLLABI TO ANSWER OUR QUESTIONS (INTERPRETATION CRITERIA) After syllabi were collected, each was analyzed with respect to the four cluster areas (characteristics, assessment, remediation, and management), to determine where course content might address these four generic competencies across handicaps. Judgments about the extent to which existing curricula addressed generic clusters were based upon descriptions of the clusters themselves from current literature and from federal regulations concerning decriptions of program personnel. That is, the ideal, again, was compared to the real, and discrepancies were noted. (This was true, of course, only insofar as actual classroom activity was reflected in course outlines and syllabi.)

ANALYZING/ INTERPRETING—HOW CAN WE TELL IF OUR CONCLUSIONS WILL STAND UP? (ANALYSIS) Based on conclusions about where a course lacked training addressed to specific clusters, recommendations were made concerning what might be added when the new curriculum was designed. Where syllabi were not clear, individual faculty members responsible for specific courses were interviewed to discover the nature of clinical activities or content covered. The purpose of this cross-check was validation of exactly what was taught and what was expected of graduates of the program. With those two sources in hand—course syllabi and verifying interviews and conversations—the Phase II task forces (four in all) were able to determine exactly where the program needed strenghthening in terms of the generic clusters.

Articulation across all courses was not attempted in this phase. Rather, that process remained for Phases V, VI, VII, and VIII. Analysis of the core courses and analysis of missing elements was the singular objective of this particular phase. The standard against which any course (or set of courses) was judged was the extent to which it addressed the four generic clusters identified in the Phase I literature search and review.

FOCUS—HOW CAN WE TELL WHAT COMPETENCIES ARE NEEDED? (QUESTIONS) During Phase III, a set of competencies was defined by each of the four "generic skills" teams. (See Figure 2 for the Specification Model the teams used.) Each of the competencies identified in Phase III was analyzed and rated with respect to the *role of the teacher* (resource, itinerant, self-contained), *level of schooling* (preschool, elementary, secondary), and *type of handicap* (e.g., deaf, learning disabled, mental retardation, orthopedically handicapped). The competencies which were then evaluated as most crucial for the four areas could be displayed in the form of a cube (Figure 4).

ANALYZING/ INTERPRETING—HOW CAN WE TELL IF WE'VE DONE A GOOD JOB OF SPECIFYING COMPETENCIES? (INTERPRETATION CRITERIA) The competencies were evaluated in brainstorming sessions with the task forces, through use of literature searches, and by surveying other departments of special education. Validation of the competencies was left to Phase IX, when consumer Validation Teams were called in for a plausibility/credibility check. Faculty generally felt they would rather over-specify than under-specify and miss some competencies.

EVALUATION, COMMITMENT AND IMPLEMENTATIONS

FOCUS—HOW CAN WE ARRANGE A CURRICULUM THAT WILL TEACH THE COMPETENCIES? (QUESTIONS) The Spring 1977 (Phase V) Retreat was devoted to the delivery of content. The faculty had gained experience applying evaluation techniques to determine what the content of the curriculum should be given their goals of a revised curriculum. The process was moving well, and enough was known about the proposed content to begin faculty members wondering about who should teach what, when, and how.

COLLECTING—HOW CAN WE TELL WHICH CURRICULAR OPTIONS TO SELECT? (INFORMATION NEEDED) During this particular phase (V), options and alternatives to traditional course structure and delivery were developed. Alternative modes of delivery were explored and evaluated for their adequacy in delivering the generic competencies in assessment, characteristics, remediation, and management as well as the roll-, level-, and handicap-specific competencies. It was decided in Spring of 1977 to incorporate as many generic competencies and skills as possible into existing course structure and to spend the coming summer

ANALYZING/ INTERPRETING—ARE THERE DISCREPANCIES BETWEEN WHAT WE ARE DOING AND WHAT WE THINK WE SHOULD BE DOING? (INTERPRETATION CRITERIA) and fall semsters (called Phases VI and VII) constituting the revised curriculum and new course structure. Where discrepancies between current practice and projected practice occurred and could be addressed immediately, changes were made. There was no wait for the "totally revised curriculum" to be put into place, but rather the faculty proceeded with some changes at once.

FOCUS—WHAT DECISIONS DO WE HAVE TO MAKE? (PURPOSES) Phases V, VI and VII were guided by their own evaluation/decision-making questions. These included:

1. What were alternatives to the traditional course structure and delivery system? Which of these alternatives and options offered the "best fit" with the competencies identified in terms of philosophy, mode of presentation, opportunities for skill acquisition and demonstration, opportunities for clinical or *in situ* experiences (in addition to student teaching) and adaptation to role, level, and handicap-specific competencies?

2. What objectives and activities in the current course structure met revised curriculum requirements?

3. How were content and competency items developed in Phases III, IV and VI to be evaluated, synthesized and organized into the set of "working competencies" which would form the new and revised curriculum?

4. What types of decisions would need to be made about who would teach what and when?

MANAGEMENT—WHO IS TO DO WHAT AND BY WHEN? (TASKS/SCHEDULES) In each of these latter phases, individual faculty members, curriculum structure teams (partly elected by the special education faculty, and in part appointed by the chairperson), and occasionally the faculty as a whole, worked on the phases and addressed the problem of how to answer the questions. In the Spring of 1978, a Program Standard Team was elected from among the department faculty. Their task was two-fold: to develop curriculum review guidelines and to establish evaluation guidelines as standards for grading practices on a department-wide basis. This particular phase (Phase VII) was a benchmark. Since the curriculum review and evaluation process initially undertook the revision of just baccalaureate offerings and master's-level programs, the development of curriculum review guidelines and standards for

DESIGN—HOW CAN WE MAKE USE OF THE PROCESSES WE'VE LEARNED? (APPROPRIATENESS OF PROCEDURES) grading practices created and institutionalized a form that the evaluation of the doctoral programs would later take. Furthermore, extensive documentation of the evaluation and revision effort, and the internalizing of evaluation and data gathering activities assured that the process could be repeated as often as necessary to update and innovate.

COLLECTING—HOW CAN WE FIND OUT IF THE MANY DECISIONS WE'VE MADE SEEM TO BE GOOD ONES? (COLLECTION PROCEDURES) During the next two phases (IX and X, See Figure 3), consumer validation of the proposed curriculum revisions was sought, appropriate modifications and deletions were made, and priorities for instruction were ranked.

FOCUS—WHO ARE THE PEOPLE IMPORTANTLY CONCERNED WITH THE EVALUATION EFFORT? (AUDIENCES) The department advisory committee included practitioners outside the department. The committee was consulted for advice and direction in the

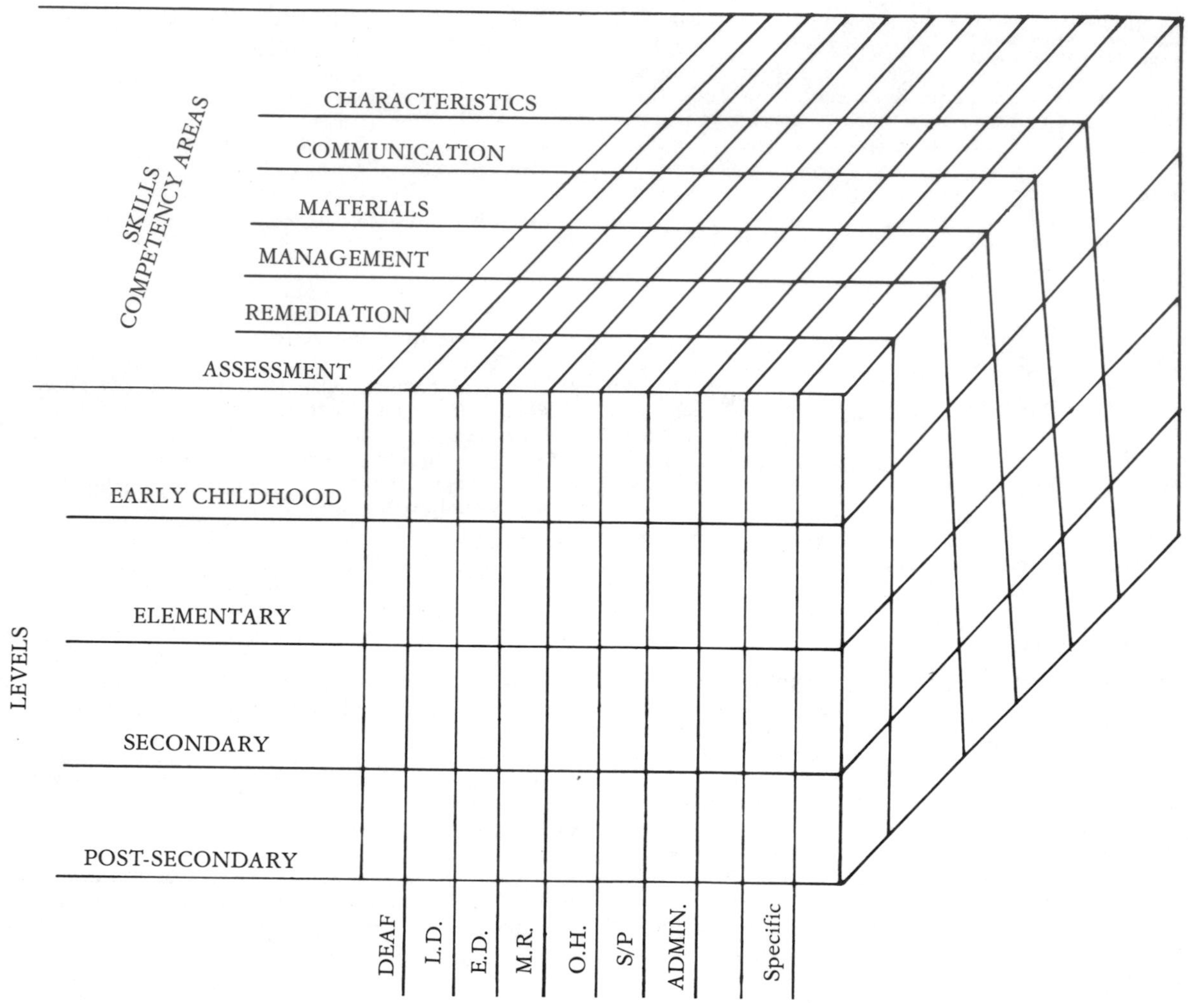
SKILLS
COMPETENCY AREAS
CHARACTERISTICS
COMMUNICATION
MATERIALS
MANAGEMENT
REMEDIATION
ASSESSMENT
LEVELS
EARLY CHILDHOOD
ELEMENTARY
SECONDARY
POST-SECONDARY
DEAF
L.D.
E.D.
M.R.
O.H.
S/P
ADMIN.
Specific

FIGURE 4

composition of the Consumer Validation Teams. The purpose of the consumer validation was both to integrate stakeholding audiences and to validate and "fieldtest" the curriculum with the people who might work with new trainees, with teachers who needed the generic skills and competencies, and with those who might direct in-service education for special education personnel. Membership varied on the several validation teams, but each included special education and regular classroom teachers, principals from elementary, middle and/or secondary schools, students in the current special education program and support person from schools.

FOCUS—WHAT QUESTIONS SHOULD WE ASK THEM? (QUESTIONS) The evaluation questions which guided the Consumer Validation Teams were principally pragmatic in nature, and were built around problems such as:

1. What do we have to do now that we were not trained to do?
2. How have the roles that special education personnel fulfill been altered by state and federal legislation?
3. Where—in what areas—could we use more training, either preservice or inservice?
4. How can support personnel augment and aid the work of special education teachers, resource room teachers, consultants or itinerant personnel?

Within the context of those and other related questions, the Consumer Validation Teams explored and examined the proposed new curriculum and suggested additions,

REPORTING—WHO MUST APPROVE THE CURRICULAR MODIFICATIONS? (AUDIENCE) deletions and modifications. The Special Education Department was responsive to this group and made the modifications recommended in group sessions throughout that semester. After that, the new curriculum was ready to be presented to the School Assembly, the body of voting faculty which gives final approval to curricular changes within the School of Education.

The project culminated in the Spring of 1978 with a total revision of all departmental offerings being approved by the assembly of the School of Education. This involved elimination of all existing courses and the design of new programs, course content, course titles, sequence of courses, and program options. Teaching assignments of faculty members were changed and a number of new initiatives emerged. For example, while no undergraduate degrees are offered, courses and practicum experiences are now open to undergraduates. An Ed.S. degree was initiated, and categorical boundaries were greatly dissolved.

The new curriculum continues to be monitored, and occasional changes are made. While other departments in the School of Education have made major changes in the curriculum, this revision process has been the only example where the total curriculum was eliminated and replaced with a new concept and new requirements.

REFLECTION ON THE CURRICULUM EVALUATION/REVISION PROCESS

FOCUS—DID THE EVALUATION EFFORT ACHIEVE ITS GOALS? (PURPOSES) Although coordination of the department's proposal for curriculum revision with the School Assembly's agenda resulted in a minor delay, the proposal was accepted with minor changes. The changes were primarily in the form of clarification. The new curriculum is now operational, and elements of the planning and evaluation structure continue. Faculty members have accepted responsibility for monitoring and evaluating the curriculum. While revisions will periodically occur it is reasonable to assume that at some time in the future the "total evaluation look" will occur again. For instance, it will arrive again within the next two years as the faculty "recycles" to examine its doctoral program. While curriculum evaluation and revision was at the heart of departmental change, other information support mechanisms (e.g., Student Management System, Faculty Evaluation) fed into the curricular effect. So it was that each project was closely aligned with the curricular development effort, and made some important contribution to it.

It is difficult in describing a project of this scope to provide detailed information on the many aspects of the project and the contributions of the people involved. To aid readers in benefiting from the case study, two summaries are provided. The first summarizes the residual benefits derived from the evaluation/revision process. The second lists the products, the "audit trail" produced during the process.

RESIDUAL BENEFITS

1. Faculty members acquired planning and evaluation skills which generalize to other areas of faculty responsibilities.
2. Curriculum evaluation/revision evolved as an on-going concern and not a project concern.
3. A definitive state of the art accounting of the department's curriculum was achieved.
4. A broad understanding of the department's program was achieved.
5. Student-Faculty relationships took on added meaning for doctoral students.
6. Strengths and weaknesses of faculty instructional resouces became evident.
7. Readiness for related evaluation activities was achieved.
8. A number of concerns, not publicly discussed previously, were dealt with in a productive manner.
9. Secretaries and other staff members gained a fuller understanding of the department's mission.
10. A more empirical attitude toward program decisions evolved.
11. The importance of data bases for planning became evident.

12. The interrelatedness of curriculum decisions with personnel, resource, and organizational evaluation decisions was reinforced.

THE AUDIT TRAIL

REPORTING—HOW WERE PEOPLE KEPT INFORMED ABOUT THE EVALUATION? (CONTEXT) A number of products in the form of position papers, reports and progress memos were developed during the planning process. Each product was the consequence of specific activities and intended for a particular purpose. Collectively, they represent a chronology of progress. Following is a listing of selected products.

1974: 1. Working papers describing trends in the education of exceptional children, issues in higher education, emerging special education roles, assumptions for personnel training and general direction for curriculum planning.
2. Preliminary statement on curriculum planning as an element within Block Grant proposals. Block Grant proposals represent major reports on evaluation, productivity, and curriculum planning.
1975: 1. Working paper setting forth an organizational structure for the curriculum planning project.
2. Data report on enrollment by course and location over a three-year period.
3. Compilation of course outlines, reading lists and content resources.
4. Annual evaluation report included in Block Grant proposal.
5. Retreat report on curriculum planning activities.
1976: 1. Specification model for detailing and organizing curriculum.
2. Reports resulting from specification process. Content areas included assessment, characteristics, remediation and management across all areas of exceptionality and levels of development. These reports primarily included listings of competencies. Competencies were stated as grades and related behavioral objectives.
3. Annual evaluation report included in Block Grant proposal.
4. Retreat report on curriculum planning activities. Specific agenda items were planned on curriculum revision.
1977: 1. Preliminary delivery model.
2. Revised specification reports with implications for course structure.
3. Team reports.
4. Annual evaluation report included in Block Grant proposal.
5. Retreat report on curriculum planning activities.
1978: 1. Final delivery model.
2. Summary progress report.
3. Course descriptions.
4. Ed.S. program descriptions.
5. Doctoral program proposed revision options.
6. Retreat report on curriculum revision activities.

7. Final proposal prepared for School of Education Curriculum Committee.

SUMMARY

The need for systematic curriculum revision was included as an agenda item in the 1974 Spring retreat. The process employed was primarily one of curriculum development rather than revision. The project began with the determination of the role(s) for which the department prepared personnel, while analysis of those roles determined major competencies, and the generation of content for the preparation of personnel. Faculty and consumer teams were organized to participate in the determination of content, the organization of content, and the verification of content. No changes were made in the existing curriculum of the department during the process of this project. The project basically amounted to the substituting of a newly designed curriculum for the existing curriculum.

The curriculum revisions represent the result of a systematic evaluative review of all departmental offerings. The organizational structure of the curriculum project involved faculty, students, and consumer representatives. The extensive time commitment to the project was due to the comprehensiveness of the changes proposed and the nature of the procedures employed.

DISCUSSION QUESTIONS AND TOPICS

1. How does the process this department went through compare to the way curricular revisions are usually done? What are some of the major similarities and differences?
2. Were the interim results of the work adequately reported? (Look especially at the "Audit Trail" at the end of the case.) Who do you suppose looked at or used the various reports?
3. The four other projects that were going on at the time of the curricular revision had, as was pointed out in the case, important influences on the curricular revision process. What were some of those influences?
4. The other four projects had something in common: they involved centralized departmental control of important departmental functions. Do you suppose that helped or hindered in obtaining faculty participation in the revision process?
5. People sometimes say that most major educational evaluation efforts occur (only) in response to external threats. To what extent does this case support that observation? What other factors, if any, do you believe contributed to attaining significant faculty involvement and cooperation in the case?

SUGGESTIONS FOR STIMULATING DISCUSSIONS

1. Have at least two persons or groups go through the case examining the "evaluation questions" raised in it. Each question should be categorized under one of these three headings: Educational Questions, Evaluation Questions,

Procedural Questions. Have the persons or groups compare their categorizations and discuss why they categorized each question as they did. (Hint: the purpose of the discussion is not to arrive at the truth of the matter but to notice that evaluators are often involved with all three types of questions:

1. Educational questions related to why the evaluation is being done, to purposes.
2. Evaluation questions which should be stated so they can be answered rather unequivocally by the data collected, and
3. Procedural questions about how to do the evaluation work (e.g. most of the questions in the case margin are of this type.)

2. Arrange a debate. Resolved: The residual benefits of the case were of more importance to the department than were the actual evaluation data collected.
3. Arrange a discussion about the strategy of making evaluation an integral part of the curricular revision process. What were some of the benefits? drawbacks? (Hint: Consider the problems sometimes reported in the literature of doing elegant evaluations no one uses vs. integrating the evaluation into the process so much that it loses its potential for providing an unbiased perspective.)

APPLICATION EXERCISES

1. Read some of the material in the *Sourcebook* indicated by the asides. Then, suggest alternative things people in the case might have done at several points in the case. Or suggest a whole new approach they might have taken.
2. Using the case as a model (and foil) and your suggested alternatives as guides, design an evaluation for a situation or problem similar to that shown in the case.
3. Using Chapter 7 of the *Sourcebook* as a guide, do a meta-evaluation and critique of the case (and/or your evaluation design).
4. Use the *Design Manual* to develop an improved evaluation design for the case.
5. Use the *Design Manual* to develop an evaluation design for a situation or problem similar to the one described in the case.